Beginning ASP.NET 1.1
with Visual C#® .NET 2003

Beginning ASP.NET 1.1
with Visual C#® .NET 2003

Chris Ullman
John Kauffman
Chris Hart
Dave Sussman
Daniel Maharry

WILEY
Wiley Publishing, Inc.

Beginning ASP.NET 1.1 with Visual C#® .NET 2003

Published by
Wiley Publishing, Inc.
10475 Crosspoint Boulevard
Indianapolis, IN 46256
www.wiley.com

Copyright © 2004 by Wiley Publishing, Inc., Indianapolis, Indiana

Published simultaneously in Canada

Library of Congress Card Number: 2004100135

ISBN: 0-7645-5708-4

Manufactured in the United States of America

10 9 8 7 6 5 4 3 2 1

1B/RW/RS/QU

About the Authors

Chris Ullman

Chris Ullman is a freelance Web developer and technical author who has spent many years stewing in ASP/ASP.NET, like a teabag left too long in the pot. Coming from a Computer Science background, he started initially as a UNIX/Linux guru, who gravitated towards MS technologies during the summer of ASP (1997). He cut his teeth on Wrox Press ASP guides, and since then he has written over 20 books, most notably as lead author for Wrox's bestselling Beginning ASP/ASP.NET series, and has contributed chapters to books on PHP, ColdFusion, JavaScript, Web Services, C#, XML and other Internet-related technologies too esoteric to mention, now swallowed up in the quicksands of the dot.com boom.

Quitting Wrox as a full-time employee in August 2001, he branched out into VB6 programming and ASP development, maintaining a multitude of sites from http://www.cuasp.co.co.uk, his "work" site, to http://www.atomicwise.com, a selection of his writings on music and art. He now divides his time between being a human punchbag for his 29-month-old son Nye, composing electronic sounds on bits of dilapidated old keyboards for his music project Open E, and tutoring his cats in the art of peaceful co-existence, and not violently mugging each other on the stairs.

Chris Ullman contributed Chapters 1, 14, 15, 16, 17, and Appendix E to this book.

John Kauffman

John Kauffman was born in Philadelphia, the son of a chemist and a nurse. He received his degrees from The Pennsylvania State University, the colleges of Science and Agriculture. His early research was for Hershey foods in the genetics of the chocolate tree and the molecular biology of chocolate production. Subsequently, he moved to the Rockefeller University, where he cloned and sequenced DNA regions that control the day and night cycles of plants.

Since 1997, John has written ten books, six of which have been on the Amazon Computer Best Seller List. His specialty is programming Web front-ends for enterprise-level databases.

In his spare time, John is an avid sailor and youth sailing coach. He represented the USA in the sailing World Championship of 1985 and assisted the Olympic teams of Belgium and China in 1996. He also enjoys jazz music and drumming and manages to read the *New Yorker* from cover-to-cover each week.

My portions of this book are dedicated to the instructors of two drum and bugle corps. These men taught me about precision, accuracy, and discipline: Ken Green and John Flowers of the Belvederes 1976 and Dennis DeLucia and Bobby Hoffman of the Bayonne Bridgemen 1978.

John Kauffman contributed Chapters 2, 3, 4, 5, 6, and Appendix B to this book.

Chris Hart

Chris Hart is a full-time .NET Developer and part-time author who lives in Birmingham (UK) with her husband James. While she's most at home in the world of the Web, she's recently been working with the .NET Compact Framework. In her spare time, Chris spends much of her time playing with beta technologies, and then attempting to write about them.

Chris has contributed many chapters to a variety of books, including *Beginning ASP.NET* (Wrox Press), *Beginning Dynamic Websites with ASP.NET Web Matrix* (Wrox Press), and most recently, *A Programmer's Guide to SQL* (Apress).

When she gets away from computers, Chris enjoys travel, especially when it involves driving along narrow winding roads to get to out-of-the-way parts of Scotland. She dreams of building her own house somewhere where she can keep a cat.

Chris Hart contributed Chapters 10, 11, 12, 13, and Appendices C and D to this book.

Dave Sussman

Dave Sussman is a writer, trainer, and consultant, living in the wilds of the Oxfordshire countryside. He's been working with ASP.NET since before it was first released and still isn't bored with it. You can contact him at davids@ipona.com.

Dave Sussman contributed Chapters 7, 8, and 9 to this book.

Daniel Maharry

Dan Maharry is a freelance writer, reviewer, speaker, and editor who has, in no particular order, taught English, Math, and Guitar, directed, crewed, acted in, and produced several plays and short films, been a film and music columnist for four years, co-founded ASPToday.com, rewritten his own at HMobius.com several times, opened an office in India, variously edited, reviewed, and written pieces of over 40 programming books, qualified as a sound engineer, and consumed enough caffeine in his lifetime to keep most of China awake for a week. Occasionally, he sleeps. Sometimes. Contact him at danm@hmobius.com.

"With deep-felt love to Jane, and in memoriam to John Kauffman's father."

Dan Maharry contributed Chapters 5 and 6 to this book.

Credits

Authors
Chris Ullman
John Kauffman
Chris Hart
Dave Sussman
Daniel Maharry

Senior Acquisitions Editor
Jim Minatel

Vice President & Executive Group Publisher
Richard Swadley

Vice President and Executive Publisher
Bob Ipsen

Vice President and Publisher
Joseph B. Wikert

Executive Editorial Director
Mary Bednarek

Project Coordinator
Mary Richards

Project Manager
Ami Frank Sullivan

Senior Production Manager
Fred Bernardi

Editorial Manager
Mary Beth Wakefield

Book Producer
Peer Technical Services Pvt. Ltd.

Contents

Introduction   **xxi**

Chapter 1: Getting Started with ASP.NET   **1**

What Is a Static Web Page?   **2**
How Are Static Web Pages Served?   **3**
   Limitations of Static Web Pages   4
   What Is a Web Server?   5
How Are Dynamic Web Pages Served?   **6**
   Client-Side Dynamic Web Pages   6
   Server-Side Dynamic Web Pages   7
What Is ASP.NET?   **9**
   How Does ASP.NET Differ from ASP?   9
   Using C# with ASP.NET   10
   I'm Still Confused about ASP, ASP.NET, and C#   11
The Installation Process   **11**
   Which Operating System Do You Have?   11
   Prerequisites for Installing ASP.NET   12
      Try It Out Installing MDAC 2.8   **13**
   Installing ASP.NET and the .NET Framework   13
      Try It Out Installing the .NET Framework Redistributable   **14**
   Installing Web Matrix   15
      Try It Out Installing Web Matrix   **16**
   Configuring Web Matrix to Run with .NET Framework 1.1   18
      Try It Out Configuring Web Matrix   **18**
   Running Web Matrix and Setting Up the Web Server   19
      Try It Out Starting the Web Server   **19**
ASP.NET Test Example   **25**
      Try It Out Your First ASP.NET Web Page   **25**
ASP.NET Troubleshooting   **28**
   Page Cannot Be Displayed: HTTP Error 403   29
   Page Cannot Be Found: HTTP Error 404   30
   Web Page Unavailable While Offline   31
   I Just Get a Blank Page   31
   The Page Displays the Message But Not the Time   31
   I Get an Error Statement Citing a Server Error   32
   I Have a Different Problem   33
Summary   **33**

Contents

Chapter 2: Anatomy of an ASP.NET Page   35

What Is .NET?   **35**
From Your Code to Machine Code   37
Introducing Two Intermediate Languages   37
Objects   38
The .NET Base Classes   39
The Class Browser   40
How ASP.NET Works   **41**
Saving Your ASP.NET Files with an ASPX Suffix   42
Inserting ASP.NET Code into Our Web Pages   42
    Try It Out Inserting Server-Side (ASP.NET) Code   **44**
    Try It Out Interweaving ASP.NET Output with HTML   **49**
ASP.NET in Action   **51**
Binding to a Database   51
    Try It Out Binding to a Database   **51**
Binding to a Simple XML File   54
    Try It Out Binding to a Simple XML Document   **54**
Summary   **57**
Exercises   **58**

Chapter 3: Server Controls and Variables   59

Forms   **60**
Web Pages, HTML Forms, and Web Forms   **60**
Request and Response in Non-ASP.NET Pages   **61**
Where ASP.NET Fits in with the .NET Framework   63
The <form> Tag in ASP.NET   64
Using ASP.NET Server Controls   **64**
<asp:Label>   65
    Try It Out Using the <asp:Label> Control   **67**
Modifying ASP.NET Controls   68
<asp:DropDownList>   69
    Try It Out Using the <asp:DropDownList> Control   **69**
<asp:ListBox>   73
    Try It Out Using the <asp:ListBox> Control   **73**
<asp:TextBox>   75
    Try It Out Using the <asp:TextBox> Control   **75**
<asp:RadioButtonList> and <asp:RadioButton>   77
    Try It Out Using the <asp:RadioButtonList> Control   **78**
<asp:CheckBox> and <asp:CheckBoxList>   79
    Try It Out Using the <asp:CheckBox> Control   **80**
Storing Information in C# Variables   **82**
Declaring Value Type Variables   82
    Try It Out Using Variables   **83**
Datatypes   **86**
Numeric   86
Text Datatypes   88
Other Datatypes   89
Naming Variables   90

Variable Scope   91
  Try It Out *Creating Block and Function-Level Variables*   **92**
Constants   **97**
Conversion Functions   **97**
Arrays   **98**
  Try It Out *Using Arrays*   **99**
Data Collections   **103**
  ArrayList   103
    Try It Out *Using an ArrayList*   **105**
  Hashtables   106
    Try It Out *Using Hashtables*   **108**
  SortedList   110
Summary   **111**
Exercises   **112**

Chapter 4: Control Structures and Procedural Programming   **113**

Operators   **113**
  Assignment Operator   114
  Arithmetic Operators   114
    Try It Out *Tax Calculator Using Arithmetic Operators*   **115**
  String Concatenation   118
  Numeric Comparison Operators   119
  Logical Operators   120
    Try It Out *Tax Calculator Using Logical Operators*   **122**
Control Structures   **125**
  Overview of Branching Structures   125
  Overview of Looping Structures   126
  Overview of Jumping Structures   126
  Uses of Control Structures   127
Branching Structures   **128**
  The if Structure   129
    Try It Out *Using the if Structure*   **134**
  The switch Structure   138
    Try It Out *Using the switch Structure*   **141**
Looping Structures   **144**
  The for Loop Structure   144
    Try It Out *Using the for Loop*   **146**
  The while Loop   148
    Try It Out *Using the while Loop*   **150**
  The do...while Structure   151
    Try It Out *Using do...while*   **152**
  The foreach...in Loop   155
Summary   **156**
Exercises   **157**

Chapter 5: Functions   **159**

Overview   **159**
Modularization   **160**

Contents

Defining and Using Functions   **161**
    Try It Out Defining and Using a Simple Function   *161*
Passing Parameters to Functions   **164**
    Try It Out Functions with Parameters   *165*
Web Controls as Parameters   **169**
    Try It Out Using Web Controls as Parameters   *170*
Return Values   **173**
    Using Return Values in Your Code   173
    Try It Out Handling Function Return Types   *175*
Value, Reference, and Out Parameters   **181**
    Try It Out Using Value, Reference, and Out Parameters   *183*
Modularization Best Practices   **188**
Summary   **189**
Exercises   **190**

Chapter 6: Event-Driven Programming and Postback   **191**

What Is an Event?   **192**
What Is Event-Driven Programming?   **192**
HTML Events   **193**
ASP.NET's Trace Feature   **195**
ASP.NET Page Events   **197**
ASP.NET Web Control Events   **199**
    Try It Out Creating Event Handlers with Web Matrix   *201*
Event-Driven Programming and Postback   **202**
    Try It Out Reacting to Events in HTML and ASP.NET   *203*
The IsPostBack Test   **205**
    Try It Out Calculator   *206*
Summary   **211**
Exercises   **212**

Chapter 7: Objects   **215**

Classes and Instances   **216**
Properties, Methods, and Events   **216**
Objects in .NET   **216**
Why Use Objects?   **217**
Defining Classes   **218**
    Try It Out Creating a Class   *218*
    Property Variables   223
    Property Types   224
    Try It Out Read-Only Properties   *224*
    Initializing Objects   226
    Try It Out Overloading a Constructor   *226*
    Implementing Methods   227
    Try It Out Adding Methods to a Class   *227*
    Consolidating Overloaded Methods   230
Advanced Classes   **231**

Shared or Static Properties and Methods   231
Inheritance   232
   Try It Out   Inheritance   **233**
Interfaces   237
   Try It Out   Creating an Interface   **238**
.NET Objects   **243**
Namespaces   243
The Class Browser   243
Summary   **245**
Exercises   **245**

Chapter 8: Reading from Databases   **247**

Understanding Databases   **247**
Tables   248
Normalization   249
SQL and Stored Procedures   251
The Web Matrix Data Explorer   **251**
   Try It Out   Connecting to a Database   **251**
Creating Data Pages   **253**
Displaying Data Using the Data Explorer   253
   Try It Out   Creating a Grid   **253**
Displaying Data Using the Web Matrix Template Pages   256
   Try It Out   Creating a Data Page   **257**
Displaying Data Using the Code Wizards   262
   Try It Out   Creating a Data Page   **262**
ADO.NET   **269**
The OleDbConnection Object   271
The OleDbCommand Object   271
   Try It Out   Using Parameters   **273**
The OleDataAdapter Object   278
The DataSet Object   278
The DataReader Object   278
   Try It Out   Using a DataReader   **279**
Summary   **281**
Exercises   **281**

Chapter 9: Advanced Data Handling   **283**

More Data Objects   **283**
The DataTable Object   284
The DataRow Object   285
   Try It Out   The DataTable and DataRow Objects **286**
Updating Databases   **288**
ADO.NET versus ADO   289
Updating Data in a DataSet   289
   Try It Out   Adding, Editing, and Deleting Rows **289**
Updating the Original Data Source   297
   Try It Out   Auto-Generated Commands   **298**
Updating the Database   301

Contents

Try It Out **Updating the Database**	**302**
Updating Databases Using a Command	307
Try It Out **Executing Commands Directly**	**307**
Summary	**310**
Exercises	**311**

Chapter 10: ASP.NET Server Controls   313

The Wrox United Application	**314**
ASP.NET Web Controls	**315**
HTML Server Controls	**316**
HTML Server Controls versus Web Controls	**318**
Web Controls	**319**
Rich Object Model	320
Automatic Browser Detection	320
Properties	320
Events	**322**
Try It Out **Creating an Event Handler**	**322**
Page Lifecycle	**324**
Page_Load()	325
Event Handling	326
Page_Unload()	326
Understanding Web Controls: The Wrox United Application	**327**
Try It Out **Wrox United Main Page – Default.aspx**	**328**
Intrinsic Controls	331
Try It Out **Wrox United – Teams.aspx**	**332**
Data Rendering Controls	340
Try It Out **Wrox United – Teams.aspx, Part 2**	**343**
Rich Controls	352
Try It Out **Wrox United – Default.aspx, Part 2, the Event Calendar**	**354**
Try It Out **Wrox United – Displaying Fixture Details**	**360**
Web Matrix Controls	366
Try It Out **Wrox United – Players.aspx and the Web Matrix MX DataGrid**	**367**
Validation Controls	372
Try It Out **Wrox United – Registering for Email Updates (Default.aspx)**	**373**
Summary	**378**
Exercises	**378**

Chapter 11: Users and Applications   381

Remembering Information in a Web Application	**382**
Cookies	383
Try It Out **Using Cookies**	**386**
Sessions	393
Try It Out **Using Session State**	**395**
Applications	**404**
How Do Applications Work?	405
Try It Out **Using Application State**	**405**
Reacting to Application and Session Events	**410**
Global.asax	410

Contents

Try it Out Global.asax – Global Settings   **411**

Caching   **413**

Try It Out Wrox United – Caching Objects   **415**

State Management Recommendations   **418**

When to Use Cookies   419

When to Use Sessions   419

When to Use Applications   419

When to Use Caching   419

Other State Management Techniques   420

Using Multiple State Management Techniques on a Page   421

Try it Out Wrox United – Adding Some Style!   **421**

Summary   **429**

Exercises   **430**

Chapter 12: Reusable Code for ASP.NET   **431**

Encapsulation   **431**

Components   **432**

Why Use Components?   434

Applying Component Theory to Applications   434

User Controls   **435**

Try It Out Our First User Control   **437**

Try It Out Wrox United – Header Control   **440**

Try It Out Wrox United – Navigation User Control   **446**

Code-Behind   **451**

Try It Out Our First Code-Behind File   **452**

Try It Out Using Code-Behind in Wrox United   **457**

Summary   **459**

Exercises   **459**

Chapter 13: .NET Assemblies and Custom Controls   **463**

Three-Tier Application Design   **464**

ASP.NET Application Design   **465**

.NET Assemblies   **466**

Try It Out Our First ASP.NET Component   **467**

What Is Compilation?   470

Try It Out Compiling Our First ASP.NET Component   **470**

Accessing a Component from within an ASP.NET Page   474

Try It Out Using a Compiled Component   **474**

XCopy Deployment   476

Accessing Assemblies in Other Locations   477

Writing Code in Other Languages   477

Try It Out Writing a Component in VB.NET   **478**

Data Access Components   482

Try It Out Encapsulating Data Access Code in a Component   **482**

Custom Server Controls   **489**

What Are Custom Controls?   490

Try It Out Our First ASP.NET Custom Control   **491**

Composite Custom Controls   499

Contents

Try It Out Wrox United – Custom Composite Control   **499**

Summary   **506**

Exercises   **507**

Chapter 14: Debugging and Error Handling   509

A Few Good Habits   **510**

Tips on Coding   **510**

Indent Your Code   511

Structure Your Code   511

Comment Your Code   512

Convert Variables to the Correct Data Types (Validation)   512

Try to Break Your Code   513

Sources of Errors   **514**

Syntax Errors   514

Try It Out Syntax Error   **515**

Try It Out Generate a Compiler Error   **516**

Logical (Runtime) Errors   518

Try It Out Generate a Runtime Error   **519**

Try It Out Catching Illegal Values   **521**

Try It Out Using RequiredFieldValidator   **524**

System Errors   525

Finding Errors   **525**

Try It Out Viewing the Call-Stack   **526**

Debug Mode   527

Try It Out Disable the Debug Mode   **527**

Tracing   529

Try It Out Enabling Trace at the Page Level   **529**

Try It Out Writing to the Trace Log   **532**

Handling Errors   **535**

Try It Out Using try...catch...finally   **542**

Try It Out Using Page_Error()   **548**

Error Notification and Logging   **550**

Try It Out Creating Error Pages   **551**

Writing to the Event Log   553

Try It Out Writing to the Windows Error Log   **554**

Mailing the Site Administrator   557

Summary   **559**

Exercises   **559**

Chapter 15: Configuration and Optimization   561

Configuration Overview   **562**

Browsing .config Files   562

The Configuration Files   564

The Structure of the Configuration Files   567

Performance Optimization   **574**

Caching   574

Try It Out Output Caching   **576**

The Cache Object   578

Contents

Expiring Information in the Cache   581
    Try It Out Creating a File Dependency   **582**
    Try It Out Creating a Key Dependency   **586**
Tips and Tricks   **590**
Summary   **591**
Exercises   **591**

Chapter 16: Web Services   593

What Is a Web Service?   **594**
    Try It Out Creating Our First Web Service   **595**
HTTP, XML, and Web Services   **598**
  HTTP GET   599
  HTTP POST   600
Simple Object Access Protocol (SOAP)   **601**
Building an ASP.NET Web Service   **603**
  Processing Directive   603
  Namespaces   603
  Public Class   604
  Web Methods   604
    Try It Out Creating a Web Service with Multiple Web Methods   **605**
  Testing Your Web Service   607
    Try It Out Conversions Test Page   **607**
  Using Your Web Service   608
    Try It Out Viewing the WSDL Contract   **609**
    Try It Out ISBN Search Web Service   **610**
Consuming a Web Service   **613**
  How Does a Proxy Work?   613
  Creating a Proxy   615
    Try It Out Accessing the ISBN Web Service from an ASP.NET Page   **615**
Creating a Web Service for the Wrox United Application   **618**
    Try It Out Adding a Results Page   **619**
    Try It Out Creating the Web Service   **621**
Web Service Discovery   **626**
Securing a Web Service   **627**
  Username-Password Combination or Registration Keys   627
    Try It Out Securing a Web Service with Username and Password   **627**
  Secure Sockets Layer (SSL)   630
  IP Address Restriction   630
  Web Services Enhancements (WSE)   631
Other Web Services Considerations   **631**
  Network Connectivity   631
  Asynchronous Method Calls   631
  Service Hijacking (or Piggybacking)   632
  Provider Solvency   633
  The Interdependency Scenario   633
Summary   **633**
Exercises   **634**

Contents

Chapter 17: ASP.NET Security   **635**

What Is Security?   **636**
The ASP.NET Security Model   **636**
Authentication   **637**
    Implementing Forms-Based Authentication   638
        Try It Out Forms-Based Authentication   *639*
    Forms-Based Authentication Using a Database   646
        Try It Out Authenticating against a Database   *646*
Authorization   **650**
        Try It Out Authorization for User@MyDomain.com   *651*
Authentication in Wrox United   **653**
        Try It Out Adding a Login Page to WroxUnited   *653*
Encryption Using SSL   **664**
        Try It Out Enabling SSL   *665*
Summary   **666**
Exercises   **666**

Appendix A: Exercise Solutions   **667**

Chapter 2   **667**
Chapter 3   **669**
Chapter 4   **672**
Chapter 5   **675**
Chapter 6   **678**
Chapter 7   **681**
Chapter 8   **684**
Chapter 9   **686**
Chapter 10   **688**
Chapter 11   **693**
Chapter 12   **697**
Chapter 13   **702**
Chapter 14   **708**
Chapter 15   **713**
Chapter 16   **715**
Chapter 17   **720**

Appendix B: Web Matrix Quick Start   **725**

What Is Web Matrix?   **725**
Starting ASP.NET Web Matrix   **727**
    The Screen   727
    How to Enter Code   730
        Try It Out Code Entry   *731*
Saving and Viewing Pages   **731**
        Try It Out Formatting Modes, Views, and Serving Pages   *733*
Reusing Code   **735**
        Try It Out Saving and Using Snippets   *735*

Contents

Class Browser **735**

> *Try It Out Class Browser Property Look-Up* *736*

What to Study Next **738**

Summary **738**

Appendix C: The Wrox United Database 741

The Database Design **741**

Players 742

Status 742

Teams 743

PlayerTeams 743

Positions 744

Games 744

GameTypes 745

Locations 745

Opponents 746

Fans 746

Installing the Database **747**

Installing the Access Database 747

Installing the MSDE Database 747

Appendix D: Web Application Development Using Visual Studio .NET 753

Creating a Web Application Project **754**

Features of the Visual Studio .NET Environment 755

Visual Studio .NET Solutions and Projects 756

Files in a Web Application Project 757

Working with Web Pages **757**

Compiling and Running Pages **761**

Adding Code to the Code-Behind Class 762

Features of Code View 763

Adding Code to Methods 763

Styling Controls and Pages in Visual Studio .NET **769**

Working in HTML View **776**

Creating User Controls **777**

Formatting Blocks of Code 782

Developing the User Control 784

Creating an XML File 786

Adding a User Control to a Page 789

Adding Custom Classes **791**

Working with Databases Using the Server Explorer **794**

Debugging in Visual Studio .NET **797**

Using Breakpoints 798

Fixing Design-Time Errors 799

Suggested Exercises and Further Reading **801**

Contents

Appendix E: Installing and Configuring IIS   803

    Try It Out Locating and Installing IIS on Your Web Server Machine   *803*

Working with IIS   **806**

    The Microsoft Management Console (MMC)   806

    Testing Your Installation   807

    Identifying Your Web Server's Name   807

    Managing Directories on Your Web Server   808

    Try It Out Creating a Virtual Directory and Setting Up Permissions   *810*

    Permissions   814

Browsing to a Page on Your Web Server   **818**

Index   825

Introduction

ASP.NET is a radical update of Microsoft's *Active Server Pages* (*ASP*). ASP.NET is a powerful server based technology designed to create dynamic and interactive HTML pages on demand for your Web site or corporate intranet. Its design improves upon nearly every feature of classic ASP, from reducing the amount of code you need to write to giving you more power and flexibility.

ASP.NET is a key element in Microsoft's .NET Framework, providing Web-based access to the immensely powerful .NET development environment. It allows us to create Web applications in a new, flexible way by placing commonly used code into reusable controls of various kinds that can fire events initiated by the users of a site.

ASP.NET branches out into many other technologies, such as Web services, ADO.NET, custom controls, and security. We will briefly touch upon its relationship with these fields throughout the book to provide a solid, comprehensive understanding of how ASP.NET can benefit your work in a practical way.

ASP.NET 1.1 itself is a fairly light update to the complete wholesale changes that occurred in ASP.NET 1.0. This book by and large covers features that are available in both 1.0 and 1.1, but it covers the pertinent new features of 1.1 in additional depth, which will be of interest to both the novice and experienced users. So if you are already running ASP.NET 1.0, you will be expected to upgrade to 1.1.

By the end of this book you will be familiar with the anatomy of ASP.NET 1.1 and be able to create powerful, secure, and robust Web sites that can collect and work with information in a multitude of ways to the benefit of both you and your users.

Who Is This Book For?

The purpose of this book is to teach you from scratch how to use ASP.NET to write Web pages and Web applications in which content can be programmatically tailored each time an individual client browser calls them up. This not only saves you a lot of effort in presenting and updating your Web pages, but also offers tremendous scope for adding sophisticated functionality to your site. As ASP.NET is not a programming language in its own right, but rather a technology (as we shall explain in the book), we will be teaching some basic programming principles in *Chapters 2* to *7* in C#, our chosen language for implementing ASP.NET.

This book is therefore ideal for somebody who knows some basic HTML but has never programmed before, or somebody who is familiar with the basics of old style ASP, but hasn't investigated ASP.NET in any detail. If you are an experienced programmer looking for a quick crash course on ASP.NET, or somebody who's worked extensively with ASP, we suggest that you refer to *Professional ASP.NET 1.1 Special Edition, Wiley ISBN: 0-7645-58900* instead, as you'll most likely find that the early chapters here just reiterate things you already know. If are not familiar with HTML, then we suggest that you master the basics of building Web pages before moving on to learning ASP.NET.

What Does This Book Cover?

This book teaches everything the novice user needs to know, from installing ASP.NET and the relevant bits and pieces to creating pages and putting together the concepts to create a whole application using ASP.NET 1.1.

Although ASP.NET 1.1 isn't a huge update on version 1.0, this book has been considerably overhauled since edition 1.0. Plenty of the old chapters have been removed and many new ones introduced. We've removed three chapters because we wanted to simplify the experience of learning ASP.NET. We've created a brand new case study – an amateur sports league Web site – which is then used throughout the latter chapters in the book to provide a more practical guide on how to implement ASP.NET applications.

If you see the previous edition, you will find this one to be more cohesive, aimed towards the complete novice *and* the developer with some ASP experience, and written with the benefit of hindsight from experienced developers who have have been employed in creating ASP.NET applications. We trust that you will find it a great improvement over the last, just as every new edition should be.

In the course of this book you will learn:

❑ What is ASP.NET

❑ How to install ASP.NET and get it up and running

❑ The structure of ASP.NET and how it sits on the .NET Framework

❑ How to use ASP.NET to produce dynamic, flexible, interactive Web pages

❑ Basic programming principles such as variables, controls structures, procedural programming, and objects

❑ How to use ASP.NET to interface with different data sources, from databases to XML documents

❑ What ready-made controls ASP.NET offers for common situations

❑ How to create your own controls

❑ How to debug your ASP.NET pages

❑ How to deal with unexpected events and inputs

❑ How to create your own Web application

❑ How to integrate your applications with Web services and how to create your own

❑ Some simple security features and how to create a login for an application

How This Book Is Structured

Here is a quick breakdown of what you will find in this book:

❑ **Chapter 1 – Getting Started with ASP.NET**: In the first chapter, we introduce ASP.NET and look at some of the reasons that you'd want to use server-side code for creating Web pages as well as the technologies that are available to do so. This done, we spend the bulk of the chapter explaining the ASP.NET installation process in detail, how to install a Web server to run ASP.NET on (we will be using the Web server that accompanies Web Matrix), along with the ancillary installation of MDAC. We finish up with a simple example ASP.NET page to check that our installation is working correctly.

❑ **Chapter 2 – Anatomy of an ASP.NET Page**: Having completed the installation in the previous chapter, we consider the structure of an ASP.NET page and the way that it functions in relation to the .NET Framework. We use examples to demonstrate how the ASP.NET module parses the page.

❑ **Chapter 3 – Server Controls and Variables**: After familiarizing ourselves with the basics of ASP.NET controls, this chapter considers the use of variables for holding data in C#. We look at how variables are implemented, what they can contain, and how they can be placed into your ASP.NET pages.

❑ **Chapter 4 – Control Structures and Procedural Programming**: This chapter takes a whirlwind tour of the key building blocks of C# in the context of an ASP.NET page. We learn how to make our ASP.NET pages more responsive through the use of C# branching and looping structures that enable us to control the order in which our program's statements execute.

❑ **Chapter 5 –Functions**: We cover *how* the modularization and reusable ASP.NET code works in this chapter. We look at functions and how they are used together with Web controls. We learn how to pass parameters within ASP.NET pages and the different ways in which ASP.NET can handle them.

❑ **Chapter 6 – Event-Driven Programming and Postback**: We talk about how ASP.NET revolves around an event-driven model, and how things occur in strict order and ways in which the ASP.NET page can react to user intervention. We also look at the concept of *postback* and how it is used to send information back from the user to the Web server for preserving the 'state' of a page.

❑ **Chapter 7 – Objects**: This chapter deals with the thorny subject of objects. ASP.NET pages derive a great deal of their flexibility and power from the object-oriented way they are structured. This chapter introduces concepts such as properties, methods, constructors, collections, and overloading with many examples related to real-world objects to aid your understanding. We also discuss the concepts that make objects very powerful to use such as *inheritance* and *encapsulation,* and how they greatly reduce the amount of code you need to use.

❑ **Chapter 8 – Reading from Databases**: At this point in the book we're familiar with the basic anatomy of ASP.NET pages and objects, so we branch out to look at ADO.NET in the context of ASP.NET. Most specifically we look at the use of the `Connection` and `Command` objects for opening data sources and retrieving information into a `DataSet`.

❑ **Chapter 9 – Advanced Data Handling**: After mastering the basics of reading data in the previous chapter, we take things further by looking in detail at the way we can manipulate the information in a `DataReader` and `DataSet` and store the results back to the data source.

❑ **Chapter 10 – ASP.NET Server Controls**: This chapter explains how ASP.NET server controls derive their properties and methods from the various classes and objects that make up the .NET Framework. It explains the syntax required to make their functionality available along with a look at the benefits that these controls can give. We also start to create the Wrox United application case study that is used throughout the rest of the book.

❑ **Chapter 11 – Users and Applications**: This chapter deals mainly with the process of tracking users across pages. We look at the objects that ASP.NET uses to enable this. We also tie this into our case study by creating the facility for adding valid email addresses and passwords to a site via an admin interface, and then we play the part of one of those users logging in and viewing pages.

❏ **Chapter 12 – Reusable Code for ASP.NET**: Here we consider the great benefits that can be achieved by encapsulating our code to make it more maintainable. Firstly, we cover the idea of user controls designed to store sections of your ASP.NET code that are repeated on multiple pages of your site. Then we go on to consider the idea of code-behind, where the `<script>` block of our ASP.NET code is placed in its own file in order to separate the page logic from its presentation.

❏ **Chapter 13 – .NET Assemblies and Custom Controls**: We continue the ideas of the previous chapter here. We cover how to compile a .NET assembly and use it from within our ASP.NET page, as well as how to encapsulate our business logic into a component that can be reused on other projects.

❏ **Chapter 14 – Debugging and Error Handling**: No matter how careful you are, things can always go wrong within your code. This chapter explains the steps you can take to minimize errors and how to recover when things go wrong.

❏ **Chapter 15 – Configuration and Optimization**: We start by explaining how ASP.NET applications can be managed from a series of XML configuration files, and then our discussion takes a more general turn as we consider the many ways to streamline and speed-up your ASP.NET applications.

❏ **Chapter 16 – Web Services**: You learn how to expose functionality from your Web site to others as a Web service. We then discuss how this functionality can be discovered by other users of the Web, and the form that the data exchange takes.

❏ **Chapter 17 – ASP.NET Security**: We conclude the book with a quick overview of some simple precautions that you can take using forms authentication and authorization to safeguard your ASP.NET pages. You can use this to ensure that they're only accessed by authorized users in the way that you want them to be accessed.

What Do You Need to Use This Book?

The only prerequisite for this book is to have a machine with the .NET Framework installed upon it. This means that you'll need to be running Windows 2000 Professional or Server, Windows XP (either Professional or Home edition), or Windows 2003 Server.

The .NET Framework itself is available as a free download from http://www.asp.net/ and http://www.gotdotnet.com. This download is known as the *.NET Framework Redistributable* and its approximate size is 20MB. It includes everything you need to run any .NET application.

Also available is another complementary free download, which might be useful to you throughout the book, although not essential. This is the .NET Framework SDK (Software Development Kit) and it contains samples and tutorials that you can refer to in order to learn more about .NET, as well as some useful tools, some of which we make use of in the book. However it doesn't include the .NET Framework itself and its size is a rather bulky 130MB.

This book is designed with Web Matrix in mind, so we strongly suggest that you download this as well. Web Matrix is a free download also available from http://www.asp.net. It will provide you with a Web server capable of running ASP.NET if you haven't already got one. However, while this book has been designed with Web Matrix in mind, you will find that all of the examples can be created, run, and understood using *any* simple text editor such as Notepad, even though the instructions in this book are geared to the point of view of someone who is running Web Matrix. You do not need Visual Studio .NET in order to use this book.

Conventions

To help you get the most from the text and keep track of what's happening, we've used a number of conventions throughout the book.

> **Boxes like this one hold important, not-to-be forgotten information that is directly relevant to the surrounding text.**

While this background style is used for asides to the current discussion.

As for styles in the text:

- ❑ When we introduce them, we *italicize* important words
- ❑ We show filenames and code within the text like so: `persistence.properties`
- ❑ We present code in different ways:

```
The Code Foreground style shows new, important, pertinent code. We indent
            the 2nd line to show you should enter both lines as one line.
```

```
The Code Background style shows code that's less important in the present
            context, or has been shown before.
```

Occasionally, code that needs to be placed all on one line is split over two because of the layout of the book, as shown in the preceding highlighted code. However, make sure you type it all on one line.

Source Code

As you work through the examples in this book, you may choose either to type in all the code manually or to use the source code files that accompany the book. All of the source code used in this book is available for download at http://www.wrox.com. Once at the site, simply locate the book's title (either by using the Search box or by using one of the title lists) and click the Download Code link on the book's detail page to obtain all the source code for the book. Because many books have similar titles, you may find it easiest to search by ISBN, which for this book is 0764557084. Once you download the code, just decompress it with your favorite compression tool. Alternately, you can go to the main Wrox code download page at http://www.wrox.com/dynamic/books/download.aspx to see the code available for this book and all other Wrox books.

Errata

We make every effort to ensure that there are no errors in the text or in the code. However, no one is perfect, and mistakes do occur. If you find an error in one of our books, like a spelling mistake or faulty piece of code, we would be very grateful for your feedback. By sending in errata you may save another reader hours of frustration, and you will be helping us provide even higher quality information.

To find the errata page for this book, go to http://www.wrox.com and locate the title using the Search box or one of the title lists. Then, on the book details page, click the View Errata link. On this page, you can view all errata that has been submitted for this book and posted by Wrox editors. A complete book list including links to each book's errata is also available at www.wrox.com/misc-pages/booklist.shtml.

If you don't spot your error on the View Errata page, go to www.wrox.com/contact/techsupport.shtml and complete the form there to send us the error you have found. We'll check the information and, if appropriate, post a message to the book's errata page and fix the problem in subsequent editions of the book.

p2p.wrox.com

For author and peer discussion, join the P2P forums at p2p.wrox.com. The forums are a Web-based system for you to post messages relating to Wrox books and related technologies and interact with other readers and technology users. The forums offer a subscription feature to email you about topics of your interest when new posts are made to the forums. Wrox authors, editors other industry experts, and your fellow readers are present on these forums.

At http://p2p.wrox.com/ you will find a number of different forums that will help you not only as you read this book, but also as you develop your own applications. You can read messages in the forums without joining P2P but in order to post your own messages, you must join the forum.

To join the forums:

1. Go to p2p.wrox.com and click the Register link

2. Read the terms of use and click Agree

3. Complete the required information to join as well as any optional information you wish to provide and click Submit

4. You will receive an email with information describing how to verify your account and complete the joining process

Once you have joined, you can post new messages and respond to messages other users' post. You can read messages at any time on the Web. If you would like to have new messages from a particular forum emailed to you, click the Subscribe to this Forum icon by the forum name in the forum listing.

For more information about how to use the Wrox P2P, be sure to read the P2P FAQs; they answer questions about how the forum software works as well as many common questions specific to P2P and Wrox books. To read the FAQs, click the FAQ link on any P2P page.

Getting Started with ASP.NET

ASP.NET is a powerful and flexible technology for creating dynamic Web pages. It's a convergence of two major Microsoft technologies, *Active Server Pages* (*ASP*) and the .NET Framework. Active Server Pages, or ASP (or *classic* ASP as it's often referred to), is a relative old-timer on the Web computing circuit and has provided a sturdy, powerful, and effective way of building dynamic Web pages for seven years or so now. The .NET Framework, on the other hand, is a whole suite of technologies designed by Microsoft with the aim of revolutionizing the way in which all program development takes place and the way companies carry out business. ASP.NET is a way of creating dynamic Web pages while making use of the innovations present in the .NET Framework.

The first important thing to know about ASP.NET is that you don't need any ASP skills to learn it. All you need is a little HTML knowledge for building Web pages. In fact, knowing ASP could be a disadvantage in some ways because you may have to unlearn some of the principles you followed earlier. ASP.NET allows you to build dynamic Web pages and tailors the HTML output to whatever browser you're using. It also comes with a great set of reusable, predefined, and ready to use controls for your ASP.NET projects. These reduce the amount of code you have to write, so you can be more productive while programming.

So what can you do with ASP.NET? It may be easier to list what you can't, as that is arguably shorter! One of the most eye-catching things about ASP.NET is the way you can use any programming language based on the .NET Framework, such as C#, JScript.NET, or VB.NET to create your Web applications. Within these applications, ASP.NET allows you to customize pages for a particular user and makes it simpler to keep track of a particular user's details as they move around.

ASP.NET makes storing information to a database or self-describing XML document faster and easier. You can alter the layout of the page using a free Web page editor – Web Matrix – designed to be used with ASP.NET, rather than positioning everything manually within code, and even alter the contents of files on your machine, if you have the correct permissions.

In addition, you can use bits and pieces of other applications without downloading the whole application. For example, you can access a zip code verifier that is part of another Web site's features without having to download the whole application or even giving your users the impression that they've left your site (*Chapter 16* will cover Web services as well as accessing specific features of your application via the Web). With ASP.NET, the applications that you create are only limited by your imagination.

This chapter will cover the installation process of ASP.NET, Web Matrix, and the .NET Framework. Let's start with a quick introduction to the world of Web servers, dynamic Web pages, and a little bit about what ASP.NET is. This will help accomplish the main aim of this chapter – to get you running a fully functional Web server with a fully functional ASP.NET installation. We will create a short ASP.NET test page to check that both the Web server and ASP.NET are working as intended. We'll also look at some of the most common pitfalls encountered, just in case things don't go as planned!

The topics discussed in this chapter are:

- ❑   Static Web pages
- ❑   Dynamic Web pages
- ❑   What is ASP.NET?
- ❑   Installing the .NET Framework
- ❑   Installing Web Matrix
- ❑   Testing and troubleshooting your installation

What Is a Static Web Page?

If you surf the Web, you'll see many *static* Web pages. Essentially, this type of Web page consists of some HTML code typed directly into a text or Web page editor and saved as an .htm or .html file. Thus, the author of the page has already determined the exact content of the page in HTML at some time before any user visits the page.

Static Web pages are often easy to spot; sometimes you can pick them out by just looking at the content of the page. The content (text, images, hyperlinks, and so on) and appearance of static Web pages is *always* the same – regardless of *who* visits the page, or *how* and *when* they arrive at the page, or any other factor.

For example, you can create a page called welcome.htm for your Web site, by writing some simple HTML like this:

```
<html>
<head><title>A Welcome Message</title></head>
<body>
  <h1>Welcome</h1>
  Welcome to our humble website. Please feel free to view our
```

```
    <a HREF="contents.htm">list of contents</a>.
    <br><br>
    If you have any difficulties, you can
    <a href="mailto:webmaster@wrox.com">send email to the webmaster</a>.
</body>
</html>
```

Whenever a client comes to your site and views this page, it will look like the screenshot depicted in Figure 1-1:

Figure 1-1

The content of the page was determined *before* the request to view the page was made – in fact, it was determined at the time the Webmaster saved the .htm file to disk.

How Are Static Web Pages Served?

Let's think for a moment about how a static, pure HTML page finds its way to a client browser (the process is depicted in Figure 1-2):

1. A Web author writes a page using only HTML and saves it within an .htm file on the Web server

2. Sometime later, a user types a *page request* (URL) into a browser, and the request passes from the browser to the Web server

3. The Web server locates the .htm page and converts it to an HTML stream

4. The Web server sends the HTML stream back across the network to the browser

5. The browser processes the HTML and displays the page

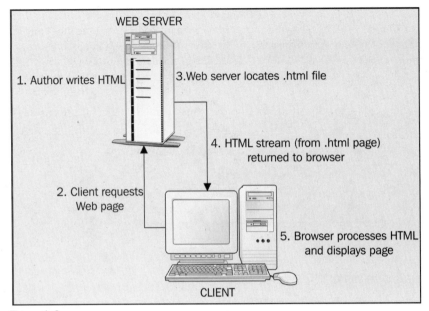

Figure 1-2

Static, pure-HTML files like `welcome.htm` make perfectly serviceable Web pages. You can even spruce up the presentation and usability of such pages by adding more HTML to alter fonts and colors. However, there are limitations with what you can achieve with pure-HTML pages, because their content is completely determined before the page is requested. There's no facility for user interaction or dynamic responses (even simple objects like forms and buttons require more than just HTML to make them work).

Limitations of Static Web Pages

Static Web pages limit you in several ways. For example, suppose you want to enhance your Welcome page so that it displays the current time or a special personalized message for each user. These are simple alterations, but they are impossible to achieve using HTML alone. If you're not convinced, try writing HTML for a Web page that displays the current time as shown in Figure 1-3:

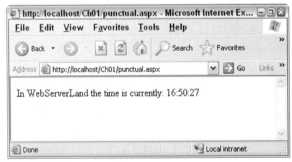

Figure 1-3

As you type in the HTML, you'll soon realize the problem – you know that the user will request the page sometime, but you don't know *what time* they will do it! Hard-coding the time into your HTML will result in a page that always shows the same time (that will almost always be wrong). In other words, you're trying to write pure HTML for a Web page that displays the time, but you can't be sure of the *exact* time that the Web page should display until the time the page is requested. This can't be done using HTML alone.

HTML offers no features for personalizing your Web pages; the same Web page is served to every user. There's also no security with HTML; the code is there for everybody to view, and there's nothing to stop you from copying somebody else's HTML code and using it in your own Web page. Static pages can be very fast, as quick as copying a small file over a network, but they cannot provide any *dynamic* features.

Since you can't create this page by saving hard-coded HTML into a file *before* the page is requested, what you need is a way to generate the HTML *after* the page is requested. There are two ways of doing this; we'll look at both of them in this chapter. However, before going any further let's make sure everybody is up to speed on the terminology we've introduced here.

What Is a Web Server?

Web servers are software that manage Web pages and make them available to client browsers – via a local network or over the Internet. In the case of the Internet, the Web server and browser are usually on two different machines, possibly many miles apart. However, in a local situation you can set up a machine that runs the Web server software, and then use a browser on the same machine to look at its Web pages.

It makes no difference whether you access a remote Web server (a Web server on a different machine from your browser) or a local one (Web server and browser on the same machine), since the Web server's function – to make Web pages available to all - remains unchanged. It may be that you are the only person with access to your own machine nevertheless the principles remain the same.

While there are many Web servers available (the common ones being Apache, *Internet Information Services* (IIS), and *iplanet Enterprise Server*) we're only going to talk about two in this book, IIS and *Web Matrix*, both of which are supplied by Microsoft. Only these Web servers run ASP.NET.

IIS

IIS Web server comes bundled with Windows 2000, Windows XP Professional, and Windows 2003 Server. IIS version 5.0 comes with Windows 2000, IIS version 5.1 with Windows XP Professional, and IIS version 6.0 with Windows 2003. However, there is little to distinguish between the different versions of IIS, so we shall treat them as the same product.

Web Matrix

Web Matrix is a free Web page editor tailored specifically for the creation of ASP.NET pages. It came late to the party as ASP.NET had already been out for a little while before Microsoft decided to release a free Web page editor to accompany it. Actually, Web Matrix wasn't exactly a new product – more an inspired resurrection of an old but not quite forgotten product for editing Web pages, namely *Visual Interdev*. While Web Matrix is quite different from Visual Interdev, there are enough similarities for people familiar with Interdev to recognize them.

However, to be able to test Web pages you also need something to run them on, so supplied with Web Matrix is an integrated Web server. This is ideal as several Windows systems aren't capable of running IIS, and until Web Matrix was released, it wasn't possible to run ASP.NET on operating systems such as Windows XP Home Edition. We have used Web Matrix for testing of Web pages throughout the book, and occasionally made use of its automatic Web page creation facilities as well – although most of the time we have created the code in the old-fashioned way, by hand.

You will learn about installing Web Matrix shortly (see *Appendix B*); however, first let's take a look at the Web server's role in creating dynamic Web pages.

How Are Dynamic Web Pages Served?

To fully understand the nature of dynamic Web pages, let's first understand what you can and can't do with a static Web page. In this book, you're only going to create dynamic Web pages on the server-side, because that's where ASP.NET resides. However, it will aid your understanding of the process to look at how content is served on the client-side because the underlying principles are similar and will give you a better overview of how Web page content is sent to the browser.

Client-Side Dynamic Web Pages

In the client-side model, modules (or plug-ins) attached to the browser do all the work of creating dynamic pages. The HTML code is typically sent to the browser along with a separate file containing a set of instructions, which is referenced from within the HTML page. However, it is also quite common to find these instructions intermingled with HTML code. The browser then uses them to generate pure HTML for the page when the user requests the page – in other words, the page is generated *dynamically* on request. This produces an HTML page, which is sent back from the plug-in to the browser.

In this model, the set of five steps that we looked at in the static pages section now becomes a set of six as depicted in Figure 1-4:

1. A Web author writes a set of instructions for creating HTML and saves it within an .htm file. The author also writes a set of instructions in a different language. This might be contained within the .htm file or within a separate file.

2. Sometime later, a user types a page request into the browser, and the request is passed from the browser to the Web server.

3. The Web server locates the .htm page and possibly a second file that contains the instructions.

4. The Web server sends both the newly created HTML stream and instructions back across the network to the browser.

5. A module within the browser processes the instructions and returns it as HTML within the .htm page – only one page is returned, even if two were requested.

6. The HTML is then processed by the browser, which displays the page.

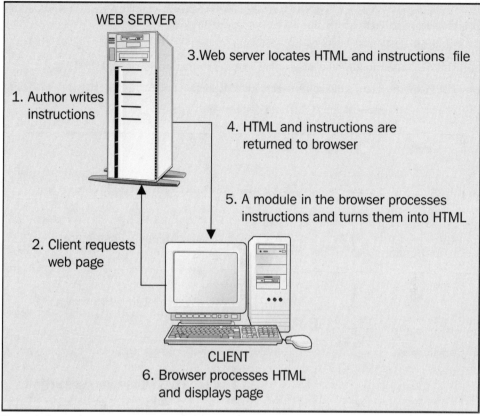

WEB SERVER

3. Web server locates HTML and instructions file

1. Author writes instructions

4. HTML and instructions are returned to browser

5. A module in the browser processes instructions and turns them into HTML

2. Client requests web page

CLIENT
6. Browser processes HTML and displays page

Figure 1-4

Client-side technologies have fallen out of favor in recent times as they take a long time to download, especially if you have to download several pages in a row that use them. A second drawback is that since each browser interprets client-side scripting code differently, you have no way of guaranteeing that all browsers will interpret and execute the code in the same way. Another drawback is the problem associated with writing client-side code that uses server-side resources such as databases, because it is interpreted at client-side. In addition, client-side scripting code isn't secure and can be easily viewed with the View I Source Code option on any browser, which is also undesirable.

Server-Side Dynamic Web Pages

With the server-side model, the HTML source is sent to the Web server with an extra set of instructions (that can be intermingled or sent separately). This set of instructions is again used to generate HTML for the page at the time the user requests the page. Once again, the page is generated dynamically upon request. The set of five steps once more becomes one with six steps, as depicted in Figure 1-5:

1.   A Web author writes a set of instructions for creating HTML and saves these instructions within a file.

2. Sometime later, a user types a page request into the browser, and the request is passed from the browser to the Web server.

3. The Web server locates the file of instructions.

4. The Web server follows the instructions in order to create a stream of HTML.

5. The Web server sends the newly created HTML stream back across the network to the browser.

6. The browser processes the HTML and displays the page.

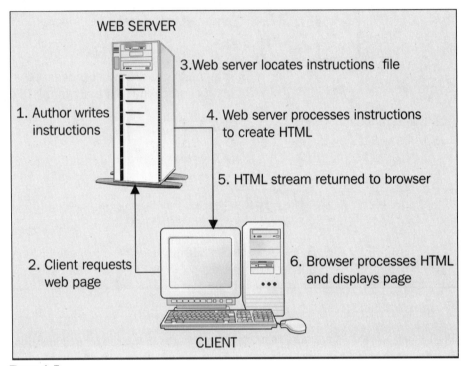

Figure 1-5

This time, there is a subtle twist regarding where the instructions are processed. The entire processing takes place on the server *before* the page is sent back to the browser. One of the key advantages this has over the client-side model is that only the HTML is sent to the browser. This means that the original page code is hidden away on the server, and you can safely assume that most browsers should be able to at least have a go at displaying it.

ASP.NET does its processing on the server-side.

While neither client-side nor server-side technologies add much in the way of complexities to the normal process for serving a static Web page (Step 5 on the client, or Step 4 on the server), this single step is crucial. Here, the HTML that defines the Web page is not generated until after the Web page has been requested. For example, you can use either technique to write a set of instructions for creating a page that displays the current time:

```
<html>
<head><title>The Punctual Web Server</title></head>
<body>
  <h1>Welcome</h1>
  In Webserverland, the time is exactly
  <INSTRUCTION: write HTML to display the current time>
</body>
</html>
```

In this case, you can compose most of the page using pure HTML. It's just that you can't hard-code the current time. Instead, you write a special code (that would replace the highlighted line here) that instructs the Web server to generate that bit of HTML during Step 5 on the client, or Step 4 on the server, at the time the page is requested. Let's return to this example later in the chapter, and see how to write the highlighted instruction using ASP.NET.

Server-side technologies are installed on the Web server and so the pages are run on the server. With client-side technologies, the Web page is run on the browser. Consequently, before the server-script can be sent back to the browser, the Web server must first translate it into HTML. The browser doesn't understand server-side code and therefore will never get to see any.

What Is ASP.NET?

The original definition of ASP.NET, right at the start of the chapter, portrayed ASP.NET as a powerful and flexible technology for creating dynamic Web pages, and this still holds true. However, as you now know, it isn't the only way to deliver dynamic Web pages, so let's refine our definition a little so it reads as follows:

> ASP.NET is a powerful and flexible *server-side* technology for creating dynamic Web pages.

Secondly, ASP.NET is only one of a set of technologies that comprise the *.NET Framework*. For now, you can think of this as a giant toolkit for creating all sorts of applications, and in particular, for creating applications on the Web. When you install ASP.NET, you will also install the .NET Framework at the same time. You will use bits and pieces of the .NET Framework throughout this book. In fact, you can also use the old versions of ASP with the .NET Framework, so why are we not using that instead?

How Does ASP.NET Differ from ASP?

ASP is restricted to using scripting languages, mainly JavaScript or VBScript (although it can be any scripting language supported by the Windows system). Scripting languages are like cut-down or junior versions of full programming languages in that they aren't as powerful and don't support all the features of full programming languages. In addition, when you add ASP code to your pages, you do it in the same way as you would do client-side script, and this leads to problems such as messy coding and restricted functionality.

ASP.NET has no such problems. It allows you to use a far greater selection of full programming languages and fully utilize the rich potential of the .NET Framework. It helps you create faster, more reliable, dynamic Web pages with any of the programming languages supported by the .NET Framework. Typical languages supported natively are C#, VB .NET and JScript.NET (a new version of Jscript). On top of this, it is expected that third party developers will create versions of Perl, Python, and many others to work in ASP.NET.

Secondly, ASP.NET comes with a far greater set of controls that you can place on a page without any extra ASP.NET coding. With classic ASP, programmers tended to rely on six objects, such as Request and Response to do everything and a couple of extra components that came with ASP. With ASP.NET, things are more *jargon free*. If you want to put a button on your page, you put an ASP.NET *Button control* on your page, and if you want a text box, you place an ASP.NET *TextBox control*. ASP.NET comes with a rich set of controls that can be applied to many common development scenarios.

A third and final reason is the separation of your ASP.NET code from your HTML. It's a commonly cited reason, if not always a well-explained one. Designers and developers play two very different roles in Web development. For instance, a developer could program a lottery number generator, but probably couldn't design a logo for a company. It makes sense to keep these two disciplines separate.

However, in ASP they aren't separate. The ASP code is sprinkled liberally between the HTML lines, like nuts over an ice cream sundae. That might be fine, unless you happen to be allergic to nuts. Now stretching this allegory a bit, it's quite common for designers to need to tinker with the actual HTML code on a Web site, but how can they alter it with confidence, if it's totally interspersed with the ASP code? In ASP.NET, you can keep the ASP code and HTML in separate files, making both the developer and the designer's life much simpler.

Using C# with ASP.NET

ASP.NET has been described as a *technology* and *not a language*, and this is an important distinction! ASP.NET pages can be made from one of many languages. However, you are not expected to know many different languages, nor are we going to teach them to you. This book uses just one language, C#, to demonstrate ASP.NET. We've chosen C# as it's arguably the most concise, and it can do just about anything that the other .NET languages can. Lastly and most importantly, C# comes free with ASP.NET – so when you install ASP.NET you get C# as well!

At this stage you may be thinking, "Hang on, I've got to figure out C#, then I've got to get a handle on ASP.NET – that sounds like an awful lot to learn." Don't worry; you won't be learning two languages. ASP.NET, as we said right from the beginning, is not a language – it is a technology. This technology is accessible via a programming language. What we're going to be doing is teaching you ASP.NET features as we teach you C#. In other words, you will be creating your Web pages using C# and using ASP.NET to drive it. However, before you rush out and get a C# book instead, remember that this book will approach the language from the angle of creating dynamic Web pages only.

> **ASP.NET is a server-side technology that lets you use fully fledged programming languages to create your Web pages.**

I'm Still Confused about ASP, ASP.NET, and C#

It's really important to get these terms separate and distinct in your mind, so before we move on to actually installing and running ASP.NET, let's go back and redefine them just to make sure:

❑ **ASP**: A server-side technology for creating dynamic Web pages that only lets you use scripting languages

❑ **ASP.NET**: A server-side technology for creating dynamic Web pages that lets you use any full-fledged programming language supported by .NET

❑ **C#**: This book's chosen programming language for writing code in ASP.NET

Now it's time to get it all installed!

The Installation Process

You're going to spend a fair amount of time on the installation process of ASP.NET, because it isn't as straightforward as ASP. Remember, if you don't get it right then you won't be able to continue to *Chapter 2* of this book!

The installation process is done in three stages:

❑ Installation of the prerequisites for .NET

❑ Installation of the .NET Framework 1.1

❑ Installation of Web Matrix (and the Web server)

Before starting the installation process let's talk about the operating system you have, because this affects some aspects of the process.

Which Operating System Do You Have?

While writing this book, we installed Web Matrix and used the server that comes with it to test code. However, Windows 2000 and Windows XP Professional already come with a Web server – IIS. You can use IIS to run ASP.NET pages on just as easily as Web Matrix's Web Server can, and you will get exactly the same results. However, we recommend that you use Web Matrix to test the examples in this book.

If you have Windows XP Home edition, you have no choice but to install Web Matrix, because it does not come with a Web server. If you have an older operating system such as Windows ME or Windows 98 then you cannot use ASP.NET or Web Matrix and will have to upgrade. Despite initial claims from Microsoft about backwards compatibility of the .NET Framework with systems as far back as Windows 95 made in the early days of the .NET Framework's beta program, the list of supported operating systems that can run ASP.NET and .NET Framework is as follows:

Supports all of the .NET Framework except Microsoft ASP.NET	Supports the entire .NET Framework	Supports Web Matrix
Windows 98	Windows 2000 (all versions – no Service Packs required)	Windows 2000
Windows 98 SE	Windows XP Professional	Windows 2003
Windows ME	Windows 2003	Windows XP Professional and Home Edition
Windows NT 4.0 (all versions – Service Pack 6a required)		
Windows XP Home Edition		

While Windows XP Home edition doesn't natively support ASP.NET, it does support Web Matrix. However, Windows 98/Windows ME do not support Web Matrix and while in theory they could both run it, we have not tested this. We will *not* be covering the use of Web Matrix with these latter two systems in this book.

If you have an operating system that comes with IIS and wish to use that instead of Web Matrix, then you need to install IIS before you install ASP.NET. However, most will probably find it easier to install Web Matrix and use it even if you have IIS already installed. To use Web Matrix correctly you need to install it after you have installed ASP.NET. The next section assumes that you have chosen to install Web Matrix and will detail the installation process. You will start by installing the prerequisites for ASP.NET followed by the .NET Redistributable.

> *If you wish to install IIS as well as Web Matrix, then you will need to jump to Appendix E found at the end of this book, where there are complete instructions for the installation and testing of IIS. If you have either the Windows 2000 Server or Windows 2003 Server operating system, then the good news is that IIS is automatically installed as part of the operating system.*

Prerequisites for Installing ASP.NET

Anybody who is familiar with ASP might be used to ASP being installed automatically with the Web server, and thereby doing it all in one step. This is true – classic ASP is still installed with the Web server; however, ASP.NET is only available as a separate download. This means you will have to download ASP.NET from Microsoft's Web site or from a CD (if you have one), even if you already have IIS installed.

Before ASP.NET or the .NET Framework is used, you will need to install the *Microsoft Data Access Components* (*MDAC*) version 2.7 or later. This is a set of components that enable you to use ASP.NET to communicate with databases and display the contents of your database on a Web page. Without these components installed, you won't be able to run any of the database examples in this book. This will affect examples as early as *Chapter 2*, so please don't skip this stage!

MDAC is a small download (roughly 5 to 6 MB) available free from the Microsoft's site at http://www.microsoft.com/data. The most recent version at the time of writing is 2.8, although version 2.7 is also adequate for this book.

The MDAC installation is quite straightforward. Version 2.7 also comes as part of the Windows Component Update of the .Net Framework and the Windows XP Service Pack, so if you've installed these you won't need to install it again.

However, in case you haven't installed either of these, we'll run through it quickly just to make sure that everything is clear.

Try It Out   Installing MDAC 2.8

1. MDAC 2.8 comes as a single file `MDAC_typ.exe` that you will need to download. Run this file to begin the installation process.

2. After agreeing to the terms of the license, it will scan your hard drive for space. If there's enough space, you will get to a dialog from which you can begin the installation by clicking Finish as shown in Figure 1-6:

Figure 1-6

3. Then the installation process will continue without requiring further intervention, although you may have to reboot the system afterwards. Once MDAC is installed, you are ready to install ASP.NET.

Installing ASP.NET and the .NET Framework

Before you install ASP.NET, you need to know a couple of important things. The first is that there have been two full release versions of the .NET Framework – 1.0 and 1.1. ASP.NET is an integral part of the .NET Framework, and so ASP.NET 1.1 accompanies the .NET 1.1 Framework. If you have previously installed .NET 1.0, then installing .NET 1.1 won't automatically erase or upgrade your 1.0 installation.

The new Framework installs alongside the old version and you can run both. You need to be aware of this because unless you have previously created applications in 1.0, it's likely that you only need the most current version (1.1) and therefore you should probably remove the previous installation using Add/Remove Programs in the Windows Control Panel. This will avoid any hiccups that may arise when running both installations together.

The second point is that while there used to be two different types of .NET installation files available from Microsoft's http://www.asp.net site, there is now only one type. In version 1.0, there was a .NET redistributable file and a .NET Framework SDK. Both files contained ASP.NET, C#, and the .NET Framework. With version 1.1, only the *.NET Framework Redistributable* contains ASP.NET, and the SDK is entirely devoted to samples, examples, and documentation. As the SDK is a hefty 108MB, don't download it unless you really want to (although one example in chapter 16 requires a tool present in the SDK). The .NET Framework Redistributable download contains everything you need to run ASP.NET and the .NET Framework. There is no accompanying extra documentation or samples in the redistributable, but this book will take you through all the necessary areas.

Also, don't worry about replacing an existing classic ASP installation, since ASP.NET will be installed alongside ASP and they will both continue to work fine without any new settings.

The next section walks you through a typical installation of the .NET Framework Redistributable. The installation process is the same on all versions of Windows, so we're only going to detail the installation process on Windows XP Home edition. Although the wizard looks a bit different on other versions of Windows, it asks for exactly the same things.

Try It Out **Installing the .NET Framework Redistributable**

1. After the download is complete, click on the installation file (currently called `dotnetfx.exe`). You are asked to agree to the license agreement and confirm your intent and after a short interval, you are taken to the setup wizard as shown in Figure 1-7:

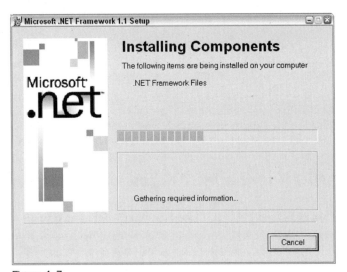

Figure 1-7

2. Check I agree to accept the License agreement and click on Install. ASP.NET will now install without further intervention.

3. You will be notified when the installation is complete. You can now move to the installation of Web Matrix.

Troubleshooting Hints and Tips

The installation process is straightforward, and works without errors on a majority of machines. However, sometimes the particular configuration of your machine will prevent it from installing. Unfortunately, this book can't cover all eventualities, but if the installation doesn't work on yours, you should check that you have enough hard disk space, as this is the most common cause of such problems. Also, try to ensure that the installation process isn't curtailed half way, as no installer is foolproof at removing all the different bits and pieces of the aborted install and this can cause problems when you try to reinstall. Additionally, check the list of newsgroups and resources later in this chapter; however, as far as I've seen, the .NET Framework rarely causes problems during installation.

> If you download the SDK as well, you must load the redistributable *first*, otherwise you will only be allowed to load the accompanying documentation and not the samples and example code.

Installing Web Matrix

You should have MDAC and .NET Framework installed on your machine so far. This leaves the last part of the equation, Web Matrix.

Web Matrix is an application development tool that you can use to create both ASP.NET and ASP pages. In previous editions of this book, we shied away from using WYSIWYG (what you see is what you get) development tools as they have a nasty tendency to add extra lines of code to your own code. For example, FrontPage, a WYSIWYG tool, allows you to create pages easily by dragging and dropping objects onto your Web page. However, it hides the HTML code away behind the interface, so you never get to understand any HTML code. Having a tool create ASP.NET code for you isn't the best way to go about learning ASP.NET – it would be trying to learn French and then getting a translator to speak all your lines for you!

This viewpoint hasn't changed, but there are some mitigating circumstances as already pointed out. The first is that without Web Matrix there is no way of running your ASP.NET pages on Windows XP Home Edition. The second is that there are circumstances under which automatically generated code can make your life a lot simpler, and it won't ultimately hinder your understanding of the way in which ASP.NET works.

Therefore, we are using Web Matrix within this book primarily for its Web serving capabilities and not its Web page creation abilities, although we will be using some of its wizards in certain appropriate situations.

You can download the latest version of Web Matrix from http://www.asp.net.

Try It Out Installing Web Matrix

1. Go to the http://www.asp.net site and download Web Matrix. Save the file to your local drive as
    shown in Figure 1-8:

Figure 1-8

2. Once the download is complete, go to Windows Explorer and run the file Web Matrix.msi. The
    wizard should start up as shown in Figure 1-9. If it doesn't, verify that you have downloaded
    the whole package, roughly 1339KB:

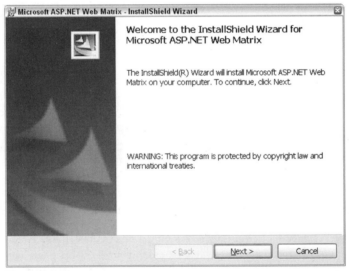

Figure 1-9

3. Click on Next and accept the terms of your license agreement. In the next dialog add your user
    name and organization details and choose whether the installation should be just for yourself or
    all users of the computer as shown in Figure 1-10:

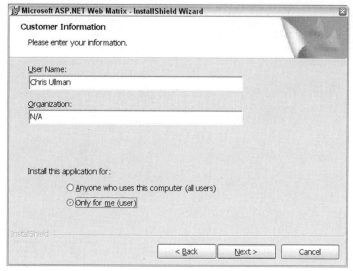

Figure 1-10

4. Click on Next again and leave the options for ASP.NET Web Matrix exactly as you find them, checking that you have enough free space on your hard drive as shown in Figure 1-11:

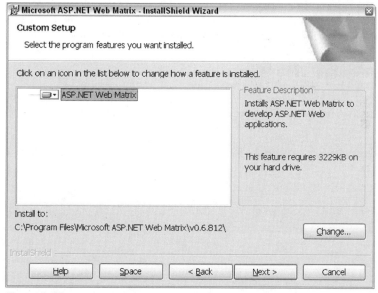

Figure 1-11

5. Click on Next and then click on Install in the final dialog to start the installation as shown in Figure 1-12:

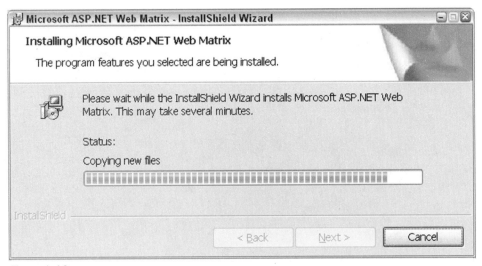

Figure 1-12

6. When Web Matrix has finished installing, you will be shown a final dialog confirming this.

Configuring Web Matrix to Run with .NET Framework 1.1

Before you can run Web Matrix, you need to configure it to use the 1.1 version of the Framework. If you have the 1.0 version of the Framework, it will automatically use that instead.

Try It Out Configuring Web Matrix

1. Open the `WebMatrix.exe.config` file that is located in your installation directory using Notepad. Typically, this will be found in `C:\Program Files\Microsoft ASP.NET WebMatrix\v0.6.812`.

2. Scroll down the file and add the following snippet immediately before the `<runtime>` section on line 18:

```
<startup>
   <supportedRuntime version="v1.1.4322" />
</startup>
```

3. After modification, the file should look like this:

```
<?xml version="1.0" encoding="utf-8" ?>
<configuration>
   ...
   </configSections>
   <startup>
     <supportedRuntime version="v1.1.4322" />
   </startup>
```

```
    <runtime>
    ...
</configuration>
```

4. Save the file.

5. Next you need to create a new text file with the name `WebServer.exe.config` and add the following code:

```xml
<?xml version="1.0" encoding="utf-8" ?>
<configuration>
  <startup>
     <supportedRuntime version="v1.1.4322" />
  </startup>
</configuration>
```

> If the file already exists then all you need do is insert the **<startup>** and **<supportedRuntime>** tags between the **<configSection>** and **<runtime>** tags as you did with **WebMatrix.exe.config**.

6. Save the file and when you run Web Matrix, the .NET Framework version should now be 1.1.x. Select the About ASP.NET Web Matrix... item from the Help menu. It should confirm this.

Running Web Matrix and Setting Up the Web Server

The next thing to do is to test the Web server to verify that it is working correctly and serving pages, as it should be. To do this, start Web Matrix and create a new folder, `BegASPNET11` (probably on your C: drive), where you can store files that you use throughout this book.

Try It Out **Starting the Web Server**

1. Go to `Program Files\Microsoft ASP.NET Web Matrix` and run Web Matrix. The screen that appears will resemble Figure 1-13:

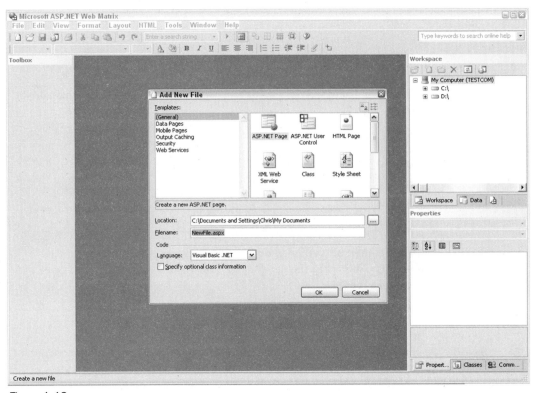

Figure 1-13

2. Change the Location so that it reads C:\BegASPNET11\and the Filename to test.aspx, and change the Language option from Visual Basic.NET to read C# as shown in Figure 1-14:

Figure 1-14

3. You are greeted with a blank page with four tabs at the foot of the page as shown in Figure 1-15:

Figure 1-15

4. Without adding any code to the dialog, click on the arrow icon (shown in Figure 1-16) which appears centrally in the toolbar above this dialog or press F5. You can also access this Start command from the View menu:

Figure 1-16

5. The dialog in Figure 1-17, will appear and enable you to start up the Web server:

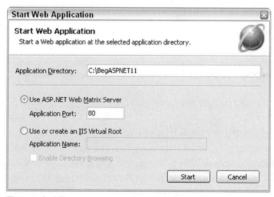

Figure 1-17

> If you have already installed IIS or another Web server that uses application port 80, then the application port may well be 8080 in this dialog and not 80; using 8080 is perfectly acceptable as well.

6. Click on Start and the browser will appear with a blank page, reading http://localhost/test.aspx. More importantly, a globe with a ring like the planet Saturn (incidently, Web Matrix was code-named Project Saturn) as shown in Figure 1-18, will appear in your taskbar:

Figure 1-18

7. This indicates that the Web server is working. Right-click on it and select Open in Web browser (Figure 1-19):

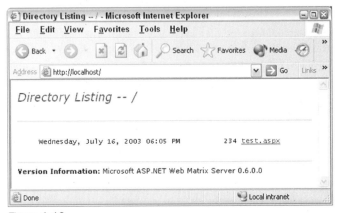

Figure 1-19

8. At this point, there should only be one file in the folder http://localhost as you've only just created it!

If you have IIS installed then you will see **http://localhost:8080** when this screen comes up. This means both Web Matrix and IIS are running simultaneously – IIS is accessible via **http://localhost** and Web Matrix via **http://localhost:8080**. From now on, you will need to add **:8080** to **localhost** if you intend to use Web Matrix as your Web server.

How It Works

You created a physical folder called BegASPNET11 and a *blank* file (it isn't literally blank as Web Matrix has auto-generated some HTML in it) called test.aspx that you placed inside your folder, and the browser was able to view this file. When you created the physical folder using Web Matrix, it automatically created a Web directory that can be accessed by a browser.

Normally when you create a new folder, it isn't automatically accessible to all and sundry on the Web. If this did happen, just about everyone would be able to see the contents of your hard drive, which would be very insecure. To allow access to files on the Web, you must place them in a specifically allotted area. Luckily, Web Matrix has done this task automatically for you!

There is something important to note about using browsers to access files as well. When you access files via the Web, you use the http:// prefix to indicate that you are looking for something on the Web. HTTP stands for *HyperText Transfer Protocol*, the protocol by which Web pages are transferred over the Internet.

The role of HTTP is discussed in the next chapter in greater depth. For now, just remember that when you use the http:// prefix you are also going to a Web server, whether on your own machine or on the Web. As ASP.NET is attached to the Web server, you must go via the Web server if you wish to use ASP.NET. For instance, you could type in C:\BegASPNET11\test.aspx into the address bar of the browser, and the browser will act like Windows Explorer, but this wouldn't let ASP.NET run your file, as you haven't gone via the Web server. When running any ASP.NET file, you must always go the http:// route.

You'll notice from the Figure 1-19 that the machine is called localhost. When you run the example on your own machine, it will also be called localhost. It is the term used to refer to your own PC. It tells the browser not to go onto the Web to search for a particular page.

This raises another question: what happens if you have two computers on the network and you wish to view ASP.NET files on one machine from the other? Simply typing in http://localhost will just go to the machine on which you're working. The answer is that each machine has a unique name. If you go to Control Panel and select the System Option, you'll find a dialog with several tabs. Choose the Computer Name tab to view a list of identifiers for your computer as shown in Figure 1-20:

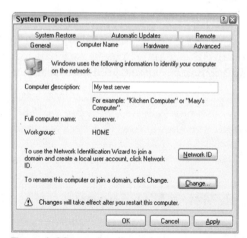

Figure 1-20

The full computer name is of particular interest, because you can use this to uniquely identify your computer on your network. My machine is named 'cuserver;' so instead of typing in http://localhost on my machine, I could have also typed http://cuserver for the same results. You can always use your machine name instead of localhost. This name is called an *alias*.

To recap, you created a folder called BegASPNET11. You can access this via the Web server by using http://localhost and can see the contents of this folder via the browser. On your own machine, you can also use your machine name to view the folder. Thus, the folder has two aliases on the Web server.

However, if you try to view your Web server via another machine, you receive an HTTP Error 403. If I logged on to another machine on my network and tried to view http://cuserver, I would receive an error as shown in Figure 1-21:

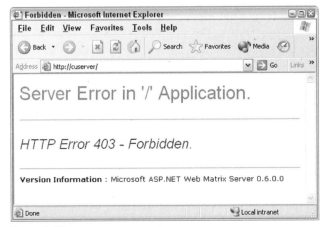

Figure 1-21

This is because the Web Matrix Web server is only intended to be used for testing purposes, and does not allow other machines on the network to access it. You can use it only to view ASP.NET files on the machine where it is installed. This has a big advantage in that it makes the server secure.

> **If you want to use a Web server that allows you to browse ASP.NET files from other machines on your network, you should use IIS. Check Appendix E for more details on how to do this.**

Troubleshooting the Web Matrix Web Server

Unfortunately, there is no guarantee that everything will install properly, but there is another tool at your disposal. Within the Web Matrix files is also a file WebServer.exe. You shouldn't need to run this file separately as it runs automatically when you start Web Matrix.exe. However, if there are any problems with the installation such as the port number that Web Matrix is trying to use (by default this is 80), being already taken by another application, then you can run this executable from the command prompt to try some other configurations.

If you run the `WebServer.exe` file from Explorer, you will get the following dialog as shown in Figure 1-22:

Figure 1-22

If you already have IIS installed, then you will probably find that you can't use the default port 80 and may need to change to another port. It should do this automatically, but to do this manually you can go to the command prompt and type in the following command from the folder in which Web Matrix was installed.

```
> WebServer /port:8080 /path:"C:\BegASPNET11"
```

You should get a popup from a planet icon confirming that you have started this instance of a Web server. If not, then it should display an error message that instructs you on what has been done incorrectly, and how it needs to be amended.

ASP.NET Test Example

Ok, you've now reached the crux of the chapter, getting your first ASP.NET page up and working!

Do you remember the 'punctual' Web server code, discussed earlier in the chapter, in which we wanted to write a Web page that displays the current time? Let's return to that example now. It's quite a simple bit of code, but should be more than enough to check that ASP.NET is working OK.

Try It Out   Your First ASP.NET Web Page

1.   Go to Web Matrix and close `test.aspx` if it is still open. Then select New File... from the File menu and in the dialog change the Location and Filename details as shown in Figure 1-23:

Figure 1-23

2. We've created another folder for this chapter's code, called `Ch01`. For each chapter, we will put the code in a corresponding folder/Web directory. Click on OK.

3. Next, select the Code tab and type in the following code, replacing the Insert code here line, taking special care to ensure that the case of each letter matches as well:

```
void Page_Load()
{
   time.Text=DateTime.Now.ToString();
}
```

4. Now select the HTML tab and add the following between the `<form>` tags:

```
   In WebServerLand the time is currently:
<asp:Label id="time" runat="server" />
```

5. Click on the arrow button or press F5 to view the page from within Web Matrix. An instance of Internet Explorer appears as shown in Figure 1-24:

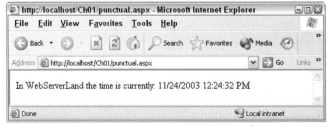

Figure 1-24

6. To view the page outside of Web Matrix, you need to start a browser and specify the URL (Uniform Resource Locator) of the ASP.NET page into the browser's Address box, as you do when browsing on the Internet. If you're using a single machine for both Web server and browser, specifying http://localhost/Ch01/punctual.aspx (or http://localhost:8080/Ch01/punctual.aspx) should be enough.

7. Notice that there is now a folder in the URL, because you added a folder in Web Matrix.

8. Click on the Refresh button of the browser and the displayed time will change as shown in Figure 1-25. In effect, the browser is showing a new and different instance of the same page:

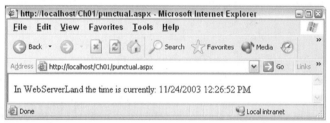

Figure 1-25

9. Now on your browser select View Source or something similar, depending on which browser you're using, to see the HTML source that was sent from the Web server to the browser. The result is shown in Figure 1-26. Notice that there is no ASP.NET code, and nothing before the first `<html>` tag. This is because what happens is the ASP.NET code is processed on the Web server. The Web server will then generate pure HTML from the ASP.NET. This HTML source is then sent back to the browser. (Here, you can see the HTML that was sent to the browser when the page was refreshed at 12.13:01.):

Figure 1-26

10. As mentioned before, you can expect this to work in any browser, because ASP.NET is processed on the Web server and not on the browser. If you have another browser available, give it a go!

How It Works

Easy, wasn't it? Even if you didn't get it to work first time, don't rush off to email technical support just yet – have a look at the next section *ASP.NET Troubleshooting*. Let's look at the ASP.NET code that makes this application tick.

There is only one block of ASP.NET code in the whole program, ignoring the server control placed under the HTML tab. It is as follows:

```
void Page_Load()
{
    time.Text=DateTime.Now.ToString();
}
```

If you ignore the `void Page_Load()` and `{ }` lines that are standard to many C# ASP.NET programs and which are discussed in *Chapter 3*, you're left with only one line:

```
time.Text=DateTime.Now.ToString();
```

This line tells the Web server to run the C# `DateTime.Now()` function on the Web server. The C# `DateTime.Now()` function returns the current time at the Web server. It returns the values of the `DateTime.Now()` function divided into hour, minute, and second values along with today's date. The result of this function is returned as part of the `<asp:Label>` control. This control is discussed in *Chapter 3*.

If the Web server and browser are on different machines, then the time returned by the Web server might not be the same as the time kept by the machine you're using to browse. For example, if this page is hosted on a machine in Los Angeles, then you can expect the page to show the local time in Los Angeles – even if you're browsing to the page from a machine in Cairo.

This example isn't wildly interactive or dynamic, but it illustrates that you can ask the Web server to do something for you and that the server can return the answer within the context of an HTML page. You can use this technique with things like HTML forms and other tools to build a more informative and responsive interface with the user.

ASP.NET Troubleshooting

If you had difficulty in executing the preceding example, perhaps you fell into one of the simple traps that commonly snare new ASP.NET programmers, but these can easily be rectified. This section will look at few common errors and reasons due to which your script might not run. If you had problems, this section may help you identify them. Common errors that you might come across include: 'Program Not Found', or the result of the ASP.NET page not getting displayed, or the browser trying to download the file that you have requested for.

You'll have this problem if you try to view the page as a local file on your hard drive with the following:

C:\BegASPNET1.1\Ch01\punctual.aspx

You'll also face this problem if you click on the file in Windows Explorer. If you have Microsoft FrontPage or Visual Studio .NET installed, then it will start up and attempt to help you to edit the code.

Otherwise, your browser may display a warning message, or (most likely) it will ask you which application you wish to use to open the ASPX file as depicted in Figure 1-27:

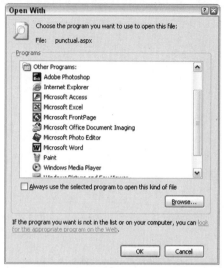

Figure 1-27

Older browsers may try to download the file. This is because you're trying to access the page in a way that doesn't cause the ASP.NET page to be requested from the Web server. Because of this, the ASP.NET code isn't processed and that's why you don't get the expected results. To call the Web page through the Web server and have the ASP.NET code processed, you need to reference the Web server in the URL. Depending on whether you're browsing to the server across a local network or across the Internet, the URL should look something like http://localhost/Ch01/punctual.aspx or http://www.distantserver.com/Ch01/punctual.aspx

Page Cannot Be Displayed: HTTP Error 403

If you get a HTTP Error 403 message as shown in Figure 1-28, it's probably because you don't have permission to execute the ASP.NET code contained within the page:

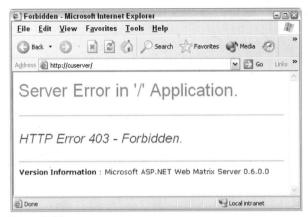

Figure 1-28

Recall that it isn't possible to view ASP.NET pages from a place other than the computer on which you have installed Web Matrix!

Page Cannot Be Found: HTTP Error 404

If you get this error message as shown in Figure 1-29, it means that the browser has managed to connect to the Web server successfully, but the Web server can't locate the page you asked for. This could be because you mistyped the URL at the browser prompt. In that case, you'll see a message as shown here. In this case, we have typed Ch02 instead of Ch01 in the URL:

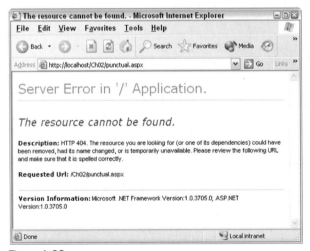

Figure 1-29

If you get this page, then you might have made the following errors:

❑　A simple typing error in the URL, such as http://localhost/BegASPNET/ch01/punctually.aspx

❑ A wrong directory name, like http://localhost/BegASPNET/punctual.aspx instead of http://localhost/ch01/punctual.aspx or http://localhost/ch01/punctual.aspx like we have above

❑ Including a directory separator (/) after the file name, like this http://localhost/ch01/punctual.aspx/

❑ Using the directory path in the URL rather than using the alias, such as http://chrisu//ch01/punctual.aspx

❑ Saving the page as .html or .htm, rather than as an .aspx

Web Page Unavailable While Offline

Very occasionally, you'll come across a message box as shown in Figure 1-30:

Figure 1-30

This happens because you've tried to request a page and you haven't currently got an active connection to the Internet. This is a misperception by the browser, unless your Web server isn't the same machine as the one on which you're working. It is trying to get onto the Internet to get your page when there is no connection, and it's failing to realize that the page you've requested is present on your local machine. One way of retrieving the page is to hit the Connect button in the dialog; but that's not the most satisfactory solution, since you might incur call charges if you are using dialup. Alternatively, you need to adjust the settings on your browser. In IE5 and IE6, select the File menu and uncheck the Work Offline option.

This could also happen if you're working on a network and using a proxy server to access the Internet. In this case, you need to bypass the proxy server or disable it for this page, as described earlier in the chapter. Alternatively, if you're using a modem and you don't need to connect, you can correct this misperception by changing the way that IE looks for pages. To do this, select the Tools | Connections option and select Never dial a connection.

I Just Get a Blank Page

If you see an empty page in your browser, it probably means that you saved your punctual.aspx page without entering any code into it or that you didn't remember to refresh the browser.

The Page Displays the Message But Not the Time

If the Web page displays the message 'In WebServerLand, the time is currently' but doesn't display the time, you might have mistyped the code. For example, you might have mistyped the name of the control:

```
time.Text=DateTime.Now.ToString();
```

and:

```
<asp:Label id="hour" runat="server" />
```

The name of the control (hour) must match the first word in the line of ASP.NET code; otherwise, the control won't be able to identify it.

I Get an Error Statement Citing a Server Error

If you get a message stating that the page cannot be displayed and citing a server error as shown in Figure 1-31, it implies that there is an error in the ASP.NET code itself:

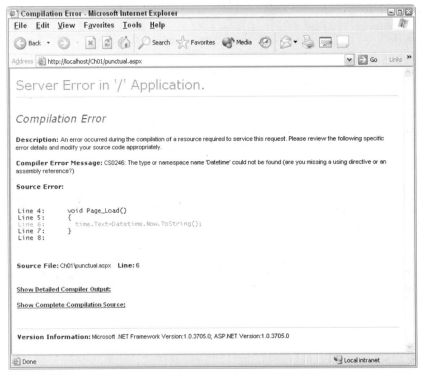

Figure 1-31

Usually, there's additional information provided with the message. For example, if you mistyped the case of the code, then you get the above error. This is because C# is recognizes a function called DateTime, but doesn't know one called Datetime. You have to be very precise when typing your code in. To verify that you haven't typed the code incorrectly, use the sample punctual.aspx page from the Wrox site at http://www.wrox.com.

I Have a Different Problem

If your problem isn't covered in the preceding sections, it's worth testing some of the sample ASP.NET pages that are supplied with the *QuickStart* tutorials at http://www.asp.net. They should help you to check that ASP.NET has actually installed properly. You can always uninstall and reinstall if necessary, although before you do this, rebooting your server might solve the problem.

You can get support from http://p2p.wrox.com, which is the Web site dedicated to support issues in this book. Alternatively, there are many Web sites dedicated to ASP and ASP.NET. In fact, you will find very few sites that focus on just one of the two technologies. Here are a few resources:

- ❏ http://www.asp.net
- ❏ http://www.asptoday.com
- ❏ http://www.asp101.com
- ❏ http://www.15seconds.com
- ❏ http://www.4guysfromrolla.com

There are many solutions, discussions, and tips on these pages, plus references to other related pages. Moreover, you can try the newsgroups available on www.asp.net such as Free For All.

By now, you should have successfully downloaded, set up, and installed both Web Matrix and ASP.NET, and got your first ASP.NET application up and running. If you've done all that, you can pat yourself on the back, make a cup of tea, and get ready to learn some of the principles behind ASP.NET in the next chapter.

Summary

This chapter started with a brief introduction to ASP.NET and dynamic Web pages in general and looked at some of the reasons you'd want to use a server-side technology for creating Web pages. You looked at some of the history behind dynamic Web pages, in the form of an overview of the other technologies. The next chapter will expand on this brief introduction to ASP.NET.

The bulk of the chapter was taken up by descriptions of the various installation processes. You will need a Web server (preferably Web Matrix), MDAC 2.7/2.8, and the .NET Framework Redistributable to be able to progress further with this book, so please don't be tempted to skip parts that might not have worked. We've listed plenty of resources that will help you get everything up and running.

The next chapter will explain in detail what ASP.NET does, what the .NET Framework is, and how the two work together.

Anatomy of an ASP.NET Page

In this chapter, we'll start by talking about the overall theory around .NET and ASP.NET. In the second half, we will get down to some coding. This chapter will not cover all the theory and won't explain every line of the examples, but at the end you will have some theoretical background about ASP.NET and a few working pages. These will provide a preliminary overview for ASP.NET that is covered in the remaining chapters in detail.

We will cover the following:

- ❑ A description of the .NET Framework and its purpose
- ❑ How ASP.NET fits into the .NET Framework
- ❑ Role of the *Common Language Runtime* (*CLR*)
- ❑ Core concepts of ASP.NET
- ❑ Some examples of ASP.NET and the .NET Framework in action

What Is .NET?

I recently attended one of Microsoft's .NET road shows, and between talks, one of the speakers was giving out free software to anyone in the audience who could answer one of several simple questions. He challenged the audience by asking them to define what they thought .NET was. Notably, in a room full of experienced developers, not a single hand was raised. He moved on quickly, and instead chose to ask what a 'delegate' in the C# language was, and was greeted with a much larger response, even though describing a delegate is a much more difficult task.

.NET is a catchall term that embraces Microsoft's core strategy, plans, and vision for the near future. At the heart of this strategy is the .NET Framework, which provides the core technology. ASP.NET is just one of the several components that are present in the Framework.

.NET is designed to help solve several fundamental problems faced by programmers:

❑ Reduces the hard work involved in building large, reliable applications

❑ Allows programmers to unify two kinds of architectures – applications that run locally on a machine and applications that are accessed over the Web

❑ Reduces overheads associated with programming frameworks – you don't need to write complex code with complicated languages to get an impressive performance out of .NET programs

❑ Allows programmers in different languages to work together on an application

❑ It has been designed with the view to accommodate various end-user tools, including desktops, PDAs, and cell phones

To sum it up, .NET provides an easier, and thus faster and cheaper way to get efficient programs into the hands of the users.

Since the aim of this book is to get you writing ASP.NET Web applications, we're not going to go into every detail of the Framework. In many cases, all you need to know is what its elements can do and what they need from you to achieve it. Some elements provide us with important functionality, and these will merit discussion. In this way, you'll gain not only a working knowledge of ASP.NET, but also a sense for how it fits in with the .NET Framework as a whole.

We can break down our discussion of the entire .NET Framework into several core concepts:

❑ **MS Intermediate Language (MSIL)**: All the code written in .NET is compiled into a more abstract, trimmed-down form before it is executed. A programmer can use any .NET language to write the code including Visual Basic (VB), C#, Jscript, and about 20 others. The result is then compiled to MSIL, the common language of .NET. This level of .NET operates without our interaction, and so, we haven't covered it in this book.

❑ **Common Language Runtime (CLR)**: This runtime is a complex system responsible for executing the MSIL code on the computer. It takes care of all the nitty-gritty tasks involved in talking to Windows and the *Internet Information Services* (*IIS*) server. This is also beyond the scope of this book.

❑ **.NET Framework class libraries**: These code libraries contain a mass of tremendously useful functionality, which we can very easily bolt onto our own applications to make complex tasks much more straightforward. We will explore these functions throughout the book.

❑ **.NET languages**: These are all the programming languages that conform to certain specific structural requirements as defined by the *Common Language Specification* (*CLS*) and can be compiled to MSIL. You can develop in any of the languages, such as C# or Visual Basic .NET, without any restrictions. This gives you the liberty to develop applications constructed from more than one of these languages. This book will discuss the application of C# to ASP.NET, and we will use only C# in all code examples.

❑ **ASP.NET**: This module of code extends the IIS so that it can implement the .NET Framework for Web pages. The chapters of this book cover almost all of the ASP.NET features.

❑ **Web services**: Web services are enabled by .NET, even though they are not a part of it. They are programs that can be accessed via the Web, and can be used within our applications. They can provide anything from news headlines, weather forecasts, and stock tickers to virus protection and operating system updates. *Chapter 16* discusses Web services in detail.

Before we go into detail, let's look at some fundamental code concepts and terminology.

From Your Code to Machine Code

Computers understand everything in terms of binary bits – sequences of ones and zeros that represent instructions and data – hence the enthusiastic use of *digital* to describe anything even vaguely related to computers. We refer to these binary instructions as *machine code*. Obviously, for most humans, it's difficult to remember even a simple binary sequence that prints "Good Morning" (let alone one that defines a sophisticated Web application). To overcome the problem, we use high-level programming languages that permit us to write code using English words.

Once we've written some code in a human-friendly language, we need to convert it into machine code. This process is called *compilation*. The compiler software translates the human-readable instructions into machine-readable instructions. Part of this compilation process involves coding information regarding the local environment into the compiled code, so that the machine code can make efficient use of all the computer resources available.

For many years, there's been a simple choice between two types of compilation that differ when it comes to compilation:

❑ **Pre-compiled code**: The code is compiled when we are done writing it and well before we need to use it. This makes for very fast execution as the compiler has the opportunity to spend time considering the full set of code and the machine it will run on. However, because pre-compiled code is for a specific machine, you are tied to using it on the same machine, or you need to set up another machine with the same system and resources that the code requires.

❑ **Interpreted code**: This code is compiled at the time of its execution (when the user requests the page). This is slower because we do a compilation for each request and the system doesn't have the chance to fully optimize the code we've written. However, the advantage is that the interpretation can adapt to the machine hosting the code.

So, developers get confused when selecting a language. They can either select slower interpreted code that is adapted to the machine, or the programmer can go with the faster pre-compiled code that does not take advantage of machine-specific benefits.

Introducing Two Intermediate Languages

.NET solves the problem by using a two-step process for compilation. When we write a program to run on the .NET Framework – generally using Visual Basic.NET or C# – we compile our human-readable code as we finish writing it. However, .NET's compilers are designed such that this only takes us halfway to the usual binary code that presents such problems of portability. .NET compiles our code into a special format, the MSIL. Some optimization can be done as part of this process, since the MSIL's structure doesn't have to be as easily human-readable as our original code. However, no machine-specific optimization is done. Thus, MSIL has the benefits of general optimization and of portability to any .NET server.

When we execute this page compiled to MSIL (when the user requests an ASP.NET page), we pass our code from MSIL to the CLR, another cornerstone of the .NET Framework. The CLR uses another compiler – the *JIT (Just-In-Time) compiler* – to compile to true machine code and make any last minute machine-specific optimizations to the program, so that it can run as quickly as possible on the local machine.

> **MSIL and the CLR together give us the best of both worlds: the structural optimization of pre-compiled code along with the portability of interpreted code.**

Most importantly, MSIL is not machine-specific, so we can execute it on any machine that has the CLR installed. In essence, once we've written and compiled some .NET code, we can copy it to any machine with the CLR installed and execute it there. While the CLR is currently only compatible with Windows (9x, NT, 2000, and XP versions), moves are already afoot to build versions for other operating systems. You can find more about one of those efforts by searching the Web for information on the *Mono Project*.

MSIL can be generated from any human-readable language that conforms to CLS. The big three are C#, VB.NET, and JScript.NET, but many more languages are now supported by MSIL compilers. We can therefore use all compliant languages *interchangeably* within our applications – once a set of files have been compiled to MSIL, they're all effectively written in the same language! This flexibility allows different teams to work on the same Web site in different languages.

Objects

In order to grasp how .NET works, you need to have a notion of what we mean when we talk about *objects*. Just about everything you come across within the .NET Framework is implemented as a software object – we can, in fact, describe .NET as an *object-oriented environment*. So what does that mean? Simply put, an object is a set of code (or data) that we develop or buy once and can easily reuse. An object is self-contained and offers a set of functions to the rest of your code. Writing code in objects and using pre-written objects has some important benefits:

- ❑ We avoid rewriting code for multiple uses.

- ❑ Objects allow us to buy functionality that may be beyond our ability or resources to develop.

- ❑ .NET objects are standardized, which means other programmers can easily discover and use an object's functionality.

- ❑ Objects can be written in any .NET-compliant language.

Thus, objects are a way to organize code so that programming is more efficient.

An object is a self-contained unit of functionality – almost like a miniature program that holds data (or code) to achieve specific tasks. Once an object is written, other code can access and manipulate the object in simple, well-defined ways. The *class definition* is the model object. We can create as many copies of the object as we need from this model. We only need to create one class definition (model object) for each particular task.

For example, consider a publishing company – there are many different jobs defined within the company, such as Manager, Editor, Proof Reader, and the Layout Assistant. Once we've established the basic jobs that an Editor needs to do (edit chapters, review chapters, send chapters to authors for rewrites), we could simply say, "Jim, please edit Chapter 2" and leave it up to him to carry out the job. We don't need to know all the details of how the Editor does this job. You could also phrase it differently and ask, "Jim, is the chapter edited yet?" and expect the Editor to give you a true or false response about the current state of the chapter.

This is essentially how objects make lives of programmers easier – in this instance, let's take the `Editor` class, which we use as a template to build an `Editor` instance called `Jim`. We can instruct the object to `Edit`, `Review`, or `Return To Author`. We can also enquire about its state, that is, whether its `EditComplete` value is set to `true` or `false`. We can create multiple copies of the `Editor` object as needed. For example, if we had three editors on books we could create three copies of the `Editor` object and name them `Jim`, `Jane`, and `Joe`. Each could handle their own project.

To sum it all up using this example, we can create as many objects as we need. We don't need to know *how* the `Jim` object edits, we can use a standard way of asking the `Editor` object to do its work or report to us, and the `Editor` object can be written in any language that is .NET compliant.

As said earlier, objects can be written or bought. Some come with the .NET Framework; Microsoft includes a group of objects called ADO.NET that can create a connection to a database and read values from tables. It would take many weeks for a programmer to write and troubleshoot similar code. Instead, we get it with ASP.NET and all we have to do is understand how to use it. As an exercise at the end of this chapter, we will be reading values from a database and writing them onto our ASP.NET Web pages.

The advantages of this type of programming are fairly obvious. First, we don't need to worry about how each object does its job, so we are free to focus on the big picture of our application. Second, we can rapidly create applications by building or buying objects and hooking them together in simple, well-defined ways. Once you understand how to use (and later, to write) objects, you will be able to produce more stable code in less time.

The .NET Base Classes

One feature of the .NET Framework that saves us from huge amounts of tedious coding is the *base class library*. This contains an enormous amount of code written by Microsoft that you can include in any of your programs. In order to take advantage of this code, you only have to know how to work with objects – there is no need to understand the inner workings of the code.

The base Framework classes cover a multitude of different functions. For instance, you'd expect to be able to display text, but what if you want to perform more specialized graphical operations, such as drawing a circle or a rectangle or adding an animated image to an ASP.NET page? These functions are

all provided in a number of base classes that are grouped together under a *namespace* called
`System.Drawing`.

> **Namespaces are used by .NET to group together classes in functionally similar
> groups. Namespaces are not unique to .NET and are found in many non-.NET
> languages as well.**

In terms of our earlier business analogy, this is equivalent to a departmental grouping. For example, all
the jobs directly involved with producing book content (Editor, Author Agent, and Project Manager) are
grouped within the Editorial namespace. Likewise, jobs involving the layout and printing of the physical
book (Layout Assistant, Cover Designer, Illustrator) would be classified within the Production
namespace.

To be able to use the classes contained within a namespace, you need to *import* the namespace first. We
can import these classes into our ASP.NET pages by simply adding a *directive* to the top of the file (before
any HTML and before the language tag). For example, to make use of all the classes defined in the
`System.Drawing` namespace, we just say:

```
<%@ Import Namespace= "System.Drawing" %>
```

This literally *directs* the Framework to apply a specific setting to the page as a whole; in this case, it
makes the classes in `System.Drawing` available to code in our page.

It is now possible to use the classes in `System.Drawing`, although you will need to reference this
namespace in front of each class name by indicating which class you want to use. So why does .NET do
this? Why can't you have access to all the classes you need, all of the time? The reason is to keep your
application small. The more you include in an application, the more bloated it becomes and the more
difficult it will be to understand, maintain, and use. It therefore, makes sense to include only the bits you
need to use. ASP.NET includes the most commonly used classes on every page by default.

*There are many varieties of .NET classes, from classes that help you in generating graphics to classes
that help simplify data access. We'll see some examples that rely on imported namespaces towards the
end of the chapter. After you've run them, try removing the import command and see the error messages
generated!*

The Class Browser

You might be wondering how to get a list of these predefined .NET classes. One great ASP.NET
application that you can use to view these classes is the .NET Framework *Class Browser*. This tool lists the
Framework classes defined on the IIS serving the page as shown in Figure 2-1. The Class Browser is
available as a part of the QuickStart tutorials that are provided along with the *.NET Framework SDK*. If
you have these installed, you'll be able to run it locally from:

http://localhost/quickstart/aspplus/samples/classbrowser/cs/classbrowser.aspx

*In case of a **Type not found** compiler error message, execute the setup procedure for QuickStart from the
`starthere.htm` (in the SDK's "version 1.1" dir). This automatically installs the required classes.*

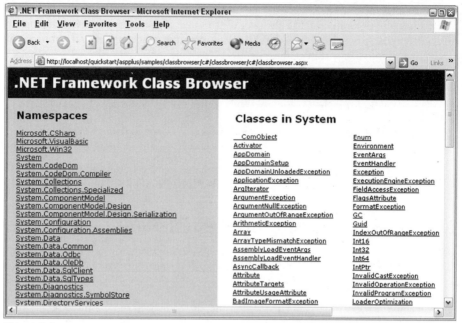

Figure 2-1

If you've only installed the *.NET Framework Redistributable,* then you won't have the Class Browser installed. It is possible, however, to access the class browser online at:

http://www.gotdotnet.com/quickstart/aspplus/samples/classbrowser/cs/classbrowser.aspx

This will list the System classes available on that site's Web server (the standard set of base classes under the System namespace). You won't be able to configure the browser application or browse any additional namespaces, such as custom namespaces or add-ins that you've installed on your server. Nevertheless, it should cover most of your needs. It really is a very handy tool for students, beginning programmers, and experienced developers alike. You'll certainly find the class browser useful in later chapters, as much of the book will be concerned with exploring .NET's various classes.

A form of the class browser is built into Web Matrix, as covered in Appendix B.

So, we have our three sections of .NET Framework: MSIL, the CLR, and the .NET language base classes. But where and how does ASP.NET fit into this model?

How ASP.NET Works

For most purposes, think of ASP.NET pages as normal HTML pages that have sections marked up for special consideration. When .NET is installed, the local IIS Web server is automatically configured to look out for files with the extension ASPX and to use the ASP.NET module (a file called aspnet_isapi.dll) to handle them.

Technically speaking, this module parses the contents of the ASPX file – it breaks them down into separate commands in order to establish the overall structure of our code. Having done this, it arranges the commands within a predefined class definition – not necessarily together and not necessarily in the order in which we wrote them. That class is then used to define a special ASP.NET Page object. One of the tasks this object performs is to generate a stream of HTML that can be sent back to IIS, and from there, back to the client. Simply put, when a user asks the IIS server to provide a page, the IIS server builds the page based on the text, HTML, and (most importantly) code on that page.

> We'll take a detailed look at various aspects of this process as we progress through the book – in particular, Chapter 7 will explore the Page object and discuss some of the things it can do for us.

For now though, we're more concerned with the immediate business of getting a page up and running. The first step is to learn to create pages that identify themselves to the Web server as ASP.NET pages.

Saving Your ASP.NET Files with an ASPX Suffix

In the last chapter, we defined an ASPX .NET page simply by saving some appropriate code in a file with an .aspx extension. This extension identifies the page as one to be processed by the ASP.NET module. Without it, IIS will just send the page to the user without executing the code.

Although you could use <script> tags in an .htm file, the code between them would not be interpreted as ASP.NET code. Instead, it will be sent to the browser for client-side execution, which is unlikely to work because the browser will only be expecting HTML and client-side script.

> Students and beginners frequently have a problem with the extension when using Notepad. They get .txt added to the extension so it looks like MyFile.aspx.txt. You can avoid this by setting the File type as All Files in the Save dialog box of Notepad. You can also change the file extension in Windows explorer after saving the file. This is not a problem when using Web Matrix because it is aware of proper extensions.

Inserting ASP.NET Code into Our Web Pages

If we place any kind of server-side code (not just ASP.NET code) within our Web page source files, we need to label it so that the server can identify it as server-side code and arrange for it to be handled correctly. There are three ways of placing ASP.NET code in your Web page:

❑ Inline code blocks

❑ Script tags

❑ Server controls

Inline code blocks (the <% %> delimiters) will seem familiar to the users of classic ASP. However, these are not the preferred technique in ASP.NET. The latter two techniques offer more robust performance and easily maintainable code.

The <script> Tags

The best way to identify ASP.NET code within the HTML and text of your pages are <script> tags with the runat attribute set to server. The default usage of the <script> tag is to enclose code to be executed on the browser (client-side), so if you're writing a server-side script, remember to specify `runat = "server"` with the double quotes.

As we discussed, ASP.NET itself is not a language, but a technology for creating dynamic pages. The technology allows us to use various programming languages within our pages. The default language for coding in ASP.NET is Visual Basic .NET. However, that is easily changed by using a `Page` directive at the top of the page:

```
<%@ Page language="C#" %>
```

To indicate a section of code, we can do the following (note the double quotes around `C#`):

```
<script language="C#" runat="server">
... C# statements go here ...
</script>
```

Since the `<%@ Page language>` tag specifies C# .NET as our language of choice, the `language` attribute of the `<script>` tag in the above example isn't essential and can be omitted. However, it serves to clarify which language we're using which makes it easier to maintain the code. The lines of code can go anywhere in the ASPX page as long as they are within `<script>` tags; in this book, we put code at the top of the page because that is how it is done by Web Matrix.

To define a page in a different language, Visual Basic for example, you can do the following:

```
<%@ Page language="VB" %>
<script language="VB" runat="server">
... Visual Basic statements go here ...
</script>
```

All code enclosed within the `<script>` element must be in the language specified. While you can have an application (multiple pages) with code in more than one language, it isn't physically possible to mix languages on one page.

Although we put code into a page, it isn't necessarily executed. Each block of code goes within a *declaration*, generally called a *function* or a *method* and indicated by the keyword `void`. A method is executed when some other code triggers it. It may be triggered once, many times, or not at all. We'll cover that idea in detail over the next few chapters.

A logical question arises: "What if we want some sort of trigger to run the code automatically as soon as a page is built for the first time?" In other words, what if we want some code to run regardless of what events may occur? When the page is created, the ASP.NET module executes any code that is written within one specific method named `Page_Load()`:

```
<script language="C#" runat="server">
  void Page_Load(source As Object, e As EventArgs)
  {
    ... Location for C#.NET code to be run when the page is started
  }
</script>
```

We won't go into detail explaining this format; suffice to say that when the page is loaded, the code block that we've labeled `Page_Load()` is triggered automatically. Any code we want to run when the page starts up should be located here.

Try It Out Inserting Server-Side (ASP.NET) Code

In this example, we're only concerned with how we insert code and not with how the ASP.NET code works, so the code is trivial. This example demonstrates how Web pages are affected by the placement of ASP.NET code.

1. Let's start with a file containing just HTML – no code for ASP to execute. Open Web Matrix and create a new ASPX page named `messageHTML.aspx` in your test directory. If you've followed the steps from *Chapter 1*, this will be `C:\BegASPNET11\Ch02\`. Go to All view, remove all existing code, and type in the following code:

```
<html>
<head>
    <title>Inserting ASP.NET code Example</title></head>
<body>
    Line1: First HTML Line<br />
    Line2: Second HTML Line<br />
    Line3: Third HTML Line<br />
</body>
</html>
```

2. Click on the arrow icon to run `messageHTML.aspx` from Web Matrix or press the F5 key. An instance of Internet Explorer appears as shown in Figure 2-2:

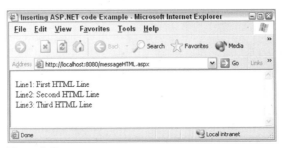

Figure 2-2

3. Now go back to Web Matrix and place the following code at the top of the page in the All view:

```
<%@ Page Language="C#" debug="true"%>
<script runat="server">

    void Page_Load()
    {
        Response.Write ("First ASP.NET Line<br />");
        Response.Write ("Second ASP.NET Line<br />");
        Response.Write ("Third ASP.NET Line<br />");
    }
```

```
</script>
<html>
<head>
    <title>Inserting ASP.NET code Example</title>
</head>
<body>
    Line1: First HTML Line<br />
    Line2: Second HTML Line<br />
    Line3: Third HTML Line<br />
    <form runat="server">
        <!-- Insert content here -->
    </form>
</body>
</html>
```

The `<script language="C#" runat="server">` line is automatically generated by Web Matrix for every ASPX page that is created from the C# template, so we never have to put it in manually. Even if you delete it, it will automatically reappear! However, if you are using a text editor for you pages, you need to insert this line at the top of all your ASPX pages.

4. Run this file in your browser by typing in the following URL: http://localhost:8080/messageASPXtop.aspx. You should get a result similar to that shown in Figure 2-3. However, this time we can see the results from the ASP.NET code we just added above the HTML:

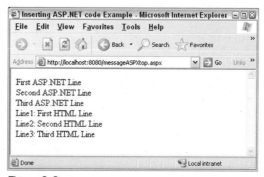

Figure 2-3

5. Return to your editor and save the file as `messageASPXbottom.aspx`. Now copy the code between the `<script>` tags (including the `<script>` and `</script>` tags), and paste it at the end of the body section as follows:

```
<html>
  <head>
    <title>Inserting ASP.NET code Example</title>
  </head>
  <body>
    Line1: First HTML Line<br />
    Line2: Second HTML Line<br />
    Line3: Third HTML Line<br />
```

```
<script runat="server" Language="C#" >

    void Page_Load()
    {
      Response.Write ("First ASP.NET Line<br />");
      Response.Write ("Second ASP.NET Line<br />");
      Response.Write ("Third ASP.NET Line<br />");
    }

</script>
  </body>
</html>
```

6. Call up `messageASPXbottom.aspx` in your browser. Notice that the browser still displays the ASP.NET code first, as shown in Figure 2-4:

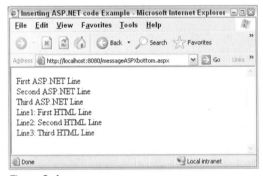

Figure 2-4

How It Works

The first thing to note is that although this is ASP.NET code, we're not actually creating a dynamic Web page that can display different pages to different users. All we're doing is demonstrating the order in which ASP.NET code and HTML are executed. The next point is that all three examples use the `.aspx` suffix despite the fact that the first page, `messageHTML.aspx`, contained only HTML code. So, as far as the Web server is concerned, all three pages are ASP.NET pages and will be checked for script to be executed. This also demonstrates that HTML is treated in the same way in both pure HTML pages and ASP.NET pages.

The code in the first page, `messageHTML.aspx`, just displays some HTML lines and some plain text. When the code is parsed in your browser, the lines are displayed in order, as you would expect.

```
<html>
  <head>
    <title>Inserting ASP.NET code Example</TITLE>
  </head>
  <body>
    Line1: First HTML Line<br />
    Line2: Second HTML Line<br />
    Line3: Third HTML Line<br />
```

```
    </body>
</html>
```

In the second Web page, `messageASPXtop.aspx`, we have a combination of some pure HTML, some plain text, and a little server-side script. By using `runat="server"`, we specified that the following script should be processed on the server, before the page is sent to the browser:

```
<script language="C#" runat="server">
    void Page_Load()
    {
        Response.Write ("First ASP.NET Line<br />");
        Response.Write ("Second ASP.NET Line<br />");
        Response.Write ("Third ASP.NET Line<br />");
    }
</script>
```

Whenever ASP.NET loads a page, it executes any code contained within the `Page_Load()` method first. So if you place code that writes to the page in this method, that text will always precede any text from the HTML part of the file even if you had physically put the code after the HTML lines (as in `messageASPXBottom.aspx`). The ASP.NET code uses a `Response.Write` statement to display three ASP.NET lines. We'll talk more about `Response.Write` in *Chapter 3*.

Take a moment here to understand another important ASP.NET concept. Open `messageHTML.aspx` in your browser and look at the source (in Internet Explorer, go to View | Source). You will see a page that starts with the following line:

```
First ASP.NET Line<br />Second ASP.NET Line<br />Third ASP.NET Line<br />
<html>
...
```

The ASP.NET module on the server interprets the code `Response.Write` and performs that writing to the page on the server. IIS only sends plain HTML to the browser. Thus, no special plug-ins or interpreters are needed on the browser. Because no browser modifications are needed, any browser can display the results of ASP.NET code.

Finally, we moved the ASP.NET code to follow the HTML lines. The browser still displays the ASP.NET code first. The Web server first scans the file to see if there is a `<script runat="server">` tag. In case some script exists, ASP.NET arranges for the script to be processed first. Because the ASP.NET code is in the `Page_Load()` subroutine, which always runs as soon as the page is loaded (created), the ASP.NET output always appears first, even if the `<script>` tag is not at the top of the code page. In other words, the server takes no notice of the position of the `<script>` tag relative to other elements of the page.

There's an important lesson to be learned here – if you place ASP.NET code in the `Page_Load()` method within the `<script>` tag, it will always be processed before the HTML code. Later we will learn how to execute other methods and functions.

Inline Code Blocks (the <% %> Delimiters)

We now know how to output text to a browser using ASP.NET. Unfortunately, anything we output from ASP.NET in the `Page_Load()` sub procedure will always write to the page before the rest of the HTML.

This is pretty awkward if we want to insert ASP.NET output anywhere lower on the page. Thus, we will now look at a couple of ways we can interweave ASP.NET output with HTML.

It's possible to incorporate code into our pages much more directly. If we specify a *render code block* (also known as an *inline code block*), any code it contains is executed as part of the page rendering process. This is the process by which we get our `Page` object to send back HTML for the browser to display. If you try coding the following block, save it as `messageASPXmiddle.aspx`. We can write render code blocks as follows (available as `Demo-inLineCodeBlock.aspx` from http://www.wrox.com/):

```
<html>
<head>
</head>
<body>
<%
Response.Write ("Hello!<br>");
%>
<html>
  <body>
    Line1: First HTML Line<br />
    <% Response.Write ("First ASP.NET Line<br />"); %>
    Line2: Second HTML Line<br />
    <% Response.Write ("Second ASP.NET Line<br />"); %>
    Line3: Third HTML Line<br />
    <% Response.Write ("Third ASP.NET Line<br />"); %>
  </body>
</html>
<%
Response.Write ("Goodbye!");
%>
</body>
</html>
```

This gives the result shown in Figure 2-5:

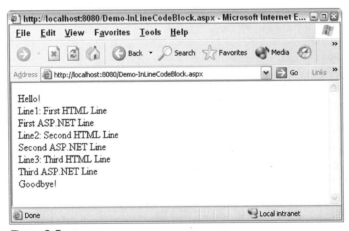

Figure 2-5

We can thus write code that executes wherever you put it, whether it's inside the HTML `<head>` tags, inside the `<body>` tag, or even at the end of the page. Also note in the following line that we can write both text as well as HTML tags, such as "Hello!" and `<br>`, in an ASP.NET `write` statement:

```
Response.Write ("Hello!<br>")
```

Server Controls

Although using the `<% %>` inline code delimiters saves on keystrokes, it ultimately produces rather intractable code. This was one of the problems of classic ASP – the pages became a jumble of text, HTML tags, and scripting statements, and it was very difficult to follow objectives and troubleshoot. Therefore, you are encouraged to use alternatives wherever possible, and we'll devote quite a lot of time in *Chapter 3* look at one very powerful way of doing this, using *server controls*.

Separating the ASP.NET code from the HTML and text makes the code easier to read. It also makes it much easier to strip out either part and reuse it in another page. As we'll see later on in the book, we can separate code and HTML blocks even further into separate files. For now, we'll keep them in one file for clarity. We recommend (and will actively practice throughout the book) placing the ASP.NET code in a declarative code block near the top of the file, just before the first `<html>` tag, as follows (this is done automatically when you use the Web Matrix editor):

```
<script language="C#" runat="server">
... ASP.NET code here ...
</script>
<html>
... HTML code here ...
</html>
```

Try It Out   Interweaving ASP.NET Output with HTML

You may still be wondering, "How do we intersperse static content with dynamic content if the code and the HTML are separated like this?" Let's take a quick look at how to get round this problem; you'll soon realize that this doesn't restrict us nearly as much as you might think.

1.   Enter the following code into a new page and save it as `messageServerControl.aspx`:

```
<script runat="server" language="C#">

    void Page_Load()
    {
        Message.Text="The ASP.NET line";
    }

</script>

<html>
<head>
  <title>Inserting ASP.NET code Example</title>
</head>
<body>
  First HTML Line<br/>
  <asp:Label id="Message" runat="server"/> <br />
  Second HTML Line<br/>
```

```
    <form runat="server">
        <!-- Insert content here -->
    </form>
</body>
</html>
```

2.   Point your browser to `messageServerControl.aspx` to see Figure 2-6:

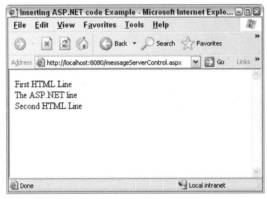

Figure 2-6

How It Works

You might have noticed that we completely avoided the use of `<%...%>` delimiters to create inline code blocks. First, we have a difference in the HTML code. Notice that we have added a special `<asp:Label>` tag, which creates an HTML tag with the `id` set to `message`:

```
<html>
<head>
  <title>Inserting ASP.NET code Example</title>
</head>
<body>
  First HTML Line<br/>
  <asp:Label id="Message" runat="server"/> <br />
  Second HTML Line<br/>
</body>
</html>
```

This named object is now available for manipulation by our ASP.NET code. Instead of having `Response.Write` statements that send text to the browser as we did in the previous example, we have code that sets a property (or attribute) of a `Label` control. This contains text that the label will display:

```
<script runat="server" language="C#">

    void Page_Load()
    {
        Message.Text="The ASP.NET line";
    }

</script>
```

50

First, the following HTML has a special tag known as a *server control* created by the `<asp:Label...>`. That control has a `runat="server"` attribute, which instructs that the code be executed by the ASP.NET module in IIS and not on the browser:

```
<asp:Label id="Message" runat="server"/> <br />
```

Second, we have a method named `Page_Load()` that changes the text of the label from nothing to `"The ASP.NET line"`. This leaves us with much cleaner code that is easier to write and easier to maintain.

ASP.NET in Action

This has been a very theoretical chapter until now. Let's now see a couple of examples. Since we've still not looked at much of ASP.NET code, the commands in these examples won't make a lot of sense at this stage. However, you will get an overview of the basic tasks that the code performs, and later in the book you can build up a more detailed picture of the syntax as your understanding grows. We'll do two exercises, of which both read data and display the information on your ASP.NET page. The first reads from an Access (`.mdb`) file, and the second from an XML file.

Binding to a Database

For most people, the key reason for using ASP.NET is the ability to connect a Web page to a database, and then read and update data from the browser. ASP.NET does this task more easily than classic ASP. In classic ASP, *binding* a page to data took many lines of code. ASP.NET provides a set of server controls that significantly cuts the amount and complexity of coding.

Try It Out   Binding to a Database

1. In this exercise, we'll use one of the example databases provided with the .NET Framework, the `grocertogo` database (MS Access format), to build a quick Web page that allows us to browse the contents of the `Products` table. There's a copy of `grocertogo` in the code download from http://www.wrox.com/, but you'll have to alter the path name to point to where you've saved it on your system. If you don't have the `grocertogo` database, modify the lines beginning with `strConnect += @"Data Source=` to point to any database that you have on your system.

2. If you cannot find the database, search your drives for `grocertogo.mdb`. Alternatively, you can download it from http://www.wrox.com/. If you want to become familiar with the database, you can open it in Access but that is not necessary for this exercise. Copy the `.mdb` file into the `C:\BegASPNET11` folder. As we will use it for more then one chapter, do not store it in the `Ch02` subfolder.

3. Open Web Matrix, create `DataControlMDB.aspx`, and type in the following:

```
<%@ Page Language="C#" %>
<%@ import Namespace="System.Data" %>
<%@ import Namespace="System.Data.OleDb" %>
<script runat="server">

    void Page_Load(Object sender, EventArgs e)
    {
```

```
        OleDbConnection objConnection;
        OleDbDataAdapter objCommand;
        String strConnect;
        String strCommand;
        DataSet DataSet1 = new DataSet();

        strConnect =  @"Provider=Microsoft.Jet.OLEDB.4.0;";
        strConnect += @"Data Source=C:\BegASPNET11\grocertogo.mdb;";
        strConnect += @"Persist Security Info=false";

        strCommand = "SELECT ProductName, UnitPrice FROM Products";

        objConnection = new OleDbConnection(strConnect);
        objCommand = new OleDbDataAdapter(strCommand, objConnection);
        objCommand.Fill(DataSet1, "products");
        DataGrid1.DataSource=DataSet1.Tables["Products"].DefaultView;
        DataGrid1.DataBind();
    }

</script>
<html>
<head>
    <title>Data Grid Control example</title>
</head>
<body>
    <asp:DataGrid id="DataGrid1" runat="server"></asp:DataGrid>
</body>
</html>
```

4.   Open `DataControlMDB.aspx` in your browser as shown in Figure 2-7:

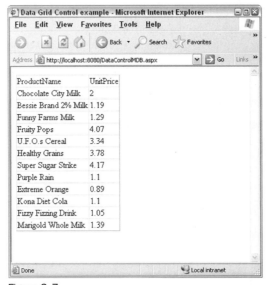

Figure 2-7

How It Works

The ASP.NET code looks quite daunting, but we can understand it when we examine the different sections. First, let's look at the `<body>` tag:

```
<body>
  <asp:DataGrid id="DataGrid1" runat="server"  />
</body>
```

We have a tag here that creates a `DataGrid` object named `DataGrid1` in the page. This will be an object that we can manipulate in our code, but when the page is requested by a user and built by the ASP.NET module in IIS, the `DataGrid` object will create in its place the `<table>`, `<th>`, `<tr>`, and `<td>` HTML tags so that a table appears in the browser.

Now let's go back up in the code and examine the `Page_Load()` method. We'll not enter into a detailed discussion about all of these lines (see *Chapters 8* and *9*). However, we can break it into several parts.

We start by establishing our language. Second, we import the namespaces (collections of objects) that we will need for working with the data:

```
<%@ Page Language="C#" debug="true"%>
<%@ import Namespace="System.Data" %>
<%@ import Namespace="System.Data.OleDb" %>
```

Then we enter our function and create some variables to hold information that we will need:

```
    void Page_Load(Object sender, EventArgs e)
    {
       OleDbConnection objConnection;
       OleDbDataAdapter objCommand;
       String strConnect;
       String strCommand;
       DataSet DataSet1 = new DataSet();
```

Next, we create a string of text in a variable called `strConnect`, which will inform the connection what kind of database we are using (the Microsoft Jet provider in the case of Access), where to find the file, and how to handle security settings:

```
       strConnect =  @"Provider=Microsoft.Jet.OLEDB.4.0;";
       strConnect += @"Data Source=C:\BegASPNET11\grocertogo.mdb;";
       strConnect += @"Persist Security Info=false";
```

Next, ASP.NET needs query that it can use to retrieve data from the database. This is written as a SQL statement. You don't need to know SQL at this point because the general syntax is obvious. We want to read (`SELECT`) values from two fields (`ProductName` and `UnitPrice`) located in the `Products` table:

```
       strCommand = "SELECT ProductName, UnitPrice FROM Products";
```

The next three lines take the information above and use it to create two objects (`Connection` and `Command`) and fill our `DataSet1` object with data read from `grocertogo`:

```
        objConnection = new OleDbConnection(strConnect);
        objCommand = new OleDbDataAdapter(strCommand, objConnection);
        objCommand.Fill(DataSet1, "products");
```

Lastly, we use two lines to instruct the `DataGrid` (from the HTML section) to use `DataSet1` as the source of its values as follows:

```
        DataGrid1.DataSource=DataSet1.Tables["Products"].DefaultView;
        DataGrid1.DataBind();
    }
</script>
```

As always, with ASP.NET, this code is interpreted on the server by the ASP.NET module of IIS to render the page from pure HTML, which sent to the browser. If you open `datacontrol.aspx` in your browser and then view the source, you will see only standard HTML table tags but none of the ASP.NET code.

Binding to a Simple XML File

ASP.NET is not limited to connecting with relational databases. We'll now look at how we can use the data controls to connect to a short XML document. This book does not go into the theory of XML. In case you are not familiar with the standard, XML is a format for holding data normally in a text file. The file is self-describing in that each piece of data has a label that identifies its classification in the scheme of records and fields. XML is becoming the standard for data exchange. To learn more about XML, refer to *Beginning XML, 2nd Edition (ISBN 0-7645-4394-6)* by *Wrox Press*.

Let's create a short XML document and then an ASPX page that demonstrates the technique to create a `DataGrid` control and bind it to the contents of an XML document. Overall, the procedure is even easier than connecting to a database.

Try It Out   Binding to a Simple XML Document

1.   Open up your Web page editor and create a document named `artists.xml` in your `Ch02` folder. Type in the following XML document. Alternatively, you can download the file from http://www.wrox.com/:

```
<?xml version="1.0" encoding="utf-8" ?>
<artists>
  <artist>
    <name>Vincent Van Gogh</name>
    <nationality>Dutch</nationality>
    <movement>Post Impressionism </movement>
    <birthdate>30th March 1853</birthdate>
  </artist>
  <artist>
    <name>Paul Klee </name>
    <nationality>Swiss </nationality>
    <movement>Abstract Expressionism </movement>
    <birthdate>18th December 1879</birthdate>
  </artist>
  <artist>
    <name>Max Ernst </name>
    <nationality>German </nationality>
```

```
        <movement>Surrealism </movement>
        <birthdate>2nd April 1891</birthdate>
      </artist>
  </artists>
```

2. Keeping your Web page editor open, create a second file named `DataControlXML.aspx` containing the following lines:

```
<%@ Page Language="C#" runat="server" debug="true"%>
<%@ import Namespace="System.Data" %>
<%@ import Namespace="System.Xml" %>
<script runat="server">

    void Page_Load()
    {
      String xmlFilename = @"C:\BegASPNET11\ch02\artists.xml";
      DataSet newDataSet = new DataSet();
      newDataSet.ReadXml(xmlFilename);
      DataGrid1.DataSource = newDataSet;
      DataGrid1.DataBind();
    }

</script>
<html>
  <head>
    <title>Data Grid Control example</title>
  </head>
  <body>
    <asp:DataGrid id="DataGrid1" runat="server"  />
  </body>
</html>
```

3. View this page in your browser; the result should look like Figure 2-8:

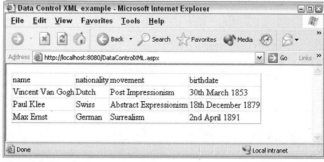

Figure 2-8

How It Works

Our XML file is pretty much like a database table. We've kept it simple, so that you can see what is happening. The first line notifies users that the file is an XML file. An overall pair of tags, `<artists>`, encapsulates all of the data:

```
<?xml version="1.0" encoding="utf-8" ?>
<artists>
...
</artists>
```

There are three artists. Each artist's individual entry is held with a single set of item tags structured as follows:

```
<artist>
  <name>Vincent Van Gogh</name>
  <nationality>Dutch</nationality>
  <movement>Post Impressionism </movement>
  <birthdate>30th March 1853</birthdate>
</artist>
```

Within each artist, we can see four elements (which are like fields or columns in other data systems), one each for `name`, `nationality`, `movement`, and `birthdate`. Notice that each data value is inside a pair of tags and that the same set of tag names is used for each artist. Even without knowledge of XML, it is easy to see how the file is organized.

Now let's look at the `datacontrolXML.aspx` ASP.NET page. At the top of the page, we must establish the language and import the namespaces that hold objects we will need to work with XML data:

```
<%@ Page Language="C#" runat="server" debug="true"%>
<%@ import Namespace="System.Data" %>
<%@ import Namespace="System.Xml" %>
```

Next, jump down to the `<body>`, where we use the `DataGrid` control to format and display the information as an HTML table. Again, the code is very neat and simple. It is crucial to include the attribute `runat="server"` for ASP.NET to work. Furthermore, every control must have a name (specified using the `id` attribute); in this case `DataGrid1`.

```
<body>
  <asp:DataGrid id="DataGrid1" runat="server"  />
</body>
```

Last, we will examine the ASP.NET code. Because it is in the `Page_Load()` method, it is automatically executed when the page is created. The first few lines record the name of the file into a variable:

```
<script runat="server">

    void Page_Load()
    {
        String xmlFilename = @"C:\BegASPNET11\ch02\artists.xml";
```

Then we make a `DataSet` and read into it the contents of the XML file:

```
        DataSet newDataSet = new DataSet();
        newDataSet.ReadXml(xmlFilename);
```

Last, we identify that `DataSet` as the source of information for the `DataGrid` control:

```
        DataGrid1.DataSource = newDataSet;
        DataGrid1.DataBind();
    }
</script>
```

As you can see, reading from an XML file is even simpler than the code we used for connecting to a database. However, at this point do not be concerned about the details of each line of code. We will discuss the exact meaning of each statement in *Chapters 8* and *9*.

Summary

This chapter has been mostly theoretical, but contained simple applications ranging from a simple display of text up to two types of data connections. You should now understand several basic points about .NET and ASP.NET.

The .NET Framework is a guideline and standard for the tools that Microsoft produces for programmers. It is flexible across languages and is suitable for both desktop and Web-based applications.

.NET is based on objects, a programming convention which puts related code together in a structure that represents an entity in the real world. The model from which objects are copied is called a class and a group of related classes is called a namespace.

ASP.NET is a module that adds on to IIS. ASP.NET checks pages for code and executes that code to create an HTML page. The resulting pages are pure HTML and require no add-ins for the browser because of which they can be viewed on any browser.

After writing an ASP page, it is partially compiled to MSIL and stored on the server. When requested, the page is run through the CLR for a final compilation. This two-stage compilation gives both performance advantages and optimization for different servers.

When we write an ASP.NET page, we must include several key parts, such as:

❑　The .aspx filename extension

❑　A directive to import namespaces and a directive designating the language

❑　HTML and text

❑　ASP.NET controls such as <asp:Label> that have an id and runat="server" attributes

❑　Code scripts

Although scripts can be designated in line by <% %>, it is better to designate them by <script> tags. Within the script, we create functions and methods. The one we have studied so far is named Page_Load(), which it automatically executes when an .aspx page is requested. Any Write commands from Page_Load() will appear on the page above HTML and text.

Once created and named, an object can be manipulated. For example, we used script to change the text that was displayed by an <asp:Label>. We also observed how easy it is to create and manipulate objects that Microsoft provides for working with data such as a database connection, command, and

`DataGrid` objects. However, before exposing objects to this type of manipulation, we must designate both the script and the control as `runat="server"`.

We can now move on to discuss in detail the various components of the pages we tested. We will start with how to hold and display information (*Chapter 3*), and then move on to controlling the lines of code that are executed (*Chapters 4 to 6*).

Exercises

1. Describe what .NET Framework provides for programmers.

2. What encompasses more code, a class or a namespace?

3. The ASP.NET module of code adds on to which part of Windows?

4. What special modifications to the browser are required on the client-side in order to view an ASP.NET page?

5. Why does an ASP.NET page get compiled twice?

6. Why does the first display of an ASP.NET page take several seconds but subsequent views appear in only milliseconds?

7. What two attributes should always be included in all ASP.NET Web controls?

Server Controls and Variables

One of the most common tasks for any Web developer is collecting and storing of information from the user. It could simply be a name or an email address, but whatever be the information that you want to gather, the processing cannot be performed within the confines of HTML on the browser alone. You need to send the information to the Web server for processing or storage.

Information is transmitted via Web pages by a *form*. HTML forms contain controls such as textboxes, checkboxes, and dropdown lists, all of which aid the passage of information from the user to the server. Moreover, ASP.NET adds its own extra controls for dealing with forms. With these, ASP.NET introduces some new concepts to the control of forms, such as remembering the text that you've typed into a textbox or the selection that you have made in a listbox between page refreshes, which must be carried out on the server.

During the manipulation of user data, variables are used to persist data from one command to another. C# is a *strongly typed* language, which means each variable has a datatype associated with it, such as string, integer, or date. This chapter will look at the main datatypes available in C# as well as the importance of assigning each variable a particular datatype and the types of errors you might encounter if you don't. We will also discuss how to use ASP.NET to create powerful forms with very little programming, and then holding data in variables.

We will cover:

- ❑ Forms
- ❑ Client-server model of the Web
- ❑ ASP.NET server controls (or Web controls)
- ❑ Theory and practice of variables
- ❑ Datatypes
- ❑ Arrays and collections

Forms

The focus of this chapter is on forms and on the transfer of data from the browser to the server. Before delving into the inner workings of forms, let's see a few situations in which forms would be required in the business world. If you look at commercial Web sites, you'll find that most forms are for the same kind of situation. For example:

❏ To obtain information from a user for the purpose of registration, the purchase of a product, or joining an email list, forum, or a newsgroup

❏ To take note of a user's preferences so that we can customize other pages in the site to include just the relevant information

❏ To act as the front-end for a forum or newsgroup, where a user can enter and edit their input online

❏ To capture business transaction and display reports and related information in e-commerce applications

Let's start with a quick overview of forms, and see the effects that ASP.NET has on them.

Web Pages, HTML Forms, and Web Forms

With the introduction of any new technology comes new terminology and jargon. ASP.NET is no different in this respect. With ASP.NET, even the terms you use to describe a simple Web page have been updated to more accurately describe the processes that are going on within them. To avoid confusion, let's start by defining familiar concepts and their ASP.NET equivalents.

A *Web page* is a bundle of ASCII characters including HTML code, text to be marked up and beginning and ending with `<html>` and `</html>` tags. The Web page is placed on a machine known as a *Web server*, which sends the page to any requestors (users). HTML pages are typically saved with the suffix `.html` or `.htm`.

An *HTML form* is a Web page that contains one or more *form controls* (grouped together inside an HTML `<form>` element) that allow the user to enter information on the Web page and send that information back to the Web server. Commonly used form controls include buttons, textboxes, checkboxes, and dropdown lists. The user fills in details and generally presses a button to send their data back to the Web server.

Although you don't need anything more than HTML to send form data to the server, the server needs some sort of extra technology (in this case, ASP.NET) to actually work with the information it receives.

ASP.NET introduces a new concept, the *Web form*. Behind the scenes, a Web form is much easier and faster to program than HTML forms. Technically speaking, the term Web form refers to the grouping of two distinct blocks of code:

❑ **HTML template** containing page layout information and ASP.NET server controls. This is responsible for the presentation of the Web form on the browser.

❑ **ASP.NET code** that holds a script containing the Web form's processing logic. This is responsible for generating dynamic content to be displayed within the Web form. This content is typically exposed via server controls defined in the HTML presentation block.

When you start using ASP.NET to create Web forms, you can use a new breed of ASP.NET *server controls* within your HTML. Not only do they duplicate the functionality of many HTML elements (including the form controls), but they also provide additional features. A server control has the appearance of an *HTML* element, but it only marks a point in the page at which the server needs to generate a corresponding true-HTML element. We will be discussing in-depth how to use ASP.NET server controls.

> **Although a Web form may also be an HTML form (there's nothing to stop you using `<form>` elements inside an ASPX page), remember that these two entities are defined in quite distinct terms. An HTML form can only use standard HTML tags while a Web form can use the more powerful ASP.NET server controls.**

It is possible for Web forms to use normal HTML form controls, but ASP.NET also comes with its own set of Web form controls that are run on the server. You will be using these most of the time, because they offer other advantages, such as being able to remember the state of the different controls. These ASP.NET controls are run within specially modified HTML `<form runat="server">` tags, and are *ASP.NET forms*.

Let's review the four terms just introduced:

❑ **Web page**: Any page that contains HTML and they can also contain script or other languages not covered by this book. In this book, a Web page will refer to pages containing only HTML.

❑ **HTML form**: An HTML element that contains HTML form controls.

❑ **Web form**: Any page that combines ASP.NET code with an HTML template.

❑ **ASP.NET form**: A form that contains ASP.NET server controls inside a Web form.

Let's start by considering the whole process of data transmission on the Web to understand the role of forms.

Request and Response in Non-ASP.NET Pages

Chapter 1 discussed the installation of ASP.NET and the concept of a Web server, which makes your Web pages available to users. Another job of the Web server is to provide an area (typically in a directory or folder structure) to organize and store your Web pages or the whole Web site.

When a user views a Web page, they will automatically be making contact with a Web server. The process of submitting the URL is called making a *request* to the server. The server receives the request and locates the corresponding page on the disk drive. In the case of a simple page (HTML and text only), the Web server sends the page back to the user as a *response*. The browser then takes the code it has received from the Web server and compiles a viewable page from it. The browser is referred to as a *client* in this interaction, and the whole interaction as a *client-server relationship*. If the Web server cannot find the requested page, it issues a response that features an appropriate error message and dispatches the error to the browser.

The term client-server describes the working of the Web by outlining the distribution of tasks. The server (the Web server) stores pages, interprets scripts, and distributes data (that is compiled into Web pages), and the client (browser) accesses the server to get at the data.

The Internet is a network of interconnected nodes. It is designed to carry *information* from one place to another. When the user tells the browser to fetch a Web page, a message is sent from the browser to the Web server. This message is sent using HTTP. The World Wide Web uses HTTP for transfer of information from one machine to another. (When you see a URL prefixed with http://, you know that the Internet protocol being used is HTTP, as it is the default protocol used by Web browsers.)

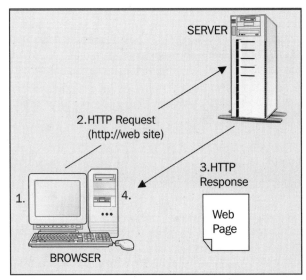

Figure 3-1

The process illustrated in Figure 3-1 is as follows:

1. The client requests a Web page by typing a URL into the browser and clicking GO.

2. The Web server hosting that URL locates the HTML page that was requested on its hard drive. The page is read into a stream of characters.

3. The server sends the stream to the browser.

4. The browser interprets (converts) the HTML code and text into a displayed Web page.

HTTP is known as a *stateless* protocol. This is because it doesn't know whether the request that has been made is part of an ongoing correspondence or just a single message (just the same way your postman won't know whether a letter is the first from your friend or the fifteenth). HTTP is stateless because it was only intended for the simple task of retrieving pages for display.

The Internet would be very slow and might even collapse if permanent connections (states) needed to be maintained between clients and servers, as people moved from one page to another. Statelessness makes the Internet faster, but the downside is that HTTP by itself can't distinguish between different users. A Web server based on pure HTML will treat all requests with the same status, that of an *unknown user*. Obviously, the modern needs of the Internet require that you can identify users and track their moves through the various pages needed for accomplishing a task on a Web site. As seen later in the book, ASP.NET creates a state that can be used by programmers.

Where ASP.NET Fits in with the .NET Framework

ASP.NET adds a step to the request-response mechanism; after the server receives the request, it reads the page from the hard drive. But rather then containing just text and HTML tags, an ASP.NET page also contains script that is interpreted to build features into the page.

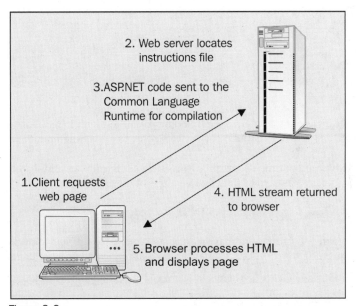

Figure 3-2

The process is illustrated in Figure 3-2 and can be explained as follows:

1. The client requests a Web page by typing an URL into the browser and clicking GO.

2. Web server locates on its hard drive the page that was requested.

3. If the name of the Web page has an .aspx extension, the server processes the page – it runs the script code. If the ASP.NET code hasn't been compiled before, it is compiled now. The code is executed to create a pure HTML stream.

4. The HTML stream is returned to the client.

5. The client browser interprets (converts) the HTML code and text into a displayed Web page.

The addition of ASP.NET implies that the HTML is created *dynamically*. This has many advantages: you can return information to the user based on their responses in a form, customize Web pages for a particular browser; or even personalize information for each user. All of this is possible because the code you write is converted into an HTML page when it is requested.

Now that you have a basic understanding of how ASP.NET pages compare to plain HTML pages, it's time to start studying forms. Mastery of the concepts of forms allows us to obtain information from users. The subsequent chapters will discuss manipulation of this information and saving it to databases.

The <form> Tag in ASP.NET

ASP.NET has a set of form controls that are similar to HTML form controls. The main difference is that ASP.NET controls are actually constructed dynamically on the server at the time of request, and then sent out. The ASP.NET version requires only a few characters of coding:

```
<form ID="MyForm" runat="server">
... ASP.NET form...
</form>
```

It takes only one attribute (runat="server") to tell the Web server that it should *process* the form itself, rather than just sending it out to the browser. If you have worked with HTML forms you may wonder about which METHOD is used. All ASP.NET forms are sent by the POST method.

The <form> tag allows you to process form controls (such as checkboxes and dropdown lists) on the server. ASP.NET introduces its own customized versions of these controls.

There are several advantages to using the ASP.NET form controls:

❑ .NET automatically creates and handles a sense of state for us. This allows us to know if the person requesting the form is the same person that requested another page.

❑ ASP.NET offers some very sophisticated controls including calendars and grids for the display of data.

❑ The content of the controls can be generated from databases or business logic.

❑ The information entered by users into controls can be validated to avoid data entry mistakes.

Using ASP.NET Server Controls

This section demonstrates how some of the ASP.NET server controls work and compares the way in which they are used to the way in which information is passed in their equivalent HTML form control. It also shows the separation of the presentation code (HTML) from the code that provides the content (ASP.NET).

ASP.NET server controls are also called *Web Controls*, a term that we'll be regularly using throughout this book.

All Web controls have two required attributes. The first is `runat="server"`, which instructs ASP.NET to handle the control at the server and thus, implement all of the ASP.NET features for the control including the creation of state. The second is the `id="MyControlName"`, which manipulates the control in code.

Before going into the details, let's take a look at the most commonly used ASP.NET server controls. We've included a comparison to the HTML form tags that you have used in the past.

ASP.NET Web Control	Similar HTML Form Tag	Purpose
`<asp:Label>`	`<Span>`, `<Div>`, simple text	Display text
`<asp:ListBox>`	`<Select>`	Offer the user a list of items from which to select.
`<asp:DropDownList>`	`<Select>`	Offer the user a list of items from which to select in a compact format
`<asp:TextBox>`	`<Input Type="Text">`	Accept typed input from user
`<asp:RadioButton>` and `<asp:RadioButtonList>`	`<Input Type="Radio">`	Allow user to make one selection from a list of options.
`<asp:CheckBox>` and `<asp:CheckBoxList>`	`<Input Type="CheckBox">`	Allow user to turn a feature on or off
`<asp:Button>`	`<Input Type="submit">`	Send the user's input to the server

<asp:Label>

Let's start with a small but very useful control, the `<asp:Label>` control. This control provides an effective way of displaying text on your Web page in ASP.NET, similar to the HTML `<span>` tag. By having a control for text, you can manipulate its contents and visibility from your ASP.NET code.

<asp:Label> Attributes

The `<asp:Label>` control is just like any normal HTML form control, in that, it has a collection of attributes you can set; the `runat="server"` and `id` attributes are used in every ASP.NET control. Other attributes are optional including:

❑   `Text`: Sets the text that you want the label to display

❑   `Visible`: Sets the visibility of the label on the page (`true` or `false`)

❑   `BackColor`: Sets the background color of the label

❑   `ForeColor`: Sets the foreground color of the label

❑   `Height`: Sets the height in pixels of the label

❑   `Width`: Sets the width of the label

You can use the class browser mentioned in Chapter 2 to see all the properties of any control.

\<asp:Label\> Examples

The basic syntax of `<asp:Label>` is simple:

```
<asp:Label id="lblMyLabel" runat="server">Sale Ends May 2nd</asp:Label>
```

The `<asp:>` prefix indicates that this control is part of the set of built-in ASP.NET controls. It is possible to create custom controls that have prefixes of the developer's choice. We will look at this in *Chapter 13*.

In the context of a Web page, the `<asp:Label>` control looks like the following (refer to the file Ch03\Demo-Label01.aspx in the code download):

```
<html>
<head>
    <title>ASP.NET Controls Demo</title>
</head>
<body>
Demo of the asp:Label control<br />
  <form id="frmDemo" runat="server">
      <asp:Label id="lblGreeting1" runat="server">Text of asp:Label</asp:Label>
  </form>
</body>
</html>
```

The `id` attribute is used to uniquely identify this control so that you can refer to it in your ASP.NET code. The `runat="server"` attribute tells the server to process the control and generate HTML code to be sent to the client. The text between the opening and closing labels provides the characters to show up in the label.

Alternatively, you can specify the text in an attribute. This way, everything can be contained within the opening tag, in which case, you need to close the tag in the following way:

```
<asp:Label id="lblGreeting3" runat="server" text="Internal Greeting" />
```

Here, the closing tag is omitted, and instead a closing / is supplied within the tag itself to indicate that the tag is closed. Throughout the book we will use this latter notation in preference to having a closing tag. Let's look at an example to set the color of a text message to red as follows (download file Ch03\Demo-Label02.aspx):

```
<asp:Label id="lblGreeting2" forecolor="red"  text="Red Text" runat="server"
/>
```

Let's now look at an example of how you can use the `<asp:Label>` control to display some text for a tourism company. In this example, it's assumed that the values of the user's name and desired destination have already been passed to the server, and that all you need to do is display a message that confirms that you have received the user's details.

Try It Out Using the `<asp:Label>` Control

1. Open ASP.NET Web Matrix and create a new folder named Ch03 within C:\BegASPNET11. Within that folder, create a new item of the type ASP.NET page named TIO-Label.aspx. Enter code as needed to create the following page. Some lines are pre-typed for you by Web ASP.NET Web Matrix. (You can learn basic techniques for working with ASP.NET Web Matrix in Appendix B.)

```
<html>
<head>
    <title>Label Control page</title>
</head>
<body>
    <h1>Feiertag Holidays
    </h1>
    <form runat="server">
        <asp:Label id="Message1" runat="server" text="Chris"></asp:Label>,
        you have selected to receive information about
        <asp:Label id="Message2" runat="server" text="Oslo"></asp:Label>.
        The information package will be sent to you.
    </form>
</body>
</html>
```

2. View it from your browser, the page should be displayed as shown in Figure 3-3:

Figure 3-3

How It Works

The text of your `<asp:Label>` that appears on the page is the same as that obtained as a result of typing it in a standard HTML `<span>` tag. More interestingly, take a look at the source code by selecting View |

Source from your browser and notice two things. First, the ASP.DLL has processed your `<asp:Label>` controls into `<span>` tags. Second, ASP.NET has added an extra tag of `name="_VIEWSTATE"` to your form with its value set to a long string of characters. The `VIEWSTATE` tag will be discussed shortly.

Modifying ASP.NET Controls

Although this exercise works, it still does not give us the ability to modify the text in code. Recall from *Chapter 2* where you used code in a `Page_Load()` event that affected controls. You can do the same here (you might want to save this file as `TIO-Label2.aspx`). First delete the `Text` attribute (shown in bold in the following code listing) at the end of both `<asp:Label>` controls:

```
<asp:Label id="Message1" runat="server" text="Chris"></asp:Label>
  , you have selected to receive information about
<asp:Label id="Message2" runat="server" text="Oslo"></asp:Label>
  . The information package will be sent to you.
```

Now add the following ASP.NET script block before your HTML code:

```
<script runat="server" Language="C#">
    void Page_Load()
    {
      Message1.Text = "Vervain";
      Message2.Text = "Madrid";
    }

</script>
```

If you run the example again, you'll see that the output has changed to that shown in Figure 3-4:

Figure 3-4

The `Page_Load()` section is executed whenever the page is requested or refreshed; we will discuss this in more detail in *Chapter 6*. Let's ignore this statement for now, it's the code it contains that's important. The following line refers to the text contained by your first `<asp:Label>` control. Here we're changing the `Text` attribute of `Message1` to `Vervain`.

```
Message1.Text = "Vervain"
```

This example allowed you to change the contents of an `<asp:Label>` control by modifying code. Future chapters will discuss how to modify the values in more sophisticated ways, including changing the text to be values read from a database. All of the ASP.NET control attributes (properties) can be changed in the code in the same way. For example:

```
Message1.Text = "Vervain"
Message1.backcolor = Drawing.color.red
Message1.font.italic=true
Message1.font.size = FontUnit.large
```

<asp:DropDownList>

Before moving onto the `<asp:DropDownList>` control, let's pause to look at its HTML form control equivalent. Dropdown listboxes are a series of `<option>` tags within a pair of `<select>` tags as shown:

```
<select name="lstCities">
  <option>Madrid</option>
  <option>Oslo</option>
  <option>Lisbon</option>
</select>
```

The `<asp:DropDownList>` control will produce the same output when coded in the following way:

```
<asp:DropDownList id="lstCities" runat="server">
  <asp:ListItem>Madrid</asp:ListItem >
  <asp:ListItem >Oslo</asp:ListItem >
  <asp:ListItem >Lisbon</asp:ListItem >
</asp:DropDownList >
```

The three important differences between the ASP.NET control and the HTML form control are:

❑ The `<asp:DropDownList>` tag directly replaces the `<select>` tag

❑ The `<asp:ListItem>` tag replaces the `<option>` tag

❑ The `id` attribute replaces the `name` attribute

Visually, the `<asp:DropDownList>` control is identical to the HTML dropdown list control; it's what goes on behind the scene that is different. The best way to explain this is to look at an example. Let's create a form that asks the user to select the particular holiday destination they wish to know more about.

Try It Out   Using the `<asp:DropDownList>` Control

1. Create a new ASP.NET page called `TIO-DropDownList.aspx` in Web Matrix and type in the following. As always with ASP.NET Web Matrix, some lines are pre-typed for you.

```
<script runat="server" Language="C#">
   void Page_Load()
   {
   if (Page.IsPostBack)
```

```
        lblMessage.Text = "You have selected " + list1.SelectedItem.Value;
      }
</script>
<html>
<head>
  <title>Drop Down List Example</title>
</head>
<body>
  <asp:Label id="lblMessage" runat="server"/><br/>
  <form runat="server">
    Which city interests you?<br />
    <asp:DropDownList id="list1" runat="server">
      <asp:ListItem>Madrid</asp:ListItem>
      <asp:ListItem>Oslo</asp:ListItem>
      <asp:ListItem>Lisbon</asp:ListItem>
    </asp:DropDownList>
  <input type="Submit">
  </form>
</body>
</html>
```

2. Run this file in your browser and the page should be displayed as shown in Figure 3-5:

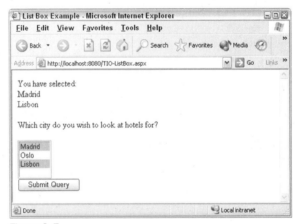

Figure 3-5

3. Select Oslo and click on Submit Query.

4. Now click on View | Source. You should see something like the following; don't worry if your version isn't exactly the same – the code is tailored to your personal browser:

```
<html>
<head><title>Drop Down List Example</title></head>
<body>
  <span id="lblMessage">You have selected Oslo</span><br/>
  <form name="_ctl0" method="post" action="TIO-DropDownList.aspx" id="_ctl0">
<input type="hidden" name="__VIEWSTATE"
value="dDwtMTMyNTU5Mzc0Njt0PDtsPGk8MT47PjtsPHQ8cDxwPGw8VGV4dDs+O2w8WW91IGhhdmdmU
```

```
        gc2VsZWN0ZWQgT3Nsbzs+Pjs+Ozs+Oz4+Oz4qihTIIzJYjhyzz+oJsyJ1gevEaQ==" />

      Which city interests you?<br />
      <select name="list1" id="list1">
        <option value="Madrid">Madrid</option>
        <option selected="selected" value="Oslo">Oslo</option>
        <option value="Lisbon">Lisbon</option>
      </select>
    <input type="Submit">
    </form>
  </body>
</html>
```

How It Works

As you can see, everything that has been sent to the browser is HTML code and text; there are no proprietary tags or script to run on the browser. Also note that this is a one-page solution, in contrast to the old two-page approach with HTML forms. This form page submits to itself. To explain how it works, we're going to reference the source code that we can view in our browser, and compare it to our original ASPX code.

Let's start from the <form> section of the script. The <form runat="server"> attribute is set that tells ASP.NET to execute the form on the server. If you compare this line to what has been returned to the browser, you can see a large difference:

```
<form name="ctrl0" method="post" action="listpage.aspx" id="ctrl0">
```

ASP.NET has generated four new attributes. The name and id attributes serve a similar purpose - to uniquely identify the form. However, it's the other two that are of interest. HTML forms require a page to receive the form data and a method of transmission. We didn't specify either of these in our ASPX code, so ASP.NET specified them for us by default to be the same page. It also specifies the POST method by default.

The main item on the form is the <asp:DropDownList> control:

```
Which city interests you? <br />
  <asp:DropDownList id="list1" runat="server">
    <asp:ListItem>Madrid</asp:ListItem>
    <asp:ListItem>Oslo</asp:ListItem>
    <asp:ListItem>Lisbon</asp:ListItem>
  </asp:DropDownList>
```

It's crucial to note how this is rendered. If you view the source code that's sent back to the browser, you should see the following:

```
<input type="hidden" name="__VIEWSTATE"
value="dDwtMTMyNTU5Mzc0Njt0PDtsPGk8MT47PjtsPHQ8cDxwPGw8VGV4dDs+O2w8WW91IGhhdm
Ugc2VsZWN0ZWQgT3Nsbzs+Pjs+Ozs+Oz4+Oz4qihTIIzJYjhyzz+oJsyJ1gevEaQ==" />
    Which city interests you?<br />
    <select name="list1" id="list1">
      <option value="Madrid">Madrid</option>
```

```
        <option selected="selected" value="Oslo">Oslo</option>
        <option value="Lisbon">Lisbon</option>
    </select>
```

It's the first line that is of particular note. It contains a hidden control called VIEWSTATE, which contains an encoded representation of the overall state of the form when last submitted. This is used by ASP.NET to keep track of all the server control settings from one page refresh to another. Without this record of the state of the page controls, the dropdownlist would revert to its default setting every time you submitted a value.

It may not be immediately obvious how useful this can be – consider a non-ASP.NET registration form in which you have to enter a full set of personal details. If you forget to fill in a required field, and then submit the form, you may well be prompted with the same empty form again. ASP.NET solves this problem for us with the VIEWSTATE; all that data is automatically persisted through to the refreshed page, and you have barely raised a finger to code this functionality!

The string of characters contained in the value attribute is a condensed and encoded depiction of each control on the page as it was when the submit button was clicked. When this information is sent back to IIS on a subsequent submit, it is decoded and ASP.NET can work with the values.

The second half is just a `<select>` HTML form control; this is the HTML output of a `<dropdownlist>`. Note that it had one of the `<option>` tags altered to reflect the selection you made before submitting the form.

How ASP.NET Code Works

We've seen that the ASP.NET server control passes form values to the ASP.NET code. Now let's see how you can use a control's values in your code. Assume that we have a label named lblMessage and a dropdown list named DropList1 (you can download this code in the file Demo-HowAspNetCodeWorks.aspx):

```csharp
<script runat="server" language="C#">
  void Page_Load()
  {
    if(Page.IsPostBack)
      lblMessage.Text = "You have selected " + DropList1.SelectedItem.Value;
  }
</script>
```

There are three lines of code here inside Page_Load(). The first line of code (the if(Page.IsPostBack) condition) checks whether the page has been returned by the user before. This check involves using the Page object, which keeps a record of whether this is the first time a form is shown or it is being displayed after a submit.

If the form has been submitted, IsPostBack returns true, otherwise false. The code inside if() will only be run if the form has been posted back by the user. So, if this is the first time the user has seen the form (Page.IsPostBack would equal false), then ASP.NET will jump over to the second line and, in this case, end. The page would not show any text in the message control. However, if the user has submitted the page, then the following line will be run first:

```
This line lblMessage.Text = "You have selected " +
DropList1.SelectedItem.Value
```

This code has two parts: the right side of the equals sign picks up the option that the user clicked in the dropdown list and the left side identifies where to put that text, namely the `<asp:Label>` control. Note that the `SelectedItem.Value` keeps a record of the items that the user selects. On both sides we refer to the server control by its `id` value.

<asp:ListBox>

The `<asp:ListBox>` server control resembles the dropdown list control, except that it doesn't drop down and is capable of multiple selections. The `<asp:ListBox>` has the following syntax:

```
<asp:ListBox id="list1" runat="server" selection mode = "multiple">
  <asp:ListItem>Madrid</asp:ListItem>
  <asp:ListItem>Oslo</asp:ListItem>
  <asp:ListItem>Lisbon</asp:ListItem>
</asp:ListBox>
```

The `selectionmode` attribute is used to determine whether you can select multiple or only select single items from the listbox. By default it is set to single. Let's alter our previous example to use a listbox that allows multiple selections.

Try It Out Using the `<asp:ListBox>` Control

1. Create the `TIO-ListBox.aspx` file in the `Ch03` folder, and enter the following code:

```
<%@ Page Language="C#" %>
<script runat="server">
    void Page_Load()
      {
      string msgCitiesList = "";

      if (Page.IsPostBack == true)
        if (list1.Items[0].Selected == true)
        {
          msgCitiesList = msgCitiesList + list1.Items[0].Text + "<br />";
        }
        if (list1.Items[1].Selected)
        {
          msgCitiesList = msgCitiesList + list1.Items[1].Text + "<br/>";
        }
        if (list1.Items[2].Selected)
        {
          msgCitiesList = msgCitiesList + list1.Items[2].Text + "<br />";
        }
        if (msgCitiesList != "")
        {
          Message.Text = "You have selected: <br />" + msgCitiesList;
        }
        else
        {
          Message.Text = "";
```

```
            }
          }
  </script>
  <html>
    <head>
      <title>ListBox Example</title>
    </head>
    <body>
      <asp:Label id="Message" runat="server"/><br/>
      Which city do you wish to look at hotels for?<br/>
      <form runat="server">
        <asp:ListBox id="list1" runat="server" selectionmode="multiple">
          <asp:ListItem>Madrid</asp:ListItem>
          <asp:ListItem>Oslo</asp:ListItem>
          <asp:ListItem>Lisbon</asp:ListItem>
        </asp:ListBox><br/>
        <input type="Submit">
      </form>
    </body>
  </html>
```

2. Run this page in your browser, use the Ctrl or Shift key to select multiple choices, and then click on Submit Query to see the page as depicted in Figure 3-6:

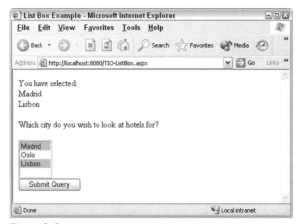

Figure 3-6

How It Works

The controls in this example have hardly changed from the previous `listpage.aspx` example. All we've done is switched from `DropDownList` to a `ListBox` and set the `selectionmode` attribute to allow multiple selections:

```
<asp:ListBox id="list1" runat="server" selectionmode="multiple">
```

However, we've had to completely overhaul the ASP.NET code to accommodate the possibility of several cities selected. We will build the list to be displayed in a variable named `msgCitiesList`:

```
string msgCitiesList = "";
```

Then for each possible city choice, we check if it was selected; if yes, we add the city name to the `msgCitiesList` variable. The trick here is to understand that the choices are numbered (indexed) in the listbox, and if they are selected, the `selected` property is switched to `true`. Finally, we assign the value of the variable `msgCitiesList` (a string of text and HTML) to the `Text` attribute of the `Message` label so that it can be seen on the page. This is slightly more complicated than handling the results of single selections.

<asp:TextBox>

This control is ASP.NET's version of the HTML `<textbox>` and `<textarea>` controls. In fact, textareas are simply textboxes that feature multiple lines, thus allowing you to input larger quantities of text. The `TextBox` control also provides the functionality of an HTML form password control. To enable these variations the `<asp:TextBox>` control needs some extra attributes:

❑ `textmode`: Specifies whether you want the control to have one line (not set), many lines (set to `multiline`), or have a single line of masked content (set to `password`)

❑ `rows`: Specifies the number of rows you want the textbox to have and will only work if `textmode` is set to `multiple`

❑ `columns`: Specifies the number of columns you want the textbox to have and will only work if `textmode` is set to multiple

If you wish to provide any default text that appears in the control, you can either place it between the opening and closing tags or set it in the `text` attribute of the control:

```
<asp:TextBox id="text1" runat="server">Default text here...</asp:TextBox>
<asp:TextBox id="text1" runat="server" text="Default text here..."/>
```

Let's look at an example that uses the `TextBox` control to ask for the name and address of the user, and a password as well. Previously in HTML, this would require three different types of controls; here we shall only use the `<asp:TextBox>` control.

Try It Out Using the `<asp:TextBox>` Control

1. In the `Ch03` folder, create `TIO-TextBox.aspx` and type in the following code:

```
<script runat="server" language="C#">
void Page_Load()
{
  if (Page.IsPostBack)
  {
    lblName.Text = "";
    lblAddress.Text = "";
    lblPassword.Text = "";
  }

  if (txtName.Text !="")
    lblName.Text = "You have entered the following name: " +  txtName.Text;

  if (txtAddress.Text !="")
    lblAddress.Text = "You have entered the following address: " +
                      txtAddress.Text;
```

```
    if (txtPassword.Text !="")
        lblPassword.Text = "You have entered the following password: " +
                            txtPassword.Text;

}
</script>

<html>
  <head>
    <title>Textbox Example</title>
  </head>
  <body>
    <asp:Label id="lblName" runat="server" /><br />
    <asp:Label id="lblAddress" runat="server" /><br />
    <asp:Label id="lblPassword" runat="server" /><br />
    <form runat="server">
      Please enter your name:
      <asp:TextBox id="txtName" runat="server" />
      <br /><br />
      Please enter your address:
      <asp:TextBox id="txtAddress" runat="server" textmode="multiline" rows=5
                                                     />
      <br/><br />
      Please enter your password:
      <asp:TextBox id="txtPassword" runat="server" textmode="password" />
      <br /><br />
      <input type="Submit">
    </form>
  </body>
</html>
```

2. Open `TIO-TextBox.aspx` in your browser, type in some details, and then click on **Submit Query** to see the results as shown in Figure 3-7:

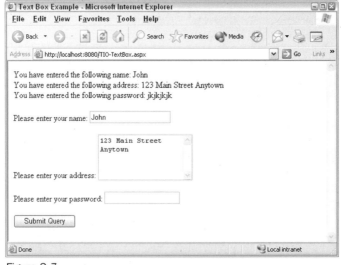

Figure 3-7

How It Works

Within the form, we have created three types of `TextBox` controls:

```
<asp:TextBox id="txtName" runat="server" />
<asp:TextBox id="txtAddress" runat="server" textmode="multiline" rows=5 />
<asp:TextBox id="txtPassword" runat="server" textmode="password" />
```

The first is identified as `txtName`, and requires no attributes other than `id` and `runat`. This is displayed as a single text field. The second control, `txtAddress`, is a multiline textbox, and requires the `textmode` attribute to be set to `multiline` so that we can set the number of rows we wish this textbox to have. Here, we have set it to 5 for the address. Lastly, we create a third control, `txtPassword`, in which the `textmode` attribute is set to `password`. This, again, will display a single line text field, but any text typed into will be masked by asterisks.

To display the results from the three controls, we have used three separate `<asp:Label>` controls:

```
<asp:Label id="lblName" runat="server" /><br />
<asp:Label id="lblAddress" runat="server" /><br />
<asp:Label id="lblPassword" runat="server" /><br />
```

Each one is identified with a different `id` attribute so that we can refer to them individually in other lines of our code. The job of assigning text values to these three label controls falls to the ASP.NET code contained within `<script>` tags at the top of the page.

```
lblName.Text = "";
lblAddress.Text = "";
lblPassword.Text = ""; }
```

First we make sure that blank values are assigned to each of the `<asp:Label>` controls in the first three lines. This is because once the page has been posted back, it will display the old messages, unless we clear them.

Then we check if `txtName` is not empty (that is if its text value is something other than `""`) and display the contents in `lblName` along with some hard coded text. This is repeated for the other labels.

<asp:RadioButtonList> and <asp:RadioButton>

The `<asp:RadioButtonList>` control works in the same way as its HTML forms equivalent or the Windows interface. Choice of one button excludes the selection of another button within the group. Note that the identifier for the whole group is set only once in the `id` attribute of the `<asp:RadioButtonList>` control:

```
<asp:RadioButtonList id="radSample" runat="server">
  <asp:ListItem id="option1" runat="server" value="Option A" />
  <asp:ListItem id="option2" runat="server" value="Option B" />
  <asp:ListItem id="option3" runat="server" value="Option C" />
</asp:RadioButtonList>
```

You can programmatically find out the option that was selected by the user by using `radSample.SelectedItem.Value`; if Option A is selected, the value returned will be `"Option A"`.

The following example uses a group of radio buttons to find out the destination selected by a user on an HTML form, and relays that information back to the user.

Try It Out   Using the <asp:RadioButtonList> Control

1.   Create `TIO-RadioButtonList.aspx` within the `Ch03` folder and enter the following code:

```
<%@ Page Language="C#" %>
<script runat="server">
  void Page_Load()
  {
    if (Page.IsPostBack)
    Message.Text = "You have selected " + radCity.SelectedItem.Value;
  }
</script>

<html>
  <head>
    <title>Radio Button List Example</title>
  </head>
  <body>
    <asp:Label id="Message" runat="server" />
    <br /><br />
    Which city interests you? <br /><br />
    <form runat="server">
      <asp:RadioButtonList id="radCity" runat="server">
        <asp:ListItem id="optMadrid" runat="server" value="Madrid" />
        <asp:ListItem id="optOslo" runat="server" value="Oslo" />
        <asp:ListItem id="optLisbon" runat="server" value="Lisbon" />
      </asp:RadioButtonList><br />
      <input type="Submit">
    </form>
  </body>
</html>
```

2.   View it in your browser as shown in Figure 3-8, select a city, and click on **Submit Query**:

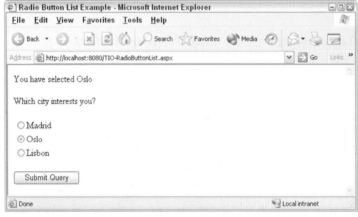

Figure 3-8

How It Works

The `TIO-RadioButtonList.aspx` page has a form with three radio buttons in a single group with the ID `radCity`. Note that we use a different ID and value for each option:

```
<form runat="server">
  <asp:RadioButtonList id="radCity" runat="server">
    <asp:ListItem id="optMadrid" runat="server" value="Madrid" />
    <asp:ListItem id="optOslo" runat="server" value="Oslo" />
    <asp:ListItem id="optLisbon" runat="server" value="Lisbon" />
  </asp:RadioButtonList><br />
  <input type="Submit">
</form>
```

In the `Page_Load()` section, we have used the three familiar lines to return information from the user to the form. We can get the selected option by reading the `SelectedItem.Value` property, which is similar to reading the selected value in a listbox:

```
if (Page.IsPostBack)
  Message.Text = "You have selected " + radCity.SelectedItem.Value;
```

If a radio button is selected, then the label named `Message` will have its text set to "You have selected" followed by the user's choice returned by `SelectedItem.Value`.

<asp:CheckBox> and <asp:CheckBoxList>

Checkboxes are similar to radio buttons in that they present multiple choices from a group of buttons. However, `<asp:CheckBox>` is for a *single* option (say, for the answer to, "Do you want to pay $5 more for quick shipping?") whereas with the `<asp:CheckBoxList>` control, a user can select more than one option (for the answer to, "Which free catalogs can we send you: Sports, Clothing, or Shoes?"). Most of the same principles that you followed in the `<asp:RadioButtonList>` example apply to checkboxes. The main difference is the syntax – radio buttons use `<options>` whereas checkboxes use `<ListItems>`. A solo `<asp:CheckBox>` has a single ID:

```
<asp:CheckBox id="chkQuickShipping" runat="server" />
```

An array of checkboxes can be contained inside an `<asp:CheckBoxList>` control. You need to set an `id` attribute for the `<asp:CheckBoxList>` control itself, and create a `<asp:ListItem>` control for each option inside the control as shown here:

```
<asp:CheckBoxList id="chkCatalogs" runat="server">
  <asp:ListItem id="itmSports" runat="server" value="Sports" />
  <asp:ListItem id="itmClothes" runat="server" value="Clothes" />
  <asp:ListItem id="itmShoes" runat="server" value="Shoes" />
</asp:CheckBoxList>
```

The next example is a tweaked version of the previous *Try-It-Out*, where the user is now allowed to select more than one holiday destination option.

Try It Out **Using the <asp:CheckBox> Control**

1. Open up the `TIO-RadioButtonList.aspx` and save it in the `Ch03` folder as `TIO-CheckBoxList.aspx` and change the highlighted code as follows:

```
<script runat="server" language="C#">
 void Page_Load()
  {
   string msg = "You have selected the following items:<br />";
   if (chkCities.Items[0].Selected)
      msg += chkCities.Items[0].Text + "<br />";
   if (chkCities.Items[1].Selected)
      msg += chkCities.Items[1].Text + "<br />";
   if (chkCities.Items[2].Selected)
      msg += chkCities.Items[2].Text + "<br />";
    lblCities.Text = msg;
  }
</script>
<html>
<head>
  <title>Checkbox List Example</title>
</head>
<body>
  <asp:Label id="lblCities" runat="server" /><br /><br />
  Which city do you wish to look at hotels for?<br /><br />
  <form runat="server">
    <asp:CheckBoxList id="chkCities" runat="server">
      <asp:ListItem id="optMadrid" runat="server" value="Madrid" />
      <asp:ListItem id="optOslo" runat="server" value="Oslo" />
      <asp:ListItem id="optLisbon" runat="server" value="Lisbon" />
    </asp:CheckBoxList><br /><br />
    <input type="Submit">
  </form>
</body>
</html>
```

2. Open `TIO-CheckBoxList.aspx` in your browser and select several options as shown in Figure 3-9; click on **Submit Query**:

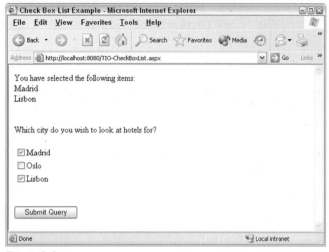

Figure 3-9

How It Works

Very little has changed with your page – all you've done is changed an HTML control to an `<asp:CheckBoxList>` and changed its ID. Notice that within checkbox groups the choices are labeled as `<ListItem>` rather than `<options>`.

Our ASP.NET code is the same as that used for the TIO ListBox example except that here it refers to a checkbox rather than a listbox. The syntax has also been modified to join the city name onto the end of the value in `msg`. Note that we can use the syntax `msg+=` to get the same result as the syntax `msg=msg+`.

```
void Page_Load()
{
  string msg = "You have selected the following items:<br />";
  if (chkCities.Items[0].Selected)
      msg += chkCities.Items[0].Text + "<br />";
  if (chkCities.Items[1].Selected)
      msg += chkCities.Items[1].Text + "<br />";
  if (chkCities.Items[2].Selected)
      msg += chkCities.Items[2].Text + "<br />";
  lblCities.Text = msg;
}
```

With this section, we have covered a set of basic ASP.NET server controls. You have seen how to use them to gather information from the user and then use that information in your code. In a number of pages you have used variables; for example, `msg` in the radio button and checkbox pages. You have also used control structures such as `if ()`.

> All ASP.NET controls start with `<asp: >`, contain the attribute `runat="server"`, and each control has an `id` attribute.

Before going on to chapters with other ASP.NET features, let's pause to look more closely at how to use variables in ASP.NET pages. Then we will take a closer look at the control structures in the logic being used.

Storing Information in C# Variables

Variables are fundamental to programming – they let you store information in memory. Once the information is stored, you can perform mathematical functions, calculate new dates, manipulate text, count the length of sentences, and perform many such functions. This book discusses the techniques of using variables in C#. The syntax would be different if you work in VB.NET or another language, but the theory is very similar.

A *variable* is a space in memory that is allocated a name and given a datatype by the programmer. These spaces in memory can be used to store pieces of information that will be used in the program. Think of variables as you might think of boxes or repositories for information. Different datatypes require different sizes and shapes of boxes – with different amounts of memory. Any variable is empty until you put information into it (although the memory space is *reserved* while the code runs). You can then view the information inside the variable, get the information out, or replace the information with new data. Variables have four parts: a name, a space in memory, a datatype, and the value that they hold.

C# is a *strongly typed* language, which means that every variable has a datatype associated with it, such as string, integer, or date. Typing tells C# how to deal with the data so that, for example, dates can be seen as proper dates and not a long 'division' operation such as 5/10/2003.

Declaring Value Type Variables

Good programming practice requires that you explicitly create or *declare* variables before you use them. In C#, the simplest type of variable declaration for value types is made with the datatype followed by the name of the variable. In the following case `int` implies that we want a variable of the datatype integer. We will talk at length about the different datatypes later in this chapter.

```
int NumberOfStates;
```

This statement performs three tasks. First, the name of the variable is established, second the datatype is noted, and third a space is allocated in the memory. Until the variable is assigned a value, it contains *nothing* (bear in mind that 0 *is* a value, so it won't contain zero or even a blank space). You can check if a string variable contains a value by using the following conditional check (`MyVariable == null`), which returns true if the variable is empty and false if the variable has a value.

While naming a variable, you have to remember the following rules:

❑ All variable names must begin with a letter (not a number or symbol)

❑ They may not contain an embedded period (full-stop) or a space

❑ They cannot be the same as C# reserved words (keywords) such as `if` and `void`

In C#, variable names are case sensitive. In the following example, the first line declares a variable as a `string` type with the name `strCarType`; the second line assigns a string value to that variable:

```
string strCarType;
strCarType = "Buick";
```

It's also possible to declare a variable and assign a value to it on a single line:

```
string strCarType = "Buick";
```

If you have several variables of the same type, you can set them up with one line of code (see `Demo-VariableDeclare.aspx` in the code download):

```
string strCarType1, strCarType2, strCarType3;
strCarType1 = "Buick";
strCarType2 = "Cadillac";
strCarType3 = "Pontiac";
```

You can also initialize and assign values to them on one line as follows:

```
string strCarType1 = "Buick", strCarType2="Cadillac", strCarType3="Pontiac";
```

However, you can not *mix* datatypes in one line of initialization or filling. The following line will not work:

```
string strCarType1, int strCarType2,  date strCarType3;
```

Now let's use our knowledge of variable declaration and assignment in an example. We'll take the code above and combine it with ASP.NET server controls.

Try It Out Using Variables

1. Create a file called `TIO-Variable1.aspx` and type in the following:

```
<%@ Page Language="C#" debug="true"%>
<script runat="server">

    void Page_Load()
    {
        string CapitalCityOfUK;
        int NumberOfStates;
        DateTime IndependenceDay;

        CapitalCityOfUK = "London";
        NumberOfStates = 50;
        IndependenceDay = Convert.ToDateTime("7/4/1776");

        lblCapital.Text = CapitalCityOfUK;
        lblNumStates.Text = Convert.ToString(NumberOfStates);
        lblDateIndependence.Text = Convert.ToString(IndependenceDay);
    }
</script>
```

```
<html>
<head>
<title>Creating Variables Example</title>
</head>
<body>
  The contents of CapitalCityOfUk is:
  <asp:Label id="lblCapital" runat="server" />
  <br>The contents of NumberOfStates is:
  <asp:Label id="lblNumStates" runat="server" />
  <br>The contents of IndependenceDay is:
  <asp:Label id="lblDateIndependence" runat="server" />
</body>
</html>
```

2. Open `TIO-Variable1.aspx` in your browser as shown in Figure 3-10:

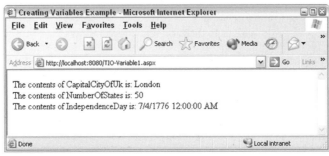

Figure 3-10

3. Add to the following line to the code, which uses a variable (`NumberofDaysInJuly`) that we have not declared:

```
CapitalCityOfUK = "London";
NumberOfStates = 50;
IndependenceDay = Convert.ToDateTime("7/4/1776");
NumberOfDaysInJuly = 31;
```

4. Save this file as `TIO-Variable2.aspx` and run the example. What you get is an error message as shown in Figure 3-11:

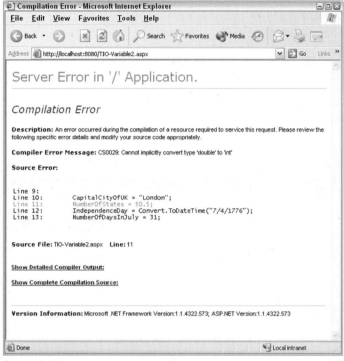

Figure 3-11

How It Works

The first section of code declares each of the variables we wish to use in the example. Note the difference in type to match the data we will store:

```
string CapitalCityOfUK;
int NumberOfStates;
DateTime IndependenceDay;
```

Having declared the variables, you can assign values to each. We will cover the details of the syntax (especially for DateTime) when we look at each datatype later in this chapter.

```
CapitalCityOfUK = "London";
NumberOfStates = 50;
IndependenceDay = Convert.ToDateTime("7/4/1776");
```

> **The value for a string datatype must be enclosed within double quotes while numbers should not be enclosed at all. Dates must be typed as a string within double quotes, and then that 'string' must be converted to the C# format used to store dates.**

In the last section, we've created three `<asp:Label>` controls. We then set the `Text` values of these labels to the contents of our variables. Note below that only a string type can go directly into a `Text` property. Both numbers and dates must be converted using the `ToString()` function of the `Convert` class.

```
lblCapital.Text = CapitalCityOfUK;
lblNumStates.Text = Convert.ToString(NumberOfStates);
lblDateIndependence.Text = Convert.ToString(IndependenceDay);
```

Your Web form duly displays the contents of your variables. You might be wondering what stops a control from displaying the literal text `CapitalCityOfUK`. The answer is the absence of quotation marks. Anything inside quotation marks is interpreted as literal text. Anything not contained in quotes is treated as a variable, numeric value, or object. You then amended your example to add another line:

```
NumberOfDaysInJuly = 31;
```

This line looks perfectly okay, but this causes an error – because you haven't declared the variable prior to using it. Variables cannot simply appear within your script or code – they must be explicitly declared and assigned. An error is generated because the `NumberOfDaysInJuly` variable used in the script is not declared.

You've seen how important datatypes are in your ASP.NET Web forms. Let's discuss the C# datatypes and when you should use them.

Datatypes

C# supports about two-dozen data types. These datatypes can be roughly divided into three groups: numeric, text, and miscellaneous datatypes.

Numeric

Numeric datatypes represent eleven of the C# datatypes. They are divided into three groups: integers, floating-point, and decimals.

Integers

Integers are whole numbers (numbers without a decimal component). Examples of integers are 3, -12, and 0. The various storage formats for integers vary with the size of integer that needs to be stored. You can use these types as per your requirements to make optimal use of memory resources:

❑   `int`: The integer datatype is referred to as `int` in code; can store whole numbers up to about 2 billion (`2,147,483,648`), both positive and negative.

❑   `uint`: Stores integers from 0 to 4 billion, but this range can consist of *only positive* numbers.

❑   `byte`: Can be used to store integers between the range 0 to 255, but negative values are not allowed. It's a useful type because a variable can easily be stored by the computer within a single byte – a computer's basic storage unit – and any processing or arithmetic done with them is therefore faster.

❑ sbyte: Same as byte but allows negatives, so the range is reduced to –128 to +127.

❑ short: As the name implies, can only accept a limited range of values, from – 32,768 to +32,767.

❑ ushort: is like uint and can be used for unsigned (positive) numbers; since memory space is not used for the sign, the value can go up to 65,535.

❑ long: Similar to the int type, but supports a much larger range; can contain a value up to 9,223,372,036,854,775,808 (that is 9 x 10^19), either positive or negative.

❑ ulong: Allows positives up to about 18 x 10^18.

Floating-Point Numbers

Floating point datatypes can store numbers with decimal places. The various floating point datatypes supported by C# are:

❑ float: Holds single precision floating-point numbers. The float type supports values within the range -3.402823E38 to -1.401298E-45 (for negative values), and 1.401298E-45 to 3.402823E38 (for positive values).

❑ double: Holds double precision floating-point numbers. The range of double is - 1.79769313486232E308 to -4.94065645841247E-324 (for negative values), and 4.94065645841247E-324 to 1.79769313486232E308 (for positive values).

Decimal

The decimal type accepts numbers with about 28 digits, which you can allocate between the left and right side of the decimal point. With zero decimal places, it can support large positive or negative numbers with up to 27 following zeros. Alternatively, you can store a very accurate number with about 27 digits to the right of the decimal point.

Selecting the Correct Numeric Datatype

Given the wide range represented by these eleven types, here is a short guide to selecting the correct type for your needs. Your code will be most efficient if you use the smallest and simplest type that will do the job.

❑ If you must use decimal numbers and you need less than 28 digits, you can use decimal. If you need decimal places and more digits, go to float, and if you need even more, then go to double. Currency is generally stored as a decimal type.

❑ If you don't need decimal places, then start with byte (0 to 255). Keep in mind that byte does not handle negative values. If you need to use larger numbers or negative values, then first use short, then go on to integer, and finally use the long type. If you will only use positive numbers, then consider the unsigned versions, where you might be able to settle for a smaller datatype.

If you have violated the limits of a Numeric type you will get an error such as "CS1021: Integral constant is too large" or "Cannot convert...."

Text Datatypes

Normally text datatypes store words or letters, but you can also use them to store symbols and numbers. At the same time, you should not store numbers that you plan to use in arithmetic. For example, a `string` variable called `MyString` can hold values like "2.0" or "July 4, 2004". However, you will not be able to perform any calculations on these values. Numbers usually go into one of the numeric datatypes.

An exception to this is a number that you will not perform any math with, such as telephone numbers, social security numbers, and catalog numbers that may contain a mix of numbers and letters; these are usually better stored as strings.

There are just two datatypes for storing text. The `string` datatype is almost always used. The other, `char`, stores only one character of text and it is in an encoded form.

String

The `string` type identifies its stored value as text, even if you supply it with a mixture of text and numerical data, numerical data alone, or even date information. A `string` variable will grow or shrink to accommodate any number of characters. However, it does not inherently contain any formatting like line breaks. See the following example on the `string` datatype (see `Demo-VariableStringAndChar.aspx`):

```
string CarType;
string CarEngineSize;
string CarModel;
string DatePurchased;

CarType = "Buick";
// this is normal
CarEngineSize = "2.0";
// this works, but is not normal
CarModel = "123-Z-456";
// OK because these numbers do not have a mathematical values
DatePurchased = " July 4, 1999";
// this works, but it is better to use the date type
```

As mentioned earlier, `string` values are encapsulated in double quotation marks, so they can be differentiated visually from numerical values without having to reference their actual declarations.

> **We use double quotation marks to encapsulate strings, and never single quotation marks, because they imply the use of the `char` datatype.**

The .NET Framework provides a number of special methods by which you can manipulate strings. These methods allow you to measure the length of a string, truncate a string at the beginning or end, return certain characters from a given string, or even convert a string into its numerical equivalent. String manipulation and conversion requires the use of the .NET `String` object, which will be discussed in later chapters.

Char

The char data type is a bit of a strange one, because it stores text as a number! This means you place a single character in a variable defined as a char, and it is stored as a number between 0 and 65535. The large storage capacity provides the ability to store characters from non-English languages. You store the value as follows (see Demo-VariableStringAndChar.aspx in the code download for this chapter):

```
Char MyLetter;
MyLetter = 'Q';
```

When you display the contents of a char variable, you see a text character despite the fact that it is stored as a code number.

> **For Western languages, almost all characters are represented by integers ranging from 0 to 255. This is the ASCII format of representation. However, to support additional languages (like Chinese) with a large number of characters, we need more space to store them. Therefore we use 256 squared = 65536 possible characters in a system called UNICODE.**

Other Datatypes

The next few datatypes don't really fit together, as they have nothing in common other than the fact that they are not numeric or text.

Date

The date datatype is treated differently than the text or numeric types. You must be accurate in entering and reading data. The date cannot be entered directly as a string. Rather, it must be converted using a function Convert.ToDateTime(). Within the parenthesis, place the date string in the format set by the Server's Windows Regional settings. For example, in the USA, this would be mm/dd/yy, dd/mm/yyyy in the UK, and dd.mm.yyyy in Germany. Conversely, when reading a date from a variable, you need to convert it to a string if you want to display it in a label:

```
DateTime MyDateTime;     //declares the variable
MyDateTime = Convert.ToDateTime(txtDateIn.Text);  //fills the variable
lblDateOut.Text = Convert.ToString(MyDateTime);   //reads the variable

// alternate formats for input
 MyDateTime = Convert.ToDateTime("1/1/2005");
 MyDateTime = Convert.ToDateTime("4:25:05 PM");
 MyDateTime = Convert.ToDateTime("16:25:05");
 MyDateTime = Convert.ToDateTime("1/1/2005 16:25:05");

// following line fails - use 24 hour time or AM/PM but not both
 MyDateTime  = Convert.ToDateTime("16:25:05 PM");
```

Boolean

Boolean variables can be set to one of two values: `true` or `false`. There are no acceptable alternatives such as 0 or 1 like in other languages. Note that `true` or `false` as a value should *not* be in quotes and must be all lower case as shown here:

```
bool MyBool;     //'my variable to indicate membership
MyBool = true;   // note lower case, no quotes
```

Naming Variables

As we've seen earlier, there are four basic rules for naming variables. First, all variable names must begin with a letter (not a number or symbol). Second, they may not contain an embedded period (or full-stop) or a space. Third, they cannot be the same as C# reserved words (keywords), such as `if` and `void`. Lastly, C# variables are case sensitive. Some programmers use the following kinds of non-descriptive variable names:

```
int i;
bool varBoolean;
int Counter;
DateTime Date;
```

This is a sloppy way of coding because such variable names increase the cost of creating and maintaining an application. At the same time, excessively long variable names are unwieldy and easy to mistype. Good programming practice is to use suitable names for variables that are meaningful to those who subsequently read the code.

When your variable name has more than one word, you can use two techniques. Some people like to separate the words with underscores like `Name_ First`. Some prefer to use 'Pascal case', wherein letters are lower case except the first of each word used in the variable, like `NameFirst`. You could also use 'Camel case,' which is the same as Pascal case, but with the first letter of the variable name in lowercase. Here are some additional naming tips:

❑   `DataStart` and `DateEnd` are better than `StartDate` and `EndDate`, as these two related variables will then come next to each other in an alphabetically sorted search.

❑   Variables like `Price`, `Name`, and `Number` are confusing because there are usually more than one of these. It is better to use a `NounAdjective` combination like `NameFirst` and `NameLast`.

❑   Variable names that coincide with datatypes aren't allowed.

❑   Avoid confusing and non-intuitive abbreviations, such as `FDOM` for first day of month –FDOM could stand for anything.

❑   Never use the same variable name for two different variables in a Web site, no matter how sure you are that they will not conflict.

A very common mistake occurs in programming when a variable of one type is used as if it is of another type. For example, a line of code tries to subtract a string from a date and throws an error. The sensible answer is to use a naming convention that identifies the type of a variable. The most common convention, called the *Hungarian notation*, is to use the first three letters of a variable's name to distinguish the type. The fourth letter of the variable is then typed in uppercase, to indicate that this is where the actual variable name starts. There are variations to this convention that are used by programmers. The following table lists some examples of the usage of this notation:

Datatype	Prefix	Example
bool	bln	blnMember
byte	byt	bytDaysInMonth
char	chr	chrWang
DateTime	dat	datDatePurchased
double	dbl	dblPi
decimal	dec	decSalary
float	Flt	fltRate
int	int	intDistanceToSun
long	lng	lngDistanceToStar
short	sho	shoNumberOfAtoms
string	str	strNameFirst

Variable Scope

A few simple questions arise when we consider using variables. How widely available is a variable? If a variable is created, can it be used by other events and methods on the page? Can it be seen by other pages, or can other users visiting the same Web site see it? These are the issues of *scope* – a definition of how widely a variable can be used. We will study three levels of variables: *block*, *function*, and *global*. It is important to create your variables with the least amount of scope to do the job. Then, when a variable is no longer needed it is destroyed and memory is freed up. Remember that the more limited the scope of variables, the faster your programs will run.

> You can't have two variables with the same name within the same scope. To be safe, avoid duplicating a variable name anywhere within a Web site. Do not rely on differences in case to differentiate between two variables.

Block-Level Variables

The block-level scope is the most limited in nature. A set of statements enclosed by curly braces after an `if` (or `while`) statement is considered a block (these structures are discussed in detail in *Chapter 4*). Variables created within the block scope can be used only within that block. When the block ends (say, after the last loop), the variable is destroyed. In the following example, the scope of the variable `strBlockLevelVariable` within the highlighted code and `strBlockLevelVariable` can no longer be referenced when execution passes out of the block, so `lblMessage1.Text` would contain nothing. (See `Demo-ScopeBlockLevel.aspx` and `Demo-ScopeBlockLevel-Fixed.aspx` in the code download.)

```
if(1==1)
{
    string strBlockLevelVariable;
    strBlockLevelVariable = "Very Short Lived!";
} // end if(1==1)
// nb: block-level variables now out of scope
lblMessage.Text = strBlockLevelVariable; //This statement will not execute
```

However, if we try to use `strBlockLevelVariable` within the block where it was created, as follows, then our `lblmessage` shows the message.

```
if(1==1)
{
    string strBlockLevelVariable;
    strBlockLevelVariable = "Very Short Lived!";
    lblMessage.Text = strBlockLevelVariable;
} // end if(1==1)
// nb: block-level variables now out of scope
```

The advantage of block variables is that they save resources for variables not needed outside the block. The disadvantage is that if you aren't careful, you can accidentally declare a variable inside a block and then try to access it outside the block scope. For this reason, many programmers avoid block declaration of variables.

Function-Level Variables

The next wider level of scope is the function-level variable. These variables are available to all of the code within a function (for example, the `Page_Load()` method). They can also be called *local* variables because they are local to the function that created them. Outside that function, the local variable has no value; this is because the lifetime of the variable ends when the subroutine ends.

Try It Out   Creating Block and Function-Level Variables

1.   In the `Ch03` folder, create the `TIO-VariableScope1.aspx` file and enter the following code:

```
<%@ Page Language="C#" Debug="true" %>
<script runat="server">
  void Page_Load()
  {
    string strMyFuncVariable = "Function-Level Variable";
    if(Page.IsPostBack)
    {
        string strMyBlockVariableUsedInside = "Block Variable Used In Block";
        lblMessageBlockInBlock.Text = strMyBlockVariableUsedInside;
        lblMessageFunction.Text = strMyFuncVariable;
    }   //end if pagepostback

  }   //end pageload
```

```
    </script>

<html>
<head>
    <title>Variable Scope</title>
</head>
<body>
    <form runat="server">
        <asp:Label id="lblMessageBlockInBlock" runat="server"
                   text="DEFAULT - BlockInBlock"></asp:Label>
        <br />
        <asp:Label id="lblMessageFunction" runat="server"
                   text="DEFAULT - Function"></asp:Label>
        <br />
        <asp:Button runat="server" Text="Submit"/>
    </form>
</body>
</html>
```

2.   Open it in your browser as shown in Figure 3-12 prior to the click:

Figure 3-12

3.   Add the following highlighted lines of code to declare a block variable inside a block but use it outside the block. Rename the file (and later save) as `TIO-VariableScope2.aspx` and view the page in your browser. Note the **strMyBlockVariable2** not declared error as seen in Figure 3-13:

```
<%@ Page Language="C#" Debug="true" %>
<script runat="server">

  void Page_Load()
  {
    string strMyFuncVariable = "Function Variable";
    if(Page.IsPostBack)
    {
      string strMyBlockVariableUsedInside = "Block Variable Used In Block";
      string strMyBlockVariableUsedOutside= "Block Variable Used After Block";
      lblMessageBlockInBlock.Text = strMyBlockVariableUsedInside;
      lblMessageFunction.Text = strMyFuncVariable;
    }   // end if(postback)
        // note - block variables now out of scope
    lblMessageBlockOutBlock.Text = strMyBlockVariableUsedOutside;
  }   // End page_load
```

```
    </script>

<html>
<head>
<title>Variable Scope</title>
</head>
<body>
  <form runat="server">
    <asp:Label id="lblMessageBlockInBlock" runat="server"
                 text="DEFAULT - BlockInBlock"></asp:Label>
    <br />
    <asp:Label id="lblMessageBlockOutBlock" runat="server"
                 text="DEFAULT - BlockOutBlock "></asp:Label>
    <br />
    <asp:Label id="lblMessageFunction" runat="server"
                 text="DEFAULT - Function"></asp:Label>
    <br />
    <asp:Button runat="server" Text="Submit"/>
    </form>
</body>
</html>
```

Figure 3-13

5. Move the offending line up into the block as follows, and modify the following lines of code in the file. Save the file as `TIO-VariableScope2Fixed.aspx`; the variable is now available for use:

```
void Page_Load()
{
  string strMyFuncVariable = "Function Variable";
  if(Page.IsPostBack)
  {
    string strMyBlockVariableUsedInside = "Block Variable Used In Block";
    string strMyBlockVariableUsedOutside= "Block Variable Used After Block";
    lblMessageBlockInBlock.Text = strMyBlockVariableUsedInside;
    lblMessageFunction.Text = strMyFuncVariable;
    // moving next line inside block solves the out-of-scope problem
    lblMessageBlockOutBlock.Text = strMyBlockVariableUsedOutside;
  }   //End If(postback)
}   //End Page_Load

  <form runat="server">
    <asp:Label id="lblMessageBlockInBlock" runat="server" text="DEFAULT -
    BlockInBlock"></asp:Label>
    <br />
    <asp:Label id="lblMessageBlockOutBlock" runat="server" text="DEFAULT -
    BlockOutBlock - fixed "></asp:Label>
    <br />
    <asp:Label id="lblMessageFunction" runat="server" text="DEFAULT -
    Function"></asp:Label>
    <br />
    <asp:Button runat="server" Text="Submit"/>
  </form>
</body>
</html>
```

6. Open the page in your browser as shown in Figure 3-14:

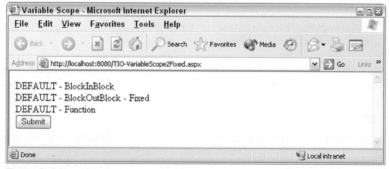

Figure 3-14

How It Works

Let's start with the `<form>` section where we have two labels to show variables in different situations: a block variable used in a block and a function-level variable. Note that they have a default text, so if we do nothing we will see the DEFAULT message:

```
<form runat="server">
  <asp:Label id="lblMessageBlockInBLock" runat="server" text="DEFAULT -
  BlockInBlock"></asp:Label>
  <br />
  <asp:Label id="lblMessageFunction" runat="server" text="DEFAULT -
  Function"></asp:Label>
  <br />
  <asp:Button runat="server" Text="Submit"/>
</form>
```

Now let's look at our `Page_Load()` method. We start by declaring a variable within a method (but outside a block), so this will be a function-level scope (or local) variable. We will use it later towards the end of the function and it works fine:

```
void Page_Load()
{
  string strMyFuncVariable = "Function Variable";
  if(Page.IsPostBack)
  {
    string strMyBlockVariableUsedInside = "Block Variable Used In Block";
    lblMessageBlockInBlock.Text = strMyBlockVariableUsedInside
    lblMessageFunction.Text = strMyFuncVariable
  }   //end if pagepostback

}   //end pageload
```

Then we have a block that is used if `Page.IsPostBack` is true. So the first time the code is run, you will just see the default text from the label. However, after clicking on **Submit**, this other block will run and the contents of the two variables will be put into the labels.

In step three, we changed three things: we added a new label, declared a variable inside a block, and, assigned a variable's contents to the new label. However, we performed that assignment outside the block and thus created an error.

In step five we moved the assignment line inside the block, so now the variable would be available, and this time the code runs without problems.

Global Variables

If variables created in subroutines are local to the subroutine that created them, how do we go about ensuring that the value of a variable persists after a subroutine is done and is still available to other subroutines on the page? The answer comes in the form of a *global* variable that is simply declared outside any individual method (this is in `Demo-VariableGlobal.aspx` in the download files):

```
<%@ Page Language="C#" debug="true"%>
<script runat="server">
```

```
string strVariableGlobal = "Use me anyplace on the page";
void Page_Load()
{
} //end Page_Load
```

The lifetime of a global variable begins at the start of the ASP.NET page, ends at the end of the page, and spans all functions within script. In ASP.NET, you can also create variables with a scope beyond the page, for example, for a user's session or for all of the users at a Web site. These techniques are covered in *Chapter 11*.

Constants

There will be occasions when you want the value assigned to a variable to remain constant throughout the execution of the code, for example sales tax percentage. This value will rarely change, yet when calculating the total of a shopping basket, you'll probably need to refer to it several times. Even if the tax is changed, you would not need to change the value during the code execution – rather, you would change it manually during a design mode edit of the code. C# allows you to store unchanging data in a *constant*. The main reason you'd assign a value to a constant is to prevent its alteration by a mistakenly written line of code.

In C#, we create a constant with the Const keyword followed by the datatype, generally outside of a function or method like a global variable. By convention, constants are named in uppercase:

```
Const int ABSOLUTEZERO = -273
Suppose we tried to assign another value to ABSOLUTEZERO, such as:
ABSOLUTEZERO = 0
```

This change would be rejected and an error message will be produced. Constants remain in force for the duration of the script, just as global variables do. It isn't possible to amend their value once they have been set. Constants make code easier to read and maintain, as they require less updating. Also, if you choose a self-explanatory name, they make your code easily understandable. They also give a performance increase over variables.

Conversion Functions

A common variable problem in ASP.NET programming arises when a value of one type could be used as another type, but C# will not allow the crossover. For example, if you have a textbox where a user enters a date like 1/1/2005, you will not be able to directly use that as a date in C# commands. This is because textboxes deliver the user's input as string data.

To overcome this problem, C# offers a class of functions that convert data from one type to another. This class is called Convert and the members all start with 'To' followed by the resulting datatype that you want to cast a variable to. Put the original value into the parenthesis and the function will return the cast value (see Demo-ConvertDataType.aspx file in the code download):

```
DateTime MyDate;
MyDate = Convert.ToDateTime(txtInput.Text);
```

There are over a hundred methods in the Convert class, all logically named. You can convert any variable to any type to any type that makes logical sense. The list is available in ASP.NET Web Matrix by clicking on the class browser in the lower right, then typing **Convert** in the search box. Select the Convert Class from the System Namespace and then in the middle of the screen expand the Methods folder. Note that the group of methods named ToInt32 is the way we normally convert to a number (ToInt16 and ToInt64 are beyond the scope of this book). Most commonly used conversions include:

```
MyStringVariable = Convert.ToString(a Number or Boolean or DateTime)
MyLabelControl.Text = Convert.ToString(a Number or Boolean or DateTime)
MyIntegerVariable = Convert.ToInt32(a string from a text control)
MyDateVariable = Convert.ToDateTime(a string from a text control)
```

Arrays

Arrays are like variables but can store a series of related values. Each value has an identifying number called an *index*. You could use an array to store the names of the Marx brothers, for instance (in the code bundle, see Demo-Array.aspx):

```
string[] strMarx = new string[6];    // '6' means we can hold six members
strMarx[0] = "Groucho";
strMarx[1] = "Harpo";
strMarx[2] = "Chico";
strMarx[3] = "Zeppo";
strMarx[4] = "Gummo";
strMarx[5] = "Karl";
lblMarx.Text = strMarx[3];
```

The first thing to note is that when we declare an array in C#, we state the size of the array variable in terms of the number of elements. As with variables, you must declare which type of data (string, integer, date, and so on) goes into the array. For example, the string[6] declaration creates a string array with six elements. However, when we refer to the members within code, we use a zero-based count; the first member has an index of zero and *not* one. There are actually six Marx brothers here (even if one isn't related by family!), and they occupy the positions 0 to 5 in the array. It's not mandatory to store a value in each item of the array, or to store values sequentially:

```
string [] strFriends = new string[5]; // up to 5 members
strFriends[1] = "Mr. Jones";
strFriends[4] = "Mr. Goldstein";
strFriends[3] = "Mrs. Soprano";
lblFriend.Text = strFriends[4];
```

All of the values in an array must be of the same datatype. For example, you could set up an array to have 50 entries, one for each of the states in the US with the following statement:

```
string[] StatesInUS = new string[50]
```

Arrays are particularly useful if you want to manipulate a whole set of data items as though they were one. The next chapter will discuss looping that can make changes to all the values in an array with just a few lines of code.

> *We establish space for 50 states. However, the numbering of the members starts at zero, so the last state would be number 49.*

The following simple page allows a user to submit a shipping company code and get back the actual name of the shipper. We will hold the shippers' names in an array where a shipper's code number is the same as its index number in the array.

Try It Out   Using Arrays

1. Create a new page named `TIO-Array.aspx` in the `Ch03` folder and enter the following lines:

```
<%@ Page Language="C#" Debug="true" %>
<script runat="server">

void Page_Load()
{
  if (Page.IsPostBack)
  {
     string[] VendorShipping = new string[4];
     VendorShipping[0] = "no shipping";
     VendorShipping[1] = "Canada Post";
     VendorShipping[2] = "UPS";
     VendorShipping[3] = "FedEx";
     string[] VendorShipping = new string[4];
     lblShipper.Text = "Shipper is " +
     VendorShipping[Convert.ToInt32(txtShipNum.Text)];
     lblShipper.Visible = true;
  }    //End if (Page.IsPostBack)
}    // End Page_Load

</script>
<html>
<head>
    <title>Array Example</title>
</head>
<body>
    <form runat="server">
        Please enter your shipper code number from your invoice<br />
        (should be between 0 and 3)
        <asp:TextBox id="txtShipNum" runat="server"
                     width="30px"></asp:TextBox>
        <br />
        <asp:Button id="Button1" runat="server" Text="Submit"></asp:Button>
        <br />
        <asp:Label id="lblShipper" runat="server"></asp:Label>
    </form>
</body>
</html>
```

2. View this page in the browser, then enter a number between 0 and 3, both inclusive, and submit it to see the results as seen in Figure 3-15:

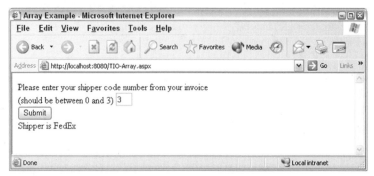

Figure 3-15

3. Try some test values that are likely to give you an error such as:

❑ Try entering '5' and note the error message that states that the index is outside the bounds of the array.

❑ Note the results of submitting with no number at all.

❑ Modify your code so that the array entry with the index 2 is not filled, and then ask for it. You can do that by adding slashes to make a comment as follows:

```
// VendorShipping[2] = "UPS";
```

Reactivate the index entry for 2 and save the file again so that it works when you review this chapter.

How It Works

Let's start on the form where the three controls are seen. The first allows the user to enter their shipper code number and the second submits the form. The third control, a label, displays the answer:

```
<form runat="server">
    Please enter your shipper code number from your invoice<br/>
    (should be between 0 and 3)
    <asp:TextBox id="txtShipNum" runat="server" width="30px"/><br />
    <asp:Button id="Button1" runat="server" Text="Submit"/><br />
    <asp:Label id="lblShipper" runat="server"/>
</form>
```

Now, we use the `Page_Load()` method in the script, but we only run the code if the page is a *postback*. A postback page means that the page is shown *after* the user clicks on a submit button (as opposed to the first time it is requested by the browser's URL Address input tool). Thus, the entire process of creating and filling the array only occurs with postback. Likewise, the `lblShipper` only appears on the page in a postback, not at the first request:

```
<script runat="server">
```

```
void Page_Load()
{
  if (Page.IsPostBack)
  {
    string[] VendorShipping = new string[4];
    VendorShipping[0] = "no shipping";
    VendorShipping[1] = "Canada Post";
    VendorShipping[2] = "UPS";

    lblShipper.Text = "Shipper is " +
    VendorShipping[Convert.ToInt32(txtShipNum.Text)];
    lblShipper.Visible = true;
  }    //End if (Page.IsPostBack)
}    // End Page_Load

</script>
```

We will assume that the user has entered a number. In the following line, we will set the text of lblShipper to some value, plus a value from the VendorShipping array. The index will be whatever number was typed into the txtShipNum. The TextBox control returns text but the index of the array only accepts an integer. So we run the text control input through the Convert.ToInt32() function to get an integer.

```
lblShipper.Text = "Shipper is " +
VendorShipping[Convert.ToInt32(txtShipNum.Text)];
```

We then looked at three kinds of errors. The first was the result of C# trying to look up an index number (5) that was not in the array. This is common and requires that you validate user data before trusting it as an index value. Likewise, you can never assume that a given textbox will actually have data. The error from the missing index (2) was a little more subtle. Like a variable, an array when created does not have data. If you request the value of an empty index you will get back nothing.

The Array class also provides us with an IndexOf() method, which returns an integer representing the first occurrence of a value in a specified array, but only works on single-dimension arrays. For example, to find out which element contains the first occurrence of the "FedEx" string, we use the following expression (see Demo-ArrayIndexOf.aspx in the code bundle for this chapter):

```
IntShipperCode = Array.IndexOf(VendorShiping, "FedEx")
```

Note that this matching is case sensitive, and if there is no match, C# will return -1.

Multi-Dimensional Arrays

If you need to keep information of a two-dimensional nature, you can do it by declaring a two-dimensional array. For instance, you might want to store a set of related information separately, such as a first name, last name, and employee number. A normal (one-dimensional) array would be unsuitable because all three pieces of information would have to be in one string. You can achieve far better results by adding another parameter to your array declaration:

```
string [] strClient = new string[4,3]; // 4 people, 3 properties each
```

This will set up a two-dimensional array of up to 4 by 3, which can hold a total of 12 values. You can assign values to a multi-dimensional array by referencing each element of the array through its two-value index. For example, you could use such an array to store first and last names and the phone numbers for four people (download `Demo-ArrayMultidimensional.aspx`):

```
strClient[0,0] = "John";
strClient[0,1] = "Buck";
strClient[0,2] = "111-111-1111";

strClient[1,0] = "Jane";
strClient[1,1] = "Doe";
strClient[1,2] = "222-222-2222";

strClient[2,0] = "Jill";
strClient[2,1] = "Fawn";
strClient[2,2] = "333-333-3333";

strClient[3,0] = "Jade";
strClient[3,1] = "Cervid";
strClient[3,2] = "444-444-4444";
```

The first dimension stores the information that is related to one person, while the second dimension holds data of the same type for each different person. To get the last name of the first client you use `strClients[0,1]`, which is 'Buck'.

You can also think of the data stored in a table where the first index represents columns and the second index represents rows. Therefore, the value in `strClient[0,1]` represents the value in the first column and the second row, which would be 'Buck'.

Array Index	0	1
0	John	Jane
1	Buck	Doe
2	111-111-1111	222-222-2222

Benefits of Arrays

Arrays are a very popular way to group elements together and they have some very important benefits:

❑ **Easy to use:** Arrays are very easy to use and used in almost every programming language – if you have done any programming earlier, you will almost certainly have come across them

❑ **Fast to alter elements**: Arrays are just a consecutive list of items, so altering the items is extremely fast and pretty easy as we can easily locate any element

❑ **Fast to move through elements**: Because an array is stored continuously in memory, it's quick and easy to cycle through the elements one-by-one from start to finish in a loop

❑ **You can specify the type of the elements**: When you create an array, you can *define* the datatype

Limitations of Arrays

However, as we noted earlier, arrays also have some distinct limitations:

❑ **Fixed size**: Once you have created an array, it will not automatically resize if you try to add more items onto the end.

❑ **Inserting elements mid-way into a filled array is difficult**: If you wanted to add an element between two existing elements, it can be quite challenging. First, you may have to increase the size of the array to make space. In addition, you then have to move all the existing elements up by one index count to make space for a new element.

Data Collections

All in all, arrays are quite simple to understand and very easy to use. However, we often need more sophisticated ways to group items together. These advanced techniques in C# are grouped as *collections* and include the `ArrayList`, the `HashTable`, and the `SortedList`. Collections are characterized by:

❑ A collection can contain an *unspecified* number of members.

❑ Elements of a collection need to be *related* only by the fact that they exist in the collection.

❑ Elements of a collection do not have to share the same *datatype*.

❑ An object's *position* in a collection can change whenever a change occurs in the collection as a whole. Therefore, the position of a specific object in the collection can vary.

ArrayList

The `ArrayList` is a special array that provides us with some functionality over and above that of the standard `Array`. Most importantly, you can dynamically resize it by simply adding and removing elements. Let's see how an `ArrayList` measures up.

Benefits of ArrayLists

The benefits of ArrayList are as follows:

❑ **Supports automatic resizing**: When creating an `ArrayList`, you do not need to specify the array bounds (size) – as we add elements, the array automatically ensures there's enough space.

❑ **Inserts elements**: An `ArrayList` starts with a collection containing no elements. You can add them as you choose (and in any position you choose for) them.

❑ **Flexibility when removing elements**: You can remove elements from an `ArrayList` very easily.

❑   **Easy to use**: Using an `ArrayList` requires you to learn some new commands but they are intuitive.

Limitation of ArrayLists

There is one major limitation to an `ArrayList`. Given that the `ArrayList` control seems to offer so much more than arrays, you may be wondering why we bother using arrays at all – the reason is simply a matter of speed. The flexibility of an `ArrayList` comes at a cost, and since memory allocation is a very expensive business (in performance terms at least), the fixed structure of the simple array makes it a lot faster to work with.

Using ArrayLists

We create objects from the `ArrayList` by using a general type of syntax that will be covered in detail later. Since an ArrayList is an object, we create it as follows:

```
ArrayList ShippersArrayList = new ArrayList();
```

You can use whatever name you want instead of `ShippersArrayList`, but it must follow the rules defined for naming variables. We use the `new` keyword since we are creating a new instance of the `ArrayList` object. As you can see, you don't need to specify how large it should be. Once you have an empty `ArrayList` object, you can use the `Add()` method to add elements to it:

```
ShippersArrayList.Add("none");
ShippersArrayList.Add("Canada Post");
ShippersArrayList.Add("UPS");
```

Each new item in the `ArrayList` is added to the end of the list, so it has the largest index number. If we want to insert an item into the middle of the list (in the example below, this is location 2), we can use `Insert()` with a numeric argument as follows:

```
myArrayList.Insert(2,"MyDataNew");
```

> **myArrayList.Add()** puts the new member at the end. **myArraylist.Insert()** lets you specify a location in the list to insert the new member.

You can also remove members of an `ArrayList` using either of the following syntaxes. In the following code snippet, `"MyData2"` would be the actual data such as `"UPS"`. Notice they use slightly different keywords; if you are providing an index number, you need to use `RemoveAt()`:

```
myArrayList.RemoveAt(2);
myArrayList.Remove("MyData2");
```

Let's create a page that creates an `ArrayList` of shippers and then shows them in a dropdown listbox. This will introduce us to some data binding concepts covered later, but they are not difficult.

Try It Out **Using an ArrayList**

1. In your `Ch03` folder, create `TIO-ArrayList.aspx` and enter the following code:

```
<%@ Page Language="C#" Debug="true" %>
<script runat="server">

    void Page_Load()
    {
        ArrayList ShippersArrayList = new ArrayList();
        ShippersArrayList.Add("none");
        ShippersArrayList.Add("Canada Post");
        ShippersArrayList.Add("UPS");

        ShippersArrayList.Insert(1,"FedEx");

        MyDropDownList.DataSource = ShippersArrayList;
        MyDropDownList.DataBind();
    }   //End Page_Load()

</script>
<html>
<head><title>ArrayList Example</title></head>
<body>
  <form id="Form1" method="post" runat="server">
    <asp:DropDownList id="MyDropDownList" runat="server" />
  </form>
</body>
</html>
```

2. Run it in your browser as shown in Figure 3-16:

Figure 3-16

How It Works

There are just two changes here from when we used a simple array. First, we are using an array list that requires us to use the special syntax for creating objects:

```
ArrayList ShippersArrayList = new ArrayList();
```

Note that we don't specify a length or a datatype. This is because the elements will be assigned dynamically (as and when we need them) and can be of any type.

Next, we use the object's Add() method to add three strings as elements that are added to the end:

```
ShippersArrayList.Add("none");
ShippersArrayList.Add("Canada Post");
ShippersArrayList.Add("UPS");
```

Now we test the Insert by adding one to the second position (index number 1, since first position is index number 0):

```
ShippersArrayList.Insert(1,"FedEx");
```

Finally, we specify that ShippersArrayList is a data source for the dropdown list, and bind the data:

```
MyDropDownList.DataSource = ShippersArrayList
MyDropDownList.DataBind()
...
<asp:DropDownList id="MyDropDownList" runat="server" />
```

Obviously, an ArrayList is much more amenable to manipulation than a simple array, even if it is slower and a more resource intensive. Read on for an option that moves us completely away from the use of index numbers.

Hashtables

In some respects, the Hashtable object is quite similar to an ArrayList, except that we don't have to use a numerical index. Instead, we can use a *key* that can be numeric, textual, or even in form of a date. For example, we might want our index to be the text of country codes (such as US and UK) rather than numbers. Some people refer to Hash keys as an 'index', but it is best to leave the term index for arrays and arraylists.

Benefits of Hashtables

The benefits of Hashtables are as follows:

- ❑ **Non-numeric indexes allowed**: Because you can use text, numbers, or dates as your key (index), the Hashtable object is flexible for looking up data.

- ❑ **Inserting elements**: When you use a Hashtable, you can add as many pairs of key/value elements as necessary. You do not have to specify the size ahead of time (as simple arrays require).

- ❑ **Removing elements**: You can remove items from Hashtable objects very easily.

- ❑ **Fast Lookup**: The Hashtable collection provides very fast lookup.

Limitations of Hashtables

The limitations of Hashtables are:

❑ **Performance and speed**: Although the lookup is very quick, each time we add and remove items from a `Hashtable`, .NET has to do quite a bit of work in order to keep its lookup mechanism optimized. This work ultimately makes `Hashtable` objects *slower* to update but *faster* to use in a look-up than `ArrayList` objects.

❑ **Keys must be unique**: An array automatically keeps the index values unique. In a `Hastable` we must monitor the key uniqueness. If you expect to have duplicate keys (like more then one person as a salesman for a given company), you should consider using a relational database for storage of information.

❑ **No useful sorting**: The items in a Hashtable are sorted internally to make it easy to find objects very quickly. But it's not done by using the keys or values, so for our purposes, the items may as well not be sorted at all.

Using a Hashtable

You can create a `Hashtable` object by using the same syntax as an `ArrayList` (download `Demo-Hashtables.aspx`):

```
Hashtable myHashtable = new Hashtable();
```

Once it's created, you can then add the *key-value* pairs. Remember that the key is like an index for the entry and the value is the data we're storing. We store each element using the `Add()` method with the following syntax:

```
myHashtable["UK"] = "United Kingdom";
myHashtable["US"] = "United States";
```

Hashtables with numbers or dates for the keys are written as follows. In general, it is best to use only one datatype for the index of a hashtable:

```
myHashtable[Convert.ToDateTime("1/1/2005")] = "Event on January 1st 2005";
```

> You need to convert **DateTime** index values when they are used as an index for a Hashtable.

To read an element, you just need to specify the key and the value is returned. The following code puts the value `United Kingdom` into a variable named `CountryName`. Remember that the keys are *case-sensitive*, so the fourth line in the following code snippet would put nothing into `CountryName`:

```
string CountryName;
CountryName = Convert.ToString(myHashtable["UK"]);   // works fine
// next line fails because incorrect case won't find a match so returns a
blank
CountryName = Convert.ToString(myHashtable["uk"]);
lblOut.Text = CountryName;
```

Let's look at an example page that uses Hashtables. Let's build a page that allows users to find out who is performing on a given date of a concert series.

Try It Out Hashtables

1. In the Ch03 folder, create TIO-HashTable.aspx and enter the following code:

```
<%@ Page Language="C#" Debug="true" %>
<script runat="server">

  void Page_Load()
  {
    lblShow.Visible = false;
    if (Page.IsPostBack)
    {
      DateTime datDateIn;
      Hashtable hashConcerts = new Hashtable();
      hashConcerts[Convert.ToDateTime("1/3/2005")] = "Bridgemen";
      hashConcerts[Convert.ToDateTime("1/4/2005")] = "Vanguard";
      hashConcerts[Convert.ToDateTime("1/2/2005")] = "Blue Devils";
      hashConcerts[Convert.ToDateTime("1/1/2005")] = "Belevederes";

      datDateIn = Convert.ToDateTime(txtDateIn.Text);
      lblShow.Text = "On this date enjoy the: ";
      lblShow.Text += hashConcerts[datDateIn];
      lblShow.Visible = true;
    }    //End if (Page.IsPostBack)
  }    //End  Page_Load

</script>
<html>
<head>
    <title>HashTable Example</title>
</head>
<body>
    <form runat="server">
        <h3>2005 Drum and Bugle Corps Concert
        </h3>
        Please enter a date between 1/1/2005 and 1/4/2005
        <asp:TextBox id="txtDateIn" runat="server"></asp:TextBox>
        <br />
        <asp:Button id="Button1" runat="server" Text="Look up"></asp:Button>
        <br />
        <asp:Label id="lblShow" runat="server"></asp:Label>
    </form>
</body>
</html>
```

2. Call up the page in your browser, and enter some dates as shown in Figure 3-17:

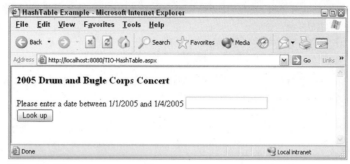

Figure 3-17

How It Works

In the form, we have a textbox to receive a date and a label that displays the performer:

```
<form runat="server">
    <h3>2005 Drum and Bugle Corps Concert</h3>
    Please enter a date between 1/1/2005 and 1/4/2005
    <asp:TextBox id="txtDateIn" runat="server"></asp:TextBox>
    <br />
    <asp:Button id="Button1" runat="server" Text="Look up"></asp:Button>
    <br />
    <asp:Label id="lblShow" runat="server"></asp:Label>
</form>
```

Up in the script, we start by hiding the lblShow label until we know a date has been requested. We then check if this is a postback. If not, we don't do anything:

```
void Page_Load()
{
    lblShow.Visible = false;
    ...
    ...
}   //End Page_Load
</script>
```

However, if the page is displayed as the result of a postback, it should have a date. We start with two declarations: the first will hold the incoming date and the second will create our Hashtable:

```
DateTime datDateIn;
Hashtable hashConcerts = new Hashtable();
```

Then we fill our Hashtable by using dates as the keys. Note that you must enclose the dates in quotation marks. Also note that you can add items in any order because .NET will find them by their keys:

```
hashConcerts[Convert.ToDateTime("1/3/2005")] = "Bridgemen";
hashConcerts[Convert.ToDateTime("1/4/2005")] = "Vanguard";
hashConcerts[Convert.ToDateTime("1/2/2005")] = "Blue Devils";
hashConcerts[Convert.ToDateTime("1/1/2005")] = "Belevederes";
```

Now we have to take the text that comes from `txtDateIn` and convert it to a date using the `ToDateTime()` function:

```
datDateIn = Convert.ToDateTime(txtDateIn.Text);
```

We put some default display text into the label and then add the value returned from the Hashtable to it. Now we can show the label with the performer:

```
lblShow.Text = "On this date enjoy the: ";
lblShow.Text += hashConcerts[datDateIn];
lblShow.Visible = true;
```

SortedList

A `SortedList` is another collection that stores key-value pairs, in which we can not only insert and remove items at will, but can also rely on the items being efficiently ordered. In fact it's really just like a `Hashtable` object in which the elements are automatically sorted according to their keys. Just like the `ArrayList` and `Hashtable` objects, the `SortedList` class lives in the `System.Collections` namespace.

Since the items in a `SortedList` are always stored in a well defined order, we get the best aspects of a `Hashtable` object (the ability to use key-value pairs) along with the best aspects of an `ArrayList` (the ability to sort the items). Remember, however, that the items in a `SortedList` are sorted on the key, and not on the value. A `SortedList` is most useful when we have to sort a list of key-value pairs for which the ordering of the key is what matters, rather than the order of the values. For example, we might use a sorted list to hold entries in a dictionary.

We create and use a `SortedList` collection in the same manner as a `HashTable`. Remember that we have to use the `new` keyword when creating the object. Adding items to a `SortedList` is exactly the same as with a `Hashtable`, the only difference being that each item is automatically inserted in the correct position in the list, according to the key-based sort order. A value can be read from the `SortedList` as follows (you can see this in action in `Demo-SortedList.aspx` available in the code download):

```
SortedList stlShippers = new SortedList();

stlShippers["cp"]="Canada Post";
stlShippers["fe"]="Federal Express";
stlShippers["us"]="United State Postal Service";
lblOut.Text = "The full name of shipper = " + stlShippers[txtCodeIn.Text];
```

The last dozen pages of this chapter covered four ways to handle sets of related data. First, we used an array, which gave us indexed access to a group of data. Although fast, it is limited in capabilities. Then we used the `ArrayList` object, which gives us more power to arrange the order of items but still within a numeric index system. The `Hashtable` object broke free of numeric indexing by using a key, which can be of numeric, text, or date type. And finally, we used the `SortedList` object, which added automatic maintenance of the order of keys that are similar to a Hashtable, but at a performance price.

Summary

The chapter started with a discussion of the difference in the ways in which an HTML and ASPX page are handled on the server as well as the additional interpretation step required for an ASPX page. ASPX pages enable building a Web page per request.

Further in the chapter, ASP.NET server controls were introduced and their server-side capabilities demonstrated. All of these controls require you to use the specific <asp:...> tag and to include the runat="server" attribute. You should make it a habit to always include the id="ControlName" attribute so that you can refer to the control in code.

When using a control in code, you can refer to it with the syntax ControlName.Property, where property is usually Text. All controls have three basic properties: runat, id, and visible in addition to properties such as text, backcolor, and width.

The most common mistakes with ASP.NET controls arise from radio buttons and list controls. You need to be careful and use <asp:RadioButtonList> if there is more than one option (as opposed to <asp:RadioButton>), so that you have one id attribute for the list. Also ensure that you add a different id for each option. You can use ListBoxes to obtain multiple selections from a user by setting the control to be in the multiple selection mode.

Creating variables results in four events: creation of a variable name, creation of space in memory for the variable, allocation of a datatype to the variable, and assigning a value to the variable. When you name a variable, you must start with a letter and not have spaces or periods (full stops) in the name. It is best to keep the names descriptive but short. You could consider the use of camel case and you *must* avoid using a variable name twice in an application.

We then discussed the types of variables in C#. Three types of numeric datatypes support decimals: (from smallest to largest) decimal, float, and double. Numeric types that support only integers (no decimals) include (again, smallest to largest) byte, short, int, and long. These also come in unsigned types. The ushort, uint, and ulong datatypes can hold only positive numbers but larger in value as compared to the signed counterpart. Always select the smallest numeric type that will do the job; for currency, use the decimal type.

Text information is stored in a string type variable. Strings are also used for numeric characters that are identifiers or codes that have no arithmetic value (for example telephone numbers). When assigning a text value, you need to enclose it in double quotation marks.

Any true/false data is stored in a Boolean variable (referred to as bool in code). Both dates and times are stored in the Date variable. Dates are converted prior to storage using the Convert.ToDateTime(); numbers do not require quotes while assignment to variables. The conversion functions (such as Convert.ToDateTime, Convert.ToInt32 and Convert.ToString) allow you to change data so that it can be used as a different type.

We also covered the scope of variables. Scope establishes the amount of time for which a variable will exist, or to put the idea another way, defines limitations on the code that can use the variable. Block variables are declared within a block and only available to that block. Function-level (local) variables are limited to the function in which they are declared. Global variables, declared outside of any function, are available to the entire page. Always use the smallest scope possible.

We studied four ways to store related groups of information of the same datatype. The simplest and fastest is the array, which tracks members by an index number. `ArrayLists` have more capabilities to sort, add, and remove members, but still use a numeric index. A `HashTable` allows you to use non-numeric identifiers called keys, such as text or dates, but is slower than an array. Finally, you can use `SortedLists` which are even slower, but hold the members in the order of the keys.

Exercises

1. Explain the difference between `<form>` and `<form runat="server">` and describe how each is handled.

2. What is a variable, and how is it related to datatypes in C#?

3. Use variables of the `string`, `numeric`, and `date` type to create an ASPX file that displays your name, age, and date of birth.

4. Arrange the following into groups of numeric, textual, and miscellaneous datatypes. Rank the numeric datatypes according to the size number they can hold. Give an example of a value and use for each:

   ❑ `integer`, `char`, `byte`, `uint`, `short`, `boolean`, `string`

   ❑ `long`, `sbyte`, `float`, `double`, `ushort`, `date`, `decimal`, `ulong`

5. Create an array containing five of your favorite singers. Concatenate the elements of your array into one string, and after the opening sentence "My 5 favorite singers are:", display them in a clear way using the `<asp:Label>` control.

6. Describe a situation in which you would use each of the following and state why that choice is the best:

   ❑ Arrays

   ❑ ArrayLists

   ❑ Hashtables

   ❑ SortedLists

Control Structures and Procedural Programming

In this chapter, we continue to explain programming techniques in C#. In the last chapter, we focused on obtaining and holding information in variables or server controls. Now we will work on manipulating that data using lines of code. Specifically, we want to know how to control the order of execution of those lines of code.

First, we will cover the basics of creating expressions. Then we will study two of the three groups of control structures: *branching* and *looping*. We will cover the third group, *jumping*, in the next chapter.

This chapter will cover:

- ❑ Assignments, arithmetic operators, and string concatenation
- ❑ Comparison operators
- ❑ Logical operators
- ❑ Overview of control structures
- ❑ Branching structures: `if` and `switch`
- ❑ Looping Structures: `for`, `while`, `do...while`, and `foreach...in`

Operators

We use *operators* to manipulate values. An operator is a symbol that carries out a predefined operation on the operands and generates a result. If X=1+2, then X is a variable (or control property value), = and + are operators and 1 and 2 are operands. We have already seen many examples of basic data manipulation using operators in the last two chapters, but in this section, we'll introduce the concepts more formally.

Assignment Operator

The familiar equals sign (=) *assigns* a value to a variable or control value. (Note that the symbol = = is a test for equality, different from an assignment.) The variable *name* goes on the left; the variable *value* goes on the right. C# doesn't enforce spaces on either side of the equals sign, but you may prefer to include some to make your code easier to read:

```
intMyVariable = 2;
lblMyLabel.Text = "Sale Ends January 15.";
```

You can also use the assignment operator to change values of variables using the following syntax:

```
intMyVariable = 2;
intMyVariable = intMyVariable + 1
```

At the end of these two lines, `intMyVariable` equals three. Mathematicians will be scratching their heads, wondering how `intMyVariable` can be equal to `intMyVariable` plus 1; it's similar to saying 2 = 2 +1, which is impossible. In C#, variable values are calculated on the right, and then stored on the left of the equals sign. Thus in this example `intMyVariable + 1` is evaluated first, and *assigned* to `intMyVariable` at the end, replacing the old value in `intMyVariable`.

C# also offers a shorter syntax to perform the above task, at the end of which `intMyVariable` equals three:

```
intMyVariable = 2
intMyVariable += 1
```

Arithmetic Operators

The arithmetic operators available in C# are:

Operator	Symbol
Addition	+
Subtraction	−
Multiplication	*
Division	/
Exponentiation	^
Negation	−
Modulus	%

Here is a very simple example that assigns values to the variables `intNumber1` and `intNumber2` before adding them together, and assigns the result to a third variable `intNumber3` (See download file in Chapter 04 folder `Demo-Operators.aspx`):

```
int intNumber1;
int intNumber2;
int intNumber3;
intNumber1 = 14;
intNumber2 = 12;
intNumber3 = intNumber1 + intNumber2;
lblResult1.Text = Convert.ToString(intNumber3);
```

Because of this, `intNumber3` will contain the value 26.

You can also use brackets (parentheses) to influence the order in which a calculation is performed. For example, in the following code we divide the variable `intNumber2` by 6 and add the result to the variable `intNumber1`:

```
int intNumber4;
int intNumber5;
int intNumber6;
intNumber4 = 14;
intNumber5 = 18;
intNumber6 = intNumber4 + (intNumber5/6);
lblResult2.Text = Convert.ToString(intNumber3);
```

First, the computer evaluates the contents of the brackets, following normal mathematical procedure: `intNumber2` is divided by 6 and yields the result 3. This is added to the value of `intNumber1`, and the result of this is 17, which is assigned to the variable `intNumber3`.

As a quick reminder, normal mathematical procedure is to start inside the innermost pair of parentheses and work from left to right performing exponentiation. Within these parentheses, go left to right performing multiplication and division and then finally go left to right performing addition and subtraction. Then repeat the previous steps again for the next innermost set of parentheses, until you've calculated the expression. All programming languages use these rules for performing arithmetic operations. Using parentheses is a good idea to make your code more readable, even when they may not be technically required for the evaluation to occur correctly.

Let's have a go at a quick example that performs a simple tax calculation. To do this you need to create three variables, one for earnings, one for the tax percentage, and one for the total. We're going to deduct the earnings by whatever percentage the tax rate is set to, and display the output in the familiar `<asp:label>` control.

Try It Out   Tax Calculator Using Arithmetic Operators

1.   Create a folder named `C:\BegAspNet11\Ch04` and within this folder create a new file called `TIO_CalculateTax.aspx`. Enter the following code in the All view (deleting the existing code):

```
<%@ Page Language="C#" Debug="true" %>
<script runat="server">

    void Page_Load()
```

```
            {
        if (Page.IsPostBack)
        {
          lblTax.Text = "Your tax bill would be $";
          lblTax.Text +=
          Convert.ToString(Convert.ToInt32(txtEarnings.Text)*
          Convert.ToInt32(txtTaxRate.Text)/100);
          lblTax.Visible=true;
        }   //end if (Page.IsPostBack)
      }// End  Page_Load()

</script>
<html>
<head>
    <title>Calculate Tax Bill</title>
</head>
<body>
    <h3>Tax rates
    </h3>
    <form runat="server">
        Please enter your earnings: $
        <asp:TextBox id="txtEarnings" runat="server"
          width="80px"></asp:TextBox>
        <br />
        Please enter your tax rate, for example enter '7' for 7%
        <asp:TextBox id="txtTaxRate" runat="server"
          width="30px"></asp:TextBox>
        <br />
        <asp:Button id="Button1" runat="server" Text="Submit"></asp:Button>
        <br />
        <asp:Label id="lblTax" runat="server" visible="false"></asp:Label>
        <br />
    </form>
</body>
</html>
```

2. View this in your browser. Note that the output label does not appear. When you enter some values and click Submit, the calculation is made and the label appears as shown in Figure 4-1:

Figure 4-1

How It Works

The form has two `asp:textbox` controls to receive data. There is a `Submit` button and a `Label` for output interspersed with some explanatory text. Note that the label is set to be invisible:

```
<form runat="server">
    Please enter your earnings: $
    <asp:TextBox runat="server" ID="txtEarnings" width="80px"/><br/>
    Please enter your tax rate, for example enter '7' for 7%
    <asp:TextBox runat="server" ID="txtTaxRate" width="30px"/><br/>
    <asp:Button runat="server" Text="Submit"/><br/>
    <asp:Label runat="server" ID="lblTax" visible=false/><br/>
</form></body></html>
```

In the script, we execute the code during page load, but only if it is a postback. If it's not a postback, the user has requested the page and thus the input textboxes would be empty:

```
<%@ Page Language="C#" Debug="true" %>
<script runat="server">

    void Page_Load()
    {
        if (Page.IsPostBack)
        {
```

In the next line, we put some boilerplate text into the `lblTax.text`:

```
        lblTax.Text = "Your tax bill would be $";
```

Then we do the calculation inside the parentheses. That result is then converted to a string because a label can have difficulty with non-string data types:

```
lblTax.Text += Convert.ToString(Convert.ToInt32(txtEarnings.Text)*
               Convert.ToInt32(txtTaxRate.Text)/100);
```

Finally, we make the label visible:

```
lblTax.Visible=true;
}    //end if (Page.IsPostBack)
}// End  Page_Load()

</script>
```

Some find the modulo operator difficult to understand. Its symbol is the percent sign (%). Modulo will return the remainder of a division. For example, 10 mod 3 = 1 because 10 divided by 3 gives 3 with a remainder of 1. It is the value of the remainder that is returned by the modulo operator.

Modulo is useful when you want to identify every *nth* occurrence. For example, if you numbered your site visitors using `intUser` you could identify every 100th visitor with `intUser % 100 == 0`. This expression would be true for every hundredth visitor. Each visitor would have their number divided by 100 and most would have a remainder. Only the visitors numbered 0, 100, 200, 300, and so on would exactly divide by 100 and leave no remainder (modulo = 0). We will present an example later in the chapter where it fits in nicely into the `while` loop exercise. For now, you might want to look at the file `Demo-ModuloSimple.aspx` that is available for download at **www.wrox.com**.

String Concatenation

Programmers frequently need to append new text to old, as you did with the contents of `lblTax`. You appended the dollar amount to the end of the string to get "Your tax bill would be $". Programmers speak of "adding" strings, but that is only a manner of speaking, as there is no mathematical addition involved. The proper term is *concatenation*, which means to join or link strings together to make a larger string. In .NET there are two ways to concatenate strings.

To concatenate two strings, use the plus operator (+). You can concatenate the strings "`Spring`" and "`Sale`", as follows (see this in action in `Demo-Concatenation.aspx` available at **www.wrox.com**):

```
string strSaleNote1;
strSaleNote1 = "Spring" + "Sale";
```

Here, the result of the concatenation is the string "`SpringSale`", which will be assigned to the variable `strSaleNote`, of type `String`. You should note that C# doesn't automatically put in spaces. You can concatenate any number of strings within the same expression. You can also concatenate the contents of non-string variables, however you should covert them to string using Convert.ToString(). Here, you'll concatenate three strings, one of which is a space (also a string, since a space is a character):

```
string strSaleNote2;
DateTime datSaleSpring = Convert.ToDateTime("3/3/2005");
strSaleNote2 = "Spring" + " " + "Sale begins " +
Convert.ToString(datSaleSpring);
```

C# handles the text value of a control in the same way as a variable or literal string, as follows:

```
txtSaleEnd.Text = "Spring" + " " + "Sale begins " +
Convert.ToString(datSaleSpring);
<asp:TextBox runat="server" ID="txtSaleEnd"/>
```

What if you already have information in a variable and want to add to that? As with numeric addition, you can use the original contents of a variable on the right side of the assignment as follows.

```
StrSaleNote4 = "Sale starts on 3/1/2005";
StrSaleNote4 = strSaleNote4 " and ends on " + txtSaleEnd.Text;
```

However, there is a better technique to do this.

Concatenation by Assignment

In addition to the (+) operator, C# supports a second method to concatenate strings, the (+=) operator:

```
string strSaleNote5;
strSaleNote5 = "Sale starts on 3/1/2005 and ends on ";
strSaleNote5 += txtSaleEnd.Text;
```

strSaleNote will then contain the string Sale starts on 3/1/2005 and ends on followed by the value entered by the user in txtSalesEnd.

> String concatenations can be slow. It is recommended that you study and use the .NET StringBuilder class if you perform many of these operations.

Numeric Comparison Operators

When you get to control structures in the second half of this chapter, you will have to create expressions that use comparison operators as follows:

Operator	Symbol
Equality	==
Less than	<
Less than or equal to	<=
Inequality	!=
Greater than	>
Greater than or equal to	>=

> The equality operator (used for a comparison) is a double equals sign (==). The single equals sign is the assignment operator which fills a variable or object property with a value. They are not interchangeable and if interchanged, will cause errors.

For example, to test if something is true, you can use:

```
datDatDOB == Convert.ToDateTime("1/1/2005")
intCode == 36
strNameFirst == "John"
```

These statements say, "If the date value in DatDOB is the date equivalent of "1/1/2005" then consider this expression to be true." Later you will build control structures that make decisions based on whether an expression is true or false.

Other comparison operators work in the same way. If you want to compare two numbers to check whether one is greater than the other, you could do the following:

```
number1 > number2
```

This would test whether the first number was greater than the second, and the expression would evaluate to either `true` or `false`, depending on the contents of the variables.

For dates, < means earlier and > means later (test and observe code from the file Demo-DateComparison.aspx available for download at www.wrox.com). For strings, things are a little trickier since the comparison is by ASCII code. In general, ASCII codes are lowest for numeric characters, then they increase through the uppercase letters to the lowercase letters and finish with European diacritics. The symbols are sprinkled throughout the numbering system. Download and try Demo-StringComparison.aspx to test various combinations of letters, numbers and symbols. It also generates a list of ASCII numbers as shown in Figure 4-2:

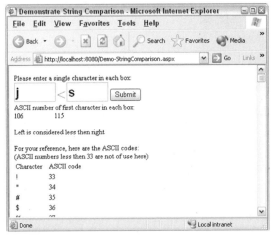

Figure 4-2

Logical Operators

C# also provides a set of three common logical operators you can use in your code:

- ❏   `&&`: used for AND
- ❏   `||`: used for OR
- ❏   `!`: used for NOT

Logical operators are used in the same way as comparison operators and the whole expression evaluates to a Boolean value:

```
intNumber1 == 1 && intNumber2 == 2
```

In the above line, if `intnumber1` is 1 and `intnumber2` is 2, then the whole phrase `intNumber1 = 1 AND intNumber2 = 2` will evaluate to `true` and the line will become "If true Then" and the code for true will be executed.

When using `&&` (AND), *both* expressions have to be `true` for the whole expression to be true. When using OR, only *one* out of the two conditions has to be `true` for the expression to be true:

```
intNumber1 == 1 || intNumber2 == 2
```

> A common logical operator mistake is an incomplete syntax such as:
> `intNumber1 == 1 || 2`. This line fails because C# requires a complete expression on
> each side of the logical operator. The correct syntax is:
> `intNumber1 == 1 || intNumber1 == 2`

The third logical operator, NOT, simply implies the reverse of the condition. If `number1` isn't equal to 1 then the expression is true. For example, you have been using a property of the page called `IsPostBack`. If the page is posted back then this property will be `true`. You can use NOT to give a `false` when the page is posted back, as follows:

```
!Page.IsPostBack
```

If you are using the `!` to apply to an entire expression, it is recommended that you put the expression in parenthesis and the `!` before it.

```
!(intNumber1 == 2)
```

When a statement contains more than one logical operator, C# decides which operator to execute first according to a simple rule. Operators are executed in the following order, known as the order of *operator precedence*:

- ❑ NOT
- ❑ AND
- ❑ OR

Consider the following code:

```
if (  number1 == 5 || !(number2 == 1) && !(number3 == 1)  )
```

What does this expression actually test? Well, first it checks that `number2` is not equal to 1, and that `number3` is not equal to 1. It then evaluates the AND operation and uses the result to evaluate the OR operation. Beware of these kinds of logical 'traps' in the same way as you would with mathematical operators. Let's look at how the above expression is solved. Assume the following values:

```
number1 = 1          number2 = 2          number3 = 3
```

We replace the variable names with their values as follows:

```
(  1 == 5 || !(2 == 1) && !(3 == 1)  )
```

We then evaluate the equalities:

```
(   false   || !(false) && !(false)  )
```

We execute the logical operators in the order NOT, AND, OR. Perform the two NOT operators as follows:

```
(   false   ||   true   &&   true   )
```

We perform the AND operations:

```
(   false   ||          true  )
```

Finally, we perform the OR operations:

```
(          true          )
```

You can check that result, and test others, in the file named `Demo-LogicalOperators.aspx` that is available for download at www.wrox.com

> **To ensure that your code works as intended, use parentheses wherever possible.**

Let's now look at three examples. We will create three pages, each demonstrating a logical operator to determine whether an input date is in the year 2005 or not.

Try It Out   Tax Calculator Using Logical Operators

1. In your Ch04 folder create a file named `TIO-LogicalAND.aspx` as follows:

```
<%@ Page Language="C#" %>
<script runat="server">

    void Page_Load()
    {
        if (IsPostBack)
         DateTime datInput;
         datInput = Convert.ToDateTime(txtIn.Text);

            if ( datInput>=Convert.ToDateTime("1/1/2005")
              &&
             datInput<=Convert.ToDateTime("12/31/2005")
             )
           lblOut.Text = "Date inside year 2005. " + datInput;
        }
     }

</script>
<html>
<head>
     <title>Logical AND Example</title>
```

```
    </head>
    <body>
        <form runat="server">
            Please enter a date, first in 2005.
            <br />
            Next try a date not in 2005
            <br />
            <asp:TextBox id="txtIn" runat="server"></asp:TextBox>
            <br />
            <asp:Button id="Button1" runat="server" Text="Submit"></asp:Button>
            <br />
            <asp:Label id="lblOut" runat="server"></asp:Label>
            <br />
        </form>
    </body>
</html>
```

2. Now save the file as `TIO-LogicalNOT.aspx` and change the code to the following. Carefully check the two lines of `lblOut.text` and the >+ and <+ symbols:

```
void Page_Load()
{
    if (IsPostBack)
    {
        lblOut.Text="Date inside year 2005";
        DateTime datInput;
        datInput = Convert.ToDateTime(txtIn.Text);
        if ( ! ( (datInput>=Convert.ToDateTime("1/1/2005")) &&
            (datInput<=Convert.ToDateTime("12/31/2005")) ) )
        {
        lblOut.Text = "Date outside year 2005.";
        }
    }
}
```

3. Now save the file as `TIO-LogicalOR.aspx` and change the code to the following. Carefully check the two lines of `lblOut.text` and the >+ and <+ symbols:

```
void Page_Load()
{
    if (IsPostBack)
    {
        lblOut.Text="Date inside year 2005";
        DateTime datInput;
        datInput = Convert.ToDateTime(txtIn.Text);
        if (
            Convert.ToDateTime(datInput)<Convert.ToDateTime("1/1/2005")
            ||
            Convert.ToDateTime(datInput)>Convert.ToDateTime("12/31/2005")
            )
        {
        lblOut.Text = "Date outside year 2005.";
        }
    }
}
```

4. View and test all three pages in your browser. The `TIO-LogicalAND.aspx` page is shown in Figure 4-3:

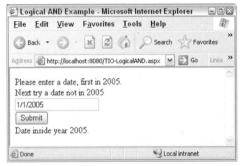

Figure 4-3

How It Works

In the form, we simply pick up a user's date input, offer a Submit button, and create a label for output. Up in the script we have the lines of interest. There are several points germane to all three pages.

❑ We reset the text of the output label with every page response so that there is no hangover of text from the last update of the page.

❑ Since all of the `lblOut.Text` is inserted in script, we do not have to worry about making the label invisible. When the `Page.IsPostBack` is `false`, the script does not run and the label is empty and thus effectively invisible.

❑ The `if` block either changes the `lblOut.Text` or leaves it the same.

❑ Fourth, since we are working with dates, we put the literal dates within double quotation marks and use the `Convert.ToDateTime()` function to convert the string input to the `Date` data type.

Now let's look at the code for `TIO-LogicalAND`:

```
if (datInput>=Convert.ToDateTime("1/1/2005") &&
    datInput<=Convert.ToDateTime("12/31/2005"))
  lblOut.Text = "Date inside year 2005. " + datInput;
}
```

To be within the year 2005, a date must meet two criteria: it must be *after* (greater than or equal to) January 1, 2005, and *before* (less then or equal to) December 31, 2005. In other words, both of these conditions must be true in order for a date to be within 2005. Thus we use the logical AND comparator.

In `TIO-LogicalNOT`, we can reverse the situation with a single logical word, and a reversal of the label text values. We change the default text to `inside year 2005` and the text executed by the `if` block to `outside year 2005`. Then we merely add a NOT around the entire comparison we did on the AND page. For dates that are in the year 2005, the NOT reverses the TRUE into FALSE.

In `TIO-LogicalOR`, we start with a text of `Date inside year 2005`, and want to run code that changes the text to `outside year 2005` if the expression is true. Our expression will test if the date is before 1/1/2005, and after 12/31/2005. If either is true, the date is not in 2005. Only one has to be true in order to know that the date is *not* in the year 2005. Thus we can use the `OR` operator.

As a last note on logical operators, the `NOT` works to change control properties that are true or `false`. For example, you may want use certain actions to switch the visibility of a control between `visible=true` and `visible=false`. Within the action just include the line: `MyControl.Visible = !myControl.Visible`. This is shown in `DemoLogicalNotToggle.aspx` available for download at www.wrox.com.

Having looked at the types of operators you can use with control structures, it's time to look at the structures in more detail.

Control Structures

In C# (or just about any other computer language), we have three types of structures (groups of control statements) to control the order in which the lines of code are executed. These are branching structures, looping structures, and jumping structures. We'll look at each of these in detail.

- ❑ **Branching structures:** decide which of two or more sections of code to run, for example, you can display either "Good Morning" or "Good Afternoon" depending on the time of day.

- ❑ **Looping structures:** consecutively repeat a section of code as many times as needed – for example, you can write a line to a schedule page repeatedly, once for each upcoming event.

- ❑ **Jumping structures:** move out of the code sequence and execute sections of code in another part of your script – for example, on a library receipt page we run the same few lines to calculate the due date for each item borrowed. This topic is covered in *Chapter 5*.

Overview of Branching Structures

Branching structures work by first performing some kind of test. Based on the test results, one set of code is executed and other sets of code are skipped. Consider a real life example. Imagine you're in a car and pull up to a set of traffic lights. If the lights are red, you'll have to stop the car and maybe switch it off, and wait until the lights change before proceeding. If the lights are green, you can drive straight through. The course of action you take is determined by the result of the test condition (the color of the traffic light).

C# offers two types of branching structures:

- ❑ `if else`: is generally used to select one of two or more sets of lines of code depending on a condition. For example, in a Web page featuring news stories, you could choose whether to display the international or regional news headlines, depending on a user's preferences. `if` `else` is also used for complicated comparisons, such as expressions using the terms && (AND), || (OR), and ! (NOT).

❏ `Switch:` is generally used to select which lines to execute based on many possibilities. For example, in a page featuring news stories, we could choose which of several icons to include in the page next to the story, depending on whether the story was about politics, business, sport, entertainment, or technology.

Overview of Looping Structures

Looping structures allow the same block of code to run repeatedly. Instead of skipping code, we *repeat* code. Let's go back to our previous real life example. I frequently go to the airport in my car to pick up my brother. I don't like to pay the parking fee, so he comes out the door to the street for pick up. I go around the terminal road past the door and check if he is there. If yes, I stop and pick him up and we go home. However, if he is not out yet I do another loop around the terminal and re-check the door. I continue to loop (both literally and procedurally) until he comes out the door.

In the holiday booking site example of *Chapter 3*, you could use a looping structure to generate a page for each person who is going to be staying at a hotel. The construction of those lines (print the description, print the quantity, print the price, put in a line break) would be looped to produce one line for each item ordered:

❏ `for:` is used to repeat line(s) when, at the beginning of the repetitions, you know exactly how many repetitions you want. Alternatively, you can use a test, such as the `sizeof()` function to determine the number of repetitions needed. For example, if you know there are five trucks needing a wash, you could repeat the set of steps involved in successfully washing a single truck.

❏ `while:` is used to repeat line(s) when you don't know exactly how many repetitions you want at the time the code is written. You build a test condition into the loop that is checked after each iteration. The loop will repeat as long as this condition is `true`.

❏ `do...while:` is similar to the `while` loop except that the condition is tested after the loop is performed. Thus the loop is performed atleast once even if the condition is `false`.

❏ `foreach...in:` is a convenient alternative to `for` when you have a defined collection of items, but don't know how many, and want to repeat the loop for every item in the collection.

Overview of Jumping Structures

Jumping structures allow the programmer to pause the execution of the current code and jump to another named code block. For example, we may need directions during our car trip. Therefore, we have a procedure that is to pull over, dial our friend on the cell phone, write down the directions, and then proceed. It is good to have this type of code in a separate section for the following reasons.

❏ First, you may never need it.

❏ Second, you might have to perform the code several times but probably not consecutively (thus it is not amenable to a loop).

❑ Third, it makes sense to have a discrete job such as this in its own section, not mixed into the main code. This makes the code easier to maintain

For example, a Web page may have a block of code called `ShowOrder` that produces lines to show the customer the goods they ordered. Whenever you want C# to show those lines you don't have to rewrite or copy all of that code. Instead, just have C# jump out of the current code, execute `ShowOrder` and then come back and continue executing the original code. The only jumping control (that we cover in this book) is:

❑ **Procedures (also called Methods):** run the statements in the subroutine, and then return control to the line that called them. They may accept information (called parameters) to perform the job. Procedures may also return information to the main code. For example, a procedure could change information in a database. Or a procedure could calculate the total of an order and then return that value to the main block of code.

Branching, looping, and jumping form the backbone of just about every program or application you will come to write in C# on your ASP.NET pages. This chapter will cover branching and looping and the next chapter will cover jumping.

Many find it difficult to decide which type of structure to use. This is understandable for several reasons. First, there are numerous choices. Second, there is some overlap in their functionality. Third, in some cases the decision of which structure to use is entirely the programmer's discretion, so studying one set of code may not match the tactics of another code sample. In this chapter, we will spend a lot of time comparing the options and guiding you in making wise selections.

Uses of Control Structures

The following table lists several programming objectives and suggests which type of structure will help us achieve the desired results:

Situation	Solution	Why?
I want ASP.NET to show page A or page B.	Branching `if`	You want to perform only one of two possible events.
I need to show the user one of several meetings they should attend. The meeting displayed is based on which department they belong to.	Branching `switch`	You want to write to the page only one out of several possible meeting locations.
I want C# to list each member of a club. The data about each member is held in essentially the same manner, with a name, photo, address, and other contact information.	Looping `do...while`	You will be performing the same set of code (that retrieves a member's name) many times (once for each member, until all members are listed).

Situation	Solution	Why?
I want to present a known number of records of data in a table.	Looping `for`	You will perform the same code (make a row for a table) repeatedly until you have built all of the rows needed.
After placing an item that I describe in a catalog page, I want to put in a few lines of information about 'How to Order'. There will be several items across several pages that I need to do this for.	Jumping Function	You want to pause the main code and perform several lines of *another* set of code that describes 'How to Order'. Then you want to resume execution of the main code. Since the 'How to Order' set of code will be performed at various times across the page, it is best to write it once and call that one piece of code as needed.
I need to calculate prices in several places on each page. The prices will be set according to input from a user form.	Jumping Function	You will pause building the page, jump out to execute code that calculates the price of an item, and then return to building the page and return the calculated amount. Since you will calculate many prices it is best to write the formula once and have it called when needed.

Let's recap what we've discussed so far. Three kinds of statements control your code's execution:

❑ Branching statements perform a test and then execute some lines of code, but not others.

❑ Looping statements execute a set of code repeatedly.

❑ Jumping statements pause the execution of the current code, jump over to another set of code, and then return to where they started, sometimes bringing values back with them.

Let's look at branching statements in detail, and see what we can do with them.

Branching Structures

Branching controls perform some type of test called an *expression*. Based on the test results, a set of code is executed and other sets of code are skipped. C# offers two techniques for branching. `if` is used when there are only a few choices of outcome. Bear in mind that the more lines you use in `if`, the more difficult your code will become to follow. It is better to use `Switch` when there are several outcomes.

For example, if you are making a decision on how to proceed having asked the user "Do you want a confirmation by telephone?", the outcome is either "Yes" (`true`) or "No" (`false`), so you would perform the branch using `if else`. However, if you ask the user "Do you want confirmation by telephone, fax, FedEx, e-mail, voicemail, or telepathy?" given the number of outcomes, it is better to use `Switch`.

The if Structure

The basic `if` statement has three parts:

- ❑ An expression: a test that evaluates to either `true` or `false`
- ❑ An "`if true`" section of code
- ❑ An (optional) "`if false`" section of code

The first part is the expression, which can be a combination of keywords, operators, variables, and constants. The expression must be Boolean, and evaluates to either `true` or `false`. If the test evaluates `true`, then only the lines of code in the 'if true' section are executed. If the test evaluates `false`, then only the lines of code in the 'if false' section are executed. After either the 'true' or 'false' section is executed, the execution jumps down to the ending statement and continues with the next line of code. There is never a situation where both the true *and* false sections are executed in a given case.

There are four ways of building `if` statements. Selection of proper syntax depends on two critera:

- ❑ Do I want to do anything if the test is `false`?
- ❑ Do I want to execute *more than one statement* if the test is `true`?

if()

The first and the simplest syntax is useful if you only want to run one statement in the case of a `true` condition. Using this method, you will not be able to execute any statements if your expression evaluates to `false`. For example, if a user checks a box to inform you that they have a fax, you want them to enter the number. If they don't check the box then you want to take no action. In this case, you can use a simple one-line syntax:

```
if (expression) one line of code to execute if expression is true;
if (chkFaxConfirm.Checked = true) lblFax.Text = "We will confirm by fax.";
```

A two-line form works the same.(note that in this case, there is no need for braces { }).

```
if (chkFaxConfirm.Checked = true)
lblFax.Text = "We will confirm by fax.";
```

if() {}

The next most complex syntax is where you want to execute more than one statement in the case of `true`, but still nothing if the test is `false`. For example, if the user wants a telephone confirmation, you would display a confirmation message and make visible a text box for the user to enter a phone number. In this case, write the `if` with these changes from the syntax outlined above. Since there is now more than one line for the `if` code, you must use a set of braces:

```
if (expression)
{
  code to execute if true - line 1;
  code to execute if true - line 2;
}
```

We might want to add text and make visible a label (two commands) when an expression is true:

```
if (chkTelConfirm.Checked == true)
{
  lblTel.Text = "We will confirm by telephone. Please enter your
                number";
  txtTel.Visible =true;
}
```

if()...else

The third level is where you want to execute one or more statements in the case of `true`, and one or more lines of code if the test is `false`. For example, if the user has requested a fax confirmation then ask for the fax number and jump over to the fax entry page. If they haven't requested a fax, then show a line that says that a fax will not be sent. In this situation, write the `if` with a line containing the word `else` to separate the code that will run in the `true` case from the code that will run in the `false` case. For each section you must include braces if there is more then one line of code in that section.

```
if (expression)
{
  code to execute if true - line 1;
  code to execute if true - line 2;
}
else
{
  code to execute if false - line 1;
  code to execute if false - line 2;
}
```

An actual example would be as follows.

```
if (chkShipByGovernment.Checked == true)
{
  lblAddress.Text = "Please enter your post office box number";
  txtAddress.Visible=true;
}
else
{
  lblAddress.Text = "Please enter your street address";
  txtAddress.Visible=true;
}
```

C# supports an alternate syntax for `if...else` called the Ternary Operator. This construction saves typing several keywords and reduces the number of lines in the code in the case where you will only execute one statement for true or one statement if false.

```
expression ? Statement to execute for true : Statement to execute for false;
```

The syntax has three parts separated by two symbols. First, is the expression, then a question mark, then the statement to execute for true, then a colon, and finally the statement to execute for false. Although not necessary, putting the entire structure in parenthesis helps readability. The same goes for putting the expression in parenthesis. For example, we could set the text of lblOut depending on the size of the number entered in txtIn:

```
lblOut.Text = Convert.ToInt32(txtIn.Text)>100 ? "large" : "small";
```

Or

```
lblOut.Text = (Convert.ToInt32(txtIn.Text)>100 ? "large" : "small");
```

Or

```
lblOut.Text = (   (Convert.ToInt32(txtIn.Text)>100) ? "large" : "small"   );
```

The Ternary form employs a different syntax compared to other if structures. You do not use the keyword if, and you do not code an entire statement to be executed. Rather, the Ternary returns one of two values to be used by the rest of the command line. If you have to execute full statements, use the full if...else syntax. A particularly useful application for this syntax is when you need to modify grammar in a string, for example:

```
lblOut.Text = "… your product" + (intNumberOfProducts>1 ? "s." : ".");
```

if()...else if()

The fourth level is quite complex but there are some situations where it cannot be avoided. It allows you to choose between several different pieces of code to execute according to multiple expressions. To do this, you need to separate each new expression with the keywords else if(). You can also include a non-expression else clause that will be executed if none of the other cases were chosen.

```
if(expression1)
{
    statement to execute if expression1 is true - line1;
    statement to execute if expression1 is true - line2;
}
else if(expression2)          //only tested if expression1 is false
{
    statement if expression1 is false and expression2 is true - line1;
    statement if expression1 is false and expression2 is true - line2;
}
else
{
    statement if expression1 is false and expression2 is false - line1;
    statement if expression1 is false and expression2 is false - line2;
}
```

Here we test the data to see if it meets expression1. If it doesn't, we test it to see if it meets expression2. If it doesn't meet that either, we execute the code under the else. For example, we might have two rules about getting free tickets. Members and students get free tickets. So, we have to test two different conditions, membership and age. This can be done two ways. First would be a single test which uses the || OR operator. Alternatively we can use the if…else if discussed in this section, as shown below (see download file Demo-ifElseif.aspx)

```
<form runat="server">
  <asp:TextBox id="txtAge" runat="server" / >
  <asp:CheckBox id="chkIsMember" runat="server" / >
  <asp:Label id="lblOut" runat="server" / >
</form>

if(Page.IsPostBack)
{

  if(chkIsMember.Checked==true)
  {
     lblOut.Text = "Members get a free ticket";
     lblOut.BackColor=System.Drawing.Color.LightPink;
  }
  else if(Convert.ToInt32(txtAge.Text)<=18)
  {
     lblOut.Text = "Students get a free ticket";
     lblOut.BackColor=System.Drawing.Color.LightPink;
  }
  else
  {
     lblOut.Text = "Price is ¥500";
     lblOut.BackColor=System.Drawing.Color.LightSeaGreen;
  }
}   //end if(Page.IsPostBack)
```

These if structures are demonstrated in the download file, Demo-if.aspx. There is an alternative structure (switch), which provides a simpler solution in some cases, and we'll be looking at this shortly. Generally, if you are testing to see if a variable contains one of several values, you will use Switch rather than if...else if. The following table contains a summary of the four if control structures:

Situation	Syntax	Example
If expression is True do one statement Otherwise do nothing	if (expression) statement	if (age < 18) Message.Text = "You must be 18 or older to order by credit card."
If the expression is true do two or more statements If the expression is false do nothing	if expression { true code line 1; true code line 2; ... }	if (age < 18) { discount = true; Message.Text = "You are eligible for the student rate of $49."; }

Situation	Syntax	Example

If the expression is true
 	
do one or more statements
 	
If the expression is false
 	
do a different set of one or more statements
	`if`
	`(expression)`
	`{`
	` true code`
	`line 1;`
	` true code`
	`line 2;`
	`}`
	`else`
	`{`
	` false code`
	`line 1;`
	` false code`
	`line 2;`
	`}`
		`if (age < 18) {`
		` discount = true;`
		
		` Message.Text = "You are`
		`eligible for the student rate of`
		`$49.";`
		`}`
		`else`
		`{`
		` Message.Text = "The fee for`
		`this service is $59."`
		`}`

If the first expression is `true`
 do one or more statements
 	
Else if the second expression is `true`
 	
do a different set of
one or more statements
 	
If all expressions are `False` do
 	
do a different set of
one or more statements
	`if`
	`(expression)`
	`{`
	
	` true code`
	`line 1;`
	` true code`
	`line 2;`
	
	`else`
	`if(expressio`
	`n)`
	
	` True code`
	`line 1;`
	` True code`
	`line 2;`
	
	`else`
	` false code`
	`line 1;`
	` falseTrue`
	`code line 2;`
	
	`}`
		`if (age < 18) {`
		` discount = true;`
		
		` Message.Text = "You are`
		`eligible for the student rate of`
		`$49.";`
		`}`
		`else if (age > 65) {`
		` discount = true;`
		
		` Message.Text = "You are`
		`eligible for the senior rate of`
		`$49.";`
		`}`
		`else`
		`{`
		` Message.Text = "The fee for`
		`this service is $59.";`
		`}`

> **When executing a single command for an expression case, you do not need braces.**
> **If there is more then one command, you must put them within braces.**

Try It Out **Using the if Structure**

It's time for a quick example that involves a number guessing game. The computer 'thinks' of a number between one and five and you have to guess what it is.

1.   In folder Ch04 create a file named TIO-if.aspx and type in the following:

```
<%@ Page Language="C#" %>
<script runat="server">

    void Page_Load()
    {
        int theNumber, theGuess;
        Random objRandom;

        objRandom = new Random();
        theNumber = Convert.ToInt32(objRandom.Next(5)) + 1;

        if (Page.IsPostBack)
        {
          theGuess = Convert.ToInt32(Guess.SelectedItem.Value);

          if (theGuess > theNumber)
          {
            message.Text = "<BR><BR>Guess was too high<BR>Try again - it was "+
                            theNumber;
          }

          if (theGuess < theNumber)
          {
            message.Text = "<BR><BR>Guess was too low<BR>Try again - it was " +
                            theNumber;
          }

          if (theGuess == theNumber)
          {
            message.Text = "<BR><BR>Guess was correct!";
          }

        }    //end if (Page.IsPostBack)
    }    //end Page_Load()

</script>
<html>
<head>
    <title>IF THEN example - solution 1</title>
</head>
<body>
    <form runat="server">
        What number am I thinking of?
        <asp:dropdownlist id="Guess" runat="server">
            <asp:listitem>1</asp:listitem>
            <asp:listitem>2</asp:listitem>
```

```
                <asp:listitem>3</asp:listitem>
                <asp:listitem>4</asp:listitem>
                <asp:listitem>5</asp:listitem>
        </asp:dropdownlist>
        <br />
        <br />
        <input type="submit" value="Submit guess" />
        <asp:label id="message" runat="server"></asp:label>
    </form>
</body>
</html>
```

2. Open `TIO-if.aspx` in your browser, choose a number, and click Submit guess. See Figure 4-4:

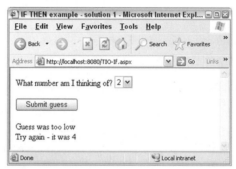

Figure 4-4

How It Works

As it's such a simple example, it doesn't require too much code. We get the user to enter a guess into the Web form with the `<asp:dropdownlist>` control:

```
<asp:dropdownlist id="Guess" runat="server">
  <asp:listitem>1</asp:listitem>
    ...
  <asp:listitem>5</asp:listitem>
</asp:dropdownlist>
```

Using a dropdown list ensures that you get a valid response from the user, as they can only choose from what you place in the list. You can then interrogate the dropdown list box via its name (`Guess`), directly through the code.

The actual C# code is quite interesting. You start by defining two variables:

```
<%@ Page Language="C#" %>
<script runat="server">

void Page_Load()
{
      int theNumber, theGuess;
```

The two variables above contain the randomly generated number and the user's guess:

```
Random objRandom;
objRandom = new Random();
theNumber = Convert.ToInt32(objRandom.Next(5)) + 1;
```

Next, above, we create an object, which will be of the type `Random` (this reserves the name and memory space). Then we instantiate (actually fill the memory space with a new copy of the Random object). Last, we generate a number with the `Random` object's `Next()` method. To get a random number between 1 and 5, we tell the `Random.Next()` method to generate a number that is 5 or less, which will generate a number between 0 and 4.999... (not 5 itself). We use the `ConvertToInt32()` function to cut off the decimal part so we have a whole number between 0 and 4. We add 1 to it, giving us what we need: a number from 1 to 5. Any range of random integers in C# can be generated with the following equation:

```
RandomNumber = Convert.ToInt32(objRandom.Next(UpperBound)) + 1
```

So we've generated our random number, we've got the guess from the user stored in the variable (`Guess`); so all we need to do now is compare them, right? Well, not quite! As this is a Web form with just one single page, you need to check whether the user has ever been there before. On their first arrival they won't have entered a number, and you don't want to test the random number against an empty variable.

The first time the page is run the user hasn't guessed yet, so `Page.IsPostBack` will return `false` and not run the code contained within. The page execution will jump to the end of the `if` structure, marked by the closing brace. However, when the user submits a guess, there will be a value and `Page.IsPostBack` will be `true`.

There are three separate `if` structures inside this code. You can see how useful it is to indent your code in these structures to keep track of which closing brace applies to which `if` structure:

```
if (Page.IsPostBack)
{
  theGuess = Convert.ToInt32(Guess.SelectedItem.Value);

  if (theGuess > theNumber)
  {
    message.Text = "<BR><BR>Guess was too high<BR>Try again - it was "
    + theNumber;
  }

  if (theGuess < theNumber)
  {
    message.Text = "<BR><BR>Guess was too low<BR>Try again - it was "
                   + theNumber;
  }

  if (theGuess == theNumber)
  {
    message.Text = "<BR><BR>Guess was correct!";
  }
```

```
}      //end if (Page.IsPostBack)
```

These are all ignored the first time around because `IsPostBack` has returned `false`. Second time around, the `Page.IsPostBack` is true (and we assume the user has submitted a guess) so the code inside will be run. It's worth noting that if the user has not selected a number then the page will process the default value of `1`. Each structure is considered to be a separate test in its own right. Before we do the test, we set our `theGuess` variable to be equal to the contents of the `SelectedItem.value` of the dropdown list box, to save us a bit of typing each time we refer to the user's guess:

```
theGuess = Convert.ToInt32(Guess.SelectedItem.Value);
```

The first test checks to see whether the guess is bigger than the number:

```
if (theGuess > theNumber)
{
   message.Text = "<BR><BR>Guess was too high<BR>Try again - it was " +
                  theNumber;
}
```

If so, it sets the `<asp:label>` control to display a message informing the user that their guess was too high, along with the number that the user failed to guess.

The second test checks whether the guess is smaller than the number:

```
if (theGuess < theNumber)
{
   message.Text = "<BR><BR>Guess was too low<BR>Try again - it was "
                  + theNumber;
}
```

In this case, we then display a message saying that the guess was too low, and display the number.

The last test checks to see whether the number is correct, and displays an appropriate message in the `<asp:label>` control:

```
if (theGuess == theNumber)
{
   message.Text = "<BR><BR>Guess was correct!";
}
```

You may be wondering how C# knows that this is the correct ending brace, as there are several in the code. The answer is that they have been *nested* inside each other. When there is an `if` statement inside the block of code belonging to another `if` statement, the inner `if` statement has to have a matching end brace, before the outer block can be ended. This means that `if` blocks can be treated as completely separate self-contained entities:

There are other ways to use `if` and achieve the same goals, for example (`TIO-ifAlternate.aspx`):

```
<%@ Page Language="C#" %>
<script runat="server">
```

```
void Page_Load()
{
    int  theNumber, theGuess;
    Random r = new Random();
    theNumber = Convert.ToInt32(r.Next(5)) + 1;

    if (Page.IsPostBack)
    {
        theGuess = Convert.ToInt32(Guess.SelectedItem.Value);
        if (theGuess > theNumber)
        {
            message.Text = "<BR><BR>Guess is too high<BR>Try again - it was"+
                            theNumber;
        }
        else if (theGuess < theNumber)
        {
            message.Text = "<BR><BR>Guess is too low<BR>Try again - it was"+
                            theNumber;
        }
        else
        {
            message.Text = "<BR><BR>Guess is correct!";
        }
    }
}
</script>
```

This alternative logic uses the `elseif` clause for `if` to perform the second test and assumes that negatives from the first two tests will result in a correct guess.

The switch Structure

The disadvantage with `if...else` is that it can start getting unwieldy after more than three possible outcomes. What happens if you want to show a different page to visitors from each of five departments? What happens if you want to do a calculation based on the user providing one of twelve salary grades? Or if you have different procedures for confirming an order by telephone, fax and e-mail? Your `if` structure code is going to become difficult to maintain with more then a few nested `else if` code blocks. In addition, code with many layers of nesting runs slow.

The switch structure is a better alternative for handling branching and it caters much more neatly for these situations by providing a better structure, better performance, and extra readability.

> Use `switch` when you need to make a choice among several answers (more than just `true` or `false`).

The syntax for `switch` has four parts:

❑   The statement of a value to be tested against (the "test value")

❑   The statement of a 'possible value' and what to do if that possible value matches the test value (this part is repeated for all possible values)

❑   An optional catchall `default`, in case the variable matches a value you haven't anticipated

The following example carries out one of three actions depending on what is contained in the variable confirmation (see entire page in download file `Demo-Switch1.aspx`):

```
string confirmation = txtIn.Text;
switch(confirmation)
{
    case "fax":
    lblOut.Text = "Fax confirmation takes 12 hours.";
    break;

    case "telephone":
    lblOut.Text = "Telephone confirmation takes 24 hours.";
    break;

    case "email":
    lblOut.Text  ="Email  confirmation takes 1 hours.";
    break;
}
```

From the first line, C# knows that you want to compare the answers to the contents of the variable confirmation. Next, it will begin testing the contents of the variable against the values shown in the Case lines. When C# finds a match, it executes the following code up to the next break line, and then jumps down to the first line after the closing brace, which defines the end of the cases.

The previous if example used a drop down list to ensure that the user could only enter a valid answer. When checking user input using switch we often need to do the same thing, as string comparisons in C# are case-sensitive. If you allow the user to enter text in response to a Yes/No question, be prepared to handle the fact that **Yes**, **yes**, and **YES** will all be handled differently. Additionally, prepare to handle unexpected inputs (like the user entering **Yeah**) as well. This can be done using the `default` statement as shown here:

```
switch (txtIn.Text)
{
  case "yes":
    lblOut.Text= "Details will be sent.";
    break;

  case "YES":
    lblOut.Text= "Details will be sent.";
    break;

  case "Yes":
    lblOut.Text= "Details will be sent.";
    break;

  case "no":
    lblOut.Text= "We will not contact you.";
```

```
      break;

   case "NO":
      lblOut.Text= "We will not contact you.";
      break;

   case "No":
      lblOut.Text= "We will not contact you.";
      break;

   default:
      lblOut.Text = "Your answer " + txtIn.Text + " is not recognized.";
      break;
   } //end switch (txtIn.Text)
```

In this example, a user who decides to type **Yeah** will receive a custom error message.

You can further refine this code by having C# test for more than one result on each **case** line. As an example, for both **yes** and **YES** we would do the same thing, so we can handle them together (download file `Demo-SwitchYesNo2.aspx`):

```
switch (txtIn.Text)
{
        case "yes":
        case "YES":
        case "Yes":
        case "Y":
        lblOut.Text= "Details will be sent.";
        break;

        case "no":
        case "NO":
        case "No":
        case "N":
        lblOut.Text= "We will not contact you.";
        break;

        default:
        lblOut.Text= "Your answer " + txtIn.Text + " is not recognized.";
        break;
  }    //end switch (txtIn.Text)
```

This will work fine, but do you really want to spend all that time dreaming up possible case variations? C# offers a completely different way to solve the case problem. If you change all input text to uppercase before testing, you can reduce the number of tests needed. Any string object (variable typed as string or object property that is of string type) has a `ToString()` method that can be added to the end of its name. In this case, we will apply it to the text entered in the `txtIn` control (download file `Demo-SwitchYesNo3.aspx`):

```
switch (txtIn.Text.ToUpper())
        {
        case "YES":
```

```
        case "Y":
        lblOut.Text= "Details will be sent.";
        break;

        case "NO":
        case "N":
        lblOut.Text= "We will not contact you.";
        break;

        default:
        lblOut.Text= "Your answer " + txtIn.Text + " is not recognized.";
        break;
}    //end switch (txtIn.Text)
```

We've managed to cut down on the number of test statements. However, in some situations, such as the previous random number guessing example, it proved more beneficial to use a dropdown list control to limit the range of possible answers.

Let's look at an example that uses `switch` to make a more detailed set of selections. In *Chapter 3*, we used an example that showed how the user could select a holiday from a set of destinations. We're now going to go one better and provide a brief sales pitch depending on which destination the user selects. We will use `switch` to decide which pitch to use.

Try It Out Using the switch Structure

1. Create `TIO-Switch.aspx` in the `Ch04` folder and type the following code in the All view:

```
<%@ Page Language="C#" debug="true"%>
<script runat="server">

    void  Page_Load()
      {
      if (Page.IsPostBack)
        {
        switch(radDestination.SelectedItem.Value)
          {
          case "Barcelona":
            lblMessage.Text = "You selected Spain's lively Catalan city";
            break;
          case "Oslo":
            lblMessage.Text = "Experience the majesty of Norway's capital
                               city";
            break;
          case "Lisbon":
            lblMessage.Text = "Portugal's famous seaport and cultural hub";
            break;
          default:
            lblMessage.Text = "you did not select a destination we travel
                               to";
            break;
        }   //End switch
      }     // end if (Page.IsPostBack)
    }   //end Page_Load()
```

```
</script>
<html>
<head>
    <title>Switch Example</title>
</head>
<body>
    <form runat="server">
        Select your choice of destination:
        <br />
        <br />
        <asp:radiobuttonlist id="radDestination" runat="server">
            <asp:listitem>Barcelona</asp:listitem>
            <asp:listitem>Oslo</asp:listitem>
            <asp:listitem>Lisbon</asp:listitem>
        </asp:radiobuttonlist>
        <br />
        <br />
        <input type="submit" value="Submit Choice" />
        <br />
        <br />
        <asp:label id="lblMessage" runat="server"></asp:label>
    </form>
</body>
</html>
```

2. View this in your browser, make a choice, and click on Submit Choice as shown in Figure 4-5:

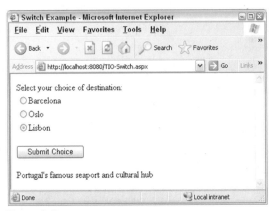

Figure 4-5

How It Works

There's a lot of code here, but it's actually simpler than the last example you studied. The form has a radiobuttonlist control called destination, which allows the user to select a holiday destination:

```
<asp:radiobuttonlist id="radDestination" runat="server">
    <asp:listitem>Barcelona</asp:listitem>
```

```
            <asp:listitem>Oslo</asp:listitem>
            <asp:listitem>Lisbon</asp:listitem>
        </asp:radiobuttonlist>
```

The `Page.IsPostBack` test checks whether the page has been run before, as in the last example. If it hasn't, there will be nothing in either of these values, and you can skip to the end of the program and wait until the page is run again. If it has been posted back, then you take the contents of the radio button's `SelectedItem.Value` and test it for various values:

```
if (Page.IsPostBack)
{
    switch(radDestination.SelectedItem.Value)
    {
      case "Barcelona":
          lblMessage.Text = "You selected Spain's lively Catalan city";
          break;
        case "Oslo":
          lblMessage.Text = "Experience the majesty of Norway's
                             capital city";
          break;
        case "Lisbon":
          lblMessage.Text = "Portugal's famous seaport and cultural
                             hub";
          break;
      }  //End switch           }
} // end if (Page.IsPostBack)
```

As the page contains one question with three options, we deal with all of these possibilities within our single `switch` structure. So if the user selects **Oslo** then only the code in the `Case "Oslo"` section will run.

There is a `default` case at the end. This should never be executed unless you have made a mistake in matching up the cases you can handle with the options presented to the user:

```
            default:
              lblMessage.Text = "you did not select a destination we
                                 travel to";
            break;
          }  //End switch          }
```

If they don't select anything, then no message at all is displayed, as this is caught by the default structure. It's a simple example, but it demonstrates the potential power of case structures. Most importantly, it should be obvious how easy it is to add additional cases to a structure of this type, particularly compared to adding additional code to an if...else structure. There is a major drawback of `switch`. It doesn't support comparison operators. You can only check for different equality in each `case`. You cannot write `case >3`. This means switching may not work in some situations (such as our age-range selector previously shown) and you must revert to an unwieldy if...elseif... structure.

Looping Structures

C# has several types of looping structures:

❑   `for`

❑   `while`

❑   `do..while`

❑   `foreach..in`

If you *can* determine the number of loops at the point where the loop begins (for example, the loop will always be performed exactly ten times, or you have the number of loops stored in a variable), then use `for`. If you *do not* know how many loops you want to perform at design time, and will have to decide after each loop whether to continue, then use a `while` or `do while` loop.

`for...each` is used only in the case when you have a collection and need to loop through each member. In this sense, the term 'collection' has a specific definition (not just any old group) such as the collection objects `ArrayList` and `HashTable` that were discussed in *Chapter 3*.

Technique	When Used
`for`	The code knows before the first loop how many loops will be performed
`while`	The code does not know how many loops to perform and thus must decide at the end of each loop whether to perform another loop. Expression tested before first loop, so possible for no loops to be done.
`do...while`	The code does not know how many loops to perform and thus must decide at the end of each loop whether to perform another loop. Expression tested after first loop, so first loop is always done.
`foreach...in`	Only used for collections. Performs one loop for each member of the collection.

The for Loop Structure

The `for` structure has three parts. The first is a line that describes how many times to repeat the loop. Next, a set of lines with action statements that carry out the task you want repeated. Finally, a brace indicating the end of the action statements. It also tells C# to go back and repeat the action statements again:

```
for(CounterInitialize; expression; CounterIncrement)
{
  lines of code to repeat;
```

```
    }
```

Here is a simple example to get started. In the holiday example discussed earlier, some of the adventure holidays require participants to be over a certain age and so we need a signed age declaration form from each traveler. The trip organizer wants to get a Web page with a blank line for each person and then print that page to use as the sign-in sheet. If you imagine we needed a sheet for groups that always have five people you could use the following code(see download file `Demo-for.aspx`):

```
for(int intCounterAttendees=0;intCounterAttendees<5;intCounterAttendees++)
{
   Message1.Text += "Attendee Name _____<br />";
   Message1.Text += "Attendee Age _____<br /><hr /><br />";
} //end for
```

Going by the information on the first line, C# begins the process of running the loop five times. In order to keep count we provide a variable called `intcounter`. The lines that will be repeated are contained between the braces ({ }). In this case, two statements are needed to create lines for an attendee to write their name and their age as shown in Figure 4-6:

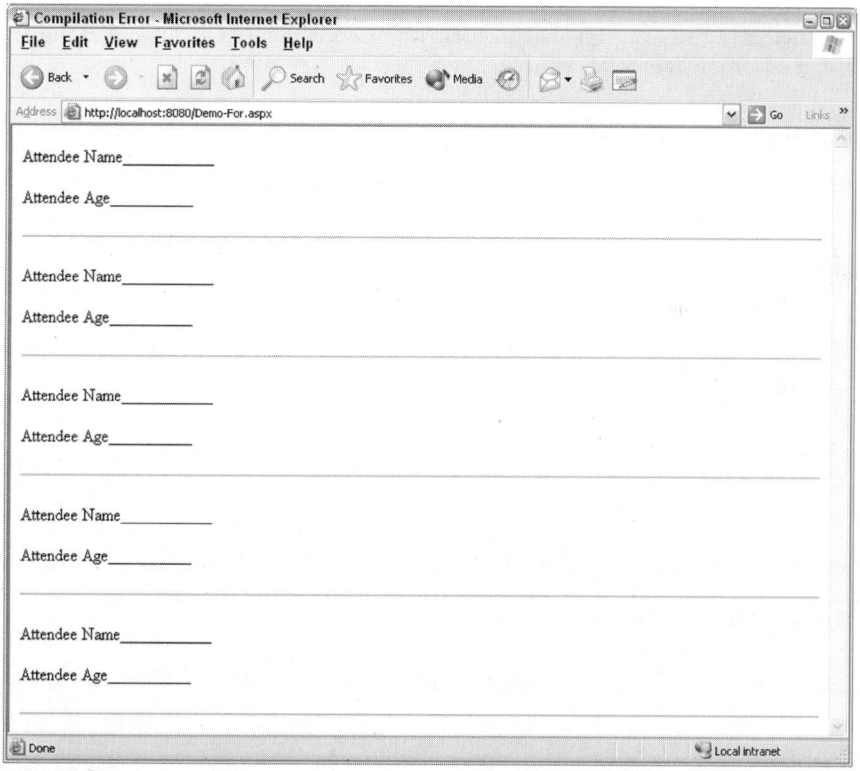

Figure 4-6

One quick point to note in the preceding code is that to get the `<asp:label ID="Message1">` control to display five sections for signatures you concatenated the next name to the contents of `Message1.Text`. This is because if you simply assigned the string to `Message1.Text` each time around the loop it would replace the previous contents and you would end up with just one line of text.

This example assumes that you would always have five attendees. What if that number varied? In that event, you could have a list box that asks for the number of attendees, for example, `lstNumberAttendees`, and then use that number to determine how many lines to print. You can use `for` (instead of `while`) because when you start the loop you know how many loops to make. You may not know at design time, but will know when you run the code. A sample follows:

```
for(int intLineLoopCounter = 1;
    intLineLoopCounter<=Convert.ToInt32(NumberAttendees.SelectedItem.Value);
    intLineLoopCounter++)
{
  lblMessage1.Text += "Attendee Name _____<br /><br />";
  lblMessage1.Text += "Attendee Age _____<br /><br />
                      <hr /><br />";
  number = numberAttendees.SelectedItem.Value
```

Let's implement this code into a page that takes a number from the user and supplies the requisite amount of signature/age lines for a printout.

Try It Out   Using the for Loop

1.   Within the folder `Ch04` create a file `TIO-for.aspx` and type in the following:

```
<%@ Page Language="C#" Debug="true" %>
<script runat="server">

    void Page_Load()
    {
      if(Page.IsPostBack)
      {
          lblMessage1.Text = "";
          for(int intLineLoopCounter = 1;
intLineLoopCounter<=Convert.ToInt32(NumberAttendees.SelectedItem.Value);
          intLineLoopCounter++)
          {
            lblMessage1.Text += "Attendee Name <br /><br />";
            lblMessage1.Text += "Attendee Age <br /><br /><hr /><br />";
          }    //end for intLineLoopcounter
      }    //end if(Page.IsPostBack)
    }    //end Page_Load

</script>
<html>
<head>
    <title>For Example</title>
</head>
<body>
    <form runat="server">
        Select the number of attendees:<br />
```

```
        <br />
        <asp:dropdownlist id="NumberAttendees" runat="server">
            <asp:listitem>1</asp:listitem>
            <asp:listitem>2</asp:listitem>
            <asp:listitem>3</asp:listitem>
        </asp:dropdownlist>
        <br />
        <br />
        <input type="submit" value="Submit Query" />
        <br />
        <br />
        <asp:label id="lblMessage1" runat="server"></asp:label>
    </form>
</body>
</html>
```

2. Open and view this page in your browser. Select a number and check that the sheet that appears looks like the Figure 4-7:

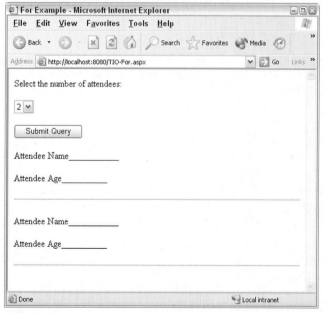

Figure 4-7

How It Works

The form should not be a problem for you by now – it is a simple `<asp.dropdownlist>`. This control makes the selection available to our code as `numberAttendees.SelectedItem.Value`.

We start by checking for postback, and if `true`, we blank out whatever was in our `lblMessage`.

```
void Page_Load()
{
  if(Page.IsPostBack)
  {
    lblMessage1.Text = "";
```

We then create a loop by filling in the three arguments of the `for()` as shown below. The first creates an integer counter, which starts at zero. The second is the test for when to stop the loop. The third is how to increment the counter:

```
for(int intLineLoopCounter = 1;
    intLineLoopCounter<=Convert.ToInt32(NumberAttendees.SelectedItem.Value);
    intLineLoopCounter++)
{
  lblMessage1.Text += "Attendee Name _____<br /><br />";
  lblMessage1.Text += "Attendee Age _____<br /><br />
                      <hr /><br />";
}    //end for intLineLoopcounter
```

Each time the loop is executed, C# automatically increases `intLineLoopCounter` by one. If that number is not greater than the value in `NumberAttendees.SelectedItem.Value`, then the loop runs again. When the number of the counter goes above the number held in the value C# jumps past the closing brace } and moves on to the statement after.

The value held in `intLineLoopCounter` (and automatically increased with each loop) is available to you just like any other variable. Recall from your study of HTML that `<br/>` puts in a line break and `<hr/>` adds a horizontal line. Try changing your `Message1.Text` as follows (`TIO-forNumbered.aspx`):

```
for(int intLineLoopCounter = 1;
    intLineLoopCounter<=Convert.ToInt32(NumberAttendees.SelectedItem.Value);
    intLineLoopCounter++)
{
  lblMessage1.Text += Convert.ToString(intLineLoopCounter) + ": ";
  lblMessage1.Text += "Attendee Name _____<br /><br />";
  lblMessage1.Text += "Attendee Age _____<br /><br />
<hr /><br />";
```

In the highlighted line shown above, C# adds the loop number (which equals the attendee number) to the `lblMessage.Text`.

The while Loop

We briefly mentioned the `while` loop earlier in the chapter. It's used in cases where the number of iterations it has to carry out is unknown when the loop begins. A Boolean test is made at the beginning of each cycle. So, it performs a test before each loop, and continues looping as long as the specified condition is true. If the condition is false from the start, the loop will not perform even a single cycle. The syntax is written as follows.

```
while (condition)
{
  // looping code here
```

```
}
```

The while loop is perfect for tasks where it is impossible to know how many times you are going to have to execute the loop. For example, we could write a page which simulates rolling a dice (by coming up with a random number between one and six) – and keeps rolling it until it gets a six. However, we don't know at the time of writing our C# code (or even before we roll the dice), how many rolls we need to get a six. So, for example, we could write:

```
Random r = new Random();
int diceRoll = 0;
while (diceRoll != 6)
{
   diceRoll = Convert.ToInt32(r.Next(6)) + 1;
   message1.Text = message1.Text + "Rolled a: " + diceRoll + "<br />";
}
```

The code begins by setting up a variable (diceRoll) that will track the value of our last dice roll. We initialize it to zero at declaration. We have to do this because we immediately test its value in the while statement, and if it were to have no value, the code would not compile because the diceRoll variable is unassigned at the point that it is used.

Next, we begin the loop. In order to avoid an infinite loop, we have to make sure that the loop can end by providing a way for the diceRoll variable to equal 6. We do this by rolling the dice (or more truthfully, by creating a random number between 1 and 6 using the random number generator we met earlier) and storing the value in diceRoll. Then we print some text from the loop.

After the loop has executed once, the test is executed again, this time using the value rolled inside the loop. If it is not a six, then the loop is run again. If it is a six, then the loop exits.

There is a serious trap that every novice programmer (and plenty of more experienced ones, too!) falls into: if you start a loop and do not provide the means for it to stop, it will continue forever in an infinite loop. You must include a way for the condition to change to false (somewhere down the line). Most current servers will eventually cut off a given ASP.NET page, since the server needs to attend to other visitors and must optimize its resources. If a page seems to be hung and not loading properly, it could be due to an infinite loop, and it can effectively cause the web server not to respond to page requests.

Here is an example of an infinite loop in pseudocode (code that explains the idea but does not use proper syntax). We want to print the names of all the members of our club. In *Chapter 8,* we will discuss how to connect to the database. Then we would write code along these lines:

```
. . .Code to connect to database
. . .Code to read the names into a set of records (RecordSet)
do while Not EndOfRecordSet
   LblMEssage += (RecordSet.currentrecord.Name) & "<br/>"
   Move to next record
Loop
```

When we start the loop, we do not know how many cycles we need to perform. However, at the beginning of each cycle we do a test as follows. First, we read the true/false property of the EndOfRecordset. If we are not at the end then this property returns a false. Since it is not at the end, we want to execute the loop, so we change the `false` into a `true` using `NOT`. With that `true` returned to C#, it would execute the loop.

Note the second line within the loop – if we don't move to the next record we would just keep printing the name from the first record. However, with the `Move` we get, at some point, to the end of the records and `EndOfRecordSet` returns a `true`. That is turned into a `false` by the `NOT` and when the `do...while` sees a `false` in its text expression, it ends looping and jumps down to the next line of code below the loop. We are not ready to read from databases, but we can code a page that involves chance and thus we do not know the number of loops to execute.

Try It Out **Using the while Loop**

1. Open your web page editor and type in the following:

```
<script language="C#" runat="server">
void Page_load()
    {
      Random r = new Random();
      int diceRoll = 0;
      while (diceRoll != 6)
      {
        diceRoll = Convert.ToInt32(r.Next(6)) + 1;
        message1.Text = message1.Text + "Rolled a: " + diceRoll + "<br />";
      }
    }
</script>

<html>
<head>
<title>While Loop Example</title>
</head>
<body>
   <asp:label id="message1" runat="server"/>
</body>
</html>
```

2. Save this as `Demo-While.aspx`. and view it in your browser. You will see Figure 4-8:

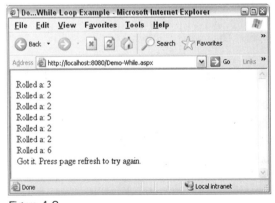

Figure 4-8

How It Works

We started by declaring a random number, and a variable to hold our `diceroll` number:

```
void Page_load()
{
    Random r = new Random();
    int diceRoll = 0;
```

Then we run the loop. If the last dice roll is anything other than a six, we want to roll again, so we use the inequality operator to tell C# to keep running the loop, so long as the dice roll is not equal to six. We do this because we want the loop to stop once we have a six:

```
while (diceRoll != 6)
{
  diceRoll = Convert.ToInt32(r.Next(6)) + 1;
    message1.Text = message1.Text + "Rolled a: " + diceRoll + "<br />";
  }
}
```

When `diceRoll` equals 6 the condition will resolve to false, and the while loop will stop looping. In this case it is the closing brace that will end the C# code. It is possible for this code to enter an infinite loop. However, it is highly unlikely that the computer will keep on selecting random numbers forever without selecting a six at some point.

The do...while Structure

You're not restricted to having the condition at the beginning of your loop. If you want your condition at the end use the `do...while` syntax. In this case the loop will be run at least once because C# tests the condition after the loop.

```
do
{
  // looping code here
} while (condition);
```

Once thing you should note about this syntax is the semicolon after the `while` statement. It is required for the code to compile (and is easily forgotten, if, say, you are converting a while loop into a do...while loop). So, if you go back to the previous example, you can amend it as follows:

```
void Page_load() {
  Random r = new Random();
  int diceRoll;
  do
  {
    diceRoll = Convert.ToInt32(r.Next(6)) + 1;
    message1.Text = message1.Text + "Rolled a: " + diceRoll + "<br />";
  } while (diceRoll != 6);
}
```

Note that you do not have to assign a dummy value to the `diceRoll` variable before the loops runs. This is because the variable is set during the first (and possibly only) run of the loop and is tested afterwards.

If you save your amended `Demo-While.aspx` file as `Demo-DoWhile.aspx`, you will see exactly the same sort of output (but with different numbers, naturally) as shown in Figure 4-9:

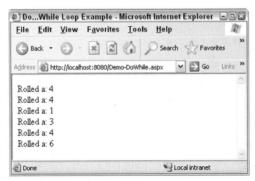

Figure 4-9

We will write a page that simulates rolling a dice (by coming up with a random number between one and six) – and keeps rolling it until it gets a six. A label on the page tells us the results of each try that was made. However, we don't know – at the time of writing our C# code, or even before we roll the first dice – how many times we'll have to roll the dice to get a 6. So, we must use a `do...while` loop.

Try It Out Using do...while

1. Create a new page `TIO-DoWhileLoop.aspx` in `Ch04` folder and type in the following:

```
<%@ Page Language="c#" Debug="true" %>
<script runat="server">

    void Page_load() {
        Random r = new Random();
        int diceRoll;

        message1.Text = "Lets get started. <br>";

        do
        {
            diceRoll = Convert.ToInt32(r.Next(6)) + 1;
            message1.Text = message1.Text + "Rolled a: " + diceRoll + "<br />";
        } while (diceRoll != 6);

        message1.Text += "There is our six.";

    }

</script>
```

```
<html>
<head>
<title>Do While Loop Example</title>
</head>
<body>
  <asp:label id="message1" runat="server"/>
</body>
</html>
```

2. View this page in your browser as shown in Figure 4-10 and click the Refresh button several times:

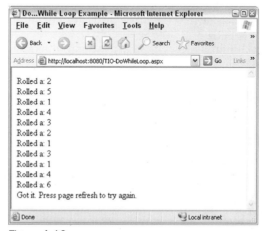

Figure 4-10

How It Works

We started by declaring a variable that will hold the result of the diceRoll. Then we put some text into Message1.text. This line mainly demonstrates a line before a loop – it will only be executed once. When you start building complex pages you will need to keep a clear idea of what is inside and outside of the loop:

```
<script runat="server">
  void Page_load()
  {
    Random r = new Random();
    int diceRoll;
    message1.Text = "Lets get started. <br>";
```

Then we run the loop. If the last dice roll was anything other than a 6, we want to roll again, so we use the inequality operator to tell C# to keep running the loop, so long as the dice roll is not equal to six. We do this because we want the loop to stop once we have a six. We finish with a demonstration of a line after the loop

```
    do
    {
```

```
        diceRoll = Convert.ToInt32(r.Next(6)) + 1;
        message1.Text = message1.Text + "Rolled a: " + diceRoll + "<br
                        />";
    } while (diceRoll != 6);
  }
  message1.Text += "There is our six.";

</script>
```

When `diceRoll` equals six, it will stop and not execute the contents of the loop, instead jumping to the next statement beyond the loop.

> Use do...while when actions within the loop absolutely have to occur at least once no matter what the result of the expression. Use while when there are actions within the loop that should not execute if the expression is false.

Modulo example

You came across the modulo (%) operator in the last chapter, and early on in this chapter. Recall that modulo returns the remainder of a division. You can refer to these sections to jog your memory about what modulo can do. Here we will apply this operator to our dice example. Open TIO-WhileLoop.aspx, change the code as shown and save as Demo-Modulo.aspx. This modification will give the user an encouragement message with every third roll:

```
<%@ Page Language="C#" debug="true"%>
<script runat="server">

void Page_Load()
{
    // demo of modulo where every third try displays an encouraging message
    Random objRandom = new Random();
    int  DiceRoll = 0;
    byte bytRollCounter = 0;
    Message1.Text = "Lets begin. We'll keep trying until we get a six.<br/>";

    while (DiceRoll != 6)
    {
        // check if we need to show the 'keep trying' message

        if(bytRollCounter%3 == 0 && !(bytRollCounter==0))
        {
            Message1.Text += "   Keep trying! <br>";
        }    // End If

        bytRollCounter +=1;
        DiceRoll = Convert.ToInt32(objRandom.Next(6)) + 1;
        Message1.Text += "Rolled a: " + DiceRoll + ."<br />";
    }    // end Loop
    Message1.Text += "Got it. Press page refresh to try again.";
}    //end void Page_Load()

</script>
```

```
<html>
<head>
    <title>Modulo example (using a While Loop)</title>
</head>
<body>
    <asp:label id="Message1" runat="server"></asp:label>
</body>
</html>
```

Test it with several refreshes until a try takes at least three rolls. In this code, we start by creating a variable that will count our rolls. We can use byte data type with the assumption that we will roll a six in less then 255 tries. Then in each loop, we increase the value in `bytRollCounter`. Then we check if `bytRollCounter` is evenly divisible by 5, in other words the remainder is zero. If true, we concatenate the encouragement message as shown in Figure 4-11:

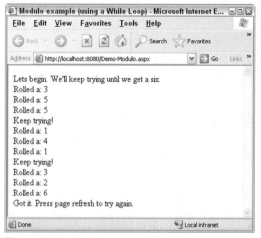

Figure 4-11

The foreach...in Loop

C# has a cousin of the `for` statement named `foreach`. It works in a similar way to `for`, except that it's only used for elements inside an array or a collection. It is a lot like `while`, since we don't have to know the number of members in the collection. We've met several collections in the last chapter: `Arrays`, `ArrayLists`, `Hashtables`, and `SortedLists`. For example, we could read all elements of a simple array into a label as follows (see the download file named `Demo-forEach.aspx`)

```
void page_Load()
{
  string[] arrCities = new string[3];
  arrCities[0]=("London");
  arrCities[1]=("Paris");
  arrCities[2]=("Munich");

  foreach (string item in arrCities)
  {
```

```
        lblOut.Text += item + "<BR>";
    }    //end foreach
}    //end page_Load()
```

It looks almost identical to the for structure. The only difference is that you don't have to specify the number of items you want to loop through; C# will simply start with the first item in the array and then repeat the loop until it reaches the last item.

Summary

This chapter introduced C# control structures, the tools used to determine the order of execution of lines of code. Sometimes we use a branching control to choose only one of several alternatives of lines to execute. At other times, we use a looping structure to consecutively repeat lines of code. We may also use jumping structures, which are covered in the next chapter.

We started with operators. The equal sign (=) assigns a value into a variable or object property. We can also use += to make an addition to the existing value in a variable or property. We also covered the concatenation operator, +, which appends a string of text onto an existing string of text.

We then covered the basic math operators for addition, subtraction, etc. Always keep in mind the precedence of execution if you have many terms: start in the parentheses, work left to right with multiplication and division, then left to right with addition and subtraction. Then C# moves to the next higher level of parentheses. Using parentheses often makes the calculation easier to write and maintain. Modulo provides the remainder value from a division.

There are three commonly used logical operators. && means AND, which uses two complete expressions and requires both to be true in order to return a value of true. || means OR, which also uses two complete expressions but only one has to be true in order to get an overall answer of true. ! means NOT which reverses the logical value of whatever follows it (if the expression is complicated, it is best to put it in parenthesis).

if allows us to execute just one of two sets of code. The simplest form only takes one line, but can only execute one statement for the true case. Adding the braces allows multiple lines to be executed in the case of the expression being true. If you also use else then you can execute lines in the case where the expression resolves to false. When you have many possible values for a variable then you can use the switch structure rather than heavily nested if structures.

When looping you must decide on (if you know, at the time the loop starts) the number of loops you intend to execute. If you can determine the number of loops needed to be performed, use the for loop structure. Be careful about the lines that go in the loop and the ones that should be before or after the loop. If you do not know the number of iterations required, you use the while or do loops that perform a test at each cycle and either loop again, or stop. It never executes a loop if the expression is false. The do...while looping structure always executes at least once because the test is not performed until the end of the first loop. If you need to loop through code that affects each member of a collection (arraylist, hashtable, etc.) then use foreach...in looping structure. C# will automatically perform the loop once on each member of the collection.

This chapter covered branching and looping structures. The next chapter will cover jumping structures

Exercises

1. For each of the following Boolean expressions, say for what integer values of A each of them will evaluate to `true` and when they will evaluate to `false`:

- ❏ NOT A=0
- ❏ A > 0 OR A < 5
- ❏ NOT A > 0 OR A < 5
- ❏ A > 1 AND A < 5 OR A > 7 AND A < 10
- ❏ A < 10 OR A > 12 AND NOT A > 20

2. Suggest a loop structure that would be appropriate for each of the following scenarios and justify your choice:

- ❏ Displaying a set of items from a shopping list stored in an array
- ❏ Displaying a calendar for the current month
- ❏ Looking through an array to find the location of a specific entry
- ❏ Drawing a chessboard using an HTML table

3. Write a page that generates ten random numbers between two integers provided by the user in text boxes.

Functions

In the last chapter, we mentioned three ways to sequence the execution of C# code within your ASP.NET page: branching, looping, and jumping. We have already discussed branching and looping and will now discuss jumping structures. *Jumping* is used when we want to leave the execution of our main code midway and jump over to execute another block of code. After executing the block, we return to our main code.

Jumping makes it easier to create and maintain code for many reasons, and is therefore, an important skill for programmers. This chapter will cover the following topics:

❑   Defining and using simple functions

❑   Passing parameters to functions

❑   Using the return value from a function

❑   Passing parameters by value and by reference

❑   Good practices

Overview

Jumping structures allow the programmer to halt the execution of the main code and jump to another block of code. This block of code is called a *function*. ("Later, when we look at classes in *Chapter 7*, we will also refer to it as a *method*.") After the function has run, execution returns to the main code again. Functions will come in handy as you write more and more ASP.NET code, and begin to find that you need to use the same code in more than one place. Then you just write a function containing that particular code, and execute it as many times as you like.

For example, you may have written a function called ShowOrder() that displays the goods that a customer has ordered. For C# to display this output, you don't have to rewrite or copy all of that code into the body of code. Instead, just have C# jump out of your current code, execute the ShowOrder() function, and then come back and continue executing the original code.

Modularization

The process of dividing one large program into several smaller, interlocking parts is called *modularization*. This term can be applied to several instances; for example, we already modularize our page into an HTML section and a script section. Within the script section, we can further modularize our code by creating functions as described in this chapter. Later, we will discuss moving code to its own page (covered in *Chapter 12*). An additional level of modularization is to move code out into objects that exist completely independently of the page, something that we will cover in *Chapter 7*. Let's take a moment to discuss the advantages of modularization.

❏   **Easier to write**: Instead of trying to organize an entire project in your mind, you can focus on just code that performs a specific job in a module. Then, you can move on to the specific job of another module. Many studies show that this type of programming, if properly planned, results in better code with development done sooner and cheaper.

❏   **Easier to read and maintain**: A programmer looking at the code for the first time can quickly grasp the objectives of each section if sections are independent. Not only is each module clearer, but a reader also has an easier time tracing the flow of a program from section to section.

❏   **Facilitates testing and troubleshooting**: You can test modules independently without worrying about errors introduced by the rest of the code. If you know a particular module works without error and then plug it into an untested module, you can narrow down the causes of any errors to the untested module or to the interface between the two.

❏   **Multiple programmers can work together**: Each group of programmers can focus on one objective that will be self-contained within a module. The important management issue is to have each module clearly defined in terms of its purpose, input, and output. In more advanced forms of modularization (particularly objects), different teams can even work in different languages. .NET provides for a common interface for modules to interchange information.

❏   **Code reuse**: Many tasks (such as the display of a shopping cart's current value) must be repeated at many points on a page or on a Web site. If you put 100 lines of code in one module and call it ten times in your code, that's 890 lines of code you've saved.

❏   **Good stepping stone**: Ultimately, you will want to use the more sophisticated techniques of code-behind and objects, but before you get there, it is a good practice to think and act modular within your simple script tags.

Programmers must keep their designs straight especially if their code calls functions. These calls can be several layers deep and are easy to conceptualize with a diagram such as Figure 5-1:

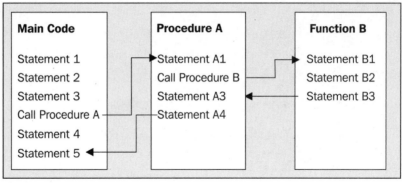

Figure 5-1

Defining and Using Functions

Functions are easy to write; let's look at a simple example where we write a function in our Web page and call it. We'll start with a basic function that doesn't exchange any information with the rest of the page and then move on to more complex code.

Try It Out **Defining and Using a Simple Function**

1. Create a new ASP.NET page called `SimpleFunction.aspx` and save it in your `Ch05` folder.

2. Add the following code to the file in the All view:

```
<%@ Page Language="C#" Debug="true" %>
<script runat="server">

    void Page_Load()
    {
        lblMessage.Text = "First Line";
        InsertLinebreak();
        lblMessage.Text += "Second Line";
        InsertLinebreak();
        lblMessage.Text += "Third Line";
        InsertLinebreak();
    }

    void InsertLinebreak()
    {
        lblMessage.Text += "<br><hr>";
    }

</script>
<html>
<head>
    <title>Simple Function Example</title>
</head>
```

```
<body>
    <form runat="server">
        <asp:Label id="lblMessage" runat="server"></asp:Label>
    </form>
</body>
</html>
```

3. Save the code and see the page in your browser (Figure 5-2):

Figure 5-2

How It Works

The layout of `SimpleFunction.aspx` is very straightforward. It is a blank page containing only a `Label` control called `lblMessage`.

```
<body>
    <form runat="server">
        <asp:Label id="lblMessage" runat="server"></asp:Label>
    </form>
</body>
```

In the `<script>` block, we define a function called `InsertLinebreak()` to insert a horizontal line and a line break at the end of the text string displayed in `lblMessage`.

```
void InsertLinebreak()
{
    lblMessage.Text += "<br><hr>";
}
```

When the page is loaded, ASP.NET calls `Page_Load()` and the first line of the code is executed. When the second line of code is executed, `Page_Load()` calls (or *invokes*) our function `InsertLinebreak()`. *Call* is the term for one line of code running another block of code, after which execution returns to the calling code.

```
void Page_Load()
{
    lblMessage.Text = "First Line";
```

```
        InsertLinebreak();
        lblMessage.Text += "Second Line";
        InsertLinebreak();
        lblMessage.Text += "Third Line";
        InsertLinebreak();
    }
```

The line of code in `InsertLinebreak()` is executed, and then control returns to the next line in `Page_Load()`. This switching of execution continues until the end of `Page_Load()`, and then control is handed back to ASP.NET. `InsertLinebreak()` will be called three times every time `Page_Load()` executes.

Now if we want to change the style of the line break in `SimpleFunction.aspx`, we only need to change the code in `InsertLinebreak()`. If we had not used a function, we would have had to rewrite the line creation code three times in the main code. Even in such a simple example, we can see the advantages of using functions.

You would have noticed that `Page_Load()` looks remarkably similar to `InsertLinebreak()` in terms of its structure:

```
void InsertLineBreak()
{
    ...
}

void Page_Load()
{
    ...
}
```

This is because `Page_Load()` is, in fact, a function, although of a special type because ASP.NET already knows about it without any help from us. Inside ASP.NET, there are several functions that can be executed at times without a call from your code. `Page_Load()`, for example, is automatically called whenever a page is loaded from the server. These pre-defined functions are associated with *events* and will be discussed in the next chapter.

Before moving on, there are a few more basics to be aware of while using functions:

❑ All function definitions have the same basic structure as `Page_Load()` and `InsertLinebreak()`, although they are usually a little more complicated. The following snippet shows the general structure of a function in C#:

```
<accessType> <returnType> FunctionName (<parameter1, parameter2, ...,
                                        parameterX>)
{
    ...
}
```

You'll learn more about return types and parameters later on in this chapter. The top line of a function's definition is called the function's *signature*.

❑ You can give functions any name you like provided it begins with a letter and only contains letters, numbers, and underscore characters. So `InsertLinebreak()`, `tequila()`, and `z12_y32()` are fine, but `_hello()`, and `28DaysLater()` are not. Also, try to give them sensible and easy to remember names pertinent to the code functionality. Note also that C# *is* case-sensitive. This means that calling `HELLOMUM()` will execute only if the function called is `HELLOMUM()`, and not `HelloMum()` or `hellomum()`!

❑ Parentheses are used both in the function definition and when we call the function. Their presence is mandatory. If you don't use them, the page won't run.

The ( ) characters are referred to as parentheses in American English and as brackets in European English. In American English, brackets imply [ ]. However, we will use the term parentheses in this chapter to refer to ( ), which are the characters of interest for writing functions.

❑ If you have more than one function in a `<script>`, include a line of documentation in your code so that it is apparent what they do and how they do it. C# uses two slashes (`//`) to delineate a single line of documentation and `/* ... */` to denote multiple lines. For example:

```
// InsertLineBreak adds a line break and horizontal rule to the text
void InsertLineBreak()
{
    ...
}
```

```
/* Page_Load is a special type of function. It is associated with a
     pre-defined event. In this case it writes some text to a Label control
*/
void Page_Load()
{
    ...
}
```

❑ You cannot nest function definitions within one another. Therefore, they go inside our script tags at the same level as our `Page_Load()` code.

Right then! On to slightly more complex functions. Our `SimpleFunction.aspx` example above has a weakness in that it is inflexible. We can't use it to insert two lines at once or reuse it to change the contents of any other label. Also, the code will work only when we have a `Label` control named `lblMessage`. Our `InsertLinebreak()` function is of no use if we want lines added to the text of another `Label` control, say `lblMessageTwo`. Passing parameters can solve this problem.

Passing Parameters to Functions

You can make functions more versatile by including parameters. A *parameter* (also called an *argument*) is a piece of data that is passed to the function. This allows the behavior of the function to be varied from one execution to the next. The result of calling the function will depend on data sent from the code when you make the call.

The basic syntax is not too difficult. When creating a function that uses a parameter, we simply declare the name of the parameter and its type inside the parentheses following the function's name. For example, you could define a function that takes an integer parameter called `MyInteger`. The value of this parameter is then available for use within the function:

```
void SomeFunction(int MyInteger)
{
    ... code that uses the value held in MyInteger
}
```

When you call a function that expects an argument, place the value of the argument in the parentheses after its name. For example, you could pass the integer 1050 to a function, say, `SomeFunction()` as follows:

```
SomeFunction(1050);
```

1050 will be stored in the block variable named `MyInteger`. Functions can receive more than one argument as long as a comma separates each parameter – a combination of both name and datatype. In the following example, the code at the bottom calls `MyFunction()` and passes two values – the first, a string (in quotes) and the second, a number:

```
void MyFunction(string MyParameter1, int MyParameter2)
{
    ... code that uses the values held in MyParameter1 and myParameter2
}

MyFunction("myText", myNumber);
```

As you can see, variables or strings can both be used as parameters for functions – in fact, you can use anything that can be evaluated to a value – mathematical or logical expressions, numbers, or an object's property (like the `Text` property of a `TextBox` Web control).

Let's try this out with an example. We're going to expand on our previous example here by giving `InsertLinebreak()` two parameters to work with. These will determine the number and width of horizontal rules to generate between lines.

Try It Out   Functions with Parameters

1. Create a new ASP.NET page called `FuncWithParameters.aspx` and save it in your `Ch05` folder.

2. Add the following code to your page in the All view:

```
<%@ Page Language="C#" Debug="true" %>
<script runat="server">

    void Page_Load()
    {
        if (IsPostBack)
        {

            lblMessage.Text = "First Line";
            InsertLinebreak(Convert.ToInt32(NumberOptions.SelectedItem.Value),
```

```
                        Convert.ToInt32(WidthOptions.SelectedItem.Value));
            lblMessage.Text += "Second Line";
            InsertLinebreak(Convert.ToInt32(NumberOptions.SelectedItem.Value),
                        Convert.ToInt32(WidthOptions.SelectedItem.Value));
        }
    }

    void InsertLinebreak(int NumLines, int Width)
    {
        for (int i=1; i<=NumLines; i++)
        {
            lblMessage.Text += "<br><hr width='" + Width.ToString() +
                        "' align='left'>";
        }
    }
}
</script>
<html>
<head>
    <title>Using Functions with Parameters</title>
</head>
<body>
    Choose the number and width of the linebreaks and then press submit
    <form runat="server">
        <asp:RadioButtonList id="WidthOptions" runat="server">
            <asp:ListItem value="100">100 pixels wide</asp:ListItem>
            <asp:ListItem value="300">300 pixels wide</asp:ListItem>
            <asp:ListItem value="600">600 pixels wide</asp:ListItem>
        </asp:RadioButtonList>
        <asp:DropDownList id="NumberOptions" runat="server">
            <asp:ListItem value="1">1 Line</asp:ListItem>
            <asp:ListItem value="2">2 Lines</asp:ListItem>
            <asp:ListItem value="3">3 Lines</asp:ListItem>
        </asp:DropDownList>
        <asp:Button id="Button1" runat="server" text="Submit"></asp:Button>
        <br />
        <br />
        <asp:Label id="lblMessage" runat="server"></asp:Label>
    </form>
</body>
</html>
```

3. Save the code and open the page in your browser. It should appear as in Figure 5-3:

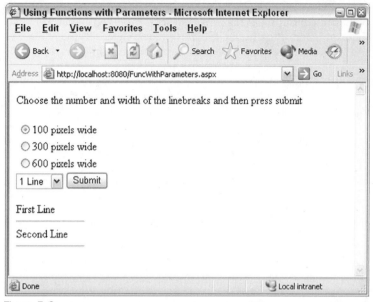

Figure 5-3

How It Works

This example builds on the SimpleFunction.aspx page you saw in the previous Try-It-Out section. It has the same Label control, lblMessage, but more sophisticated input controls have been added to get the user's preference for how to format the horizontal rules. (Later these will be passed to the function that creates the rules.) The radio button group offers a choice of widths and the drop down list provides a choice of the number of lines to produce:

```
<form runat="server">
    <asp:RadioButtonList id="WidthOptions" runat="server">
        <asp:ListItem value="100">100 pixels wide</asp:ListItem>
        <asp:ListItem value="300">300 pixels wide</asp:ListItem>
        <asp:ListItem value="600">600 pixels wide</asp:ListItem>
    </asp:RadioButtonList>
    <asp:DropDownList id="NumberOptions" runat="server">
        <asp:ListItem value="1">1 Line</asp:ListItem>
        <asp:ListItem value="2">2 Lines</asp:ListItem>
        <asp:ListItem value="3">3 Lines</asp:ListItem>
    </asp:DropDownList>
```

There's also a button that needs to be clicked to indicate that the choices have been made:

```
    <asp:Button id="Button1" runat="server" text="Submit"></asp:Button>
    <br />
    <br />
    <asp:Label id="lblMessage" runat="server"></asp:Label>
</form>
```

Now let's take a look at the function in the page. Note that it is within the `<script>` tags but *not* inside any other functions. Furthermore, it has the correct structure as noted earlier. The first line is of interest because this is where our parameters are set up. The first parameter sets the number of lines to create and the second sets the line widths. Both parameters are marked as integers. Within the function we do a simple loop that appends text to the end of `lblMessage.Text`.

Note how the value from the `Width` parameter is first cast from an integer into text, and then appended directly to the string so that it becomes a valid HTML attribute of the `<hr>` tag:

```
void InsertLinebreak(int NumLines, int Width)
{
    for (int i=1; i<=NumLines; i++)
    {
        lblMessage.Text += "<br><hr width='" + Width.ToString() +
                           "' align='left'>";
    }
}
```

Now that we have input and output controls on the form and a function to do the work, we are ready to call the function from our main code. We do this from `Page_Load()` since we know that it will execute automatically. `Page_Load()` first checks if we are in postback mode, which implies that the choice of the number and width of lines has been made. We then write `First Line` into `lblMessage.Text` and call `InsertLinebreak()` to add our lines, remembering to pass the two parameters that it requires.

The first parameter for the number of lines to display is *the value of the item selected in the drop down list*. The second parameter for the width of the lines is *the value of the selection in the Radio button group*. Note that both values are initially strings and must be converted to integers before they are passed to the function:

```
void Page_Load()
{
    if (IsPostBack)
    {

        lblMessage.Text = "First Line";
        InsertLinebreak(Convert.ToInt32(NumberOptions.SelectedItem.Value),
                        Convert.ToInt32(WidthOptions.SelectedItem.Value));
```

We then write `Second Line` into `lblMessage.Text` and call `InsertLinebreak()` again.

```
        lblMessage.Text += "Second Line";
        InsertLinebreak(Convert.ToInt32(NumberOptions.SelectedItem.Value),
                        Convert.ToInt32(WidthOptions.SelectedItem.Value));
    }
}
```

This example demonstrated several points. First, we looked at the syntax of a function that uses parameters. We also looked at a couple of Web controls (a radio button group and a dropdown list) that can be used to get information and pass it as a parameter. Within the function, we practiced how to use this data in code.

Finally, we saw that the values we gave our parameters had to be of the same type as we defined in the function's signature. In fact, when we call a function, the parameters must exactly match the definitions specified in the function signature. This means matching the parameter types, the number of parameters, and the order of the parameters. Thus the following call to `InsertLinebreak()` is valid:

```
InsertLinebreak (5, 120);
```

However, the following calls to `InsertLinebreak()` are not valid:

```
InsertLinebreak("five", 120);
InsertLinebreak(5, 120, now!);
```

There is a technique known as *overloading functions* that can get around this problem (discussed in *Chapter 7*). Likewise, the problem of not knowing how many parameters a function will be sent can be resolved by using a parameter array in your function definition, but that is outside the scope of this book.

For more information on function overloading and parameter arrays, take a look at Beginning Visual C# by Karli Watson, Wrox Press, ISBN 0-7645-4382-2.

Web Controls as Parameters

It's worth noting that when you want to pass the name of a Web control object to a function as a parameter, you need to be on your toes. Let's say you want to write a generic function that will change the font size of a `Label` control and that this function will accept one parameter, the name of the control. At first, you might think that you need to pass a string containing the name of the `Label` control to the function. No. All the function will get is the literal text `lblMyLabel`. Rather, you want the reference to be to the `Label` control object itself.

When passing a Web control reference, you must declare its type as one of the Web controls:

```
void MyFunction(TextBox target)
void MyFunction(Label target)
void MyFunction(Button target)
void MyFunction(CheckBox target)
```

Within the function, after we declare a Web control type we can refer to the Web control by the name we gave it within parentheses. In the following case, this name would be `target`:

```
void MakeFancy(Label target)
{
    target.BackColor = Drawing.Color.Red;
    target.Font.Size = FontUnit.Large;
}
```

Let's try this out in an example. In this example, we're going to create a simple page containing three `Label` controls that already contain text. The text of any of these controls can be changed to italics according to the state of a checkbox. The process of changing a label's style to italic should be coded once in a function. This single function can then be used to change any of the three labels to italics:

Try It Out Using Web Controls as Parameters

1. Create a new ASP.NET page called `ParameterWebControl.aspx` and save it in your `Ch05` folder.

2. Add the following code to this page:

```
<%@ Page Language="C#" Debug="true" %>
<script runat="server">

    void Page_Load()
    {
        MakeItalic(Label1, CheckBox1.Checked);
        MakeItalic(Label2, CheckBox2.Checked);
        MakeItalic(Label3, CheckBox3.Checked);
    }

    void MakeItalic(Label TargetLabel, bool ItalicYN)
    {
        TargetLabel.Font.Italic = ItalicYN;
    }

</script>
<html>
<head>
    <title>Chapter 5 : Parameter Web Controls</title>
</head>
<body>
    <form runat="server">
        <table>
            <tbody>
                <tr>
                    <td>
                        <asp:CheckBox id="CheckBox1"
                                        runat="server"></asp:CheckBox>
                    </td>
                    <td>
                        <asp:CheckBox id="CheckBox2"
                                        runat="server"></asp:CheckBox>
                    </td>
                    <td>
                        <asp:CheckBox id="CheckBox3"
                                        runat="server"></asp:CheckBox>
                    </td>
                </tr>
                <tr>
                    <td>
                        <asp:Label id="Label1" runat="server"
                                    text="apple"></asp:Label></td>
                    <td>
                        <asp:Label id="Label2" runat="server"
                                    text="banana"></asp:Label></td>
                    <td>
```

```
                     <asp:Label id="Label3" runat="server"
                                  text="carrot"></asp:Label></td>
              </tr>
          </tbody>
      </table>
      <asp:Button id="Button1" runat="server"
                     Text="Change Font Style"></asp:Button>
    </form>
  </body>
</html>
```

3. Save the code and open the page in your browser (see Figure 5-4):

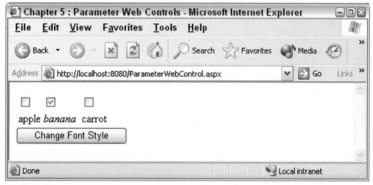

Figure 5-4

How It Works

In this example, we've used a table to align the checkboxes with their corresponding labels. The first row consists of checkboxes:

```
<form runat="server">
    <table>
        <tbody>
            <tr>
                <td>
                    <asp:CheckBox id="CheckBox1"
                                    runat="server"></asp:CheckBox>
                </td>
                <td>
                    <asp:CheckBox id="CheckBox2"
                                    runat="server"></asp:CheckBox>
                </td>
                <td>
                    <asp:CheckBox id="CheckBox3"
                                    runat="server"></asp:CheckBox>
                </td>
            </tr>
```

The second row contains labels displaying the names of fruits. Make a mental note of their IDs – these are used to refer to the controls in your code:

```
<tr>
    <td>
        <asp:Label id="Label1" runat="server"
                        text="apple"></asp:Label></td>
    <td>
        <asp:Label id="Label2" runat="server"
                        text="banana"></asp:Label></td>
    <td>
        <asp:Label id="Label3" runat="server"
                        text="carrot"></asp:Label></td>
    </tr>
    </tbody>
</table>
```

Also notice that underneath the table is a button to notify ASP.NET that you've made your choice of labels to change:

```
<asp:Button id="Button1" runat="server"
            Text="Change Font Style"></asp:Button>
</form>
```

Our `MakeItalic()` function receives two parameters and can be found inside the `<script>` tags. The first parameter is a reference to an ASP.NET `Label` Web control; therefore it must be of the datatype `Label`. The second parameter is a Boolean value that will be used to toggle the italicization of the text:

```
void MakeItalic(Label TargetLabel, bool ItalicYN)
```

Inside the function, we can refer to the label by using the name assigned to it in the function signature, in this case, `TargetLabel`. Observe that we must use the C# object model syntax to refer to the label's properties. Therefore, we use `TargetLabel.Font.Italic` to set the style of the label's text rather than HTML attribute syntax such as `<p style="font-style: italic;">`.

Lastly, notice how the second parameter has been used. The `ItalicYN` property has only two settings, `true` or `false`. Since a Boolean variable comes in as `true` or `false`, we can directly use that as the value for a Web control property:

```
{
    TargetLabel.Font.Italic = ItalicYN;
}
```

Now it is time to actually call the function. As we've seen, we need to pass two variables to `MakeItalic()`. The first is the name of the `Label` control that it should modify. The second is a Boolean value that conveys whether we want the italicization turned on or off. Conveniently, the `CheckBox` Web control's `Checked` property contains a `true` if the check is on and a `false` if the check is off, so we do not need to do any testing or transformation; we just need to type the `object.property` reference into the parameter and its value is passed to the function:

```
void Page_Load()
{
    MakeItalic(Label1, CheckBox1.Checked);
    MakeItalic(Label2, CheckBox2.Checked);
    MakeItalic(Label3, CheckBox3.Checked);
}
```

A good question arises when you study this code. In the form, instead of three independent CheckBox controls, why not use a asp:CheckBoxList and then have the three calls made to MakeItalic() in a loop with the counter equal to CheckBoxList.Item()? The problem is that we want to present the page in a table, and table tags like <td> do not co-exist well with code to add items to a CheckBoxList. An alternate solution would be to use a DataGrid bound to an array. (See *Chapter 8* and *9* for more on a DataGrid.)

Return Values

So far in this chapter, we've only looked at functions that perform a job without returning a value. Now it's time to look at those that perform a job and then send a piece of information back to the calling code. If you'll recall, the generic structure of a function looks like this:

```
<accessType> <returnType> FunctionName (<parameter1, parameter2, ...,
    parameterX>)
{
    ...
}
```

So then, in order to define a function that returns a value to the calling code, you need to replace <returnType> with the type of the value the calling code will receive. Previously, we've used void to indicate there is no return value. We'll also now need to include the return keyword to end the function and send the return value back to the calling code. As an example, here is a function that adds two integer parameters together and returns the result:

```
int Add(int IntegerOne, int IntegerTwo)
{
    return IntegerOne + IntegerTwo;
}
```

Note that functions return only a *single* piece of data. A common error that a beginning programmer makes is attempting to write a function that returns multiple values, which isn't possible. It is possible, however, to return a single custom object that has multiple properties and, consequently, multiple values. We'll look at this further in *Chapter 7*.

Using Return Values in Your Code

You can call a function that returns a value by typing its name followed by a pair of parentheses, just like any other function:

```
MyFunction();
```

However, unless you handle the returned value, by assigning it to a variable for example, your code will not compile and return an error:

```
MyVariable = MyFunction();
```

Another mistake, frequently seen with beginners developing functions, is that they fail to handle the returned value. A function call cannot exist by itself on a line if it returns a value; the returned value *must* go into something. The most common receivers of a function's return value are:

- ❏ A variable
- ❏ A property of an object
- ❏ An argument for another function
- ❏ An expression in a control structure

Let's look at an example of each of the four ways to use a function's return value in pseudo code, and then we will try them out in an exercise. To cut down on space we won't present the forms below. You can assume that we have various labels and text boxes in a form as needed by the code. In addition, the lower portion of each example would be within Page_Load(). Of course the functions would be outside Page_Load() because we cannot nest one function inside another. However, all the functions would be within the <script> tags.

The following example demonstrates allocating the return value of a function *to a variable* named WholesalePrice:

```
decimal WholesaleCostLookUp(int CatalogNumber)
{
... code that takes a catalog number and looks up the price in the database
... code that will RETURN the price
}
...
decimal WholesalePrice = WholesaleCostLookUp(txtCatalogNumber.Text);
```

In the following example, we assign the return value of a function *to the value of an object's property,* namely the Text property of lblItemName. Notice that the function expects an integer in the parameter, but the TextBox.Text property is a string. It must be converted to an integer prior to using it as an argument for our custom-built function NameLookUp():

```
string NameLookUp(int CatalogNumber)
{
... code that takes a catalog number and looks up the item's name in the
        database
... code that will RETURN the name
}
...
lblItemName.Text = NameLookUp( Convert.ToInt32(txtCatNumber.Text) );
```

The following example demonstrates how the return value of a function can be used as *an expression in a control structure*. Note that the value returned is Boolean and can be used as a whole expression; there's no need for an additional value=true expression:

```
bool IsMember(int maybeNumber)
{
```

```
... code that looks up a number and sees if it is a true member number or not.
... code that will RETURN a Boolean
}
...
if (IsMember(SomeNumber))
{
    lblMember.Text = "You are a member";
}
else
{
    lblMember.Text = "You are not a member";
}
```

Our last example demonstrates how the return value of a function can be used as an *argument* for another function. In this case, the function retrieves a user's password (because he has forgotten it). In the latter half of the code, the result of the function (the password) is used as an argument for the function named `EmailPassword()` that sends the password to the user through email. `EmailPassword()`, in turn, returns a Boolean value to say whether it has completed its task or not and so must have a receiver for its output, which in this case is the Boolean `EmailOnItsWay` variable:

```
string GetPassword(string UserName)
{
... code which retrieves the users password
... code that will RETURN a string
}
...
bool EmailOnItsWay = EmailPassword( GetPassword(user), EmailAddress );
```

Having seen the pseudo code of several function examples, let's move on to a working exercise. Our objective in this exercise is to write and use functions that will demonstrate different ways of handling the results of a function, as explained earlier: assigning the results to a variable, allocating the results to an object's property, using the result as the argument for another function, and using the result as an expression in a control structure.

Try It Out Handling Function Return Types

Note that the entire exercise is run on four parallel tracks: four functions, four output labels, and four sections of code that call the functions. For input, we have just two text boxes and a Submit button.

1. Create a new ASP.NET page called `Functions.aspx` and save it in your `Ch05` folder.

2. Add the four functions to your page. The first function is named `Disguise()`, and its return value will be put into a variable. `Disguise()` performs a simple encoding on a string of characters by moving each character one up in turn. So for example, a becomes b, b becomes c, and so on. The input parameters and output are of the `string` datatype. The results will be displayed in the `lblDisguised` control:

```
<%@ Page Language="C#" Debug="true" %>
<script runat="server">

    // 'Disguises' a string by adding one to each characters ASCII value
    string Disguise(string String1)
```

```
{
    string DisguisedString;
    Byte[] myBytes = System.Text.Encoding.ASCII.GetBytes(String1);
    for (int i=0;i<myBytes.Length;i++)
    {
        myBytes[i] += 1;
    }
    char[] myChars=System.Text.Encoding.ASCII.GetChars(myBytes);
    DisguisedString = new string(myChars);
    return DisguisedString;
}
```

3. The second function is named `JoinWithDash()`, and its return value will be put into an object's property. `JoinWithDash()` takes two text strings and concatenates them with a dash in the middle. Input parameters and the output are of type string. We use `JoinWithDash()` to join the two strings in the textboxes and then we display the results using `lblJoinedText`:

```
// Returns a concatenation of two texts with a separating hyphen
string JoinWithDash(string String1, string String2)
{
    return String1 + " - " + String2;
}
```

4. The third function is named `Blank()`, and its return value will be used as an the argument of another function. `Blank()` returns a string of asterisks that is the same length as the string it receives as a parameter. Both input and output parameters are of type `string`. We use `JoinWithDash()` to join the two strings in the textboxes and then use that long string as the argument for `Blank()`. The result is displayed using `lblJoinedAndBlanked`:

```
// Returns the string, replacing all characters with asterisks
string Blank(string String1)
{
    string BlankString = "";
    for (int i=1; i <= String1.Length; i++)
    {
        BlankString += "*";
    }
    return BlankString;
}
```

5. The fourth and final function is named `IsString1Longer()`, and its return value will be put into an expression used within a control structure. `IsString1Longer()` returns a `true` or `false` – `true` if the first string parameter is longer then the second string parameter, and false if the first string is smaller or equal in length to the second parameter. `IsString1Longer()` has two input parameters of type `string` and it returns a Boolean value:

```
// Checks if string1 is longer than string2. Returns true if this is so.
bool IsString1Longer(string String1, string String2)
{
    return (String1.Length > String2.Length);
}
```

6. To finish our code, we need to add the `Page_Load()` function to call our functions and the various controls we require to feed our functions and display the results:

```
void Page_Load()
{
    if (IsPostBack)
    {
        // Assign the result of Disguise() to a variable named
        //DisguisedWord
        string DisguisedWord = Disguise(txtIn1.Text);
        lblDisguised.Text = DisguisedWord;

        // Assign the result of JoinWithDash() to the property of an
        //object
        lblJoinedText.Text = JoinWithDash(txtIn1.Text, txtIn2.Text);
        // Use the result of JoinWithDash() as the argument of Blank()
        lblJoinedAndBlanked.Text =
            Blank(JoinWithDash(txtIn1.Text, txtIn2.Text));

        // Use the result of IsString1Longer() as the expression
        // in a control structure
        if (IsString1Longer(txtIn1.Text, txtIn2.Text))
        {
            lblCompareLengths.Text = "String one is longer than string
                                                        two.";
        }
        else
        {
            lblCompareLengths.Text =
                "String one is shorter than or the same length as string
                                                        two.";
        }
    }
}
</script>
<html>
<head>
    <title>Chapter 5 : Using Functions Which Return Values</title>
</head>
<body>
    <form runat="server">
        <asp:TextBox id="txtIn1" runat="server"></asp:TextBox>
        <br />
        <asp:TextBox id="txtIn2" runat="server"></asp:TextBox>
        <br />
        <asp:Button id="Button1" runat="server" Text="Submit"></asp:Button>
        <br />
        Function used in a variable:
        <asp:Label id="lblDisguised" runat="server"></asp:Label>
        <br />
        Function used as value for an object property:
        <asp:Label id="lblJoinedText" runat="server"></asp:Label>
        <br />
        Function used as an argument in another function:
        <asp:Label id="lblJoinedAndBlanked" runat="server"></asp:Label>
```

```
        <br />
        Function used as an expression:
        <asp:Label id="lblCompareLengths" runat="server"></asp:Label>
    </form>
</body>
</html>
```

7. Save the code and open the page in your browser (Figure 5-5)

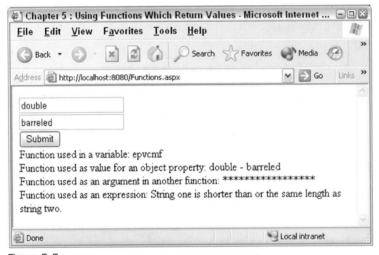

Figure 5-5

How It Works

Carefully read the documentation in the earlier section, *Using Return Values In Your Code*, because that explains our overall purpose and approach. Remember that the code is written in four parallel tracks, one for each way to use a function's results. We have four functions, four output labels, and four sections that use the functions. In addition, as good modularization requires good documentation, we have documented the purpose of each function.

Let's take a quick look at the form. We use two textboxes for accepting input and a Submit button:

```
<form runat="server">
    <asp:TextBox id="txtIn1" runat="server"></asp:TextBox>
    <br />
    <asp:TextBox id="txtIn2" runat="server"></asp:TextBox>
    <br />
    <asp:Button id="Button1" runat="server" Text="Submit"></asp:Button>
    <br />
```

Next, let's look at the four functions and how they are used. In each case, we will look at how the function is called, the function itself, and then the label used to display output.

In the first case, our objective is to demonstrate how to use a variable as a receiver for the function Disguise(). The function receives a string that is then converted into an array of bytes (numbers between 0 and 255). Each byte represents the ASCII value for every character in the string. Then we loop through the array and add one to each value. Finally, we convert the ASCII values back into characters and assemble them into a string.

Disguise() is called by Page_Load(), which takes its return value and puts it into a variable called DisguisedWord. This variable is used as the source for the value in lblDisguised.Text:

```
// Assign the result of Disguise() to a variable named DisguisedWord
string DisguisedWord = Disguise(txtIn1.Text);
lblDisguised.Text = DisguisedWord;

...

// 'Disguises' a string by adding one to each characters ASCII value
string Disguise(string String1)
{
    string DisguisedString;
    Byte[] myBytes = System.Text.Encoding.ASCII.GetBytes(String1);
    for (int i=0;i<myBytes.Length;i++)
    {
        myBytes[i] += 1;
    }
    char[] myChars=System.Text.Encoding.ASCII.GetChars(myBytes);
    DisguisedString = new string(myChars);
    return DisguisedString;
}

...

Function used in a variable:
    <asp:Label id="lblDisguised" runat="server"></asp:Label>
```

In the second example, we use the output of the JoinWithDash() function to set the value in an object's property. Here our function performs the simple task of taking two string parameters and concatenating them with a hyphen in the middle. Therefore the text at the top of the following listing must pass two parameters to the function:

```
// Assign the result of JoinWithDash() to the property of an object
lblJoinedText.Text = JoinWithDash(txtIn1.Text, txtIn2.Text);

...

// Returns a concatenation of two texts with a separating hyphen
string JoinWithDash(string String1, string String2)
{
    return String1 + " - " + String2;
}

...

Function used as value for an object property:
    <asp:Label id="lblJoinedText" runat="server"></asp:Label>
```

The third example joins together the two input texts with `JoinWithDash()` and uses the output as the argument of another function called `Blank()`. This function requires a string as input. Instead of providing a literal string (like "apple") we provide our string as the return value from the `JoinWithDash()` function. `Blank()` works by using a `for` loop to create a string called `BlankString`, which contains the same number of asterisks as the number of characters in the input string:

```
// Use the result of JoinWithDash() as the argument of Blank()
lblJoinedAndBlanked.Text = Blank(JoinWithDash(txtIn1.Text, txtIn2.Text));

...

// Returns the string, replacing all characters with asterisks
string Blank(string String1)
{
    string BlankString = "";
    for (int i=1; i <= String1.Length; i++)
    {
        BlankString += "*";
    }
    return BlankString;
}

...

Function used as an argument in another function:
    <asp:Label id="lblJoinedAndBlanked" runat="server"></asp:Label>
```

The last example is the most interesting because it uses the output of a function as a very small and clean expression. The function `IsString1Longer()` takes in two strings. If the number of characters in the first string is greater than the number of characters in the second string, it returns a Boolean value of true. If not, it returns `false`:

```
// Use the result of IsString1Longer() as the expression
// in a control structure
if (IsString1Longer(txtIn1.Text, txtIn2.Text))
{
    lblCompareLengths.Text = "String one is longer than string two.";
}
else
{
    lblCompareLengths.Text =
        "String one is shorter than or the same length as string two.";
}

...

// Checks if string1 is longer than string2. Returns true if this is so
bool IsString1Longer(string String1, string String2)
{
    return (String1.Length > String2.Length);
}

...

Function used as an expression:
<asp:Label id="lblCompareLengths" runat="server"></asp:Label>
```

Note that we do not have to write = or > in the `if` statement expression. Since `IsString1Longer()` returns either `true` or `false`, it is sufficient for the `if` statement to perform its branch.

In addition, bear in mind that it is often worth returning a value even when there isn't a logical result to return. For example, let's say you wrote a function for adding some values to a database. You could just say the return type is `void`, but it could be more useful to return a value indicating the successful completion of its task. For example, your database function might return a positive integer value indicating the number of records it successfully affected or an error code of a negative value to reflect that the task failed. When your main code runs the function, it checks the return value for a positive or negative value and either carries on or goes into an error-reporting mode.

Value, Reference, and Out Parameters

So far in this chapter, all functions we have written have behaved in the same way. When a value is passed as a parameter, the value is copied and the copy is passed into a parameter and assigned to an internal variable. Any changes made to the value in the function have no effect on the value in the original source. This is known as passing a parameter *by value*. There are, however, two other ways to use parameters that we shall investigate.

In the second method, the parameter is passed *by reference*, which means that instead of passing the actual value into the function, we just pass a pointer to the original value in the calling code. Any changes made to the value in the function are actually made to the value in the calling code.

In the third method, the parameter is an *out parameter*. This is much like a parameter passed by reference in that any changes made to the value in the function are also made to the value in the calling code but with a couple of differences.

❑   An out parameter need not have been assigned a value before it is passed to the function. One passed by reference must necessarily have a value.

❑   Even if it does have a value, the function initially treats it as though it has no value. Any prior value that an out parameter has in the calling code is lost. However, the function must assign a value to the out parameter before it finishes executing.

Let's look at some examples and the implications for each of these techniques.

By default, simple data values are passed to functions by value in C#. This means that when the parameter variables are created inside the function, they are all set up to have the value that was passed in. This may seem like it goes without saying, but has some subtle consequences. Effectively, it means that inside a function, we are working with a *copy* of the original data. Look at the following code (available in code download as `PassingByValue.aspx`):

```
<%@ Page Language="C#" %>
<script runat="server">

    void Page_Load()
    {
        int a = 1;
        Increment(a);
```

```
                lblMessage.Text = a.ToString();
        }

        void Increment(int Number)
        {
            Number += 1;
        }

</script>

<html>
<head>
    <title>Chapter 5 - Demonstration of Passing a Parameter by Value</title>
</head>
<body>
    <asp:Label id="lblMessage" runat="server"></asp:Label>
</body>
</html>
```

This is a function that takes an integer as a parameter and increments it. When you use this function from `Page_Load()`, a variable containing the number 1 is passed in, but when you display the contents of this variable, you'll find that it hasn't been incremented. This is because the data is passed by value. Passing by value means that a copy is made for the function to play with and that the data in the calling code is left untouched.

When `Increment(a)` is called in the preceding code, the value stored in the variable a (which is 1) is copied into a new variable (called `Number`) inside the `Increment()` function. `Increment()` then adds 1 to the value stored in this variable, but the value stored in a is left untouched. If the `Number` variable were called a instead, it would still be a new variable.

What happens if you wanted the calculation within your function to affect the calling code's contents? Well, then you could pass the parameter by reference. Let's amend the `Increment()` function to pass parameters by reference (available in the code download as `PassingByReference.aspx`):

```
void Page_Load()
{
    int a = 1;
    Increment(ref a);
    lblMessage.Text = a.ToString();
}

void Increment(ref int Number)
{
    Number += 1;
}
```

Note that you need to use the `ref` keyword to denote a parameter passed by reference, and that it must be present in both the function definition and any calls made to that function. Running this amended code now results in the number 2 as the value of a. When `Increment(ref a)` is called, instead of a copy of the value of a, a second variable is created that points to the variable a. This way, whenever the code inside the function makes a change to the `Number` variable, it is actually changing the data in the a variable as well.

Let's try to get the same effect using an out parameter. The syntax for using out parameters is very similar to passing values by reference, with the out keyword replacing ref in the function definition and calls:

```
void Page_Load()
{
    int a = 1;
    Increment(out a);
    lblMessage.Text = a.ToString();
}

void Increment(out int Number)
{
    Number += 1;
}
```

However, this doesn't have the desired effect. If you try and run this code, you'll get an error telling you that Increment() has tried to 'use the unassigned local variable 'Numbers'. Indeed, we've overlooked the fact that a function always treats an out parameter as an unassigned variable whether or not it had a value in the calling code. Trying to add 1 to it the way that the Increment() function does makes no sense unless we assign it a value first. In order to get the same result as in the earlier examples, we must change the code as follows (available in code download as PassingOutParameters.aspx):

```
void Page_Load()
{
    int a = 1;
    int b;
    Increment(a, out b);
    lblMessage.Text = b.ToString();
}

void Increment(int Number, out int Result)
{
    Result = Number + 1;
}
```

Increment() now has a second parameter, Result, which is an out parameter and is not originally initialized in Page_Load(). It is however assigned a value inside the function. It's this value we reflect on screen, and as expected, it equals 2.

Let's put this into practice. In this last example, we will create a simple page that demonstrates the effects of passing parameters by value and reference, and also by using out parameters.

Try It Out Using Value, Reference, and Out Parameters

1. Create a new ASP.NET page called ValRefOut.aspx and save it in your Ch05 folder.

2. Add the following code to the file and save it:

```
<%@ Page Language="C#" Debug="true" %>
<script runat="server">
```

```
    void Page_Load()
    {
        if (IsPostBack)
        {
            string s = txtInVal.Text;
            byValue(s);
            lblAfterValue.Text = s;

            byReference(ref s);
            lblAfterReference.Text = s;

            string o; // o need not be initialised
            byOut(s, out o);
            lblAfterOut.Text = s;
            lblOutValue.Text = o;
        }
    }

    void byValue(string strIn)
    {
        strIn += " after byValue";
    }

    void byReference(ref string strIn)
    {
        strIn += " after byReference";
    }

    void byOut(string strIn, out string outValue)
    {
        strIn += " after byOut";
        outValue = strIn;
    }
</script>
<html>
<head>
    <title>Chapter 5 : Passing Parameters By Value and By Reference</title>
</head>
<body>
    <form runat="server">
            Type a string
            <asp:TextBox id="txtInVal" runat="server"></asp:TextBox>
            <br />
            <asp:Button id="Button1" runat="server"
                                        Text="Submit"></asp:Button>
            <br />
            After calling byValue, the string =
            <asp:Label id="lblAfterValue" runat="server"></asp:Label>
            <br />
            After calling byReference, the string =
            <asp:Label id="lblAfterReference" runat="server"></asp:Label>
            <br />
            After calling byOut, the string =
```

```
            <asp:Label id="lblAfterOut" runat="server"></asp:Label>
            <br />
            and the output parameter =
            <asp:Label id="lblOutValue" runat="server"></asp:Label>
    </form>
</body>
</html>
```

3. View this in your browser. You will see a screen similar to Figure 5-6:

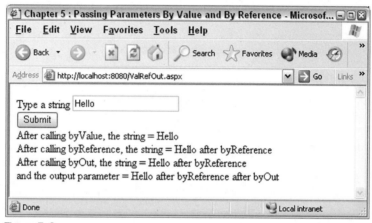

Figure 5-6

How It Works

Let's start with a quick glance at the form, which should be self-explanatory. We have a `TextBox` for input and four `Label` controls for output. The extra `Label` is to show the values of both parameters after calling the function with an out parameter:

```
<form runat="server">
        Type a string
        <asp:TextBox id="txtInVal" runat="server"></asp:TextBox>
        <br />
        <asp:Button id="Button1" runat="server"
                    Text="Submit"></asp:Button>
        <br />
        After calling byValue, the string =
        <asp:Label id="lblAfterValue" runat="server"></asp:Label>
        <br />
        After calling byReference, the string =
        <asp:Label id="lblAfterReference" runat="server"></asp:Label>
        <br />
        After calling byOut, the string =
        <asp:Label id="lblAfterOut" runat="server"></asp:Label>
        <br />
        and the output parameter =
        <asp:Label id="lblOutValue" runat="server"></asp:Label>
    </form>
```

185

Now we'll take a look at the three functions written. They all concatenate a short bit of text to an incoming string parameter. However, they differ in how the parameter is passed to the function.

The first function receives its parameter by value. Thus the original value remains intact in the calling code. A copy of the value is created in the `strIn` variable:

```
void byValue(string strIn)
{
    strIn += " after byValue";
}
```

The second function receives its data by reference. In other words, `strIn` does not hold a string. Rather it holds a pointer to a variable or object property in the calling code:

```
void byReference(ref string strIn)
{
    strIn += " after byReference";
}
```

Finally, the third function receives a parameter by value and uses an out parameter to make a note of the result.

```
void byOut(string strIn, out string outValue)
{
    strIn += " after byOut";
    outValue = strIn;
}
```

As we start to examine the code that uses these functions, it's worth noting a slight difference here between VB.NET and C#.

> **In VB.NET, you can pass the property of an object by reference and as an out parameter, but you cannot do this in C#.**

So, for example, instead of calling:

```
byReference(ref txtInVal.Text)
```

we need to first assign the value of that property to a variable and pass that by reference instead. This is the method we use in the examples below.

Now we can examine the code that uses the routines. It picks up text from a `TextBox` and assigns it to a `string` variable that each of the functions will use. The results of the functions are then stored in their respective labels.

```
void Page_Load()
{
    if (IsPostBack)
    {
        string s = txtInVal.Text;
```

In the first case (passing by value), the function modifies a copy of the string that was passed to it and not the string itself. Thus the string in s remains unaltered and the result in lblAfterValue.Text is the same as that typed into txtInVal by the user:

```
byValue(s);
lblAfterValue.Text = s;
```

In contrast, the second call is by reference. Within the byReference() function, the concatenation occurs with the actual text held in s. Therefore, we see a different result. First s is modified, and then the text in lblAfterReference.Text as well.

```
byReference(ref s);
lblAfterReference.Text = s;
```

The third call is by value but uses an out parameter o to retrieve the altered string. Because s is passed by value, it does not reflect the concatenation made inside byOut() once the function has ceased to execute. We can see this in the value of lblAfterOut.Text. However, the result of the concatenation is assigned to the out parameter o before byOut() finishes executing, and so we see a different result in lblOutValue.Text:

```
            string o; // o need not be initialised
            byOut(s, out o);
            lblAfterOut.Text = s;
            lblOutValue.Text = o;
        }
    }
```

Before we leave this topic, let's do a final comparison between passing parameters by value and parameters by reference.

❑   By default, all parameters can be passed by value except for objects (for example, a Web control Label object), which are passed by reference.

❑   Passing parameters by value makes a copy of the actual data within the function block. If the data is large and thus uses a lot of resources, passing by reference saves resources by simply pointing to the original holder of the data.

❑   You may not directly name object properties as parameters to be passed by reference in C#. You may pass them by value however.

❑   Passing parameters by value leads to fewer conflicts in complex pages. Several different functions using parameters passed by reference (perhaps even written by different authors) could be changing the original contents of a variable. Programmers may not be sure at a given moment of the actual value that is supposed to be in a variable.

For example, you may run a DateDue() function that checks if the due date falls on a day the business is open. That would best be done by value so that programmers writing other processes that are looking at the date won't be confused if another function modifies this date. On the other hand, if you write a procedure that modifies the grayscale of a bitmap image, it would be better to pass the entire image by reference to avoid multiple copies of the large file.

Modularization Best Practices

This section describes several guidelines for breaking your code up into functions, a process we've referred to as modularization. *Chapter 7* covers custom objects, another form of modularization, for which many of these same ideas apply.

Modularization is good. Whenever practical, *divide your code into smaller parts* that each perform a single job. As you improve your skills, try to move your modularization practices into higher levels. Start with functions and then move to code-behind (*Chapter 12*) and custom objects.

Successful modularization requires *careful planning and definition*. You must ensure that each task in your project can be performed and that all modules have the same definition of data that is passed among them. Diagramming is often helpful in the planning stages. As a part of the plan, there needs to be a clear statement of input and output of each module as well as the task that the module performs.

Good modules contain *extensive internal documentation* – at a minimum, note the purpose of the module, its creation date, version number, and author. Code maintenance is cheaper if you also include notes on the purpose of variables. Comments do not slow down execution of code (they are removed at compilation) so there is no performance overhead for internal documentation.

Much of the planning for modularization can be done with *software design and authoring tools*. Basic tools come with Web Matrix, such as the ability to save snippets of code like function signatures and insert them in code that will call those functions. More sophisticated tools are available in Visual Studio and third-party software.

Avoid using *message boxes* or other *interfaces* which pop-up outside of the HTML page. When you deploy your code on a server, you may have thousands of pop-ups occurring on a server that isn't even connected to a monitor.

Avoid variable name conflicts by *having a unique naming system*. Be especially wary of very common terms like *Price* and *Date*. Scope variables as narrowly as possible. Pass parameters by value to reduce the chances of a module making a change that is not expected by another module.

Within a function, avoid specific reference to a Web control by name. It is almost always better to use a parameter to pass to a function than a reference to a Web control.

Passing a parameter by reference is more likely to cause errors in the page as a whole. Therefore, *explicitly document code when parameters are being passed by reference*.

In the end, the objective of your main code is to call a series of modules to go through a task. *The leaner the main code the better*. The only time to skip modularization is when there is a single, simple, and short operation executed in the code of a page.

Summary

Modularization is the process of breaking the code for a project into smaller, independent groups of code. The benefits include faster development, easier testing, and cheaper maintenance. Frequently used code is written and tested once, put in a module, and can then be reused often. Furthermore, advanced forms of modularization permit different programmers to work in different languages, according to their preferences or the best language to achieve a goal.

This chapter covered one of three modularization techniques: functions. The other two are code-behind (*Chapter 12*) and custom objects (*Chapter 7*).

Functions perform a task in a block of code that is separate from the main body of code. The code in a function is executed when it is called. The function may or may not return a value to the calling code once it has finished execution.

All function definitions have the same structure. It begins with a function signature that declares the function's name, its return type, and required parameters. The code for the function is then written within a block surrounded by curly braces { }. Good practice dictates that each function start with some comments identifying its purpose, creation date, author, as well as restrictions on incoming data.

Function definitions and function calls must include parentheses after the function's name, regardless of whether or not the function has any parameters.

If a function has a return value, it must have a receptacle in the calling code. The receiver for a function's return can be a variable, an object property, an argument for another function, or an expression in a control structure. Functions that return a Boolean value can be an entire expression; there is no need to compare them to `true` or `false`.

Information can be passed into functions by using parameters. Incoming values are assigned a name, and datatype upon receipt within the function. They are then available within the function as block-level variables. Web controls, such as a `Labels` or a `TextBox`, can be passed as parameters into a function and their property values may change within the function.

Data passed by value to a function is copied into a block variable. Any operations occur only on the copy and the original is untouched. Data passed into a function by reference creates a block variable that points to the original source of data. Operations within the function will actually modify the contents of the original holder of the data that is outside the function.

Out parameters work much like parameters passed by reference but their value is always reset when they are passed into a function. That function must then assign a value to these parameters before it terminates. Data is passed to a function by value by default, and this is generally best left unchanged unless there is a need to improve performance.

Exercises

1. Determine whether a function will return a value for each of the following scenarios and justify your choice:

   ❑ Calculate the due date of a book being checked out of a library

   ❑ Find out the day of the week on which a certain date falls on in the future

   ❑ Display a string, which is determined by the marketing department and stored in a text file, as a `Label`

2. List where and when values are held when a variable is a parameter passed by value. Do the same for a variable is a parameter passed by reference.

3. Write a function that generates a set of random integers. Build an ASP.NET page that allows you to enter the lower and upper bounds, and then generate a set of random numbers within that range.

Event-Driven Programming and Postback

A fundamental change from ASP to ASP.NET is the implementation of a robust, event-driven programming model. In ASP, we had to write many lines of code for reacting to a user's click on a submit button. With ASP.NET, much of that work is automatically performed for us and we can focus on writing just the code that implements our business goals.

ASP.NET supports three major groups of events. The first comprises HTML events that are executed on the browser. The second group includes the ASP.NET page-level events that allow you to automatically run code at certain stages while the page loads. A particularly important page-level event is a *postback*, which is triggered whenever a page is resubmitted to the server after the user clicks on a submit button. Lastly, you have a group of ASP.NET server control events that allow you to react to the user clicking on or typing into controls on the Web page.

The great range of events available in ASP.NET improves the user experience, reduces the amount of code you write, and makes the resulting code much easier to maintain.

This chapter will look at:

❑   The definition of an event

❑   HTML events

❑   ASP.NET page events

❑   ASP.NET Web control events

❑   Event-driven programming

❑   `IsPostBack`

What Is an Event?

Let's start by comparing an event to actions in real life. A fictional employee, Joe Public, sits in his cubicle in the marketing department of his company, staring out the window. The phone rings. Joe reacts by picking it up and answering it with his name. A customer says, "We need to order ten cans of beans." Joe reacts by placing the order and hanging up the phone. Joe then goes back to staring out the window. Note the sequence of actions: the ringing of the phone is an *event*, Joe responds to the event with a set of *actions* (answers the phone, states his name, and takes the order), and then the event *concludes* (hangs up the phone). After the event is finished, Joe returns to a state of waiting for the next event to occur.

In event-driven programming, we have the same scenario. Your page sits on the browser waiting for the user to interact. An event occurs when the user clicks on or types into the page. Your program reacts by executing code to perform some task in reaction to the event. When your code is done executing, the page goes back to waiting for the next event.

> An *event* is an action taken on your application by some force outside of your code. This external force is usually the user, but could be another program. An event can hold code that will run when the action occurs.

Therefore, you can break down your event-driven environment into four chronological sections:

- **An event occurs**: The user clicks on a button
- **The system detects the event**: ASP.NET registers that an event has occurred
- **The system reacts to the event**: Some code is executed
- **The system then returns to its original state**: Waits for the next event

Knowing this series of activities allows us to understand the usage of events when programming.

What Is Event-Driven Programming?

Event-driven programming is a fundamental change in the nature of the traditional programming model. We leave behind the idea of sequential pages being processed on a server, and look at a model of programming where the server responds to events triggered by the user.

Before event-driven programming, your programs would execute from top to bottom as follows:

```
Line 1
Line 2
Line 3
Line 4
```

Broadly speaking, traditional programming languages (those over ten years old) start with the first line of your code, process it, move on to the second line, process that, and then move on to the third. There is no stopping, pausing, or waiting for interaction with the user. Even when functions are used, they don't change the timing of execution as one function calls another, which calls another, and so on. There is still an uninterrupted sequence of execution.

The concept of event-driven programming changes all of this; with events, the sequential way of execution is no longer necessary. The timing of code execution depends on interactions with the user. Consider the Windows Operating System, which is event-driven. It doesn't execute in a sequential fashion. Windows starts and waits for an event to occur, such as a user clicking on Start. As soon as an event occurs, Windows takes appropriate action to deal with that event. If you click on a menu, Windows provides the menu, and then waits for another user action. Windows is a collection of numerous sets of code, each waiting to be executed when called by an event.

Similarly, ASP.NET pages display in the browser and wait for user action. When the user types or clicks on the page, ASP.NET responds by executing some code. After the code execution ends, the page goes back to waiting for the next user action.

In event-driven programming, when something happens to your page, such as a user's click, the user typing some text, or the page being served by IIS, an event occurs. An *event handler* – a function that is run in reaction to (or *fired by*) the event – then handles the event.

There are two differences between an event handler and functions. First, the way in which you should name handlers is different. You can use almost any name, such as `MyFunction()`, for a handler. Microsoft recommends creating the handler's name such that it includes the object and the name of the event it caters to separated by underscores; for example, `MyButton_Click()`. This logical approach makes the names easy to remember. The second difference is how an event handler is called. A non-event handler is executed when it is called from other code. An event handler is executed automatically in response to its event.

ASP.NET supports three groups of events:

❏   The first group contains HTML events that can occur on the page and are handled by the browser on the client-side. For example, pop-up tool tips or menu expansions typically run on the client-side JavaScript. You'll see an example later in this chapter.

❏   The second group contains several events that occur automatically when ASP.NET generates a page. There is no user involvement; they occur before the user even sees the page. We use these events to build the page.

❏   The last group is the largest, and contains all the events that occur due to user interaction with the page.

HTML Events

Let's briefly discuss the events that execute in HTML on the browser (client) that are not part of ASP.NET. Client-side events are written within pure HTML tags such as `<input>`. The language is usually JavaScript or VBScript. An interpreter built into the browser executes the code and there is no transfer of information to or action on the part of the server.

In the demonstration code that follows (`OnClickEventDemo.htm`), we create a page that contains only HTML. For HTML input button tags there is an event called `onclick`. When the user clicks on the button, it executes the short line of code within the tag's `onclick` attribute. For this HTML event to work, you must be using a modern version of a browser (*at the least* IE 4.0, Netscape 6.0, or Opera 5.0).

```html
<html>
<head>
    <title>HTML Browser Event Example</title>
</head>
<body>
    <form>
        <input onclick="alert('You have raised an event!')"
               type="button" value="Click Me" />
    </form>
</body>
</html>
```

The code results in the screen shown in Figure 6-1:

Figure 6-1

In this case, the code for the event handler is inside the `onclick` attribute rather than in a separate function called inside the `onclick` attribute. Most HTML tags can react to many events:

Event	Occurs When
onmouseup	A mouse button is released while clicking over an element
onmousedown	A mouse button is pressed and held over an element
onmouseover	A mouse is moved over an element
onmousemove	A mouse moves over an element

Event	Occurs When
onclick	A mouse is clicked over an element
ondblclick	A mouse is double-clicked while hovering over an element
onkeyup	A key is released over an element
onkeypress	A key is pressed and released over an element
onkeydown	A key is pressed and held down while over an element

For the events triggered by the keyboard, be sure to have the focus on the button before you strike the keys to test. We could change the earlier code so that our button reacts to a different event; here, we've changed it to the OnMouseOver event (OnMouseOverEventDemo.htm):

```
<html>
<head>
    <title>HTML Browser Event Example</title>
</head>
<body>
    <form>
        <input onmouseover="alert('You have raised an event!')"
               type="button" value="Click Me" />
    </form>
</body>
</html>
```

ASP.NET can handle events similar to HTML. However, .NET gives us much more functionality and the ability to utilize server-side resources such as database connections.

ASP.NET's Trace Feature

Before we dive into the two groups of ASP.NET events, let's preview a technique for debugging, which will be discussed in detail in *Chapter 14*. By adding Trace="true" in the Page directive, we can have ASP.NET create a log of how it built the page. The log is appended to the bottom of the page. Trace does not conflict with Debug="true".

```
<%@ Page Language="C#" Debug="true" Trace="true" %>
```

For example, open the ParameterWebControl.aspx page from *Chapter 5* and save it as TraceDemo.aspx in the Ch06 folder. You can then turn on the trace by adding Trace="true" in the Page directive and get to the screen depicted in Figure 6-2:

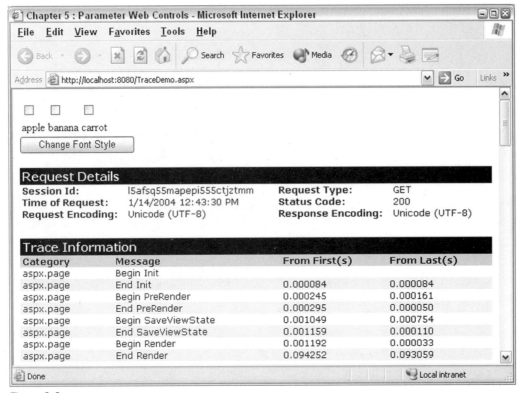

Figure 6-2

In the Trace Information, note the beginning and ending of events such as Init() and PreRender() under the Message column. We can put a custom message into the trace log with the following lines of code (TraceDemoWithNotes.aspx):

```
<script runat="server">
    void Page_Load()
    {
        Trace.Write("NOTE - First line of Page_Load");
        MakeItalic(Label1, CheckBox1.Checked);
        MakeItalic(Label2, CheckBox2.Checked);
        MakeItalic(Label3, CheckBox3.Checked);
    }

    void MakeItalic(Label TargetLabel, bool ItalicYN)
    {
        Trace.Write("NOTE - First Line of MakeItalic");
        TargetLabel.Font.Italic = ItalicYN;
    }
</script>
```

Our Trace.Write notes will show up in the log in the order they are executed. You can see in Figure 6-3 that the 'NOTE – First line of MakeItalic' occurs three times as MakeItalic() was called thrice:

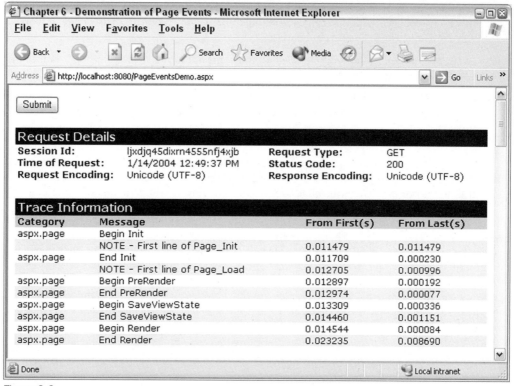

Figure 6-3

You can turn off the Trace by setting it to false in the Page directive, thus removing all of your diagnostic aids in one change. The Trace.Write() methods can remain in the code, they will have no effect on the output or performance of the page. This is a big advantage for those of us who programmed in classic ASP and had to remove scores of diagnostic Response.Write notes. We'll talk more about using Tracing in *Chapter 14*, but for now we only need to know *when* events occur and *how* our page reacts to those events.

ASP.NET Page Events

This section will address a group of events that are automatically run by ASP.NET when a page loads. Everything in ASP.NET comes down to objects, and in particular, the Page object mentioned in *Chapter 2*. Each Web form you create is a Page object in its own right. You can think of the entire Web form as an executable program with HTML output. Every time a page is called, the object goes through a series of stages – initializing, processing, and displaying information. These events occur with every round trip to the server.

When you request your ASP.NET Web form, a series of events automatically occur on your Web server as follows:

❑ The `Page_Init` event occurs when the page is initialized. You can use the `Page_Init()` function associated with it to run code before .NET displays controls on the page. It works in a way similar to `Page_Load()`, but earlier.

❑ `Page_PreRender()` and `Page_Render()` and some additional events support advanced topics such as transactions. We will not discuss them in this book.

❑ `Page_Load()` occurs when the whole page is visible for the first time (when the page has been read into memory and processed), but after some details about server controls have been initialized and displayed by `Page_Init()`.

❑ `Page_Unload()` occurs when the page is unloaded from IIS memory and is sent out to the browser. This occurs after all control events have been executed and is an ideal place to shut down database connections. The name is misleading because this event does not occur when the user in the browser leaves the page or turns off the browser. The term *unload* is from the perspective of IIS, not the browser.

Notice the usage of the word *event* in the preceding list. An *event* occurs – a page is served up by IIS – and calls the `Page_Load()` *event handler*. The process of an event firing an event handler can be implied by other terms such as *execute, start, invoke, initiate,* and somewhat misleadingly, *call.*

If you want code to execute on your page before anything else occurs, you need to put it within a `Page_Init()` event handler. The event of the page loading will automatically fire the `Page_Load()` event handler.

The syntax along with some trace writes (`PageEventsDemo.aspx`) is as follows:

```
<%@ Page Language="C#" Debug="true" Trace="true" %>
<script runat="server">

    void Page_Init()
    {
        Trace.Write("NOTE - First line of Page_Init");
    }

    void Page_Load()
    {
        Trace.Write("NOTE - First line of Page_Load");
    }

</script>
<html>
<head>
    <title>Chapter 6 - Demonstration of Page Events</title>
</head>
<body>
    <form runat="server">
        <asp:Button id="Button1" runat="server" Text="Submit"></asp:Button>
        <br />
    </form>
</body>
</html>
```

This code results in the screen shown in Figure 6-4:

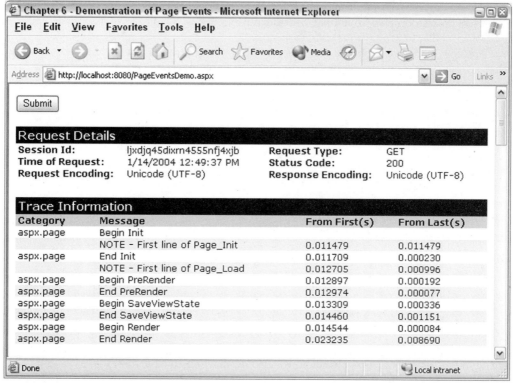

Figure 6-4

The `Page_Unload()` event fires automatically but when IIS unloads the page from its working space and sends it to the browser. The `Page_Unload()` event occurs after all other tasks have been performed to create the page and can be used to free resources used by the page, such as database connections. As `Page_Unload()` executes after the rest of the ASP.NET page has been completed, you cannot use `Page_Unload()` to change ASP.NET controls.

ASP.NET Web Control Events

Now we reach the third and richest group of events – those that are associated with ASP.NET Web controls such as `<asp:TextBox>` and `<asp:Button>`. There are three important reasons why ASP.NET Web control events are more powerful than HTML events run on the browser:

❑ You can execute the event handler code on the server, which means that you have all the server resources available for the event handler. This includes custom-built objects and connections to other servers and databases.

❑ You don't have to rely on the browser's capability to recognize and handle HTML events because the ASP.NET Web server sends only pure HTML back to the browser.

❑ You can write code for an event handler in any language that is supported by .NET instead of just the scripting languages that browsers can execute.

You add events to ASP.NET controls in two steps. First, in the control's tag you add an extra attribute with the name of the event and set its value to an event procedure. For example, in the following code, a function named `Button1ClickEventHandler()` will execute when a user clicks on `button1`.

```
<asp:Button id="button1"
  runat="server"
  text="Click me"
  onclick="Button1ClickEventHandler"
  />
```

Second, you create the *event handler*, which is the function that runs when invoked by an event. The small difference between this and other handlers we've seen so far is that you have to specify two incoming parameters (arguments) with the *exact* syntax as follows:

```
<script runat="server">
    void Button1_Click(object sender, EventArgs e)
    {
        ... Code to handle the click event here ...
    }
</script>
```

The arguments passed to an event handler provide information to the handler. The first argument – `sender` – provides a reference to the object that raised the event. The second – e – is an event class that captures information regarding the state of the event being handled, and passes an object that's specific to that event.

A common mistake is to not match the handler's name with the name specified as the value for the event's attribute in the control's tag. The result is that *nothing* will happen when the event is triggered. You can call the function whatever name you want, as long as you are consistent in using the same name in the server control and within the `<script>` tags. If adding 'EventHandler' or 'EH' to the name helps you remember the purpose of the function, then do it. Don't forget to document the event handler as well. You saw how to document functions in *Chapter 5*.

ASP.NET Web controls have a reduced set (compared to HTML) of events that can be added to controls as attributes. Those common to all Web controls are as follows:

Event Name	Occurs When
ondatabinding	A control is bound to a data source (see *Chapter 8*)
ondispose	A control is no longer needed and is being removed from a window or frame
onload	A control has loaded into the window or frame

Event Name	Occurs When
onunload	A control has been removed from a window or frame
oninit	The Web page is first initialized
onprerender	Just before the control is rendered

The difference between HTML controls and ASP.NET Web controls is the way in which they're handled. With HTML form controls, when the event is raised, the browser handles it by itself. However, with Web controls, the browser raises the event and the client sends a postback message to the server so that it can handle the event.

It doesn't matter what kind of event is raised, the client will always return a single postback event to the server. However, some events such as key presses or mouseovers are impossible to deal with on the server and there are no equivalent ASP.NET events for these. They will not be passed onto the server and will have to be handled by the client. We've seen the syntax to add event handlers to ASP.NET server controls in the section above. If you use Web Matrix, it's even easier. In the following *Try It Out*, we'll demonstrate just how simple this is.

Try It Out Creating Event Handlers with Web Matrix

  1. In Web Matrix, create a new ASP.NET page called EventsInWebMatrix.aspx and save it in your Ch06 folder. In **Design View**, drag a Label control and a Button control onto the blank page. Now select the Button control with your mouse. In **Design View**, drag a Label control and a Button control onto the blank page. Now select the Button control with your mouse.

  2. The Properties box on the right hand side of the Web Matrix window displays information about the control you have selected. Click on the icon that looks like a bolt of lightning near the top of the box. The Properties box will now show a list of all the events that you can handle for this control. In Figure 6-5, you can see the possible events for an <asp:Button> control:

Figure 6-5

4. Click on the blank box next to Click and press Enter. Web Matrix adds the `onclick` attribute to the `<asp:Button>` tag and generates an empty function called `Button1_Click()` to handle the event. Fill in this function with the following code:

```
void Button1_Click(object sender, EventArgs e)
{
    Label1.Text = "Web Matrix helped me handle the clicking of this button.";
}
```

5. Now save this code and run it. When the page loads, click the button. The `Label` displays the message as we had expected.

How It Works

The events window in the Web Matrix Properties box lets you hook up events to event handlers in three different ways. It generates a new handler function for you (as per the recommended naming guidelines discussed earlier) if you just click into the space next to an event and press Enter. If you haven't written a function yet but have a specific name for it, say `MyButtonEventHandler()`, you can just type the name `MyButtonEventHandler` into the space next to the event that it will handle and press Enter. Note that while typing this name you do not need to include parentheses. Web Matrix will create a blank function with that name and hook it up to the control as you ask. Finally, if you have written the handler function already, you will be able to select it from the drop down box on the right hand side of the box after which you need to press Enter. This function will be wired up automatically, and Web Matrix will not create a new function for you.

On the page itself, when you click the button, the browser posts back to the server to say that the `Click` event has occurred and the server responds by resending the page, but altered by the `Click` handler function.

Event-Driven Programming and Postback

So far, the issue of postback architecture has not been discussed in detail. In this section, we're going to consider the theory and practical application of postback in more detail, and then do an exercise that utilizes multiple buttons and event handlers.

Postback is the process by which the browser sends information back to the server so that the server can handle the event. The server executes the code in the event handler and sends the resulting HTML back to the browser again. Postback only occurs with Web forms that have the `runat="server"` attribute set. In addition, only ASP.NET Web controls post information back to the server.

> **Postback is not available in HTML forms and is implemented only weakly in ASP.**

Note that ASP.NET doesn't look after the processing of all events. It is still necessary to handle some events (such as `onmouseover`) on the client-side because a round trip to the server couldn't possibly react to them as quickly as the user expects. Ideally, you need a mix of server-side and client-side event functions in your Web application.

In the following Try It Out, we will create two pages. The first has only simple HTML events and you will see that there is no postback as the event is handled on the browser. We will then modify the page to support ASP.NET Web controls and see the postback to the server in effect.

Try It Out   Reacting to Events in HTML and ASP.NET

1. Create a new ASP.NET page called `NoPostbackInHTML.htm` and save it in your `Ch06` folder and add the following code to the page:

```html
<html>
<head>
    <title>No Postback In HTML</title>
</head>
<body>
    <h2>No Postback In HTML
    </h2>
    <form method="get">
        Select either A, B or C and click the button at the bottom<br />
        A<input type="radio" value="a" name="test" />
        <br />
        B<input type="radio" value="b" name="test" />
        <br />
        C<input type="radio" value="c" name="test" />
        <br />
        <br />
        <input onclick="alert('Button Click event occurred in HTML')"
               type="submit" value="Click Me" />
    </form>
</body>
</html>
```

2. Save the page, and ensure you use the HTML suffix. View it in your browser to arrive at the screen shown in Figure 6-6 and click on a choice. After the click you will be shown an alert that says "Button Click event occurred in HTML". Click on the OK button and you will lose your selection on the page:

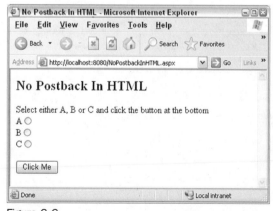

Figure 6-6

3. Go back to your editor and save the file as `PostbackInAspNet.aspx`. Check that the file extension is `.aspx`. Make the following changes to convert the HTML code to ASP.NET code:

```
<%@ Page Language="C#" %>
<html>
<head>
    <title>PostBack In ASP.NET</title>
</head>
<body>
    <h2>Postback In ASP.NET</h2>
    <form runat="server">
        Select either A, B, or C and click the button at the bottom<br />
        <asp:RadioButtonList id="test" runat="server">
            <asp:listitem id="option1" value="a" runat="server" />
            <asp:listitem id="option2" value="b" runat="server" />
            <asp:listitem id="option3" value="c" runat="server" />
        </asp:RadioButtonList>
        <br />
        <br />
        <input onclick="alert('Button Click event occurred in HTML')"
            type="submit" value="Click Me" />
    </form>
</body>
</html>
```

4. Save the file (double check the extension) and surf to `PostbackInAspNet.aspx` using your browser. Select an option and click the button to see that option remains selected. You will see that the page state has been retained by the postback.

5. After clicking the button take a look at the source (in IE, click on View | Source) as shown in Figure 6-7:

Figure 6-7

How It Works

In the HTML form, you noted the loss of selection when the button was clicked. However, the browser appended a query string to the request as follows:

http://localhost:8080/NoPostbackInHTML.htm?test=b

However, the server has no intrinsic mechanism to pass that selection through to the refreshed page. This is normal behavior for HTML.

In our second page, we use ASP.NET postback. Postback is turned on because we use an ASPX extension on the file name and the `form` and `RadioButtonList` controls use the `runat="server"` attribute. When you view the source, you will see a new `<input>` tag:

```
<input type="hidden" value="dDw0MDk5MTgxNTU7Oz4WyuRHDZk+oHVRnH+Vueg8zM7fnQ=="
       name="__VIEWSTATE" />
```

When postback is used, information about the state of the form is sent back in an associated hidden control called _VIEWSTATE. This information in `_VIEWSTATE` is generated by ASP.NET by encrypting the values of the old state of the form. That state includes user selections for each ASP.NET Web control. ASP.NET is able to look at the old version and compare it to the current version. With this information, ASP.NET can persist the state of Web controls between page submissions. If there are differences, such as a different radio button being selected, internal events are generated by ASP.NET in response to the difference and the DLL runs code to create a 'current' version of the form. The string of characters contained in the `value` attribute will differ.

There are three points to remember about _VIEWSTATE:

❑ It is crucial to ASP.NET for remembering the state of controls between page submissions without actually maintaining a `Page` object or HTTP connection throughout.

❑ You never have to program or interpret `_VIEWSTATE` at all; it is a fully automated part of ASP.NET.

❑ `_VIEWSTATE` is passed to the browser as a standard HMTL `<input type=hidden>` control. There is no need for any special plug-in or interpretive software on the browser.

The IsPostBack Test

Let's discuss the `IsPostBack` test introduced in *Chapter 3*. This test determines whether a user has returned a form with data or whether it is the first time the form had been displayed. In other words, our `IsPostBack` test just checks to see whether any postback information has been generated by an event. If it hasn't, this test generates `false`; otherwise it generates `true`. The syntax is as follows:

```
if (IsPostBack){
    //Code to run to check for and use data
}
else{
    //Code to run assuming there is no data
}
```

It is not necessary to have code to run in both cases. Many times we do not have code to run if IsPostBack=false. This is logical since we probably don't have any data to feed into code.

Let's look at an example that draws together all the things we've looked at in the chapter and utilizes event-driven programming. We'll build a simple calculator on a page. It contains two textboxes to take numbers from the user, and will perform a calculation depending on whether the user selects the add, subtract, divide, or multiply button. It will also highlight the button to indicate the type of calculation just performed. Note that multiple button forms force us to write specific event handlers for the clicking of each button, as opposed to writing a form with a single button.

In the second part of the example, we will tighten up the code by using a single event handler.

Try It Out **Calculator**

1. Create a new ASP.NET page called Calculator.aspx and save it in your Ch06 folder with the following code:

```
<%@ Page Language="C#" Debug="true" %>
<script runat="server">

    void Page_Load()
    {
        btnAdd.BackColor = System.Drawing.Color.LightGray;
        btnSubtract.BackColor = System.Drawing.Color.LightGray;
        btnMultiply.BackColor = System.Drawing.Color.LightGray;
        btnDivide.BackColor = System.Drawing.Color.LightGray;
    }

    void Add(object sender, EventArgs e)
    {
        double answer = Convert.ToDouble(txtInput1.Text) +
                        Convert.ToDouble(txtInput2.Text);
        lblAnswer.Text = answer.ToString();
        btnAdd.BackColor = System.Drawing.Color.Yellow;
    }

    void Subtract(object sender, EventArgs e)
    {
        double answer = Convert.ToDouble(txtInput1.Text) -
                        Convert.ToDouble(txtInput2.Text);
        lblAnswer.Text = answer.ToString();
        btnSubtract.BackColor = System.Drawing.Color.Yellow;
    }

    void Multiply(object sender, EventArgs e)
    {
        double answer = Convert.ToDouble(txtInput1.Text) *
                        Convert.ToDouble(txtInput2.Text);
        lblAnswer.Text = answer.ToString();
        btnMultiply.BackColor = System.Drawing.Color.Yellow;
    }
```

```
    void Divide(object sender, EventArgs e)
    {
        double answer = Convert.ToDouble(txtInput1.Text) /
                        Convert.ToDouble(txtInput2.Text);
        lblAnswer.Text = answer.ToString();
        btnDivide.BackColor = System.Drawing.Color.Yellow;
    }

</script>
<html>
<head>
    <title>Chapter 6 - Calculator example v1</title>
</head>
<body>
    <form runat="server">
        <h2>Calculator Version 1
        </h2>
        <asp:TextBox id="txtInput1" runat="server"></asp:TextBox>
        <asp:Button id="btnAdd" onclick="Add"
                runat="server" Text=" + "></asp:Button>
        <asp:Button id="btnSubtract" onclick="Subtract"
                runat="server" Text=" - "></asp:Button>
        <br />
        <asp:TextBox id="txtInput2" runat="server"></asp:TextBox>
        <asp:Button id="btnMultiply" onclick="Multiply"
                runat="server" Text=" x "></asp:Button>
        <asp:Button id="btnDivide" onclick="Divide"
                runat="server" Text=" ÷ "></asp:Button>
        <br />
        <strong>Answer = <asp:Label id="lblAnswer" runat="server"></asp:Label>
        </strong>
    </form>
</body>
</html>
```

2. Open `Calculator.aspx` in your browser – it should be as shown in Figure 6-8. Enter two numbers in the textboxes and select a button to perform a calculation. Note that only the operation corresponding to the button clicked is performed. Also, notice that the executed operation's button is highlighted in yellow:

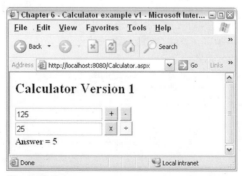

Figure 6-8

If you don't enter a number into any of the boxes before selecting an operator, you will get an error. Error handling will be discussed in *Chapter 14*.

3. After performing a calculation, take a look at the source code and note the existence of a _VIEWSTATE. You may want to take a look at the _VIEWSTATE after several calculations and notice the difference in the encrypted value. Do not try to discern a pattern, just note that it responds to changes in your activities as a user of the page.

4. Now save the page as CalculatorV2.aspx and make the following changes. Start by deleting the four operator functions and replacing them with a single one as follows:

```
<%@ Page Language="C#" Debug="true" %>
<script runat="server">

    void Page_Load()
    {
        btnAdd.BackColor = System.Drawing.Color.LightGray;
        btnSubtract.BackColor = System.Drawing.Color.LightGray;
        btnMultiply.BackColor = System.Drawing.Color.LightGray;
        btnDivide.BackColor = System.Drawing.Color.LightGray;
    }

    void Calc(object sender, EventArgs e)
    {
        double answer;
        Button PressedButton = (Button)sender;
        switch (PressedButton.ID)
        {
            case "btnAdd":
                answer = Convert.ToDouble(txtInput1.Text) +
                        Convert.ToDouble(txtInput2.Text);
                lblAnswer.Text = answer.ToString();
                break;
            case "btnSubtract":
                answer = Convert.ToDouble(txtInput1.Text) -
                        Convert.ToDouble(txtInput2.Text);
                lblAnswer.Text = answer.ToString();
                break;
            case "btnMultiply":
                answer = Convert.ToDouble(txtInput1.Text) *
                        Convert.ToDouble(txtInput2.Text);
                lblAnswer.Text = answer.ToString();
                break;
            case "btnDivide":
                answer = Convert.ToDouble(txtInput1.Text) /
                        Convert.ToDouble(txtInput2.Text);
                lblAnswer.Text = answer.ToString();
                break;
        }
        PressedButton.BackColor = System.Drawing.Color.Yellow;
    }
</script>
```

5. Change the code for each button control so that the new handler function is fired when it is clicked. View the file in your browser and you'll notice that there is no change in behavior:

```
<html>
<head>
    <title>Chapter 6 - Calculator example v2</title>
</head>
<body>
    <form runat="server">
        <h2>Calculator Version 2</h2>
        <asp:TextBox id="txtInput1" runat="server"></asp:TextBox>
        <asp:Button id="btnAdd" onclick="Calc"
                    runat="server" Text=" + "></asp:Button>
        <asp:Button id="btnSubtract" onclick="Calc"
                    runat="server" Text=" - "></asp:Button>
        <br />
        <asp:TextBox id="txtInput2" runat="server"></asp:TextBox>
        <asp:Button id="btnMultiply" onclick="Calc"
                    runat="server" Text=" x "></asp:Button>
        <asp:Button id="btnDivide" onclick="Calc"
                    runat="server" Text=" ÷ "></asp:Button>
        <br />
        <strong>Answer = <asp:Label id="lblAnswer"
runat="server"></asp:Label>
        </strong>
    </form>
</body>
</html>
```

How It Works

In `Calculator.aspx`, we created a function which fires automatically from the `Page_Load()` event. This function merely returns all buttons to their original color:

```
void Page_Load()
{
    btnAdd.BackColor = System.Drawing.Color.LightGray;
    btnSubtract.BackColor = System.Drawing.Color.LightGray;
    btnMultiply.BackColor = System.Drawing.Color.LightGray;
    btnDivide.BackColor = System.Drawing.Color.LightGray;
}
```

Next, look at how we set events to be handled when a button is clicked. These functions are called by the four ASP.NET button controls we have created:

```
<asp:Button id="btnAdd" onclick="Add"
            runat="server" Text=" + "></asp:Button>
<asp:Button id="btnSubtract" onclick="Subtract"
            runat="server" Text=" - "></asp:Button>
....
<asp:Button id="btnMultiply" onclick="Multiply"
            runat="server" Text=" x "></asp:Button>
```

```
<asp:Button id="btnDivide" onclick="Divide"
            runat="server" Text=" ÷ "></asp:Button>
```

Each button has a symbol corresponding to its equivalent mathematical operation, and it calls the relevant event handler function. All four functions work in an identical way. Let's closely look at the `Add()` function:

```
void Add(object sender, EventArgs e)
{
    double answer = Convert.ToDouble(txtInput1.Text) +
                    Convert.ToDouble(txtInput2.Text);
    lblAnswer.Text = answer.ToString();
    btnAdd.BackColor = System.Drawing.Color.Yellow;
}
```

The code is wired to the add button's `Click` event by the `onclick` attribute of `btnAdd`. It accepts two parameters – the contents of the two `TextBox` controls. Inside the handler, we get the contents of `txtInput1` and `txtInput2` by referring to their `Text` attributes. Because the `Text` attribute returns its information as a string, we use `Convert.ToDouble()` to convert the `string` to a `double`. We can then perform a mathematical operation on these two pieces of data, effectively calculating:

```
txtInput1 + txtInput2
```

We store our data in the `<asp:Label>` control, `lblAnswer`. We can access its `Text` attribute, but instead of getting the information, we need to set it:

```
lblAnswer.Text = txtInput1 + txtInput2
```

This result is displayed on the screen. The other three handler functions work in the same way, and will only be executed if the particular button associated with them is clicked.

In `Calculator.aspx`, ASP.NET reacts in a different way to each of the buttons on the page by having four different event handlers for each button. In `CalculatorV2.aspx`, we build a single event handler that is called by all four buttons. A click on `btnAdd` fires the `Calc()` event handler, not `Add()`:

```
<asp:Button id="btnAdd" onclick="Calc"
            runat="server" Text=" + "></asp:Button>
```

In order to perform the correct calculation, `Calc()` needs to know which button was pressed. If you recall from earlier, the `sender` parameter passed into an event handler provides a reference to the object that raised the event. However, it is just a generic object when passed into the handler and must be cast back to the correct type of server control – a `Button` – before we can discover which button triggered the event.

```
void Calc(object sender, EventArgs e)
{
    Button PressedButton = (Button)sender;
```

Now we can find out which button triggered the event by looking at the ID attribute of the button passed to Calc(). We can use that information in a switch statement to perform the correct operation on the two values from the TextBox controls and display the result in lblAnswer:

```
double answer;
switch (PressedButton.ID)
{
    case "btnAdd":
        answer = Convert.ToDouble(txtInput1.Text) +
                    Convert.ToDouble(txtInput2.Text);
        lblAnswer.Text = answer.ToString();
        break;
    case "btnSubtract":
        answer = Convert.ToDouble(txtInput1.Text) -
                    Convert.ToDouble(txtInput2.Text);
        lblAnswer.Text = answer.ToString();
        break;
    case "btnMultiply":
        answer = Convert.ToDouble(txtInput1.Text) *
                    Convert.ToDouble(txtInput2.Text);
        lblAnswer.Text = answer.ToString();
        break;
    case "btnDivide":
        answer = Convert.ToDouble(txtInput1.Text) /
                    Convert.ToDouble(txtInput2.Text);
        lblAnswer.Text = answer.ToString();
        break;
}
```

Finally, we change the background color of the button that fired the Calc() event:

```
PressedButton.BackColor = System.Drawing.Color.Yellow;
```

In this exercise, you saw two ways to handle multiple buttons. The first is to have individual event handlers for each button. If the different buttons have parallel tasks, we can employ the second technique where we create one handler that behaves differently depending on the object that triggers it.

Summary

This chapter presented the theory and practical aspects of event-driven programming. Traditional code ran all at once through to the end. In event-driven programming, different parts of our code are run at different times depending on user interactions with the page.

We started with a brief look at HTML events that provide one way of handling user action. HTML events are executed on the browser and are generally written in VBScript or JavaScript. They are useful for implementing reactions to events that would take too long to process on a round trip to the server; for example, the display of tooltips. However, HTML events do not tap the power of the server.

When you use event-driven programming associated with ASP.NET, you execute your code on the server. You create blocks of code in functions. The page loads and runs some functions automatically. Then the page sits and waits for user actions called *events*. Each event runs the code of an event handler to perform the desired tasks. When the event handler is finished, the page returns to a state of waiting for the next user-created event.

We looked at a group of events that occur automatically when a page is created on the server. The most commonly used event is Page_Load() to populate list boxes and to respond to the user input if the page displayed is the result of a postback. Postback pages are those that have already been shown to the user and are now being refreshed, usually with data entered by the user into the ASP.NET Web controls.

We saw another group of events that do not fire automatically. The Web control events are only executed when a user interacts with the controls. These controls will execute the event handlers specified in their tag, typically an attribute like onclick="MyOnClickHandler". A handler function named MyOnClickHandler() *must* exist on the page for the event to be handled. These event handlers are written as standard functions; thus, they need a valid function signature and their code should be enclosed inside curly braces {}. Like any other function, they cannot be nested inside any other function and must be written within the <script> tags on the page. They must also be written to handle two incoming parameters: object sender and EventArgs e. The former contains a pointer to the object that invoked the event handler. The latter is used for passing some special parameters; we haven't covered these in this chapter.

The OnClick event of the asp:Button is a commonly used event. It triggers a postback, which is a request to the server to refresh the page. Included in the request is a ViewState (the _VIEWSTATE attribute) that defines, in a compact and encrypted form, the status of each ASP.NET Web control on the page. This process only works when the page filename ends in .aspx, and each form and control contains the runat="server" attribute. Multiple buttons on a page can have their events handled by multiple event handlers or by one handler that behaves differently depending on the object that triggered the event.

Exercises

1. Explain why event-driven programming is a good way of programming for the Web.

2. Modify an HTML form to add a set of ASP.NET Web controls so that the information in the form is retained when the submit button is pressed.

3. Add a Page_Load() event handler to the ASPX code you've just created in Exercise 2 to confirm the selections made in the following format:

   Thank you very much _____.

   You have chosen ____ for breakfast. I will prepare it for you _____.

4. Create a very basic virtual telephone using an ASPX file that displays a textbox and a button named Call. Configure your ASPX file so that when you type a telephone number into the textbox and press Call, you are:

❑   Presented with a message confirming the number you are calling

❑   Presented with another button called Disconnect, which when pressed, returns you to your opening page, enabling you to type another number

Objects

When I started writing this chapter, I was struggling for a concise definition of an object. After all, everything is an object. A door is an object. So is an aardvark. So, being the computer geek that I am, I went online to one of the numerous dictionary sites, and what I first got was the etymology:

"Middle English, from Medieval Latin objectum, from Latin, neuter of objectus, past participle of obicere to throw in the way, present, hinder, from ob- in the way + jacere to throw." I didn't understand any of that, so I tried elsewhere and got this:

"\Ob"ject\, n.: That which is put, or which may be regarded as put, in the way of some of the senses; something visible or tangible."

OK, that makes a little more sense. So an object is something we can see, feel, hear, touch, taste or smell. Not much use in the virtual world of computer programming, so here's a more suitable definition:

An object is a self-contained entity that is characterized by a recognizable set of characteristics and behaviors.

Taking this concept further, how do you tell the difference between various objects? Well, you do so through their recognizable characteristics and behaviors. Take a cow for an example, where you could have the following:

Characteristics	Behaviors
They have four legs	They moo
They have udders	They eat grass
Size	They make milk
Color	
Breed	

These are fairly distinctive characteristics – if you described these everyone should be able to tell you are describing a cow. What you are describing is not any single cow, but all cows – the template that specifies the characteristics of a cow. What you need to consider is what makes one cow different from another.

Classes and Instances

In the world of *Object Oriented - Programming (OOP)*, the following two terms are used:

❑   **Class**: This is the template for an object and defines the characteristics of the object. In our bovine example it's what defines the characteristics of a cow.

❑   **Instance**: This is a real life object – the thing you can interact with. Thus, you only have one class defining a cow but many instances of it.

Therefore, cows don't exist until they each have an instance created. This is when their characteristics come into play. A good analogy is making cookies – the cookie cutter is the class (it defines the size and shape of the cookie), and once cut, the cookie is the instance. In this case, multiple instances are a good thing.

Properties, Methods, and Events

In OOP, the following terms are used to describe the characteristics of an object:

❑   **Property**: This is a noun and describes some feature of the object. A cow has a `Breed` – this property describes the breed to which a cow belongs, which, in turn, might be indicative of other characteristics. For example, the Holstein breed produces beer instead of milk. Actually I made that up, but it's a nice idea, isn't it? In fact, the Holstein is the best milk-producing breed.

❑   **Method**: This is a verb and describes something the object can do, or that you want the object to do. The cow can be milked and therefore might have a `Milk()` method.

❑   **Event**: This is also a verb and describes something that the object does in response to some stimuli. For example, your cow would have an event called `Moo`, which might happen when it is being milked. Or perhaps a `Sleep` event for when it's dark or the cow is tired.

The following sections show how these definitions apply to .NET.

Objects in .NET

.NET uses a lot of objects – in fact everything is an object. Variables were discussed in *Chapter 3*, and in .NET even these are objects. You don't really need to understand why or how (it's just the way .NET is built), but it's worth remembering that everything you deal with is an object. Consider the following:

You are actually declaring an object. Just like the real world, where objects are something specific, the `Name` variable is also something specific; it's a `String` – in fact, it's an instance of the `String` class. The

`String` class defines characteristics that our `Name` variable possesses, some of which are shown as follows:

Property	Method
Chars	ToUpper()
Length	StartsWith()
	Trim()

It has a `Length` property so we can see how many characters make up the string, and a `ToUpper()` method to allow us to convert the characters to uppercase. These are just a few of the methods, but are enough to give you an idea that a string is an object. Notice that there are no events – the `String` class doesn't have any events. This is an important point – classes don't need to have properties, methods, or events. In this chapter, we'll see how to build up a class in stages, adding the characteristics as you need them.

Why Use Objects?

Many people think OOP and Object-Oriented Design is a complex subject, but in reality, it's quite simple and can be explained in four simple terms: *abstraction, encapsulation, polymorphism,* and *inheritance.* *Chapter 12* discusses encapsulation in detail, but it's worth having an idea about the other terms as well, so that when you do more complex programming you'll understand the concepts:

❑   **Abstraction**: This is the process of hiding the complexity and the inner workings of a class, so that users don't have to know how it operates. For example, you don't have to know how a TV works if you only wanted to view a picture; you just switch it on and get the picture. The On/Off switch abstracts the actual operation. In the `String` example, you have a `Trim()` method that strips off any blank space at the beginning and the end of a string. You don't need to know how it actually does it – just that it does.

❑   **Encapsulation**: This is the process of every object containing everything it needs to be able to operate. Thus, they don't have to rely on other objects to be able to perform their own actions. For example, a cow contains everything it needs to produce milk – teeth to chew the grass, a stomach (four of them in fact), udders and so on. A `String` doesn't have to go elsewhere to convert all its characters into uppercase when you use the `ToUpper()` method.

However, encapsulation doesn't mean that you include absolutely everything in your class that it needs. For example, a class that uses strings would not define its own string object; it would reuse the standard one. This is acceptable because the `String` class is a part of the base classes supplied by .NET. It wouldn't be sensible to rely on a class that might not be present.

❑   **Polymorphism**: This is the term given to different objects being able to perform the same action, but through their own implementation. For example, our cow might have a `Chew()` method. For that matter, even a `Person` class could have a `Chew()` method, but the under-the-hood implementation might be different.

❑ **Inheritance**: This defines how classes can be related to one another and share characteristics. Inheritance works by defining classes and subclasses, where the subclass inherits all of the characteristics of the parent class. For example, if an `Animal` class were to define the base characteristics of an animal, there could be subclasses of `Cow`, `Dog`, `Human`, and so on. Each subclass would not only inherit the characteristics of the `Animal` class, but could also define new characteristics.

The importance of inheritance is that it enforces conformance across classes of a similar type, and allows shared code. If you decide to create a new class called `Mouse`, you don't have to reinvent all of the characteristics of the parent class. Inheritance will be discussed in more detail later in the chapter.

Defining Classes

It's now time to put some of this theory into practice. We're going to create a `Person` class, with the following characteristics:

❑ **Properties**: `Name, Age, EyeColor`

❑ **Methods**: `Walk(), Talk(), Chew()`

This will be done in stages, so that you fully understand each part of the class before moving on. You'll be creating the class as part of an ASP.NET page and you'll look at how to create classes as separate files later in the chapter. You can use Web Matrix for these examples if you like (or any other editor as we're not using any specific Web Matrix features). However, using Web Matrix means you don't have to bother with any Web server settings as it handles it all for you.

Try It Out **Creating a Class**

1. Create a new ASP.NET page called `FirstClass.aspx` in the Ch07 folder. If you are using Web Matrix you can pick the ASP.NET page template – make sure you pick the correct **Location** for the file and **Filename** as shown in Figure 7-1:

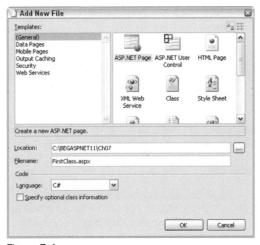

Figure 7-1

2. In Web Matrix select the All tab and delete everything that is in the file before adding the following code:

```
<%@ Page Language="C#" %>

<script runat="server">

  public class Person
  {
    private string  _Name;
    private int _Age;
    private string  _EyeColor;

    public Person() {
    }

    public string  Name {
      get {
        return _Name;
      }
      set {
        _Name = value;
      }
    }

    public int Age {
      get {
        return _Age;
      }
      set {
        _Age = value;
      }
    }

    public string EyeColor {
      get {
        return _EyeColor;
      }
      set {
        _EyeColor = value;
      }
    }
  }

  void Page_Load(object Sender, EventArgs E) {

    Person myPerson = new Person();
    myPerson.Name = "Susan";
    myPerson.Age = 25;
    myPerson.EyeColor = "Blue";

    Name.Text = myPerson.Name;
    Age.Text = myPerson.Age.ToString();
```

```
        EyeColor.Text = myPerson.EyeColor;
    }
</script>

<html>
<head>
</head>
<body>
    <form runat="server">
        Name: <asp:Label runat="server" id="Name" /><br />
        Age:  <asp:Label runat="server" id="Age" /><br />
        Eye Color: <asp:Label runat="server" id="EyeColor" />
    </form>
</body>
</html>
```

3. Save this file, and run it by hitting the **F5** key. You should see the result similar to Figure 7-2:

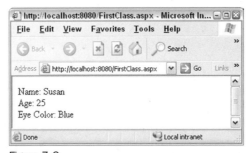

Figure 7-2

Nothing spectacular – it just shows the name, age, and eye color – but you are using a custom class. Let's see how this works.

How It Works

The first couple of lines define the language used in the page and the start of the server script. This is where your code will go:

```
<%@ Page Language="C#" %>
<script runat="server">
```

Next you see the definition of the class:

```
    public class Person
```

Unlike variables, where the variable type defines an object, only the `class` keyword followed by the class name (in this case, `Person`) has been used. This is because we are creating a new class. If you refer to the discussion on variables in *Chapter 3*, `public` implies that the class will be available to all other programs. This is necessary because an ASP.NET page will need to use it.

The lines that initialize the class follow next. This method, called the *Constructor*, is always named the same as the class and has no data type. It is the procedure that is run when you create an instance of a class, and it is a good place to set default values or perform any processing that the class itself requires. These will be discussed in more detail later.

```
public Person () {
}
```

Next in the code are some `private` variables that will be used to store the properties of the class such as the `Name`, `Age`, and `EyeColor`:

```
private string  Name;
private int  Age;
private string  EyeColor;
```

As these variables are `private`, they cannot be accessed from outside your class. How in such cases would one allow external access to them? For this, the code uses the following way of defining properties:

```
public string Name {
  get {
    return _Name;
  }
  set {
    _Name = value;
  }
}
```

Let's break this statement down, starting with the declaration:

```
public string Name {
```

As mentioned earlier, `public` implies that the property can be accessed from outside the class – that's what we need. We then have the data type (in this case a `string`), followed by the name of the property.

Next we have the `get` statement, which is the code that runs when the property is read. Here we just return the value of the private property variable:

```
get {
  return _Name;
}
```

The second part of the property is the `set` statement, which is the code that runs when we want to store a value in the property:

```
set {
  _Name = value;
}
```

Here we just set the private property variable to the value passed in. The `set` statement is unusual in that you don't have to define an argument to hold the value you are setting the property to – it's automatically catered for, and the value is available within the property `set` code as the variable named `value`. For example, consider the following:

The value `Susan` is passed into the property automatically, and is stored in the `value` variable.

Next we have the property definitions for the `Age` and `EyeColor` properties; these follow the same pattern as `Name`:

```
public int Age {
  get {
    return _Age;
  }
  set {
    _Age = value;
  }
}

public string  EyeColor {
  get {
    return _EyeColor;
  }
  set {
    _EyeColor = value;
  }
}
```

Next we have the line that ends the class:

```
}
```

Now we come to that part of the page that will use the class, starting with the `Page_Load()` method that runs when the page is loaded:

```
void Page Load(object Sender, EventArgs E) {
```

When the page loads, an instance of the `person` class needs to be created; this is done in a manner similar to that of declaring variables:

```
Person myPerson = new Person();
```

We declare the class instance exactly as we would for any other class, by defining the variable type, and then creating a new instance by using the `new` keyword followed by the class name. At this stage we have an instance of the class. But because it doesn't contain anything we set the property values to the following:

```
myPerson.Name = "Susan";
myPerson.Age = 25;
myPerson.EyeColor = "Blue";
```

Now the class instance has some values for its properties. We can read them out and display them in label controls:

```
Name.Text = myPerson.Name;
Age.Text = myPerson.Age;
EyeColor.Text = myPerson.EyeColor;
```

The last bit of code is the end of the `Page_Load()` routine and the end script tag:

```
  }
</script>
```

Finally, there are the HTML and server controls: three `Label` controls used to display the property values:

```
<html>
<head>
</head>
<body>
  <form runat="server">
    Name: <asp:Label runat="server" id="Name" /><br />
    Age: <asp:Label runat="server" id="Age" /><br />
    Eye Color: <asp:Label runat="server" id="EyeColor" />
  </form>
</body>
</html>
```

That's all there is to it – you've now created and used your first custom class. Let's look at the reasons behind using private variables for properties.

Property Variables

Why do you need to define variables that are private and then have property statements to allow access to them? Wouldn't it be easier to just have `public` variables such as the following:

```
public string _Name;
```

Yes it would, but this would break one of the key object oriented features mentioned earlier – abstraction. The whole idea is that you abstract the inner workings of a class; using the above code doesn't achieve that. It explicitly exposes how the properties are stored. Therefore, we use `private` variables and the property method, ensuring that all access to the property details is controlled.

This also allows you to add any processing, such as validation, to the property. For example, consider the `Age` property, where you may wish to add validation:

```
public int Age {
  get {
    return _Age;
  }
  set {
    if (value < 1)
```

```
            _Age = 1;
        else
            _Age = value;
    }
}
```

This validation checks whether the age is less than zero, and sets it to 1 if it is. This sort of processing wouldn't be possible had the property method not been used.

Property Types

As of now, the EyeColor property can be both read from and written to. In the real world, you can't change the color of your eyes (except by using contact lenses, but that's not really *changing* the color) so why should your class allow it? You'd certainly want some way of *setting* the eye color, but a property can't be the answer, as this would allow the eye color to be *changed*. However, the property can't be done away with either; we still want to be able to read the value.

One way to achieve a value that can only be read is to utilize a feature of properties that allows us to decide whether they can be read from or written to. To allow only reading of a property, we remove the set section of the property. Similarly, to allow only writing to a property, we remove the get section. The following code snippets show how this could be applied to the EyeColor property. For a read-only property, you would use:

```
public string EyeColor {
  get {
    return _EyeColor;
  }
}
```

For a write-only property you would use:

```
public string EyeColor {
  set {

    _EyeColor = value;
  }
}
```

Let's try making EyeColor a read-only property.

Try It Out   Read-Only Properties

1.   Edit FirstClass.aspx, and change the property for the EyeColor to the following:

```
public string EyeColor {
  get {
    return _EyeColor;
  }
}
```

2.   Save the file and run it; you should see something similar to Figure 7-3:

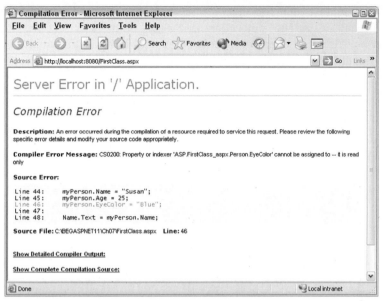

Figure 7-3

Oops, an error! This is fairly obvious because we've made the property read-only and thus can't set the value.

3. From the `Page_Load()` method, take out the line that sets the `EyeColor` and modify the class constructor so that it looks like the following:

```
public Person() {
  _EyeColor = "Blue";
}
```

4. Save the file and run it. The error will disappear and the eye color will be displayed.

How It Works

The key to this is simply the removal of the `set` section of the property, which has the effect of turning the property into a read-only one. Thus, we can only read the value from the property and not set it. To set the value, we modify the constructor so that it uses the private variable to set the eye color:

```
public Person() {
  _EyeColor = "Blue";
}
```

Remember that the constructor is run when the class is instantiated. So when we do the following:

```
Person MyPerson = new Person();
```

The `new` keyword specifies that the object is being created therefore causes the constructor to be run.

225

Although we can set the eye color by using the internal private variable, it's not a very flexible object, as the color is hardcoded into the class – this means that the user of the class can't change the eye color. Thus, every person will have eyes of the same color (and think how dull that would be)! There needs to be some way to set the color as the object is created, and to do that you need to look at what happens when objects are initialized.

Initializing Objects

In the previous code, you've seen the following method of creating objects:

```
Person myPerson = new Person ();
```

You might also see this sort of coding:

```
Person myPerson = Person();
myPerson = new Person();
```

This has the same effect as the single line version, but it is subtly different. The first line declares a variable of type `Person`, but doesn't instantiate it. It's only on the second line, when `new` is used, that the object instance is created. It's important to understand this so that you know when your object is actually created. For this example, an object that accesses a database and fetches a lot of data could take a long time to create, therefore knowing when it happens is important.

None of this, however, solves our problem of being able to set the eye color as the object is created. You can do this by creating another constructor that allows you to specify the eye color.

Try It Out   Overloading a Constructor

1. Open the `FirstClass.aspx` file and add the following code, just below the existing constructor:

```
public Person(string EC) {
  _EyeColor = EC;
}
```

2. Change the line that instantiates the class (the `Person myPerson = new Person();` line in the `Page_Load()` method) to:

```
Person myPerson = new Person("Green");
```

3. Save the file and run it. Notice that the eye color is now displayed as **Green**.

How It Works

This technique works because .NET allows the same method to be declared more than once as long as the argument types are different. The description of a method (its name and the number and data types of its arguments) is called the method *signature*. In our case we have the method declared twice – once with no arguments, and once with a single `String` argument, therefore the method has two signatures. This is called *overloading*, and thus both of the following lines are valid:

```
public Person()
public Person(string EC)
```

What you can't have in addition to the above lines, however, is the following:

```
public Person(string NM)
```

The reason is that it has the same signature as the declaration that accepts `EC` as its argument. Note that it's the argument type rather than its name that is important. A different data type indicates a different signature, but the same data type (even if the variable name is different) is the same signature. So what you can do is this:

```
public Person (string NM, string EC)
```

This declaration has a different signature, and is therefore allowed.

> **Class constructors always have the same name as the class.**

Implementing Methods

Our class doesn't do much so we need to add some methods to round it out. You've already seen methods – the constructor is one. Adding a method is just the same, although unlike the constructor, you can pick the method name. A method is simply a `public` function within the class and follows the same rules discussed in *Chapter 5*, so we don't need to cover the basics again. However, it's worth looking at them within the context of a class, so let's give it a go.

Try It Out Adding Methods to a Class

1. Edit the `FirstClass.aspx` file, and remove the text and labels from the HTML `<form runat="server">` section. We are using a different form of displaying data in this example.

2. Add the following code to the `Person` class, just before the end of the class:

```
public string Walk() {
   return _Name +
      ": you are now walking forwards";
}
```

3. Change the `Page_Load()` event so that it looks like the following:

```
void Page_Load(object Sender, EventArgs E) {
   Person Susan = new Person("Green");
   Susan.Name = "Susan";

   Response.Write(Susan.Walk());
```

```
      Response.Write("<br/>");
    }
```

4. Save the file and run it. You'll see the name of the person and the direction they are travelling in displayed on the screen, as shown in Figure 7-4:

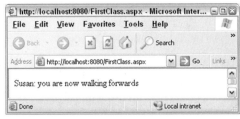

Figure 7-4

This is all very well, but what if you want to specify the direction of travel? You can use overloading for this (as you did with the constructor).

5. Switch back to your editor and add the following code, just underneath the previous `Walk()` method:

```
public string Walk(string Direction) {
   if (Direction == "Back")
      return _Name +
        ": you are now walking backwards";
   else
      return _Name +
        ": you are now walking forwards";
}
public string Walk(int Direction) {
   if (Direction > 0)
      return _Name +
        ": you are now walking forwards";
   else
      return _Name +
        ": you are now walking backwards";
}
```

6. Change the `Page_Load()` event so that it looks like the following:

```
void Page_Load(object Sender, EventArgs E)
{
   Person Susan = new Person("Green");
   Susan.Name = "Susan";

   Response.Write(Susan.Walk());
   Response.Write("<br/>");

   Person Sam = new Person("Blue");
   Sam.Name = "Sam";
   Response.Write(Sam.Walk("Back"));
```

```
        Response.Write("<br/>");
        Response.Write(Sam.Walk(1));
        Response.Write("<br/>");
    }
```

7. Save the file and run it again, and you'll see Figure 7-5:

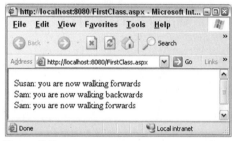

Figure 7-5

How It Works

The changes made to the `FirstClass.aspx` class were very simple – just the addition of an overloading methods. The first variant has no arguments, and just returns a string consisting of the name of the person and some text indicating that the person is walking forwards:

```
public string Walk() {
    return _Name +
        ": you are now walking forwards";
}
```

The second variant takes a string as its argument and uses it to decide upon the direction of travel. If the string is `"Back"`, the person is deemed to be walking backwards, otherwise it indicates walking forwards:

```
public string Walk(string Direction) {
    if (Direction == "Back")
        return _Name +
            ": you are now walking backwards";
    else
        return _Name +
            ": you are now walking forwards";
}
```

The third variant also takes an argument to determine the direction of travel, but this time it's a number. A value greater than `0` implies that the person is travelling forwards, and a negative number as travelling backwards:

```
public string Walk(int Direction) {
    if (Direction > 0)
        return _Name +
            ": you are now walking forwards";
```

```
        else
           Return _Name +
             ": you are now walking backwards";
    }
```

Overloading can be useful if you can provide several signatures for a method, and therefore allowing the method to be called in a variety of ways. One good example of the application of overloading methods is when you need to look up items in lists. You might have an overloaded method that allows lookup by name (a string) or by position in the list (a number).

Using these methods is simple, as seen in the `Page_Load()` event:

```
    void Page_Load(object Sender, EventArgs E)
    {
      Person Susan = new Person("Green");
      Susan.Name = "Susan";

      Response.Write(Susan.Walk());
      Response.Write("<br/>");

      Person Sam = new Person("Blue");
      Sam.Name = "Sam";
      Response.Write(Sam.Walk("Back"));
      Response.Write("<br/>");
      Response.Write(Sam.Walk(1));
      Response.Write("<br/>");
    }
```

Here we create two instances of the `Person` object – `Susan` and `Sam`. For the `Susan` instance, we use the first `Walk()` method without any arguments and indicate that this instance is walking forwards. For the `Sam` instance, we use the other two `Walk()` methods (the string and the numeric ones).

This example also uses `Response.Write` to output strings directly onto the page and display them. Generally, you wouldn't use this method to interact with the page as you'd use server controls, but using `Response.Write` allows you to output any amount of text without worrying about creating controls.

Consolidating Overloaded Methods

Using overloaded methods can be beneficial, but it can also lead to repetition of code in the implementation. As developers, you'd want to minimize the repetition of code in an application:

❑   It saves time – the quicker you can develop applications, the better.

❑   If you want to change any functionality, you have to change it in all the methods.

❑   The more code there is, the greater are the chances of errors.

In the preceding example, we have repeated the following (or similar) code in all methods:

```
    Return _Name + ": you are now walking forwards";
```

You could just create a private method that performs the actions necessary for walking, which is not accessible outside of the class. You can then call this method from the three public methods within the class.

You can also call one overloaded method from another overloaded method. For example, the methods in the previous example could become:

```
public string  Walk() {
  return Walk(1);
}

public string  Walk(string  Direction) {
  if ( Direction == "Back" )
    return Walk(-1);
  else
    return Walk(1);
}

public string  Walk(int Direction) {
  string dir;

  if ( Direction > 0 )
    dir = "forwards";
  else
    dir = "backwards";

  return _Name +
        ": you are now walking " +
        dir;

}
}
```

The actual functionality in this example is contained within just one method – the one that takes an integer as its argument. This method in turn is called by the other methods. All code is in one place and therefore, can easily be tested or changed if required.

Advanced Classes

So far this chapter has dealt with the basics of classes, which probably covers most of what you'll need and use. However, it would be worth mentioning a few advanced topics here; they can be useful, and you may well see them used elsewhere.

Shared or Static Properties and Methods

The chapter began with a discussion on classes and instances, and about how you need to create an instance of a class before using it. However, the creation of an instance isn't always necessary because you can create properties and methods that can be used without a class instance. These are called *static* properties or methods, and are implemented using the static keyword in C#. For example, consider a Tools class that contains some central methods, such as error logging. Using the techniques shown earlier, it could be defined as:

```
public class Tools {
  public void Log(string error) {
    // error logging code goes here
  }
}
```

To use this class, we would need the following code:

```
Tools t = new Tools();
t.Log("Something went wrong");
```

The use of a class here is just for abstraction and encapsulation purposes – providing a simple way to log errors and hiding how it's actually done (writing to a file or database, for example). Since this is a single operation with no other properties or methods involved, the `Log()` method can be made static:

```
public class Tools {
  public static void Log(string error) {
    // error logging code goes here
  }
}
```

To use this static method, you no longer need to instantiate an object and the `Log()` method can be called directly as follows:

```
Tools.Log("Something went wrong");
```

This technique should be restricted to methods and properties that require no other references – properties that haven't yet been initialized. It is ideal for "helper" type methods, such as the `Log()` method shown above, where the class simply provides a wrapper for the method.

Inheritance

Inheritance was mentioned at the beginning of the chapter when describing why objects are used and how you can create subclasses that inherit properties from the parent. This is best described with an example.

Consider an `Animal` class that defines the `Legs` and `BodyHair` properties and a `Walk()` method. Let's look at two instances of this class:

Property / Method	Instance 1	Instance 2
Legs	4	2
BodyHair	Yes	No
Walk()	Yes	Yes

You can make an intelligent guess as to what these two instances could be in real life. Something with lots of body hair and four legs could be a dog, and something without body hair and two legs is probably a human being. There could be other shared characteristics, but more importantly, there could be characteristics that aren't shared and need to be different for each instance. Therefore, you need to create two new classes (`Dog` and `Person`) that inherit from the `Animal` class and also define distinct characteristics. For example:

Dog	Person
Bark()	Talk()
Bite	
Wag	

As you can see, dogs `Bark()`, `Bite`, and `Wag` their tails, unlike people, who can `Talk()`. However, since both classes inherit from the `Animal` class, they both have its properties and methods – `Legs`, `BodyHair`, and `Walk()`. Because `Dog` and `Person` inherit from `Animal`, they don't have to implement the methods and properties of `Animal` again.

This has several benefits:

❑   You can create a hierarchy of objects by implementing any functionality where it is most appropriate. For example, all ASP.NET server controls inherit from a control called `WebControl`. This isn't used directly and is simply a way to define all of the common functionality for server controls. For example, it has a `BackColor` property to set the background color of a control, and `Height` and `Width` properties to set its height and width. It doesn't, however, have a `Text` property because *not* all server controls require text (the `Label` and the `TextBox` controls do for example, but the `Image` and the `Panel` controls don't).

❑   Functionality only needs to be implemented once, in the parent or *base* class as it is often called. This not only reduces time, but also reduces the testing time and the possibility of errors.

❑   You can enforce functionality on subclasses by providing base functionality. For example, consider using a set of classes to provide access to databases. You can code all of the base functionality, such as security, into the base class and enforce it so that classes inheriting from the base class have to use it. This would ensure that all the data is accessed in a secure manner.

Although the remainder of the book doesn't involve extensive usage of inheritance, it is an invaluable technique – give it a go and see how easy it is.

Try It Out   Inheritance

1.   Create a new ASP.NET page called `Inheriting.aspx`.

2.   Add the following class within the server code block just after the `<script runat="server">` line:

```
public class Animal {

  private int _Legs;
  private string _BodyHair;

  public int Legs {
    get {
      return _Legs;
    }
    set {
      _Legs = value;
    }
  }

  public string BodyHair {
    get {
      return _BodyHair;
    }
    set {
      _BodyHair = value;
    }
  }

  public string Walk() {
    return "I'm walking on " +
        _Legs + " legs";
  }
}
```

3. Add the Dog class underneath the Animal class:

```
public class Dog : Animal {

  public Dog() {
    Legs = 4;
  }

  public string Bark() {
    return "Woof";
  }

  public string Bite() {
    return "Chomp Chomp";
  }

  public string Wag() {
    return "Wag Wag";
  }
}
```

4. Now, add the Person class underneath the Dog class:

```
public class Person : Animal {
  public Person() {
```

```
      Legs = 2;
    }

  public string  Talk() {
    return "yadda yadda yadda";
  }
}
```

5. Add the `Page_Load()` event that consists of code that will use our classes:

```
void Page_Load(object Sender, EventArgs E) {

  Dog Rover = new Dog();
  Response.Write(Rover.Walk());
  Response.Write("<br />");
  Response.Write(Rover.Bark());
  Response.Write("<br />");

  Person  Susan = new Person();
  Response.Write(Susan.Walk());
}
```

6. Save the file and run it. You'll see the following output as shown in Figure 7-6:

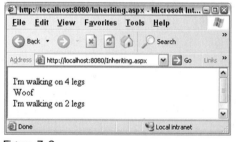

Figure 7-6

How It Works

Let's start by looking at the base class, `Animal`. It has two properties, `Legs` and `BodyHair`, and one method, `Walk()`:

```
public class Animal {

  private int _Legs;
  private string  _BodyHair;

  public int Legs {
    get {
      return _Legs;
    }
    set {
```

```
      _Legs = value;
    }
  }
  public string  BodyHair {
    get {
      return _BodyHair;
    }
    set {
      _BodyHair = value;
    }
  }
  public string  Walk() {
    return "I'm walking on " +
          _Legs + " legs";
  }
}
```

Next comes the class declaration for the Dog class:

```
public class Dog : Animal {
```

Notice the use of the colon (:) here. This indicates that you are inheriting from the Animal class, which automatically gives the Dog class the properties and methods defined in that class. This is obvious when we look at the constructor:

```
public Dog() {
   Legs = 4;
}
```

Notice that this class uses the Legs property without declaring it. That's because it's part of the base class. Note that you can't use the _Legs *variable* because that's private to the Animal class, but you can use the Legs *property*.

The methods are simple, each returning a string. These have been added to show that you can have methods additional to those provided by the base class:

```
public string  Bark() {
   return "Woof";
}

public string  Bite() {
   return "Chomp Chomp";
}

public string  Wag() {
   return "Wag Wag";
}
}
```

You then defined the Person class, again inheriting from the Animal base class with the Legs property set to 2:

```
public class Person : Animal {

  public Person() {
    Legs = 2;
  }

  public string  Talk() {
    return "yadda yadda yadda";
  }
}
```

Finally you create the `Page_Load()` event where the classes are used:

```
void Page_Load(object Sender, EventArgs E) {
```

Within this event, you first create an instance of the Dog class, and then call the Walk() and Bark() methods:

```
Dog Rover = new Dog();
Response.Write(Rover.Walk());
Response.Write("<br />");
Response.Write(Rover.Bark());
Response.Write("<br />");
```

Then you create an instance of the `Person` class and call the `Walk()` method:

```
Person Susan = new Person();
Response.Write(Susan.Walk());
}
```

The `Walk()` method is called in both the `Dog` and the `Person` classes, even though they do not implement it. It's the base class that implements this class, but because they both inherit from the base class they can use the `Walk()` method. As you can see, the same functionality is available in multiple classes despite being implemented only once.

A class can inherit from only *one* other class.

Interfaces

An *interface* is a special type of class, but one that doesn't implement any methods or properties – it defines what a class *does*, rather than what a class *is*. The term interface is used to describe the public view of a class – the public methods and properties.

Why is an interface useful? While developing a large application, you may have a set of classes that all need to perform some similar action(s). An interface specifies what that similar action should be but does not implement it. This is different from the concept of inheritance, where the implementation is at the base class level.

Good examples of interfaces are some of the data handling classes that .NET provides. Data can be stored in different types of databases and there are special classes for handling data. There are two main sets of classes – one for Microsoft SQL Server and one for other databases. Despite the fact that these databases might require special handling, the data handling classes need to provide a common implementation. This allows similar code to be used irrespective of the database. This reduces not only the techniques you need to learn, but also the complexity of code you need to write. Let's look at a simple example.

Try It Out   Creating an Interface

1.   Create a new ASP.NET page called `Interfaces.aspx`.

2.   Add the following code that defines the interface below the `<script runat="server">` line:

```
public interface IAnimal {

   int Legs { get; set; }

   string  Walk();
}
```

3.   Add the following code to define the `Person` class:

```
public class Person : IAnimal {

   private int _Legs;

   public Person() {
      _Legs = 2;
   }

   public int Legs {
      get {
         return _Legs;
      }
      set {
         _Legs = value;
      }
   }

   public string  Walk() {
      return "I'm walking on " +
            _Legs + " legs";
   }
}
```

4.   Add the code for the `Dog` class:

```
public class Dog : IAnimal {

   public int Legs {
      get {
         return 4;
      }
      set {
      }
```

```
    }

    public string Walk() {
      return "I want to run";
    }
  }
```

5. And finally, add the code for using these classes:

```
void Page_Load(object Sender, EventArgs E)
{
  Dog  Rover = new Dog();
  Response.Write(Rover.Walk());
  Response.Write("<br />");


  Person  Susan = new Person();
  Response.Write(Susan.Walk());

}
```

6. Save the file and run it – you'll see the following output:

Figure 7-7

How It Works

The code is simple even if the concept seems a little strange. Let's start by looking at the `Interface`:

```
public interface IAnimal {

  int Legs { get; set; }

  string Walk();
}
```

It's similar to the way a class is defined, except that you need to use the `interface` keyword before the interface name. By convention, the classname starts with an uppercase I. The properties and methods are defined within the interface. Notice that there is no implementation – all you are doing is defining what the interface does and *not* how it does it. The use of `get` and `set` in the `Legs` property here imply the read and /write characteristics of the property, respectively. We also have the `Walk()` method that returns a `string`.

Once the interface is defined, you can use a class to implement it in the same manner as inheritance:

```
public class Person : IAnimal {
```

This tells .NET that we have a `Person` class, and that apart from its own properties and methods, it should also implement the properties and methods defined by the `IAnimal` interface. Therefore we first define a private variable to store the number of legs, and then the constructor to set a value for it as follows:

```
private int _Legs;

public Person() {
  _Legs = 2;
}
```

Now consider the properties defined in the interface. The definition is the same as for normal properties except that the interface has already specified this property making its implementation mandatory:

```
public int Legs {
  get {
    return _Legs;
  }
  set {
    _Legs = value;
  }
}
```

There's nothing special you have to do to specify that this code is implementing a property defined in the interface. The C# compiler knows when you are implementing an interface and matches the properties (and methods) accordingly. The same technique applies to the method:

```
public string  Walk() {
  return "I'm walking on " +
        _Legs + " legs";
}
```

Now let's look at the `Dog` class, which also implements the `IAnimal` interface:

```
public class Dog : IAnimal {
```

The `Legs` property is implemented next. Note that the following implementation is completely different from that of the `Person` class. There is no private variable to store the number of legs, setting the property doesn't do anything, and reading the value always returns 4.

```
public int Legs {
  get {
    return 4;
  }
    set {
  }
}
```

The same applies to the `Walk()` method, which has an implementation different from that of the `Person` class:

```
public string Walk() {
  return "I want to run";
}
}
```

Finally, we have the code that uses the classes. Notice that we can still call the `Walk()` method on both classes in exactly the same manner as in previous examples:

```
void Page_Load(object Sender, EventArgs E)
{
    Dog Rover = new Dog();
    Response.Write(Rover.Walk());
    Response.Write("<br />");


    Person  Susan = new Person();
    Response.Write(Susan.Walk());

}
```

The key to understanding interfaces is remembering that the interface defines what a class can do, not how it does it. That's clearly seen from the implementation of the `Person` and `Dog` classes, where the `Legs` property and `Walk()` method have been implemented differently. The external view of these classes is the same.

Interfaces as Types

Interfaces could be useful in a scenario where you need to write some generic routines to handle class instances. For example, consider a function that accepts an object as an argument, does some processing, and then calls a method on that object. Using the `Dog` class, you could have the following:

```
Dog Rover = new Dog();
GoForAWalk(Rover);

public void GoForAWalk(Dog inst) {
  // do some processing
  ...
  // go for a walk
  inst.Walk();
}
```

Here you've created an instance of `Dog`, and passed that into the `GoForAWalk()` function as an `int` argument. This function simply calls the `Walk()` method of the `Dog` class instance. What happens if you now want to have the same sort of thing for a `Person` object? You could expand your code as follows:

```
public void GoForAWalk(Dog inst) {
```

```
      // do some processing
      ...
      // go for a walk
      inst.Walk();
   }
   public void GoForAWalk(Person inst) {
      // do some processing
      ...
      // go for a walk
      inst.Walk();
   }
```

The only difference in the second routine is the argument definition. All other code is repeated.

A better solution is to realize that both Dog and Person implement IAnimal, and we can use the interface name as our argument type:

```
   public void GoForAWalk(IAnimal inst)
   {  // do some processing
      ...
      // go for a walk
      inst.Walk();
   }
```

We now have a single routine that applies to both the Dog and Person objects. In fact it applies to all objects that implement IAnimal, so if another class is created (Cat for instance), the GoForAWalk() routine doesn't need to be changed.

The key points are that interfaces:

❑ Provide a class definition that is enforced upon classes that implement the interface. This ensures that all classes that implement the interface are guaranteed to have the set of properties and methods defined in the interface.

❑ Don't enforce the implementation, as that is left up to the individual class.

❑ Allow generic routines, because interfaces are data types. This means that instead of using the actual class as the data type, we can use the interface name, thus allowing the routine to work with any object that implements the interface.

The last point will be discussed in the next couple of chapters where the topic of data access is addressed.

Implementing Interface Methods and Properties

One important point to remember is that when implementing an interface in a class, you *must* implement all methods and properties of that interface. For example, you cannot implement just the Walk() method, and not the Legs property. Everything defined in the interface has to be implemented in the class. If you don't, you'll get a compilation error.

.NET Objects

So far, this chapter has looked at creating classes and objects. Earlier, we talked about everything in .NET being an object. This is a core point to remember because it will aid you considerably in understanding .NET. Let's look at a couple of topics to understand how objects are organized and used within .NET.

Namespaces

Namespaces provide a logical separation for classes. The first step towards understanding objects in .NET is to understand namespaces. If you look at the number of classes that come as a part of .NET, you'll see why – there are more than 3000 classes! Having that number of classes without any form of structure would be really difficult to manage, especially when searching through documentation. There are a couple of places you can look at the available namespaces. The first is the documentation that comes with .NET as shown in Figure 7-8:

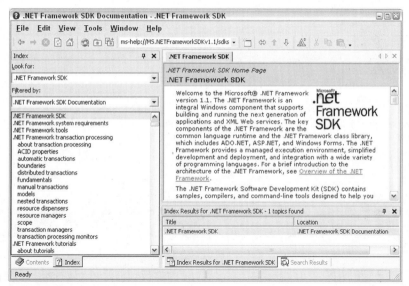

Figure 7-8

Observe the number of namespaces and how they have been broken down. Knowing the classes that belong in which namespace is essential, not only to help you look up documentation, but also to know about the namespaces to import into an ASP.NET page.

The Class Browser

Another useful tool is the class browser application, which is available if you have installed and configured the .NET Framework SDK samples. To access this, navigate to http://localhost/quickstart/aspplus and scroll to the bottom where you'll see a link to Sample Applications and A Class Browser Application. Running this sample shows Figure 7-9:

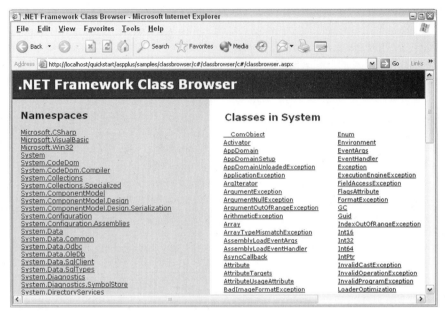

Figure 7-9

On the left you see the namespace; selecting one of these will display the classes in the namespace on the right side of the screen. Selecting an individual class will show its members. See Figure 7-10:

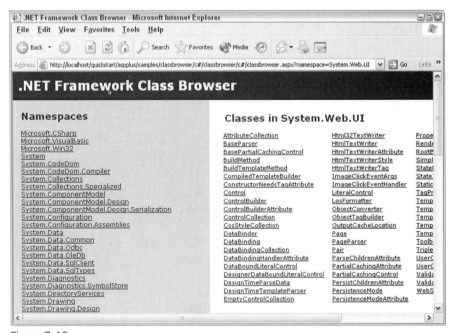

Figure 7-10

This figure shows all the members of a class – the constructors, properties, methods, and events. It also shows the object hierarchy (the inheritance used) and the implementation (classes implemented).

Summary

This chapter covered the fundamentals and some complex topics surrounding classes. You could go deeper into objects and other complex topics, but these are really outside the scope of the book. We've looked at what objects are, and how OOP is beneficial.

Features such as inheritance and abstraction provide many benefits to programmers, such as reduction in development time, improved stability of applications, and better structure. These techniques were used to create some sample classes to show how they work and to see how properties and methods can easily be added to a class.

This chapter also discussed advanced topics such as overloading and interfaces. The chapter ended with a quick look at how classes are organized in .NET, and how you can find out what is in a namespace and a class.

Now it's time to turn attention to data; the next chapter will look at how data can be retrieved from a database and displayed in your pages.

Exercises

1. The examples covered in the chapter have modelled some simple characteristics of real - world objects, such as animals. Think about other real world objects that, when turned into classes, would be useful in programming.

2. In the `Animal` class, where the `Walk()` method accepts an argument of type `int`, expand this to use this integer as the speed of walking. Think about how you'd store that speed and what you'd do with it.

3. With the results of Exercise 2, think about how you'd add validation to the speed to ensure that it doesn't exceed certain set limits.

4. Describe the main differences between class inheritance and interfaces. When would you use one over the other?

5. Create a class called `PieceOfString` with a single read/write property (of type `int`) called `Length`. Create an instance of the class and set the `Length` to `16`. Now you can answer that age old question "How long is a piece of string?"

Reading from Databases

So far, you've learnt a lot about programming, and seen those techniques in use in a variety of Web pages. Now it's time to turn our attention to one of the most important topics of building Web sites – data. Whatever the type of site you aim to build, data plays an important part. From a personal site (perhaps a vacation diary or a photo album), to a corporate e-commerce site, *data is key!*

There are numerous ways to store data, but most sites use a *database*. In this chapter, we're going to look at data stored in databases, and show how easily it can be used on Web pages. For this we are going to use ADO.NET, which is the data access technology that comes as part of the .NET Framework.

If the thought of databases sounds complex and scary, don't worry. We're going to show you just how easy this can be. In particular, we'll be looking at:

- ❑ Basics of databases and how they work
- ❑ How to create simple data pages using Web Matrix
- ❑ Different ADO.NET classes used for fetching data
- ❑ Basics of ADO.NET and how it fetches data
- ❑ How to use Web Matrix to simplify developing data access pages

Let's develop some basic understanding of databases first.

Understanding Databases

Understanding some basics about databases is crucial to using data in your pages. You don't need to be a database expert, but there are certain things you will need to know in order to work with data in .NET. For a start, you need to understand how data is stored. All types of data on a computer are stored in files of some sort. Text files, for example, are simple files and just contain plain text. Spreadsheets, on the other hand, are complex files containing not only the entered text and numbers, but also details about the data, such as what the columns contain, how they are formatted, and so on.

Databases also fall into the category of complex files. When using Microsoft Access, you have an MDB file – this is a database file, but you can't tell anything about the data from the file itself. You need a way to get to the data, either using Microsoft Access itself, or as we are going to do, using the .NET data classes. Before you can access the data, you need to know how it is stored internally.

Tables

Within a database, data is stored in *tables* – these are the key components of all databases. A table is like a spreadsheet, with *rows* and *columns*. You generally have multiple tables for multiple things – each distinct type of data is stored separately, and tables are often linked together.

Let's look at an example that should make this easier to visualize. Consider an ordering system, for example, where you store details of customers and the goods they've ordered. The following table shows rows of customer orders, with columns (or *fields*) each piece of order information:

Customer	Address	Order Date	Order Item	Quantity	Item Cost
John	15 High Street Brumingham England UK	01/07/2003	Widget	10	3.50
John	15 High Street Brumingham England UK	01/07/2003	Doodad	5	2.95
John	15 High Street Brumingham England UK	01/08/2003	Thingy	1	15.98
Chris	25 Easterly Way Cradiff Wales UK	01/08/2003	Widget	1	3.50
Dave	2 Middle Lane Oxborough England UK	01/09/2003	Doodad	2	2.95

Customer	Address	Order Date	Order Item	Quantity	Item Cost
Dave	3 Middle Lane Oxborough England UK	01/09/2003	Thingamajig	1	8.50

This is the sort of thing you'd see in a spreadsheet, but there are a couple of big problems with this. For a start, we have repeated information. John, for example, has his address shown three times. What happens if he moves house? You'd have to change the address everywhere it occurs. Dave has two addresses, but notice they are slightly different. Which one is correct? Are neither correct?

To get around these problems, we use a process called *Normalization*.

Normalization

This is the process of separating repeated information into separate tables. There are whole books dedicated to database design, but we only need to look at the simplest case. A good beginner book on database design is *Database Design for Mere Mortals: A Hands On Guide to Relational Database Design, by Michael J. Hernandez*

What we need to do is split the previous table into three tables, one for each unique piece of information – Customers, Orders, and OrderDetails. To link the three new tables together, we create ID columns that uniquely identify each row. For example, we could create a column called CustomerID in the Customers table. To link the Customers table to the Orders table, we also add this CustomerID to the Orders table. Let's look at our tables now.

The Customers table is as follows:

CustomerID	Customer	Address
1	John	15 High Street Brumingham England UK
2	Chris	25 Easterly Way Cradiff Wales UK
3	Dave	2 Middle Lane Oxborough England UK

The Orders table is as follows:

OrderID	CustomerID	OrderDate
1	1	01/07/2003
2	1	01/08/2003
3	2	01/08/2003
4	3	01/09/2003

The `OrderDetails` table is as follows:

OrderDetailsID	OrderID	Order Item	Quantity	Item Cost
1	1	Widget	10	3.50
2	1	Doodad	5	2.95
3	2	Thingy	1	15.98
4	3	Widget	1	3.50
5	4	Doodad	2	2.95
6	4	Thingamajig	1	8.50

We now have three tables that can be linked together by their ID fields as shown in Figure 8-1:

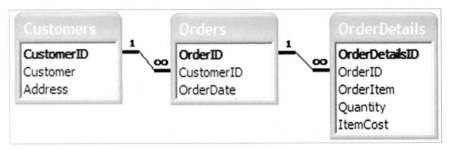

Figure 8-1

We now have links between the tables. The `CustomerID` field in the `Orders` table is used to identify which customer the order is for. Similarly, the `OrderID` field in the `OrderDetails` table identifies which order a particular order line belongs to.

The unique key in a table is defined as its *Primary Key* – it's what uniquely defines a row. When used in another table it is called the *Foreign Key*, so called because it's a key, but one to a foreign table. The foreign key is simply a column that is the primary key in another table. Because the values of the primary key and the foreign key will be the same, we can use them to link the tables together. This linking of the tables is done in *Structured Query Language (SQL)*, usually as a query or a stored procedure.

SQL and Stored Procedures

Queries are the way in which we deal with data in a database, either to extract data or to manipulate it. We can use an SQL statement or a stored procedure, which is an SQL statement wrapped to provide a simple name. It's worth noting that a stored procedure is actually more than just wrapping an SQL statement in a name, but that's a good enough description for what we need.

In *Chapter 5* when we looked at functions, we had a function name encapsulating some code statements. Think of a stored procedure in a similar way – it wraps a set of SQL statements, allowing us to use the name of the stored procedure to run those SQL statements. We're not going to focus much on this topic as it's outside the scope of this book.

To learn more about SQL, read *SQL for Dummies (ISBN 0-7645-4075-0) by John Wiley & Sons Inc.*

Here are a few reasons why you should always use stored procedures instead of direct SQL:

❑ **Security:** Using the .NET data classes with stored procedures protects you against certain forms of hacking.

❑ **Speed:** Stored procedures are optimised the first time they are called, and then the optimised code is used in subsequent calls.

❑ **Separation:** It keeps the SQL separate from your code.

In the remainder of this book, we'll actually be using a mixture of SQL and stored procedures for the simple reason that sometimes it's easier to use SQL in the context of an example. Remember, our focus is on ASP.NET. We'll be using Microsoft Access for the samples, and although Access doesn't support stored procedures, its use of stored queries is equivalent.

Let's get on with some examples.

The Web Matrix Data Explorer

You've already seen how powerful Web Matrix is for creating Web pages, and this power extends to working with data. Where you've used the Workspace Explorer in the top right hand corner of Web Matrix to work with files, you can use the Data Explorer to work with data. This provides ways of creating databases, connecting to existing ones, and working with tables and queries. Let's give this a go.

Try It Out **Connecting to a Database**

1. Select the Data Explorer tab, and click the Add Database Connection button – the one that's second in from the right, and will be the only one highlighted, as shown in Figure 8-2, if you haven't already got a database connection open:

Figure 8-2

2. Select Access Database from the window that appears and press OK.

3. Enter the following into the Data File text area (use a central location for the database, so that we can reuse it later in the book):

```
C:\BegASPNET11\data\Northwind.mdb
```

4. Press OK to connect to the database. This is the Northwind database, one of the sample databases that ships with Microsoft Access.

5. Figure 8-3 shows the tables contained in this database:

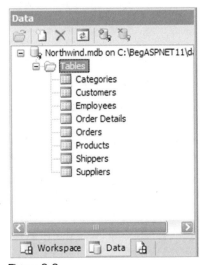

Figure 8-3

You can double-click on these to open the table, and see and change the data. One thing you might notice is that you don't see any queries – that's because Web Matrix doesn't support queries in Access. When connecting to SQL Server, you'll see the stored procedures – you can even create and edit them – but for Access, you are limited to tables only.

How It Works

There's nothing really to explain about how it works. What we are doing is simply creating a connection to a database that Web Matrix can use. This isn't required for ASP.NET to fetch data from databases, but Web Matrix has some great ways to generate code for you, so you don't have to do as much coding.

Creating Data Pages

Pages that display data can be created in a number of ways, and let's first look at the three ways that Web Matrix uses to save you coding. This is the quickest way to get data into your pages and saves a great deal of time. However, what it might not do is give you the knowledge to access databases without using Web Matrix. After we've seen the easy ways, we'll look at the .NET classes that deal with data. This way you'll have techniques to work with and without Web Matrix.

Displaying Data Using the Data Explorer

You've already seen how easy connecting to a database is using the Data Explorer. Creating pages directly from this explorer is even easier – all you have to do is drag the table name and drop it onto a page. This will automatically create a connection on the page and a fully functional data grid. Let's give this a go.

Try It Out Creating a Grid

1.   Create a new ASP.NET page called Grid1.aspx.

2.   From the Data Explorer, drag the Suppliers table onto your empty page as shown in Figure 8-4:

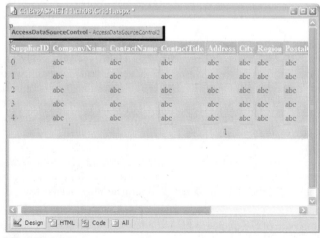

Figure 8-4

3. Save the page and run it as shown in Figure 8-5:

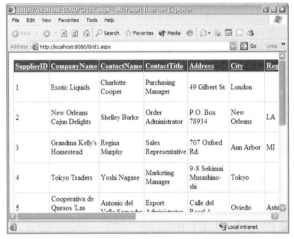

Figure 8-5

Amazing! A sortable grid full of data and you didn't have to write even a single line of code!

How It Works

The workings rely on two controls – the `AccessDataSourceControl` that provides the connection to the database, and an `MxDataGrid`, which is a Web Matrix control (also covered in *Chapter 10*) that displays the data. Looking at the HTML view for these controls gives you a good idea of what they do.

Let's start with the `AccessDataSourceControl`:

```
<wmx:AccessDataSourceControl id="AccessDataSourceControl2"
    runat="server" SelectCommand="SELECT * FROM [Suppliers]"
    ConnectionString="Provider=Microsoft.Jet.OLEDB.4.0; Ole DB Services=-4;
Data Source=C:\BegASPNET11\data\Northwind.mdb"></wmx:AccessDataSourceControl>
```

The first thing to notice is the way the control is declared. You're used to seeing `asp:` at the beginning of controls, but not `wmx:`. This prefix is the namespace – remember the previous chapter where we said that namespaces provide a separation between classes. In this case, these controls are part of Web Matrix, and have thus been given a namespace that is different from the standard server controls.

Apart from the `id` and `runat`, two other attributes provide the details regarding which database to connect to and what data to fetch:

❑ The `SelectCommand`: Defines the SQL that will return the required data – in this case, it's all rows and columns from the `Suppliers` table. This is the default since we dragged this table, but we can customize the `SelectCommand` to return only selected rows or columns.

❑ The `ConnectionString`: Defines the OLEDB connection string. You only need to worry about the bit with the path of the database file – the `Data Source` bit (if you move the file, you'll need to change this). The other parts of the `ConnectionString` just define the type of database and some database specific features. You don't need to know about these specifically (they are fully documented in the .NET help files); just copy them if you ever need to use them again.

At this stage, you have enough details to connect to a database and fetch data, but don't have any way to *display* it. For that we are going to use the `MxDataGrid` control:

```
<wmx:MxDataGrid id="MxDataGrid2" runat="server"
  DataSourceControlID="AccessDataSourceControl2" BorderColor="#CCCCCC"
  AllowSorting="true" DataMember="Suppliers" AllowPaging="true"
  BackColor="White" CellPadding="3" DataKeyField="SupplierID"
  BorderWidth="1px" BorderStyle="None">
    <PagerStyle horizontalalign="Center" forecolor="#000066"
      backcolor="White" mode="NumericPages"></PagerStyle>
    <FooterStyle forecolor="#000066" backcolor="White"></FooterStyle>
    <SelectedItemStyle font-bold="true" forecolor="White"
      backcolor="#669999"></SelectedItemStyle>
    <ItemStyle forecolor="#000066"></ItemStyle>
    <HeaderStyle font-bold="true" forecolor="White"
      backcolor="#006699"></HeaderStyle>
</wmx:MxDataGrid>
```

This may seem complex but is actually very simple. Let's look at all of the attributes:

Attribute	Description
DataSourceControlID	This contains the ID of the data source control from which data will be fetched. In this case, it's the ID of the `AccessDataSourceControl` we described earlier.
BorderColor	This is the color of the grid border.
AllowSorting	Indicates whether or not the grid will support sorting.
DataMember	This contains the database table name.
AllowPaging	Indicates whether or not the grid supports paging. The default number of rows in a page is 10, and this can be changed with the `PageSize` attribute.
BackColor	This is the background color for the grid.
CellPadding	This defines the amount of padding between grid cells. A higher number means the cells will be spaced further apart.
DataKeyField	This is the primary key of the table.
BorderWidth	This is how wide the border of the grid is. Here it is 1 pixel (px stands for pixel), which is a thin border.
BorderStyle	This is the style of the border.

As part of the grid, we also have some style elements:

❑ PagerStyle: Defines the style of the pager section. In our grid, this is the last row showing the page numbers, but it appears before the footer if a footer row is being shown.

❑ FooterStyle: Defines the style of the footer row. In our grid, we aren't showing a footer, but the style is set so that the footer will look correct if it is shown.

❑ SelectedItemStyle: Defines the style of items when they are selected. Our grid isn't selectable by default, but like the FooterStyle the default style is set in case item selection is added.

❑ ItemStyle: Defines the style for each row of data in the grid.

❑ HeaderStyle: Defines the style for the header row, where the column names are shown.

That's all there is to this example – two controls that are linked together. When the page is loaded, the AccessDataSourceControl connects to the database and runs the command. The MxDataGrid then fetches the data stored by the data source control and constructs a grid around it. In fact, the grid is the most complex piece of code here because of all the properties being set - purely to change the look. At its simplest, you could have the following:

```
<wmx:MxDataGrid id="MxDataGrid2" runat="server"
  DataSourceControlID="AccessDataSourceControl2">
</wmx:MxDataGrid>
```

This only contains the attributes required to display data.

Displaying Data Using the Web Matrix Template Pages

You've probably noticed a number of *template pages* when you add a new page in Web Matrix – some of those are for data reports. These provide a simple way to get more functionality into grids than the example earlier used.

The supplied template pages are as follows:

❑ Simple Data Report: Gives a simple grid without paging or sorting

❑ Filtered Data Report: Gives a grid with a filter option, so you can select the rows displayed

❑ Data Report with Paging: Gives a grid with paging enabled

❑ Data Report with Paging and Sorting: Gives a grid with paging and column sorting enabled

❑ Master – Detail Grids: Gives two grids, representing a master table and a child table

❑ Editable Grid: Gives a grid allowing updates to the data

❑ Simple Stored Procedure: Gives a grid that uses a stored procedure for its data source

All of these supplied templates connect to a SQL Server database, and need modification if they are to be used with a different database. However, they provide a quick way to get pages constructed, allowing you to make a few simple changes to get what you need, rather than coding from scratch.

Let's look at one of these - the report with paging and sorting.

Try It Out Creating a Data Page

1. Create a new page using the **Data Pages** templates. Pick the **Data Report with Paging and Sorting**, and call it `SortPage.aspx`.

2. In the design window, select the **All** tab and change this line:

```
<%@ import Namespace="System.Data.SqlClient" %>
```

To:

```
<%@ import Namespace ="System.Data.OleDb" %>
```

If this is not done, errors will be encountered while loading the page.

3. In the design window, select the **Code** tab, find the `BindGrid()` subroutine, and change the code so it looks like the following:

```
void BindGrid()
{
  // TODO: update the ConnectionString value for your application
  string ConnectionString = "Provider=Microsoft.Jet.OLEDB.4.0; " +
                            "Data Source=C:\BegASPNet11\data\Northwind.mdb";
  string CommandText;

  // TODO: update the CommandText value for your application
  if (SortField == String.Empty)
    CommandText = "select * from Suppliers order by CompanyName";
  else
    CommandText = "select * from Suppliers order by " + SortField;

  OleDbConnection myConnection = new OleDbConnection(ConnectionString);
  OleDbDataAdapter myCommand = new OleDbDataAdapter(CommandText,
                                                    myConnection);

  DataSet ds = new DataSet();
  myCommand.Fill(ds);

  DataGrid1.DataSource = ds;
  DataGrid1.DataBind();
}
```

Use a different path if you've installed the samples in a directory other than `C:\BegASPNET11`.

4. Save the file and run it; you'll see something like Figure 8-6:

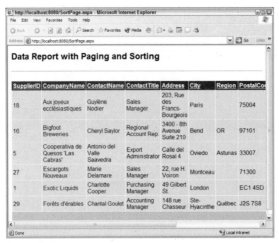

Figure 8-6

This isn't much different from the drag and drop approach we used in the first example, but it uses the .NET data classes and a `DataGrid` control, rather than the Web Matrix controls (`AccessDataSourceControl` and `MxDataGrid`). It means this technique will work even if Web Matrix isn't installed on the server running the page. Let's see how it works.

How It Works

The first thing to look at is the namespace change:

```
<%@ import Namespace="System.Data.OleDb" %>
```

By default, the data pages are configured to use SQL Server and therefore use the `SqlClient` namespace. Since we are using Access, we have to use the `OleDb` namespace.

Now let's look at the declaration of the grid itself. We won't show all the properties, as some are to do with the visual style. Instead, we'll concentrate on those that are related to the code we'll see:

```
<asp:datagrid id="DataGrid1" runat="server"
    AllowPaging="true" PageSize="6" OnPageIndexChanged="DataGrid_Page"
    AllowSorting="true" OnSortCommand="DataGrid_Sort">
```

Here we have the following properties defined:

❑ `AllowPaging`: When set to `true`, allows the grid to page the results. This works in a way similar to the `MxDataGrid` where the page numbers are shown at the bottom of the grid.

❑ `PageSize`: Defines the number of rows to show per page.

❑ `OnPageIndexChanged`: Defines the event procedure to call when the page number is changed. When a page number link is clicked, the procedure defined here is run.

❑   `AllowSorting`: Allows the grid to sort the rows on the basis of column selections. Setting this to `true` enables links on the column headings.

❑   `OnSortCommand`: Defines the event procedure to call when a column heading is clicked.

Now let's look at the code that uses this grid, starting with the `Page_Load()` event:

```
void Page_Load(object sender, EventArgs e)
{
  if (!Page.IsPostBack) {

    // Databind the data grid on the first request only
    // (on postback, rebind only in paging and sorting commands)

    BindGrid();
  }
}
```

Here we are calling the `BindGrid()` routine, but only if this is the first time the page has been loaded. This ensures that the grid, in its initial state, displays data in a default sort order. You'll see how this works as we go through the code.

Next, we have two events for the grid. The first is for when a page is selected on the grid, and is the event procedure defined in the `OnPageIndexChanged` attribute:

```
void DataGrid_Page(object sender, DataGridPageChangedEventArgs e)
{
  DataGrid1.CurrentPageIndex = e.NewPageIndex;
  BindGrid();
}
```

Notice that the second argument to this procedure is of type `DataGridPageChangedEventArgs`. This is automatically sent by ASP.NET and contains two properties, of which we are interested in only one – `NewPageIndex`. This identifies the number of the page selected, so we set the `CurrentPageIndex` property of the grid to the selected page number. We then call the `BindGrid()` routine to re-fetch the data and bind it to the grid. Later, we'll look at why you need to do this.

The second event procedure is for sorting the grid, and is defined in the `OnSortCommand` attribute:

```
void DataGrid_Sort(object sender, DataGridSortCommandEventArgs e)
{
  DataGrid1.CurrentPageIndex = 0;
  SortField = e.SortExpression;
  BindGrid();
}
```

The second argument for this procedure is of type `DataGridSortCommandEventArgs`, which contains the expression on which the grid is being sorted. In this case, this is automatically set by the `DataGrid` as the column headings are sortable, and so contains the column name.

The first line sets the `CurrentPageIndex` of the grid to 0, having the effect of starting the grid at page 1. We do this because we are re-sorting. We then set `SortField` to the sorted field, and rebind the grid.

Notice that `SortField` hasn't been declared as a variable – in fact it's a property. This might seem confusing because properties are always attached to objects, prompting the question what object is this one attached to. Well, since it hasn't got a named object, ASP.NET takes this as being a *property* of the current Page. By default, a Page doesn't have a SortField property, so we define one:

```
protected String SortField {

  get {
    object o = ViewState["SortField"];
    return (o == null) ? String.Empty : (String)o;
  }
  set {
    ViewState["SortField"] = value;
  }
}
```

The interesting point is that we haven't defined a class. Because we are coding within an ASP.NET page, the Page *is* a class, so all we are doing is adding a property to the page (for the purpose of referencing the sorted field later when we bind the grid). When the page is run, ASP.NET adds your code to the class for the page. It's not like the examples in the previous chapter, where we were creating a separate class – here we want our property to be part of the same class as the rest of the code.

The get part of the property first fetches the sort value from the ViewState into an object variable (all items in ViewState are returned as objects), and then checks to see if the object is null. This would be the case if the sort hasn't been defined, such as the first time the page is loaded. If it is null, then an empty string is returned, otherwise the object is converted to a string with the (String) cast and that is returned. This is a perfectly safe conversion because we know that the ViewState for this item only contains a string, as that's what the set part of the property does. ViewState was covered in *Chapter 6*.

> Using String.Empty *is a special way of defining an empty string, and avoids having to use open and close quotation marks next to each other, where it's often difficult to see if there is a space between the quotation marks.*

Now let's look at the BindGrid() routine:

```
void BindGrid() {
```

The first two lines define string variables to hold the connection string and the text for the command to run. Notice that the connection string has been changed to an Access one:

```
string ConnectionString = "Provider=Microsoft.Jet.OLEDB.4.0; " +
              "Data Source=C:\BegASPNet11\data\Northwind.mdb";
string CommandText;
```

The use of the @ symbol before part of the string tells the C# compiler to treat the string exactly as it is typed. We need to do this because in C#, the backward slash character (\) is treated as an escape sequence, indicating that the following character is something special. To avoid this we can either use to slash characters together (\\), meaning we really want a slash character, or use the @ symbol. Later in the chapter, you'll see examples of the \\ style.

Next, we check the SortField property to see if we are sorting the data in the order selected by the user (that is, if the user has clicked one of the column headings). This is accessing the SortField property of the Page and therefore calls the get part of the property. If the sort order hasn't been defined, the String.Empty is the value of SortField. So we set the command string to order by the CompanyName. If a sort string has been set, then we use that as the sort order. In either case, we are simply selecting all rows and columns from the Suppliers table:

```
      if (SortField == String.Empty)
        CommandText = "select * from Suppliers order by CompanyName";
      else
        CommandText = "select * from Suppliers order by " + SortField;
```

These commands use SQL statements, but we could equally have used stored queries or stored procedures. In practice, you should use stored queries, but using SQL directly here means we don't have to create the stored query – since we're concentrating on ASP.NET we don't want to distract ourselves with the stored procedure. We'll be looking at stored procedures later in the chapter.

Now we come to the part where we connect to the database. Don't worry too much about this code – although we are going to explain it, we're not going to go into too much detail in this section, as we'll be going over the theory later. To define the connection we use an `OleDbConnection` object, and as part of the instantiation we pass in the connection string details. This tells ASP.NET which database to connect to, but doesn't actually open the connection. It defines *where* to connect to when we are ready to connect:

```
      OleDbConnection myConnection = new OleDbConnection(ConnectionString);
```

Now we use an `OleDbDataAdapter` to define the command to run – this will be the SELECT query to fetch the data. The data adapter performs two functions. It provides the link between the database and the `DataSet`. It is also how data is fetched from and sent to the database (we'll be looking at the `DataAdapter` in detail in the next chapter). The two arguments we pass in are the command text to run the SQL statement, and the connection object. These define which command to run and which database to run it against:

```
      OleDbDataAdapter myCommand = new OleDbDataAdapter(CommandText,
                                                        myConnection);
```

Note that we still haven't connected to the database and fetched any data, as we've nowhere to store that data. For that we use a `DataSet` object, which you can think of as a mini database (it's not actually a mini database, but that descriptions works well for the moment). It provides a place for the data to be held while we manipulate it:

```
      DataSet ds = new DataSet();
```

Now that we have all of the pieces in place (the connection, the command to run, and a place to put the data), we can go ahead and fetch the data. For that we use the `Fill()` method of the data adapter, passing in the `DataSet`. This opens the database connection, runs the command, places the data into the `DataSet`, and then closes the database connection.

```
      myCommand.Fill(ds);
```

The data is now in our `DataSet` so we can use it as the `DataSource` for the grid, and bind the grid:

```
      DataGrid1.DataSource = ds;
      DataGrid1.DataBind();
    }
```

This may look like a complex set of procedures, but it's actually a simple set of steps that is used many times when you need to fetch data. You'll be seeing this many times during this book, and we'll go over its theory later so you really understand what's happening. For now though, let's look at another way to save time, by using the Web Matrix *Code Wizards*.

Displaying Data Using the Code Wizards

There are times where both the drag and drop from the Data Explorer and the template pages cannot provide you with exactly what you need. Perhaps you'd like to customize the query, or just add a routine to fetch data to an already existing page. The code wizards allow you to add code routines to a page, giving you a finer control of the data being fetched or updated. Let's give this a go.

Try It Out   Creating a Data Page

1. Create a new blank ASP.NET page called `CodeWizard.aspx`.

2. Switch to Code view and you'll notice that the Toolbox now shows Code Wizards as shown in Figure 8-7:

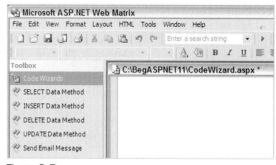

Figure 8-7

3. Pick the SELECT Data Method and drag it from the Toolbox, dropping it into your code window. This starts the wizard, and the first screen as shown in Figure 8-8 is where you pick the database to connect:

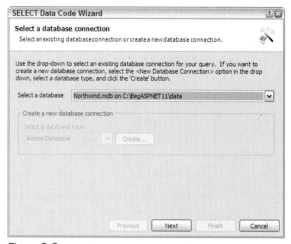

Figure 8-8

4. The drop-down list shows configured data sources (from the Data Explorer) as well as an option to create a new connection. Pick the existing connection and press Next to go to the screen shown in Figure 8-9:

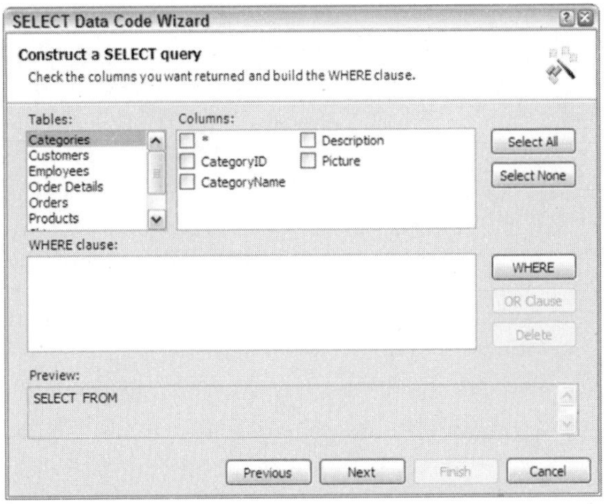

Figure 8-9

Now you can select the columns you wish to show. You can pick multiple columns (the * means all columns from the table) from multiple tables. You simply select them individually. However, when picking columns from multiple tables, you must join the tables. Remember our discussion of linked tables and keys from the beginning of the chapter – you need the primary and foreign key to join the tables.

5. Select the Products table and the ProductName column, and the Categories table and the CategoryName column. Notice the Preview pane at the bottom of the window shows the SQL statement, but without the tables joined together, as shown in Figure 8-10:

Preview:

SELECT [Products].[ProductName], [Categories].[CategoryName] FROM [Products], [Categories]

Figure 8-10

6. To join these tables together, we need a WHERE clause, so press the WHERE button to open the WHERE Clause Builder window.

7. Select your options the same as shown in Figure 8-11:

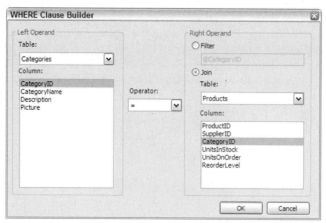

Figure 8-11

8. Click OK and you'll see the WHERE clause part of the window is filled in as shown in Figure 8-12:

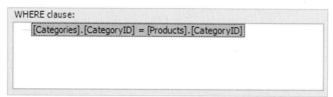

WHERE clause:

[Categories].[CategoryID] = [Products].[CategoryID]

Figure 8-12

9. Press the Next button, and on the Query Preview window press the Test Query button:

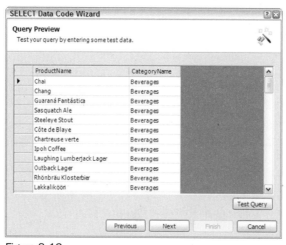

Figure 8-13

You can see just the required columns in Figure 8-13.

10. Press Next.

11. From the **Name Method** window, change the name textbox to `GetProductsDataSet`. Make sure the radio button at the bottom is set to `DataSet` and press **Finish**. We'll look at the `DataReader` later in the chapter.

12. Once the code has been added, you want a way to display it. You can do this by switching to **Design** view and dragging a **DataGrid** onto the page.

13. Switch to **Code** view and add the following code, after the `GetProductsDataSet` function:

```
void Page_Load(Object sender, EventArgs e)
{
  DataGrid1.DataSource = GetProductsDataSet();
  DataGrid1.DataBind();
}
```

14. Save the page and run it – you should see Figure 8-14:

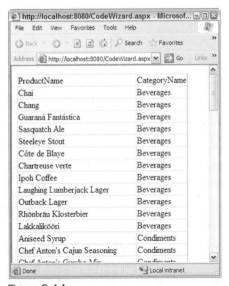

Figure 8-14

You can see how we now only have two columns and from two different tables. Let's see how this works.

How It Works

The key to this is the wizard that allows you to build up an SQL statement. This is great if you are a newcomer to SQL as you don't have to understand how the SQL language works. Perhaps the most important part of this wizard is the WHERE Clause Builder shown in Figure 8-11.

This is where (pun intended) we add the WHERE part of the SQL statement, and this is what filters the rows and joins tables together. We've selected the Join option allowing us to specify the primary key (CategoryID in the Categories table) and the foreign key (CategoryID in the Products table). The WHERE clause becomes:

```
WHERE [Categories].[CategoryID] = [Products].[CategoryID]
```

If we wanted to add a third table, perhaps Suppliers, we could use an AND clause. Once you've declared one WHERE clause, the WHERE button has a different name – **AND Clause** as shown in Figure 8-15:

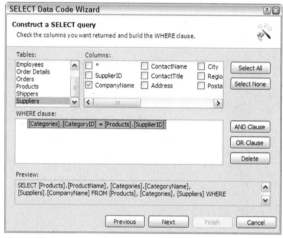

Figure 8-15

Pressing the **AND Clause** button shows the same **WHERE Clause Builder**, but this time you'd set the link between the Suppliers and Products tables as shown in Figure 8-16:

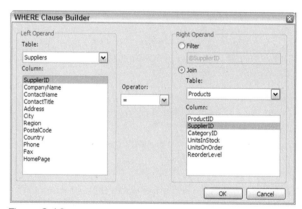

Figure 8-16

Now when you look at the WHERE clause section you see two tables joined together as in Figure 8-17:

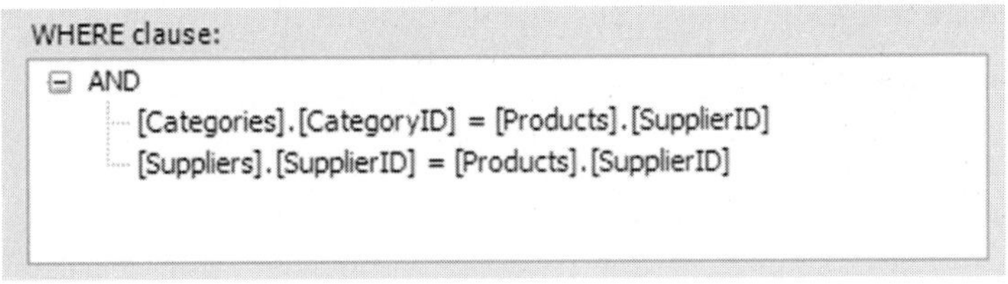

```
WHERE clause:
⊟ AND
      [Categories].[CategoryID] = [Products].[SupplierID]
      [Suppliers].[SupplierID] = [Products].[SupplierID]
```

Figure 8-17

The WHERE Clause Builder can also be used to filter data so that only *selected* rows are shown; we'll look at that later. For now though, let's look at the code the wizard created for us (it may look slightly different in your page – we've wrapped it so it's easier to read):

```
System.Data.DataSet GetProductsDataSet() {
   string connectionString = "Provider=Microsoft.Jet.OLEDB.4.0; " +
         "Ole DB Services=-4; Data Source=C:\\BegASPNET11\\" +
         "data\\Northwind.mdb";
   System.Data.IDbConnection dbConnection =
         new System.Data.OleDb.OleDbConnection(connectionString);

   string queryString = "SELECT [Products].[ProductName], " +
         "[Categories].[CategoryName] FROM [Products], [Categories] " +
         "WHERE ([Categories].[CategoryID] = [Products].[CategoryID])";
   System.Data.IDbCommand dbCommand = new System.Data.OleDb.OleDbCommand();
   dbCommand.CommandText = queryString;
   dbCommand.Connection = dbConnection;

   System.Data.IDbDataAdapter dataAdapter =
         new System.Data.OleDb.OleDbDataAdapter();
   dataAdapter.SelectCommand = dbCommand;
   System.Data.DataSet dataSet = new System.Data.DataSet();
   dataAdapter.Fill(dataSet);

   return dataSet;
}
```

Let's tackle this systematically. First, we have the function declaration:

```
System.Data.DataSet GetProductsDataSet() {
```

This is defined as type `System.Data.DataSet`, which means it's going to return a `DataSet` (we'll look at this in detail in the next chapter). You'll notice that the declaration has the `System.Data` namespace before it. This is done because, while declaring variables or functions, ASP.NET needs to know where the type is stored.

Normally we use the `<%@ import Namespace="..." %>` page directive to indicate the namespaces being used in a page, and thus we don't have to specify the namespace when declaring variables. The wizard isn't sure what namespaces have been set at the top of the page, so it includes the full namespace just-in-case, ensuring that the code will compile under all situations.

Next, we have the connection string that simply points to our existing database:

```
string connectionString = "Provider=Microsoft.Jet.OLEDB.4.0; " +
        "Ole DB Services=-4; Data Source=C:\\BegASPNET11\\" +
        "data\\Northwind.mdb";
```

Notice that this uses two backward slash characters to avoid the problem of the single slash character being an escape sequence. In our earlier example we used the @ symbol.

Now we have the connection object:

```
System.Data.IDbConnection dbConnection =
        new System.Data.OleDb.OleDbConnection(connectionString);
```

One thing that's immediately obvious is the fact that this example doesn't use the `OleDbConnection` type to define the connection to the database; it uses `IDbConnection`. If this seems confusing, refer to the discussion of interfaces in the previous chapter, where we talked about generic routines.

`IDbConnection` is an interface that defines what the `Connection` class must do, and since the wizard is building a generic routine, it uses this interface. This is because the wizard allows you to connect to different database types. This is seen on the first screen and is the same as the **Data Explorer** allowing you to pick either Access or SQL Server database. To make the wizard simpler, it uses the generic interface as the type rather than having to use the type for a specific database.

The Interface simply enforces the correct signature on a class implementing the interface. There's no actual requirement for the implementation to do anything. You could have a class that implements the Open() method but that actually does something else instead of opening a connection. It would be dumb, but it could be done.

Next we have the SQL string, as built up by the wizard:

```
string queryString = "SELECT [Products].[ProductName], " +
        "[Categories].[CategoryName] FROM [Products], [Categories] " +
        "WHERE ([Categories].[CategoryID] = [Products].[CategoryID])";
```

Now we have the definition of the command object. In previous examples, we passed the command text directly into the `OleDbDataAdapter`. Underneath, ASP.NET actually creates another object – a `Command` object. However, you don't see that `Command` object, as it is used internally. The wizard creates the `Command` object directly, by making use of the `CommandText` property to store the SQL command, and the `Connection` property to store the database connection. As with the connection that used the interface as its type, the command is also defined as an interface type (`IDbCommand`).

```
System.Data.IDbCommand dbCommand = new System.Data.OleDb.OleDbCommand();
dbCommand.CommandText = queryString;
dbCommand.Connection = dbConnection;
```

Now we have the definition of the data adapter, and as with the connection, the type of the variable is the interface type:

```
System.Data.IDbDataAdapter dataAdapter =
        new System.Data.OleDb.OleDbDataAdapter();
```

We mentioned earlier that the data adapter is the link between our page and the data. As part of this link, the adapter provides not only data fetching, but also data modification. It does so with different command objects, exposed as properties of the adapter. These allow the different commands to run depending upon the action being performed. In this example, we are fetching data so we use the `SelectCommand` property (so named because we are selecting rows to view).

```
dataAdapter.SelectCommand = dbCommand;
```

If you use the data adapter directly, without explicitly creating a `Command`, this is what it does behind the scenes.

To fetch the data, we then create a `DataSet` and use the `Fill()` method of the adapter:

```
System.Data.DataSet dataSet = new System.Data.DataSet();
dataAdapter.Fill(dataSet);
```

And finally, we return the data:

```
    return dataSet;
}
```

This code is more complex than the previous example, but it follows a similar path. It creates a connection, creates a command, creates a data adapter, and then a `DataSet`. A look at these objects and their relationships in more detail will give you a clearer picture of how they work together.

> *To find out more about the `DataAdapter`'s properties and methods consult the .NET Documentation. The `OleDbDataAdapter` is in the `System.Web.OleDb` namespace and the `SqlDataAdapter` is in the `System.Web.SqlClient` namespace.*

ADO.NET

All of the data access we've seen so far is based upon ADO.NET – the common name for all of the data access classes. We'll only be looking at a few of these, and the ones you'll use most are:

- ❑   `Connection`: Provides details of connecting to the database
- ❑   `Command`: Provides details of the command to be run
- ❑   `DataAdapter`: Manages the command, and fetchs and updates data
- ❑   `DataSet`: Provides a store for data
- ❑   `DataReader`: Provides quick read-only access to data

ADO.NET is designed to talk to multiple databases, so there are different objects for different database types. To keep the separation, ADO.NET classes are contained within different namespaces:

- ❑   `System.Data`: Contains the base data objects (such as `DataSet`) common to all databases.

❏ `System.Data.OleDb`: Contains the objects used to communicate to databases via OLEDB. OLEDB provides a common set of features to connect to multiple databases, such as Access, DBase, and so on.

❏ `System.Data.SqlClient`: Provides the objects used to communicate with SQL Server.

For some of the objects there are two copies – one in the `OleDb` namespace, and one in the `SqlClient` namespace. For example, there are two `Connection` objects – `OleDbConnection` and `SqlConnection`. Having two objects means they can be optimized for particular databases. Look at Figure 8-18 to see how they relate to each other:

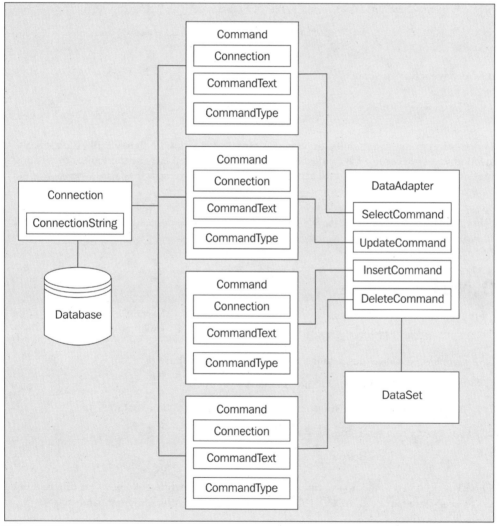

Figure 8-18

On the left we have the database and the connection, in the middle we have four Command objects, and on the right a DataAdapter and a DataSet. Notice that the DataAdapter contains four Command objects:

❑   SelectCommand: Fetches data

❑   UpdateCommand: Updates data

❑   InsertCommand: Inserts new data

❑   DeleteCommand: Deletes data

Each of these Command objects has a Connection property to specify which database the command applies to, a CommandText property to specify the command text to run, and a CommandType property to indicate the type of command (straight SQL or a stored procedure).

As we said earlier, if you don't explicitly create Command objects and use the DataAdapter directly, a Command is created for you using the details passed into the constructor of the DataAdapter, and this Command is used as the SelectCommand.

We'll be looking at the UpdateCommand, InsertCommand, and DeleteCommand in the next chapter.

Let's look at these objects in a bit more detail, concentrating on the OleDb ones as we're using Access. If you want to use SQL Server, you can simply replace OleDb with SqlClient in the object names; just change the connection string, and continue working.

The OleDbConnection Object

As we've said earlier, the Connection object provides us with the means to communicate to a database. Probably the only property you'll use is the ConnectionString property that can either be set as the object is instantiated:

```
string connectionString = "Provider=Microsoft.Jet.OLEDB.4.0; " +
         "Data Source=C:\\BegASPNET11\\data\\Northwind.mdb";
OleDbConnection conn = new OleDbConnection(connectionString);
```

or it can be set with the property:

```
string connectionString = "Provider=Microsoft.Jet.OLEDB.4.0; " +
         "Data Source=C:\\BegASPNET11\\data\\Northwind.mdb";
OleDbConnection conn = new OleDbConnection();
conn.ConnectionString = connectionString;
```

The two main methods you'll use are Open() and Close(), which (unsurprisingly) open and close the connection to the database. When used as we have so far, there is no need to do this explicitly since the Fill() method of a DataAdapter does it for you.

The OleDbCommand Object

The OleDbCommand has several properties that we'll be looking at:

Property	Description
CommandText	Contains the SQL command or the name of a stored procedure.
CommandType	Indicates the type of command being run, and can be one of the CommandType enumeration values, which are:

	StoredProcedure	To indicate a stored procedure is being run.
	TableDirect	To indicate the entire contents of a table are being returned. In this case, the CommandText property should contain the table name. This value only works for Oledb connections.
	Text	To indicate a SQL text command. This is the default value.

Property	Description
Connection	The Connection object being used to connect to a database.
Parameters	A collection or Parameter objects, which are used to pass details to and from the command.

The three main methods of the command you'll use are the execute methods:

Method	Description
ExecuteNonQuery()	This executes the command but doesn't return any data. It is useful for commands that perform an action, such as updating data, but don't need to return a value.
ExecuteReader()	This executes the command and returns a DataReader object.
ExecuteScalar()	This executes the command and returns a single value.

In the examples so far, we haven't used these methods as the execution of the command is handled transparently for us. You'll see the ExecuteReader() method in action when you look at the DataReader, and the ExecuteNonQuery() method in action in the next chapter.

The Parameters Collection

A parameter is an unknown value – a value that ADO.NET doesn't know until the page is being run, and is often used to filter data based upon some user value. For example, consider a page showing a list of products, with a drop-down list showing the product categories. The user could select a category so that only those categories are shown.

The `Parameters` collection contains a `Parameter` object for each parameter in the query. Thus, a command with three parameters would have objects looking like in Figure 8-19:

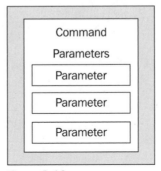

Figure 8-19

Let's look at an example to see how this works.

Try It Out   Using Parameters

1. Create a new blank ASP.NET page called `Parameters.aspx`.

2. Add a Label and change the `Text` property to `Category:`.

3. Add a DropDownList next to the label and change the `ID` property to `lstCategory`.

4. Add a Button next to the DropDownList and change the `Text` property to `Fetch`.

5. Add a DataGrid underneath the other controls. Your page should now look like Figure 8-20:

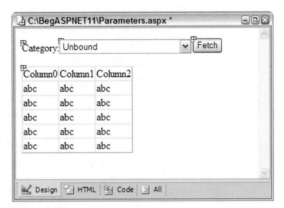

Figure 8-20

6. Double-click the Fetch button to switch to the `Click` event procedure. Add the following code:

```
void Button1_Click(object sender, EventArgs e) {
  DataGrid1.DataSource =
GetProducts(Convert.ToInt32(lstCategory.SelectedValue));
  DataGrid1.DataBind();
}
```

7. Underneath that procedure, add the following code:

```
void Page_Load(Object Sender, EventArgs e)
{
  if (!Page.IsPostBack) {
    lstCategory.DataSource = GetCategories();
    lstCategory.DataValueField = "CategoryID";
    lstCategory.DataTextField = "CategoryName";
    lstCategory.DataBind();
  }
}
```

8. Underneath the preceding block of code, drag a SELECT Data Method wizard from the toolbox onto the page. Pick the current database connection and select the `CategoryID` and `CategoryName` columns from the `Categories` table. Call the procedure that you have created `GetCategories` and have it return a `DataSet`.

9. Drag another SELECT Data Method wizard onto the page, underneath the SELECT Data Method wizard that you just created. Pick the current database connection, and select `ProductName`, `QuantityPerUnit`, `UnitPrice`, and `UnitsInStock` from the `Products` table.

10. Click the WHERE button and pick the `CategoryID` from the `Products` table making it Filter on `@CategoryID`, as shown in Figure 8-21:

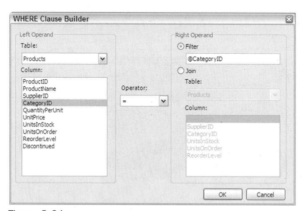

Figure 8-21

11. Click OK and Next to get to the Name Method screen.

12. Call the procedure `GetProducts` and have it return a `DataSet`. Press Finish to insert the code.

13. Save the file and run it.

14. Select a category and then click Fetch to see only the products for that category shown in Figure 8-22:

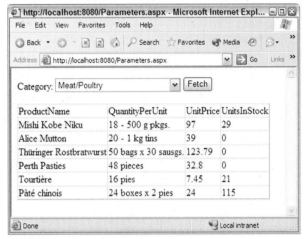

Figure 8-22

What you've achieved here is two things. First, you've used two controls that are bound to data – the list of categories and the grid of products. Second, you only fetched the products for a selected category – you've filtered the list. Let's see how this works.

How It Works

Let's start the code examination with the `Page_Load()` event, where we fill the `Categories` list:

```
void Page_Load(Object Sender, EventArgs e) {
```

We only want to fetch the data and bind it to the list the first time the page is loaded, so we use the `IsPostBack` property of the page to check if this is a postback. If it isn't, it must be the first load, so we fetch the data. We don't need to do this on subsequent page requests as the list itself stores the data.

```
if (!Page.IsPostBack) {
   lstCategory.DataSource = GetCategories();
```

Instead of calling the `DataBind` straight away, we want to tell the list which columns from the data to use. A `DropDownList` stores two pieces of information – one is shown on the page (the text field), and the other is hidden (the value field). The text field is used for what the user needs to see, while the value field often contains an ID – what the user doesn't need to see. The `DropDownList` doesn't automatically know which columns contain these pieces of information, thus we use the `DataValueField` and `DataTextField` properties. The `DataValueField` is the `CategoryID`, the unique key for the category, and this will be used later in our code:

```
        lstCategory.DataValueField = "CategoryID";
        lstCategory.DataTextField = "CategoryName";
        lstCategory.DataBind();
    }
}
```

When the Fetch button is clicked, we need to get the value from the `DropDownList`. For this, we use the `SelectedValue` property, which is new to ASP.NET 1.1. This contains the ID of the selected category, and we pass this into the `GetProducts` routine, which will return a `DataSet` of the products.

However, we can't pass this value directly into `GetProducts` as an integer value is expected, and the `SelectedValue` returns a string. So we have to convert it first using the `ToInt32` method of the `Convert` class. This is a static class method (which doesn't require an instance of the `Convert` class) and simply takes a single string argument. The return value from `ToInt32` is an integer representation of the string passed in.

The `DataSet` returned from `GetProducts` is set to the `DataSource` of the grid and the `DataBind` method is called to bind the data:

```
void Button1_Click(object sender, EventArgs e) {
  DataGrid1.DataSource =
                    GetProducts(Convert.ToInt32(lstCategory.SelectedValue));
  DataGrid1.DataBind();
}
```

There are two routines to fetch data, but one of them is the same as we've already seen – using a simple `DataSet` to fetch data (in this case the `Categories`). What we want to see is the `GetProducts` routine, which gets *filtered* data. The first thing to notice is that it accepts an `int` argument – this will contain the `CategoryID`, passed in from the button click event:

```
System.Data.DataSet GetProducts(int categoryID) {
```

Next, we define the connection details, as we've seen in previous examples:

```
string connectionString = "Provider=Microsoft.Jet.OLEDB.4.0; " +
        "Ole DB Services=-4; Data Source=C:\\BegASPNET11\\" +
        "data\\Northwind.mdb";
System.Data.IDbConnection dbConnection =
        new System.Data.OleDb.OleDbConnection(connectionString);
```

Then we define the query:

```
string queryString = "SELECT [Products].[ProductName], " +
                     "[Products].[QuantityPerUnit], [Products].[UnitPrice],"+
                     "[Products].[UnitsInStock] FROM [Products] " +
                     "WHERE ([Products].[CategoryID] = @CategoryID)";
```

Note that the `WHERE` clause is filtering on `CategoryID`. However, the value used for the filter (`@CategoryID`) is not a real value but a *placeholder*. This tells ADO.NET that the value will be supplied by a parameter.

Once the query string is set, we define our command to run the query, as follows:

```
System.Data.IDbCommand dbCommand = new System.Data.OleDb.OleDbCommand();
dbCommand.CommandText = queryString;
dbCommand.Connection = dbConnection;
```

Now we come to the definition of the parameter. Like many of the other examples, this uses a database specific object – an `OleDbParameter`, which defines what is being passed into the query:

```
System.Data.IDataParameter dbParam_categoryID =
    new System.Data.OleDb.OleDbParameter();
```

We then set the properties of the parameter. The `ParameterName` indicates the name of the parameter, and we set the value to be the same as the placeholder. The `Value` property stores the value for the parameter, and is set to the `CategoryID` passed into the procedure from the button click event – it's the ID of the category selected from the list. The `DbType` property indicates the database type – `Int32` is the database equivalent of an `Integer`:

```
dbParam_categoryID.ParameterName = "@CategoryID";
dbParam_categoryID.Value = categoryID;
dbParam_categoryID.DbType = System.Data.DbType.Int32;
```

At this point, even though we have a `Parameter` object, it's not associated with the command, so we add it to the `Parameters` collection of the command:

```
dbCommand.Parameters.Add(dbParam_categoryID);
```

When ADO.NET processes the command, it matches parameters in the collection with the placeholders in the query and substitutes the placeholder with the value in the parameter.

The rest of the code is as we've seen it before. We create a `DataAdapter` to run the command, and use the `Fill()` method to fetch the data into our `DataSet`:

```
System.Data.IDbDataAdapter dataAdapter =
            new System.Data.OleDb.OleDbDataAdapter();
dataAdapter.SelectCommand = dbCommand;
System.Data.DataSet dataSet = new System.Data.DataSet();
dataAdapter.Fill(dataSet);

return dataSet;
}
```

As you can see, there really isn't that much code; even though we've introduced a new object, much of the code remains the same.

Filtering Queries

There's a very important point to know about filtering data, as you may see code elsewhere that uses a bad method of doing it – it simply builds up the SQL string (as we've done), but instead of using parameters, it just appends the filter value to the SQL string. For example, you might see this:

```
string queryString = "SELECT [Products].[ProductName], "
                "[Products].[QuantityPerUnit], [Products].[UnitPrice]," +
                "[Products].[UnitsInStock] FROM [Products] " +
                "WHERE ([Products].[CategoryID] = " + CategoryID + ")";
```

This simply appends the CategoryID value (from the function argument) into the SQL string. Why is this bad when it achieves the same objectives while using lesser code? The answer has to do with hacking. This type of method potentially allows what are known as *SQL Injection Attacks*, which are 'very bad things' (do a Web search for more details on SQL Injection). If you have a scale for 'bad things to do', then this is right up there, at the top!

Using Parameters protects you from this. Although it has the same effect, the processing ADO.NET does secure you against this type of attack.

Although using Parameters involves a little more work, it's much safer and should always be used.

The OleDataAdapter Object

The OleDbDataAdapter contains the commands used to manipulate data. The four Command objects it contains are held as properties; SelectCommand, UpdateCommand, InsertCommand, and DeleteCommand. The SelectCommand is automatically run when the Fill() method is called. The other three commands are run when the Update method is called – we'll be looking at this in the next chapter.

The DataSet Object

While the other objects we've looked at have different classes for different databases, the DataSet is common to all databases, and is therefore in the System.Data namespace. It doesn't actually communicate with the database – the DataAdapter handles all communication.

The DataSet has many properties and methods; we'll look at them in the next chapter. Since this chapter is concentrating on displaying data, all you need to remember is that when we fetch data it is stored in the DataSet, and then we bind controls to that data.

The DataReader Object

The DataReader, an object that we haven't come across yet, is optimised for reading data. When dealing with databases, connecting to them and fetching the data can often be the longest part of a page, therefore we want to do it as quickly as possible. We also want to ensure that the database server isn't tied up – we want not only to get the data quickly, but also stay connected to the database for as little time as possible.

For this reason we aim to open the connection to the database as late as possible, get the data, and close the connection as soon as possible. This frees up database resources, allowing the database to process other requests. This is the technique that the DataAdapter uses when filling a DataSet. If you manually open a connection, it isn't automatically closed.

Many times, when fetching data we simply want to display it as it is, perhaps by binding it to a grid. The `DataSet` provides a local store of the data, which is often more than we need, so we can use an `OleDbDataReader` to stream the data directly from the database into the grid. Let's give this a go.

Try It Out **Using a DataReader**

1. Create a new blank ASP.NET page called `DataReader.aspx`.

2. Drag a DataGrid control from the Toolbox onto the page.

3. Switch to Code view and start the code wizard by dragging the SELECT Data Method onto the code page.

4. Select the existing database connection from the first screen and press Next.

5. Select the Products table, and from the Columns select ProductName, QuantityPerUnit, UnitPrice, and UnitsInStock.

6. Click Next, and Next again, to go past the Query Preview screen.

7. Enter `GetProductsReader` as the method name, and select the DataReader option on the Name Method screen.

8. Press Finish to insert the code into your page.

9. Underneath the newly inserted method, add the following:

```
void Page_Load(Object sender, EventArgs e) {
  DataGrid1.DataSource = GetProductsReader();
  DataGrid1.DataBind();
}
```

10. Save the page and run it.

You'll see a grid containing just the selected columns. This doesn't look very different from the other examples, but it's how the data is fetched that's important. Let's look at this.

How It Works

Let's start by looking at the code that the wizard generated for us. The declaration of the function returns an `IDataReader` – the interface that data readers implement:

```
System.Data.IDataReader GetProductsReader() {
```

Next we have the connection details – these are the same as you've previously seen (although they might look different in your code file, as this has been formatted to fit on the page):

```
string connectionString = "Provider=Microsoft.Jet.OLEDB.4.0; " +
          "Ole DB Services=-4; Data Source=C:\\BegASPNET11\\" +
          "data\\Northwind.mdb";
  System.Data.IDbConnection dbConnection =
        new System.Data.OleDb.OleDbConnection(connectionString);
```

Next, we have the query string and the command details:

```
string queryString = "SELECT [Products].[ProductName], " +
      "[Products].[QuantityPerUnit], [Products].[UnitPrice], " +
```

```
               "[Products].[UnitsInStock] FROM [Products]";
        System.Data.IDbCommand dbCommand = new System.Data.OleDb.OleDbCommand();
        dbCommand.CommandText = queryString;
        dbCommand.Connection = dbConnection;
```

Once the command details are set, we can open the database connection:

```
        dbConnection.Open();
```

Even though the database connection has been opened for us when using a `DataSet`, we still have to open it manually because we are using an `OleDbCommand` and a data reader.

Next, we declare the data reader. It is of type `IDataReader` and the object is created by the return value of the `ExecuteReader()` method of the command:

```
        System.Data.IDataReader dataReader =
              dbCommand.ExecuteReader(System.Data.CommandBehavior.CloseConnection);
```

Remember that the command has the SQL statement, so `ExecuteReader()` tells ADO.NET to run the command and return a data reader. The argument indicates that as soon as the data is finished with the connection to the database, the connection should be closed. When using `ExecuteReader()`, you should always add this argument to make sure the connection is closed as soon as it is no longer required.

Finally, we return the reader object:

```
        return dataReader;
    }
```

To bind to the grid, we simply use this function as the `DataSource` for the grid. Since the function returns a stream of data, the grid just binds to that data:

```
    void Page_Load(Object sender, EventArgs e) {
        DataGrid1.DataSource = GetProductsReader();
        DataGrid1.DataBind();
    }
```

DataReader Methods and Properties

The `DataReader` exists as `SqlDataReader` (for SQL Server) and `OleDbDataReader` (for other databases), as well as a common `IDataReader` interface. If you are not using generic code, you can create the reader as follows:

```
    System.Data.OleDbDataReader dataReader = new _
    dbCommand.ExecuteReader(System.Data.CommandBehavior.CloseConnection);
```

Using data readers is the most efficient way of fetching data from a database, but you don't have to bind to a grid. You can use the properties and methods to fetch the data directly. If you do this, it's best to use the `OleDbDataReader` rather than the interface, as the `OleDbDataReader` contains more properties that make it easier to use. For example, consider the following code:

```
System.Data.OleDbDataReader dataReader = new _
dbCommand.ExecuteReader(System.Data.CommandBehavior.CloseConnection);

if (!dataReader.HasRows)
  Response.Write("No rows found");
else
  while (dataReader.Read())
    Response.Write(dataReader("ProductName") + "<br />";

dataReader.Close();
```

This first uses the `HasRows` property to determine if there are any rows, and then uses the `Read` method to read a row. This is done within a loop, with `Read` returning the `true` if there is a current row and moving onto the next, and `false` if there are no rows.

Summary

The results of the examples in this chapter have been relatively simple, but you've actually learned a lot. The first three main topics looked at how to use the Web Matrix to reduce your development time, taking away much of the legwork you'd normally have to do. We looked at the using the **Data Explorer** to drag and drop tables directly onto page, using the Web Matrix template pages, and using the code wizards.

After looking at the quick way of getting data, you saw the theory behind it, examining the objects. Even though we continued to use the wizards to generate code, you were now able to see how this wizard code worked (just because we understand how it works doesn't mean we abandon anything that makes our job easier).

Now it's time to look at taking your data usage one step further by showing how to update data, and how to manage your data-handling routines.

Exercises

1. In this chapter we created a page that showed only the products for a selected category. Try and think of ways to enhance this to show products for either a selected category or all categories.

2. In Exercise 1, we wanted to bind data from a database to a `DropDownList` as well as manually add an entry. There are two ways to solve this issue – using techniques shown in this chapter, and using techniques not yet covered. Try and code the solution using the known technique, but see if you can think of a way to solve it using a new technique.

Advanced Data Handling

In the previous chapter, we looked at various ways of reading data, how Web Matrix saves us some of the effort involved in writing code, and how ADO.NET objects work. Displaying data on a Web page is only half the story, as there are many times when you want to update the data as well. As we saw in the previous chapter, there are several ways in which this can be achieved; some more suitable in certain situations than others.

In this chapter, we will look at ways of updating data, as well as some advanced topics that didn't really fit in the previous chapter. In particular, this chapter covers:

❑   A close look at the `DataTable` and `DataRow` objects

❑   Updating data in a `DataSet`

❑   Using the `DataSet` to update the original database

Let's start with a detailed look at some of the ADO.NET objects.

More Data Objects

In the previous chapter, we looked at the `DataSet`, but didn't really examine it in depth. It was used as a repository of data to which we could bind grids. In this chapter, we will not only discuss `DataSet` in detail, but also look at the objects that the `DataSet` contains. In the examples until now, we've only fetched one set of data from a database, but the `DataSet` has the ability to hold more than one set of data. It does this by having a `Tables` collection containing a `Table` object for each set of data. Each table in turn has a `Rows` collection with a `Row` object for each row of data. Let's look at this in more detail.

The DataTable Object

The `DataTable` object is held in the `Tables` collection as part of the `DataSet`, as shown in Figure 9-1:

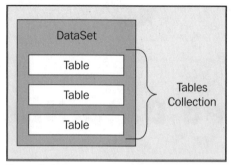

Figure 9-1

In the previous chapter, our `DataSet` contained just a single table; we need to know how to get more than one table into a `DataSet`. This is done by using different text for the command to be run, and calling the `Fill()` command of the `DataAdapter` again – if the table name in the command text is different then a new table in the `DataSet` will be created. For example, you can do this:

```
string connectionString = "Provider=Microsoft.Jet.OLEDB.4.0; " +
        "Ole DB Services=-4; Data Source=C:\\BegASPNET11\\" +
        "data\\Northwind.mdb";
System.Data.IDbConnection dbConnection =
        new System.Data.OleDb.OleDbConnection(connectionString);

string queryString = "SELECT * from Products"
System.Data.IDbCommand dbCommand = new System.Data.OleDb.OleDbCommand();
dbCommand.CommandText = queryString;
dbCommand.Connection = dbConnection;

System.Data.IDbDataAdapter dataAdapter = new
System.Data.OleDb.OleDbDataAdapter();
dataAdapter.SelectCommand = dbCommand;
System.Data.DataSet dataSet = new System.Data.DataSet();
dataAdapter.Fill(dataSet);

dataAdapter.SelectCommand.CommandText = "SELECT * FROM Employees";
dataAdapter.Fill(dataset);
```

Most of this code is exactly as you've seen it in the previous chapter – creating a connection and setting the command before using `Fill()`. However, we then change the `CommandText` of the `SelectCommand` to a new SQL command and call the `Fill()` method again. This gives two tables to our `Tables` collection, and we could access them as follows:

```
DataTable tblProducts = data.Tables[0];
```

Here we are just indexing into the `Tables` collection to get the first table. To make this easier to read, we could name the tables as they are filled from the data adapter. For example:

```
dataAdapter.Fill(dataset, "Products");
dataAdapter.SelectCommand.CommandText = "SELECT * FROM Employees"
dataAdapter.Fill(dataset, "Employees");
```

This form of `Fill()` takes two arguments. The first is the same as before – the `DataSet` into which the data is put, and the second is the name of the table, once it's in the collection. Realizing that each table in the `DataSet` has a name allows us to do the following:

```
DataTable tblProducts = data.Tables["Products"];
```

There's no difference between this version and the one where we access the table by its index number, but this version is clearer – it's much easier to see which table you are dealing with in the collection. To use this method of accessing the `Tables` collection, you don't have to specify the name when you use the `Fill()` method. If you leave it out, the name of the source table is used as the name in the collection. Thus the SQL string `SELECT * FROM Products` would result in `Products` being used as the table name.

Since `Tables` is a collection, you can also loop through it if required:

```
foreach (DataTable tbl in data.Tables)
  DoSomethingToTable(tbl);
```

So far in our examples, we've used a `DataGrid` bound to a `DataSet`:

```
DataGrid1.DataSource = data;
DataGrid1.DataBind();
```

This automatically binds to the first table in the collection. To bind to an explicit table, simply specify the table name:

```
DataGrid1.DataSource = data.Tables["Products"];
DataGrid1.DataBind()
```

In fact, because the `DataSet` contains multiple tables, they can each be bound to different controls:

```
DataGrid1.DataSource = data.Tables["Products"]
DataGrid1.DataBind();

DataGrid2.DataSource = data.Tables["Employees"];
DataGrid2.DataBind();
```

The DataRow Object

In the same way that the `DataSet` contains a `Tables` collection, each `DataTable` contains a `Rows` collection, as shown in Figure 9-2:

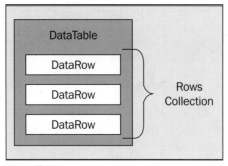

Figure 9-2

Like the `Tables` collection, the `Rows` collection can be indexed:

```
DataRow row = data.Tables["Products"].Rows[0];
```

They can also be enumerated in a loop:

```
foreach (DataRow row in data.Tables["Products"].Rows)
  DoSomethingToRow(row);
```

Let's now look at an example using these two objects.

Try It Out   The DataTable and DataRow Objects

1. Create a blank ASP.NET page called `TableAndRow.aspx` into a new directory called `Ch09`.

2. In the All view, add the following code at the top of the page:

```
<%@ Import Namespace="System.Data" %>
<%@ Import Namespace="System.Data.OleDb" %>
```

3. Add the following code to the server code block:

```
void Page_Load(Object sender, EventArgs e) {
  string connectionString = "Provider=Microsoft.Jet.OLEDB.4.0; " +
    "Ole DB Services=-4; " +
    "Data Source=C:\\BegASPNET11\\data\\Northwind.mdb";
  OleDbConnection dbConnection = new OleDbConnection(connectionString);
  string queryString = "SELECT * FROM Categories";
  OleDbCommand dbCommand = new OleDbCommand();
  dbCommand.CommandText = queryString;
  dbCommand.Connection = dbConnection;
  OleDbDataAdapter dataAdapter = new OleDbDataAdapter();
  dataAdapter.SelectCommand = dbCommand;
  DataSet data = new DataSet();
```

```
    dataAdapter.Fill(data, "Categories");
    dataAdapter.SelectCommand.CommandText = "SELECT * FROM Shippers";
    dataAdapter.Fill(data, "Shippers");
    DataGrid1.DataSource = data.Tables["Categories"];
    DataGrid1.DataBind();
    DataGrid2.DataSource = data.Tables["Shippers"];
    DataGrid2.DataBind();
    Label1.Text = data.Tables["Categories"].Rows[1]["CategoryName"].ToString();
    Label2.Text = data.Tables[1].Rows[2][2].ToString();
}
```

4. Switch to **Design** view and drag the two `DataGrid` controls onto the page. Also drag two the `Label` controls onto the page and position them as headings to describe the contents of the `Datagrid` controls.

5. Save the page and run it to see the result shown in Figure 9-3:

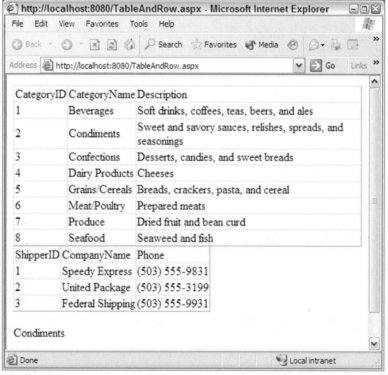

Figure 9-3

How It Works

You have seen most of this code in *Chapter 8*, so let's concentrate on the new bits of it, starting with the filling of the `DataSet`:

```
dataAdapter.Fill(data, "Categories");

dataAdapter.SelectCommand.CommandText = "SELECT * FROM Shippers";
dataAdapter.Fill(data, "Shippers");
```

Here we fill the `DataSet` with the first table, change the `CommandText`, and then fill the `DataSet` with the next table, binding both tables to different grids:

```
DataGrid1.DataSource = data.Tables["Categories"];
DataGrid1.DataBind();
DataGrid2.DataSource = data.Tables["Shippers"];
DataGrid2.DataBind();
```

Next we extract some details from the individual lines. The code demonstrates two different ways of indexing into the `Tables` and `Rows` collections, so you can see them in practice:

```
Label1.Text = data.Tables["Categories"].Rows[1]["CategoryName"].ToString();
Label2.Text = data.Tables[1].Rows[2][2].ToString();
```

For the first line we use the table name to get to the correct table, and then pick the second row (remember that collections in .NET are zero-based). This gives us:

```
data.Tables["Categories"].Rows[1]
```

At this stage we are pointing to an individual row. The `DataRow` can be indexed allowing us to extract the column, so we just specify the column name and then use the `ToString()` method to convert this to a string.

The second line does exactly the same thing, but in a different way:

```
Label2.Text = data.Tables[1].Rows[2][2].ToString();
```

Instead of using names for collection indexes, we are using numbers. So we pick the second table in the `Tables` collection and find the second row. You can use either form but using column names makes it clearer to read as well as not relying upon the column order, so it's probably best to stick to this form.

Updating Databases

Pages that display data are all very well, but we also often need to update data. There are two main ways to do this – by modifying data in the `DataSet` and using the `DataAdapter` to send the data back to the database, or by simply running a SQL command to update the data directly.

Which method you should pick depends on what you are doing. If you are making several changes to multiple rows, the `DataSet` method is best. Using this translates into less work for you because you only have to specify the commands and tell the `DataAdapter` to perform the update. If you are only making changes to a single row, the direct command method is often the best.

ADO.NET versus ADO

One thing that you must know is that ADO.NET works in a disconnected manner. This means that when you have a `DataSet`, you are completely disconnected from the database. You can make changes, add rows, and so on, but you are only working within the `DataSet`, and until you explicitly force those changes back onto the database, it remains unchanged. This means that even in something like a grid, where it seems natural to use a `DataSet` because you might change multiple rows, you are only changing a single row at a time.

This is also similar to the way Web applications work – remember they are stateless, meaning that the server doesn't remember things between requests. If you change some data in a `DataSet` and then postback to the server, those changes will be lost.

The reason for designing such a (disconnected) model is better performance – the less time you spend connected to the database, the better the database can run. This is not the way ADO worked, where (unless explicitly stated) you were always connected to the database, and thus the database generally had to do more work. Although you can work in a fully connected mode with ADO.NET, you can only read data this way, but cannot update data.

This disconnected model is an important point to remember about ADO.NET. Let's look at this in detail, starting with the `DataSet` method.

Updating Data in a DataSet

Updating data in a `DataSet` is a two-step process. First, you need to know how to get access to the data within the `DataSet` and then alter it. This doesn't just mean changing values, but also includes adding and deleting rows. Then you have to know how to get those changes back into the database. We'll be doing the following example in stages, showing three simple ways to manipulate the data held in a table.

These examples change the data in the database, so rerunning them will fail unless the data is reset. To reset the data, the downloadable samples for this chapter contain an ASP.NET page called `DataReset.aspx`.

Try It Out   Adding, Editing, and Deleting Rows

1.   Create a new file called `EditingData.aspx` in the Ch09 folder and in the All view delete the existing code, and add the following code:

```
<%@ Page language="C#" %>
<%@ Import Namespace="System.Data" %>
<%@ Import Namespace="System.Data.OleDb" %>
```

```
<script runat="server">

  void Page_Load(Object sender, EventArgs e) {
    string connectionString;
    string queryString;
    DataSet data = new DataSet();
    OleDbConnection dbConnection;
    OleDbDataAdapter dataAdapter;

    connectionString = "Provider=Microsoft.Jet.OLEDB.4.0; " +
                       "Data Source=C:\\BegASPNet11\\data\\Northwind.mdb";
    queryString = "SELECT FirstName, LastName FROM Employees";
    dbConnection = new OleDbConnection(connectionString);
    dataAdapter = new OleDbDataAdapter(queryString, dbConnection);

    dataAdapter.Fill(data, "Employees");

    DataGrid1.DataSource = data;
    DataGrid1.DataBind();

    // -------------------------------------------------------
    // Marker 1

    // -------------------------------------------------------
    // Marker 2

    // -------------------------------------------------------
    // Marker 3
  }
</script>

<html>
 <body>
  <table width="100%">
   <tr>
    <td>Original Data</td>
    <td>Data with new Row</td>
    <td>Data with edited Row</td>
    <td>Data with deleted Row</td>
   </tr>
   <tr>
    <td valign="top"><asp:DataGrid id="DataGrid1" runat="server" /></td>
    <td valign="top"><asp:DataGrid id="DataGrid2" runat="server" /></td>
    <td valign="top"><asp:DataGrid id="DataGrid3" runat="server" /></td>
```

```
        <td valign="top"><asp:DataGrid id="DataGrid4" runat="server" /></td>
      </tr>
    </table>
  </body>
</html>
```

The Marker 1, 2, and 3 comments will help you add code as we expand this example.

2. Run the file and you'll see the result shown in Figure 9-4:

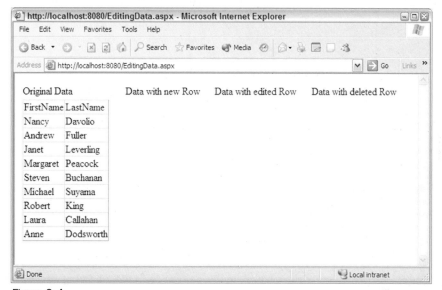

Figure 9-4

This is no different from some of the examples you saw in the previous chapter, but it serves as a foundation for showing the changes we'll be making.

3. Switch to your editor and add the following code after `Marker 1`. This will add a row to the table and display it in another grid:

```
DataTable table;
DataRow newRow;

table = data.Tables["Employees"];
newRow = table.NewRow();
newRow["FirstName"] = "Norman";
newRow["LastName"] = "Blake";
table.Rows.Add(newRow);
// bind the second grid to the new data
DataGrid2.DataSource = table;
```

```
DataGrid2.DataBind();
```

4. In the browser, click the Refresh button (or F5) to see the new page, as shown in Figure 9-5:

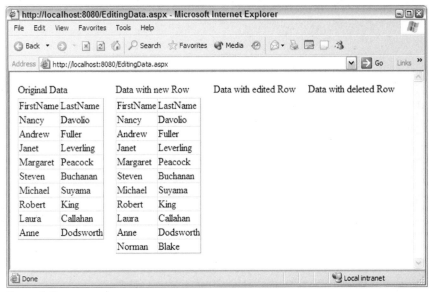

Figure 9-5

Here you can see that another row has been added to the end of the table.

5. Let's look at editing a row. Switch back to the code and add the following after `Marker 2`:

```
DataRow[] selectedRows;

// find the row to change
selectedRows = table.Select("FirstName='Margaret' AND
                             LastName='Peacock'");
selectedRows[0]["FirstName"] = "John";
selectedRows[0]["LastName"] = "Hartford";

// bind the third grid to this new data
DataGrid3.DataSource = table;
DataGrid3.DataBind();
```

6. Back in the browser, click the Refresh button (or F5) to see the new page as shown in Figure 9-6:

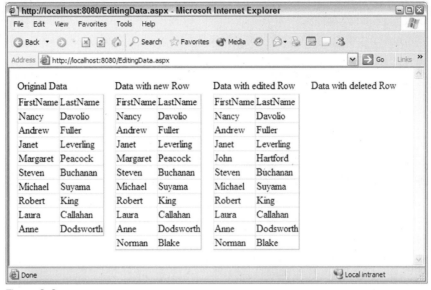

Figure 9-6

You can see that the row for **Margaret Peacock** has been changed to **John Hartford**.

7. Make the last addition to the code by adding the following after `Marker 3`:

```
// The Rows collection is 0 indexed, therefore
// this deletes the sixth row
table.Rows[5].Delete();

// bind the fourth grid to the new data
DataGrid4.DataSource = table;
DataGrid4.DataBind();
```

8. Back in the browser, click the **Refresh** button (or F5) to see the new page as shown in Figure 9-7:

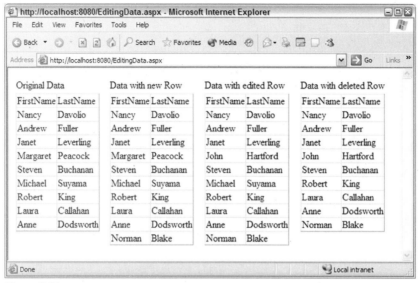

Figure 9-7

Here you can see that the row for **Michael Suyama** has been deleted, and doesn't appear in the fourth table.

Let's see how all this code works. We don't need to examine the code that gets the data from the database or binds it to the grid, as it's the same as the code we used in the previous example. We concentrate here on how we changed the data and the code fragments we put in the markers to do that.

How It Works – Adding Rows

The first section of code adds a new row to the table. The first thing we do is to declare two variables – one to point to the DataTable containing the data, and another to hold the data for the new row:

```
DataTable table;
DataRow newRow;
```

We point the `table` variable to the `Employees` table:

```
table = data.Tables["Employees"];
```

Next, we use the `NewRow()` method of the `DataTable` object to create a new `DataRow`:

```
newRow = table.NewRow();
```

This doesn't create a new `DataRow` in the table – it just provides a new `DataRow` object into which we can add data. We can then add this new row to the table once the data is filled. Note that you could add the empty row and then fill in the details – doesn't matter which way round you do it, but I prefer this way. The new row we've just created is empty, so we need to add some details. The rows in our table only hold first and last name information, but if you have tables with more columns, you can just fill in their values too. The `DataRow` has only those columns requested in the `SelectStatement` when we filled the `DataSet`:

```
newRow["FirstName"] = "Norman";
newRow["LastName"] = "Blake";
```

Now that we've filled in the details, we need to add the new row to the existing table. Using the `NewRow()` method only creates a new `DataRow` object for us, and we have to add it to the table ourselves. This isn't done automatically as ADO.NET doesn't know what we want to do with the new row, so it leaves us to make the choice. If you flip back to Figure 9-2, you'll notice that each `DataTable` has a `Rows` collection. The collection has an `Add` method, into which we pass the `DataRow` that we want to add to the table:

```
table.Rows.Add(newRow);
```

Now that the new row is in the table, all that's left to do is bind the table to the second `DataGrid` on the page, allowing us to see the results:

```
DataGrid2.DataSource = table;
DataGrid2.DataBind();
```

One thing to remember is that you are still disconnected from the database. This means that if your database has constraints, they won't be enforced when adding the data to the `DataSet`. It's only when you update the original data store (which we'll discuss later) that this becomes an issue. You can also create constraints on the `DataSet`, but we won't be covering it here.

> **Constraints are rules held in the database to ensure that the data is correct. For example, a constraint would stop you from deleting an order if there were order lines attached to it.**

How It Works – Editing Rows

The first thing we do in this code section is to declare a variable that can hold the rows we want to edit:

```
DataRow[] selectedRows;
```

Notice that this is an array, because the method we use to find selected rows returns an array of `DataRow` objects.

Next we use the `Select()` method of the table to find the row we want:

```
selectedRows = table.Select("FirstName='Margaret' AND
                             LastName='Peacock'");
```

The string we pass is the same as a SQL `WHERE` clause.

Finally, we update the data for the selected row. There could be many rows returned by the `Select()` method, so we index into the array. In this case we know that there is only one row returned:

```
selectedRows[0]["FirstName"] = "John";
selectedRows[0]["LastName"] = "Hartford";
```

It isn't necessary to use the `Select()` method, since you can edit the data directly, but using this method here makes it clear which row we are editing. What you can also do is just index into the `Rows` collection, using this code:

```
DataRow row;

row = table.Rows[3];

row["FirstName"] = "John";
row["LastName"] = "Hartford";
```

First we declare a variable to hold the row to be edited:

```
DataRow row;
```

Now you can point this variable at the row we are going to edit by indexing into the `Rows` collection. It's important to note that the `Rows` collection (like any other collection) is zero-based, so the following line of code refers to the fourth row:

```
row = table.Rows[3];
```

Once the row variable is pointing to the correct row, we can just update the values for the appropriate columns:

```
row["FirstName"] = "John";
row["LastName"] = "Hartford";
```

Now that the data has been changed, we bind the data to a new grid so we can see the results:

```
DataGrid3.DataSource = table;
DataGrid3.DataBind();
```

How It Works – Deleting Rows

Deleting a row from a table is simple – just use the `Delete()` method of the `DataRow`. In the following code we index into the `Rows` collection (each member of which is a `DataRow`), specifying the row number as the index. Once again, remember that the `Rows` collection is zero-based, so this removes the sixth row:

```
table.Rows[5].Delete();
```

And as we saw before, we bind the data to a new grid:

```
DataGrid4.DataSource = table;
DataGrid4.DataBind();
```

As you saw in the *Editing Rows* section of this Try-It-Out, we could have used the `Select()` method of the table to return the rows to delete.

Updating the Original Data Source

Now that you've seen how to change data with a `DataSet`, you need to get that data back into the database, and to do that we use the `DataAdapter`. Remember in the previous chapter we said that the `DataAdapter` contains a `Command` object for each type of database operation, as shown in Figure 9-8:

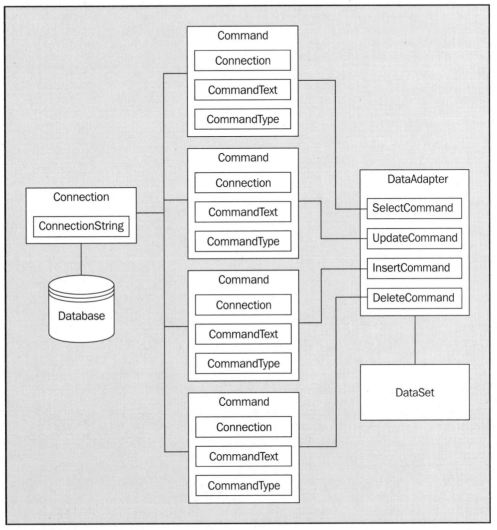

Figure 9-8

The question is how to set these commands, and what to set them to. You've seen the `SelectCommand` being used, but what about the other commands? Well, instead of learning SQL and worrying about this you can automate the process by using the `CommandBuilder`.

The `CommandBuilder` object automatically generates SQL commands using the `SelectCommand` as basis. This way you can concentrate on just coding without worrying about the actual way the commands are constructed.

> *The `CommandBuilder` is good for simple scenarios, but more advanced SQL code may pose a problem. For a good description of these problems go to MSDN (http://msdn.microsoft.com/) and search for the article titled 'Weaning Developers from the CommandBuilder'.*

Let's see in an example, how easy it is to use `CommandBuilder` object:

Try It Out Auto-Generated Commands

1. Create a new blank ASP.NET page called `CommandObjects.aspx`.

2. Switch to All view and delete everything on the page.

3. Add the following code:

```
<%@ Page Language="C#" %>
<%@ import Namespace="System.Data" %>
<%@ import Namespace="System.Data.OleDb" %>
<script runat="server">

  void Page_Load(Object sender, EventArgs e) {

    string connectionString;
    string queryString;
    DataSet data = new DataSet();
    OleDbConnection dbConnection;
    OleDbDataAdapter dataAdapter;
    OleDbCommandBuilder commandBuilder;

    connectionString = "Provider=Microsoft.Jet.OLEDB.4.0; " +
                       "Data Source=C:\\BegASPNet11\\data\\Northwind.mdb";
    queryString = "SELECT EmployeeID, FirstName, LastName FROM Employees";

    // open the connection and set the command
    dbConnection = new OleDbConnection(connectionString);
    dataAdapter = new OleDbDataAdapter(queryString, dbConnection);


    // set the other commands
    commandBuilder = new OleDbCommandBuilder(dataAdapter);
    dataAdapter.UpdateCommand = commandBuilder.GetUpdateCommand();
    dataAdapter.InsertCommand = commandBuilder.GetInsertCommand();
    dataAdapter.DeleteCommand = commandBuilder.GetDeleteCommand();

    // now display the CommandText property for each command
    lblSelectCommand.Text = dataAdapter.SelectCommand.CommandText;
    lblUpdateCommand.Text = dataAdapter.UpdateCommand.CommandText;
    lblInsertCommand.Text = dataAdapter.InsertCommand.CommandText;
    lblDeleteCommand.Text = dataAdapter.DeleteCommand.CommandText;
  }
```

```
    </script>
  <html>
  <head>
  </head>
  <body>
    <form runat="server">
      <table width="100%" border="1">
        <tr>
          <td>Command</td>
          <td>CommandText</td>
        </tr>
        <tr>
          <td>SelectCommand</td>
          <td><asp:Label id="lblSelectCommand" runat="server" />
        </tr>
        <tr>
          <td>UpdateCommand</td>
          <td><asp:Label id="lblUpdateCommand" runat="server" />
        </tr>
        <tr>
          <td>InsertCommand</td>
          <td><asp:Label id="lblInsertCommand" runat="server" />
        </tr>
        <tr>
          <td>DeleteCommand</td>
          <td><asp:Label id="lblDeleteCommand" runat="server" />
        </tr>
      </table>
    </form>
  </body>
  </html>
```

4. Save the file and run it to see the result as shown in Figure 9-9:

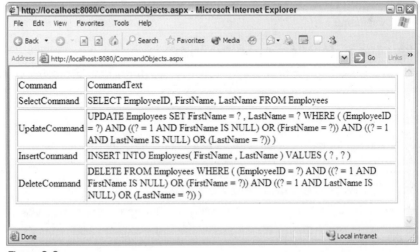

Figure 9-9

You can see that the SQL statements that perform updates have been generated automatically. Let's see how this works.

How It Works

The start of this code is the same as we've seen before – creating a connection and an adapter. The only difference is the declaration of an `OleDbCommandBuilder` object. Like the `DataAdapter`, this deals directly with databases and therefore is in the `OleDb` namespace:

```
OleDbCommandBuilder commandBuilder;
```

Now create the `CommandBuilder` object, using the `DataAdapter` as the argument to the constructor. This ensures that the `CommandBuilder` picks up the `SelectCommand`:

```
commandBuilder = new OleDbCommandBuilder(dataAdapter);
```

Next we use the `Get` methods to fill the other commands – there is a `Get` command for each type of `Command` object that we need to generate:

```
dataAdapter.UpdateCommand = commandBuilder.GetUpdateCommand();
dataAdapter.InsertCommand = commandBuilder.GetInsertCommand();
dataAdapter.DeleteCommand = commandBuilder.GetDeleteCommand();
```

Finally we display the `CommandText` for each of the `Command` objects:

```
lblSelectCommand.Text = dataAdapter.SelectCommand.CommandText;
lblUpdateCommand.Text = dataAdapter.UpdateCommand.CommandText;
lblInsertCommand.Text = dataAdapter.InsertCommand.CommandText;
lblDeleteCommand.Text = dataAdapter.DeleteCommand.CommandText;
```

You can see that the `GetUpdateCommand` simply generates a SQL UPDATE statement, and so on. Let's look at these in more detail.

How It Works - The SelectCommand Property

You've already seen this before, but there is a reason we need to further talk about this. Our initial `SelectCommand` contained:

```
SELECT EmployeeID, FirstName, LastName FROM Employees
```

A unique key is required for the command builder to generate the other commands, so this time we have included the `EmployeeID` in the `SelectCommand`.

How It Works - The UpdateCommand Property

The `UpdateCommand` is built to use a SQL UPDATE statement, for updating a row of data:

```
UPDATE Employees
SET FirstName = ?, LastName = ?
WHERE ((EmployeeID = ?)
AND ((? = 1 AND FirstName IS NULL)
  OR (FirstName =   ?))
```

```
AND ((? = 1 AND LastName IS NULL)
   OR (LastName = ?)) )
```

This consists of three parts:

❑ The UPDATE command followed by the table.

❑ The SET command indicating fields that are to be updated. Here we are updating the FirstName and LastName fields (the EmployeeID field is a primary key and therefore can't be updated). The question marks are placeholders into which ADO.NET will place the updated values.

❑ The WHERE clause that filters data, ensuring that the correct row is updated.

How It Works - The InsertCommand Property

The InsertCommand property is built to use a SQL INSERT statement, for inserting a new row of data:

```
INSERT INTO Employees(FirstName, LastName) VALUES(?, ?)
```

This consists of two parts:

❑ The INSERT INTO statement, specifying the table name and, in parenthesis, the columns being updated.

❑ The VALUES statement, where the question marks are placeholders into which ADO.NET will place the column values for the new row.

How It Works - The DeleteCommand Property

The DeleteCommand is built to use a SQL DELETE statement, for deleting a row of data:

```
DELETE FROM Employees
      WHERE ((EmployeeID = ?)
      AND ((? = 1 AND FirstName IS NULL)
        OR (FirstName =  ?))
      AND ((? = 1 AND LastName IS NULL)
        OR (LastName = ?)) )
```

This consists of two parts:

❑ The DELETE FROM statement followed by the table name.

❑ The WHERE clause, which filters the data, ensuring that the correct row is deleted.

Updating the Database

Our examples so far have shown us how to modify data within a DataSet and how to generate the commands that will force these changes back to the database. What we now need to consider is how the database is actually updated. We've previously said the DataAdapter does this, and it's the Update method we need to use. So let's combine the examples in this page.

In the following Try-It-Out, you'll update some data, use the `CommandBuilder` to generate the update commands, and then send those changes back to the database.

Try It Out — Updating the Database

1. Create a new blank ASP.NET page called `UpdateDatabase.aspx`.

2. Switch to All view and delete everything that's there.

3. Add the following code (or if you're all fingers and thumbs like me, download it from www.wrox.com):

```
<%@ Page language="C#" %>
<%@ import Namespace="System.Data" %>
<%@ import Namespace="System.Data.OleDb" %>
<script runat="server">

  void Page_Load(Object sender, EventArgs e) {


      string connectionString;
      string queryString;
      DataSet data = new DataSet();
      OleDbConnection dbConnection;
      OleDbDataAdapter dataAdapter;


      connectionString = "Provider=Microsoft.Jet.OLEDB.4.0; " +
          "Ole DB Services=-4; " +
          "Data Source=C:\\BegASPNET11\\data\\Northwind.mdb";
      queryString = "SELECT EmployeeID, FirstName, LastName FROM Employees";

      // set the connection and command
      dbConnection = new OleDbConnection(connectionString);
      dbConnection.Open();
      dataAdapter = new OleDbDataAdapter(queryString, dbConnection);

      // fetch the data
      dataAdapter.Fill(data, "Employees");

      // display the data
      DataGrid1.DataSource = data.Tables["Employees"];
      DataGrid1.DataBind();

      // -------------------------------------------------------------
      // start transaction
      //   only to ensure example can be run multiple times
      OleDbTransaction dbTrans = dbConnection.BeginTransaction();

      //-------------------------------------------------------------
      // add a new row to the table
      DataTable table;
      DataRow newRow;
```

```
table = data.Tables["Employees"];
newRow = table.NewRow();
newRow["FirstName"] = "Norman";
newRow["LastName"] = "Blake";
table.Rows.Add(newRow);

// add another new row. We'll be deleting the one above later
// and we can't delete existing rows from the database because
// of referential integrity (every employee also has orders)
newRow = table.NewRow();
newRow["FirstName"] = "Beth";
newRow["LastName"] = "Hart";
table.Rows.Add(newRow);

// bind the second grid to the new data
DataGrid2.DataSource = table;
DataGrid2.DataBind();


//----------------------------------------------------------
// edit an existing row in the table
DataRow row;

// the Rows collection is 0 indexed
// so this will change the fourth row
row = table.Rows[3];
row["FirstName"] = "John";
row["LastName"] = "Hartford";

 // bind the third grid to the new data
 DataGrid3.DataSource = table;
 DataGrid3.DataBind();


//----------------------------------------------------------
// delete a row from the table
table.Rows[table.Rows.Count - 2].Delete();

 // bind the fourth grid to the new data
 DataGrid4.DataSource = table;
 DataGrid4.DataBind();


//----------------------------------------------------------
// generate the update commands
OleDbCommandBuilder commandBuilder = new
```

```
                                          OleDbCommandBuilder(dataAdapter);
    dataAdapter.UpdateCommand = commandBuilder.GetUpdateCommand();
    dataAdapter.InsertCommand = commandBuilder.GetInsertCommand();
    dataAdapter.DeleteCommand = commandBuilder.GetDeleteCommand();


    //---------------------------------------------------------
    // updqate the data store
    dataAdapter.Update(data, "Employees");



    //---------------------------------------------------------
    // refresh the data in the DataReader and bind it to a new grid
    // to prove that the data store has been updated

    queryString = "SELECT EmployeeID, FirstName, LastName FROM Employees";
    dbConnection.Open();
    OleDbCommand cmd = new OleDbCommand(queryString, dbConnection);

    DataGridUpdated.DataSource =
            cmd.ExecuteReader(CommandBehavior.CloseConnection);
    DataGridUpdated.DataBind();

  // ---------------------------------------------------------
  // Rollback transaction, to reset the data
  dbTrans.Rollback();
  }

</script>
<html>
<head>
</head>
<body>
  <form runat="server">
    <table width="100%">
      <tr>
        <td>Original Data</td>
        <td>Data with new Row</td>
        <td>Data with edited Row</td>
        <td>Data with deleted Row</td>
      </tr>
      <tr>
        <td valign="top"><asp:DataGrid id="DataGrid1" runat="server" /></td>
        <td valign="top"><asp:DataGrid id="DataGrid2" runat="server" /></td>
        <td valign="top"><asp:DataGrid id="DataGrid3" runat="server" /></td>
        <td valign="top"><asp:DataGrid id="DataGrid4" runat="server" /></td>
```

```
      </tr>
    </table>
    <hr />
    Data fetched from the database after the update:<br />
    <asp:DataGrid id="DataGridUpdated" runat="server" />
  </form>
</body>
</html>
```

4.   Save the page, run it, and you'll see the results as shown in Figure 9-10:

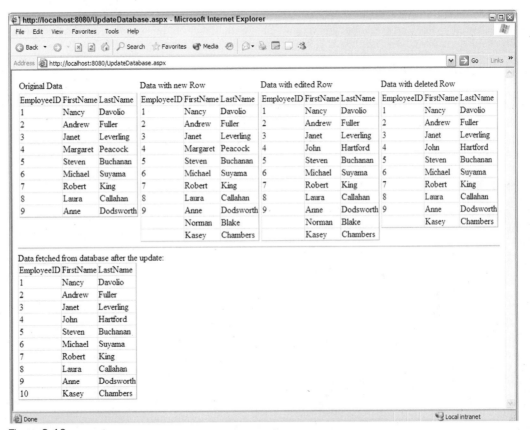

Figure 9-10

How It Works

You've seen most of this code before; the only new parts are the data update and the transactions. Let's look at the update first, since this is what actually changes the data in the database

```
dataAdapter.Update(data, "Employees");
```

Calling the `Update()` method of the `DataAdapter` sends any pending changes back to the database. The two arguments are:

- ❏ The `DataSet` containing the pending changes
- ❏ The name of the table within the `DataSet`

This actually looks through the table for rows that have changed, and then executes the appropriate `Command` object. If a new row has been added, the `InsertCommand` is run using the values from the new row.

In reality, you wouldn't update your data in the `Page_Load()` event – you'd probably have a button on the page allowing the users to send their edits back to the database, and you'd have an event procedure for that button. It's at that stage that you'd update the data. However, this example works fine for the purpose of explaining how simple it is to send the changes back to the database.

How It Works – Transactions

Transactions are not part of the example we are focusing on, but we need to explain what they are and why they've been used. In operations involving multiple actions, a transaction ensures that either *all* the actions of an operation complete, or *none* of them complete. For example, consider a bank transaction, where you transfer money from one account to another. This actually involves two distinct actions – the removal of the money from one account, and the addition of the money to the other. Either both parts must take place, thus ensuring the money has moved, or neither must take place, in which case the money hasn't moved. You can't have a situation where only one part happens!

In databases, transactions work in the same manner. We can wrap many database actions within a transaction to ensure that they all take place. The way this works is:

1. Start a transaction.
2. Make changes to the database.
3. If *all* changes are correct, commit all the changes.
4. If *all* changes are *not* correct, abandon all the changes.

In our example, we actually want to abandon all of the changes. Although we are modifying data in this example, we want to be able to run the sample several times. One way to achieve this would be to reset the data by changing it back to the way it was by running commands again – adding in the deleted rows, etc.

A simpler way however, is to wrap our actions in a transaction. Before we modify any data, we start the transaction, which tells the database that we are performing multiple changes, and that the database should keep track of those changes. The changes are actually made in the database, but because they have been kept track of, we can abandon them if necessary. After we have finalized our changes, we tell the database that we do want to abandon the changes, so the data is returned to its state when the transaction started. It's a simple way to perform multiple changes but not keep any of them permanently.

The transaction is started with this code:

```
OleDbTransaction dbTrans = dbConnection.BeginTransaction();
```

This defines a new `OleDbTransaction` object, which is the transaction started from the connection's `BeginTransaction` method. Transactions can only be started on an open connection, which is why we explicitly opened the connection (it was automatically opened for us in earlier examples). Once the transaction is started, we can perform data edits until we want to abandon the changes, where we use the following line of code:

```
dbTrans.Rollback();
```

This tells the database to rollback the changes to the point at which the transaction started. If we wanted to commit those changes, we would have used the `Commit` method of the transaction.

In the real world, you wouldn't automatically rollback changes, as you'd only do it if some exception occurred. This topic is really outside the scope of this book. Check the .NET Documentation for more details on transactions.

Updating Databases Using a Command

The preceding examples show the modification of data by use of a `DataSet` and a `DataAdapter`, but this isn't the only way it can be done. In the previous chapter, you saw the use of the `Command` object for running SQL commands and we mentioned the use of the `ExecuteNonQuery` method. Let's look at how to use this.

Try It Out   Executing Commands Directly

1. Create a new blank ASP.NET page called `CommandExecute.aspx`.

2. Add a `Label` and a `TextBox` control. Change the `Text` property of the `Label` to `First Name`, and the `ID` property of the `TextBox` to `txtFirstName`.

3. Underneath the first two controls add a second `Label` and a second `TextBox` control. Change the `Text` property of the `Label` to `Last Name`, and the `ID` property of the `TextBox` to `txtLastName`.

4. Underneath these add a button, changing the `Text` property to `Run` and the `ID` property to `btnRun`. Your page should look like Figure 9-11:

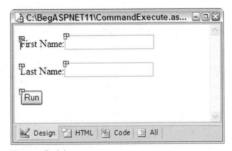

Figure 9-11

5. Double-click the Run button to create the event handler and add the following code:

```
void btnRun_Click(object sender, EventArgs e) {

string connectionString = "Provider=Microsoft.Jet.OLEDB.4.0; "+
   "Ole DB Services=-4; " +
   "Data Source=C:\\BegASPNET11\\data\\Northwind.mdb";
OleDbConnection dbConnection = new OleDbConnection(connectionString);
dbConnection.Open();

string commandString = "INSERT INTO Employees(FirstName, LastName) " +
                       "Values(@FirstName, @LastName)";

OleDbCommand dbCommand = new OleDbCommand(commandString, dbConnection);

OleDbParameter fnParam =
              new OleDbParameter("@FirstName", OleDbType.VarChar, 10);
fnParam.Value = txtFirstName.Text;
dbCommand.Parameters.Add(fnParam);

OleDbParameter lnParam =
              new OleDbParameter("@LastName", OleDbType.VarChar, 20);
lnParam.Value = txtLastName.Text;
dbCommand.Parameters.Add(lnParam);

dbCommand.ExecuteNonQuery();

dbConnection.Close();
}
```

6. Switch to All view and add the following, either at the top of the page, or underneath the `<%@ Page %>` directive:

```
<%@ Import Namespace="System.Data.OleDb" %>
```

7. Save the file and run it.

8. Enter a first and last name and press the button.

9. Switch to Web Matrix and open the Data Explorer. Pick the `Employees` table, open it, and you'll see the newly added data, as shown in Figure 9-12:

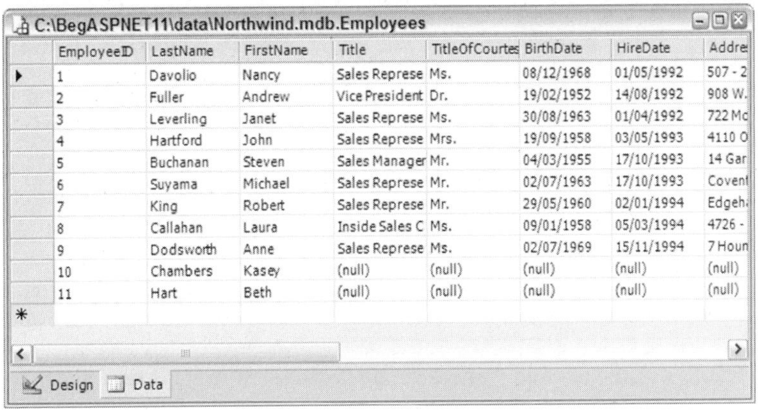

C:\BegASPNET11\data\Northwind.mdb.Employees

EmployeeID	LastName	FirstName	Title	TitleOfCourtes	BirthDate	HireDate	Addre
1	Davolio	Nancy	Sales Represe	Ms.	08/12/1968	01/05/1992	507 - 2
2	Fuller	Andrew	Vice President	Dr.	19/02/1952	14/08/1992	908 W.
3	Leverling	Janet	Sales Represe	Ms.	30/08/1963	01/04/1992	722 Mc
4	Hartford	John	Sales Represe	Mrs.	19/09/1958	03/05/1993	4110 O
5	Buchanan	Steven	Sales Manager	Mr.	04/03/1955	17/10/1993	14 Gar
6	Suyama	Michael	Sales Represe	Mr.	02/07/1963	17/10/1993	Covent
7	King	Robert	Sales Represe	Mr.	29/05/1960	02/01/1994	Edgeh
8	Callahan	Laura	Inside Sales C	Ms.	09/01/1958	05/03/1994	4726 -
9	Dodsworth	Anne	Sales Represe	Ms.	02/07/1969	15/11/1994	7 Houn
10	Chambers	Kasey	(null)	(null)	(null)	(null)	(null)
11	Hart	Beth	(null)	(null)	(null)	(null)	(null)

Design Data

Figure 9-12

You can see that I entered Kasey Chambers and Beth Hart as my new names (I just happen to be listening to their albums at the moment!).

How It Works

You've seen most of the code before, but there are a couple of differences. We first start with the connection, which we open explicitly. That's because we are going to run a command directly, which needs the connection to be open:

```
string connectionString = "Provider=Microsoft.Jet.OLEDB.4.0; "+
  "Ole DB Services=-4; " +
  "Data Source=C:\\BegASPNET11\\data\\Northwind.mdb";
OleDbConnection dbConnection = new OleDbConnection(connectionString);
dbConnection.Open();
```

We then define the command we are going to run. Notice that although this is an SQL `INSERT` statement, it uses placeholders for parameters. We do so because the user is going to supply the values, and using parameters is the secure method of doing this:

```
string commandString = "INSERT INTO Employees(FirstName, LastName) " +
                       "Values(@FirstName, @LastName)";
```

We then create the `Command` object, using the command string shown earlier and the opened connection:

```
OleDbCommand dbCommand = new OleDbCommand(commandString, dbConnection);
```

Now we can define our parameters. The first argument defines the parameter name and must match one of the parameter names defined in the SQL statements. The second argument defines the type of the parameter, and in this case, they are both character strings (`VarChar` is what we use for general strings that have a variable length). The final argument is the length of the column.

Once the parameter object has been created, we set the `Value` property to be the contents for that parameter, and these are the values of the `TextBox` controls:

```
OleDbParameter fnParam =
                new OleDbParameter("@FirstName", OleDbType.VarChar, 10);
fnParam.Value = txtFirstName.Text;
dbCommand.Parameters.Add(fnParam);

OleDbParameter lnParam =
                new OleDbParameter("@LastName", OleDbType.VarChar, 20);
lnParam.Value = txtLastName.Text;
dbCommand.Parameters.Add(lnParam);
```

Now we run the command using its `ExecuteNonQuery()` method. This simply instructs ADO.NET to run the command but without expecting a result. This way it doesn't have to worry about creating a `DataSet` or a `DataReader` for the data. This gives us a slight performance increase – if no data is going to be returned, there's no point creating an object just in case some data is returned.

```
dbCommand.ExecuteNonQuery();
```

Finally, we close the connection:

```
dbConnection.Close();
```

As you can see, this method is much simpler than the `DataSet` method of updating data, and is certainly the best method to use for small amounts of data.

Note that we haven't used transactions in this example so that you can see the newly added rows in the Web Matrix Data Explorer. You therefore might like to delete any new rows you've added, just to keep your database data clean.

Summary

In this chapter, we extended our knowledge of ADO.NET, moving from data reading to advanced topics in data handling. We looked at the `DataSet` in more detail, seeing how it's really a container object, having a collection of `Tables`, and it's these tables, which provide us with access to the data by way of the `Rows` collection. We also saw that data can be updated within the `DataSet`, but is still disconnected from the database.

We then looked at ways in which to update the data in database, first using the changes made to a `DataSet`, and then by using commands to directly update data.

Now it's time to combine the techniques we've seen in this book, as we move on to creating a sample application.

Exercises

1. Load a `DataSet` with the `Shippers` table from Northwind and add the following data into it:

- ❑ Company Name: FastShippers

- ❑ Phone: (503) 555-9384

2. Using the `CommandBuilder` object, create an `InsertCommand` to insert this new data, and send the changes back to the database.

3. Using direct SQL commands change the phone number of FastShippers to (503) 555-0000.

4. Use the Web Matrix data templates to create an Editable DataGrid. Have a look at the code and see how many familiar techniques you see.

ASP.NET Server Controls

So far the book has covered a lot of theory about how to create Web pages and use .NET's object-oriented approach to create some interesting pages, including those that display data from a database. While creating these pages, we've used some common server controls (the `Button` and `Label` controls, for example). However, we haven't explored their characteristics in great detail – now's our chance! In this chapter we'll start building a simple Web site using a wide variety of controls.

You should now be familiar with the fact that ASP.NET has a *control-based*, *event-driven* architecture. Pages are built using controls (textboxes, buttons, data lists, grids, and so on), and these controls generate and can react to events (the clicking of a hyperlink, the selecting of items). This chapter concentrates on two key concepts: *controls* and *events*, and how they are an integral part of every ASP.NET application you will write.

Server controls are reusable components that can render plain output to the browser, just like standard HTML tags, but they have the additional ability to be processed on the server and can be accessed like any other .NET object. They can respond to events, get and set properties, and so on. These controls are processed on the server. For example, data from a data source can be retrieved and combined with a server control when the page is compiled. When that page is requested, the appropriate HTML or JavaScript content is sent back to the browserthat displays the finished page. This process is known as *rendering*.

There are two main types of server controls available to us: *Web controls* (the `<asp:Button ... >` control) and *HTML server controls* (simple HTML elements with a `runat="server"` attribute). This chapter will concentrate on Web controls for the most part, though we'll briefly discuss how HTML server controls work.

Web controls are declared using tag syntax like normal HTML tags but with a stronger adherence to XML formatting rules. The following example declares an ASP.NET `Button` control and assigns values to three of the control's properties:

```
<asp:Button id="SampleButton" runat="server"
            Text="I'm A Sample Button!"/>
```

One of the unique qualities of Web controls is that even though their tag syntax is different from that of HTML tags, every Web control is *rendered* (processed and converted) to standard HTML after being processed on the server. Some of the Web controls also provide the ability to render rich Web content – for example, a `Calendar` control for displaying dates, a `DataGrid` control for displaying data, as well as other controls that will be explored later in this chapter.

As we delve into the world of controls and events, you would benefit greatly from having a copy of ASP.NET Web Matrix installed on your system. Web Matrix is a superb tool for putting together simple sites, like the one we will create soon.

In this chapter, we will look at:

❑ A review of the syntax and benefits of Web controls

❑ A brief recap of the lifecycle of an ASP.NET page

❑ Using a variety of Web controls on a Web form that starts the Wrox United application that we'll be developing in the following chapters

❑ Introducing data rendering controls – a very powerful group of controls for displaying data

❑ Using rich controls like the `Calendar` control to render complex HTML with minimal code

❑ The extra controls offered by Web Matrix that we could use in our applications

❑ Validating user input using validation controls

Server controls are such a major part of ASP.NET that we won't be able to cover everything here, but you will gain a good understanding of how they work and how to use them.

The Wrox United Application

Whether you call it soccer or football, you'll no doubt be familiar with this game – eleven players, a ball, two goals, and a legion of dedicated supporters! Our application will be the Web site of a fictitious soccer team known as Wrox United that competes in a small league. Figure 10-1 shows the finished application home page:

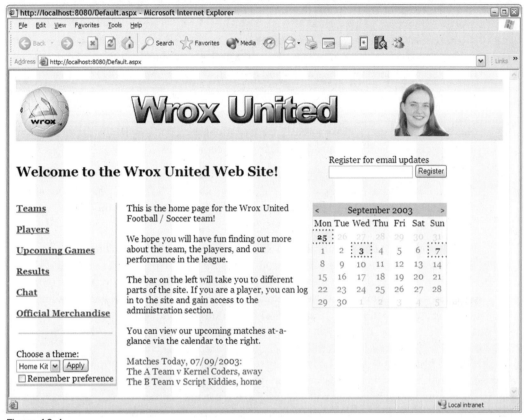

Figure 10-1

As we work through this chapter and the following three chapters, we'll build up the core of this site using Web Matrix. In *Appendix D*, we will duplicate some of the features of the Wrox United application when we discuss creating Web applications using Visual Studio .NET.

ASP.NET Web Controls

Day-to-day usage of the different types of controls is possibly the best way to realize how useful they are. Whenever we add a single line of code to an ASP.NET page to add a simple control, we're actually adding a lot of functionality that has been hidden away from us. The end result is that the complicated inner workings of the control are abstracted away from us, leaving us to worry about designing pages, without having to write mountains of code to make pages functional. Anyone who has experience of developing with older Web technologies like ASP will appreciate how simple Web development becomes when they have a full set of controls at their fingertips!

ASP.NET has a broad set of Web controls that can be grouped into four broad categories:

❑ **Basic controls**: This group (sometimes referred to as *intrinsic* controls) contains controls that, when rendered, look and feel like standard HTML elements but are processed on the server. They have a standard set of properties and events that are common to all of these controls and can be accessed by the server. Examples include the `Button`, `CheckBox`, and `TextBox` controls, all of which have `Text`, `Font`, `ForeColor`, and `Visible` properties among many others.

❑ **Data rendering controls**: These controls are used for binding and displaying data from a data source; for example, the `DataGrid` and `DataList` controls.

❑ **Rich controls**: These controls have no direct HTML counterparts. Rich controls like the `Calendar` control are made up of multiple components, and the HTML generated typically consists of numerous HTML tags (as well as client-side script) to render the control in the browser.

❑ **Validation controls**: These controls are designed to improve user interaction with pages. They can be used in a wide range of situations, from ensuring that a password is entered correctly to ensuring that only valid data is entered into textboxes and submitted to a database server. Hackers can bring down entire sites that use Textboxes to get data into databases without applying any validation logic! Examples of validation controls include the `RequiredFieldValidator` that can be used to ensure that data is provided in all mandatory fields. We'll see these controls in action in the next chapter.

As you start to build the Wrox United example in this chapter, you will gain experience of working with each type of control listed above. You will also learn to write event handlers for the various events raised by each of these controls, for example, the clicking of a button, or the selection of an item in a drop down box.

The introduction briefly mentioned that you can add a `runat="server"` attribute to HTML tags to process them on the server, so let's take a look now at what this means and how it works. We'll then compare HTML server controls with Web controls.

HTML Server Controls

HTML server controls are simple HTML tags with a `runat="server"` attribute, which enables developers to access them programmatically and work with them in a similar way to Web controls. So, why include these types of controls when we have Web controls? Well, HTML server controls do have some advantages over Web controls, including:

❑ Web developers coming from an ASP3 or similar background may prefer to work with the HTML-style of control that they're used to

❑ Developers can convert existing HTML tags to HTML server controls fairly easily, thus gaining some server-side programmatic access to the control

When a `runat="server"` attribute is added to an HTML tag, the tag *becomes* a control. Each of these controls derives its functionality from the `System.Web.UI.HtmlControls.HtmlControl` base class.

Compare the following lines of code:

```
<input id="MyHTMLTextBox" type="text"
       name="MyHTMLTextBox">
```

```
<input id="MyHTMLTextBox" type="text"
       name="MyHTMLTextBox" runat="server">
```

The first tag is a simple HTML tag that the server doesn't particularly care about; it will be rendered exactly as it appears here. The second snippet of code adds the magic words `runat="server"`, which means that the following code can be added to our page:

```
void Page_Load()
{
  MyHTMLTextBox.Value = "Hello world!";
}
```

This would produce the output shown in Figure 10-2:

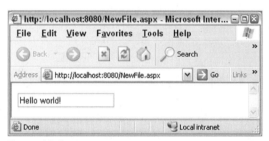

Figure 10-2

There is an HTML server control object for every corresponding HTML tag, so any standard HTML tag, from a `<div>` to an `<img>`, can be processed on the server.

> Note that you always need to add an identifier for all server-side controls (for example, id="`MyHTMLTextBox`") to provide a unique name for the object, which enables you to reference it in your server-side code.

Like Web controls, HTML server controls offer a variety of features that include:

❑ **Programmatic object model**: HTML server controls can be accessed programmatically on the server. Each HTML server control is an object and you can access its various properties and get (and /set) them in your method or event-handler code.

❑ **Event processing**: HTML server controls provide a mechanism to write event handlers in much the same way as you would for a client-based form. The only difference is that the event is handled in the server code.

❑ **Automatic value caching**: When form data is posted to the server, the values that the user enters into the HTML server controls are automatically maintained when the page is sent back to the browser. The magic behind this functionality is the result of a property called *ViewState* that all ASP.NET Web controls inherit.

❑ **Custom attributes**: You can add any attribute you need to an HTML server control. The .NET Framework will render them to the client browser without any changes. This enables you to add browser-specific attributes to your controls.

❑ **Validation**: You can actually assign an ASP.NET validation control to do the work of validating an HTML server control. Validation controls are covered in the next chapter.

One situation where you might consider using HTML server controls in your ASP.NET pages is when you have an existing HTML page that you would rather not rewrite from scratch but would like to write some server-side code to access properties of the various controls on the page.

> **A neat trick – if you want to edit the properties of a plain HTML tag on your Web page using the Web Matrix properties editor, you can add a `runat="server"` attribute to the tag you want to edit, which makes the control appear in the list of available controls in the** Properties **pane. All you have to do then is select the control and edit the properties. When you have finished, you can simply remove the `runat="server"` attribute to change the control back into a tag.**

HTML Server Controls versus Web Controls

Given that Microsoft has provided two categories of server controls (HTML and Web), with both sets sharing some functionality, you may be a bit confused as to which set of controls you should use within your Web forms. The short answer is simply: you can use both! It's perfectly fine to mix the usage of HTML server controls and ASP.NET server controls within your Web forms – using one set of controls does not restrict you to that control type. Despite the overlap in functionality, there are some clear distinctions between these controls that you should be aware of when developing your ASP.NET pages:

Control Feature	HTML Server Control Behavior	ASP.NET Web Control Behavior
Control abstraction	Provide a one-to-one mapping with a corresponding HTML tag and offer no real abstraction.	Offer a high level of abstraction – they don't necessarily map directly to any existing HTML control. For example, an ASP.NET Calendar control has no equivalent HTML control– it's actually made up of a collection of several controls. As such, you will often hear the phrase *Rich control* associated with many ASP.NET server controls.

Control Feature	HTML Server Control Behavior	ASP.NET Web Control Behavior
Object model	Utilize a very HTML-centric object model. In addition, the HTML attribute convention is not strongly typed, so you could set `<div width="huge" ...>`. This would be sent to the browser, but the browser would not be able to render it to be "huge" (there is no such attribute) and it will revert to a standard width.	Provide a consistent and type-safe programming model, meaning that the server will prevent an invalid page from being rendered. An error page will be displayed when you run a page that contains a control with a property that is set to an invalid value. In addition, code design environments such as Web Matrix or Visual Studio won't let you set the properties in the Properties panel to an invalid value (for example, attempting `<asp:panel width="huge"...>` will cause an error message to be displayed in the designer). All ASP.NET Web controls inherit a set of base properties and methods (such as `ForeColor`, `BackColor`, `Font`, and so on).
Target browser	Cannot automatically detect the capabilities of the browser loading the page. It's up to you to make sure that the HTML controls you use are compatible with the browsers that might be rendering your page.	Automatically detect the client browser requesting the page and render the controls based on the browser's capabilities.
How the control renders	Provide complete control over what gets rendered and is sent to the client browser.	Provide a higher level of abstraction in terms of how the controls are rendered. The properties you choose to set for a control how it is actually rendered, but the process of rendering is handled by the ASP.NET runtime. If you really need complete control over the output, you can dig deep into .NET and customize controls or write your own – a topic that is briefly covered in *Chapter 13*.

Web Controls

ASP.NET's Web controls are the building blocks for creating ASP.NET Web forms. Like their HTML counterparts, Web controls provide all the basic controls necessary for building Web forms (`Button`, `ListBox`, `CheckBox`, `TextBox`, and many more), as well as a collection of rich controls, such as the `Calendar` and `DataGrid` controls. As we discussed earlier, these controls have a rich object model, such as the ability to detect which browser is displaying them and a set of properties and events that we can use as we develop sites.

Rich Object Model

Web controls draw from the rich features of the .NET Framework. As such, they inherit their base methods, properties, and events from either the `System.Web.UI.WebControls.Control` or `System.Web.UI.WebControls.WebControl` base classes.

As discussed in *Chapter 7*, inheritance is a key feature of object-oriented design and programming. When instantiating a Web control, you're really creating an instance of an object that gives you access to the properties, methods, and events of its base class and interface. Web controls have style properties that are instances of `CssStyle` objects. We can set colors using standard .NET `Color` objects, and specify dimensions using strongly typed Web measurement objects. By comparison, HTML controls generally have weakly-typed properties mapping to their attributes, allowing any string to be set as a value.

Automatic Browser Detection

Web controls detect client browser capabilities and create the appropriate HTML and client-side script for the client browser. The difference in rendering won't be apparent with a control such as a `Button` control, but you might find that a script-rich control such as a validation control renders differently on different browsers. Or you may find that older non-CSS compliant browsers may have style rendered as old style attributes, instead of `style=""` attributes. The HTML (or the script) rendered for different browsers is all handled by the Web control, and by and large, the developer does not have to worry too much about client browser capabilities or limitations.

Properties

All Web controls share a common set of base properties and also have their own class-specific properties. These properties allow you to change the look and behavior of the control. Some of the common base class properties shared by all ASP.NET server controls include:

❑ `BackColor`: The background color of the control, for example, `AliceBlue`, `AntiqueWhite`, or even a hexadecimal value like `#C8C8C8`.

❑ `ForeColor`: The foreground color of the control.

❑ `BorderWidth`: The width of the border of the control, in units of either exs, ems, pixels, points, picas, inches, centimeters (or millimeters), or a percentage value.

❑ `Visible`: If set to `true` (the default for all controls), the control will be displayed. If set to `false`, the control will be hidden. This property is useful for when you want to hide a particular control on the Web form. For example, if you were obtaining details from a user, and in one control they had declared their nationality as British, you might want to hide another control that asks them for their Social Security Number (or SSN; only US residents have an SSN) while displaying a third that asks for their National Insurance number (only UK residents have an NI number).

❑ `Enabled`: Whether on not the control is enabled. If set to `false`, the control will appear grayed out and will not process or respond to events until its `Enabled` property is set to `true`.

❑ `Height`: Height of the control.

❑ `Width`: Width of the control.

❑   `ToolTip`: Hover text displayed dynamically on mouse rollover. Typically used to supply additional help without taking up space on the form.

❑   `Font-Size:`–The font size of the control.

The above properties are merely an abbreviated listing; many more common properties are available (you can investigate these in depth in the SDK documentation).

The following code snippet is an example of an ASP.NET `Button` Web control with several of the common base class properties assigned to give it a distinctive look:

```
<asp:Button id="MyButton" runat="server"
            Text="I'm an ASP.NET server control Button!"
   BackColor="purple"
   ForeColor="white"
   BorderWidth="4"
   BorderStyle="Ridge"
   ToolTip="Common Properties Example!"
   Font-Name="Tahoma"
   Font-Size="16"
   Font-Bold="true"
/>
```

When rendered and displayed in the client browser, the button will look something like Figure 10-3:

I'm an ASP.NET server control Button!

Figure 10-3

The HTML generated for this control (for Internet Explorer 6.0) looks like this:

```
<input type="submit" name="MyButton"
        value="I'm an ASP.NET server control Button!"
        id="MyButton" title="Common Properties Example!"
        style="color:White;background-color:Purple;
            border-width:4px;border-style:Ridge;
            font-family:Tahoma;font-size:16pt;font-weight:bold;" />
```

To look at the HTML, just select View | Source from your browser.

As an alternative method of adding styles, all Web controls have a `style` property. This property acts in a similar manner to the `style` attribute of an HTML tag, and makes it possible to apply any CSS-compatible style to a control. Using this property, the code used to generate this control would be as follows:

```
<asp:Button id="MyButton" runat="server"
            Text="I'm an ASP.NET server control Button!"
            style="color:White;background-color:Purple;
                border-width:4px;border-style:Ridge;
                font-family:Tahoma;font-size:16pt;font-weight:bold;"
/>
```

Note that this code looks very similar to the code produced when the control is rendered.

Finally, you can also use the `CssClass` attribute of any Web control to specify that the control inherits styling information from the appropriate class in the underlying stylesheet for the page. For example, the button could also have been written as follows:

```
<asp:Button id="MyButton" runat="server"
            Text="I'm an ASP.NET server control Button!"
            CssClass="StylishButton"
/>
```

The appropriate CSS stylesheet would then need to contain the following declaration:

```
.StylishButton{
  color:White;
  background-color:Purple;
  border-width:4px;
  border-style:Ridge;
  font-family:Tahoma;
  font-size:16pt;
  font-weight:bold;
}
```

These three variations on the same button are included in the code download for this chapter, along with a very simple stylesheet. They demonstrate that despite the code written in each of the three cases being different, the rendered appearance is the same.

Events

As seen in *Chapter 3*, an event handler is essentially the code you write to respond to a particular event. For example, a `Button` control raises a `Click` event after being clicked; a `ListBox` control raises a `SelectedIndexChanged` event when its list selection changes; a `TextBox` control raises a `TextChanged` event whenever its text has changed and the active focus on the form changes, and so on. ASP.NET Web controls support the ability to assign event handlers that execute specific code in response to specific events raised by an ASP.NET Web control.

Events and event handlers are extremely useful to Web developers because they provide a mechanism for responding dynamically to events in our Web pages. For example, let's say you were asked to write a page containing a button that listed the current date and time to the latest second. For demonstration purposes, when the user clicks on the button, you might want the date and time to be displayed as the button's new text. To achieve this result, you'll need to "wire up" an event handler for our `Button` control. Let's do this in Web Matrix.

Try It Out Creating an Event Handler

1. Fire up Web Matrix and create a new ASP.NET page called `SimpleButton.aspx` within your `C:\BegASPNET11\Ch10` folder. Switch to HTML view, and enter the following code:

```
<form runat="server">
```

```
<asp:Button id="CurrentTimeButton" runat="server"
    Text="Click for current time..." OnClick="UpdateTime" />
</form>
```

2. Switch to **Code** view and add the following method to handle the clicking of the button:

```
void UpdateTime (object sender, EventArgs e)
{
  // update the button text with current time
  CurrentTimeButton.Text = DateTime.Now.ToLongTimeString();
}
```

3. If you run the code in your browser, you'll see the button we created, and when you click on it you'll see the current time, as shown in Figure 10-4:

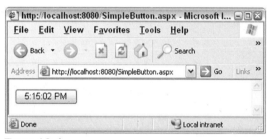

Figure 10-4

How It Works

In this example, we added a Button control to a form and named it CurrentTimeButton. We also set its Text property to Click for current time..., which is the first thing you see when you run the page:

```
<asp:Button id="CurrentTimeButton" runat="server"
    Text="Click for current time..." OnClick="UpdateTime" />
```

In addition, we set the OnClick property to UpdateTime, the name of the method that we added to handle the Click event. We then added the event handler to update the button text with the current time whenever the button is clicked:

```
void UpdateTime (object sender, EventArgs e)
{
  // update the button text with current time
  CurrentTimeButton.Text = DateTime.Now.ToLongTimeString();
}
```

The body of this method has just one line of code, which assigns the value DateTime.Now.ToLongTimeString () to the Text property of the CurrentTimeButton. This is basically saying, "when the UpdateTime() method is run, display the current time in the Text property of CurrentTimeButton (which is a string datatype)."

The DateTime *class is a standard .NET class, which has a* Now() *method that returns the current date and time. This date/time value can be displayed in many ways by using different methods, including* ToShortDateString() *and* ToLongTimeString().

Page Lifecycle

Let's take a moment to consider the series of events that occur whenever an ASP.NET page is requested, how it is loaded, when the events are raised, and when controls are rendered. When you create a page, you are really creating a new Page object (instantiating a new instance of the Page class). The Page class defines a series of methods, properties, and events that are available to all ASP.NET pages. When loading a page for the first time, you might, for example, want to preload the Page object controls with values from a database, or set property values of various controls on the page dynamically.

Let's quickly look at the order of events that happen on the server every time a page is requested. This is shown in Figure 10-5:

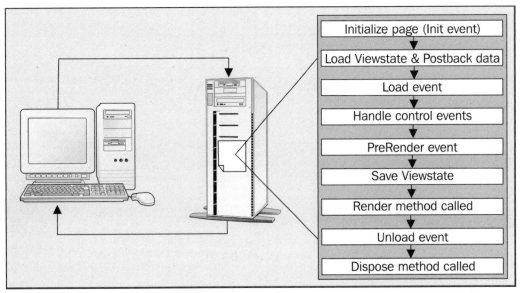

Figure 10-5

When a page is requested, the server runs through the page lifecycle as it prepares the page for the browser. Let's quickly run through the main items in this list:

❑ **Init event**: This is the first stage in the page lifecycle. If you so want, you could add code to the Page_Init() method to handle this event. The code in this method will then be processed before any code in the Page_Load() method and before any event handlers are processed. You can use it to initialize variables or objects that you may need later.

❑ **Load ViewState and Postback data**: This stage is at which any data sent back from the client related to the state of the page and the information being requested is handled.

❑ **Load event**: The `Page_Load()` method handles the `Load` event of the page and usually contains any code that needs to be processed each time the page is loaded. We'll soon look at this in more detail.

❑ **Handle control events**: From the clicking of a button to the selection changing in a listbox, this is the stage where any event handler method is processed. We've seen many of these events in action already and we'll soon see many more. Remember that at this point any code in your `Page_Load()` method will have already been run.

❑ **PreRender event**: The `Page_PreRender()` method is processed when this event is fired. You can add code here to perform any last minute processing after all the control events are processed. We'll see an example of how to use this event in the next chapter.

❑ **Render method called**: At this stage, the ASP.NET processor starts converting the ASP.NET code into HTML. It's at this stage that the HTML sent to the browser is produced. It's possible to add code to cause controls to be rendered differently, thereby customizing their appearance. We'll look at this in detail when we learn more about creating custom server controls in *Chapter 13*.

❑ **Unload event**: This stage is used for last minute cleanup of any objects that you may have used, such as database connections. We'll see an example of this in just a moment. Note that because this event is handled *after* the render method is called, you can't now affect the appearance of the page.

❑ **Dispose method called**: This is where the page object that was processed is removed from the .NET managed memory space on the Web server. This method is called behind the scenes when any .NET object falls out of scope and is no longer needed. Therefore, once a page is sent to the client, the server can forget about how that page was rendered on that occasion and free up memory.

The following code listings provide an overview of some methods that are commonly overridden in an ASPX `Page` object implementation that allow you to perform processing during the various stages of the page's lifetime.

Page_Load()

The `Page_Load()` method is invoked anytime the ASP.NET page is requested – in other words, when the page is loaded for the first time, refreshed, or reloaded. The following is a sample implementation of the `Page_Load()` method:

```
void Page_Load(object sender, EventArgs e)
{
  if (!Page.IsPostBack)
  {
    // First time page loads -
    // perform initialization here!
  }
}
```

The most interesting part of the preceding listing is the reference to the `Page` object's `IsPostBack` property. The `IsPostBack` property is significant because it can be used to distinguish whether a page is being loaded for the very first time, or if it's being loaded as the result of a postback. If a `Button` control was clicked, a `Click` event would be raised and the form data would be posted (sent) *back* to the server – hence the term postback. You have already used this technique several times in the past few chapters.

The most common uses of implementing the `Page_Load()` method in your ASPX pages are to:

❏   Check whether this is the first time the page is being processed, or to perform processing after the page is refreshed

❏   Perform data binding the first time the page is processed, or re-evaluate data binding expressions on subsequent round trips to, for example, display the sorted data differently

❏   Read and update control properties

You'll often use the `if (!Page.IsPostBack)` construct in your pages when binding data to controls on a page. Minimizing the number of times you query a database is essential for a site with good performance, and in many cases you will only want to bind data once because the data is stored in the page's ViewState.

Event Handling

The next major part in the lifecycle of a page is the event handling stage. After an ASPX page is loaded and displayed, additional event handlers are invoked when control events are raised. For example, after a user clicks an ASP.NET `Button` control, the `Click` event is raised, which causes a postback to the server so that the event can be handled. If an event handler is written and assigned to process the `Click` event for that particular control, it will be invoked whenever the `Button` control is clicked.

Not all controls perform this type of automatic posting-back to the server when an event is raised. For example, the `TextBox` control does not, by default, post back notification to the server when its text changes. Similarly, the `ListBox` and `CheckBox` server controls do not, by default, post back event notifications to the server every time their selection state changes. For these controls, the `AutoPostBack` property (which can be set to either `true` or `false`) needs to be explicitly set to `true` in the control's declaration (or set programmatically within the code) to enable automatic post back of events (or state changes) to the server for processing.

> *If you create an ASP.NET Web control that performs server-side processing whenever the control's state changes (such as when a `CheckBox` is checked), and you don't seem to be getting the results you expect, check if the control has an `AutoPostBack` property and whether it is set to `true`. This property typically defaults to `false` if not explicitly declared when the control is defined.*

Page_Unload()

`Page_Unload()` serves the opposite purpose to the `Page_Load()` method. The `Page_Unload()` method is used to perform any cleanup just before the page is unloaded. You would want to implement the `Page_Unload()` method in cases where any of the following actions need to be performed:

❏   Closing files

❏   Closing database connections

❏   Any other cleanup or discarding of server-side objects or resources

The following is an example implementation of the `Page_Unload()` method:

```
void Page_Unload(object sender, EventArgs e)
{
    // Perform any post-load processing here!
}
```

One thing to note is that the unloading of a page doesn't occur when you close the browser or move to another page. The `Page_Unload()` event occurs after the page has been processed by ASP.NET and before it's sent to the browser, by which time it is too late to do anything that will affect the appearance of the page.

Right then – now that we've spent time looking at how pages and basic controls work, let's put it together by starting our Wrox United application.

Understanding Web Controls: The Wrox United Application

The Wrox United application that we'll be building up over the next few chapters has a database with some sample data and a series of pages that query and display that data. We'll be using a variety of controls and events, and examine each of these in turn as we encounter them.

Let's take a quick look at the database structure for the application. This is shown in Figure 10-6:

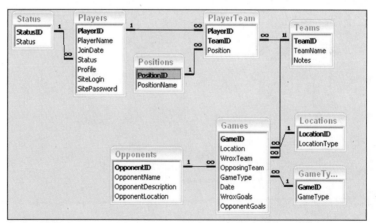

Figure 10-6

The key tables in this database are `Players`, `Teams`, `Games`, and `Opponents`. Players have a `Status` (Active, Injured, or Retired), and can play in different positions in more than one Wrox team (they can be a forward in one team, and a goalkeeper in another). Each team has many players. Games are held between one of the Wrox teams and an opposing team. Each game can take place either at home (at the

Wrox location) or away (at the opposing team's ground). Finally, games can be either friendly or league games.

For a more thorough investigation of the Wrox United database and its data structures, and creating it, please refer to Appendix C – *The Wrox United database*. The Access and MSDE versions of this database are available for download from the Wrox Web site.

So, let's have a go at displaying some of this data using some server controls.

> **To run this code, you need to download the Wrox United database. Download the version of the database that you prefer (the samples in the book assume you are using the Access version) before starting this exercise. For more information on the Wrox United database, refer to Appendix C.**

Try It Out | Wrox United Main Page – Default.aspx

The first page we'll build in our site is the `Default.aspx` page. This page will be the first thing that visitors will see when they visit the site. For now, don't worry too much about styling – as you work through these chapters, we'll refine this page step by step until it looks and feels like a Web site. For now, let's start by adding a heading or two and some links to other pages that we'll be building.

1. Open up your ASP.NET Web Matrix editor, and create a new ASP.NET page called `Default.aspx` in a folder that lives within your `BegASPNET11` directory (`C:\BegASPNET11\WroxUnited`, for example), as shown in Figure 10-7. Web Matrix will then display this page in the main window, ready to be worked on:

Figure 10-7

2. Start off in Design view. Type in Wrox United and make this text Heading 1 style, using the block format drop-down menu on the main toolbar at the top of the environment. On a new line, change the paragraph style back to Normal and type in Welcome to the Wrox United Website! Please select one of the following:

3. Select the Web Controls tab on the left (if it isn't already selected), and drag four Hyperlink controls onto your form, pressing the Return key after each link to place them on separate lines. Your page screen should appear as shown in Figure 10-8:

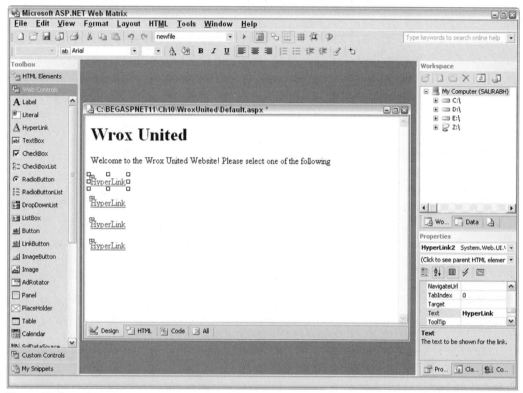

Figure 10-8

4. Notice that when you select one of the Hyperlink controls, the properties available for that control appear in the Properties pane on the right hand side. Select each Hyperlink control in turn and assign the following properties using the Properties pane:

Property	Link 1	Link 2	Link 3	Link 4
Text	Teams	Players	Upcoming Games	Results
ID	lnkTeams	lnkPlayers	lnkGames	lnkResults
NavigateUrl	Default.aspx	Default.aspx	Default.aspx	Default.aspx

5. As we continue to build pages in this site, we'll add a separate `NavigateUrl` property for each of these controls, but for now we keep them all pointing to the same page. If you run this page now, you will see that these controls are rendered almost exactly like an HTML `<a href ...>` hyperlink would be; see Figure 10-9:

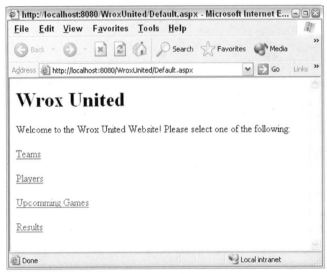

Figure 10-9

How It Works

In Web Matrix, go to the HTML view and you will see that the following code has been created:

```
<h1>Wrox United
</h1>
<p>
Welcome to the Wrox United Website! Please select one of the following:
</p>
<p>
  <asp:HyperLink id="lnkTeams" runat="server"
              NavigateUrl="Default.aspx">Teams</asp:HyperLink>
</p>
<p>
  <asp:HyperLink id="lnkPlayers" runat="server"
              NavigateUrl="Default.aspx">Players</asp:HyperLink>
</p>
<p>
  <asp:HyperLink id="lnkGames" runat="server"
              NavigateUrl="Default.aspx">
    Upcoming Games
  </asp:HyperLink>
</p>
<p>
  <asp:HyperLink id="lnkResults" runat="server"
              NavigateUrl="Default.aspx">Results</asp:HyperLink>
</p>
```

This isn't a lot of code, but we would have had to type it all by hand, so we've saved time by using the Web Matrix editor (with the added advantage of no typos).

Now, view the page in your browser, and select View | Source from the main menu. You will see the following code:

```
<h1>Wrox United
</h1>
<p>
Welcome to the Wrox United Website! Please select one of the following:
</p>
<p>
   <a id="lnkTeams" href="/Default.aspx">Teams</a>
</p>
<p>
   <a id="lnkPlayers" href="/Default.aspx">Players</a>
</p>
<p>
    <a id="lnkGames" href="/Default.aspx">Upcoming Games</a>
</p>
<p>
   <a id="lnkResults" href="/Default.aspx">Results</a>
</p>
```

The ASP.NET Hyperlink control is one of the simplest Web controls in our toolbox and acts in a very similar way to the <a href ... > HTML anchor control. As you can see, the changes between the code we've created and the rendered code are very small, but this is not always the case.

When you click on each link in turn, notice that the browser window flickers as it follows the link to the page. These controls don't cause a postback to the server in the same way as a Button control does – these controls simply transfer you to a new page, without firing any server-side events. We didn't need to add an OnClick attribute like we did with the Button control.

So what's so useful about the ASP.NET Hyperlink control? First, they have the same basic set of properties that every Web control has. Second, they're simple and just as easy to use as a normal anchor tag. Later on, we'll use the Visible property of the Hyperlink controls to display or hide links, depending on whether or not you're logged in as a user – a very useful trick!

Let's take a quick look at several other simple controls available to you for developing ASP.NET pages.

Intrinsic Controls

These are controls that correspond directly to HTML tags and include the Button, Checkbox, DropDownList, and TextBox controls. By now you must be familiar with these controls, as they've been used throughout the book. Here is a list to remind you of the controls that fall into this group:

Control	Purpose
Button	General-purpose button – you typically use the Click event handler
CheckBox	Single check box
DropDownList	Drop-down list box, also known as a combo box, for selecting from a list of items
Hyperlink	Similar to the HTML <a> </a> tag for displaying a hyperlink
Image	Displays a GIF, JPG, or other image files
Label	Provides a way to display text on a page; corresponds to the HTML <span> tag
ListBox	Provides a scrollable list of items, single or multiple selection
Panel	Similar to the <DIV> tag – typically serves as a container for other controls
RadioButton	Single radio button, similar to a checkbox, except that you need to handle its de-selection programmatically
Table	Similar to an HTML table
TableCell	A cell within a table
TableRow	A row within a table
TextBox	Text box – single or multiple lines – similar to an <input ... > or a <textarea ... > control

Let's take a look at some more interesting controls. Here we'll create the Teams.aspx page, and examine a different type of control, the DataList control. This control enables you to display repetitive elements on a page based on rows of data that are stored in a database.

Try It Out Wrox United – Teams.aspx

1. Create a new ASP.NET page and call it Teams.aspx. On this page, in the Design view, add a Heading 1 that displays the text Wrox United again. Underneath that, add a Heading 2 that displays the text Teams. On a new line, switch back to Normal paragraph style. Now you can add some content.

2. You can add a simple table to the form to lay the form out a bit more clearly. Navigate to the HTML menu and select Insert Table. Create a 1-row, 2-column table, with no specified width or height, as shown in Figure 10-10:

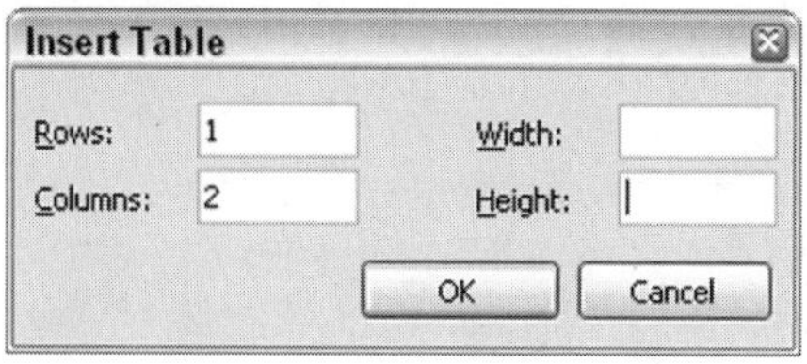

Figure 10-10

3. Drag a `DataList` control into the first cell of the table from the **Web Controls** panel on the left, as shown in Figure 10-11:

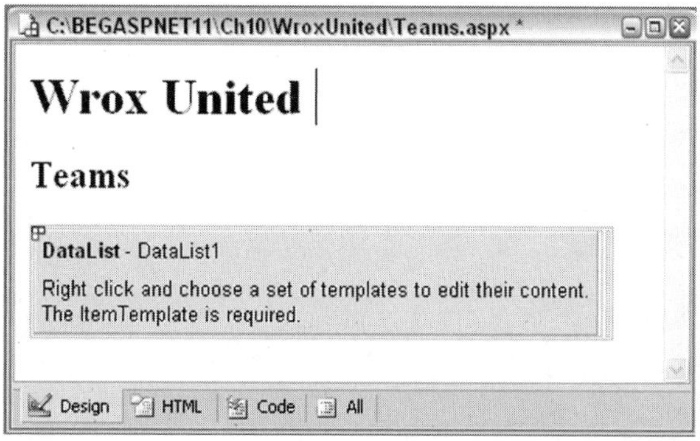

Figure 10-11

4. Let's do some work on the code in the page. First, switch to **HTML** view and enter the following code:

```
<asp:DataList id="TeamList" runat="server">
  <ItemTemplate>
    <asp:linkbutton
        text='<%# DataBinder.Eval(Container.DataItem, "TeamName") %>'
        CommandArgument='<%# DataBinder.Eval(Container.DataItem, "TeamID") %>'
        id="TeamNameLink" style="color:darkred" runat="server" />
    <br />
    <asp:Label text='<%# DataBinder.Eval(Container.DataItem, "Notes") %>'
        id="teamnotes" runat="server" />
  </ItemTemplate>
  <SeparatorTemplate>
    <br />
    <hr color="#b0c4de" width="200px"/>
  </SeparatorTemplate>
</asp:DataList>
```

We've entered some data binding expressions in here, but not yet created a data source for this control. Next, you'll need to grab the name of each of the teams from the database, and create an ID for each team. This ID will come in handy when you need to get more information about each of the teams. In addition, you'll need to grab data from the Notes field that describes each of the teams. Both of these tasks will be carried out next.

> **If you are using Microsoft Access, ensure that a copy of the database is placed into the `BegASPNET11\WroxUnited\Database` folder (you need to create this folder if it doesn't already exist).**

5. The first step is to add some data source information to the page. We're going to use the neat data wizard feature of Web Matrix to generate some database access code. In Code view, drag a `SELECT` Data Method wizard onto the page from the Code Wizards panel on the left, which shows up as shown in Figure 10-12:

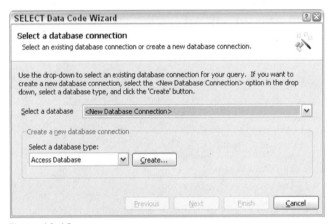

Figure 10-12

6. Create a new database connection to the `WroxUnited` database by selecting your preferred database type, and clicking on the Create button. If you are using Access, you will be prompted to enter the path to the database. If you are using MSDE, you will be prompted to select the `WroxUnited` database from your database list; see Figures 10-13, 10-14, and 10-15:

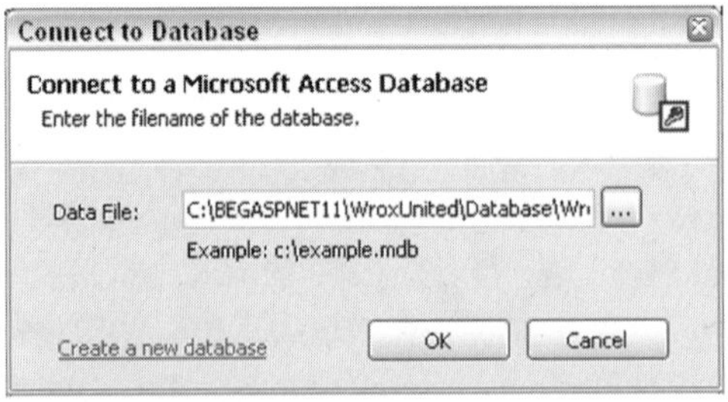

Figure 10-13

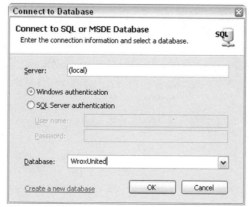

Figure 10-14

> In this book, the examples use the Access version of the database, but you can obviously use the SQL Server version. In fact, in Appendix D, a SQL Server connection has been used instead.

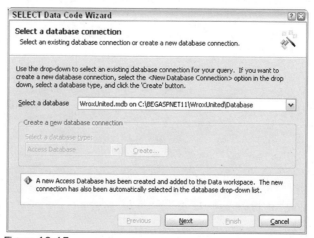

Figure 10-15

Now that you have a connection to your database, you can go ahead with the Code Wizard.

7. Click Next, and the Code Wizard is launched. All you need is data from the Teams table, so select the Teams table, then select each field from that table, as shown in Figure 10-16:

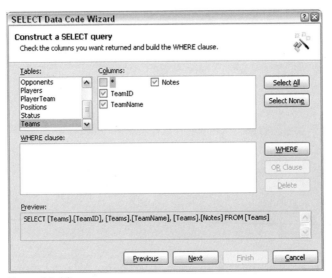

Figure 10-16

8. Click Next, and you can test out the query. You should see a screen similar to Figure 10-17:

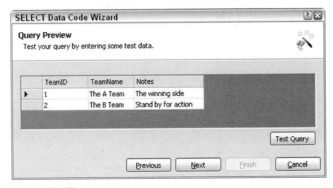

Figure 10-17

9. In the final screen, save this method as GetTeams(), ensure that the **DataReader** type is selected, and then click Finish, as shown in Figure 10-18:

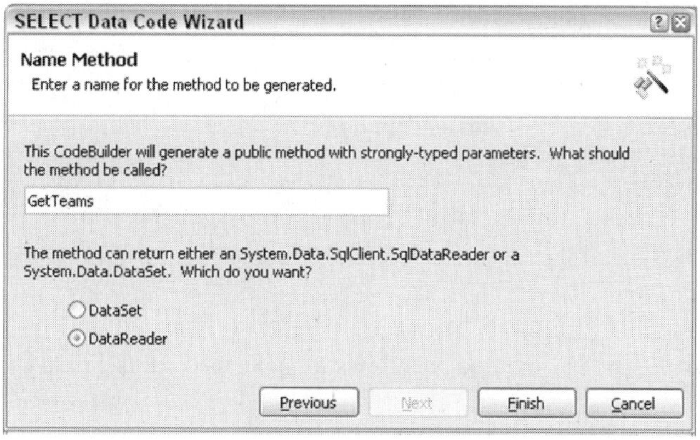

Figure 10-18

Back in Code view, you will now see the following:

```
System.Data.IDataReader GetTeams()
{
  string connectionString =
    "Provider=Microsoft.Jet.OLEDB.4.0; Ole DB Services=-4;" +
    "Data Source=C:\\BegASPNET11\\WroxUnited\\Database\\WroxUnited.mdb";
  System.Data.IDbConnection dbConnection = new
                          System.Data.OleDb.OleDbConnection(connectionString);
  string queryString = "SELECT [Teams].[TeamID], [Teams].[TeamName], " +
                        "[Teams].[Notes] FROM [Teams]";
  System.Data.IDbCommand dbCommand = new System.Data.OleDb.OleDbCommand();
  dbCommand.CommandText = queryString;
  dbCommand.Connection = dbConnection;
  dbConnection.Open();
  System.Data.IDataReader dataReader =
    dbCommand.ExecuteReader(System.Data.CommandBehavior.CloseConnection);

  return dataReader;
}
```

Phew – that's a lot of code! These code builders are very useful, and we'll be using these quite often as we build up the site. We now have a function that returns a DataReader object that we can use to populate the `DataList` control. However, before we continue, we need to change this code a bit. The database connection string can be stored in a central location in the `web.config` file. Since we'll be doing a fair amount of database work for this application, let's change the code so that we use this technique.

10. Create a new `web.config` file for your Wrox United application and in the code that is generated, add the highlighted line of code.

> **Due to page width limitations, the highlighted line in the following code snippet has been wrapped to two lines. You must ensure that the following statement is not wrapped in your code and is all on one line!**

```
<?xml version="1.0" encoding="UTF-8" ?>

<configuration>

  <appSettings>
    <add key="ConnectionString"
        value="Provider=Microsoft.Jet.OLEDB.4.0; Ole DB Services=-4;
        Data Source=C:\BegASPNET11\WroxUnited\Database\WroxUnited.mdb"/>
  </appSettings>

    <system.web>
```

11. Modify the `GetTeams()` method as follows to make use of this global connection string:

```
System.Data.IDataReader GetTeams()
{
  string connectionString =
    ConfigurationSettings.AppSettings["ConnectionString"];
  System.Data.IDbConnection dbConnection = new
    System.Data.OleDb.OleDbConnection(connectionString);
...
```

12. Add the following code block above the `GetTeams()` function:

```
void Page_Load()
{
  TeamList.DataSource = GetTeams();
  TeamList.DataBind();
}
```

That's it for this page. Run the page; the output is as shown to Figure 10-19:

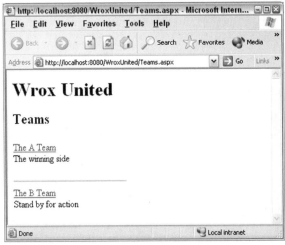

Figure 10-19

How It Works

This exercise used many different types of ASP.NET controls to display team information on the page. Let's look at each of these controls, in turn, starting with the DataList control.

The DataList control is a powerful way to display repeated values from a database. It uses templates to present the data. In this example, we added content for the ItemTemplate and SeparatorTemplate elements within the DataList.

The ItemTemplate section is used to display each row of data retrieved and gives you the option of adding some layout and styling code:

```
<asp:DataList id="TeamList" runat="server">
  <ItemTemplate>
    <asp:linkbutton
        text='<%# DataBinder.Eval(Container.DataItem, "TeamName") %>'
        CommandArgument='<%# DataBinder.Eval(Container.DataItem, "TeamID") %>'
        id="TeamNameLink" style="color:darkred" runat="server" />
    <br />
    <asp:Label text='<%# DataBinder.Eval(Container.DataItem, "Notes") %>'
        id="teamnotes" runat="server" />
  </ItemTemplate>
```

The SeparatorTemplate is where we added a horizontal line to clearly separate the results:

```
<SeparatorTemplate>
  <br />
  <hr color="#b0c4de" width="200px"/>
</SeparatorTemplate>
</asp:DataList>
```

Inside the ItemTemplate, we used two different controls – an ASP.NET LinkButton control and a Label control. Let's first look at the LinkButton control:

```
<asp:linkbutton
    text='<%# DataBinder.Eval(Container.DataItem, "TeamName") %>'
    CommandArgument='<%# DataBinder.Eval(Container.DataItem, "TeamID") %>'
    id="TeamNameLink" style="color:darkred" runat="server" />
```

The Text property is set to display the value stored in the TeamName field for each row in the database. The CommandArgument property stores the TeamID that represents the currently selected team. This property will be very useful later on when we use the LinkButton control to display more information on the page. Later in this chapter, we'll use it to retrieve a list of players that play for the selected team.

Now, let's look at the Label control:

```
<asp:Label text='<%# DataBinder.Eval(Container.DataItem, "Notes") %>'
    id="teamnotes" runat="server" />
```

This control is a little simpler than the `LinkButton` control. The interesting bit is the `Text` property that is set to the value stored in the database for the notes for the currently selected team.

Each of these controls will be rendered once for each row in the database. Six teams would result in six links and six notes. Each result will have the same separator between items.

The code used to access the data stored on the database should be familiar to you from working through the exercises in *Chapters 8* and *9*. The Web Matrix data wizard takes a lot of hard work away and produces neat functions that you can use in your code. However, the Web Matrix wizards don't allow you to specify a centralized database connection string, so we added a line to the default `web.config` file created for this exercise:

```
<add key="ConnectionString"
   value="Provider=Microsoft.Jet.OLEDB.4.0; Ole DB Services=-4;
   Data Source=C:\BegASPNET11\WroxUnited\Database\WroxUnited.mdb"/>
```

Once this was added, the `connectionString` created by the data access wizard was changed as follows:

```
string connectionString =
   ConfigurationSettings.AppSettings["ConnectionString"];
```

This line of code looks up the value stored in the central `web.config` file and uses that value to connect to the database.

Linking to the Teams.aspx Page

Before you finish this example completely, flip back to `Default.aspx` and change the following line of code as shown:

```
<asp:HyperLink id="lnkTeams" runat="server" NavigateUrl="Teams.aspx">
   Teams
</asp:HyperLink>
```

Changing the `NavigateUrl` property means that you can link to the newly created `Teams.aspx` page from the main front page.

The `DataList` control is one of the numerous data controls available to ASP.NET developers. Here's a quick look at the other controls available to us.

Data Rendering Controls

These controls are extremely feature-rich (they have numerous properties to choose from) and greatly simplify the work of displaying a variety of data, particularly database-related data. The definition of data in the context of these controls is very broad. It could include database records, an `ArrayList`, an XML data source, or even custom collection of objects containing custom class instances. There are two important concepts you need to know:

❑ **Data binding**: This is the term used to describe the process of associating a server control with information in a data store. Binding data to a server control is a two-step process in ASP.NET – first assign the server control's `DataSource` property to the data you want to bind to and then call the control's `DataBind()` method. Controls can be bound to a variety of data sources, ranging from tables retrieved from the database to values stored in an object, such as an Array or a Hashtable.

❑ **Templates**: These are used to define the various layout elements of a particular control. Templates describe how data is displayed in the browser.

The following table lists the available data controls:

Control	Purpose
DataGrid	Creates a multi-column, data-bound grid. This control allows you to define various types of columns, lay out the contents of the grid, and add specific functionality (edit button columns, hyperlink columns, and so on).
DataList	Displays items from a data source by using templates and renders them as a structured table. You can customize the appearance and contents of the control by manipulating the templates that make up its different components.
Repeater	The `Repeater` control is very similar to the `DataList`, except that results are not rendered in a table. Each row in the data source is rendered in a format that you specify in the `ItemTemplate`. Given the lack of structure in the rendered output, you may find that you use the `ItemSeparatorTemplate` more often. Unlike `DataList`, the `Repeater` control does not have any built-in selection or editing support.

The DataGrid Control

The `DataGrid` control provides a wealth of functionality for displaying data in columns and rows and has many properties that you can use to control the layout of your grid. For example, you could alternate the colors for the rows of data being displayed. Some useful properties for the `DataGrid` control include:

❑ `AllowSorting`: Allows you to dynamically sort and re-display the data based on the values in a selected column. For example, if you have a table in a database containing employees' surnames and salaries, enabling sorting would allow you to sort the rows in your table according to either column.

❑ `AllowPaging`: Allows you to view subsets of the data called by the `DataGrid` control on different pages. The number of items displayed on the page is determined by the `PageSize` property.

❑ `AlternatingItemStyle`: Sets the style (such as background color) of every other item listed.

❑ `ItemStyle`: The style of individual items. If no `AlternatingItemStyle` is defined, all the items will render with this style.

❑ `FooterStyle`: The style of the footer (if any) at the end of the list.

❑ `HeaderStyle`: The style of the header (if any) at the beginning of the list.

To use the `DataGrid` control, declare it like the other server controls you've seen (using the `<asp:DataGrid>` start and end tags), set the relevant properties, define the columns in your table, and then apply the relevant template for those columns. Within the template tags, include the information to which the template must be applied:

```
<asp:DataGrid id="EventData"
   AllowSorting="true"
     <Columns>
       <asp:TemplateColumn HeaderText="Column1">
         <ItemTemplate>
           <%# DataBinder.Eval(Container.DataItem, "ShortDesc") %>
         </ItemTemplate>
       </asp:TemplateColumn>
       <asp:TemplateColumn HeaderText="Column2">
         <ItemTemplate>
           <%# DataBinder.Eval(Container.DataItem, "DetailDesc") %>
         </ItemTemplate>
       </asp:TemplateColumn>
     </Columns>
</asp:DataGrid>
```

The DataList Control

The `DataList` control used in the previous example is useful for displaying rows of database information (which can become columns in `DataGrid` tables) in a format that you can control using *templates* and *styles*. Manipulating various template controls changes the way your data is presented. The `DataList` control enables you to select and edit the data that is presented. Here is a list of the supported templates:

Templates	Purpose
ItemTemplate	This is a required template that provides the content and layout for items referenced by DataList.
AlternatingItemTemplate	If defined, this template provides the content and layout for alternating items in the DataList. If it is not defined, ItemTemplate is used.
EditItemTemplate	If defined, this template provides editing controls, such as text boxes, for items set to 'edit' in the DataList. If it is not defined, ItemTemplate is used.
FooterTemplate	If defined, the FooterTemplate provides the content and layout for the footer section of the DataList. If it is not defined, the footer section will not be displayed.
HeaderTemplate	If defined, this provides the content and layout for the header section of the DataList. If it is not defined, the header section will not be displayed.
SelectedItemTemplate	If defined, this template provides the content and layout for the currently selected item in the DataList. If it is not defined, ItemTemplate is used.
SeparatorTemplate	If defined, this provides the content and layout for the separator between items in the DataList. If it is not defined, a separator will not be displayed.

You can actually make a DataList render like a DataGrid by arranging data in columns. You can do this by changing the RepeatDirection property from Vertical to Horizontal. We recommend trying this out yourself and taking a look at the source for the rendered page – you'll soon see where you need to add or remove layout data to customize the appearance of your data.

The Repeater Control

The Repeater control is very similar to the DataList control with one very important distinction: the data displayed is always *read-only*. You cannot edit the data being presented. It is particularly useful for displaying repeating rows of data. Like the DataGrid and DataList controls, it utilizes templates to render its various sections. The templates it uses are generally the same as the ones used with the DataList control, with a similar syntax. The next Try-It-Out illustrates the Repeater control in action.

We've completed the first part of the Teams page, but it would be really useful to see the players on each team. For that part of the example, we'll work with some more Web controls (including a Repeater control) that bind to data.

Try It Out   Wrox United – Teams.aspx, Part 2

In this example, we'll make the TeamNames from the previous example "clickable", so that when a team is selected, the players of that team are listed on the right-hand side of the table.

1. Reopen `Teams.aspx`, and go straight to Code view. We need to get some more data from the database. Start by dragging another SELECT query onto the page and launching the wizard.

2. This time, select `PlayerName` from the `Players` table and `PositionName` from the `Positions` table as the two columns to be displayed, as shown in Figure 10-20:

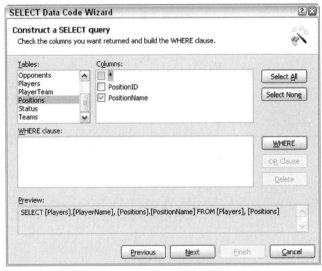

Figure 10-20

3. Before you can exit the wizard, you need to add some WHERE clause data to link the data that you're gathering. This data comes from two different tables, `Players` and `Positions`. You also need to ensure that player data is only retrieved for the specific team that you're interested in.

4. Click the **WHERE** button to start adding a WHERE clause, which selects only those rows where the `PlayerID` column in the `PlayerTeam` join table matches the `PlayerID` column in the `Players` table as shown in Figure 10-21:

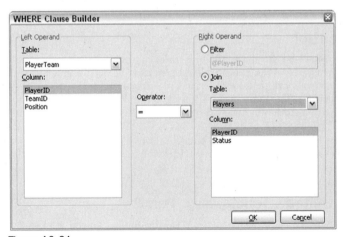

Figure 10-21

5. Repeat this process to join the following sets of tables and columns: the `Position` column in the `PlayerTeam` table to the `PositionID` column in the `Positions` table, and the `TeamID` column in the `PlayerTeam` table to the `TeamID` column in the `Teams` table.

6. Finally, set the `TeamID` column in the `PlayerTeam` table to be equal to the `TeamID` parameter, as shown in Figure 10-22. This will be passed in when the function is called:

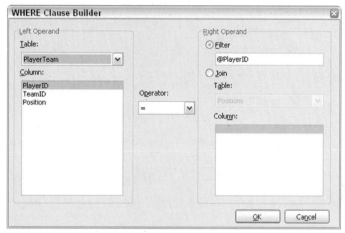

Figure 10-22

You should now see the screen shown in Figure 10-23:

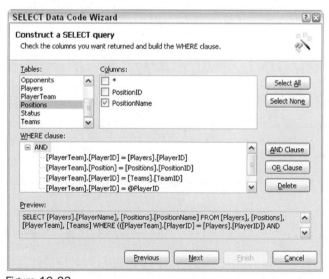

Figure 10-23

7. Click Next to test the query. When prompted, enter an integer that corresponds to a valid `TeamID`, as shown in Figure 10-24 (1 is a safe bet!):

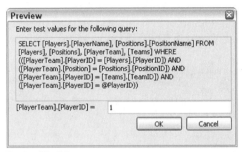

Figure 10-24

You should now see the screen shown in Figure 10-25:

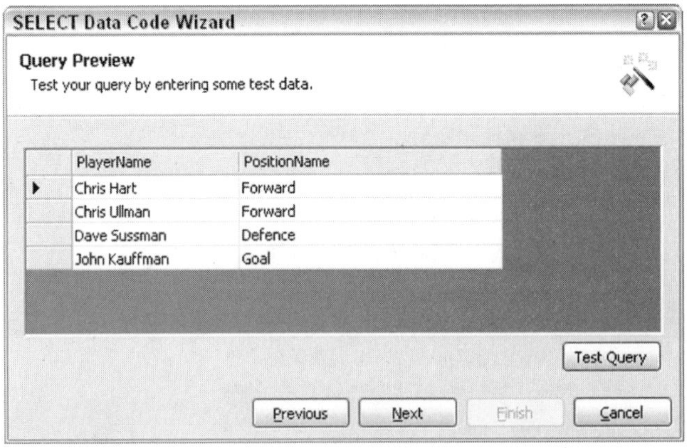

Figure 10-25

8. Save the query as a **DataReader** called `GetPlayersByTeam`. You can now exit the wizard. The following code should have been inserted (we've added a few line breaks in the longer strings to make it easier to read):

```
System.Data.IDataReader GetPlayersByTeam(int teamID)
{
  string connectionString =
    "Provider=Microsoft.Jet.OLEDB.4.0; Ole DB Services=-4; " +
    "Data Source=C:\\BegASPNET11\\WroxUnited\\Database\\WroxUnited.mdb";
  System.Data.IDbConnection dbConnection =
    new System.Data.OleDb.OleDbConnection(connectionString);

  string queryString =
    "SELECT [Players].[PlayerName], [Positions].[PositionName] " +
    "FROM [Players], [Positions], [PlayerTeam], [Teams] "+
```

```
        "WHERE (([PlayerTeam].[PlayerID] = [Players].[PlayerID]) " +
          "AND ([PlayerTeam].[Position] = [Positions].[PositionID]) " +
          "AND ([PlayerTeam].[TeamID] = [Teams].[TeamID]) " +
          "AND ([PlayerTeam].[TeamID] = @TeamID))";
    System.Data.IDbCommand dbCommand = new System.Data.OleDb.OleDbCommand();
    dbCommand.CommandText = queryString;
    dbCommand.Connection = dbConnection;

    System.Data.IDataParameter dbParam_teamID =
      new System.Data.OleDb.OleDbParameter();
    dbParam_teamID.ParameterName = "@TeamID";
    dbParam_teamID.Value = teamID;
    dbParam_teamID.DbType = System.Data.DbType.Int32;
    dbCommand.Parameters.Add(dbParam_teamID);

    dbConnection.Open();
    System.Data.IDataReader dataReader =
      dbCommand.ExecuteReader(System.Data.CommandBehavior.CloseConnection);

    return dataReader;
}
```

Again, the wizard has done a great job of creating complex code with only a few mouse clicks! You need to make one slight adjustment though, so that the code uses the centralized connection string added to the web.config file earlier. Change the following highlighted line of code to use this central connection string:

```
System.Data.IDataReader GetPlayersByTeam(int teamID)
{
  string connectionString =
    ConfigurationSettings.AppSettings["ConnectionString"];
  Dim dbConnection As System.Data.IDbConnection = _
    New System.Data.OleDb.OleDbConnection(connectionString)
```

Now, add some controls that can use this code. Switch back to HTML view and add another cell to the table that contains a Repeater control:

```
</td>
<td style="vertical-align:top">
  <asp:Repeater id="PlayersList" runat="server">
    <ItemTemplate>
      <asp:linkbutton
          text='<%# DataBinder.Eval(Container.DataItem, "PlayerName") %>'
          style="color:darkred" runat="server"
          width="120"/>
          
      <asp:Label
          text='<%# DataBinder.Eval(Container.DataItem, "PositionName") %>'
          id="playerposition" runat="server" /><br/>
    </ItemTemplate>
    <headerTemplate>
      Players in: <%= SelectedTeam %>
      <hr color="#b0c4de" width="200px">
```

```
        </headerTemplate>
        <footerTemplate>
          <hr color="#b0c4de" width="200px">
        </footerTemplate>
      </asp:Repeater>
    </td>
  </tr>
</table>
```

With this, you've got a `Repeater` control and a function to fill it with data. However, a few things are missing. The `Repeater` control should only be filled with data when a team is selected. We do this in three steps. First, you wire up an event handler so that when the name of the team is clicked, the respective team players will be displayed. Then, you pass the `TeamID` parameter to the `GetPlayerByTeam()` function. Here, you should remember the name of the team that has been selected, so that you can display it in the Repeater's header template.

9. Head back to the `DataList` control and edit the `LinkButton` control as follows:

```
<asp:linkbutton
    text='<%# DataBinder.Eval(Container.DataItem, "TeamName") %>'
    CommandArgument='<%# DataBinder.Eval(Container.DataItem, "TeamID") %>'
      id="TeamNameLink" style="color:darkred"
        CommandName="ShowTeam" runat="server" />
```

10. Add the following to the `DataList` control tag:

```
<asp:DataList id="TeamList" runat="server"
              OnItemCommand="TeamList_ItemCommand">
```

11. Add the following line of code outside all the methods in the page (this is a public variable):

```
string selectedTeam;
```

12. Finally, add the following code in the Code view of the page:

```
void TeamList_ItemCommand(object sender, DataListCommandEventArgs e)
{
  if (e.CommandName == "ShowTeam")
  {
    LinkButton button = (LinkButton)e.CommandSource;
    selectedTeam = button.Text;
    PlayersList.DataSource =
      GetPlayersByTeam(int.Parse((string)e.CommandArgument));
    PlayersList.DataBind();
  }
}
```

The page is now ready, so run the page in your browser. You should see the screen shown in Figure 10-26:

Figure 10-26

How It Works

We extended the first part of the example to incorporate an event handler that runs some specific code when the name of a team is clicked. This code is used to populate the `Repeater` control. Let's run through it bit-by-bit:

```
<asp:DataList id="TeamList" runat="server"
              OnItemCommand="TeamList_ItemCommand">
```

Adding the `OnItemCommand` property to the `DataList` control ensures that when the `LinkButton` within the `DataList` is clicked, the `ItemCommand` event of the `Repeater` is raised and code in the `TeamList_ItemCommand()` event handler is run. However, we need to pass the `CommandArgument` of the `LinkButton`, so we assign a `CommandName` property to the `LinkButton`:

```
<asp:linkbutton
   text='<%# DataBinder.Eval(Container.DataItem, "TeamName") %>'
   CommandArgument='<%# DataBinder.Eval(Container.DataItem, "TeamID") %>'
     id="TeamNameLink" style="color:darkred"
     CommandName="ShowTeam" runat="server" />
```

In the event handler that runs when the `ItemCommand` event is fired, we can use the `CommandArgument` property of the `LinkButton`:

```
void TeamList_ItemCommand(object sender, DataListCommandEventArgs e)
```

The event handler takes two parameters. `e` is an object of the type `DataListCommandEventArgs`. This means that we can access certain properties of `e` in our code that relate back to the control that originally fired the event.

349

First, we can use the `CommandName` property of the `LinkButton` that was set to `ShowTeam` earlier:

```
if (e.CommandName == "ShowTeam")
{
```

We test whether the argument passed into the event handler has a `CommandName` set to `ShowTeam`. If it does, we process some more code. The next two lines extract the name of the currently selected team. This is used to set the value of the public string variable `selectedTeam`:

```
LinkButton button = (LinkButton)e.CommandSource;
selectedTeam = button.Text;
```

Notice that we first have to create a new LinkButton object and use it to work with the properties of the button that originally fired the method. We can identify the button that the request originated from by using the `CommandSource` property of the `EventArgs` (e) passed into the method. Once we have the newly-created button object, we can access its `Text` property.

The next section binds data to the `PlayersList` `Repeater` control. Here, we access the `CommandArgument` property of the e object, which is the `CommandArgument` property of the `LinkButton` control that raised the event and is passed into the event handler. Because this argument is passed across as a string and we require an integer, we must first specify that the argument is a string and then convert it to an integer:

```
PlayersList.DataSource =
    GetPlayersByTeam(int.Parse((string)e.CommandArgument));
PlayersList.DataBind();
  }
}
```

> This event handler is quite complicated, but is a great example of how to handle events raised by child controls (the `LinkButton`) via a parent control (the `DataList`). This is a process known as *Event Bubbling*, in which the events raised by the child control *bubble up* to their parent control where they can be intercepted and handled.

We've seen how the event is handled. Now let's look at the control that is populated when the event handler runs:

```
<asp:linkbutton
    text='<%# DataBinder.Eval(Container.DataItem, "PlayerName") %>'
    style="color:darkred" runat="server"
    width="120"/>
    
<asp:Label
      text='<%# DataBinder.Eval(Container.DataItem, "PositionName") %>'
      id="playerposition" runat="server" /><br/>
</ItemTemplate>
```

This control contains a `LinkButton` and a `Label` control in its `ItemTemplate`. We also define a header and footer for our player list. Notice that the string value stored in the `SelectedTeam` variable adds the name of the team to the header of the control:

```
      <headerTemplate>
        Players in: <%= SelectedTeam %>
        <hr color="#b0c4de" width="250px">
      </headerTemplate>
      <footerTemplate>
       <hr color="#b0c4de" width="250px">
      </footerTemplate>
    </asp:Repeater>
```

The data for the items in the `Repeater` control comes from the `GetPlayersByTeam()` method:

```
System.Data.IDataReader GetPlayersByTeam(int teamID)
{
  string connectionString =
    "Provider=Microsoft.Jet.OLEDB.4.0; Ole DB Services=-4; " +
    "Data Source=C:\\BegASPNET11\\WroxUnited\\Database\\WroxUnited.mdb";
  System.Data.IDbConnection dbConnection =
    new System.Data.OleDb.OleDbConnection(connectionString);
```

This method contains the following large SQL statement to retrieve the data we're interested in:

```
  string queryString =
    "SELECT [Players].[PlayerName], [Positions].[PositionName] " +
    "FROM [Players], [Positions], [PlayerTeam], [Teams] "+
    "WHERE ((([PlayerTeam].[PlayerID] = [Players].[PlayerID]) " +
       "AND ([PlayerTeam].[Position] = [Positions].[PositionID]) " +
       "AND ([PlayerTeam].[TeamID] = [Teams].[TeamID]) " +
       "AND ([PlayerTeam].[TeamID] = @TeamID))";
```

This query is followed by some code that creates a `Command` object, and a parameter that passes the `TeamID`.

```
  System.Data.IDbCommand dbCommand = new System.Data.OleDb.OleDbCommand();
  dbCommand.CommandText = queryString;
  dbCommand.Connection = dbConnection;

  System.Data.IDataParameter dbParam_teamID =
    new System.Data.OleDb.OleDbParameter();
  dbParam_teamID.ParameterName = "@TeamID";
  dbParam_teamID.Value = teamID;
  dbParam_teamID.DbType = System.Data.DbType.Int32;
  dbCommand.Parameters.Add(dbParam_teamID);
```

> **Using a parameter ensures that the data passed into the method doesn't violate any database constraints. For example, using a parameter removes our obligation to escape text that would be invalid in a SQL statement, worry about inserting dates in an unsuitable format, and so on. Catching data type errors in code before data is passed to the database is a good way to work.**

Finally, the data is read from the database and the `DataReader` object is returned by the function:

```
dbConnection.Open();
System.Data.IDataReader dataReader =
  dbCommand.ExecuteReader(System.Data.CommandBehavior.CloseConnection);

return dataReader;
}
```

Our page is a bit more interesting now. Try clicking on different teams and see how the list of players changes. You could also add more code that responds to the clicking of the link button in the `PlayersList` control, which transfers the user to more information about the selected player, but we recommend that you this yourselves.

The `Repeater` control has produced results similar to the `DataList` control, and in many cases, you might find yourself wondering which controls to use for different purposes. The end result is subtly different. The `DataList` control actually renders as an HTML table with cells for each item in the template. The `Repeater` is much less structured and simply spits back rendered versions of exactly what was put into the templates with no extra hidden tags. This is why we had to add a line break to this control to split the content onto different lines (we could also have used a separator template).

The only functionality difference between the two is that the `DataList` can be used to edit data, whereas the `Repeater` is always read-only. For more information and some great examples, refer to *Professional ASP.NET 1.0, Special Edition, Wrox Press, ISBN 0-7645-4396-2*.

> *Data-oriented controls have many different properties and events that we could discuss in depth here, but it's time to move on and look at other topics. I highly recommend that you play and experiment with these controls. Check out the rendered HTML in your browser using* **View | Source** *– you'll find that it's a great way to understand how the rendering process works, and how you can optimize your code to work with, not against, the ASP.NET compiler to produce the results you want.*

You've now gained some experience of using a `DataList`, a `Repeater`, and a `LinkButton` while putting together one of the pages in the site. As you saw at the end of the previous example, the `DataList` control is a *data rendering control*. The `LinkButton` control, however, is a rich control. Let's find out more about this type of control.

Rich Controls

Rich controls are compound in nature and provide extended functionality. In other words, rich controls are typically combinations of two or more simple or *intrinsic* controls that compose a single functional unit, for example, an `AdRotator` control. Another distinguishing trait of these controls is that they don't have a direct correlation to any single HTML control, even though they render to HTML when displayed in the client browser. The following table discusses various rich controls and their functions:

Control	Purpose
AdRotator	Displays advertisement banners on a Web form. The displayed advertisement is randomly changed each time the form is loaded or refreshed.
Calendar	Displays a one-month calendar for viewing/selecting a date, month, or year.
CheckBoxList	Multiple-selection checkbox group; can be dynamically generated with data binding.
ImageButton	Provides a clickable image with (optional) access to the clicked coordinates to support image-map functionality.
LinkButton	Hyperlink-style button that posts back to the page of origin. We've seen a couple of these in action already.
RadioButtonList	Mutually exclusive radio button group. Can be dynamically generated with data binding.

The nice thing about this family of rich controls is that they are just as easy to use as the other ASP.NET server controls. They may boast of more features and properties, but the basic way of defining them and interacting with them is programmatically the same as for all the other ASP.NET server controls.

The Calendar Control

The `Calendar` control produces some really complex HTML when rendered, but you'll find that adding this control to a Web page is as simple as adding any other Web control! This control is designed to present date information in the form of a calendar and allows a user to select a particular date. You can configure the control via the `SelectionMode` property to allow the user to select a range of dates. You can also completely customize how this control is presented using the many different properties that it has access to. Let's take a quick look at some of these properties:

```
FirstDayOfWeek=[Default|Monday|Tuesday|Wednesday|
Thursday|Friday|Saturday|Sunday]
```

The `FirstDayOfWeek` property enables you to choose the day of the week your calendar starts from. Some calendars default to Sunday as the first day of the week. For business purposes, however, it's more practical to have the week starting from Monday.

```
SelectionMode=[None|Day|DayWeek|DayWeekMonth]
```

By default, the `Calendar` control's `SelectionMode` defaults to `Day`. This is useful when you want your user to be able to select only a single day. However, you can select multiple days by setting the `SelectionMode` property to either `DayWeek`, which will allow you to select a single day or an entire week, or `DayWeekMonth`, which will allow you to select a single day, an entire week, or the entire month.

The `Calendar` control's `SelectMonthText` and `SelectWeekText` properties enable you to customize the HTML that is rendered at the browser – use these properties if you're really going for a customized look:

```
SelectMonthText="HTML text"
SelectWeekText="HTML text"
```

You need not define all of the properties of the ASP.NET `Calendar` control to display the control. In fact, the following declaration will create an efficient ASP.NET `Calendar` server control that looks good and displays quite well:

```
<asp:Calendar id="MyCalendarControl" runat="server" />
```

When delivered to the client browser, the result is an HTML calendar as shown in Figure 10-27 that enables you to navigate through the various days, months, and years:

Figure 10-27

Take a look at the HTML that ASP.NET produced to create this page – over 100 lines of HTML and JavaScript, while you wrote only a single line!

Let's now add a calendar that will highlight the days on which matches are scheduled and then display the details of those matches when that date is selected.

Try It Out Wrox United – Default.aspx, Part 2, the Event Calendar

1. Reopen `Default.aspx` and add the following HTML table in the HTML view to change the layout of the new and improved front page:

```
<p>
    Welcome to the Wrox United Website! Please select one
```

```
    of the following:
</p>
<table style="WIDTH: 800px">
  <tr>
    <td style="WIDTH: 200px">
      <p>
        <asp:HyperLink id="lnkTeams" runat="server"
                       NavigateUrl="Default.aspx">
          Teams
        </asp:HyperLink>
      </p>
...
      <p>
        <asp:HyperLink id="lnkResults" runat="server"
                       NavigateUrl="Default.aspx">
          Results
        </asp:HyperLink>
      </p>
    </td>
    <td style="VERTICAL-ALIGN: top; width: 350px;"> </td>
    <td style="VERTICAL-ALIGN: top; width: 250px;"></td>
  </tr>
</table>
</form>
```

2. Switch to **Design** view and drag a `Calendar` control into the third cell of the table, as shown in Figure 10-28. Name this calendar `EventCalendar`:

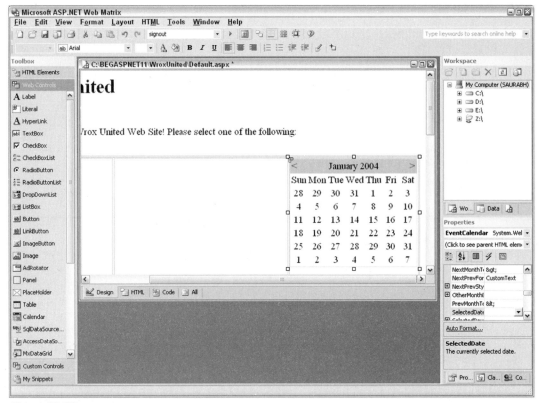

Figure 10-28

3. Click the lightning bolt in the **Properties** pane to display the available events, and double-click on the `DayRender()` event's textbox to be taken back to **Code** view, where you need to enter more code. Before filling in the `DayRender()` event handler, let's take a moment to consider what we're trying to achieve. We want to highlight the days of the games and store dates of the games in the `Games` table in the database. If we want to display more information about a particular day, we also need to store the `GameID` so that we can again query the database later.

4. The next task is to add another `DataReader` to this page using the wizard, and then store that data in a *Hashtable* (where we can store details of dates and games in key-value pairs, as we saw in *Chapter 8*). At the top of the page, add the following line of code:

```
System.Collections.Hashtable DateList;
```

5. Drag a `SELECT` data wizard onto the page. Select the `GameID` and `Date` fields from the `Games` table, save this function with the name `Dates()`, and specify that it returns a `DataReader` object:

```
System.Data.IDataReader Dates()
{
  string connectionString = "Provider=Microsoft.Jet.OLEDB.4.0; " +
```

```
            "Ole DB Services=-4; Data Source=C:\\BegASPNET11\\" +
            "WroxUnited\\Database\\WroxUnited.mdb";
        System.Data.IDbConnection dbConnection = new
            System.Data.OleDb.OleDbConnection(connectionString);

        string queryString = "SELECT [Games].[Date], [Games].[GameID] FROM [Games]";
        System.Data.IDbCommand dbCommand = new System.Data.OleDb.OleDbCommand();
        dbCommand.CommandText = queryString;
        dbCommand.Connection = dbConnection;

        dbConnection.Open();
        System.Data.IDataReader dataReader =
            dbCommand.ExecuteReader(System.Data.CommandBehavior.CloseConnection);

        return dataReader;
}
```

6. Change the following code to use the central connection string stored in `web.config`:

```
System.Data.IDataReader Dates()
{
    string connectionString =
        ConfigurationSettings.AppSettings["ConnectionString"];
    System.Data.IDbConnection dbConnection = new
        System.Data.OleDb.OleDbConnection(connectionString);
```

7. Add a `Page_Load()` event handler to the page, just below the hashtable declaration:

```
public void Page_Load(object sender, EventArgs e)
{
    DateList = new System.Collections.Hashtable();

    // we need to run this each time the page is loaded, so that
    // after a date is selected and the page is posted back, the
    // active dates will still be highlighted.
    System.Data.IDataReader DateReader = Dates();

    while (DateReader.Read())
    {
        DateList[DateReader["Date"]] = DateReader["Date"];
    }
    DateReader.Close();
}
```

8. Finally, add code to the `DayRender()` event handler that checks if a match has been scheduled for a specific day and highlights it in such a case:

```
public void EventCalendar_DayRender(object sender, DayRenderEventArgs e)
{
    if (DateList[e.Day.Date] != null)
    {
        e.Cell.Style.Add("font-weight", "bold");
        e.Cell.Style.Add("font-size", "larger");
```

```
    e.Cell.Style.Add("border", "3 dotted darkred");
    e.Cell.Style.Add("background", "#f0f0f0");
  }
  else
  {
    e.Cell.Style.Add("font-weight", "lighter");
    e.Cell.Style.Add("color", "DimGray");
  }
}
```

9. Run the page. You should see the screen shown in Figure 10-29:

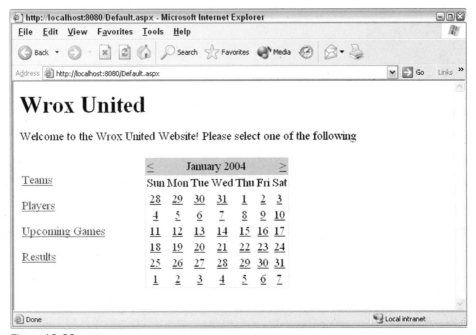

Figure 10-29

How It Works

The `Calendar` control is one of the most complex controls in the ASP.NET toolbox, and without writing too much code, we've managed to get the calendar to highlight dates that are stored in a database! Let's take a look at how we did this, and consider how this code can be improved.

First, we added a `Calendar` control to our page by simply dragging it onto the page and then wired it up to an event handler:

```
<asp:Calendar id="EventCalendar" runat="server"
          OnDayRender="EventCalendar_DayRender"></asp:Calendar>
```

The OnDayRender property ensures that when each day is rendered in the calendar, the event handler is fired. This means that we can test each date as it is rendered, and compare it with the dates stored in the database. Let's take a look at the event handler:

```
public void EventCalendar_DayRender(object sender, DayRenderEventArgs e)
{
   if (DateList[e.Day.Date] != null)
   {
```

This is where we check whether the date being rendered (e.day.date) matches a date in the DateList hashtable that is declared at the top of the page.

```
      e.Cell.Style.Add("font-weight", "bold");
      e.Cell.Style.Add("font-size", "larger");
      e.Cell.Style.Add("border", "3 dotted darkred");
      e.Cell.Style.Add("background", "#f0f0f0");
   }
```

If a matching date is found, some formatting is added to the cell as shown in the preceding code. We make the date slightly larger, bold, and add a border and background shading.

However, if the date being rendered doesn't match, we apply different formatting as follows:

```
   else
   {
      e.Cell.Style.Add("font-weight", "lighter");
      e.Cell.Style.Add("color", "DimGray");
   }
}
```

At the top of the page, as mentioned earlier, is the hashtable declaration:

```
System.Collections.Hashtable DateList;
```

Adding this to the top of the page implies that all methods in the code have access to the data stored in the hashtable for as long as the page exists.

```
public void Page_Load(object sender, EventArgs e)
{
   DateList = new System.Collections.Hashtable();

   // we need to run this each time the page is loaded, so that
   // after a date is selected and the page is posted back, the
   // active dates will still be highlighted.
   System.Data.IDataReader DateReader = Dates();
```

The first part of the Page_Load() method is where we create a new DataReader using the Dates() function that is built using the wizard. We can then loop through this data, and store key and value pairs in the Hashtable. In this case, we can store just the date information in both the key and the value parts of the Hashtable:

```
   while (DateReader.Read())
```

```
  {
     DateList[DateReader["Date"]] = DateReader["Date"];
  }
  DateReader.Close();
}
```

As the comment in the code states, we need to run this code each time the page is loaded, because the values in the Hashtable do not persist between postbacks. The problem with this method is that every time the page is loaded, we have to go back to the database to get the same data over and over again, which isn't very efficient! In the next chapter, we'll look at a better way to store this data, when we introduce the Cache object.

The function that retrieves the data from the database is really quite simple and looks very similar to the code we've seen previously – let's just recap the SQL that was generated to get the data we're interested in:

```
string queryString = "SELECT [Games].[Date], [Games].[GameID] FROM [Games]";
```

In the final example of this chapter, we'll extend the calendar example so that the details of the match are displayed whenever the selected date corresponds to a match day.

Try It Out   Wrox United – Displaying Fixture Details

In this example, we need to respond to a different type of event to display the details of a match. The Calendar control has many different events that can be handled, and the one we need to handle in this example is the SelectionChanged() event, which fires whenever a date is selected. The user should be able to click on a highlighted date in the calendar and view the details of any matches scheduled for that day. Clicking on a different date will cause the SelectionChanged() event to fire, which we can handle and add code to display the data for the selected day.

1.   Let's start by adding some more controls to the page for displaying the results. Start by adding a paragraph and an ASP.NET Panel control. Set the Panel ID to pnlFixtureDetails, and its Visible property to false:

```
<asp:Calendar id="EventCalendar" runat="server"
              OnDayRender="EventCalendar_DayRender"></asp:Calendar>
<p>
  <asp:Panel id="pnlFixtureDetails" runat="server" visible="false">
  </asp:Panel>
</p>
```

2.   Inside the Panel control, add the following Repeater control:

```
<asp:Repeater id="MatchesByDateList" runat="server">
  <headertemplate>
    <span style="width:110px;height:25px">Date: </span>
    <span style="width:135px;height:25px">
      <%# EventCalendar.SelectedDate.ToShortDateString() %>
    </span> <br />
  </headertemplate>
```

```
      <itemtemplate>
        <span style="width:110px">Wrox Team</span>
        <span style="width:135px">
          <%# DataBinder.Eval(Container.DataItem, "TeamName") %>
        </span><br />
        <span style="width:110px">Opposing Team</span>
        <span style="width:135px">
          <%# DataBinder.Eval(Container.DataItem, "OpponentName") %>
        </span><br />
        <span style="width:110px">Venue</span>
        <span style="width:135px">
      <%# Venue((string)DataBinder.Eval(Container.DataItem, "OpponentLocation"),
                     (int)DataBinder.Eval(Container.DataItem, "Location")) %>
        </span><br />
      </itemtemplate>
      <separatortemplate>
        <hr color="#b0c4de" width="200" />
      </separatortemplate>
    </asp:Repeater>
```

We will bind this control to some data to display it on the page. As there could be more than one match on a certain day, we need to use a repeater control to display all the matches on that day. One last item to note at this stage is the last span in the ItemTemplate:

```
        <span style="width:135px">
      <%# Venue((string)DataBinder.Eval(Container.DataItem, "OpponentLocation"),
                   (int)DataBinder.Eval(Container.DataItem, "Location")) %>
        </span><br />
```

Another piece of code needs to be added to render an appropriate value for the match venue. We'll add a venue function in just a moment, and we'll examine why we need this in the *How It Works* section.

3. While you're in the HTML view, modify the Calendar control to add an event handler for the SelectionChanged() event:

```
<asp:Calendar id="EventCalendar" runat="server"
              OnDayRender="EventCalendar_DayRender"
              OnSelectionChanged="EventCalendar_SelectionChanged">
</asp:Calendar>
```

4. Add the following event handler to the page:

```
public void EventCalendar_SelectionChanged(object sender, EventArgs e)
{
  if (DateList[EventCalendar.SelectedDate] != null)
  {
    MatchesByDateList.DataSource = GamesByDate(EventCalendar.SelectedDate);
    pnlFixtureDetails.Visible = true;
    MatchesByDateList.DataBind();
  }
  else
  {
```

```
      pnlFixtureDetails.Visible = false;
    }
  }
```

5. Add the `Venue()` function:

```
public string Venue(string OpponentLocation, int MatchVenue)
{
  if (MatchVenue == 1)
  {
    // match is at home
    return "Wroxville";
  }
  else
  {
    return OpponentLocation;
  }
}
```

6. Finally, we need to add a function that gets the data that we're interested in. We need to display:

   1. The name of the team (the `TeamName` field from the `Teams` table)

   2. The name of the opposing side (the `OpponentName` field from the `Opponents` table)

   3. The location of the game (the `Location` field from the `Games` table)

   4. The home location of the opposing team (the `OpponentLocation` from the `Opponents` table)

   We also need to add some `WHERE` clauses to link together the related tables, so select the `WHERE` clause and add the following relationships:

   1. `OpponentID` from the `Opponents` table is equal to the `OpposingTeam` field in the `Games` table

   2. `TeamID` from the `Teams` table is equal to the `WroxTeam` field in the `Games` table

   3. `Date` from the `Games` table is equal to a parameter that we input called `@Date`

   Save the method as `GamesByDate()`, and have it return another `DataReader` object. If it all goes according to plan, you will end up with the following code:

```
System.Data.IDataReader GamesByDate(System.DateTime date)
{
  string connectionString = "Provider=Microsoft.Jet.OLEDB.4.0; Ole DB
Services=-4; Data Source=C:\\BegASPNET11\\" +
"WroxUnited\\Database\\WroxUnited.mdb";
  System.Data.IDbConnection dbConnection =
    new System.Data.OleDb.OleDbConnection(connectionString);

  string queryString =
    @"SELECT [Teams].[TeamName], [Opponents].[OpponentName], " +
```

```
      "[Games].[Location], [Opponents].[OpponentLocation] " +
    "FROM [Teams], [Opponents], [Games] " +
    "WHERE (([Opponents].[OpponentID] = [Games].[OpposingTeam]) " +
      "AND ([Teams].[TeamID] = [Games].[WroxTeam]) " +
      "AND ([Games].[Date] = @Date))";
System.Data.IDbCommand dbCommand = new System.Data.OleDb.OleDbCommand();
dbCommand.CommandText = queryString;
dbCommand.Connection = dbConnection;

System.Data.IDataParameter dbParam_date =
  new System.Data.OleDb.OleDbParameter();
dbParam_date.ParameterName = "@Date";
dbParam_date.Value = date;
dbParam_date.DbType = System.Data.DbType.DateTime;
dbCommand.Parameters.Add(dbParam_date);

dbConnection.Open();
System.Data.IDataReader dataReader =
  dbCommand.ExecuteReader(System.Data.CommandBehavior.CloseConnection);

return dataReader;
}
```

7. Change this code to use the central connection string as follows:

```
System.Data.IDataReader GamesByDate1(System.DateTime date)
{
  string connectionString =
    ConfigurationSettings.AppSettings["ConnectionString"];
  System.Data.IDbConnection dbConnection =
    new System.Data.OleDb.OleDbConnection(connectionString);
```

8. Run the page and take a look at the results; they should be as seen in to Figure 10-30:

Figure 10-30

How It Works

We've added another panel to the page to display details of matches on a specific day. We first added the
`Panel` control itself, and then started to build up another `Repeater` control:

```
<asp:Panel id="pnlFixtureDetails" runat="server" visible="false">
  <asp:Repeater id="MatchesByDateList" runat="server">
    <headertemplate>
      <span style="width:110px;height:25px">Date: </span>
      <span style="width:135px;height:25px">
        <%# EventCalendar.SelectedDate.ToShortDateString() %>
      </span> <br />
    </headertemplate>
```

To write out the selected date in the header of the control, we use the `SelectedDate` property of the
calendar, and write it out as a short date. After the header template comes the item template. Here, to
render the results, we add plain HTML `<span>` tags as follows:

```
<itemtemplate>
  <span style="width:110px">Wrox Team</span>
  <span style="width:135px">
    <%# DataBinder.Eval(Container.DataItem, "TeamName") %>
  </span><br />
```

Notice how the text within the span contains a data binding expression that takes the `TeamName` column from the data source and places it as text within the control.

We repeat the process of building up the template for the rest of the columns:

```
<span style="width:110px">Opposing Team</span>
<span style="width:135px">
  <%# DataBinder.Eval(Container.DataItem, "OpponentName") %>
</span><br />
<span style="width:110px">Venue</span>
<span style="width:135px">
<%# Venue((string)DataBinder.Eval(Container.DataItem, "OpponentLocation"),
                 (int)DataBinder.Eval(Container.DataItem, "Location")) %>
</span><br />
```

In the final item in the list, we call the `Venue()` function that we declared in our code, which displays text detailing the location of the game (depending on whether it's a home or away match). We pass two parameters into the function – the location of the opponent's pitch and the location flag from the `Games` table that states whether the game is at home (Wrox location) or away (opponent's location).

Finally, after finishing with the items in the `Repeater`, we add a `SeparatorTemplate`:

```
      </itemtemplate>
      <separatortemplate>
        <hr color="#b0c4de" width="200" />
      </separatortemplate>
    </asp:Repeater>
  </asp:Panel>
```

Let's head back to the `Venue()` function and look at how it works:

```
public string Venue(string OpponentLocation, int MatchVenue)
{
```

The function takes two input parameters – the location of the opposing team's pitch and the flag that states whether the match is at home or away. It returns a string that writes out either the name of the home pitch, or the name of the opposing teams pitch:

```
if (MatchVenue == 1)
{
  // match is at home
  return "Wroxville";
}
else
{
  return OpponentLocation;
}
}
```

The rest of the code for this exercise deals with getting the match data from the database and displaying it when an event happens. We want to display details when the currently selected date in the calendar changes, so we added an `OnSelectionChanged` attribute to the `Calendar` control:

```
                          OnSelectionChanged="EventCalendar_SelectionChanged">
```

Then we added the event handler code:

```
public void EventCalendar_SelectionChanged(object sender, EventArgs e)
{
  if (DateList[EventCalendar.SelectedDate] != null)
  {
    MatchesByDateList.DataSource = GamesByDate(EventCalendar.SelectedDate);
    pnlFixtureDetails.Visible = true;
    MatchesByDateList.DataBind();
  }
  else
  {
    pnlFixtureDetails.Visible = false;
  }
}
```

In this event handler, we call the GamesByDate() function to retrieve match details by passing the selected date as a parameter. This function will retrieve the information and the resulting DataReader will be used as the data source for the MatchesByDateList repeater control. The DataReader in the panel is data bound only if matches *are* scheduled for the selected date – if not, the panel is hidden.

The actual code that retrieved the data included quite a substantial SELECT query:

```
string queryString =
    "SELECT [Teams].[TeamName], [Opponents].[OpponentName], " +
      "[Games].[Location], [Opponents].[OpponentLocation] " +
    "FROM [Teams], [Opponents], [Games] " +
    "WHERE (([Opponents].[OpponentID] = [Games].[OpposingTeam]) " +
      "AND ([Teams].[TeamID] = [Games].[WroxTeam]) " +
      "AND ([Games].[Date] = @Date))";
```

Because we are gathering data from multiple tables, the query used is a bit long-winded. As the end result, it retrieves the required data fields from three tables and displays them on the page. There are two more types of controls that we need to look at in this chapter. First, we're going to look at the Web-Matrix-specific controls, and produce another quick and simple ASP.NET page. In the second example, we'll take a quick look at validation controls.

Web Matrix Controls

There are some extra controls that you can use when working with Web Matrix to develop Web applications. They are designed to make life very simple when you want to create data-driven pages.

The MX DataGrid

This control is a lot like a normal DataGrid control, except that you can use it in conjunction with a Web Matrix DataSource control. There are two data source controls, one for SQL Server connections and one for Access connections. There is only one extra property on the MX DataGrid control – the DataSourceControlID property. This is how you tell the MX grid to get its data from the appropriate data source control.

The Data Source Controls

These controls have three simple properties:

- ❑ `ConnectionString`: The string for connecting to the database

- ❑ `SelectCommand`: The SQL used to get the data into the grid

- ❑ `EnableViewState`: To determine whether the data stored in the control has persisted between postbacks

Let's see a quick example of this in action.

Try It Out   Wrox United – Players.aspx and the Web Matrix MX DataGrid

1.   Create a new ASP.NET page and call it `Players.aspx`. In the Design view, add a Heading 1 that displays the text Wrox United. Underneath this, add a paragraph underneath a Heading 2 that displays the text Players. On a new line, switch back to the Normal paragraph style. Now we can add some content. Then in in the Workspace I Data panel at the top left of the Web Matrix environment, switch to Data view. Now drag the `Players` table onto the form, below the two headings as shown in Figure 10-31:

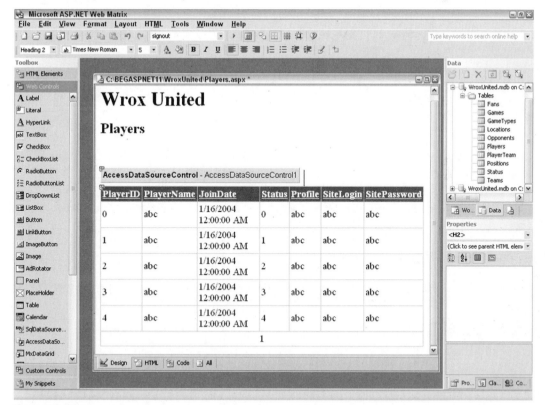

Figure 10-31

You can actually run the page at this stage – with one click and drag operation, you can display an entire table of data on the screen. If you run the page now, you will see the screen shown in Figure 10-32:

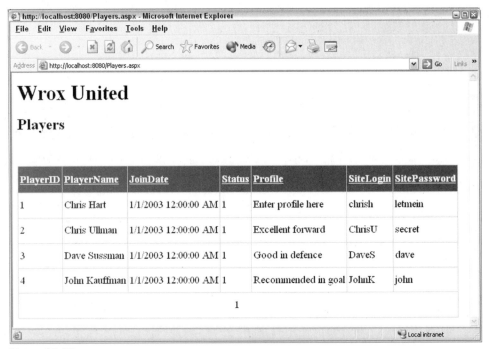

Figure 10-32

Although this is very cool, we don't necessarily want just anyone to view the site login or password details. Also, a status flag of 1, 2, or 3 doesn't mean much whereas **Active**, **Injured**, or **Retired** would mean more to visitors. Let's amend the example slightly.

3. Switch to **Design** view in Web Matrix, select the `DataSource` control, and in the **Properties** panel set the `SelectCommand` to the following:

```
SELECT PlayerID, PlayerName, Profile, JoinDate FROM [Players]
```

4. Select the `MxDataGrid` control and change the `AutoGenerateFields` property to `false`, then back to `true` to refresh the grid. Run the page again to see the screen shown in Figure 10-33:

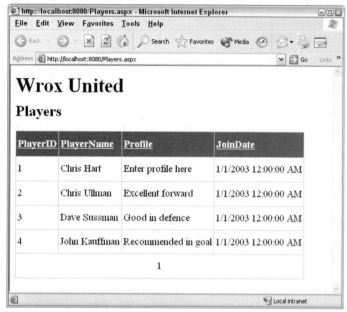

Figure 10-33

How It Works

This simple example demonstrates how Web Matrix can make life easy for us! The results of this quick and simple page aren't exactly brilliant, but the information we want to display is on the form with minimal fuss. The `MxDataGrid` control can be customized to a great extent like the .NET `DataGrid` control, so that you can better control how the data is rendered.

Let's take a quick look at the code that was generated for us:

```
<wmx:AccessDataSourceControl id="AccessDataSourceControl1"
  runat="server"
  ConnectionString="Provider=Microsoft.Jet.OLEDB.4.0; Ole DB Services=- 4;
  Data Source=C:\BegASPNET\WroxUnited\Database\WroxUnited.mdb"
  SelectCommand="SELECT PlayerID, PlayerName, Profile, JoinDate FROM
[Players]">
</wmx:AccessDataSourceControl>
```

The first control added to the page was the `DataSourceControl` that is either a `SQLDataSourceControl` or an `AccessDataSourceControl`, depending on the database that you are using. This control contains a connection string, and a `SELECT` statement to retrieve the data that we're interested in. This control is accompanied by the `MxDataGrid`:

```
<wmx:MxDataGrid id="MxDataGrid1" runat="server" BorderStyle="None"
  BorderWidth="1px" DataKeyField="PlayerID"
  CellPadding="3" BackColor="White" AllowPaging="true"
  DataMember="Players" AllowSorting="true"
  BorderColor="#CCCCCC"
```

```
  DataSourceControlID="AccessDataSourceControl1">
  <SelectedItemStyle font-bold="true" forecolor="White"
    backcolor="#669999">
  </SelectedItemStyle>
  <ItemStyle forecolor="#000066"></ItemStyle>
  <FooterStyle forecolor="#000066" backcolor="White"></FooterStyle>
  <HeaderStyle font-bold="true" forecolor="White"
    backcolor="#006699"></HeaderStyle>
  <PagerStyle horizontalalign="Center" forecolor="#000066"
    backcolor="White" mode="NumericPages"></PagerStyle>
</wmx:MxDataGrid>
```

As you can see, this control contains templates just like any other repetitive data-bound control. In addition, this grid has a few properties different from the `DataGrid` control:

❑   `DataKeyField`: The unique identifier for each row in the table

❑   `DataMember`: The name of the table you want to view

❑   `DataSourceControlID`: The name of the control that contains the data

Also included in the default implementation of this grid is a considerable amount of styling information that you might want to remove. When it comes to styling a site, it makes sense to remove this information to ensure that all pages follow the same style sheet.

To further improve this page, you could manually specify the columns that appear in the grid and add formatting information for the `JoinDate` field. For example, you might want to remove the time portion of the date.

To try this out, you can manually set the `AutoGenerateFields` property to `false` and then specify each field individually using the `Fields` collection editor. You could also alter the code as follows:

```
<wmx:MxDataGrid id="MxDataGrid1" ...
AutoGenerateFields="false">
  <SelectedItemStyle font-bold="true" forecolor="White"
    backcolor="#669999"></SelectedItemStyle>
  <ItemStyle forecolor="#000066"></ItemStyle>
  <FooterStyle forecolor="#000066" backcolor="White"></FooterStyle>
  <HeaderStyle font-bold="true" forecolor="White"
    backcolor="#006699"></HeaderStyle>
  <PagerStyle horizontalalign="Center" forecolor="#000066"
    backcolor="White" mode="NumericPages"></PagerStyle>
  <Fields>
    <wmx:BoundField Visible="false" DataField="PlayerID">
    </wmx:BoundField>
    <wmx:BoundField DataField="PlayerName" HeaderText="Name">
    </wmx:BoundField>
    <wmx:BoundField DataField="Profile" HeaderText="Profile">
    </wmx:BoundField>
    <wmx:BoundField DataField="JoinDate" HeaderText="Join Date"
      DataFormatString="{0:d}">
    </wmx:BoundField>
  </Fields>
```

```
</wmx:MxDataGrid>
```

This will change the appearance of the page as shown in Figure 10-34:

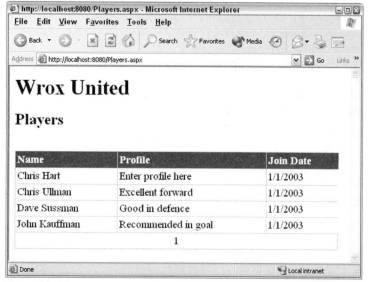

Figure 10-34

If you want to use the centralized connection string, you could alter the code as follows:

```
<wmx:AccessDataSourceControl id="AccessDataSourceControl1" runat="server"
SelectCommand="SELECT PlayerID, PlayerName, Profile, JoinDate FROM [Players]"
ConnectionString='<%# ConfigurationSettings.AppSettings("ConnectionString")%>'
</wmx:AccessDataSourceControl>
```

For this code to work correctly, you need to call the `DataBind()` method of the page object – you can do this by adding a simple `Page_Load()` method to your page as follows:

```
void Page_Load()
{
  Page.DataBind();
}
```

Before we finish this section, flip back to `Default.aspx` and alter the following line of code as shown here:

```
<asp:HyperLink id="lnkPlayers" runat="server"
    NavigateUrl="Players.aspx">
  Players
</asp:HyperLink>
```

With this code, we can now link to the `Players.aspx` page from the main front page of the site.

371

Let's move on to the final part of this chapter, where we take a brief look at validation controls.

Validation Controls

Validation controls are designed to help ensure that data entered into a form conforms to some specific criteria. This reduces the chances of random gibberish being sent back to the server. Validation controls also demonstrate how ASP.NET Web controls abstract common tasks. Without validation controls, we would typically need to write our own client-side validation code (for example, client-side JavaScript) – a time consuming task indeed!

By using validation controls within ASP.NET Web forms, our work is greatly simplified. Although validation involves a bit of overhead and some thought (for instance, what type of validation control to use and some knowledge of how to implement it), the benefits are that we end up with:

❑ Easier code base to maintain

❑ Better control over the user interface and the data that gets passed to our servers

❑ Better experience for our users or customers

For example, using these controls, you can ensure that a user registration form contains valid data in all appropriate fields. This is done using the `RequiredFieldValidator` control before posting it to the server. You can also verify that an email address is in a valid format.

The following is a complete list of validation controls that will give you an idea of what is possible:

Control	Purpose
`CompareValidator`	Compares a user's entry against a constant value (less than, equal to, greater than, and so on). For example, you can use this to check that a Password and a Confirm Password textbox contain identical data.
`CustomValidator`	Checks the data entered by the user using validation logic from a custom method that you write – processed on the server or the client.
`RangeValidator`	Checks that data entered by the user falls between specified lower and upper boundaries. Checks for ranges between pairs of numbers, alphabetic characters, and dates. Boundaries can be expressed as constants or as values derived from another control.

Control	Purpose
RegularExpressionValidator	Checks that the entry matches a pattern defined by a regular expression. This type of validation allows you to check for predictable sequences of characters, such as those in social security numbers, e-mail addresses, telephone numbers, postal codes, IP addresses, and so on.
RequiredFieldValidator	Ensures that the user does not skip an entry.

Let's take a quick look at how we can add validation controls to the site.

Try It Out Wrox United – Registering for Email Updates (Default.aspx)

We are going to add a textbox to the front page of the Web site to collect email addresses of fans who may want to receive information about upcoming events or emails containing match reports. In this example, we will simply add the textbox, a button for submitting the data, and some validation controls. We won't store the email address in this part of the example, since we'll be coming back to this example in the next chapter.

1. Start by re-opening `Default.aspx`. At the moment, we have code that displays a welcome message:

```
<p>
  Welcome to the Wrox United Website! Please select one of the following:
</p>
```

2. Change the following section of code as shown here:

```
<table width="800">
  <tr>
    <td width="580">
      <h2>Welcome to the Wrox United Website! Please select one of the
following:
      </h2>
    </td>
    <td width="220" border="1">
    </td>
  </tr>
</table>
```

3. Switch back to Design view and you will see the screen shown in Figure 10-35:

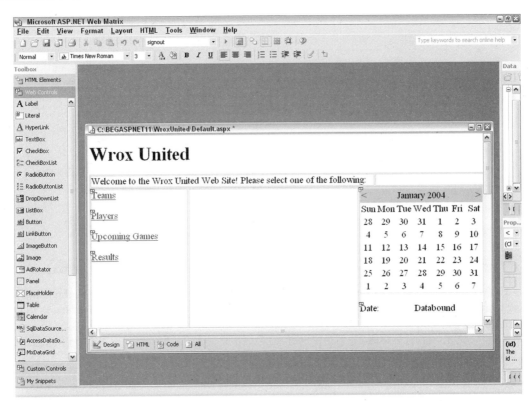

Figure 10-35

4. Drag a `Label` control into the second cell of the top table, then a `TextBox` control, a `Button` control, and finally a `RegularExpressionValidator` control. Set their properties as follows:

Control	Property	Value
Label	Id	lblRegister
	Text	Register for email updates
TextBox	Id	txtEmailAddress
Button	Id	btnRegister
	Text	Register
	Width	60
RegularExpressionValidator	Id	validEmail
	ErrorMessage	Please enter a valid email address
	ControlToValidate	txtEmailAddress

Notice that when you set the `ControlToValidate` property of the `RegularExpressionValidator`, the property box displays a combo box that lists all the available controls that can be validated (in this case, the only control that can be validated by this control is `txtEmailAddress`).

5. We need to enter a validation expression, or else, not much will happen when we run the page. In the properties for the `validEmail` control, select the `ValidationExpression` property and click the ... button in the box to go to the expression builder.

Select Internet E-mail Address from the list, as shown in Figure 10-36, and click OK:

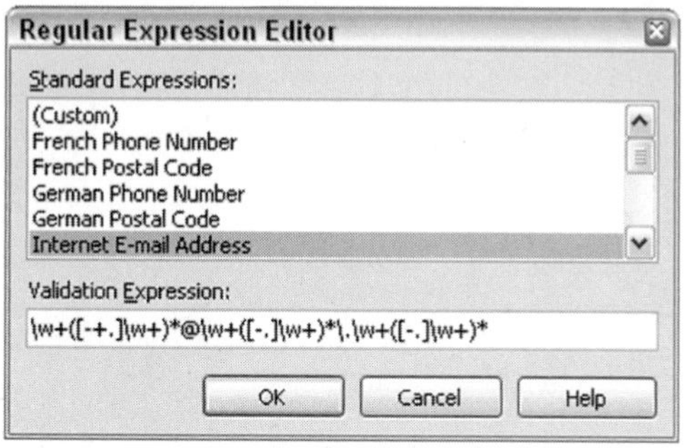

Figure 10-36

You should now have the following code on your page:

```
<asp:Label id="lblRegister"
           runat="server">Register for email updates</asp:Label>
<asp:TextBox id="txtEmailAddress" runat="server"></asp:TextBox>
<asp:Button id="btnRegister" runat="server" Text="Register"
            Width="60px"></asp:Button>
<asp:RegularExpressionValidator id="validEmail" runat="server"
    ErrorMessage="Please enter a valid email address"
    ControlToValidate="txtEmailAddress"
    ValidationExpression="\w+([-+.]\w+)*@\w+([-.]\w+)*\.\w+([-.]\w+)*">
</asp:RegularExpressionValidator>
```

6. Run the page and try to enter different values into the textbox. You'll notice that if you enter some text that is not a valid email address, an error message appears when you click the button as shown in Figure 10-37. Also notice that the page doesn't reload when you click the button – the error message is generated using client-side script!

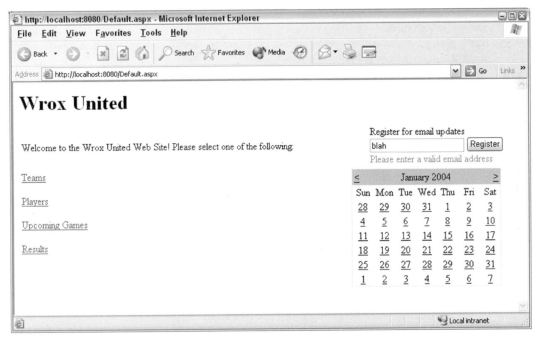

Figure 10-37

Alternatively, if you enter a valid email address, you will notice that a postback occurs when you click the button but no new information displays on the form. This is because we haven't yet handled the button click event on the server.

How It Works

Once again, we managed to create quite an interesting result using minimal code. Let's look at the code that was created when we added the validation control:

```
<asp:RegularExpressionValidator id="validEmail" runat="server"
    ErrorMessage="Please enter a valid email address"
```

The first interesting property is the `ErrorMessage` property, which contains the text that is displayed if the validation fails.

```
ControlToValidate="txtEmailAddress"
```

The `ControlToValidate` property is quite self-explanatory. Notice, that the only control we could select in the Web Matrix Properties pane was the textbox. The textbox is the only control on the form that allows free text input, so it is the only one that can possibly be validated by this control.

The final property contains the validation expression that we saw briefly when we were using the expression browser. The `RegularExpressionValidator` control works by comparing text that has been entered against this pattern. If it matches the rules specified by the pattern, validation is successful. If the text does not match this pattern, validation will fail:

```
ValidationExpression="\w+([-+.]\w+)*@\w+([-.]\w+)*\.\w+([-.]\w+)*">
```

While a full explanation of regular expressions would take a long time, let's quickly look at what this expression means:

- ❑ \w+ match one or more alphanumeric characters
- ❑ (...) * match zero or more instances of the contents of the brackets:
  - ❑ [-+.] match a hyphen, a plus sign, or a period
  - ❑ \w+ match one or more alphanumeric characters
- ❑ @ matches an @ sign
- ❑ \w+ match one or more alphanumeric characters
- ❑ (...) * match zero or more instances of the contents of the brackets:
  - ❑ [-.] an instance of a hyphen or a period
  - ❑ \w+ match one or more alphanumeric characters
- ❑ \. matches a period
- ❑ (...) * match zero or more instances of the contents of the brackets:
  - ❑ [-.] an instance of a hyphen or a period
  - ❑ \w+ match one or more alphanumeric characters

Ok, so no one said these things were going to be too easy! However, a lot of this expression is repeated, and it means that all the following (and many more) are valid:

- ❑ me@here.com
- ❑ someone-else@somewhere.co.uk
- ❑ thing.2@elsewhere-thing.com

> If you are a full time developer, it's definitely worth spending time looking at how regular expressions work – they are extremely powerful and extremely useful. The .NET Framework SDK includes information on all of the regular expression patterns available to .NET developers.

Summary

In this chapter, we spent a fair bit of time looking at different types of controls and how they work. We've started putting together a small Web site using these controls, and we'll be building on this Web site in the next few chapters. Let's take a look at what we've achieved in this chapter.

❑ We looked at what a Web control is, and we discussed the relative merits of both Web controls and HTML controls (HTML tags with a `runat="server"` attribute).

❑ We saw how a page is rendered and looked at when (and how) events are handled.

❑ We looked at some simple intrinsic controls, particularly the `Hyperlink` control, which we used to add some links to the Wrox United application. We returned to this control twice to add links to the `Players` and `Teams` pages.

❑ We used a `DataList` control and a `Repeater` control to display information about teams, and we covered Event Bubbling and saw how to handle events raised by controls that live within other controls.

❑ We used the `Calendar` control to display date information on our pages and learned about two of the events it raises that we can handle, thus providing a customized appearance and behavior.

❑ We looked at validation controls, particularly the `RegularExpressionValidator` control. We'll be learning more about these controls in the following chapters.

We've covered a lot of information, but given that ASP.NET is designed to work around controls and events, it's understandable that there's still a lot to discuss! The in-built-in controls provide us with a lot of rich functionality that we can use in our sites to display data, arrange information, and make the site user friendly.

In the next chapter, we'll look at different methods of storing information outside the scope of a page (including that hashtable of dates from the `Calendar` control that we saw earlier). We'll also look at adding other validation controls, as well as extending the `Default.aspx` page to actually store an email address when the `Register` button is clicked.

Exercises

1. Consider the use of an HTML tag with `runat="server"` in the Wrox United application instead of one of the existing Web controls and explain why the HTML control is able to achieve the same result as the Web control.

2. Add some code to `Default.aspx` that makes sure that only match days (days when there is a match scheduled) are selectable in the calendar. You may find that the `Day.IsSelectable` property comes in handy here.

3. Add another event handler to the `Teams.aspx` page that reacts to the selection of the name of a player and takes the reader to the `Players.aspx` page.

4. Have a go at customizing `Players.aspx` and change the field to displays the name of the player as a hyperlink. When clicked, this hyperlink should reveal a panel lower in the page that lists the team or teams that the selected player is a member of. You will find that the **Fields** editor of the `MxDataGrid` is very useful for this (select the **Fields** property builder when in **Design** view). You need to ensure that the clicking of the player name is handled correctly. You also need to add another method to extract team information (you will find that the `DataReader` function that returned the list of teams from the `Teams.aspx` page is useful here).

Users and Applications

Moving from a series of Web pages connected together by links to a fully functional Web application is an essential step when developing a site. Once you can share information across all the pages in a site, the term *application* really starts to take hold. From the users' perspective, whenever they log in to a site, they receive some amount of personalization in the pages they view. From a developer's point of view, once users log in, certain details related to them can be tracked as they navigate the site. All this is made possible using centralized configuration settings with reusable code, reducing development time and increasing reusability.

This chapter will look at tracking users across pages using sessions, and will start to add some application-specific configuration. We will work with the Wrox United application started in the previous chapter and add extra functionality and features to demonstrate key concepts.

ASP.NET stores information about a user session in a `Session` object. From the moment the user first starts to browse a site, you can access any code with the Session scope and use this, for example, to store information about the currently logged-in user. You can also add code that will remain in memory as long as the application is running. This could contain some in-memory data objects that are accessed frequently but don't often change. This technique protects the database from repeat requests for the same data, thereby improving the performance of the application.

Another means of remembering information is using cookies – small text files that are created and stored on the client computer (assuming cookies are enabled on the client). A cookie can store information such as the number of times that a user has visited a site, whether the user has registered to receive email notifications, and so on. You can also add Application or Session scope configuration information that can store global settings, such as the length of a session until it expires or the connection string to a database. This information is stored in the `web.config` file. In addition, the application's security model can be configured using the information stored in this file.

This chapter will cover:

- ❑ Using a cookie to store user-related information
- ❑ Remembering information relating to user actions as they browse the Web site

❑ Storing data in a variable that is accessible by any piece of code in the Web application

❑ Storing commonly used data in memory to improve application performance

❑ Writing code that will respond to application or session events

❑ Adding some skinning functionality to the Wrox United site by using state management techniques discussed in the chapter

Remembering Information in a Web Application

Whenever you browse to a Web page, you establish a connection with the Web server for a brief moment while the page is sent to your browser. After this, the Web server forgets all about you. This is because HTTP, the protocol used for surfing the Web, is a *stateless* protocol. A stateless protocol is used where it is impractical to maintain a constant connection between the server and the client. Messages are sent back and forth using a request-response mechanism. The client makes requests and the server sends responses. After each response is sent by the server, the connection is dropped.

Unless some external mechanism is in place to associate a client with a known list of clients stored on the server, proactive client-specific communication from the server is not possible. One of the reasons for which HTTP is stateless is that it would be impossible for a Web server to remember everything about every single visitor to the site – imagine how the BBC news Web site would cope with remembering the details of every one of the millions of readers that visit to catch up with the headlines! Statelessness essentially means that you cannot log in to a site using only HTTP. Thankfully, there are tools available that make it possible for the Web server to remember information.

When you browse any Web site, you leave a trail of information with the Web server about the pages you are viewing and where you are connecting from. This information, combined with some code on the server (and some help from the client), enables Web servers to remember visitor information. What Web servers do with that data depends on how you configure them, but as a user, you are most likely to see the result of this process in the form of a personalized browsing experience. For example, you can buy stuff from online stores or log in to community Web sites and participate in online forums. Personalization comes as a result of being able to remember user information and making it useful.

It's not just information about users that needs to be stored – often you might need to access common code that uses data stored in memory from every page on the site. This data could be any kind of object, from a simple string variable to a `DataSet`. Because of the stateless mechanism used to serve pages to browsers (the HTTP protocol), pages have a limited lifespan. Thus, persisting information is a problem you are likely to encounter as you develop ASP.NET sites. Learning to overcome the stateless nature of HTTP is important, and not very difficult, as you'll see when you work through examples in this chapter.

There are four different mechanisms for remembering information:

❑ **Cookies**: Identifying previous visitors to a site by storing data on the client machine

❑ **Sessions**: Remembering information for the duration that a user browses a site

❑ **Applications**: Remembering information that exists for as long as the application runs

❑ **Caching**: Storing data for as long as is necessary to improve performance

Each of these mechanisms fulfills a different purpose, so it is important to understand *which* mechanism should be used to remember information and not just *how* each mechanism works. Let's start the discussion by looking at how cookies work.

Cookies

Cookies are used throughout the Web to store small pieces of information on the client machine. They are small text files that usually store persistent data, which is useful whenever you revisit a site. This can be data such as user preferences and login tokens, whether a user has voted in an online poll, details of the last time you browsed a site, and so on. In short, cookies contain dat that allows a Web server to identify users based on their visiting history. Cookies are designed so that only the site that created them can read them. If you look at the `<drive>\Documents and Settings\<UserName>\Cookies` folder on your hard drive, you'll notice that many cookies reside on your system. Each of them has some kind of identifier in its name that indicates the site that created them.Figure 11-1 shows that I've visited the BBC, Computer Manuals, and Firebox.com sites. You can open a cookie using MS Notepad. The information contained in any of these cookies, usually some text, will give you clues about the site that created it.

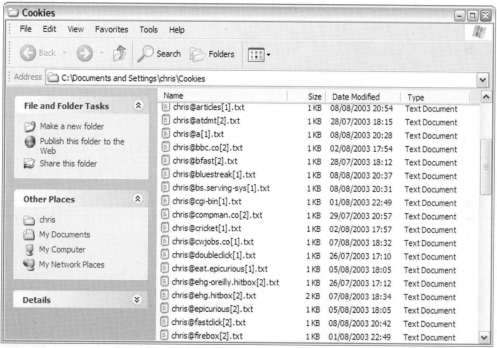

Figure 11-1

Taking the BBC news site as an example, I've in the past checked a button to say that I'm in the UK (so I get the UK front page by default whenI visit the site). I've also specified that when I view the http://www.bbc.co.uk/weather site, my hometown be set to Birmingham, UK. If I look inside the BBC cookie, I can see bits and pieces of text (among the other text) that look as if they correspond to those choices:

```
... BBCNewsAudienceDomestic ... BBCWEACITYuk1045 ...
```

If I change the default page preference to BBC News Audience International and the hometown to Nottingham, the relevant information in the cookie changes as follows:

```
... BBCNewsAudienceInternational ... BBCWEACITYuk2803 ...
```

By modifying preferences on the Web site, a file on my hard drive has been updated. This means that when I next visit the site, it will remember my preferences. Let's look at how this happens.

How Do Cookies Work?

Cookies are linked to the request-response mechanism of HTTP and are passed back and forth along with other data between the client and the server. Let's look at what happens where a site uses cookies to remember whether a user wants a certain popup when they visit a site.In Figure 11-2, Stage 1 is about a user visiting a page on the site. Stage 2 is when the contents of that site are sent to the browser. These contents happen to include a popup. At Stage 3, anyone browsing the site could check a box on a form that states, "Do not show the advert popup again." When they click a button to submit their request, they send data back to the server. Finally, the server sends a small cookie to the client machine. Figure 11-3 represents what happens when the user requests the page again.:

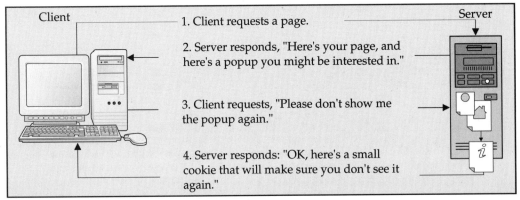

Figure 11-2

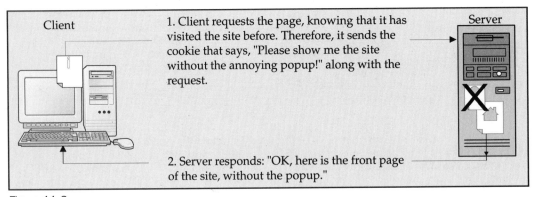

Figure 11-3

This time round, the user won't see the popup ad when browsing the site. This is because the server will have read the cookie that the client sends across while requesting the page and know that the user expressed a preference not to see the popup. The client sends this cookie each time the user visits the site.

At this point, you need to understand that the client cannot be trusted. The client may not send the cookie, send a dodgy cookie, or a cookie that has prematurely expired. Different Internet settings and browsers mean that you can't always rely on cookies. If they were reliable, you could store all kinds of login data in a cookie. However, in practice, you should treat the information contained within them as 'it would be nice if you could remember this.' For secure and reliable storage of information, use cookies in combination with features such as sessions and data stored in a database.

When you save a cookie onto the client machine, you can specify how long it should exist. Cookies can persist indefinitely, or they can be set to expire after a certain time. In the popup example, you could specify that the cookie will expire after a month, by which time a new advert will have appeared. The user will have to recreate the cookie if they wanted to block the popup.

Note that users also can manually delete cookies from their system. If you have Internet Explorer, you can delete all the cookies on your machine by selecting Tools | Internet Option from the main IE window, and then clicking Delete Cookies, as shown in Figure 11-4:

Figure 11-4

Of course, if I do this, I would need to tell the BBC site again that I wanted the UK version of the site and weather details for Birmingham. Moreover, you will find you have to log on to all the sites where you have selected the Remember my details option.

As the earlier lifecycle diagrams hinted, you can set the cookie state using the `Response` object and read the existing cookie state using the `Request` object. It's quite simple to do this, so let's look at an example and see these objects working their magic!

Try It Out   Using Cookies

In this example, we're going to add to the Wrox United application once again. In the previous chapter, we added a box that enabled the user to register for email updates about changes made to the `Default.aspx` page. However, this page didn't do anything with this information other than validate it. Let's get this working now.

1.   Open up `Default.aspx` in Web Matrix and you will see the page in its current state, as shown in Figure 11-5:

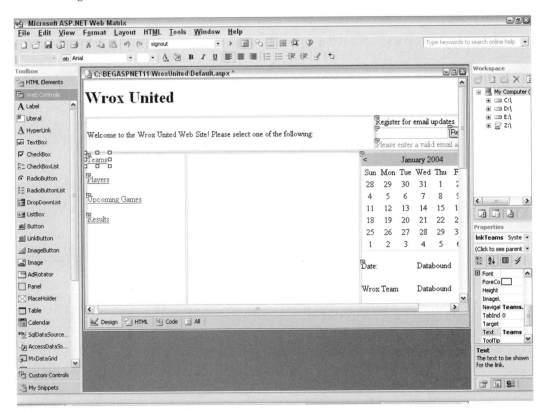

Figure 11-5

In the `WroxUnited` database there is a simple table called `Fans` that will contain email addresses of fans of the team. When the **Register** button is clicked, we need to do three things:

❑   Check that the address hasn't been added to the database. If it has, create a cookie and update the display to indicate that the user has registered for updates.

❑ If the address hasn't already been added, add it to the database, create a cookie, and indicate that the user has been registered for updates.

❑ When the page is loaded, if the client has a cookie indicating that they have already registered for updates, display a message confirming this.

2. Switch to **Code** view – it's time to add some database code to check whether a user has registered already or not. Drag a **SELECT Data Method** wizard onto the page and select the FanEmail field from the Fans table where the FanEmail field matches the @FanEmail parameter. Call this method CheckFanEmailAddresses and save it as a DataReader. Pass this into the function:

```
System.Data.IDataReader CheckFanEmailAddresses(string fanEmail)
{
  string connectionString =
   "Provider=Microsoft.Jet.OLEDB.4.0; Ole DB Services=-4; " +
   "Data Source=C:\\BegASPNET11\\WroxUnited\\Database\\WroxUnited.mdb";
  System.Data.IDbConnection dbConnection =
   new System.Data.OleDb.OleDbConnection(connectionString);

  string queryString = "SELECT [Fans].[FanEmail] FROM [Fans]" +
                       " WHERE ([Fans].[FanEmail] = @FanEmail)";
  System.Data.IDbCommand dbCommand = new System.Data.OleDb.OleDbCommand();
  dbCommand.CommandText = queryString;
  dbCommand.Connection = dbConnection;

  System.Data.IDataParameter dbParam_fanEmail =
   new System.Data.OleDb.OleDbParameter();
  dbParam_fanEmail.ParameterName = "@FanEmail";
  dbParam_fanEmail.Value = fanEmail;
  dbParam_fanEmail.DbType = System.Data.DbType.String;
  dbCommand.Parameters.Add(dbParam_fanEmail);

  dbConnection.Open();
  System.Data.IDataReader dataReader =
   dbCommand.ExecuteReader(System.Data.CommandBehavior.CloseConnection);

  return dataReader;
}
```

This code needs to be altered slightly to fit our needs. Firstly, we need to change the connection string to use the database connection details stored in the web.config file. Then we need to find out if a user has already registered, so let's modify this code to retrieve a count of the number of times that a particular email address appears in the database. If all goes well, this should never exceed 1. We can then use this value to return a Boolean true (if the user already exists) or false.

3. To alter this code, change the following highlighted lines:

```
bool CheckFanEmailAddresses(string fanEmail)
{
  string connectionString =
ConfigurationSettings.AppSettings["ConnectionString"];
  System.Data.IDbConnection dbConnection =
```

```
    new System.Data.OleDb.OleDbConnection(connectionString);
  string queryString = "SELECT COUNT([Fans].[FanEmail]) FROM [Fans]" +
                       "WHERE ([Fans].[FanEmail] = @FanEmail)";
System.Data.IDbCommand dbCommand = new System.Data.OleDb.OleDbCommand();
dbCommand.CommandText = queryString;
dbCommand.Connection = dbConnection;

System.Data.IDataParameter dbParam_fanEmail =
  new System.Data.OleDb.OleDbParameter();
dbParam_fanEmail.ParameterName = "@FanEmail";
dbParam_fanEmail.Value = fanEmail;
dbParam_fanEmail.DbType = System.Data.DbType.String;
dbCommand.Parameters.Add(dbParam_fanEmail);
int result = 0;
dbConnection.Open();
try
{
  result = (int)dbCommand.ExecuteScalar();
}
finally
{
  dbConnection.Close();
}

if (result > 0)
{
  return true;
}
else
{
  return false;
}
}
```

Notice the changes made to the return type of the function, the SQL, and the method used to query the data source. This will be discussed in a moment.

4. Switch back to the Design view and double-click the Register button at the top left to create an event handler for the Click() event of the button. Add the following code:

```
void btnRegister_Click(object sender, EventArgs e)
{
  string FanEmail = txtEmailAddress.Text;

  //Check whether the email address is already registered
  //If not, we need to register it by calling the AddNewFanEmail() method
  if (!CheckFanEmailAddresses(FanEmail))
  {
    AddNewFanEmail(FanEmail);
  }

  // Email has been registered, so update display and attempt write to cookie
  txtEmailAddress.Visible = false;
  lblRegister.Text = "You have successfully registered for email updates";
  btnRegister.Visible = false;
```

```
HttpCookie EmailRegisterCookie = new HttpCookie("EmailRegister");
EmailRegisterCookie.Value = FanEmail;
EmailRegisterCookie.Expires = DateTime.Now.AddSeconds(20);
Response.Cookies.Add(EmailRegisterCookie);
}
```

Here, make note of the call to a function called `AddNewFanEmail()` – let's create this now.

5. Drag an Insert Data Method code wizard onto the page, select the Fans table, click Next, and save the method as `AddNewFanEmail()`.

> **Don't check the box next to the `FanEmail` field when you are building this method.**
> **The correct parameter information will be created automatically if you totally ignore**
> **the field. All you need to do is select the `Fans` table, click Next, and save the method.**

Let's take a look at the code:

```
int AddNewFanEmail (string fanEmail)
{
   string connectionString =
     "Provider=Microsoft.Jet.OLEDB.4.0;Ole DB Services=-4;" +
     "Data Source=C:\\BegASPNET11\\WroxUnited\\Database\\WroxUnited.mdb";
   System.Data.IDbConnection dbConnection =
     new System.Data.OleDb.OleDbConnection(connectionString);

   string queryString = "INSERT INTO [Fans] ([FanEmail]) VALUES (@FanEmail)";
   System.Data.IDbCommand dbCommand = new System.Data.OleDb.OleDbCommand();
   dbCommand.CommandText = queryString;
   dbCommand.Connection = dbConnection;

   System.Data.IDataParameter dbParam_fanEmail =
     new System.Data.OleDb.OleDbParameter();
   dbParam_fanEmail.ParameterName = "@FanEmail";
   dbParam_fanEmail.Value = fanEmail;
   dbParam_fanEmail.DbType = System.Data.DbType.String;
   dbCommand.Parameters.Add(dbParam_fanEmail);

   int rowsAffected = 0;
   dbConnection.Open();
   try
   {
     rowsAffected = dbCommand.ExecuteNonQuery();
   }
   finally
   {
     dbConnection.Close();
   }
   return rowsAffected;
}
```

6. Change the connection string to use the central connection string:

```
int AddNewFanEmail (string fanEmail)
{
    string connectionString =
    ConfigurationSettings.AppSettings["ConnectionString"];
    System.Data.IDbConnection dbConnection =
      new System.Data.OleDb.OleDbConnection(connectionString);
```

7. Finally, check whether a cookie is present when the page is loaded, so that you can change the display if the user has already registered. Add the following to the `Page_Load()` method:

```
if (Request.Cookies["EmailRegister"] == null)
{
    txtEmailAddress.Visible = false;
    lblRegister.Text = "You have registered for email updates";
    btnRegister.Visible = false;
}
```

Run the page now, enter your email ID, and click **Register**. The message will change (as long as you enter a valid email address) to indicate that you've registered, as shown in Figure 11-6.

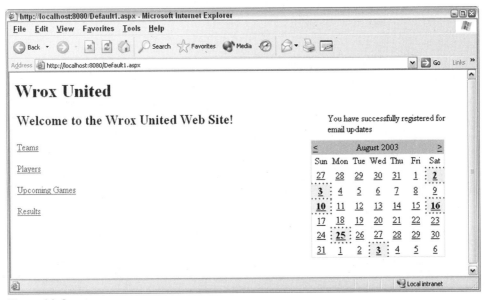

Figure 11-6

Note that the expiration time on the cookie was set to 20 seconds, which resulted in your email address not being remembered for long. Quickly close your browser and reopen the page. You should see the message shown in Figure 11-7:

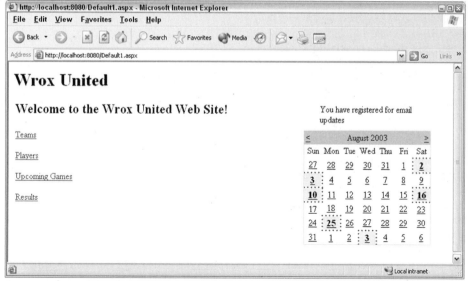

Figure 11-7

If you keep clicking Refresh after every 20 seconds, the textbox and button will reappear along with a message asking you to register.

How It Works

Let's start the discussion by looking directly at what happens when a user clicks the Register button. This is when the cookie is created on the client:

```
void btnRegister_Click(object sender, EventArgs e)
{
  string FanEmail = txtEmailAddress.Text;

  //Check whether the email address is already registered
  //If not, we need to register it by calling the AddNewFanEmail() method
  if (!CheckFanEmailAddresses(FanEmail))
  {
    AddNewFanEmail(FanEmail);
  }
```

If the email address is already stored in the database, the CheckFanEmailAddresses() method will return true. However, if it returns false, the email address is new and needs to be added to the database.

Once the email address has been stored in the database, we can go ahead and change the displayed text on the screen:

```
// Email has been registered, so update the display and attempt write to a
cookie
txtEmailAddress.Visible = false;
```

```
lblRegister.Text = "You have successfully registered for email updates";
btnRegister.Visible = false;
```

Next we attempt to add a cookie at the client end:

```
HttpCookie EmailRegisterCookie = new HttpCookie("EmailRegister");
EmailRegisterCookie.Value = FanEmail;
EmailRegisterCookie.Expires = DateTime.Now.AddSeconds(20);
Response.Cookies.Add(EmailRegisterCookie);
```

The first line of code creates a new instance of the `HttpCookie` class and names it `EmailRegister`. Once the cookie has been successfully created on the client, you can refer to the cookie by name later on in the code. The value of the cookie was set to be the email address entered into the textbox, and the `Expires` property also was set. In this example, the cookie was set to expire 20 seconds from the time at which it was created, which isn't practical in a real world application! The `Expires` property can be any `DateTime` value, so you could, for example, change this to `AddMonths(6)` so that the cookie persists for 6 months.

The `DateTime.Now` property is the easiest way to get the current date and time on the server, so by calling the `AddSeconds()` method, we can easily specify that a cookie will expire after a set amount of time from when it was created. For example, you may want to display this box every 6 months to fans in case their email address has changed, to ensure that they are registered correctly. Alternatively, you can hard-code a date (for example, if you wanted to create a monthly special).

We also added two data methods to check the status of the cookie. The first method was used to add a new email address to the database:

```
string queryString = "INSERT INTO [Fans] ([FanEmail]) VALUES (@FanEmail)";
```

The second data method queried the database to check whether the email address exists in the database. Let's look at the code:

```
bool CheckFanEmailAddresses(string fanEmail)
{
```

The first thing altered was the function return type. After all, we don't want a `DataReader` in this case – we want a simple yes or no answer to whether the email address exists already, so the return type is set to return a Boolean `true` or `false`.

The next change is to the query used:

```
string queryString = "SELECT COUNT([Fans].[FanEmail]) FROM [Fans]" +
                     " WHERE ([Fans].[FanEmail] = @FanEmail)";
```

The `COUNT` statement literally counts the number of results matched by the `SELECT` statement. You should never end up with the result of a count being more than one because this check is performed every time we attempt to add a new email address. To be on the safe side, return `true` to the calling code if you retrieve any rows at all:

```
int result = 0;
dbConnection.Open();
```

```
try
{
  result = (int)dbCommand.ExecuteScalar();
}
finally
{
  dbConnection.Close();
}

if (result > 0)
{
  return true;
}
else
{
  return false;
}
```

Hee, we added a quick test to the `Page_Load()` event handler to see if a cookie exists on the client:

```
if (Request.Cookies["EmailRegister"] == null)
{
```

The `Request` object is used to read the cookie; you can refer to a cookie by the name given to it earlier. If the cookie exists, this will return `true` and you can hide the unnecessary registration functionality:

```
txtEmailAddress.Visible = false;
lblRegister.Text = "You have registered for email updates";
btnRegister.Visible = false;
}
```

OK, so we've learned a lot about cookies and seen how to use cookies in a site. To recap, the general rules of thumb for using cookies are:

❑ Use them to store small pieces of data that aren't crucial to your application.

❑ Use them wisely – don't be tempted to store large objects in a cookie, because every request a client makes to your site will be accompanied by the cookie data.

❑ Don't rely on them for storing secure user details; instead, keep them simple to help with preliminary identification. The Amazon Web site is a good example of how to use cookies. It uses cookies to remember information about you when you visit the site, but actually to *buy* stuff, you need to retype your password details. These are passed to secure servers that authenticate you.

Sessions

A session can be thought of as the total amount of time you spend browsing a site. For example, in an online store, you first visit the site, log on, buy some stuff, and then leave. A user session pertains to the interactions that occur when a single user browses a site. Information in a session is accessible only for as long as the session is active. You could, for example, store the name of the currently logged-in user in the `Session` object specific to that user, and any of the pages in the site could then take this value and display it. Sessions are useful for features such as shopping baskets or any application that stores information on whether or not a user is logged in. They are tied in to a specific instance of a browser, so another instance of the browser on the same machine would not be able to access the same data.

It's a bit tricky to evaluate when a session ends, since when a browser closes, this information is not usually sent to the server (imagine having to wait for a 'close' signal to be sent whenever you closed a Web page!) To solve this problem, you can specify a timeout value for sessions. The default value is usually 20 minutes, which means that the session ends after 20 minutes of inactivity. This value can be changed; for example, if you created a financial Web site, you may want sessions to end after five minutes of inactivity. This minimizes the chances of sensitive information leaking even if a user forgets to log out or leaves the browser window open after a banking transaction.

How Do Sessions Work?

When a session starts, you can store data that will exist during that session. This could be simple text information about a user or an object such as an XML file. A 120-bit session identifier identifies each session. This session identifier is passed between ASP.NET and the client either by using cookies or by placing the identifier in the URL of the page (a technique that can be used for clients that have cookies turned off). Let's look at a session identifier – the following is an example of embedding a session identifier in the URL of a page:

http://www.mysite.com/(vgjgiz45ib0kqe554jvqxw2b)/Default.aspx

The extra data in the URL is only the session identifier – the actual data stored in the session is stored on the server. As a session can hold a variety of objects (a string, an `ArrayList`, even a `DataSet` object), only the identifier is passed between the client and the server. Figure 11-8 shows how sessions work:

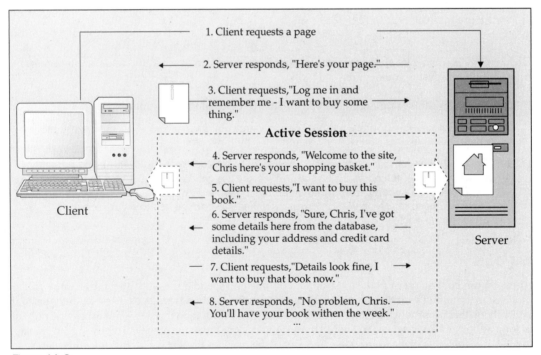

Figure 11-8

After the user logs on to an online store, the server knows who the user is and can relate each request from that user to the details specific to the user that are stored in the session. Therefore, the server can maintain a shopping basket and checkout functionality without asking the user to log back in with every request. Once the user has finished browsing the site, the server will eventually destroy the information stored in session memory and free up resources that it might need for other clients.

ASP.NET, by default, stores session information in the memory and in the same process as ASP.NET. This means that if the application crashes, session data will be lost. However, you do have the option to store session state information in a different process, on a different machine, or even in a database. This flexibility allows you to make your applications more robust in large-scale deployment scenarios.

The `Session` object has quite a few methods that you can use:

❑ `Session.Add`: Adds a new item to the `Session` object

❑ `Session.Remove`: Removes a named item from the session

❑ `Session.Clear`: Clears all values from the session but leaves the session active

❑ `Session.Abandon`: Ends the current session

Perhaps the simplest way to add data to a session is to use the following syntax:

```
Session["ItemName"] = Contents
```

After creating a new item in the session, you can use `ItemName` to refer to the contents of its corresponding `Session` object. The item is an identifying feature of the contents of the session, so you could store all the following in the session, where the first item is a simple string, the second is the string entered into a textbox, and the third is a `Hashtable` object:

```
Session["Name"] = "Chris"
Session["Email"] = txtEmailAddress.Text
Session["ShoppingBasket"] = HashtableOfBasketItems
```

Let's look at sessions in action by using an example. Before you run this example, you will need three images – `shirt.gif`, `hat.jpg`, and `mascot.jpg`. These three files are available along with the rest of the source code for this book from the Wrox Web site.

Try It Out Using Session State

1. This example will add another new page called `Merchandise.aspx` to the site. Add this new blank ASP.NET page to the Wrox United application folder.

2. Add a heading 1 with the text **Wrox United** at the top of the page, and directly underneath that, add a heading 2 with the text **Official Merchandise Store**. If you switch to HTML view, you'll see that the following code has been added:

```
<form runat="server">
  <h1>Wrox United</h1>
  <h2>Official Merchandise Store</h2>
```

3. Add an HTML table of width 600 pixels to the page, with three columns and three rows. In each row, insert an ASP.NET `Image` control, some text, and an ASP.NET `Button`, with the following properties, and you should see the **Design** view as shown in Figure 11-9

	Column 1: Image Control	Column 2: Text	Column 3: Button Control
Row 1	**ImageUrl**="images/shirt.gif"	"The Wrox United shirt, available in one size only"	**id**="btnBuyShirt" **onclick**="AddItemToBasket" **width**="100px" **text**="Buy a shirt!" **CommandArgument**="Shirt"
Row 2	**ImageUrl**="images/hat.jpg"	"The official Wrox United hat!"	**id**="btnBuyHat" **onclick**="AddItemToBasket" **width**="100px" **text**="Buy a hat!" **CommandArgument**="Hat"
Row 3	**ImageUrl**="images/mascot.jpg"	"The Wrox United cuddly mascot – a must-have for the younger supporters!"	**id**="btnBuyMascot" **onclick**="AddItemToBasket" **width**="100px" **text**="Buy a Mascot!" **CommandArgument**="Mascot"

Figure 11-9

4. In HTML view, you should have the following code generated for you automatically (alternatively, instead of dragging and dropping, you could type this lot in by hand if you wanted to):

```
<table width="600">
  <tr>
    <td><asp:Image id="imgCap" runat="server" ImageUrl="images/shirt.gif">
        </asp:Image></td>
    <td>The Wrox United shirt, available in one size only</td>
    <td><asp:Button id="btnBuyShirt" onclick="AddItemToBasket"
                    runat="server" Text="Buy a shirt!" Width="100px"
                    CommandArgument="Shirt"></asp:Button> </td>
  </tr>
  <tr>
    <td><asp:Image id="imgShirt" runat="server" ImageUrl="images/hat.jpg">
        </asp:Image></td>
    <td>The official Wrox United hat!</td>
    <td><asp:Button id="btnBuyHat" onclick="AddItemToBasket"
                    runat="server" Text="Buy the hat!" Width="100px"
                    CommandArgument="Hat"></asp:Button> </td>
  </tr>
  <tr>
    <td><asp:Image id="imgMascot" runat="server"
                   ImageUrl="images/mascot1.jpg">
        </asp:Image></td>
    <td>The Wrox United cuddy mascot - a must-have for the younger
    supporters!
    </td>
    <td><asp:Button id="btnBuyMascot" onclick="AddItemToBasket"
                    runat="server" Text="Buy the mascot!" Width="100px"
                    CommandArgument="Mascot"></asp:Button> </td>
  </tr>
</table>
```

5. Add the following code below the table, while still in HTML view:

```
<br/>
  <p>
    Your basket contains:
    <asp:label id="lblBasketMessage" runat="server"></asp:label>
  </p>
  <p>
    <asp:Repeater id="basketlist" runat="server">
      <itemTemplate>
        <asp:Label width="70" runat="server"
            text='<%# ((DictionaryEntry)Container.DataItem).Key + "s: " %>'>
          </asp:Label>
         
        <asp:Label runat="server"
          text='<%# ((DictionaryEntry)Container.DataItem).Value %>'>
          </asp:Label>
        <br />
```

```
      </itemTemplate>
    </asp:Repeater>
  </p>
  <p>
    <asp:Button id="btnCheckOut" runat="server" Text="Checkout"></asp:Button>
    <asp:Button id="btnEmptyBasket" onclick="btnEmptyBasket_Click"
                runat="server" Text="Empty Basket"></asp:Button>
  </p>
</form>
```

6. That's it for the HTML side of things! Switch to the **Code** view and enter the following methods:

Note that the method signature for the `AddItemToBasket ()` *function is already generated for you, so make sure you don't add another copy of this or the page won't compile properly.*

```
void Page_Load()
{
  if (Session["Basket"] == null)
  {
    InitializeBasket();
  }
}


void btnEmptyBasket_Click(object sender, EventArgs e)
{
  InitializeBasket();
}
```

```
void AddItemToBasket(object sender, EventArgs e)
  {
    // Each time this is run, get the CommandArgument property of the button
    //that fired the event, and use this to populate the Session object
    System.Web.UI.WebControls.Button theButton =
      (System.Web.UI.WebControls.Button)sender;
    string itemName = (string)theButton.CommandArgument;

    System.Collections.Hashtable basketTable =
      (System.Collections.Hashtable)Session["Basket"];

    // Check whether the session contains an entry for that item
    // if no entry exists, create one with value 0
    if (basketTable[itemName] == null)
    {
      basketTable[itemName] = 0;
    }

    // Increment the counter for the selected item
    int itemCount = (int)basketTable[itemName];
    basketTable[itemName] = itemCount + 1;
  }
```

```
void InitializeBasket()
{
  System.Collections.Hashtable basketTable = new
                    System.Collections.Hashtable();
```

```
    Session["Basket"] = basketTable;
}

void Page_Prerender()
{
  System.Collections.Hashtable basketTable =
    (System.Collections.Hashtable)Session["Basket"];
  basketlist.DataSource = basketTable;
  basketlist.DataBind();

  if ((basketTable.Count) == 0)
  {
    lblBasketMessage.Text = "nothing - please buy something!";
  }
  else
  {
    lblBasketMessage.Text = "";
  }
}
```

You'll notice that there are quite a few methods in here, which we'll look at in detail in just a moment; these are designed to make the application more scalable Let's see how the page works, then the purpose of these methods will become a bit clearer. It's time to run the page and try it out! You should see the screen depicted in Figure 11-10:

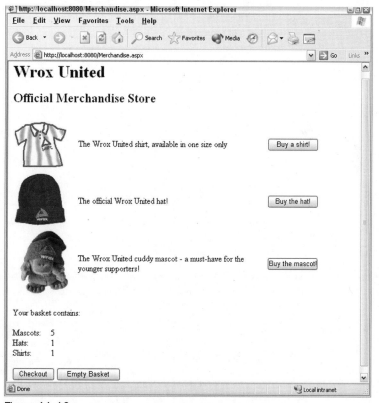

Figure 11-10

How It Works

This simple example uses quite a few techniques to store data about the items in the shopping basket. The data stored in the `Session` object is a hashtable that stores name-value pairs. The key field for the hashtable is the name of the item added to the basket and the value is the quantity of that item. The event handlers on that page all perform different actions on the data stored in the session. Let's start by looking through the added code.

First, we added an HTML table and some simple controls to the page. Notice that the `onClick` attribute of each button in the table was set to fire the same event handler – `AddItemToBasket()`. Each button has a unique `CommandArgument` property that describes what is added to the basket:

```
<table width="600">
  <tr>
    <td><asp:Image id="imgCap" runat="server" ImageUrl="images/shirt.gif">
        </asp:Image></td>
    <td>The Wrox United shirt, available in one size only</td>
    <td><asp:Button id="btnBuyShirt" onclick="AddItemToBasket"
                    runat="server" Text="Buy a shirt!" Width="100px"
                    CommandArgument="Shirt"></asp:Button> </td>
  </tr>
  <tr>
    <td><asp:Image id="imgShirt" runat="server" ImageUrl="images/hat.jpg">
        </asp:Image></td>
    <td>The official Wrox United hat!</td>
    <td><asp:Button id="btnBuyHat" onclick="AddItemToBasket"
                    runat="server" Text="Buy the hat!" Width="100px"
                    CommandArgument="Hat"></asp:Button> </td>
  </tr>
  <tr>
    <td><asp:Image id="imgMascot" runat="server"
        ImageUrl="images/mascot1.jpg">
        </asp:Image></td>
    <td>The Wrox United cuddy mascot - a must-have for the younger
        supporters!
    </td>
    <td><asp:Button id="btnBuyMascot" onclick="AddItemToBasket"
                    runat="server" Text="Buy the mascot!" Width="100px"
                    CommandArgument="Mascot"></asp:Button> </td>
  </tr>
</table>
```

Next, we added some more controls to display the contents of the basket and to provide the option of either clearing the basket or checking out via a checkout and payment process:

```
<br/>
  <p>
    Your basket contains:
    <asp:label id="lblBasketMessage" runat="server"></asp:label>
  </p>
  <p>
    <asp:Repeater id="basketlist" runat="server">
      <itemTemplate>
```

The `basketlist Repeater` control will be data-bound to a `Hashtable` object (as we'll see in just a moment). This enables us to do some interesting data binding in this control. The first label in this control includes an interesting statement:

```
<asp:Label width="70" runat="server"
        text='<%# ((DictionaryEntry)Container.DataItem).Key + "s: "%>'>
</asp:Label>
```

Notice that the `text` property has a data-binding statement in it. Here, the `Key` of the current item in the Hashtable, which is used to populate this control, is displayed in this label along with some text. In this way, we take the name of each item, and we can pluralize it by adding "s" to the end of it. The colon is there to add a neat grammatical separator between the name of the item and the quantity. So we have **Mascots: 3** as the displayed text, having obtained the key `Mascot` from the Hashtable. Notice that we have to add a cast to this statement to tell the C# compiler that the `DataItem` is of type `DictionaryEntry`, because Hashtables are collections of `DictionaryEntry` data types.

The rest of the code in the HTML view of the page includes another data-binding expression to obtain the quantity of the current item in the shopping basket.

```
       
      <asp:Label runat="server"
          text='<%# ((DictionaryEntry)Container.DataItem).Value %>'>
        </asp:Label>
      <br />
    </itemTemplate>
  </asp:Repeater>
</p>
<p>
  <asp:Button id="btnCheckOut" runat="server" Text="Checkout"></asp:Button>
  <asp:Button id="btnEmptyBasket" onclick="btnEmptyBasket_Click"
              runat="server" Text="Empty Basket"></asp:Button>
</p>
```

The online payment procedures that you would associate with the Checkout *button hasn't been implemented in the code – that's a bit beyond the scope of this chapter. For more information on online payments, you might want to consult* **www.paypal.com**, *one of many online payment service providers.*

It's time to work through the methods in the code. They are presented in roughly the same order in which they will be processed when a page is requested by the browser (following the chain of events as they correspond to the page lifecycle).

Firstly, the `Page_Load()` event handler:

```
void Page_Load()
{
  if (Session["Basket"] == null)
  {
    InitializeBasket();
  }
}
```

Each time the page is loaded, this method will check whether the `Session` object contains a basket. If it doesn't, a new empty basket is created. We'll look at the `InitializeBasket()` method that does this in just a moment.

```
void btnEmptyBasket_Click(object sender, EventArgs e)
{
  InitializeBasket();
}
```

The `btnEmptyBasket_Click()` method also calls the `InitializeBasket()` method to clear out any existing basket data. The `AddItemToBasket()` method comes next, and this one is quite interesting. For starters, *all* the three item buttons call *this* method, and they each pass a `CommandArgument` property.

```
void AddItemToBasket(object sender, EventArgs e)
{
  // Each time this is run, get the CommandArgument property of the button
     that
  // fired the event, and use this to populate the Session object
  System.Web.UI.WebControls.Button theButton =
    (System.Web.UI.WebControls.Button)sender;
  string itemName = (string)theButton.CommandArgument;
```

These two lines of code are all that's needed to get the string information that specifies which button the user clicked. Once you have this string (which is set to either `Shirt`, `Hat`, or `Mascot`), you can use it to add data to the session.

First, create a local `Hashtable` object to temporarily store the contents of the Session's basket item. This will make the code easier to understand.

> **The New keyword is not included in the Hashtable's declaration – this is very important, as you'll see in a moment!**

```
System.Collections.Hashtable basketTable =
  (System.Collections.Hashtable)Session["Basket"];
```

The remainder of the code for this method uses `basketTable`, which is the hashtable representation of the contents of the `Session` object's `Basket` item, to add items to the session. Now, the fun thing is that because you didn't add a `New` keyword to the `basketTable`, you don't get a *new* `Hashtable` object. Instead, you *refer* to an existing Hashtable object, specifically the one that is stored in the `Session` object. This is an example of working with *reference* types. Because you are working with the contents of the Session's `Basket` item via the `basketTable` Hashtable; anything you do to the `basketTable` will affect the contents of the Session.

A full discussion of value and reference types is beyond this chapter. For more information, you should read Professional ASP.NET 1.1, Wrox Press, ISBN: 0-7645-5890-0.

We check to see if the item added to the basket has been added before:

```
// Check whether the session contains an entry for that item
// if no entry exists, create one with value 0
if (basketTable[itemName] == null)
```

```
  {
    basketTable[itemName] = 0;
  }
```

If the item has never been in the basket before, it is added to the basket and initialized to 0 to make it ready to receive a new quantity. In the next piece of code, one more of the selected item is added to the basket. Thus, if there were already three Mascots in the basket, clicking this button will add another one to the basket, resulting in a basket that contains four Mascots.However, if this were the first mascot you bought, you would end up with one mascot.

```
    // Increment the counter for the selected item
    int itemCount = (int)basketTable[itemName];
    basketTable[itemName] = itemCount + 1;
  }
```

Let's look at the `InitializeBasket()` method mentioned earlier:

```
  void InitializeBasket()
  {
    System.Collections.Hashtable basketTable = new
                                               System.Collections.Hashtable();
    Session["Basket"] = basketTable;
  }
```

In just two lines of code, a new `Hashtable` object is created and the Session's `Basket` item is set to point to it. The new object doesn't have any items in it, so it will be an 'empty' basket.

If this method was called in response to clicking the Empty Basket button, it's likely that you originally had a full basket, so where do all the original contents of the basket go?

Well, the answer is that by changing the Hashtable that the `Basket` item is pointing to, we change which Hashtable is referenced by the Session. Thus, the old Hashtable (the old basket) is no longer pointed to by anything, and the .NET garbage collector sweeps the Hashtable away. The Hashtable is no longer wanted because no one is using it, so we can get rid of it to clear out some memory. New objects can now use the memory that was used by the old hashtable. The garbage collector is very efficient and gets rid of unreferenced objects on a regular basis. The memory that the old `Hashtable` object was taking up is recycled, which means that you are less likely to run out of memory.

There is one last event handler to look at. This one handles the `Prerender()` event of the page. This event is always fired when a page is loaded and is your last chance to change anything just before the page is displayed:

```
  void Page_Prerender()
  {
    System.Collections.Hashtable basketTable =
      (System.Collections.Hashtable)Session["Basket"];
    basketlist.DataSource = basketTable;
    basketlist.DataBind();
  }
```

This code uses the same Hashtable that is stored in the `Session` object's `Basket` item by pointing another Hashtable towards the same data. This data is stored in your computer's memory, so what you're doing is telling your program where to find that data. Again, any changes made to the basketTable will change the contents of the Basket (because you are changing the same object!) The basketList control is a simple Repeater control, like the ones used in the previous chapter. In this example, we bind the contents of the Hashtable to the Repeater to display the contents of the basket on the page:

```
if ((basketTable.Count) == 0)
{
    lblBasketMessage.Text = "nothing - please buy something!";
}
else
{
    lblBasketMessage.Text = "";
}
}
```

Lastly, a message is displayed if the basket is empty. If the count of all the items in the basketTable Hashtable is 0, the Hashtable or the virtual basket is empty. All this is done by the Prerender() event handler to ensure that only the most recent data is displayed after any items that may have been added.

Remember that when you click a button, a postback is initiated and the page is reloaded. If we'd have displayed the contents of the basket by adding code to the Page_Load() event handler, we would not be displaying the most current data, but the data of what happened that *last* time the button was clicked, because the Page_Load() event handler will run *before* the button click event is handled. You can easily try this out for yourself – if you move all the contents of this method into the Page_Load() event handler, you'll see that the count of the number of items in the basket is one behind the actual count.

> The actual order of events is: **Page_Load()** --> **Control Events** --> **Prerender()**

That's it for now – Sessions will be back later when we put together a fun example that adds some style to the Wrox United site. Let's move on to applications.

Applications

One step up from the session is the application. From the time an ASP.NET application is first loaded, to when the application is restarted, which could be due to a configuration change or the restarting of the Web server, you can store information related to that application in the Application object. When the application is restarted, any information stored in the Application object will be lost, so you need to decide carefully what to store in the application state.

> **It's best to only store small amounts of data in the application state to minimize memory usage on the server. Small bits of data that change frequently but don't need to be saved when the application is restarted are best kept in the Session object.**

For larger data or for data that doesn't often change, the ASP.NET Cache object can be very useful, as you'll see in the Caching section later in the chapter.

How Do Applications Work?

Applications are a bit simpler than sessions, since they run entirely on the server. When the application is running, you can use the same method of storing data in an application object as used with sessions All you need to do is enter an identifier and a value that can be of any type, even a dataset. The best way to look at how application state can be used is through an example. Let's take this opportunity to add another page to your site that has more interactivity than the previous pages!

Try It Out Using Application State

In this example, you will construct the world's simplest chat room! All you need is a new ASP.NET page on the Wrox United site, a few controls, and a bit of code, and you can then chat with anyone around the world.

1. The first step is to reopen `Default.aspx` and add a new hyperlink to the list of links on the left. Call it `lnkChat`, and set its `NavigateUrl` property to `Chat.aspx`.

2. Create a new ASP.NET page called `Chat.aspx`. Switch to HTML view and enter the following code within the `<form>` tags:

```
<h1>Wrox United
</h1>
<h2>Online Chat
</h2>
<asp:TextBox id="txtChatBox" runat="server"
            TextMode="MultiLine"
            Height="200px" Width="550px" ReadOnly="true">
</asp:TextBox>
<br />
<br />
<table width="550">
  <tbody>
    <tr>
      <td width="150">
        Enter your name:
      </td>
      <td>
        <asp:TextBox id="txtName" runat="server"></asp:TextBox>
      </td>
    </tr>
    <tr>
      <td width="150">
        Enter your message:
      </td>
      <td>
        <asp:TextBox id="txtMessage" runat="server"
                    MaxLength="100" Width="402px">
        </asp:TextBox>
      </td>
    </tr>
    <tr>
      <td>
         
      </td>
      <td>
```

```
            <asp:Button id="btnPost" onclick="btnPost_Click"
                     runat="server" Text="Post message">
         </asp:Button>
         <asp:Button id="btnClearLog" onclick="btnClearLog_Click"
                     runat="server" Text="Clear log">
         </asp:Button>
       </td>
     </tr>
   </tbody>
 </table>
```

Quickly flip to the Design view and look at the page; it should be as shown in Figure 11-11:

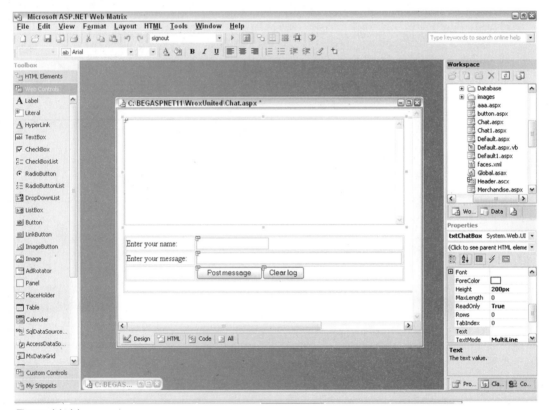

Figure 11-11

3. Switch to the Code view and enter the following code:

```
void btnPost_Click(object Sender, EventArgs e)
{
  string tab = "\t";
  string newline = "\r";
  string newMessage = txtName.Text + ":" + tab + txtMessage.Text + newline +
                  Application["ChatLog"];
```

```
  if (newMessage.Length > 500)
  {
    newMessage = newMessage.Substring(0,499);
  }

  Application["ChatLog"] = newMessage;

  txtChatBox.Text = (string)Application["ChatLog"];
  txtMessage.Text = "";
}
```

This event handler runs when someone clicks the Post message button on the page. It saves the name of the person who posted the message and the message itself in the `Application` object.

4.   Add the following two methods, followed by running the page to see Figure 11-12 (you'll be able to have a conversation with yourself!). The first is a `Page_Load()` event handler that loads the details of the current chat. The second clears the log when the Clear log button is pressed:

```
void Page_Load()
{
  txtChatBox.Text = (string)Application["ChatLog"];
}
void btnClearLog_Click(object sender, EventArgs e)
{
  Application["ChatLog"] = "";
  txtChatBox.Text = (string)Application["ChatLog"];
}
```

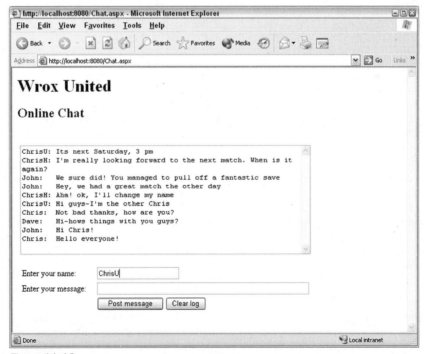

Figure 11-12

New messages in the chat will always be added at the top of the window. If you increase the size of the chat log, you could store a lot more text that would start to disappear off the bottom of the textbox (you view this by scrolling down the box). Keeping the newly added messages at the top ensures that new content is always visible.

Also notice that after a certain amount of text has appeared in the main chat window, characters start to disappear from the end of the chat – this is intentional, and it saves on server resources as we'll see in a moment. Additionally, clicking the Clear log button will wipe the entire chat log instantly. Browsers new to the page will see the current chat as soon as they get to the page.

How It Works

We've constructed a page that any visitor to the site can use to chat with their friends. There isn't a permanent store for chat logs, but you can at least get instant communication working, which could be really useful for a quick Internet team chat (especially if one member of the team works at an office where instant messaging programs like MSN Messenger or AOL Instant Messenger are banned!)

Let's look through the added code. The front-end of the site is quite simple, so let's directly look at the properties of the three textboxes on the form:

```
<asp:TextBox id="txtChatBox" runat="server"
             TextMode="MultiLine"
             Height="200px" Width="550px" ReadOnly="true">
</asp:TextBox>
```

Because the first textbox holds the entire chat transcript so far, we've made it a ReadOnly, MultiLine textbox that has a specified width and height. The second textbox is very simple indeed:

```
<asp:TextBox id="txtName" runat="server"></asp:TextBox>
```

The third textbox has an interesting feature:

```
<asp:TextBox id="txtMessage" runat="server"
             MaxLength="100" Width="402px">
</asp:TextBox>
```

We specified a maximum length for this textbox, to prevent anyone from entering really long messages.

In the Code editor, we added two button-click event handlers and a Page_Load() event handler. Let's look at them in turn:

```
void btnPost_Click(object Sender, EventArgs e)
{
  string tab = "\t";
  string newline = "\r";
  string newMessage = txtName.Text + ":" + tab + txtMessage.Text +
                      newline + Application["ChatLog"];
```

The first event handler reacts to the posting of a new message. A new String object is created to hold the message and the name of the person posting the message, and also to apply some formatting. The string displayed consists of the name of the person posting the message, followed by a colon:

```
txtName.Text + ":"
```

Then a tab character is added to space out the name from the message, before adding the message itself:

```
+ tab + txtMessage.Text
```

Finally, we add a line break followed by the current contents of the chat log. This is done in a manner such that any new message will always appear at the top of the textbox, one line above the previous message:

```
+ newline + Application["ChatLog"];
```

The existing chat log is saved in the `Application` object and is retrieved by using the following syntax:

```
Application["ChatLog"]
```

If there is no data in the log yet, this value will be null and a new message will simply contain a formatted version of the new post. You can refer to the contents of an item in the Application store by its name, in this case, `ChatLog`. This will return the contents of the item, which in this example is the string of the existing messages.

Note that you don't want to store too much data in the `Application` object or your Web server will grind to a halt! In the example, this has been limited to 500 characters. Any text beyond this point is removed (working from the oldest to the newest text):

```
if (newMessage.Length > 500)
{
   newMessage = newMessage.Substring(0,499);
}
```

The `Substring()` method grabs all the string data between the two specified points, in this case, from the first character (at index `0`) to the 500th character (at index `499`). If you want a longer log of chat transcript, increase the two larger numbers to higher values.

> Note that the end point of the substring is always one less than the length of the message because the items in the string are zero-indexed.

Finally, the new transcript is saved back to the `Application` object:

```
Application["ChatLog"] = newMessage;
```

In addition, the new transcript is displayed in the transcript textbox:

```
txtChatBox.Text = (string)Application["ChatLog"];
txtMessage.Text = "";
}
```

The application works quite well, but without any mechanism to refresh the page, other people browsing the page would have to either keep refreshing the page manually or post new messages regularly to see any new messages. The most common solution to this problem would be to split the page into two frames. The top frame could contain the chat box and the bottom frame could contain the textboxes and buttons. You could then add an auto-refresh to the top page to force it to refresh every 10 seconds or so.

Application state is quite a useful feature, as is session state, but one of the coolest things that ASP.NET has to offer when it comes to applications and sessions is the ability to react to events raised by both of these. The next section looks at this process in more detail.

Reacting to Application and Session Events

An event is fired every time an application or a session starts, ends, or when an error occurs. As an ASP.NET developer, you have the ability to intercept these events and write event handlers for them.

These event handlers have numerous useful features. For example, when an application starts, you can create an item with a default value in the application state, which can be updated later. Event handlers are placed in a special application-specific file called Global.asax.

Global.asax

This file exists at the root of a Web application and can contain event handlers for all the application- and session-level events that are fired when an application is run. If you open up Web Matrix and create a new Global.asax file, you will see the following:

```
<%@ Application language="C#" %>

<script runat="server">

  public void Application_Start(Object sender, EventArgs e)
  {
    // Code that runs on application startup
  }

  public void Application_End(Object sender, EventArgs e)
  {
    // Code that runs on application shutdown
  }

  public void Application_Error(Object sender, EventArgs e)
  {
    // Code that runs when an unhandled error occurs
  }

  public void Session_Start(Object sender, EventArgs e)
  {
    // Code that runs when a new session is started
  }

  public void Session_End(Object sender, EventArgs e)
```

```
    {
        // Code that runs when a session ends
    }

</script>
```

The helpful comments in the code give you an idea of what belongs in each part of the file. Note that you can add code that runs in these event handlers. Suppose you add the following line to the `Application_Start()` event handler:

```
public void Application_Start(Object sender, EventArgs e)
{
    Application["ChatLog"] = "Hello, and welcome to the Wrox United Chat
    page!";
}
```

Adding this one line means that the very first time the application is started, there will be some default text in the chat page.

With the event handlers available in the `Global.asax` page, you could add some global event handling code to the `Application_Error()` event handler, or you could add some cleanup code to the `Session_End` section to ensure that all memory is freed up when a session ends.

Let's add a `Global.asax` page to the application now and have a go at adding global code.

Try it Out   Global.asax – Global Settings

1.   Head back into Web Matrix and create a new file. Select the `Global.asax` file type from the options, as shown in Figure 11-13:

Figure 11-13

2. You'll find that Web Matrix automatically creates the skeleton of the file, so you don't need to add much code. In your `Global.asax` page, add the following highlighted lines of code in the appropriate event handlers:

```
<%@ Application language="C#" %>
<script runat="server">

  public void Application_Start(Object sender, EventArgs e)
  {
    Application["ChatLog"] = "Hello, and welcome to the Wrox United Chat
    page!";
  }
...
  public void Session_Start(Object sender, EventArgs e)
  {
    System.Collections.Hashtable basketTable = new
    System.Collections.Hashtable();
    Session["Basket"] = basketTable;
  }
...
</script>
```

Shut down the Web Matrix Web server. This can be done by right-clicking on the Web Matrix Web Server icon in the **System** tray at the bottom right of the screen, and then clicking **Stop**. Relaunch the `Chat.aspx` page and the application will restart and fire the Application's `Start` event. Notice that default text appears when you open the chat page for the first time, as shown in Figure 11-14:

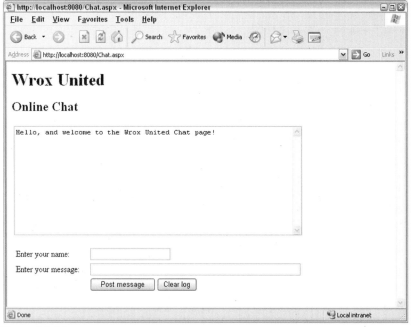

Figure 11-14

The other change made doesn't really have a discernable impact on the basket example, except that it handles the creation of a new instance of the basket Hashtable that was used in the Merchandise.aspx page. This means that you could theoretically remove the code from the Page_Load() event for the page that checks whether the basket exists or not. It will always exist, even for new sessions, if this code runs as intended without affecting the basket.

3. Once you have added this code to Global.asax, remove the contents of the Page_Load() event handler for the Merchandise.aspx page and you will find that the page will still run without errors.

How It Works

Let's quickly run through the newly added code:

```
public void Application_Start(Object sender, EventArgs e)
{
  Application["ChatLog"] = "Hello, and welcome to the Wrox United Chat
  page!";
}
```

In the Application_Start() event handler, we set the Application object's ChatLog item to have some default text. Whenever the application is restarted, there will be some text in the chat room.

Note that when you click the Clear log button on that page, the default text will not be displayed, because the application is still running. Clicking the Clear Log button clears the contents of the existing object, without reinitializing it.

The next change made was to the Session_Start() event handler:

```
public void Session_Start(Object sender, EventArgs e)
{
  System.Collections.Hashtable basketTable = new
  System.Collections.Hashtable();
  Session["Basket"] = basketTable;
}
```

In this case, we duplicated the code that was used in the InitializeBasket() method in the Merchandise.aspx page code and placed it in the event handler. This means that every new session will run this code before the user even browses to that page, so the basket will always exist for each session until the session ends (which is when all Session objects will be cleared out).

Global.asax is a very useful tool for storing default application-wide settings, but there is another way to remember information for the entire duration of an application, *caching*.

Caching

In addition to Application state, ASP.NET provides another way to share objects across an application – the Cache object. Any object, from XML data to a simple variable can be stored in the Cache object. If you are thinking that this sounds quite similar to the Application object, you are right. In general terms, you can use the `Cache` object in exactly the same way. However, the `Cache` object also has some additional features, notably the ability to store data about *dependencies*.

So, what are dependencies? Well, imagine you wanted to store the contents of a Hashtable in the cache. For example, this Hashtable could hold a set of dates corresponding to the dates when a soccer team is playing a match. You could save this to the cache with a dependency set to the value of a global variable; this could be a `DateTime` field representing when the list of dates was *last updated*. If the contents of that variable change (if a new match is scheduled), the cached hashtable would immediately expire and need to be regenerated to display the new date.

ASP.NET allows you to have dependencies between items placed in the cache and files in the file system. If a file targeted by a dependency changes, ASP.NET automatically removes dependent items from the cache. This allows for the development of fast applications where developers do not have to worry about stale data remaining in the cache.

To add an object to the cache, all you need to do in the simplest case is:

```
Cache["MyCachedThing"] = ThingToBeCached;
```

An example of this would be:

```
Cache["TeamNickname"] = txtNickname.Text;
```

In this example, you created a new item that stores a value that comes from the `Text` property of a textbox, and stored it in the `Cache` collection.

As you might be able to tell, the `Cache` stores data in the form of a collection of name-value pairs. To retrieve the value of an item in the `Cache`, all you need to do is refer to the item by its name, casting it to the appropriate type:

```
lblDisplayNickname.Text = (string)Cache["TeamNickname"];
```

To add a dependency to the object being cached, you need to add some more parameters when adding the item to the cache.

There are two ways for adding an object to the cache, with a dependency or a specified expiration (which works in a similar way to the other state management mechanisms encountered in this chapter).

The `Insert()` method adds an item to the cache. The `Add()` method also adds an item to the cache, but it returns an object representing the item you add to the cache. Let's see what this means:

```
Cache.Insert("TeamNickname", txtNickname.Text, null,
             DateTime.Now.AddMinutes(20), NoSlidingExpiration);
```

This statement will add a new entry to the cache called `TeamNickname`. The value will come from the `Text` property of a `TextBox`. There are no dependencies for this item (which is why you include null in the parameter list). The last two options are where the expiration for the item is set. In this example, the expiration is set to an absolute value (using the `DateTime` object) whereas the second parameter accepts sliding time values (specified using the `TimeSpan` object).

The Add() method works exactly the same way, except that it returns an object representing the cached item. Therefore, instead of inserting the new item into the cache on one line and using it on a following line of code, you could do the following:

```
lblDisplayNickname.Text = Cache.Add ("TeamNickname",
                              txtNickname.Text, null,
                              DateTime.Now.AddMinutes(20),
                              NoSlidingExpiration);
```

> *You can't add a new item to the cache using the Add() method if an item with the same key already exists – in that situation, you would need to use the Insert() method.*

Finally, you can be notified when an item in the cache expires, enabling you to code event handlers that react to this, a feature that could come in very handy! Let's say you cache that Hashtable of match dates in a cache object – you could intercept the event that fires when the cache expires, and automatically repopulate the cache with an updated set of data. Scheduling this sort of action for times when the site is not too busy ensures that visitors will not be inconvenienced by these updates.

> *We won't be looking at how to implement this in the examples in this book. If you are interested in learning more about this process, you should consult the documentation and learn about using the CacheItemRemovedCallback delegate. Refer to Professional ASP.NET 1.1 Special Edition, Wiley ISBN: 0-7645-5890-0 for information more on this subject.*

Let's look at an example. If you remember, in the previous chapter we added the calendar control to the front page of the site. It used a Hashtable to store the list of dates on which matches were scheduled. This Hashtable had to be refreshed every time the page was hit, which meant that each request opened up a fresh connection to the database to retrieve the active dates. However, the list of dates isn't likely to change all that often, so remembering that data for subsequent hits would be a great idea. We'll implement this functionality here.

Try It Out   Wrox United – Caching Objects

1.   Reopen Default.aspx in Web Matrix and modify the following lines of code in the Page_Load() event:

```
public void Page_Load(object sender, EventArgs e)
{
    if (Cache["DateList"] == null)
    {
      System.Data.IDataReader DateReader = Dates();

      while (DateReader.Read())
      {
        DateList[DateReader["Date"]] = DateReader["Date"];
      }

      DateReader.Close();

      Cache.Insert("DateList", DateList, null, DateTime.Now.AddMinutes(1),
        Cache.NoSlidingExpiration);

      Response.Write ("Added to cache");
```

```
  }
  else
  {
   Response.Write ("Already in cache - nothing added");
  }

...
}
```

Notice that a couple of `Response.Write` statements were added to the code – these are crude but effective ways of quickly testing whether some code worked or not, and since the caching won't really produce any visible results, you can use these to confirm that the newly implemented caching mechanism is working, then remove them at a later date.

2. Change the following highlighted line of code from the `DayRender()` event handler for the `Calendar` control:

```
public void EventCalendar_DayRender(object sender, DayRenderEventArgs e)
{
   if (((Hashtable)Cache["DateList"])[e.Day.Date] != null)
   {
     e.cell.style.add("font-weight", "bold")
...
}
```

3. Run the code and you should see Figure 11-15 the first time the page is loaded:

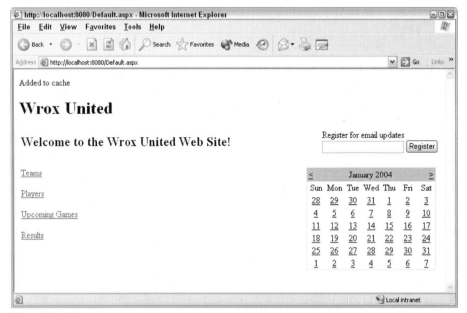

Figure 11-15

Now refresh the page or launch a new browser instance to view the page as shown in Figure 11-16:

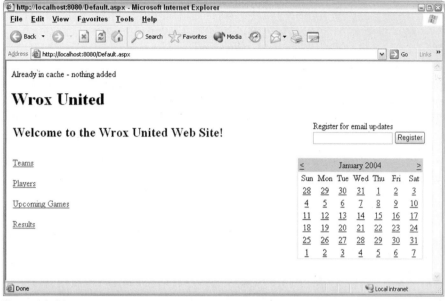

Figure 11-16

This message will appear in the top left of the page if you keep refreshing the page for a whole minute. Any hits received by the server after that minute is over will reload the Hashtable into the cache.

How It Works

Every connection opened to a database is a costly maneuver. Reducing the frequency of such actions is essential for any site to perform well under high user loads. Therefore, this simple example could considerably improve the performance of the Wrox United application.

So what did we actually do? Look at the code added to the Page_Load() event handler:

```
if (Cache["DateList"] == null)
{
```

The first addition checks whether there is an object called DateList in the cache. If there isn't one, we populate the Hashtable object like before:

```
System.Data.IDataReader DateReader = Dates();

while (DateReader.Read())
{
  DateList[DateReader["Date"]] = DateReader["Date"];
}
```

```
        DateReader.Close();
```

Then you can add this newly created Hashtable to the cache:

```
Cache.Insert("DateList", DateList, null, DateTime.Now.AddMinutes(1),
              Cache.NoSlidingExpiration);
```

In this example, we specified that the `DateList Hashtable` object should be stored in the cache with the name `DateList`. We didn't specify a dependency for this object, but we *did* specify that it only exists for one minute before expiring. In a real life situation, you could increase this to whatever you like – once every couple of hours, once a day, or whatever is appropriate depending on how often the data changes.

Finally, we added some quick debugging statements to the code to help see what was going on. Remove these or at least comment them out once you're happy with the way your code works.

```
    Response.Write ("Added to cache");
  }
  else
  {
   Response.Write ("Already in cache - nothing added");
  }
```

The only other change made was to the `DayRender()` event handler for the `Calendar` control:

```
  if (((Hashtable)Cache["DateList"])[e.Day.Date] != null)
  {
```

This statement looks a little complicated, so let's break it into pieces. Instead of referring to the Hashtable directly, we can now refer to the version stored in the `Cache` object, substituting `Cache["DateList"]` for `DateList` in the code, and adding the appropriate casting. In this case, the cache object called `DateList` is a Hashtable:

```
 ((Hashtable)Cache["DateList"])
```

We can then access an item in the Hashtable as before, using the passed in date as the key value:

```
 Hashtable[e.Day.Date]
```

Resulting in:

```
 ((Hashtable)Cache["DateList"])[e.Day.Date]
```

State Management Recommendations

In this chapter, we looked at several different methods for storing state information, but the question is, which is the right one to use? Well, it depends on what you want to achieve. The Microsoft MSDN documentation has a great discussion on this topic available to view online at

http://msdn.microsoft.com/library/default.asp?url=/library/enus/vbcon/html/vbconchoosingserverstateoption.asp
However, to round off this chapter, let's look at the important considerations to keep in mind which method to use.

When to Use Cookies

Cookies are great for storing small pieces of identification data but not complete authentication details. They can be configured to expire after any length of time, but most cookies on your system are likely to last a long time. After you log on to Amazon.com for the first time, you will be presented with a personalized front page on every subsequent trip to the site. Because cookies are stored on the client, it takes the burden off the server.

Cookies, however, can be blocked at the client end, so you can't rely on your users being able to (or even choosing to) use them. Also, cookies should never be used to store sensitive information, since cookies can be tampered with – all you have to do is open a cookie, change its contents, and save it again, and the Web site that created the cookie may not be able to use that cookie any more.

When to Use Sessions

Sessions are used to maintain information about users across a series of pages in a site. The `Session` object can store any object you choose and therefore, is a very flexible way to remember information. If you need to remember any information relating to a user session, the `Session` object is the right choice for you. You can also react to session-wide events, which gives you even more flexibility.

However, extreme flexibility comes with a price – you must take care not to store too much information in the `Session` object, because you'll quickly find it can be a drain on server resources. Store only essential data in a session.

When to Use Applications

Applications are very powerful and flexible, just like sessions. You can store any object in application state. Also, you can react to events raised (such as the `Start` and `End` of the application, as well as a global `Error` event) and add custom event handler code so that you can store information globally, and have it accessible by any code in the application.

The two main disadvantages of applications are that they too can drain your server's resources and since they don't exist after the application ends, they shouldn't be used to store anything you need to keep. You can specify default values for both the `Session` and `Application` objects using the `Global.asax` file, but if you need to store data, use something more permanent, such as a database.

When to Use Caching

Caching is often considered more of a performance-enhancement tool than a way to store application data. When you find yourself spending many precious server resources accessing the same data repeatedly, use caching instead! Caching data can bring huge performance benefits, so whenever you find that you need to frequently access data that doesn't often change, cache it in the `Cache` object and your application's performance will improve.

The trick with caching is to use the highest possible value that won't negatively impact the required behavior of the page. Taking the example we looked at earlier to both extremes (caching match dates), specifying that the cache never expires (or has a very long duration) would mean that newly added dates would not be visible to visitors to the site unless the application was restarted. On the other hand, using a very small length of time before the cache expires would mean that the performance improvements gained by using caching are reduced, since the code has to keep going back to the database to get new data.

Other State Management Techniques

Aside from the main state management methods used in this chapter, there are several other ways to remember data. Let's take a quick look at these now.

ViewState

ViewState is a concept first discussed back in *Chapter 3*, and it's been with us on every page that has server controls on it! If you use the View | Source command on any page with a Web control, you'll see a large block of code:

```
<input type="hidden" name="__VIEWSTATE" value="dDw0MTMzOTEzMDM7O2w8Y2hrUmVt
...
```

ViewState can be enabled or disabled on a control-by-control basis. The more controls you have on your page that have ViewState enabled, the more data your page will have to store in this hidden field. On complex pages, this field can grow to be quite large and will increase download times, so take care to only enable ViewState on those controls that need it. For example, if you wanted to disable ViewState on a TextBox control, you could do so using the following syntax:

```
<asp:textbox id="myTextBox" runat="server" EnableViewState="false" />
```

You'll soon find out if you need to enable ViewState for a control or not if you try disabling it for all controls on a page. If you try this and run your page, you may find that it no longer behaves as expected. At this point, you can start re-enabling it control-by-control (using EnableViewState="true"), until your site behaves as intended. This will help you understand which controls require ViewState on your site.

Hidden Form Fields

ViewState uses hidden form fields to store its data, but by default a standard hidden control is sent to the client unencrypted. Even if you do encrypt this data, the encryption methods available for such fields are not the most rigorous available, so you should never store sensitive data in them.

Database

Never underestimate the power of the database! Storing bits and pieces of data that relate to the session or application in a database is one way to move away from the standard server-based state management models. However, too much reliance on the database for this type of information could cause bottlenecks at the database-end instead of the server-end!

As you can see, most of the drawbacks to each of the methods discussed here boil down to performance. Performance enhancement techniques will be covered in *Chapter 15*.

Using Multiple State Management Techniques on a Page

Right, we've looked at many different concepts in this chapter, so let's put together one more example using a couple of those concepts. This example will use both Sessions and Cookies to add some simple skinning functionality to the Web site. Once you complete this example, you will be able to add stylesheets to improve the look of every page on the site. If you've not worked with CSS before, don't worry – it's all quite simple. Once you complete this exercise, you'll be able to alter the look of the entire site by altering the values stored in one central location.

Try it Out   Wrox United – Adding Some Style!

In this example, we're going to add some styling to the Wrox United site, and at the same time, make use of session state. It's going to take a bit of preparation, so let's work through it piece by piece.

1. Start by re-opening `Default.aspx`. Switch to HTML view and add the following line of code near the top of the page:

```
<html>
<head>
   <link id="css" href='<%= (string)Session["SelectedCss"] %>'
   type="text/css" rel="stylesheet" />
</head>
```

2. Add the following code further down the page, after the last `HyperLink` control:

```
<p>
  <asp:HyperLink id="lnkChat" runat="server" NavigateUrl="Chat.aspx">
    Chat</asp:HyperLink>
</p>
<hr /><br/><br/>
<p>
  Choose a theme: <br/>
  <asp:DropDownList id="ddlTheme" runat="server">
    <asp:ListItem Value="WroxUnited.css" Selected="true">
      Home Kit</asp:ListItem>
    <asp:ListItem Value="WroxUnited2.css">Away Kit</asp:ListItem>
  </asp:DropDownList>
  <asp:Button id="btnApplyTheme" onclick="btnApplyTheme_Click"
            runat="server" Text="Apply"></asp:Button>
  <br />
  <asp:CheckBox id="chkRememberStylePref" runat="server"
              Text="Remember preference"></asp:CheckBox>
</p>
</td>
```

3. Switch to the Design view; Figure 11-17 shows what you should see in the left hand column:

Figure 11-17

4. Double-click on the Apply button to switch back to the Code view. Notice that Sessions and Cookies have both been used in this event handler:

```
void btnApplyTheme_Click(object sender, EventArgs e)
{
    Session["SelectedCss"] = ddlTheme.SelectedItem.Value;

    if (chkRememberStylePref.Checked)
    {
        HttpCookie CssCookie = new HttpCookie("PreferredCss");
        CssCookie.Value = ddlTheme.SelectedItem.Value;
        CssCookie.Expires = DateTime.Now.AddSeconds(20);
        Response.Cookies.Add(CssCookie);
    }
}
```

5. We need to add some code to the Page Load() method to set the style for the page when it is first loaded:

```
public void Page_Load(object sender, EventArgs e)
{
    if (!Page.IsPostBack)
    {
        if (Session["SelectedCss"] == null)
        {
            if (Request.Cookies["PreferredCss"] == null)
```

```
      {
        Session["SelectedCss"] = "WroxUnited.css";
      }
      else
      {
        Session["SelectedCss"] = Request.Cookies["PreferredCss"].Value;
      }
    }
  }
```
...

That's quite a lot of Ifs! Don't worry – we will come to this in just a moment. However, before you can run the code, you need to include some stylesheets or nothing will be displayed! You will also need to make some minor adjustments to some of the code on the page, notably to the Calendar control's DayRender event handler, to make the page look a bit nicer when the stylesheet is applied.

6. First, change the DayRender event handler as follows (remove the original style settings and replace them with a single class statement):

```
public void EventCalendar_DayRender(object sender, DayRenderEventArgs e)
{
  if (((Hashtable)Cache["DateList"])[e.Day.Date] != null)
  {
    e.Cell.CssClass = "selecteddate";
    // e.Cell.Style.Add("font-weight", "bold");
    // e.Cell.Style.Add("font-size", "larger");
    // e.Cell.Style.Add("border", "3 dotted darkred");
    // e.Cell.Style.Add("background", "#f0f0f0");

    // The following line will exist in your code if you completed the
    // exercises at the end of the last chapter
    e.Day.IsSelectable = true;
  }
  else
  {
    // This line of code is part of the solution to one of the exercises at
    // the end of chapter 10
    e.Day.IsSelectable = false;
    e.Cell.CssClass = "normaldate";
    // e.Cell.Style.Add("font-weight", "lighter")
    // e.Cell.Style.Add("color", "DimGray")
  }
}
```

7. Change the code for the calendar in the HTML view:

```
<asp:Calendar id="EventCalendar" runat="server"
            OnSelectionChanged="EventCalendar_SelectionChanged"
            OnDayRender="EventCalendar_DayRender" CssClass="calendar">

  <DayStyle cssclass="normaldate"></DayStyle>
  <OtherMonthDayStyle cssclass="othermonthdate"></OtherMonthDayStyle>
```

```
</asp:Calendar>
```

8. Now create a new blank stylesheet, and call it `WroxUnited.css`, as shown in Figure 11-18:

Figure 11-18

9. In this new stylesheet, enter the following code:

```
BODY {
{
  background-image:url(images/background.gif);
  color:"#000000";
  font-family: georgia;
}

a {
  color:"#8b0000";
  font-weight:bold;
}

.selecteddate{
  font-weight: bold;
  font-size: larger;
  border: 3 dotted darkred;
  background:#f0f0f0;
}

.normaldate{
  font-weight:lighter;
  color:dimgray;
}

.calendar a{
  text-decoration:none;
  font-size: 10pt;
}
```

```
.othermonthdate{
  font-weight:lighter;
  color:#d3d3d3;
}
```

10. Save this as `WroxUnited.css` in the `WroxUnited` folder. Then, change the following lines and save the file with a different name, `WroxUnited2.css`:

```
BODY {
background-image:url(images/awaybackground.gif);
color:"#ffffff";
font-family: georgia;
}
a {
color:"yellow";
font-weight:bold;
}
.calendar a{
 text-decoration:none;
}
.selecteddate
{
 font-weight: bold;
 font-size: larger;
 border: 3 dotted white;
 background:#c0c0c0;
}
.normaldate
{
 font-weight:lighter;
 color:#d3d3d3;
}
.othermonthdate
{
 font-weight:lighter;
 color:dimgray;
}
```

11. Finally, you need to get hold of the two background images that are used in the two stylesheets, `background.gif` and `awaybackground.gif`. Both are available for download from the Wrox site. They are extremely small images, so they will not take long to download.

12. It's about time to run the page and try it out for yourself! The first style you'll see is the Home style page, as shown in Figure 11-19, the away kit that is shown in Figure 11-20, is fairly different, as you'll no doubt notice!

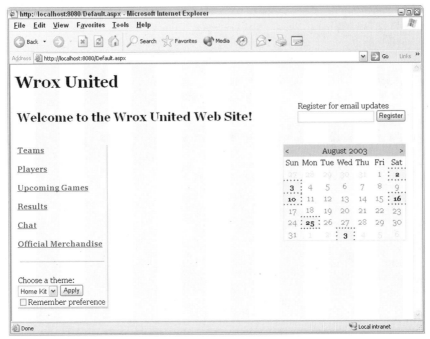

Figure 11-19:

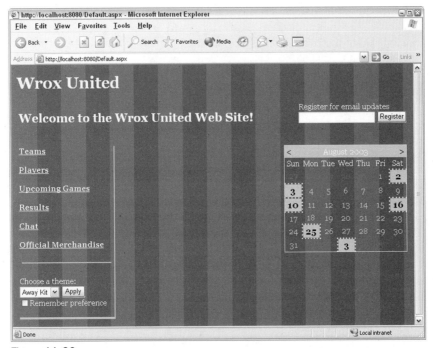

Figure 11-20

13. If you check the Remember Preference box before clicking Apply, the style you are applying will be remembered for you in a cookie. Next time you open the site, this stylesheet will be the default.

How It Works

This example rolled together two different techniques, sessions and cookies, and gave a unified look and feel that you can apply to all the pages in this site.

The first thing done was to use the contents of the `Session` object to provide a filename for the `<Link ... >` tag in the head section of the ASP.NET page:

```
<html>
<head>
    <link id="css" href='<%= (string)Session["SelectedCss"] %>'
    type="text/css"
        rel="stylesheet" />
</head>
```

You'll recall that the `<%= ... %>` syntax is used to access ASP.NET objects from the HTML side of the page. This technique is certainly adequate for this example, and is a simple way to get to the contents of the `Session` object.

The next step was to add some controls to the page to select and apply the stylesheet to the page:

```
<hr /><br/><br/>
<p>
  Choose a theme: <br/>
  <asp:DropDownList id="ddlTheme" runat="server">
    <asp:ListItem Value="WroxUnited.css" Selected="true">
    Home Kit</asp:ListItem>
    <asp:ListItem Value="WroxUnited2.css">Away Kit</asp:ListItem>
  </asp:DropDownList>
  <asp:Button id="btnApplyTheme" onclick="btnApplyTheme_Click"
            runat="server" Text="Apply"></asp:Button>
  <br />
  <asp:CheckBox id="chkRememberStylePref" runat="server"
              Text="Remember preference"></asp:CheckBox>
</p>
```

We set the details of the drop down list manually, assigning each item a `Text` property and a `Value` property. The `Text` property (the bit between the tags) is the text that displays in the control. The value is the underlying code value for the selected item, and we use this value to update the session. Clicking the `Apply` button will fire the `Click` event of the button, taking you neatly to the event handler for this event:

```
void btnApplyTheme_Click(object sender, EventArgs e)
{
  Session["SelectedCss"] = ddlTheme.SelectedItem.Value;
```

Set the value of the session to be the *value* of the currently selected drop down list item (not the displayed text). This value is the filename for the stylesheet.

```
    if (chkRememberStylePref.Checked)
    {
      HttpCookie CssCookie = new HttpCookie("PreferredCss");
      CssCookie.Value = ddlTheme.SelectedItem.Value;
      CssCookie.Expires = DateTime.Now.AddSeconds(20);
      Response.Cookies.Add(CssCookie);
    }
  }
```

If the ChkRememberStylePref checkbox is checked when the button is clicked, a cookie is added to the user's machine, specifying their preference for subsequent visits to the site. Again, we set a short expiry time for this cookie so that you can see it working and also see what happens when it expires. You can set this to be whatever time interval you prefer.

OK, so you have a session and a cookie – the next stage is to read those values in when the page is loaded:

```
public void Page_Load(object sender, EventArgs e)
{
  if (!Page.IsPostBack)
  {
    if (Session["SelectedCss"] == null)
    {
```

If the Session does not yet exist, we set a default value for the selected stylesheet using the value in the cookie if one exists on the client machine, or set it to a specific value if there is no cookie present:

```
      if (Request.Cookies["PreferredCss"] == null)
      {
        Session["SelectedCss"] = "WroxUnited.css";
      }
      else
      {
        Session["SelectedCss"] = Request.Cookies["PreferredCss"].Value;
      }
    }
  }
```

Now that we have applied the stylesheet, we need to manually alter the styling of the Calendar control (if you skip this step, you'll notice that the calendar doesn't follow the stylesheet like the rest of the page):

```
public void EventCalendar_DayRender(object sender, DayRenderEventArgs e)
{
  if (((Hashtable)Cache["DateList"])[e.Day.Date] != null)
  {
    e.Cell.CssClass = "selecteddate";
    e.Day.IsSelectable = true;
  }
  else
  {
    e.Day.IsSelectable = false;
    e.Cell.CssClass = "normaldate";
```

```
    }
  }
  ...
    <DayStyle cssclass="normaldate"></DayStyle>
    <OtherMonthDayStyle cssclass="othermonthdate"></OtherMonthDayStyle>
```

Finally, we declare some stylesheet information. Let's run through the values of just a couple of these definitions:

```
BODY {
  background-image:url(images/background.gif);
  color:"#000000";
  font-family: georgia;
}
```

The BODY tag controls the way the bulk of the page is rendered, including any background coloring or styling, as well as the font color and style.

The .selecteddate style is the style added in the DayRender() event handler for the calendar:

```
.selecteddate{
  font-weight: bold;
  font-size: larger;
  border: 3 dotted darkred;
  background:#f0f0f0;
}
```

Notice how the styles here are similar to the styles used in the code for the DayRender() event handler previously? Well, that's the joy of stylesheets! You've now centralized this code so that you only have to alter it in one place.

Summary

We covered quite a bit of ground in this chapter. We used cookies, sessions, and applications and cached data for enhancing performance. We also had some fun with interactive examples in this chapter that demonstrated these concepts.

The important points covered in this chapter are:

❑   Cookies are a neat way to store small pieces of identifying data, but cannot be relied upon (users may have them disabled in their browser preferences).

❑   Sessions are an extremely powerful way to store data that exists for as long as a user is connected to the site, and you can use them to store data for online shopping examples.

❑   Application-scope objects are accessible by any page in an application and are a great way to centralize objects that need to be shared.

❑   Caching data is crucial to improving application performance, but it's also similar to storing data in the Application object. However, the Cache object has some neat features such as linking to a dependency, and you can control when items in the cache expire and react to the events raised when those items expire.

The next chapter will look at encapsulating commonly used page elements into reusable sections known as user controls. You'll also learn how the code-behind technique can be used to cleanly separate HTML code from C# code.

Exercises

1. Add the text, Current Topic, and a label control to the Chat.aspx page above the main chat box that contains the text of the current topic (stored in the Application object). Add some default topic text to the Global.asax file, and also another box and button to the page, allowing you to change the current topic.

2. Add the session initialization code from the Stylesheet example to your Global.asax file.

3. Add a link to the Merchandise.aspx page from the front page of the site, then apply the stylesheet used in the Default.aspx page to all the other pages in the site. You will need to add the <link ... > tag to the <head ... > section of each page, and you will need to ensure that the session initialization code is correctly configured in the Global.asax file from the previous exercises.

12

Reusable Code for ASP.NET

So far, most of the ASP.NET pages we've built were quite specialized and self-contained. We've put a lot of functionality into each page, but only retained the benefits of our hard work from one page to another by copying the entire contents into a new ASPX page.

This isn't an ideal way to write functionality-rich Web sites, particularly if you're on a salary and expected to deliver results before the next millennium! We'll now look at writing reusable code for ASP.NET. Note that we're not just talking about objects here (although, yet again, objects play a crucial role in the reusability story), but about code *components* – totally independent files that encapsulate groups of useful functionality.

This chapter will look at two specific ways of using components in ASP.NET:

❑   **User control**: A Web form that is encapsulated in a reusable server control

❑   **Code-behind**: Used for separating HTML user interface design (color, aesthetics, and so on) from page code

First, let's take a careful look at what is meant by components and consider the various advantages they offer.

Encapsulation

As discussed in *Chapter 7*, an object essentially is a software construct that bundles together data and functionality. You can define interfaces to use the functionality that an object contains, for example, by creating methods and properties that can be accessed programmatically.

By hiding everything that doesn't concern task-specific usage of an object, implementation details are hidden from the consumer, which makes it a lot easier to robustly plug an object together with other objects. This makes it far easier for large teams of developers to build complex applications that don't fall prey to lots of low-level weaknesses.

Crucial information about an object is held in its class definition, and any code with access to this class should be able to instantiate an instance of this class and store it in an object. The way in which the object works is *encapsulated*, so that only the public methods and properties are available to the consumers of the class.

In a similar way, a code component is reusable code stored in a location that is accessible to many applications. Like an object, it encapsulates functionality, but while an object is an implementation unit, a component is a deployment or packaging unit. A component could be a single class or could hold multiple class definitions. Figure 12-1 considers a quick example:

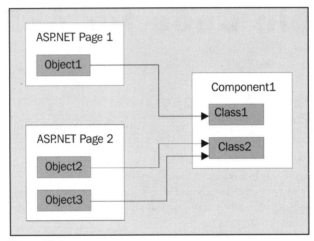

Figure 12-1

The first ASP.NET page creates a new object of type Class1 that resides within the Component1 component. The second ASP.NET page creates two new objects – one of type Class1 and one of type Class2. Class2 also resides within Component1.

All code written so far has been held in specific ASPX pages. So, what's the point in having all this reusable code if it can only be reached from within a single page? We need to break our reusable code into separate components that we can reference from other ASPX pages.

A component packages a set of classes and interfaces to isolate and encapsulate a specific functionality, and can provide a well-specified set of publicly available services. It is designed for a specific *purpose* rather than for a specific *application*.

Components

A component is a self-contained unit of functionality with external interfaces that are independent of its internal architecture. In other words, it is code packaged as a black box that can be used in as many different applications as required.

Microsoft Windows is an example of componentization. If you spend a lot of time working with Windows, you're almost certain to have come across *Dynamic Link Libraries* (*DLL*) files. These files contain components that define most of the functionality that you're likely to come across in Windows, including that of any applications you've installed.

For example, every time you start an instance of Internet Explorer, you're actually running a small program called `iexplore.exe`. This program accesses numerous DLLs that reside in your system directory (`C:\WinNT` or `C:\Windows`), and most of the browser's functionality is defined within these files. This directory also contains the `Explorer.exe` file, which is the executable for Windows Explorer. Note that both these applications feature an identical Address bar, where you type in the URL of a Web site or the path to a local directory. This user interface element has been implemented once and packaged inside a component, so that it can now be used by both programs.

What's more, if you enter the URL for a Web page in the Windows Explorer address bar, you can view that page and even browse the Web in the main pane without having to use `iexplore.exe` at all. Likewise, you can use `iexplore.exe` to view and browse your files by entering a file path in the address bar.

What we can deduce from this is that either there's a lot of duplication between the two executable files, or that the two sets of browser functionality are actually implemented as standalone components that can be accessed by both applications.

Another case to consider is the Microsoft Office suite, which features many components that are shared among individual Office applications, as also throughout Windows. For example, there is a component that handles the Save As dialog used by Word, Excel, Outlook, and the rest – this is why the Save As dialog looks the same, no matter which application you run it from. This component is actually a Windows component and the Office package uses it whenever you save or load a file. You can also use this from any other application that lets you save or load files, for example, Internet Explorer or even Microsoft Notepad as shown in Figure 12-2:

Figure 12-2

This component probably includes some presentation code for the buttons and code logic that governs what happens when you click on each of these buttons. For example, changing the selection in the Save option in dropdown box changes the files listed in the main window to show the contents of the selected directory.

Throughout this book, the `aspnet_isapi` component has been working away behind IIS to process all of our ASP.NET pages. When IIS detects a request for a page with a `.aspx` extension, it uses this component to process the page and communicate with the .NET Framework.

> *DLLs are classified as system files and are hidden by default. They can only be seen in Windows Explorer if the 'Show hidden files and folders' option in your **Folder Options** is set. The DLLs talked about in these examples are COM DLLs. .NET DLLs differ slightly in what they contain and the underlying technology, but the concept of componentization used is the same.*

Why Use Components?

You should start thinking of components as small, self-contained nuggets of functionality that can potentially make life a lot simpler when building any sort of non-trivial application. In components, behind-the-scenes functionality is encapsulated so that only certain specific interfaces are available to the programmer. It can contain class definitions that specify which objects can be created and which ones can be used for behind-the-scenes code. The benefits of using components include:

❑ An individual component is a lot simpler than a fully-blown application. It is restricted to a set of predefined functionality.

❑ As components are self-contained, they can be seamlessly upgraded (or fixed) simply by replacing one component with another that supports the same interfaces (methods, properties, and so on).

❑ Since using components is a good way of dividing your application into serviceable chunks, sometimes the functionality of a component might be reusable in other applications. You could even make it available to other programmers, or incorporate some of their components into your applications.

Ultimately, components reduce the amount of code you write and make your code easier to maintain. Moreover, you can even obtain components from third party component vendors, which is a very popular way to enhance the functionality of ASP.NET sites. For example, if you need components that utilize the drawing capabilities of .NET to their limit, and your existing knowledge does not cover this, you can consider looking for a third-party solution that you can bolt onto your application.

Applying Component Theory to Applications

Let's look at how componentization relates to our application models. So far in this book, we've made ASP.NET pages that do all sorts of things ranging from working with information input via a form to connecting to a database and working with data. Throughout the book, you've been encouraged to keep your code separated into distinct blocks – the dynamically generated content (ASP.NET code) and presentation (HTML and various controls) – so that it's easy to change the look of your page without affecting what it does. Web Matrix simplifies this process with its separate HTML and Code views.

In addition, we've written a lot of C# code in our pages for accessing and working with data stored in a central database. C# provides a framework of logical operations between the data and presentation code.

Let's consider an example. Imagine a team of developers creating a Web site that sells books. Some of these developers would be concerned with the look, feel, and usability of the site. They'd be responsible for the public image of the company on the Web, so they'd be more concerned about design, color, and usability. This group will include designers who probably use HTML and graphics tools such as Macromedia Flash for fancy loading screens. Another set of developers would be mainly interested in providing nifty blocks of code that do cool things, such as such as validating the information entered into a form by the customers when they click a button. These developers would also be responsible for generating the code required to connect to the database of different books and preparing information on individual titles for display on the site. The designers would then make use of that information and display it in an aesthetically pleasing fashion.

If you were to constantly use ASP.NET pages that had all of the code and HTML on the same page, it would be awkward for both sets of people to work on the site at once. Simple mistakes could easily be made if people overwrote each other's code. In addition, every page would have to be hand-made, and code would have to be copied, pasted, and amended as appropriate. If you made one change to the functionality of your site, you'd have to remember to make that change to all the appropriate pages.

However, if you could separate out the HTML and design-focused code from the ASP.NET code blocks, and then reuse bits of that code, it would be much easier to update a single piece of code to change functionality – every page that used it would be automatically updated.

This style of work would make everyone happy – Web designers get to play with color and layout as much as they like, and the ASP.NET developers can fine-tune their code without affecting the look and feel of the site. Code separation and reuse implies that the designers and developers can work in parallel, allowing applications to be developed much more quickly. This is called *Rapid Application Development*.

This chapter will look at two ways of dividing code into reusable sections – *user controls* and *code-behind* files. In the next chapter, we'll take this one step further and look at compiled components and custom server controls.

Let's look at user controls, the first application of this code-separation concept.

User Controls

When the ASP.NET team first devised the concept of user controls, they were called *pagelets*, a term that many people disliked. They were later renamed, but many felt that pagelet, or a mini-page, was a good descriptive term for these controls.

User controls are Web forms encapsulated into a reusable control. They hold blocks of code that are repetitively required by many pages in a Web site. For example, consider the Microsoft Web site where each page has the same header style – a menu bar and a logo. This is a common feature for many Web sites; our own http://www.wrox.com/ shown in Figure 12-3 has this kind of style, for example:

Figure 12-3

The Wrox site has the same kinds of menu bars visible on the screen at all times. These panes, panels, or frames (depending on what you call them and how you code them) form just one example of what user controls can provide.

Instead of having to copy and paste chunks of repeated code to provide the header on all of our pages, we can create a simple *user control* that will have this code inside it, ready to be used. It's a way of accessing the same functionality repeatedly throughout an application.

> *If you've ever programmed with ASP 3.0, you'll probably be familiar with include files. User controls are similar to these files, but because ASP.NET is different from ASP 3.0, these controls are now created and used in a different manner, and include advanced features such as caching (covered in Chapter 11).*

User controls can also do a lot more than simply produce headers and footers. We can give these controls the ability to look and function like ASP.NET Server controls. We can code properties so that the control can adapt according to its set attributes. A user control can be used repetitively on a site when many pages have similar blocks of functionality. Take, for example, a user login control. This control could be created as a user control by using a couple of textboxes and labels.

Another example is a menu control that applies different formatting to a page link if the page is currently being viewed, or displays a submenu for that page. A user control is saved with a `.ascx` file extension, and can be called from any of the ASP.NET pages in our application by using just two lines of code. The main principle of user controls is that you essentially cut out a portion of code from your

ASP.NET page and paste it into a user control, where it will work just fine as long as the ASP.NET page knows where to find the code and where to put it.

Let's look at a few pros and cons of using user controls in your applications. User controls are ideal for:

❏ Using repetitive elements (such as headers, menus, login controls, and so on) on pages

❏ Reducing the amount of code per page by encapsulating repetitive elements

❏ Improving page performance by using caching functionality available to user controls for frequently viewed

However, some situations aren't ideal for using user controls. These include:

❏ Separation of presentation HTML from the code blocks (use code-behind, discussed later in this chapter)

❏ Encapsulation of data access methods in a reusable package (use pre-compiled assemblies, discussed in the next chapter)

❏ Creating a control that can be reused more widely than in just your application (use custom server controls, discussed in the next chapter)

It's time to start looking at code. This chapter and the next will look at creating custom reusable elements in ASP.NET pages, showing how these elements can all be plugged together with minimal fuss, to produce a very clean .aspx file by hiding advanced functionality within reusable components. The next example demonstrates user controls in action.In this example, we will discuss a very basic example (to show the theory), which will be followed by a more complex example. We'll add a simple header control to the default page of the Wrox United application.

Try It Out   Our First User Control

1.   Start by creating a new ASP.NET user control within the Wrox United folder as shown in Figure 12-4 and name it SimpleHeader.ascx (note the different file extension – .ascx, not .aspx):

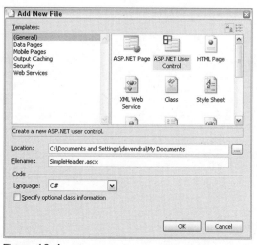

Figure 12-4

2. In the new file, switch to HTML view – notice that there is hardly anything in the file when it's first created! All you need to do here is add one line of code:

```
<h1>Wrox United</h1>
```

3. Save this file and reopen `Default.aspx` from the Wrox United application. We'll replace the heading in this page with the newly created user control. To do this, Switch to All view – notice the yellow highlighted lines (which aren't visible in any other view) at the top of the file. This is where you need to add the first piece of code. Add the following highlighted line of code:

```
<%@ Page Language="C#" %>
<%@ Register TagPrefix="WroxUnited" TagName="SimpleHeader"
                Src="SimpleHeader.ascx" %>
```

5. Switch back to HTML view. Replace the `<h1> ... </h1>` section with the highlighted code:

```
<form runat="server">
    <WroxUnited:SimpleHeader id="HeaderControl" runat="server"/>
    <table width="800">
    ...
```

6. That's about all you need to add to the code! If you switch over to the Design view as shown in Figure 12-5, you'll see that the control has been added:

Figure 12-5

7. It's time to try it out – run the page and you should see the familiar front page of the site as shown in Figure 12-6:

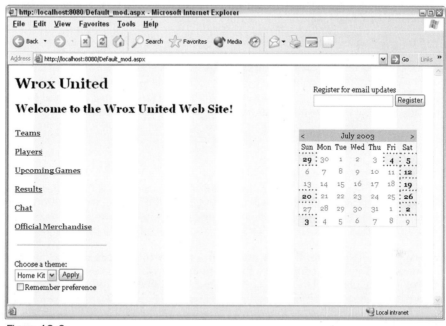

Figure 12-6

Notice that the front page looks the same as before, and the new title has the correct style applied to it as if it were still a part of the main page.

How It Works

Having completed this example, you won't see any difference in the rendered page when it is run and the page that we built in the last chapter. However, the technique that we implemented behind the scenes (changing the hard-coded HTML to a reusable control) can prove to be very useful, as you'll see for yourself later in this chapter.

If you open up `SimpleHeader.ascx` in the All view in Web Matrix, you'll see the following:

```
<%@ Control Language="C#" %>
<script runat="server">

    // Insert user control code here
    //

</script>
    <!-- Insert content here -->
    <h1>Wrox United
    </h1>
```

The default code that Web Matrix added is quite light. There are a couple of comments, an unused script block, and a special directive at the top of the code. The first line of code tells the compiler that we wrote this control in C#. The only code added to the page was the `<h1>Wrox United</h1>` line. This line of code can be displayed on any code that uses this control.Let's look at the 'consumer' of our ASCX user control, the Default.aspx page:

```
<%@ Page Language="C#" %>
<%@ Register TagPrefix="WroxUnited" TagName="SimpleHeader"
                  Src="SimpleHeader.ascx" %>
```

The first line of code links the ASCX control to the ASPX page. This tag must appear at the top of your page, before any HTML code. Two attributes have been set for the `Register` directive:

❑   TagPrefix

❑   TagName

`TagPrefix` is the collective name for our group of controls, and `TagName` is the name of this specific control. For example, to use an ASP.NET textbox control on an ASPX page, we use the syntax `<asp:textbox />`. A `TagPrefix` precedes the colon and a `TagName` follows the colon. For an ASP.NET textbox, `<asp:...>` would be the `TagPrefix`, and `<...:textbox>`would be the `TagName`.

In this example, the `TagPrefix` for the new user control was set to `WroxUnited`, and the `TagName` was set to `SimpleHeader`. To use the control on a page, you use the `<WroxUnited:SimpleHeader />` tag. You could have a whole library of `WroxUnited` tags, each identified by a different `TagName` in the code.

The final part of the directive specifies the source file of the user control. Note that ASP.NET expects this file to be in the same place as the `.aspx` file. If this is not the case, then add either a relative or an absolute path here.Then we embedded the user control into the `Default.aspx` page:

```
<WroxUnited:SimpleHeader id="HeaderControl" runat="server"/>
```

Here you can see the `WroxUnited:SimpleHeader` syntax discussed earlier. The control is added to the page using the `TagName` and `TagPrefix` specified in the attribute declaration at the top of the page.

Web Matrix can provide a preview of pages that include user controls, so you could see the output of the user control that you have added in **Design** view. The result is that the page is rendered in exactly the same way as before. The HTML code from the control is rendered within the HTML of the page.

While this user control could be implemented on every page in the site easily, this isn't exactly the most exciting control that we could use. Let's work on a visually appealing header control that can be displayed at the top of every page in the site.Let's create a user control that forms a header for the Wrox United Web site. Our example used a few images, including a team logo and pictures of the players. These images are available for download, along with the rest of the code for the book, from http://www.wrox.com/.

Try It Out   Wrox United – Header Control

1.   Open up Web Matrix and create a new ASP.NET user control called `header.ascx`. Enter the following code in the HTML view:

```
<table width="100%">
```

```
<tr style="BACKGROUND-IMAGE: url(images/headbg.gif);"><td>
    <table width="800">
      <tr style="VERTICAL-ALIGN: middle">
        <td style="TEXT-ALIGN: left" width="200">
          <a href="default.aspx"><img src="images/logo.gif" border="0"></a>
        </td>
        <td style="TEXT-ALIGN: center" width="400">
          <img src="images/teamlogo.gif" />
        </td>
        <td style="TEXT-ALIGN: right" width="200">
          <asp:AdRotator id="AdRotator1" runat="server"
                         Height="95px" Width="100px"
                         AdvertisementFile="faces.xml"></asp:AdRotator>
        </td>
      </tr>
    </table>
  </td></tr>
</table>
<h2><%= PageTitle %></h2>
```

2.   Switch to Code view and enter the following line of text:

```
public string PageTitle = "";""
```

3.   Save this file as `header.ascx`. You'll notice an ASP.NET `AdRotator` control in this file. This control depends on the contents of an XML file. Let's create this. by creating a new blank XML page called `faces.xml` and adding the following code to it:

```xml
<?xml version="1.0" encoding="utf-8" ?>
<Advertisements>

  <Ad>
    <ImageUrl>images/chrish_s_t.gif</ImageUrl>
    <NavigateUrl>players.aspx</NavigateUrl>
    <AlternateText>Player: Chris Hart</AlternateText>
    <Impressions>80</Impressions>
    <Keyword>ChrisH</Keyword>
  </Ad>
  <Ad>
    <ImageUrl>images/chrisu_s_t.gif</ImageUrl>
    <NavigateUrl>players.aspx</NavigateUrl>
    <AlternateText>Player: Chris Ullman</AlternateText>
    <Impressions>80</Impressions>
    <Keyword>ChrisU</Keyword>
  </Ad>

  <Ad>
    <ImageUrl>images/dave_s_t.gif</ImageUrl>
    <NavigateUrl>players.aspx</NavigateUrl>
    <AlternateText>Player: Dave Sussman</AlternateText>
    <Impressions>80</Impressions>
    <Keyword>Dave</Keyword>
  </Ad>
```

```
<Ad>
  <ImageUrl>images/john_s_t.gif</ImageUrl>
  <NavigateUrl>players.aspx</NavigateUrl>
  <AlternateText>Player: John Kauffman</AlternateText>
  <Impressions>80</Impressions>
  <Keyword>John</Keyword>
</Ad>

</Advertisements>
```

We'll examine how the `AdRotator` control works in just a few moments, but for now, add the new header control to the default page by altering a couple of lines.

5. Change the declaration at the top of the page in `Default.aspx`:

```
<%@ Page Language="C#" %>
<%@ Register TagPrefix="WroxUnited" TagName="Header" Src="header.ascx" %>
```

6. Change the code that embeds the header control in the page as follows:

```
<form runat="server">
  <WroxUnited:Header id="HeaderControl" runat="server"></WroxUnited:Header>
  <table width="800">
  . . .
```

7. Save the file again and view it in your browser. The page is shown in Figure 12-7:

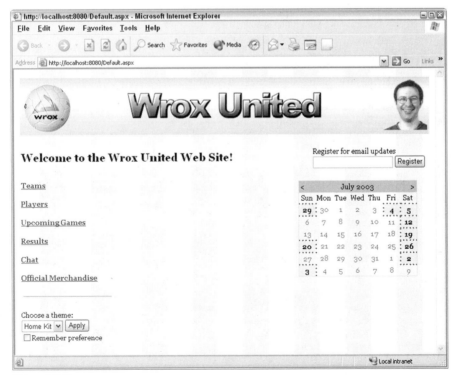

Figure 12-7

How It Works

In this example, we implemented another simple user control and introduced the `AdRotator` control. This control is traditionally used to store banner advertisements and rotate the visible advertisement according to a random algorithm. Each time the page is refreshed, an advertisement is selected for display. The frequency with which each advert appears on the page depends on the weightage we give to each advertisement. In this example, each ad is given equal weightage so adverts display for equal intervals of time but in a random fashion whenever the page is refreshed.

In this example, the `AdRotator` control was used to display images of the members of the team (instead of displaying ads) and to change the image on subsequent visits to the site. The information that controls which images to display and how often to display them is stored in an XML file.

Let's break down the code and work through what we did. First, the `header.ascx` control:

```
<table width="100%">
  <tr style="BACKGROUND-IMAGE: url(images/headbg.gif);"><td>
      <table width="800">
        <tr style="VERTICAL-ALIGN: middle">
          <td style="TEXT-ALIGN: left" width="200">
            <a href="default.aspx"><img src="images/logo.gif" border="0"></a>
          </td>
          <td style="TEXT-ALIGN: center" width="400">
            <img src="images/teamlogo.gif" />
          </td>
          <td style="TEXT-ALIGN: right" width="200">
            <asp:AdRotator id="AdRotator1" runat="server"
                           Height="95px" Width="100px"
                           AdvertisementFile="faces.xml"></asp:AdRotator>
          </td>
        </tr>
      </table>
  </td></tr>
</table>
<h2><%= PageTitle %></h2>
```

This control is made up of one large table that contains a sub-table with three cells. We applied a style to the single row in the parent table. The addition of a background image to this row resulted in this style being applied as a solid background for the whole header. The inner table helps to organize the contents of the header. The contents of the row were centered along a horizontal axis:

```
<tr style="VERTICAL-ALIGN: middle">
```

Then, each of the three cells were aligned to the left, center, or right of the vertical axis of each cell respectively:

```
<td style="TEXT-ALIGN: left" width="200">
```

In the first two cells, a couple of static images were added. Notice that the image in the first cell is wrapped in an HTML anchor (`<A ... >`) tag, which will turn the image into a hyperlink. In this case, clicking the first image would take the user to the front page, thus making it a handy 'home' button that users can use to return to the default page.

In the third cell, we added an `AdRotator` control:

```
<asp:AdRotator id="AdRotator1" runat="server"
               Height="95px" Width="100px"
               AdvertisementFile="faces.xml"></asp:AdRotator>
```

The control declaration is very simple, but the most interesting part is the link to the `AdvertisementFile` XML file, which controls how `AdRotator` works. Let's look at an extract of that file:

```
<?xml version="1.0" encoding="utf-8" ?>
<Advertisements>

  <Ad>
    <ImageUrl>images/chrish_s_t.gif</ImageUrl>
    <NavigateUrl>players.aspx</NavigateUrl>
    <AlternateText>Player: Chris Hart</AlternateText>
    <Impressions>80</Impressions>
    <Keyword>ChrisH</Keyword>
  </Ad>
  <Ad>
  ...
  </Ad>

</Advertisements>
```

The settings that control what is displayed and what functionality is available each time the page is loaded, are contained within an `<Advertisements>` ... `</Advertisements>` tag. Each displayed item is defined within an `<Ad>` ... `</Ad>` element. In this example, you can see the element definition for `Chris Hart`. Let's work through each of the tags for this player. The first tag specifies the image to be displayed for this player. Here, the image is a small one with a transparent background (available along with the code downloads for this book):

```
<ImageUrl>images/chrish_s_t.gif</ImageUrl>
```

The `<NavigateUrl>` tag specifies the path to which the browser will navigate when the image is clicked. Here we specified the `Players.aspx` page:

```
<NavigateUrl>players.aspx</NavigateUrl>
```

The `<AlternateText>` tag controls the text that is displayed when the mouse pointer hovers over the image, as well as the text that is read out to assist visually-impaired surfers:

```
<AlternateText>Player: Chris Hart</AlternateText>
```

The `<Impressions>` tag controls the weightage that affects how often this advertisement (or image) is displayed as compared to other advertisements. In this example, all players have equal weighting, but you could indicate a preference for your favorite player by increasing the number for that particular image element:

```
<Impressions>80</Impressions>
```

> **Keep the total of all the values in the `<Impressions>` tags under 2 billion to avoid a runtime error.**

The last tag controls the keyword for the advert. This element is optional, but you can use it to filter advertisements by including a `KeywordFilter` attribute to the `<ASP:AdRotator ... >` tag in your ASP.NET pages:

```
<Keyword>ChrisH</Keyword>
```

The last piece of the puzzle involves including this header on the `Default.aspx` page. You only need to make a couple of minor changes (including adding a directive at the top of the page) to specify that you want to use the new header file in the page:

```
<%@ Register TagPrefix="WroxUnited" TagName="Header" Src="Header.ascx" %>
```

You can then use the control in the page by including the following line of code:

```
<WroxUnited:Header id="HeaderControl" runat="server"></WroxUnited:Header>
```

Before we move on, don't forget that you could include this header control on all the pages of the Wrox United site in the same way. With this in mind, we added an interactive element to this header control. Recall the last line in the `Header` control itself:

```
<h2><%= PageTitle %></h2>
```

This line of text will create a Heading 2 style paragraph, and add the text contents of the `PageTitle` public variable to the page:

```
public string PageTitle = "";""
```

Take the Chat application as an example; add two lines of code to the `Chat.aspx` page to see this in action (assuming that you've already added code to add the selected CSS theme to the page). First, at the top of the page, add the following:

```
<%@ Register TagPrefix="WroxUnited" TagName="Header" Src="Header.ascx" %>
```

Then add the following tag (instead of the Heading 1 and 2 tags) to the HTML view of the page:

```
<form runat="server">
  <WroxUnited:Header id="HeaderControl" runat="server" PageTitle="Online
  Chat"></WroxUnited:Header>
  <asp:TextBox id="txtChatBox" runat="server" TextMode="MultiLine"
               Height="200px" Width="550px" ReadOnly="true"></asp:TextBox>
```

When you view this page in your browser, it should appear as shown in Figure 12-8:

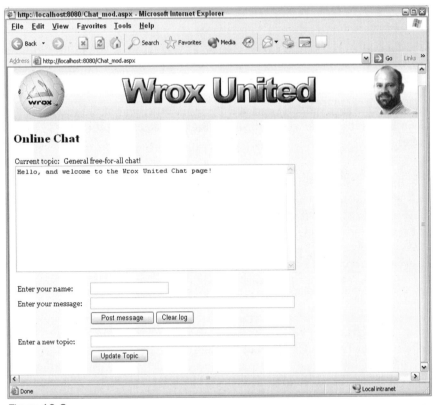

Figure 12-8

Heading 2 text has been included on the page, thanks to the `PageTitle` attribute in the control's declaration. This is a neat trick for making header controls a bit more interactive, removing standard code from the main pages, and also ensuring that the look and feel of all pages is maintained centrally.

Let's look at a slightly different type of user control. This control can be used as a navigation bar, like the links on the left of the front page. An advantage is that it can be added to all the pages in the site with minimal code reuse.

Try It Out Wrox United – Navigation User Control

In this example, we will take the ASP.NET hyperlink controls from `Default.aspx` along with the associated code from the left-hand side of the page and place it in a user control.

1. Create a new user control called `Navbar.ascx` and add the following code:

```
<div class="navbar">
</div>
```

We will add code between these tags in just a moment.

2. Reopen `Default.aspx` and head straight to the All view. Add the following highlighted line of code to the top of the page:

```
<%@ Page Language="C#" %>
<%@ Register TagPrefix="WroxUnited" TagName="Header" Src="Header.ascx" %>
<%@ Register TagPrefix="WroxUnited" TagName="NavBar" Src="NavBar.ascx" %>
```

3. Back in HTML view, find the section that contains code pertaining to the left hand column of hyperlinks (the first `<td>` element in the big layout table). This column contains the links and the CSS selector. Copy this section and paste it into `Navbar.ascx` within the `<div>` tag:

```
<div class="navbar">
<p>
  <asp:HyperLink id="lnkTeams" NavigateUrl="Teams.aspx" runat="server">
  Teams</asp:HyperLink>
</p>
<p>
  <asp:HyperLink id="lnkPlayers" NavigateUrl="Players.aspx" runat="server">
  Players</asp:HyperLink>
</p>
<p>
  <asp:HyperLink id="lnkGames" NavigateUrl="Default.aspx" runat="server">
  Upcoming Games</asp:HyperLink>
</p>
<p>
  <asp:HyperLink id="lnkResults" NavigateUrl="Default.aspx" runat="server">
  Results</asp:HyperLink>
</p>
<p>
  <asp:HyperLink id="lnkChat" NavigateUrl="Chat.aspx" runat="server">
  Chat</asp:HyperLink>
</p>
<p>
  <asp:HyperLink id="lnkMerchandise" NavigateUrl="Merchandise.aspx"
  runat="server">
  Official Merchandise</asp:HyperLink>
</p>
<hr width="95%"/>
<br />
<p>
  Choose a theme:<br />
  <asp:DropDownList id="ddlTheme" runat="server">
    <asp:ListItem Value="WroxUnited.css" Selected="true">Home
    Kit</asp:ListItem>
    <asp:ListItem Value="WroxUnited2.css">Away Kit</asp:ListItem>
  </asp:DropDownList>
  <asp:Button id="btnApplyTheme"
              onclick="btnApplyTheme_Click" runat="server" Text="Apply">
  </asp:Button>
  <br />
  <asp:CheckBox id="chkRememberStylePref" runat="server"
              Text="Remember preference"></asp:CheckBox>
</p>
</div>
```

4. Now replace the original left hand column of the main layout table in `Default.aspx` with the following:

```
<table style="WIDTH: 800px">
  <tr>
    <td style="VERTICAL-ALIGN: top; WIDTH: 200px">
      <WroxUnited:NavBar id="NavigationLinks" runat="server">
      </WroxUnited:NavBar>
    </td>
```

5. You will need to copy the event handler for the button that applies different themes. Cut and paste the `btnApplyTheme_Click()` method from `Default.aspx` and place it in the **Code** view of `Navbar.ascx`:

```
void btnApplyTheme_Click(object sender, EventArgs e)
{
  Session["SelectedCss"] = ddlTheme.SelectedItem.Value;

  if (chkRememberStylePref.Checked)
  {
    HttpCookie CssCookie = new HttpCookie("PreferredCss");
    CssCookie.Value = ddlTheme.SelectedItem.Value;
    CssCookie.Expires = DateTime.Now.AddSeconds(20);
    Response.Cookies.Add(CssCookie);
  }
}
```

In the last part of this Try-It-Out, we'll add some styling to the control. We don't have a stylesheet declaration in the code for this control, but that's not a problem. Once a control is added to a page, the control will *inherit* the current stylesheet information from the parent page.

6. Reopen `WroxUnited.css` and add the following style declaration to the bottom of the stylesheet definition:

```
.navbar{
  width:185px;
  border-bottom-width:4;
  border-bottom-color:#c0c0c0;
  border-bottom-style:solid;
  border-right-width:2;
  border-right-color:#c0c0c0;
  border-right-style:solid;
  padding-right:1;
  padding-bottom:0;
  padding-top:0;
}
```

7. Run the page and you should now see the page looking pretty much the same as it did before, except that it now has a border around the control as shown in Figure 12-9:

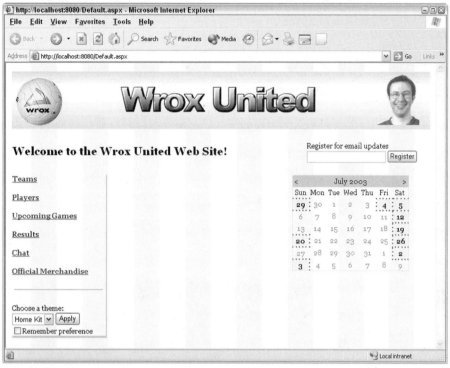

Figure 12-9

8. Add the control to the `Chat.aspx` page in exactly the same way as before. First, add the following line to the top of the page:

```
<%@ Register TagPrefix="WroxUnited" TagName="NavBar" Src="NavBar.ascx" %>
```

9. Then add the navigation bar control to the page. Note, however, that you need to add a layout table to make space for this control:

```
<form runat="server">
<WroxUnited:Header id="HeaderControl" runat="server" PageTitle="Online Chat">
</WroxUnited:Header>
```

```
<table width="800">
  <tr>
    <td width="200" style="vertical-align:top;">
      <WroxUnited:NavBar id="NavigationBar" runat="server">
      </WroxUnited:NavBar>
    </td>
    <td style="vertical-align:top;">
      <asp:TextBox id="txtChatBox" runat="server" TextMode="MultiLine"
                   Height="200px" Width="550px"ReadOnly="true">
      </asp:TextBox>
        . . .
```

```
        <asp:Button id="btnClearLog" onclick="btnClearLog_Click"
                    runat="server" Text="Clear log"></asp:Button>
        </td>
      </tr>
    </table>
  </td>
 </tr>
</table>
</form>
</body>
```

10. Once the control has been added, you can view the results of your hard work as shown in Figure 12-10:

Figure 12-10

How It Works

Once again, we've seen how to encapsulate some useful code into a reusable control and add it to our pages. Also, notice how we added a full event handler to our control, to handle the clicking of the stylesheet selector button. Go ahead and try out this button for yourself, and you'll see the stylesheet selection changes appropriately. You can then navigate back to Default.aspx and see that your selection has been saved in the Session object. If you check the box, you can also add a cookie to the client machine – if it allows cookies.

Just like in the previous examples, to add a user control to a page, you include two extra lines in the .aspx page:

```
<%@ Register TagPrefix="WroxUnited" TagName="NavBar" Src="NavBar.ascx" %>
...
...
<WroxUnited:NavBar id="NavigationBar" runat="server"></WroxUnited:NavBar>
```

In our example, the code in the ASP.NET user control also contained an event handler that was taken from `Default.aspx`. This event handler is run whenever the button in the user control is clicked. It changes in the same way as the stylesheet used on the page, on every page that includes the control. This holds true as long as each of these pages contains a stylesheet reference in the HTML view of the page:

```
<link id="css" href='<%= (string)Session["SelectedCss"] %>' type="text/css"
  rel="stylesheet" />
```

If you completed the exercises at the end of the previous chapter, you'll already have this statement at the top of each of the pages in the site.

We're now going to move on to code-behind and how to neatly separate our code into separate, manageable sections.

Code-Behind

When we were creating simple forms in *Chapter 3*, we simply created textboxes and worked with buttons that sent data on a round trip to the server. To enhance these forms, we added code that handled validating input, and so on. The extra code that enabled validation in small functions was put at the bottom of our pages to avoid cluttering the presentation code. However, there is a cleaner way of doing this – move all of this code into a *code-behind* file.

A code-behind file can be used to store all of the script blocks of an ASP.NET page. While it's perfectly possible to include this in the same page as the presentation HTML code, separating out the script blocks is a good way to separate presentation from the code. All the presentation code remains in one ASPX file (or, if you've got a couple of user controls for repetitive presentation elements, it can partly reside in ASCX files), and the code-behind code lives in a language-specific file. For example, a `.cs` file is a C# code-behind file, and a `.vb` file is a Visual Basic .NET code-behind file. The ASPX file is the central point for the application from which the code-behind file and any user controls are referenced.

Code-behind files are easy to deploy – all you need to do is copy over the code-behind file along with the ASPX page. You can even compile your code-behind files into an assembly to reuse the functionality contained within them over more than one page or application. In the next chapter, we'll introduce compilation. You'll learn how to compile components and why this is a useful technique to employ in your applications.

A code-behind file can be written in any .NET-compatible language, some good examples being C# (which we've used throughout this book so far), VB.NET, and JScript .NET. This concept will be explored in the next chapter, when we talk about .NET assemblies – don't worry if you haven't got any experience with the other languages, as we'll stick with C# for the rest of this book.

In Visual Studio .NET, Web Forms applications are always created with a code-behind file, rather than placing code on the same page. In addition, code-behind files in Visual Studio .NET are named the same as the ASPX page, with an additional `.cs` *or* `.vb` *on the end of the filename. For example,* `MyPage.aspx` *would have an associated C# code-behind page named* `MyPage.aspx.cs`.

Let's look at a simple example of a code-behind file. In this example we're going to create a very simple Web Form with a textbox and a button, and give this simple arrangement extra functionality by adding a code-behind file.

Try It Out   Our First Code-Behind File

1.   In Web Matrix, create a new C# class file and call it `SimpleCodeBehind.cs`. Set the class name to `MyCodeBehind` and the namespace to `Wrox` as shown in Figure 12-11:

Figure 12-11

2.   In this file, you will see the following generated code:

```
// SimpleCodeBehind.cs
//

namespace Wrox
{
  using System;

  /// <summary>
  /// Summary description for MyCodeBehind.
  /// </summary>
  public class MyCodeBehind
  {
    /// <summary>
    /// Creates a new instance of MyCodeBehind
    /// </summary>
    public MyCodeBehind()
    {
    }
```

```
    }
}
```

This basic code contains many comments to help you to place code in the file correctly. Let's look at the file without comments for a moment to make it a bit clearer to see what we've got:

```
namespace Wrox
{
  using System;

  public class MyCodeBehind
  {
    public MyCodeBehind()
    {
    }
  }
}
```

3. Notice how Web Matrix has put the `using` statement after the `namespace` declaration. Other editors, such as Visual Studio .NET, often place the `using` statements before the namespace declaration. This is really a matter of choice, since this code will compile and run no matter which way we have the code. To demonstrate this, switch these around by changing the order as follows:

```
using System;

namespace Wrox
{
```

4. Now change the code by adding the following highlighted lines:

```
using System;
using System.Web.UI;
using System.Web.UI.WebControls;
namespace Wrox
{
  public class MyCodeBehind : Page
  {
    public TextBox Name;
    public Label    Message;

    public void SubmitBtn_Click(object sender, EventArgs e)
    {
      Message.Text = "Hello " + Name.Text;
    }
  }
}
```

5. The `public MyCodeBehind()` method needs to be removed (notice that this method has already been removed in the preceding code listing).

The *public MyCodeBehind()* method is a constructor, a type of method used when creating a class. However, we don't need this method in a code-behind file.

6. Create a new ASP.NET page called `SimpleCodeBehind.aspx`, and save it in the same directory as the code-behind page. Switch to the **All** view and add the following code:

```
<%@ Page Language="C#" Inherits="Wrox.MyCodeBehind" Src="SimpleCodeBehind.cs"
%>

<html>
<head><title>Simple Code-Behind Page</title>
</head>
<body>
  <form runat="server">

  Please enter your name then click the button below:<br /> <br />

  <asp:textbox id="Name" runat="Server" />
  <asp:button text="ClickMe!" OnClick="SubmitBtn_Click" runat="server" />
   <br /><br />
  <asp:label id="Message" runat="Server" />
</form>
</body>
</html>
```

7. Run the ASP.NET page. You should see the page in your browser as shown in Figure 12-12:

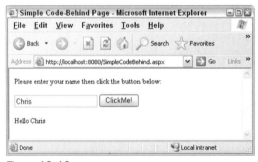

Figure 12-12

How It Works

This example did a very basic job of passing information from the `.aspx` file to the `.cs` file and back again. We entered a name into a textbox on the `.aspx` page. The `.cs` code-behind file took this name and passed it into a string along with some text, and then outputted this string to a label control that was sitting almost invisibly on our page. Let's look at the stages step-by-step to fully understand this process.

```
<%@ Page Inherits="Wrox.MyCodeBehind" Src="SimpleCodeBehind.cs" %>
```

This line of code is essential when working with code-behind. The first part of the statement specifies that we will be using the functionality in the MyCodeBehind class, which is a member of the Wrox namespace. The page will inherit the functionality defined in the `MyCodeBehind` class (refer to *Chapter 7* for more information on inheritance). The second part of this statement specifies where to find the class – in this case, in the `SimpleCodeBehind.cs` file. Only one of these declarations can be used for any given `ASPX` page.

The rest of this ASP.NET page is simple with a `textbox`, a `button`, and a `Label` control. These controls are the same as the ones introduced in *Chapter 3*:

```
<form runat="server">

Please enter your name then click the button below:<br /> <br />

<asp:textbox id="Name" runat="Server" />
<asp:button text="ClickMe!" OnClick="SubmitBtn_Click" runat="server" />
  <br /><br />
<asp:label id="Message" runat="Server" />
</form>
```

Let's move on to the code-behind file and see how this works. The syntax in this file looks different from the sort of code used so far, because this is a purely C# .NET file and not an ASP.NET page.

```
using System;
using System.Web.UI;
using System.Web.UI.WebControls;
```

This first block of code lays the foundation for the code-behind file. These three lines of code import namespaces from the .NET Class Library. These namespaces are used to access all of the functionality of ASP.NET pages. Actually, these are loaded by default into any ASP.NET page, though we never get to see this because it's all done behind the scenes. As mentioned in *Chapter 7*, these namespaces provide easy access to the classes they contain. To make use of one of their classes, you can simply refer to the class by name instead of typing out the full path that includes all of the namespace.

The next line of code assigns a `Namespace` and names the class in the code-behind file. If you remember, the first line in our ASP.NET page mentioned `Wrox.MyCodeBehind`. Well, this is what the ASP.NET page is looking for – the `MyCodeBehind` class in the `Wrox` namespace.

```
namespace Wrox
{
  public class MyCodeBehind : Page
  {
```

The second part of this line indicates that the `MyCodeBehind` class is inheriting functionality from the ASP.NET `Page` object. This means, "Take the `Page` class, combine it with the one defined below, and call it `MyCodeBehind`."

Essentially, both inheritance statements in the two files are like a kind of glue – they make the two files stick together as if they were one single file. This statement is essential when working with code-behind on an ASP.NET page.

```
    public TextBox Name;
    public Label Message;
```

These lines are simply variable declarations and mimic the names of the controls on the ASP.NET page. You need to use this technique for any code-behind file – all controls on a page that you want interacting with the code-behind file need to have a corresponding local variable.

```
public void SubmitBtn_Click(object sender, EventArgs e)
{
  Message.Text = "Hello " + Name.Text;
}
  }
}
```

We then move on to the practical details of the code-behind file. The preceding block of code is where the action happens. A method is created to handle the `onClick()` event of our **Click Me!** button. A welcome message string is built by adding some standard text to the string object, and then appending the value entered and held in the textbox by the user. The `text` attribute of the `Label` control can then be changed to display the welcome message that is constructed whenever the button is clicked.

This example was very simple, and it didn't really show off the benefits of using code-behind to the fullest. However, it did illustrate the principle of encapsulation. This technique can be used to encapsulate a lot of logic to deal with user input, thereby separating the jobs of the designer and the programmer, which is one of the goals of ASP.NET.

Code behind can be used on any ASPX page with a `<script ... >` block on it. The code portion of the page can be cleanly moved out to the code-behind file.

If you use or intend to use Visual Studio .NET, you will notice that this is the default behavior. Using code-behind is good practice since it neatly separates presentation from code – using it outside of the Visual Studio .NET environment is optional but is still a good idea.

The key steps to remember when switching to using code-behind are:

❑ Reference the code-behind file from your ASPX page by using the single line at the top of the page, specifying the class that the ASPX page is inheriting from, and the source file that contains that class definition.

❑ In the code-behind file, ensure to add : `Page` on the same line as the class definition, after the name of the class.

❑ Again, in the code-behind file, add variable declarations corresponding to each of the controls on the page that you will be working with programmatically. Ensure that you make each variable `Public` in scope.

❑ Finally, in the code-behind file, enter the code that formerly resided in the script block on the ASPX page. Ensure that all the essential `Imports` statements are added at the top of the page to reference the appropriate class libraries so that the code runs as intended.

It's worth noting that the principle of code-behind can be applied to user controls in exactly the same manner as to normal ASPX pages. All you need to do is add a statement to the top of the ASCX control, with the same syntax that the ASPX statement used in the preceding example, to link the `.ascx` to an associated `.ascx.cs` code-behind file.

Let's try using code-behind in the Wrox United site. In the next example, we'll look at how we could separate the script code contained in the Default.aspx page into a separate file.

Try It Out   Using Code-Behind in Wrox United

1. Create a new class file called Default.aspx.cs with a namespace of WroxUnited, and a class name of DefaultCodeBehind.

2. In this file, you will need to copy over all the lines of code from the Code view of Default.aspx. These are mostly methods and one public hashtable. These lines are not highlighted in the following listing (we've not included all the code from the methods in this listing; just their signatures, to give you an idea how many methods we're moving). The highlighted lines below need to be added to the code-behind page to make it work:

```
using System;
using System.Web;
using System.Web.UI;
using System.Web.UI.WebControls;
using System.Web.Caching;
using System.Collections;
using System.Configuration;

namespace WroxUnited
{
  public class DefaultCodeBehind : Page
  {

    public TextBox txtEmailAddress;
    public Label lblRegister;
    public Button btnRegister;
    public Panel pnlFixtureDetails;
    public Repeater MatchesByDateList;
    public Calendar EventCalendar;
    System.Collections.Hashtable DateList;

    public void Page_Load(object sender, EventArgs e)
    {
      ...
    }

    public void EventCalendar_DayRender(object sender, DayRenderEventArgs e)
    {
      ...
    }

    public System.Data.IDataReader Dates()
    {
      ...
    }

    public void EventCalendar_SelectionChanged(object sender, EventArgs e)
    {
      ...
```

```
        }

        public string Venue(string OpponentLocation, int MatchVenue)
        {
          ...
        }

        public System.Data.IDataReader GamesByDate(DateTime date)
        {
          ...
        }

        bool CheckFanEmailAddresses(string fanEmail)
        {
          ...
        }

        public void btnRegister_Click(object sender, EventArgs e)
        {
          ...
        }

        public int AddNewFanEmail(string fanEmail)
        {
          ...
        }
    }
}
```

Notice that all the methods are marked as `public`.

3. Once you've created the code-behind page, save the file. Ensure that you have removed all code from the Code view of the `Default.aspx` page, and then add the following line to the top of the page while in the All view:

```
<%@ Page Inherits="WroxUnited.DefaultCodeBehind" Src="Default.aspx.cs"
Language="C#" %>
```

That's it! Run the page and you shouldn't notice any difference – the page will look and feel the same, but we now have two files that store the code for the page instead of one.

How It Works

This example is a great demonstration of moving a large amount of code to a code-behind page. The main additions that had to be made were the inclusion of some additional namespace directives at the top of the file and declarations referring to the controls on the page:

```
using System;
using System.Web;
using System.Web.UI;
using System.Web.UI.WebControls;
using System.Web.Caching;
using System.Collections;
using System.Configuration;
```

```
namespace WroxUnited
{
  public class DefaultCodeBehind : Page
  {

    public TextBox txtEmailAddress;
    public Label lblRegister;
    public Button btnRegister;
    public Panel pnlFixtureDetails;
    public Repeater MatchesByDateList;
    public Calendar EventCalendar;
    System.Collections.Hashtable DateList;
```

Once these additions were made, all that remained was to transfer all the methods, ensuring that each method was marked as `public`.

If you were to now switch back to `Default.aspx`, you will find that you can't flick to the **Code** view to edit the methods that handle events like in the past. Instead, you have to open the code-behind file and edit it separately. This is a bit of a pain – why bother separating the code?

Well, for creating Web applications a natural progression is to switch to Visual Studio .NET from Web Matrix. Visual Studio .NET uses code-behind by default. Using code-behind is also good practice if you have multiple developers working on an application, because it forces you to keep presentation code separate from functionality code, leaving you with cleaner and more understandable code.

Summary

This chapter introduced two methods of encapsulating sections of code into separate files, so that our code remains as maintainable as possible:

❑ **User Controls**: Designed to hold code for sections of `ASPX` files that are repeated on numerous pages in a site

❑ **Code-behind**: Designed for containing all of the script code in one file, leaving the `ASPX` file purely for the HTML and control placement to be done by designers

These two methods are relatively straightforward, and simply involve moving code into different areas to improve readability, reduce complexity, and reduce errors caused by mixing presentation and script.

The next chapter will look at more advanced methods of encapsulating code functionality into reusable components, namely .NET assemblies and custom server controls.

Exercises

1. Add the header control and navigation bar control to each page in the site. Remember to add the following code at the top of each page:

```
<%@ Register TagPrefix="WroxUnited" TagName="Header" Src="Header.ascx" %>
<%@ Register TagPrefix="WroxUnited" TagName="NavBar" Src="NavBar.ascx" %>
```

2. Move the C# code for each page (visible in the **Code** view in Web Matrix) into an associated code-behind file, making sure each control has a corresponding declaration in the code-behind file. Note that the Players.aspx page will be a bit more tricky. Firstly, you will need to create a folder (if it doesn't already exist) within your WroxUnited directory called bin. Into this directory, you need to copy the following file: `C:\Program Files\Microsoft ASP.NET Web Matrix\v0.6.812\Framework\Microsoft.Matrix.Framework.dll`

This file contains the code that the guys at Microsoft provided for you to use if you want to deploy any of the Web Matrix custom controls, like the `MxDataGrid` that we used in the previous chapters. You'll learn more about `.dll` files and the `bin` directory in the next chapter.

3. Move the C# code from the `navbar.ascx` control (which contains an event handler) into an associated `.ascx.cs` code-behind file, following exactly the same technique that you used for the other pages on the site.

4. Create a user control for the `Merchandise.aspx` page that enables you to easily add new items to the list. You will need to copy a row of the table from `Merchandise.aspx` into a new ASCX user control file. Make the properties on the image and button controls generic, then add some public properties to programmatically set the values on each web control in the user control.

Here's some code to get you started. Firstly, here's some code that is currently in `Merchandise.aspx` that could be placed in the control:

```
<tr>
  <td>
    <asp:Image id="imgCap" runat="server" Height="100px"
      ImageUrl="images/shirt.gif" Width="100px"></asp:Image>
  </td>
  <td>
    The Wrox United shirt, available in one size only</td>
  <td>
    <asp:Button id="btnBuyShirt" onclick="AddItemToBasket" runat="server"
      Width="100px" CommandArgument="Shirt" Text="Buy a shirt!"></asp:Button>
  </td>
</tr>
```

If you change the `ImageUrl` of the image, the `Text` of the button, and the `CommandArgument` to empty strings "", then you can set those in the `Page_Load()` event. Consider the previous example – the word 'shirt' features in all three of these attributes, so you could add a property like the following that would store the name of the item (in this case, shirt), then use this value to construct the appropriate values for these attributes:

```
private string _itemName = "";

public string ItemName
{
  get{return _itemName;}
  set{_itemName = value;}
}
```

Here's an example of using this property to update another private variable:

```
if (_imageName == "")
{
    _imageName = _itemName & ".jpg";
}
```

This could be used, for example, to provide a default image name.

You would also need to move the `AddItemToBasket` method to the control because the buttons now reside within this control. Since the name of the session is globally available, it's possible to set or update session values from the control just as easily as from a page.

You will need three properties in all. The first, `ItemName` is shown in the preceding code. You can include an optional property, to override the default value (in case you want to use a .gif, for example). Finally, you need to store the text that describes the item in a `Text` property, and include the value stored in this property in the page using the following syntax:

```
<td><%=Text%></td>
```

All that remains then is to add the item to the page:

```
<WroxUnited:Product id="Shirt" runat="server"
    ItemName="Shirt"
    ImageName="shirt.gif"
    Text="The Wrox United shirt, available in one size only"/>
```

5.   Move the new code in `Product.ascx` into a code-behind file.

.NET Assemblies and Custom Controls

In the previous chapter, we discussed user controls and code-behind as two different ways to break up our code into manageable sections. These two methods are used for encapsulating commonly used chunks of ASP.NET code, and for separating the script sections of our page into separate files. In this chapter, we will concentrate on some more advanced techniques of componentization, namely, creating *.NET assemblies* and *custom server controls.*

.NET gives us the ability to pre-compile code *components* into a central location that we can then access from all the pages in a site. Each component can contain one or more classes encapsulated into a compiled *assembly*. .NET assemblies can be written in any .NET-compliant language, and are pre-compiled into a file with a `.dll` extension. ASPX pages can then reference this file to gain access to the classes and methods contained within the assembly.

An assembly can store one or many different components within one physical file on your system. You can create a separate assembly for each component if you require, enabling you to distribute your components separately. Alternatively, you can compile all of your components into one central assembly if you prefer to have fewer files to distribute with your application.

Assemblies can contain any kind of required functionality. They can be used, for example, to store a set of classes relating to accessing and working with data, all compiled into one file. Or they can even store a custom server control, which is designed to render a custom user interface element that can be used on an ASPX page as easily as an ASP.NET `Datagrid` control. An assembly is a .NET construct that contains reusable functionality required in your applications, and applies to all kinds of .NET applications, not just Web Forms.

> **.NET assemblies are groups of related classes and interface definitions encapsulated in a compiled file that can be accessed programmatically from ASP.NET Web Forms, Windows Forms, or any .NET application.**

In this chapter, we will consieder:

- ❑ What assemblies are and how they work, including details of how to compile assemblies.
- ❑ Creating an assembly that contains a data access component.
- ❑ Creating a simple custom server control that adds a Match of the Day message to the site.
- ❑ Customizing the default `calendar` control using a *composite control*.

We'll take a closer look at assemblies after we consider when and why we'd want to use them.

Three-Tier Application Design

Let us take the concept of separating content from presentation one step further. Once we've separated the elements of an application into distinct, purpose-specific categories (often referred to as layers), it becomes much easier to structure them efficiently. In many respects, everything we've said in the book so far about structured code has served as a preparation for what we're about to do – breaking out this *application logic* code into separate components that we can use both here and elsewhere. So, in traditional application design terms, our ASP.NET pages comprise the top *Presentation Layer*, a *database* stores content in a bottom *Data Layer*, and components sit in between to marshal the flow of data between them. These components provide the core logic of our application, and are collectively referred to as the *Application Logic layer*. Figure 13-1 represents the three layers we've just described:

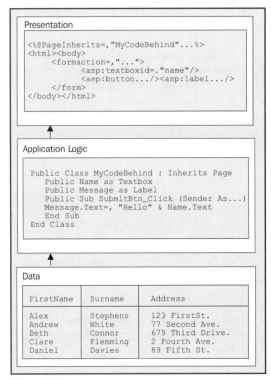

Figure 13-1

An application built using this sort of architecture is often referred to as a *three-tier application*. How do these fit together? Consider a Web site offering low priced holidays. A user might click a button on this Web site that says, "Show me all available hotels in Gran Canaria," which in a two-tier situation, would call a class in one of our application logic components that is connected to the database and query it for all hotels matching the criterion. In a three-tier scenario, this application logic may talk to data logic that, in turn, talks to the database. In either case, we're looking for hotels in Gran Canaria, but we could expand this to match hotels available on a certain date, or hotels of a certain style.

The three tiers in generic three-tier applications can be broken down as follows:

❑ **Data**: This could be any type of data store, for example, a database, an XML file, an Excel work sheet, or even a text file.

❑ **Application Logic**: This contains all the code that is used to query the database, manipulate retrieved data, pass data to the user interface, and handle any input from the UI.

❑ **Presentation**: This comprises all user interface code, containing a mixture of static HTML, text and graphics, user controls, and server controls.

Let's see how this relates to the concepts we've met so far, and how assemblies and server controls fit into the mixture.

ASP.NET Application Design

User controls are used to encapsulate frequently used sections of ASP.NET code into separate files to improve manageability and make it easier to reuse code within one application. In the previous chapter, we chose to use code-behind files to separate the code that processed our Web Form. Consider Figure 13-2:

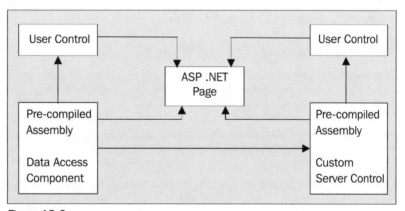

Figure 13-2

In this structure, each ASPX page as well as a user control can have a code-behind file. These user controls can be used by any of your ASP.NET pages. You can create data access components stored in assemblies that can be used by any of your user controls, ASP.NET pages, or custom server controls. You can also create custom server controls that can be used again by any of your user controls or ASP.NET pages. Your data access code can be accessed and used in your other assemblies, code-behind files, ASP.NET pages, server controls, or user controls, so the traditional three-tier application design paradigm doesn't really seem so clear. However, once you decide how you're going to structure your application, the process becomes much clearer:

1. First decide what part of your code does what. One scenario is that you keep your ASPX files purely for HTML and control elements.

2. Use code-behind to handle any page-level events (the clicking of a button, or the loading of a page).

3. You can then apply exactly the same process to the user controls, separating presentation and code as appropriate.

4. Create data access components that plug in to the ASPX and ASCX pages, which contain all your data connectivity and data processing code.

5. Finally, server controls could also make use of data-handling classes from another assembly, so you're left with a very interlinked but compact model. This process is entirely up to you.

You could theoretically keep all of your code in ASPX pages. This isn't recommended, given the benefits that encapsulating functionality into different components brings to your applications, including increased ease of manageability, increased portability, and so on.

Since we've looked at the user interface design using ASPX and ASCX files, and we've seen how we can encapsulate page logic into a code-behind file, let's look at how to encapsulate some of our application logic into a .NET assembly.

.NET Assemblies

An assembly is a logical grouping of functionality contained in a physical file. Assemblies are designed to solve the problem of versioning and make your code extremely simple to deploy. An assembly consists of two main parts:

❑   **The Assembly Manifest**: This contains the assembly metadata. This can be thought of as a table of contents that describes what's in the assembly and what it does, including the version number and culture information. It is generated when the assembly is compiled.

❑   **The MSIL (Microsoft Intermediate Language) code**: The source code (pre-compilation) is written in a .NET language, for example, VB.NET, or C#. At compile time, this source code is translated into MSIL code, which is the language .NET uses to communicate.

In the remainder of the chapter, we'll look at some examples of what can be put into assemblies. This ranges from very basic components to components containing classes that can be used to work with data. We'll also look at a simple custom server control that renders its own custom user interface. We'll do this by writing code in C#, compiling it into DLLs using the C# compiler (csc.exe), and calling it from our applications. We'll also look at how we can create an assembly in a different language that can be used in exactly the same way, so the language difference is transparent in the end result.

In our first ASP.NET assembly, we'll create a component with just one method – the SayHello() method.

Try It Out   Our First ASP.NET Component

To start with, let's create a simple component outside of the Wrox United application to demonstrate how components can be created and compiled into assemblies.

1. Ensure that you have a Chapter13 folder within your BegASPNET11 directory and then open up Web Matrix.

2. Create a new Class file called HelloWorld.cs. Set its Class property to HelloCS, and its Namespace property to WroxComponents as shown in Figure 13-3:

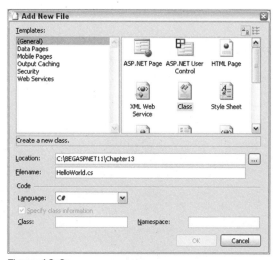

Figure 13-3

3. The file will be created when you click OK. The following code is generated automatically:

```
// HelloWorld.cs
//

namespace WroxComponents
{
  using System;

  /// <summary>
  /// Summary description for HelloCS.
  /// </summary>
```

```
  public class HelloCS
  {
    /// <summary>
    /// Creates a new instance of HelloCS
    /// </summary>
    public HelloCS()
    {
    }
  }
}
```

4. We need to make one modification to finish this example. Add the following method to the code:

```
// HelloWorld.cs
//

namespace WroxComponents
{
  using System;

  /// <summary>
  /// Summary description for HelloCS.
  /// </summary>
  public class HelloCS
  {
    /// <summary>
    /// Creates a new instance of HelloCS
    /// </summary>
    public HelloCS()
    {
    }
    /// <summary>
    /// Custom method that returns a string
    /// </summary>
    public String SayHello()
    {
      return "Hello World - I'm a C# component!";
    }
  }
}
```

5. Save the file. Let's pause for a moment and look at how this code works before continuing with the example.

How It Works

Let's take a brief look at what this simple component does, concentrating on the lines of code, ignoring the comments (lines that begin with // or ///). The first line qualifies all of the following classes into a namespace that we'll use to corral together components under a single banner:

```
namespace WroxComponents
{
```

You can use the same namespace for each of your components – as long as each method name in each component is unique, this is a good way of combining specific groups of functionality.

In this example, we've used the WroxComponents namespace. In the Wrox United application, we'll use WroxUnited as the root namespace for all of the components in the later examples.

Once the component is compiled, other pages and applications can import this namespace, and all the classes it contains can easily be accessed. It doesn't matter which DLL contains each class since ASP.NET automatically loads all classes for each application, as long as they reside in a specific location (the /bin directory) when the application is started.

The next line declares the first and only class in our component called HelloCS. Once you have imported the WroxComponents namespace into an ASPX page and created a new instance of this class, you will be able to access the HelloCS class from within an ASP.NET page:

```
public class HelloCS
{
```

Speaking of creating instances of the class, let's look at the next part of the code:

```
public HelloCS()
{
}
```

The HelloCS() method shown in the preceding code snippet is a constructor, and is called whenever a new instance of this class is created. If you wanted to, you could add code here to set some default properties or to run specific initialization code. Let's move on and look at the custom method added:

```
public String SayHello()
{
 return "Hello World - I'm a C# component!";
}
```

These lines are where our method is created. The SayHello() method is declared, and we specified that it will return a string. By declaring this function as public, we're making it available to the outside world as an interface. We'll be able to call a SayHello() method on any object derived from this class once we're in our ASPX page. We're going to be simplistic and explicitly tell our function to return the text Hello World – I'm a C# component! whenever the method is called, but in a more complex component, you can obviously do a lot more, as you will see later.

The last lines of code in our component simply close up the class declaration and the namespace declaration:

```
    }
}
```

This component must now be *compiled*, and the compiled version must be saved to the bin directory of your Web application. If the directory isn't there already, don't worry – the code you will use to compile the component will create this automatically.

Previously, when using COM, any components that were created had to be registered with the system registry. With .NET, all you need to do is save your files in the right place and compile them.

Let's take a closer look at what is meant by *compile* before compiling the component.

What Is Compilation?

When we create an ASP.NET page, we write code using an editor, and save the code as an ASPX file somewhere on our system. When that ASPX page is requested, the code is compiled into *Intermediate Language (IL)* behind the scenes when the page is first run and stored in a cache until the Web server is restarted, or until the page (the ASPX file) has been changed in some way (for example, if you added some code and re-saved the file). The cached Intermediate Language code is then *Just-In-Time (JIT)* compiled into the native machine code at runtime.

When we use an ASP.NET page, we suffer a performance hit the first time the page is accessed because the page has to be compiled to IL, and then JIT compiled. Once the page has been accessed, the process of accessing the page is much quicker because all that needs to be done then is for the JIT compiler to run. However, when we create a .NET assembly, we do the compilation to IL in advance, saving us from even more of this initial performance hit. This means that components are slightly faster than an ASPX page the first time a page is run – though subsequent page hits will perform about the same.

The compiled assembly is more discreet than the raw source code we put into it. It's much harder now to look through the compiled code and see how the classes are structured in the assembly without using a specialist tool. Simply opening the DLL in Microsoft Notepad will display gibberish, so alternative methods have to be used to see the code in its true IL form (they are outside the scope of this book).

Now let's move on to compiling our first component.

Try It Out   Compiling Our First ASP.NET Component

To compile our component, we need to create a file that will perform this compilation by running a series of specified commands.

1. Open Notepad, type in the following code, and save the file in the
    `C:\BegASPNET11\Chapter13` folder as `Compile.bat`. Remember to set the **Save as type:** to **All Files**, otherwise the file will be saved as a text file and not a batch file. We can use this batch file to execute the shell commands within it:

```
cd c:\BegASPNET11\Chapter13
md bin
csc /t:library /r:System.dll /out:bin/HelloWorldCS.dll HelloWorld.cs
pause
```

2. Double-click this file and you should see the following window:

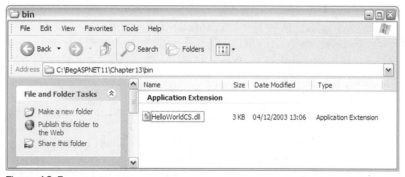

Figure 13-4

We'll examine how this works in just a moment. However, if you received any error messages when you ran this command, and the output looked different from what you can see in Figure 13-4, double check your code to make sure it's typed in correctly (especially the spacing in the .bat file).

If this doesn't solve your problem, or if you're getting an error that reads System Cannot find file csc.exe, you will need to check whether your environment variables are configured correctly. There is a tutorial on how to do this available with the code download from www.wrox.com.

How It Works

What did this do? Let's first look at what's been created, and then at the compilation batch file in detail.

If you browse your hard drive and look at the C:\BegASPNET11\Chapter13 directory, you'll notice a new folder called bin that was created as one of the steps we performed when running the compile file. Open the bin folder and you'll notice that there's the HelloWorldCS.dll file in here as shown in Figure 13-5. This is our compiled assembly, ready for use!

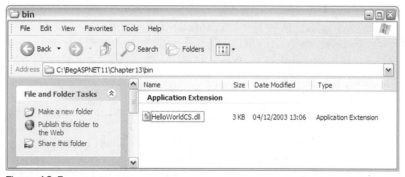

Figure 13-5

Let's look through the compilation batch file, step-by-step. First, here's the code we entered:

```
cd c:\BegASPNET11\Chapter13
md bin
csc /t:library /r:System.dll /out:bin/HelloWorldCS.dll HelloWorld.cs
pause
```

471

Let's start at the beginning. The first line of code sets the active directory for the following commands to be the directory containing the code we're using. This line means that you could place the `compile.bat` physical file anywhere on your system and run it successfully:

```
cd c:\BegASPNET11\Chapter13
```

The next line of code creates a subdirectory (if one doesn't already exist) that will contain the compiled code. This location is quite important in that it must be named `bin` and be a folder within the root of a Web application for the assemblies to be loaded correctly:

```
md bin
```

In this example, the application directory is `C:\BegASPNET11\Chapter13`, and this line of code will create a folder within here that resides at `C:\BegASPNET11\Chapter13\bin`.

The next line of code actually performs the compilation. The first part of the command is the name of the C# compiler – `csc.exe`:

```
csc /t:library /r:System.dll /out:bin/HelloWorldCS.dll HelloWorld.cs
```

The next part provides additional information that the compiler needs:

```
csc /t:library /r:System.dll /out:bin/HelloWorldCS.dll HelloWorld.cs
```

This is known as a *switch* or an *option*. We're telling the C# compiler that when it compiles, we want it to produce a *library* file or assembly, and not an executable. If we'd not included this switch, the default value would have been used instead – and the compiler would have attempted to produce an executable.

Attempting to create an executable file in this situation would have failed since EXE files must be coded so that they have a method called `Main()`. *This method is called when the EXE is run. Our code doesn't have this method in it, so we would see an error.*

Next we have a reference to the main .NET library file, `System.dll`:

```
csc /t:library /r:System.dll /out:bin/HelloWorldCS.dll HelloWorld.cs
```

The `/r:` switch indicates to the compiler that any DLL files immediately following this switch are to be referenced in the final compiled file, because they contain functionality that is necessary to the compiled assembly. The assembly referenced in this example, `System.dll`, is one of the core .NET assemblies that are installed along with .NET itself. In this example, the C# file that was compiled doesn't actually use any of the `System` classes, so this part could have been omitted, but to demonstrate a more complete example, we've kept this reference in:

```
csc /t:library /r:System.dll /out:bin/HelloWorldCS.dll HelloWorld.cs
```

This statement includes the `/out:` switch, which indicates that the code that immediately follows it is the name and location of the compiled assembly. In this case, we're creating `HelloWorldCS.dll` and placing it in the `bin` directory that we created earlier.

The last part of the statement is the name of the file we are compiling, which in our case is `HelloWorld.cs`:

```
csc /t:library /r:System.dll /out:bin/HelloWorldCS.dll HelloWorld.cs
```

The last statement in the file, `pause`, tells the operating system to wait for the user to press a key before closing the command prompt window that's popped up. This gives us the chance to wait and see what happens before the window disappears so we know that our code executed correctly, or if not, get a chance to read the error message.

When we're working with the .NET command line compiler, there are several options available to us other than those we've already seen. When we compiled our component, we used the `/t` parameter to specify the type of output the compiler would create – in our case, we used `/t:library` switch to produce a `DLL` library file. This option, a shortened form of `/target`, can also take the following arguments:

Option	Effect
`/target:exe`	Tells the compiler to create a command-line executable program. This is the default value, so if the `/target` parameter is not included, an EXE file will be created.
`/target:library`	Tells the compiler to create a `DLL` file that will contain an assembly consisting of all source files passed to the compiler. The compiler will also automatically create a manifest for this assembly.
`/target:module`	Tells the compiler to create a `DLL`, but not to create a manifest for it. This means that in order for the module to be used by the .NET Framework, it will need to be manually added to an assembly using the Assembly Generation tool (`al.exe`). This tool allows you to create the assembly manifest information manually, and then add modules to it.
`/target:winexe`	Tells the compiler to create a Windows Forms application. This is not covered in this book. (For more information about Windows Forms, you can refer to *Professional Windows Forms, Wrox Press, ISBN 1 8610 0554 7.*)

Two other compilers supplied by default with the .NET Framework are used to compile C# and JScript.net components. These compilers are in the same directory as the `csc.exe` compiler, and are called `vbc.exe` and `jsc.exe` respectively. They take the same parameters.

Accessing a Component from within an ASP.NET Page

So far, we have a simple component that contains code that displays Hello World – I'm a C# component! Let's access this from a simple ASP.NET page.

Try It Out Using a Compiled Component

1. Create a new ASP.NET page in Web Matrix called `HelloWorldExample.aspx` in the `C:\BegASPNET\Ch13` directory. In HTML view, enter the following code:

```
<form runat="server">
  <p>Our component says:</p>
  <p><asp:Label id="lblMessageCS" runat="server" /> """"</p>
</form>
```

2. Switch to Code view and enter the following code:

```
public void Page_Load()
{
  WroxComponents.HelloCS MyCSComponent = new WroxComponents.HelloCS();
  lblMessageCS.Text = MyCSComponent.SayHello();
}
```

3. Save the page and then run it in your browser to see the screen shown in Figure 13-6:

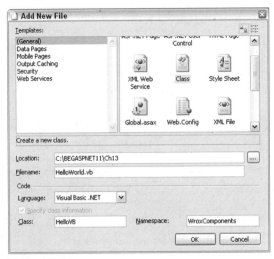

Figure 13-6

How It Works

Let's look at our ASP.NET page, starting with the code we added in HTML view:

```
<form runat="server">
  <p>Our component says:</p>
```

```
<p><asp:Label id="lblMessageCS" runat="server" /></p>
</form>
```

Within the two paragraph tags on the form, we added some text and a label control respectively. The label control's ID property was set to lblMessagecs.

In Code view, we added a Page_Load() event handler method:

```
public void Page_Load()
{
    WroxComponents.HelloCS MyCSComponent = new WroxComponents.HelloCS();
```

The first line of code in this method creates a new instance of the HelloCS class within the WroxComponents namespace. Recall that we've used syntax like this previously, whenever we created new hashtable objects or DataReader objects. Since the HelloCS class is a .NET class, and since the method within the class is an instance method, an active instance of the class needs to be created before the method within the class can be run. We instantiated a new instance of the HelloCS class by creating an object, in this case MyCSComponent, and specifying that this object will hold a new instance of the HelloCS class. MyCSComponent now has all the functionality of our class available to it as its own methods and properties. In this case, it has only one method – the SayHello() method.

The next line of code calls this method (which, as you will recall, returns a string) and uses the string value to populate the Text property of the Label control:

```
    lblMessageCS.Text = MyCSComponent.SayHello();
}
```

Returning briefly to the line of code that created the new instance of the HelloCS class, you will notice that we prefixed the HelloCS class with the namespace in which it resides. However, this could have been omitted by adding one simple line of code to the top of the page. If you switch to All view, you could add the following code:

```
<%@ Page Language="C#" %>
<%@ Import Namespace="WroxComponents" %>
<script runat="server">
...
```

Remember that this line refers to the namespace declared in the component. Back in the component, we had the following lines of code:

```
namespace WroxComponents
{
...
}
```

This is what we are referring to here. The namespace declaration is different from the class declarations in that a namespace can contain more than one class. These classes can then be referenced with the notation namespace.class, but if you use the Import Namespace command, you can simply refer to the class by name. It's a form of shorthand, and is the same as the syntax we used in the previous chapter when we imported `System.Web.UI` and similar namespaces. They act as shortcuts to commonly used classes. Note that if you use a code-behind file in conjunction with the ASPX page, the namespace would have to be imported into the code-behind file.

Once this is added, you can change the line of code that creates the object as follows:

```
HelloCS MyCSComponent = new HelloCS();
```

No doubt, some of you will be using Visual Studio. Creating and using an assembly in Visual Studio is a little different from the command line method. For a discussion on how to create components from Visual Studio .NET, please refer to Appendix D.

XCopy Deployment

If you've ever worked with Windows in detail, you've probably heard of the *Registry*. The registry is a database that holds all the information about your computer, hardware, setup, and software. It provides Windows with a way of locating `DLL` files or components. In this sense, it's a bit like the Yellow Pages of your computer. Any traditional DLL that is created has to have an entry in the registry so that the computer can locate it when it's needed. This process is called *Registration*. With basic ASP.NET components, there's no longer any need to do this – all you need to do is have the right directory in the right place, and ASP.NET will know where to look and what to do with it.

When we created our DLL, we had to place our compiled component into a `/bin` directory. This is a subdirectory of our Web application, or virtual directory.

> **Any time you need to use an assembly with .NET Web applications, the easiest way is to place your assembly in a `/bin` directory, and your ASP.NET application will now be able to use it.**

In the good old days of DOS, copying from one location to another was done with a command called `xcopy`: hence, the term that is often used when referring to deploying .NET assemblies is *XCopy deployment*.

When a component is created, it can be accessed by any Web pages in that application space. All you need to do is place the component in the correct directory, create a new instance of the component, and include an `<%@ Import Namespace ... >` declaration in your code if you want to add a shortcut to the classes contained within that namespace. If, however, you need to alter the functionality in the component in any way, all you need to do is go back to your original source file, alter the code, and recompile it. Once that process is complete, the new component will be used by any Web site hits that require it. This is very different to the scenario faced by old ASP developers, who had to stop and restart their Web application to update components, thereby losing uptime.

When a change is made to a component, ASP.NET allows any requests that are currently executing to complete, and directs all new incoming requests to the new component, so the users of a site barely notice any change.

Accessing Assemblies in Other Locations

In the previous example, we stated that all we needed to do to access our assembly was to place it within the /bin directory in the root of our Web application. What if we wanted to use an assembly in different location?

ASP.NET has a default configuration setup so that each created application knows how to access its required functionality. Occasionally, we may want to override or alter this default functionality to tailor it more to our specific application configuration. We can accomplish this using the web.config file. This file, as you will recall, resides within the root of our Web application. It can be used to help pages to find the required components.

To recap briefly, web.config is an XML-based file that specifies important configuration information that every ASP.NET application will need. It can store everything from information on debug settings and session state timeout values, to references and ASP.NET components. Being XML-based, it's human-readable, and this makes it very easy to add, remove, and change settings. Any changes to configuration that we make are instantaneous; they take effect as soon as the file is saved.

Let's take a quick look at an example of a web.config file with a directive detailing where to find an assembly:

```
<configuration>
  <system.web>
    <sessionState timeout="10" />
    <compilation>
      <assemblies>
        <add assembly="AssemblyName" />
      </assemblies>
    </compilation>
  </system.web>
</configuration>
```

> A quick word of warning – **web.config** files are case-sensitive, so all the tag names must be typed in with care.

This simple configuration file sets the session state timeout of a page to be 10 minutes, and it references an assembly called AssemblyName using the <add assembly="AssemblyName" /> tag. Here, AssemblyName refers to the assembly we require that resides outside of the bin directory. For example, we could reference System.Data if we wanted to use the classes within the System.Data namespace on a regular basis throughout our application, or c:\somedirectory\somefile.dll to locate a custom assembly in a different directory to the current working directory.

Writing Code in Other Languages

Since the .NET Framework is happily language-agnostic, we can write our components in any language. Throughout this book, we've been writing code in C#. Indeed, our first component in this chapter was written in C#. Now we'll look at that first component again, but this time written in VB.NET, to show how easy it is to work with any language to create your components.

Although the following example is written in VB.NET, don't worry if you've never looked at Visual Basic code. It's just to illustrate the cross-language compatibility of .NET and, as you'll see, there are many similarities between the two languages since they have to follow the same sorts of rules in order to be .NET-compliant.

Try It Out Writing a Component in VB.NET

1. Create a new class file `HelloWorld.vb` in Web Matrix. Set the language to **VB.NET** in the drop-down box, the **Class** name to be `HelloVB`, and the **Namespace** to be `WroxComponents` as shown in Figure 13-7:

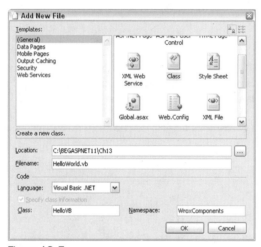

Figure 13-7

2. A chunk of standard code will be created. In this code, enter the following highlighted lines:

```vb
' NewFile.vb
'

Imports System

Namespace WroxComponents

  Public Class HelloVB

    Public Sub New()
    End Sub

    Public Function SayHello() As String
      Return "Hello World - I'm a VB.NET component!"
    End Function

  End Class
End Namespace
```

Because C# is case-sensitive, you must take particular care to copy this example letter-by-letter.

3. We need to compile this code. A simple way to do this is to reopen `Compile.bat`, amend some of the code, then save it with a new name. Amend the following code and save it as `CompileVB.bat`:

```
cd c:\BegASPNET11\Chapter13
md bin
vbc /t:library /r:System.dll /out:bin/HelloWorldVB.dll HelloWorld.vb
pause
```

4. Double-click this batch file from an Explorer window and you should see Figure 13-8:

Figure 13-8

5. Let's import the namespace for the components in this example. Open up `HelloWorldExample.aspx` and amend the file by inserting the highlighted line to the top of the page in All view:

```
<%@ Page Language="C#" %>
<%@ Import Namespace="WroxComponents" %>
```

6. Add the following line of code while in HTML view:

```
<form runat="server">
  <p>Our component says:</p>
  <p><asp:Label id="lblMessageCS" runat="server" /></p>
  <p><asp:Label id="lblMessageVB" runat="server" /></p>
</form>
```

7. Switch to Code view, modify/add the following highlighted lines, and save the file:

```
public void Page_Load()
{
  HelloCS MyCSComponent = new HelloCS();
  HelloVB MyVBComponent = new HelloVB();
  lblMessageCS.Text = MyCSComponent.SayHello();
  lblMessageVB.Text = MyVBComponent.SayHello();
}
```

Notice that we've removed the `WroxComponents` before the `HelloCS` class name and `HelloVB` class name since we added a reference to the namespace at the top of the file.

8. Reopen `HelloWorldExample.aspx` in your browser to see Figure 13-9:

Figure 13-9

How It Works

Although the syntax was somewhat unfamiliar in this example, it's not too hard to compare the two versions of our component. The lines prefixed by ' are comment lines, so ignoring those, let's look at the actual code in this example:

```
Imports System
Namespace WroxComponents
```

The `Imports` statement is the VB.NET equivalent of the C# `using` clause. The namespace declaration is no longer followed by a curly bracket. Visual Basic has a more verbose syntax, and uses pairs of statements to contain blocks of code. So, the Namespace ... End Namespace pair contain all the code in the namespace, Class ... End Class contains class code, and so on'. The next line is the start of the class block:

```
Public Class HelloVB
```

There is one default method in this class, which is the default constructor:

```
Public Sub New()
End Sub
```

Unlike C#, VB.NET uses the `New()` method to act as the default constructor for the containing class. The code within the constructor works in exactly the same way, only the name of the constructor is changed. Notice that the word `Sub` is used to declare the constructor. You'll find that VB.NET uses two different words for methods. A `Sub` (a word derived from the old Visual Basic `Subroutine`) is a method that has no return type, equivalent to a method that has a `void` return type in C#. A method that has a return value in VB.NET is declared using the `Function` keyword, and the return type is stated after the method arguments using the `As` return type syntax:

```
Public Function SayHello() As String
```

The `SayHello()` method returns a string, so the words `As String` are added to the end of the method declaration.

The next line is the body of the method:

```
Return "Hello World - I'm a VB.NET component!"
```

The `return` statement has barely changed, except for the content of the message. You'll notice that there is no semicolon at the end of the line. Where C# only finishes a line when it reaches a semicolon, VB.NET doesn't allow line wrapping, hence each physical line is the end of a line of code unless the physical line has a continuation character at the end. The VB.NET continuation character is the underscore (_).

Instead of using simple brackets to close up the method, class, and namespace respectively, the VB.NET syntax is rather more verbose:

```
    End Function

  End Class
End Namespace
```

Let's briefly look at the new lines we encountered in our ASP.NET page:

```
<p><asp:Label id="lblMessageVB" runat="server" /></p>
```

We need to add another paragraph containing another label, which we'll use to store the output of our component, just as we did with the C# component. We also added the namespace import directive to the top of the page:

```
<%@ Import Namespace="WroxComponents" %>
```

This means that we can declare the two instances of the components without having to explicitly mention which namespace the classes reside in:

```
HelloCS MyCSComponent = new HelloCS();
HelloVB MyVBComponent = new HelloVB();
```

Finally, we set the second `Label` control to display the string returned by the C# component:

```
lblMessageCS.Text = MyCSComponent.SayHello();
lblMessageVB.Text = MyVBComponent.SayHello();
```

As you'll see, the ASP.NET page hardly looks any different – there are no verbose VB.NET statements in here, because that's all held in the VB.NET version of the component. We have referenced two components, one written in VB, one written in C#, by using just one namespace import statement in our ASPX, and they've both been integrated seamlessly into our page, which only contains C# code in the script section. We could have written other components in other languages, and the results would be the same. This is one of the great features of .NET, and it's one that many developers have grown to love. Imagine, if you're a Visual Basic .NET developer, working on a project with a C# developer, and a JScript .NET developer – you could all write components to be used in ASP.NET pages, with no need to worry about which language the original component code was written in, as long as it has been compiled into Intermediate Language code.

The only way this is possible is to have a compiler that is supported by the CLR. The .NET Framework only includes a handful of compilers by default (VB.NET, C#, JScript .NET, and J#). There are many languages which have compilers for .NET, and many more are planned. For information on languages such as Perl, Python, Fortran, Cobol, along with other languages planned for use with the .NET Framework, check out the languages section of www.gotdotnet.com.

Data Access Components

A common use for components is to contain code for accessing data, or application logic. Our previous example of using an assembly didn't exactly push the boundaries very far, so in the next example, we're going to be slightly more adventurous and include some code to work with a database.

In the following example, we will create a component that combines the data access methods we've been using in the Wrox United application into a central component that can be accessed by all pages in the site. This will mean that we can reuse standard data access methods stored in this central component from any of the pages on the site. This will save us time in the long run, and it means that to change the returned data, you only need to change the code once in the central component, and not in every single page that needs to access that data.

Try It Out   Encapsulating Data Access Code in a Component

In this example, we will move some of the data access code used in the `Default.aspx` and `Teams.aspx` pages from the Wrox United site into a component. If you recall, in the previous chapter, we moved a lot of data access code from `Default.aspx` into a code-behind file called `Default.aspx.cs`. This file contains most of code that we'll be putting in the component. The rest of the methods will come from `Teams.aspx`.

1. Start by creating a new class file called `DataAccessComponent.cs` within the `BegASPNET11\WroxUnited` directory. Set its **Class** name to `DataAccessCode`, and its **Namespace** to be `WroxUnited` as shown in Figure 13-10:

Figure 13-10

2. You will see that the following code has been automatically generated for you:

```csharp
// DataAccessCode.cs
//

namespace WroxUnited
{
  using System;

  /// <summary>
  /// Summary description for DataAccessCode.
  /// </summary>
  public class DataAccessCode
  {

    /// <summary>
    /// Creates a new instance of DataAccessCode
    /// </summary>
    public DataAccessCode()
    {
    }
  }
}
```

3. The next step is to move over all the data access methods from the code-behind file to this new class. Reopen `Default.aspx.cs` and copy the following methods into this class:

- ❏ `Dates()`
- ❏ `GamesByDate()`
- ❏ `CheckFanEmailAddresses()`
- ❏ `AddNewFanEmail()`

4. You should now have the following code in your new class file (the body of each method has been omitted from the following listing to save space):

```csharp
namespace WroxUnited
{
  using System;
  using System.Data;
  using System.Collections;
  using System.Configuration;

  public class DataAccessCode
  {
    public DataAccessCode()
    {
    }

    // From Default.aspx

    //Dates() returns a DataReader containing the date and ID of every game
```

```
    public System.Data.IDataReader Dates()
    {
    ...
    }

    // GamesByDate(date) returns all games scheduled for a specified date
    public System.Data.IDataReader GamesByDate(DateTime date)
    {
    ...
    }

    // CheckFanEmailAddresses(fanEmail) verifies if an email address exists
    // in the Fans table in the database. If the email already exists, a
boolean
    // true is returned, otherwise, boolean false is returned
    public bool CheckFanEmailAddresses(string fanEmail)
    {
    ...
    }

    // AddNewFanEmail(fanEmail) adds a new email address to the Fans table.
    // The fanEmail parameter is a string representing the new email address.
    public int AddNewFanEmail(string fanEmail)
    {
    ...
    }

    // That's the last of the functions from Default.aspx'''''''''''''
    }
}
```

In the preceding code, comments have been added before each method. This is a great idea to make data components easy to use by other developers in a team, and it only takes a few minutes.

5. *Teams*.aspx also contains several methods for retrieving data, so let's add those now. You will be transferring the following methods:

❑ GetTeams()

❑ GetPlayersByTeam()

If you successfully completed the exercises at the end of the previous chapter, these methods would be in Teams.*aspx.cs*.

6. Add these two methods to the component, below the ones added previously:

```
    ...
    ''// That's the last of the functions from Default.aspx

    // From Teams.aspx

    // GetTeams retrieves the ID, Name, and Notes for each team from the
database
    // and returns them in a DataReader
```

```
    public System.Data.IDataReader GetTeams()
    {
    ...
    }

    // GetPlayersByTeam gets the details for all members of the specified team
    // The teamID parameter is an integer, and the data is returned in a
DataReader
    public System.Data.IDataReader GetPlayersByTeam(int teamID)
    {
    ...
    }
  }
}
```

7. `Default.aspx.cs` now only contains event handler methods and just one other method, `Venue()`, which is used to display the correct fixture location for either home or away matches. `Teams.aspx.cs` now only contains event handler methods.

8. The next stage is to compile this component. The easiest way to do this is to create a batch file, as we did before. Open Microsoft Notepad and enter the following lines of code. Save the file as `compile.bat`, making sure that the **Save as type** is set to **All Files**.

```
cd c:\BegASPNET11\WroxUnited
md bin
csc /t:library /r:System.dll,System.Data.dll
/out:bin/DataAccessCode.dll DataAccessCode.cs
pause
```

The two lines starting with `csc`, *shown in the preceding code snippet, should all be typed on one line with no line break in your code.*

9. Back in Windows Explorer, double-click on this file and you should see Figure 13-11:

Figure 13-11

10. If you rerun this code, you'll see a message stating that the `bin` directory already exists, but this won't affect the compile process at all, so it's worth keeping that line in to ensure that the `bin` directory always exists.

11. The data access component is now compiled, so it's time to make some changes to the ASP.NET pages so that they can still find the functions that they need! Reopen `Default.aspx.cs` and add the following lines of code:

```
using System;
using System.Web;
using System.Web.UI;
using System.Web.UI.WebControls;
using System.Web.Caching;
using System.Collections;
using System.Configuration;
using WroxUnited;

namespace WroxUnited
{
  public class DefaultCodeBehind : Page
  {

    public TextBox txtEmailAddress;
    public Label lblRegister;
    public Button btnRegister;
    public Panel pnlFixtureDetails;
    public Repeater MatchesByDateList;
    public Calendar EventCalendar;
    System.Collections.Hashtable DateList;
    public DataAccessCode Data = new DataAccessCode();

    public void Page_Load(object sender, EventArgs e)
    {
...
```

The first line is a simple namespace import; however, the second changed line of code creates a new instance of the data component that we've just created. We need to have an instance of this component before we can call any methods on this object, in the same way that we need to have instances of Web controls before we can call methods on those.

12. Now that there is an active instance of the `DataAccessCode` component on the page, we can call methods on that object. The method names are the same as they were before, but you will need to prefix each method call with the name of this object (because we are now calling methods of that object). Change the following lines of code:

In the `Page_Load()` method:

```
if (Cache["DateList"] == null)
{
    System.Data.IDataReader DateReader = Data.Dates();

    while (DateReader.Read())
    {
      DateList[DateReader["Date"]] = DateReader["Date"];
    }
```

In the `calendar` control's `SelectionChanged()` event handler:

```
public void EventCalendar_SelectionChanged(object sender, EventArgs e)
{
  if (((Hashtable)Cache["DateList"])[EventCalendar.SelectedDate] != null)
  {
    MatchesByDateList.DataSource =
      Data.GamesByDate(EventCalendar.SelectedDate);
    pnlFixtureDetails.Visible = true;
    MatchesByDateList.DataBind();
...
```

And in the `btnRegister_Click` method:

```
  if (!Data.CheckFanEmailAddresses(FanEmail))
  {
    Data.AddNewFanEmail(FanEmail);
  }
...
```

At this stage, you can view `Default.aspx` (we've not yet amended `Teams.aspx`). If you run the page, you should see the same as in Figure 13-12:

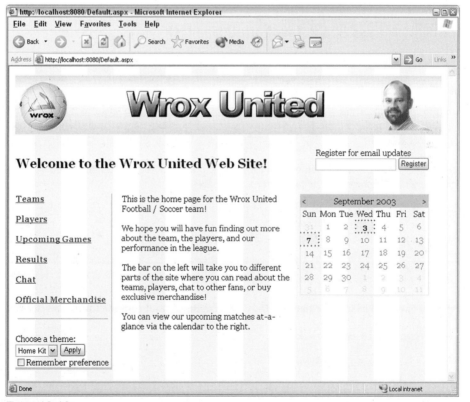

Figure 13-12

13. You need to make a couple of small adjustments to `Teams.aspx` and then the whole site should be up and running. In the code of this page (whether it's still in your ASPX page or in a code-behind page), you need to make the following changes:

```
...
using WroxUnited;
...
  public string selectedTeam;
  public DataAccessCode Data = new DataAccessCode();
...
  public void Page_Load()
  {
    TeamList.DataSource = Data.GetTeams();
    TeamList.DataBind();
  }
  public void TeamList_ItemCommand(object sender, DataListCommandEventArgs e)
  {
    if (e.CommandName == "ShowTeam")
    {
      LinkButton button = (LinkButton)e.CommandSource;
      selectedTeam = button.Text;
      PlayersList.DataSource =
      Data.GetPlayersByTeam(int.Parse((string)e.CommandArgument));
      PlayersList.DataBind();
    }
  }
}
```

14. At this point, you can run the `Teams.aspx` page, and it should look the same as before.

How It Works

This example didn't introduce any new functionality in the Wrox United site, but it did succeed in centralizing the data access methods and removing clutter from the pages themselves. Let's look through the most important parts.

At the top of the component, the namespace for the component was declared, followed by a series of using statements that referenced the necessary namespaces:

```
namespace WroxUnited
{
  using System;
  using System.Data;
  using System.Collections;
  using System.Configuration;
```

The next lines of code declared the name of the class and the default constructor for the class:

```
public class DataAccessCode
{
  public DataAccessCode()
  {
  }
```

After the default constructor was added to the code, we added all the different data access methods we've used so far from both the default and the teams pages. We won't look through these again here.

In the compilation file, we used the following statement to compile the component:

```
csc /t:library /r:System.dll,System.Data.dll
  /out:bin/DataAccessCode.dll DataAccessCode.cs
```

In this example, because we are using classes that do a lot of work with data, we need to reference the .NET `System.Data.dll` component that contains class definitions for things like the `IDataReader` interface that we've used quite often.

In the ASPX pages, we made a few changes. We added a using statement for the `WroxUnited` namespace so that we could access the `DataAccessCode` class without having to prefix it with the name of the namespace:

```
using WroxUnited;
```

We then created an instance of the new class so that we could call methods on this new object:

```
public DataAccessCode Data = new DataAccessCode();
```

Whenever we needed to call data access methods, we added the name of the object to the line of code, indicating that we were calling methods on that object:

```
        System.Data.IDataReader DateReader = Data.Dates();
...
        Data.AddNewFanEmail(FanEmail);
...
```

If you actually compare what we did in this example to what we've done in the two previous examples, you will notice that the bulk of the work has been the same – create the component, compile it, add it and instantiate it in the page, and then call methods on that object. That's all there is to it, really. Components are a convenient way to break up the code we work on to make it more maintainable and developer friendly. If you work as a full time developer, you probably encounter many components on a daily basis, so it's important to document them by adding comments, as we did in this example.

Once you understand how to put together components using class files, you can take this knowledge one step further and create custom controls. It takes a bit more coding, but the results are not just reusable code (as shown in the examples in this chapter so far), but reusable *visual* components.

Custom Server Controls

ASP.NET pages revolve around the concept of server controls. Control-based development is the new 'big thing', as you may have gathered by now. The previous chapters discussed how to use the built-in ASP.NET Server Controls, and we saw how to create our own user controls for reuse in our Web pages. Now we're going to look at what ASP.NET custom controls are, how they differ from user controls and standard components, and how they are created.

What Are Custom Controls?

Custom controls are a specific type of component – they also contain classes and are compiled. However, the main difference between a custom control and an application logic or data access component is that a custom control generates a visible user interface. When we place a server control on our page, we can see it and interact with it. As an example, consider the simple `TextBox` server control that is available to us out of the box when we create Web applications. This control was originally developed by someone at Microsoft who coded the methods and properties available to instances of that control. The .NET Framework enables us to create custom controls, which gives us the flexibility to create controls like these ourselves.

How Are Custom Controls Different from User Controls?

User controls encapsulate user interface elements of a site into easily reusable portions. However, they are usually site specific – they aren't meant to be used outside of the application in which they're based, and this is where the more universal custom control fits in. Custom controls inherit from the `System.Web.UI.Control` namespace, and are compiled. These controls can combine the functionality of other pre-existing server controls (in which case they are referred to as *composite controls*), or can be completely new controls, developed from the ground up. They are fully compiled and have no UI code contained in an ASPX page, as all rendering is controlled programmatically. They are designed to provide functionality that can be reused across many applications; for example, a tree view control for representing file systems or XML file structures.

> If you use Visual Studio .NET, you'll notice a difference between these two types of controls. A user control does not display completely in design view, and you can't set properties on this control via the property tab. However, a custom control can be coded to work with Visual Studio .NET so that you see a visual representation of the rendered page at design-time and you are able to make use of the property toolbox to work with the control at design-time.

While we won't be looking at how to achieve this here, you can see it in action whenever you drag a `TextBox`, `DataGrid`, or any other Web control onto a page – these may be built-in controls, but the theory behind them is the same as a custom control.

How Are Custom Controls Different from Standard Components?

While a standard component is designed to hold application logic or database access methods, custom controls are designed to produce viewable output. They are compiled to make it easier to deploy components on other systems or applications. They can also inherit from other assemblies and components themselves, yet their visual appearance is defined by the control-specific code they contain. A lot of functionality that is taken for granted when working with existing ASP.NET server controls, such as the ability for a control to maintain its visual state (known as its viewstate) across a postback, has to be coded by hand. This does mean a lot of coding when you get into advanced controls, but it gives the developer a very powerful reusable tool that works the way you want, rather than having to hack about to produce a less-than-ideal solution.

Let's have a go at creating a simple custom control, and displaying it in an ASP.NET page.

Try It Out **Our First ASP.NET Custom Control**

We're going to create a simple custom control that will output some text to the `Default.aspx` page on Wrox United. The text that will be displayed will be a **Match of the Day** message. We will add a small method to the `DataAccessCode.cs` class that we created earlier and recompile it. This method can then be called from within the server control, which formats the message and renders it in the browser.

1. Fire up Web Matrix and reopen `DataAccessCode.cs`. Add the following method to the class, which we'll look at in more detail once we finish the example:

```
// GetMotd() builds an Arraylist containing strings that detail any
// scheduled matches for the current day.
// If there are no matches, an appropriate message is added instead.
public ArrayList GetMotd()
{
  IDataReader myReader;
  // Call the GamesByDate function in this class
  // to retrieve fixture information for today
  myReader = GamesByDate(System.DateTime.Now.Date);

  ArrayList motdMessage = new ArrayList();
  string individualMessage = "";
  int resultCount = 0;

  while (myReader.Read())
  {
    individualMessage = (string)myReader["TeamName"] + " v " +
                        (string)myReader["OpponentName"];

    if ((int)myReader["Location"] == 1)
    {
      individualMessage += ", home";
    }
    else
    {
      individualMessage += ", away";
    }

    motdMessage.Add(individualMessage);
    resultCount = resultCount + 1;
  }

  if (resultCount < 1)
  {
    motdMessage.Add("No games scheduled today.");
  }

  return motdMessage;
}
```

2. If you like, you can recompile this class now by simply double-clicking on `Compile.bat` from explorer as you did before. If all went well, no errors will be produced. After building the custom control in this exercise, we'll add some more commands to `Compile.bat`, enabling us to compile all custom controls and classes in one step.

3. Time to build the control itself! Create a new class in Web Matrix named `CustomMotdControl.cs`, and specify that it belongs to the `WroxUnited` namespace.

4. Enter the following code into the newly created file:

```
// CustomMotdControl.cs
//

namespace WroxUnited
{
  using System;
  using System.Collections;
  using System.Web.UI;
  using WroxUnited;

  /// <summary>
  /// Summary description for MotdControl.
  /// </summary>
  public class MotdControl : Control
  {

    /// <summary>
    /// Creates a new instance of MotdControl
    /// </summary>
    public MotdControl()
    {
    }

    private string _name = "MOTD";

    public string Name
    {
      get{return _name;}
      set{_name = value;}
    }

    protected override void Render(HtmlTextWriter writer)
    {
      DataAccessCode data = new DataAccessCode();
      ArrayList motdMessages = new ArrayList();
      motdMessages = data.GetMotd();

      writer.Write("<div class='motd'>" + _name + ", " +
                   DateTime.Now.ToShortDateString() + ": <br/>");

      foreach (string message in motdMessages)
      {
        writer.Write(message + "<br />");
      }
      writer.Write("</div>");
    }
  }
}
```

5. Make sure that you save this code before you continue. Reopen `Compile.bat` and add the following highlighted line of code (again, make sure it is all on one line in your code):

```
cd c:\BegASPNET11\WroxUnited
md bin
csc /t:library /r:System.dll,System.Data.dll
/out:bin/DataAccessCode.dll DataAccessCode.cs
```

```
csc /t:library /r:System.dll,System.Web.dll,bin/DataAccessCode.dll
   /out:bin/CustomMotdControl.dll CustomMotdControl.cs
```

```
pause
```

Make sure you keep the statement that compiles the `DataAccessCode.cs` *file – this is needed in the custom control. We've added the* `DataAccessCode.dll` *file in the compile statement for the custom control – this will ensure that we can access the methods stored in the data access component from the server control.*

6. Run this file by double-clicking it in Explorer view.

7. Open `Default.aspx` and at the top of the file and the following line:

```
<%@ Register TagPrefix="WroxUnited" TagName="NavBar" Src="NavBar.ascx" %>
```

```
<%@ Register TagPrefix="WroxUnitedMotd" Namespace="WroxUnited"
            Assembly="CustomMotdControl" %>
```

8. In the central table cell (that you can use to store general introductory text), enter the following highlighted line of code:

```
The bar on the left will take you to different parts of the site. If you are
a player, you can log in to the site and gain access to the administration
section.
<br />
<br />
You can view our upcoming matches at-a-glance via the calendar to the right.
<br />
<br/>
<WroxUnitedMotd:MotdControl id="WuMotd"
                        Name="Matches today" runat="server" />
```

9. So, the extra data method has been added, the control has been created, and both components have been compiled. We've also added code to use this control from `Default.aspx`, so it's nearly time to run the page and see the results. However, before you do so, reopen `WroxUnited.css` (and `WroxUnited2.css`) and add a new element to the stylesheet.

❑ In `WroxUnited.css`, add the following:

```
.motd {
  color: #8b0000;
}
```

❑ In `WroxUnited2.css`, add the following:

```
.motd {
```

```
    color: "yellow";
}
```

10. Now it's time to run the page! If you run the page on a day when there is a game (or several games) scheduled, you'll see something like in Figure 13-13:

Figure 13-13

11. However, if you run the code on a day when no matches are scheduled, you'll see a default message saying No games scheduled today.

If you want to see different results, you can edit the contents of the Games table in the WroxUnited database. If matches are scheduled for the current day, you will see a message on the default.aspx page. However, if you change the date of each match, you can change the message that is displayed on the front page accordingly. In the above example, I manually changed the date of two scheduled matches to the previous day, in order to demonstrate what is displayed on days when there are no matches scheduled.

How It Works – The Control

We created a control with a property that rendered very limited output to demonstrate how simple custom controls can be created. Let's look at how we put it together:

```
namespace WroxUnited
{
  using System;
  using System.Collections;
  using System.Web.UI;
  using WroxUnited;
```

We added four namespaces at the top of the file. We will be using an `ArrayList` in this example, hence the `System.Collections` namespace. We will also be creating a Web control. So we've added a `using` statement for the `System.Web.UI` namespace, because we'll probably want to use classes within this namespace. We also added a using statement for the `WroxUnited` namespace, which is the namespace within which the data access class resides.

The next part of the code declares the `MotdControl` class:

```
public class MotdControl : Control
{
```

Notice that there is a `: Control` statement immediately after the class definition, indicating that this class inherits functionality defined in the `Control` class. This is an important part of custom control development, because all custom controls must inherit from either the `System.Web.UI.Control` or `System.Web.UI.WebControl` class. The `Control` class is the leaner class of the two, and while it provides a lot of basic functionality behind the scenes that any control needs in order to work, it doesn't provide many methods implemented in the `WebControl` class. This isn't a problem, because we don't need any of these methods in this example. Inheriting from `Control` means that we have more control over how the control is rendered at runtime.

The next part of the code creates the only public property of the control:

```
private string _name = "MOTD";

public string Name
{
  get{return _name;}
  set{_name = value;}
}
```

The first line of code creates a private variable called _name that is only accessible by the rest of the code in this class. The next block is where the public property is declared. This property can be set programmatically (`MyControl.Name = thing`), and also read programmatically (`thing = MyControl.Name`). The `get` and `set` blocks are used to specify how this works. Each time a new value is set via the public property, the private variable is updated. Conversely, whenever the public property is read, the returned value is stored in the private variable. The public property sits between the outside world and the internal variable. In this case, we are setting or getting the value of a string variable with some text that we'll use as we build up the displayed message. If we don't set the property in our code, the _name variable will store the default value of MOTD.

```
protected override void Render(HtmlTextWriter writer)
{
```

We're creating one method in this class. There are a couple of new terms in here that you may not be familiar with. There is a method in the `Control` class called `Render`. What we're doing here is altering how that method works by *overriding* its functionality with our own functionality. While we don't want to go too far into the world of VB programming here, you need to know that this statement is required to provide the output we specify, instead of the default output from the `Control` class. We will be using an `HtmlTextWriter` to display the output of our control.

> **The only difference between this example and the previous one is that the control is rendering (writing) the text directly to the page, while our previous tests required a `Label` control or similar to display any returned text from our components.**

However, we can render much more than just plain text using these controls. In this example, the output contains some HTML tags.

The next part of the code gets the complete set of daily match details from the data access component:

```
DataAccessCode data = new DataAccessCode();
ArrayList motdMessages = new ArrayList();
motdMessages = data.GetMotd();
```

We created a new object called `data` and set it to contain a new instance of the `DataAccessCode` class. We then created a new `ArrayList` called `motdMessages` and retrieved the `ArrayList` of the day's fixtures from the database using the `GetMotd()` method.

The next line is where the magic starts – the `Write()` method of the `writer` object that was declared in the method signature is used to write the required output to the Web page when the control is rendered:

```
writer.Write("<div class='motd'>" + _name + ", " +
             DateTime.Now.ToShortDateString() + ": <br/>");
```

This first line builds up an HTML string and inserts the string stored in the _name private variable (the one that is set programmatically using the public `Name` property), and also the current date. Notice that this HTML string is in the form of a `<div ... >` element, which has an associated class definition – this enables us to style the output of the control in a CSS file.

The remainder of this method loops through the individual strings in the `ArrayList` and adds them (and a line break after each one) to the output. The last call to the `Write()` method writes the closing `</div>` tag to the browser (a sample of the rendered HTML output is shown in just a moment):

```
foreach (string message in motdMessages)
{
   writer.Write(message + "<br />");
}
writer.Write("</div>");
    }
  }
}
```

If you view the source of `Default.aspx` you will find the following text about halfway down the page:

```
<div class='motd'>Matches today, 07/09/2003: <br/>No games scheduled
today.<br/></div>
```

This should give you a clear indication of how this code fits together. The result is clean and simple, and has been produced programmatically.

The Component

The `GetMotd()` method that we added to the `DataAccessCode` component provides the custom control with details of any matches on that particular day in the form of an `ArrayList`:

```
public ArrayList GetMotd()
{
```

The first part of this function retrieves all fixture details for the current day by passing in the current date, using the `DateTime.Now.Date` property to the `GamesByDate()` method that was created earlier:

```
IDataReader myReader;
// Call the GamesByDate function in this class
// to retrieve fixture information for today
myReader = GamesByDate(System.DateTime.Now.Date);
```

Next, we created some variables to hold various items of data, including the `ArrayList` of messages, the individual messages, and a count of how many matches are happening on the current day:

```
ArrayList motdMessage = new ArrayList();
string individualMessage = "";
int resultCount = 0;
```

Looping through the results stored in the `myReader` object, we built up a string containing details about the fixture:

```
while (myReader.Read())
{
  individualMessage = (string)myReader["TeamName"] + " v " +
                        (string)myReader["OpponentName"];

  if ((int)myReader["Location"] == 1)
  {
    individualMessage += ", home";
  }
  else
  {
    individualMessage += ", away";
  }

  motdMessage.Add(individualMessage);
  resultCount = resultCount + 1;
}
```

At this point, if there are no matches on the current day, the count of the results will still be zero; hence we can output a specific message to the array instead of match details:

```
          if (resultCount < 1)
          {
            motdMessage.Add("No games scheduled today.");
          }
```

Finally, we return the `ArrayList` of messages to the calling code:

```
          return motdMessage;
        }
```

The Batch File

The command that we used to compile this component is very similar to the one that we used to compile the `DataAccessCode.vb` file:

```
csc /t:library /r:System.dll,System.Web.dll,bin/DataAccessCode.dll
   /out:bin/CustomMotdControl.dll CustomMotdControl.cs
```

Notice that we have referenced `System.Web.dll` this time around (we needed this so that we could use the classes it contains, including the `System.Web.UI.Control` class). We also referenced the `DataAccessCode.dll` compiled assembly – needed as a reference so that the `GetMotd()` method could be called to return the required `ArrayList`. Since the `DataAccessCode` compilation statement should still be in this file, this will be compiled before the custom control is compiled, hence the custom control will be able to make use of any changes to the `DataAcccessCode` when the custom control itself is compiled.

The ASPX Page

We didn't make too many changes to the `Default.aspx` page itself – all the hard work was kept completely separate from this code file, which is exactly what we're after! Firstly, we registered the custom control so that the page knows about the assembly and the code it contains:

```
<%@ Register TagPrefix="WroxUnitedMotd" Namespace="WroxUnited"
            Assembly="CustomMotdControl" %>
```

We set a `TagPrefix` as we did with user controls, however, we do not set a `TagName` – we'll see why in a moment. We specified the namespace to be used as the `WroxUnited` namespace, and that we're using the `CustomMotdControl` assembly. Later in the code, we added the control to the page:

```
<WroxUnitedMotd:MotdControl id="WuMotd"
                            Name="Matches today" runat="server" />
```

This is where we place our control on the page. We call it by the `TagPrefix` we set earlier, followed by the class name we specified in the control. We specify a `runat="server"` attribute, set the `Name` property of the control, and close the tag. The `Name` property relates directly to the `Name` property we added to the custom control, so when we set this property, the `Set` block in the property in the custom control is run, and the local `_name` property has its value changed to the string we specify here. This value is then added to the output string, and hey presto! – we've just used our first custom control.

We mentioned earlier that one of the main reasons for using custom server controls was reusability, well, as long as our control can access a `GetMotd()` method in a class called `DataAccessCode`, we can use this control to display "message of the day" notices on a site. It's a good thing that MOTD could be an acronym for either "match" or "message" of the day!

Composite Custom Controls

In the last example, we created a completely new control that inherited some basic functionality from the `Control` base class, but the rest of the control was completely our own work. While it's possible to create all custom controls in this way, there are situations where you might find yourself saying, "Wouldn't it be great if I had a textbox that only allowed numeric input?" or perhaps, "I'd really like a custom calendar that highlighted specific dates instead of having to add event handlers and code every time!" Composite controls will solve these problems for you. A composite control is a custom control that contains an existing control within its definition, and allows you to customize how that existing control is rendered.

Let's have a look at this in action by creating a neat custom calendar class that will highlight specific dates for us automatically, and then use this as part of `Default.aspx`.

Try It Out   Wrox United – Custom Composite Control

1. Start the example by creating a new class file, setting its namespace to be `WroxUnited`, and its class name to be `CustomCalendar`. Save the file as `CustomCalendar.cs`.

2. In the file, add the following code:

```
// CustomCalendar.cs
//
namespace WroxUnited
{
  using System;
  using System.ComponentModel;
  using System.Web.UI;
  using System.Collections;
  using System.Web.UI.WebControls;

  public class CustomCalendar : Control, INamingContainer
  {
    private Calendar calendar;
    public event EventHandler SelectionChanged;
    private Hashtable _dateList;

    public Hashtable DateList
    {
      get
      {
        return _dateList;
      }
      set
      {
        _dateList = value;
      }
    }
```

```
      public DateTime SelectedDate
      {
        get
        {
          return calendar.SelectedDate;
        }
      }

      protected override void CreateChildControls()
      {
        calendar.CssClass = "calendar";
        calendar.DayStyle.CssClass = "normaldate";
        calendar.OtherMonthDayStyle.CssClass = "othermonthdate";
        this.Controls.Add(calendar);
      }

      protected override void OnInit(EventArgs e)
      {
        base.OnInit(e);

        calendar = new Calendar();

        calendar.DayRender +=
          new DayRenderEventHandler(this.EventCalendar_DayRender);
        calendar.SelectionChanged +=
          new EventHandler(this.EventCalendar_SelectionChanged);
      }

      private void EventCalendar_DayRender(object sender, DayRenderEventArgs e)
      {
        if (_dateList != null)
        {
          if (_dateList[e.Day.Date] != null)
          {
            e.Cell.CssClass = "selecteddate";
            e.Day.IsSelectable = true;
          }
          else
          {
            e.Day.IsSelectable = false;
          }
        }
        else
        {
          e.Day.IsSelectable = false;
        }
      }

      private void EventCalendar_SelectionChanged(object sender, EventArgs e)
      {
        if (SelectionChanged != null)
        {
          SelectionChanged(this, e);
        }
```

```
      }
    }
  }
```

3. We need to compile this control. In the `Compile.bat` file, add the following line of code (ensuring that this is all on one line in the file):

```
csc /t:library /r:System.dll,System.Web.dll /out:bin/CustomCalendar.dll
    CustomCalendar.cs
```

4. Double-click `Compile.bat` from an Explorer window to compile the control.

5. Add this control to the page by adding the following directive to the top of the page In `Default.aspx`:

```
<%@ Register TagPrefix="WroxUnitedCalendar" Namespace="WroxUnited"
            Assembly="CustomCalendar" %>
```

6. Add the following code in place of the original `calendar` control:

```
<td style="VERTICAL-ALIGN: top; WIDTH: 250px">
    <WroxUnitedCalendar:CustomCalendar id="EventCalendar" runat="server"
        OnSelectionChanged="EventCalendar_SelectionChanged" />
    <p>
    <asp:Panel id="pnlFixtureDetails" runat="server" visible="false">
```

7. Switch to the code-behind for this page and alter the `calendar` control declaration to refer to the new `CustomCalendar` class:

```
public TextBox txtEmailAddress;
public Label lblRegister;
public Button btnRegister;
public Panel pnlFixtureDetails;
public Repeater MatchesByDateList;
public WroxUnited.CustomCalendar EventCalendar;
System.Collections.Hashtable DateList;
public DataAccessCode Data = new DataAccessCode();
```

8. Further down the page, in the `Page_Load()` method, add the following line of code:

```
if (Cache["DateList"] == null)
{
    ...
}
else
{
    ...
}

EventCalendar.DateList = (Hashtable)Cache["DateList"];"""
```

9. Delete the `EventCalendar_DayRender` from the code-behind page – we don't need this method any more because the functionality it contained is now encapsulated in the new custom control.

10. Run `Default.aspx` in your browser and you will see the same results as before, shown in Figure 13-14. You will be able to click on the different match dates in the calendar, and see the fixture details for a particular day:

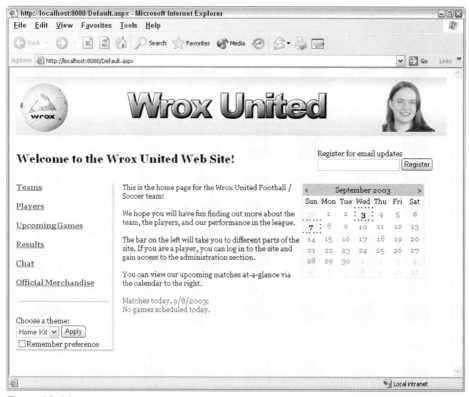

Figure 13-14

How It Works – The Control

This control may appear a bit complex at first, so let's step through it piece by piece. We start with a namespace declaration and some `using` statements:

```
namespace WroxUnited
{
  using System;
  using System.ComponentModel;
  using System.Web.UI;
  using System.Collections;
  using System.Web.UI.WebControls;
```

Next we declared the class:

```
public class CustomCalendar : Control, INamingContainer
{
```

Notice that in addition to inheriting the functionality in the Control class, we have implemented an interface called INamingContainer. This interface (a special type of class) enables ASP.NET to assign a name to the calendar that we'll be adding to this control in just a moment. Interfaces are discussed in *Chapter 7*.

The next lines of code create a new object called calendar of type WebControls.Calendar, and an event handler that will be used for the SelectionChanged() event:

```
private Calendar calendar;
public event EventHandler SelectionChanged;
```

Next comes some more familiar code. We declare a private Hashtable (which we'll use to store the dates that will be highlighted in the calendar). This Hashtable has its value set via the public property DateList:

```
private Hashtable _dateList;

public Hashtable DateList
{
  get
  {
    return _dateList;
  }
  set
  {
    _dateList = value;
  }
}
```

The next block of code creates a second property, but this time, we're only going to allow consumers of this control to read the value in this property. When you want a property to be read only, you should omit the set block:

```
public DateTime SelectedDate
{
  get
  {
    return calendar.SelectedDate;
  }
}
```

This property returns the value of the currently selected date in the calendar, which allows us to use this value to populate the panel below the calendar on the Default.aspx page.

The next part of the code is where we add the `calendar` control to the main `Parent` container. The `calendar` control is what is known as a `Child` control (it has a parent control; the custom control). To add this `Child` control, we override the `CreateChildControls` method of the `Control` class:

```
protected override void CreateChildControls()
{
```

The first part of the body of this method is where we instantiate a new `calendar` control. The reason we have added the `WebControls` prefix is that we have only imported `System.Web.UI`, not `System.Web.UI.WebControls`. Next, we specify three CSS class properties:

```
calendar.CssClass = "calendar";
calendar.DayStyle.CssClass = "normaldate";
calendar.OtherMonthDayStyle.CssClass = "othermonthdate";
```

Adding these properties to this control mean that, as long as we include a CSS stylesheet with the appropriate definitions in our pages, we'll be able to style our `calendar` control automatically. The last part of this method adds this control to the `Controls` collection of the parent control:

```
    this.Controls.Add(calendar);
}
```

The next method is necessary in any C# custom control that uses events. In order to successfully connect the control to the event handler methods (known as "wiring up" the event handlers), you need to override the page's OnInit event, as we have done here:

```
protected override void OnInit(EventArgs e)
{
    base.OnInit(e);
```

The first part of the method indicates that we'll be overriding the `OnInit()` event of the base class, which is the page on which this control is consumed. The next section is where we create a new instance of the calendar and wire up the event handlers for the two events we're dealing with:

```
    calendar = new Calendar();

    calendar.DayRender +=
        new DayRenderEventHandler(this.EventCalendar_DayRender);
    calendar.SelectionChanged +=
        new EventHandler(this.EventCalendar_SelectionChanged);
}
```

The third method in this file is the first event handler for this control, the `DayRender()` event handler:

```
private void EventCalendar_DayRender(object sender, DayRenderEventArgs e)
{
```

We then test whether any date information has been passed into the control. If it has, then _dateList will contain *something* (not `null`), and we can proceed to test whether the day that is being rendered matches any of the days in the _dateList Hashtable:

```
if (_dateList != null)
{
  if (_dateList[e.Day.Date] != null)
  {
    e.Cell.CssClass = "selecteddate";
    e.Day.IsSelectable = true;
  }
```

If the day that is being rendered is not a match day, we ensure that it isn't selectable. Likewise, if the _dateList Hashtable is empty, then we ensure that none of the dates are selectable:

```
  else
  {
    e.Day.IsSelectable = false;
  }
}
else
{
  e.Day.IsSelectable = false;
}
}
```

The final method in this control is the SelectionChanged() event handler. This method is fired whenever the calendar control's SelectionChanged() event is fired. Whenever this event is fired, we pass that event to the public SelectionChanged() event object that was declared earlier. This ensures that the SelectionChanged() event exists for the newly created custom control, and can be handled in the consuming page:

```
private void EventCalendar_SelectionChanged(object sender, EventArgs e)
{
  if (SelectionChanged != null)
  {
    SelectionChanged(this, e);
  }
}
}
}
```

After this method closes, we close up the last of the control with the last remaining closing brackets. So, time to look at the compile statement for this control!

The Batch File

The compile statement for this file isn't too different from the statements we've used in the other controls and components in this chapter:

```
csc /t:library /r:System.dll,System.Web.dll /out:bin/CustomCalendar.dll
    CustomCalendar.cs
```

This time, we only needed to reference the System.Web.dll in addition to the System.dll assembly. We didn't access any data in this example.

The ASPX Page

We made only a couple of changes to the `Default.aspx` page to use this new calendar. First, we added a reference to the new control:

```
<%@ Register TagPrefix="WroxUnitedCalendar" Namespace="WroxUnited"
Assembly="CustomCalendar" %>
```

Next, we changed the code in the page to use the custom calendar in place of the default calendar, which turned out to involve less code than before (we've added a lot of this code to the custom control already):

```
<WroxUnitedCalendar:CustomCalendar id="EventCalendar" runat="server"
                    OnSelectionChanged="EventCalendar_SelectionChanged" />
```

Notice that we still set the `OnSelectionChanged` attribute as we did before to point to the event handler that fires whenever the selection in the calendar changes.

In the code-behind page itself, we changed the `EventCalendar`'s data type from `Calendar` to `CustomCalendar`:

```
public WroxUnited.CustomCalendar EventCalendar;
```

Then we added a line to the `Page_Load()` event handler that passed in the `DateList Hashtable` (stored in the cache) to the `CustomCalendar` control. This is the data that we need to highlight specific dates!

```
EventCalendar.DateList = (Hashtable)Cache["DateList"];""
```

Summary

In this chapter, we have continued the thread from the previous one, and discussed creating .NET assemblies that can be used to store classes that handle data access code, or custom server control code. We've even seen an example of using a C# component from within a VB.NET ASPX page, demonstrating how .NET handles components written in different languages. We've also created two different custom server controls, and taken a first look into the world of custom control creation.

In this chapter, we looked at:

❑ Compiling a .NET assembly

❑ Using classes contained in a compiled assembly on a page

❑ Encapsulating data access code into a compiled component

❑ Creating simple custom controls that render custom HTML to the browser

❑ Enhancing an existing ASP.NET control using a composite control

Exercises

These exercises are separate from the Wrox United application, but you will find that concepts learned in this chapter will come in very handy when completing these exercises.

To help, we've included a tiny Access database in the code download for this chapter called Travel.mdb. It's a small database that contains a list of locations, temperatures, and weather conditions. We've also included some images that correspond to various different weather conditions.

1. Build a data access component that connects to the Travel.mdb access database and retrieves data filtered by location, about the weather at that location. You may find the following SQL useful:

```
SELECT [Locations].[LocationName], [Locations].[CurrentTemperature],
       [WeatherTypes].[WeatherType]
FROM [Locations], [WeatherTypes]
WHERE (([WeatherTypes].[WeatherTypeID] = [Locations].[CurrentWeather])
AND ([Locations].[LocationName] = @LocationName))
```

If you use the Web Matrix **SELECT** data wizard, you can create a method called GetWeatherByCity that takes the LocationName as a parameter, and returns a DataReader.

2. Add another method to this data access component called GetCities that selects all the LocationNames from the database and returns a DataReader.

3. Create a simple custom control that has one property, a temperature property that takes a temperature in Celsius and renders a string of text that displays the temperature in both Celsius and Fahrenheit:

Fahrenheit temperature = Celsius temperature * (9/5) + 32

The control should render a <span> tag that has a style=color:<color> attribute that can be used to change the color of the text for different temperature ranges. If the temperature is below 0 degrees Celsius, you should make the text blue, above 30 degrees it should be red, and all others should be orange.

4. Create another control that takes the code built in the first two examples to produce a composite control that displays temperature data stored in the database for a specific city. Your control should render the following output:

❑ The name of the city

❑ The temperature at the specified city (use an instance of the control created in the previous example)

❑ An image control <ASP:Image ...> that displays one of a series of images (available in the code download for this chapter) that represents the style of weather currently being experienced at the specified city, for example, an image of a cloud if the weather is overcast.

5. Finally, add the following to an ASP.NET page:

❑ Add a DropDownList box and databind that to the data reader returned by the GetCities method in the data access component. Enable auto-postback for this control so that a Postback occurs whenever the selection changes.

❑ Add a copy of the weather control created in the previous exercise to the page, and pass in the name of the currently selected city to the control to display the weather for that city.

Debugging and Error Handling

One of the fundamental facts about organized systems is that the more complex they become, the more likely they are to go wrong. While most of the examples in this book have been quite simple, the principles behind the .NET Framework make it easier for you to build larger and more complex systems.

Once you have planned and created your program, the steps involved in ensuring that your code runs smoothly at all times can be broken down into two main categories:

❑ **Debugging**: Regardless of the painstaking attention to detail that we give to our code, mistakes will occur. We can minimize their effects by identifying the portions of our code that are most prone to errors, and by adhering to good coding practices that facilitate troubleshooting.

❑ **Error Handling**: Even if we produce flawless code, there is no guarantee that everything will operate smoothly at runtime. Things can (and at times do) go wrong. Problems such as network connection failures or power failures may occur in the operating environment. There may be problems with unexpected data types, or data may not have been properly prepared. Third-party programs may return unexpected data. Good programming practices dictate that we anticipate as many problems as we can *before* they occur so that we may apply a graceful solution.

This chapter will help you identify problems, fix them, and prevent them from occurring in future. Specifically, we'll look at the following topics:

❑ Good coding practices

❑ Different types of errors

❑ Locating errors in the page

❑ Tracing

❑ Exceptions

Chapter 14

- ❑ Handling Exceptions
- ❑ Handling errors
- ❑ Notifying and logging errors

A Few Good Habits

Whether you're an expert developer or a beginner, you can significantly reduce the probability of an error's occurrence by adopting some very straightforward habits. Finding an error in your application is not a cause for panic – it just indicates that an effective error handling strategy is needed. We will provide you with the information needed to design and implement an effective error handling strategy.

Before getting into detail about the different kinds of errors that may afflict your code, let's talk about how you may reduce the time and effort required to identify and fix an error.

- ❑ **Understand your code**: Make a clean distinction between server-side and client-side functionality. Adopt naming conventions and use them consistently. Write headers for methods explicitly stating their purpose and give variables meaningful names. These habits will go a long way in producing self-documenting code. If sections or routines in your code are still unclear after implementing these practices , document some more. Clear and concise code will be an invaluable asset when it's time to locate where, and understand why, an error has occurred.

- ❑ **Identify where it might break**: Identify the potential problem areas before even loading the page and testing its functionality. For instance, say you have developed a page that communicates with a database and pulls a set of records. You must create a connection to the database, formulate a query, and then execute that query to retrieve the records. Connecting to the database or the execution of the query may throw an error. You need to look out for potential problems at an early stage (we will discuss different kinds of errors later in this chapter.)

- ❑ **Amend identified error conditions**: Once you have identified areas that could break within your page, the next step is to make sure that the conditions under which your error might occur are as stable as possible. Remember the old adage: an ounce of prevention is worth a pound of cure.

Mistakes in your code are not the end of the world. What matters is how quickly you can identify them and fix them. With that in mind, let's start by looking at the habits that should be cultivated.

Tips on Coding

It may not be possible to have completely error-free programs, but there are some precautions we can take to reduce or avoid common mistakes. These include indenting and structuring the code as well as adding comments to increase its comprehensibility. We will look at these and other good coding practices.

Indent Your Code

This is quite an obvious and straightforward step. Although it will not ensure an error-free program, it will really help to improve the readability of your code, for yourself *and* for others. Indenting your code will help you detect errors faster. The following example lays out some code in two different ways. See the difference for yourself:

```
<html>
<head>
<title>Syntax Error Example </title>
</head>
<body>
<form method="post" action="sytntaxerror.aspx" runat="server">
<asp:TetBox id="txtQuantity" runat="server" />
</form>
</body>
</html>
```

This code can be indented as follows to make it clearer:

```
<html>
  <head>
   <title>Syntax Error Example </title>
  </head>
  <body>
    <form method="post" action="sytntaxerror.aspx" runat="server">
    <asp:TetBox id="txtQuantity" runat="server" />
    </form>
  </body>
</html>
```

Structure Your Code

Use functions in your code to implement specific tasks. This is even more important for tasks that are used several times in your applications. For instance, consider a situation when you need to format the display of a date. The database might store a date in the form CCYYMMDD, whereas you might need to display it on the screen as MM/DD/CCYY. You could then create a function, such as the one shown below:

```
public string FormatDate(string CCYYMMDD)
{
  int intYear, intMonth, intDay;
  intYear = left(CCYYMMDD,4);
  intMonth = mid(CCYYMMDD,5,2);
  intDay = right(CCYYMMDD,2);
  return (Cstr(intMonth) &"/"& Cstr(intDay) &"/"& Cstr(intYear));
}
```

If you need to format the display of your date at different places in the program, you can simply call this function each time you need to do so, rather than writing code for the whole process repeatedly. It's fairly obvious that this will save time, but the real beauty is that if there's an error in the code (or if you need to change it), you only need to change the code once.

Comment Your Code

Commenting your code is another simple and easy-to-implement technique that increases the readability of your code. Without appropriate comments, your code will look extremely confusing. Writing comments in your code will help you remember exactly what your code is doing, which will be invaluable when you try to debug or modify it. Look again at the method from the previous section:

```
//**********************************************************************
public string FormatDate(string CCYYMMDD)
//*Purpose: convert date from CCYYMMDD format to MM/DD/CCYY format
//*Input:   String  date in the format CCYYMMDD
//*Returns: String  string that represents a date in the format MM/DD/CCYY
//**********************************************************************
{
  int intYear, intMonth, intDay;
  intYear = left(CCYYMMDD,4);
  intMonth = mid(CCYYMMDD,5,2);
  intDay = right(CCYYMMDD,2);
  return (Cstr(intMonth) &"/"& Cstr(intDay) &"/"& Cstr(intYear));
}
```

The commenting in this example may seem excessive for such a small method. However, the small investment in time that it takes adequately to comment your code will pay huge dividends upon revisiting that code. In addition, habits such as writing method headers and providing general comments facilitate the reuse of code.

Convert Variables to the Correct Data Types (Validation)

Converting the values provided in your Web page to an appropriate data type before using them in your program will prevent some compilation errors from occurring. For example, if the user assigns 12.23 for a numeric field for which you're expecting an integer value, this assignment will result in an error. To prevent this error, convert the value entered to an integer before assigning the value to a variable of integer data type. You could use the Convert class in the System namespace provided by the .NET Framework. The following table shows the syntax of using the ToString() method of the Convert class:

Conversion Function	Return Datatype
Convert.ToBoolean	Boolean
Convert.ToByte	Byte
Convert.ToChar	Char
Convert.ToDateTime	Date
Convert.ToDouble	Double

Conversion Function	Return Datatype
Convert.ToDecimal	Decimal
Convert.ToInt16	16 bit signed Integer
Convert.ToInt32	32 bit signed Integer
Convert.ToInt64	64 bit signed Integer
Convert.ToSingle	Single
Convert.ToString	String

The following code shows the syntax for using the ToString() method of the Convert class:

```
SomeVariable = Convert.ToString(SomeInteger);
'Convert Integer to String
```

Try to Break Your Code

This can be a more difficult task than expected. It is often difficult for the developer to anticipate all the unusual things a user might attempt to do with the application, such as accidentally typing in letters when numbers are required, or supplying an answer that was longer than anticipated, or even deliberately trying to break it.

So, when it is time to test your application, try to think like a user who isn't too computer literate. You can break down your testing strategy into two main approaches:

❑ **Be nice to your program**: Supply your program with legal values, or values that your program is designed to expect and handle. For instance, if your program contains an age field, supply only numbers, not letters. Watch how your program behaves – does it respond as you expect it to with the legal values supplied to it?

❑ **Try to break your program**: This is the fun part. Supply your program with illegal values. For instance, provide string values where integers are expected. This ensures that your program handles all illegal values appropriately. Depending on the kind of data you are expecting in your program, you could to do anything from a simple numeric or alphabetic check to a validity check (such as inserting invalid dates into a date field). If your program spans several pages, then surf to some of the pages out of the expected sequence.

Both these techniques can be used to help standardize and improve the readability of your code. Many basic errors can be avoided in this way. However, even if you follow all these suggestions, your code still can't be guaranteed to be bug-free. Let's look at some of the errors that may plague your code.

Sources of Errors

The errors that occur in an ASP.NET page can be grouped into four categories:

❑ **Parser errors**: These occur because of incorrect syntax or bad grammar within the ASP.NET page.

❑ **Compilation errors**: These are also syntax errors, but they occur due to statements that are not recognized by the language compiler, rather than ASP.NET itself. For example, using `If` (capital I) instead of `if`, or not providing a closing bracket to a `for` loop, will result in a compilation error. The difference between the parser error and compilation error is that the parser error occurs when there is a syntax error in the ASP.NET page, and the ASP.NET parser catches it, whereas the compilation error occurs when there is a syntax error in the C# code block.

❑ **Configuration errors**: These occur because of the incorrect syntax or structure of a *configuration file*. An ASP.NET configuration file is a text file in XML format, and contains a hierarchical structure that stores application-wide configuration settings. There can be one configuration file for every application on your Web server. These configuration files are all named `web.config`, irrespective of the application's name. There is also a single configuration file called `machine.config` that contains information that applies to every application on a single machine. We will discuss configuration files in detail in *Chapter 15*, although we do touch upon them again later in this chapter.

❑ **Runtime or logical errors**: As the name implies, these errors are not detected during compilation or parsing, but occur during execution. For example, when the user enters letters into a field that expects numbers, and your program assigns that entry to an integer variable, you will get a runtime error when the code tries to execute. These are also known as logical errors.

Now let's look at some specific examples that fall into the above categories.

Syntax Errors

As the name suggests, these errors occur when there are problems in the syntax of the code. Parser and compilation errors fall under this category. These are usually the first errors encountered when developing ASP.NET pages. There are several reasons why these errors occur:

❑ **A typo or bad grammar in the code syntax**: For example, instead of typing `<asp:textbox>` for creating a `TextBox` control in your page, you type `<asp:textbx>`, then the browser shows an error.

❑ **Incorrect code syntax**: For instance, when creating a textbox control, you might forget to close the tag (as `<asp:TextBox id="txtName" runat="server">` when it should actually be `<asp:TextBox id="txtName" runat="server" />`)

❑ **Combining or splitting keywords between languages**: I make this error quite a lot. If you've been coding in another language and come back to coding in C#, you might forget brackets, or type keywords in the wrong case.

❑ **Not closing a construct properly**: This error occurs if we forget to close a construct, such as a `for` loop or a nested `if` statement. Take a look at this example:

```
if condition1 {
```

```
    //do this
  }
  else condition2 {
    //do this
    if condition2a {
      //do this
    }
    else {
    //do this
  }
```

Did you catch the error in the above code? We're missing a closing-bracket. Imagine how difficult it would be to spot this if we had the above code block set amongst hundreds of other lines of code. It's another good argument for formatting your code correctly too. If it had been indented, it would have been easier to spot the error.

Let's look at an example of creating a syntax error (a parser error) and then see how ASP.NET responds to it.

Syntax Error

1.   Open Web Matrix and type the following lines of code into the All Window. Make a spelling mistake when creating the textbox control, as highlighted in the following code:

```
<html>
  <head>
    <title>Syntax Error Example </title>
  </head>
  <body>
    <form method="post" action="syntaxerror.aspx" runat="server">
    <asp:TetBox id="txtQuantity" runat="server" />
    </form>
  </body>
</html>
```

2.   Save this file as `syntaxerror.aspx` and load the file using a browser. You expect to see a textbox in the browser, as shown in Figure 14-1:

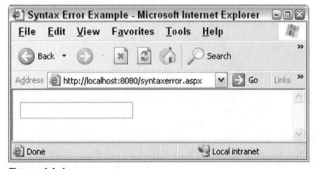

Figure 14-1

However, what you actually see is Figure 14-2:

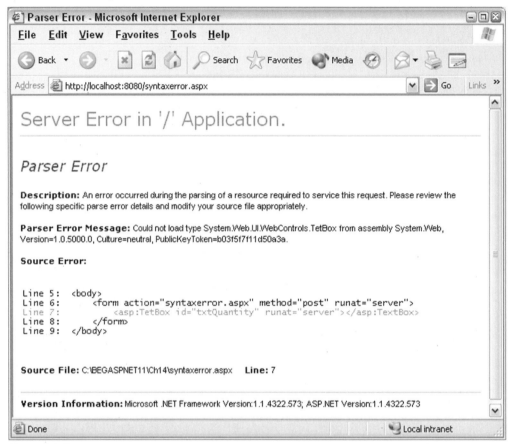

Figure 14-2

How It Works

As the error message clearly states, the ASP.NET parser points to Line 7, and asks us to check the details. You can see that a spelling mistake exists, `Tetbox` instead of `TextBox`. If you correct the spelling mistake and rerun the code, you'll get the expected result.

Errors of this kind are very common but are usually quick and easy to fix, since the error message provides a detailed breakdown of the error and the line on which it occurs.

Now we will look at a syntax error that will generate a compilation error.

Try It Out   Generate a Compiler Error

1. Create a new file called `compilationerror.aspx`, and type the following code into the Web Matrix All window:

```
<%@ Page language="C#" Debug="true" %>
<script language="C#" runat="server">

public void CompleteOrder(Object sender, EventArgs e)

{
  If (txtQuantity.Text == "")
  {
    lblOrderConfirm.Text = "Please provide an Order Quantity.";
  }
  else if (Convert.ToInt32(txtQuantity.Text) <= 0)
  {
    lblOrderConfirm.Text = "Please provide a Quantity greater than 0.";
  }
  else if (Convert.ToInt32(txtQuantity.Text) > 0)
  {
      lblOrderConfirm.Text = "Order Successfully placed.";
  }
}

</script>

<html>
  <head>
    <title>Compiliation Error Example</title>
  </head>
  <body>

    <form method="post" action="manualtrapping.aspx" runat="server">
      <asp:Label text="Order Quantity" runat="server" />
      <asp:TextBox id="txtQuantity" runat="server" />
      <br />
      <asp:Button id="btnComplete_Order" Text="Complete Order"
                                  onclick="CompleteOrder"
                                              runat="server"/>
      <br />
      <asp:Label id="lblOrderConfirm" runat="server"/>
    </form>

  </body>
</html>
```

2. Save and view the `compilationerror.aspx` file with a browser. The page displayed is as shown in Figure 14-3:

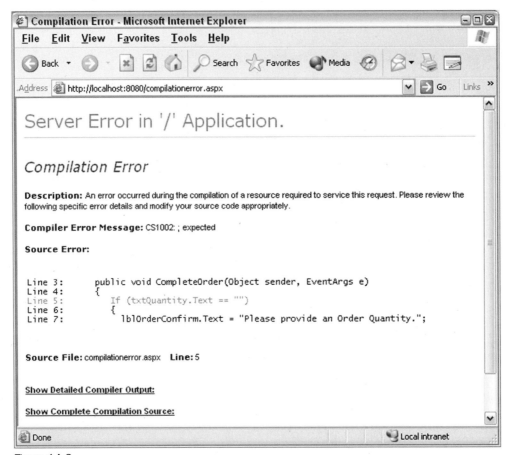

Figure 14-3

How It Works

We typed If at the beginning of our control block instead of if. As expected, when we tried to run the compilationerror.aspx file in the browser, we got an error message. It tells us we have a compiler error in Line 5 and even attempts to tell us how to fix it. (In this case it is rather misleading as it tells us we are missing a semicolon, when in fact, the if statement is the part that is incorrect!)

These are just a few common examples of syntax errors. There is no way we could provide a list of all possible syntax errors that you might encounter, but the good news is that syntax errors are easy to find and fix.

Logical (Runtime) Errors

The second type of error is the *Logical Error*. Unfortunately, it is relatively more difficult to find and fix. Logical errors become apparent during runtime. As the name implies, these errors occur due to mistakes in programming logic. Some of the more common reasons for these errors are:

❑ **Division by zero**: This dreaded error that has been around since the days of valve-based computers. It occurs when your program divides a number by zero. But why in the world do we divide a number by zero? In most cases, this occurs because the program divides a number by an integer that should contain a non-zero number, but for some reason, contains a zero.

❑ **Type mismatch**: Type mismatch errors occur when you try to work with incompatible data types and inadvertently try to add a string to a number, or store a string in a date data type. It is possible to avoid this error by explicitly converting the data type of a value before operating on it. We will talk about variable data type conversion later in this chapter.

❑ **Incorrect output**: This type of error occurs when you use a function that returns output that's different from what you are expecting in your program.

❑ **Use of a non-existent object**: This type of error occurs when you try to use an object that was never created, or when an attempt to create the object failed.

❑ **Mistaken assumptions**: This is another common error, and should be corrected during the testing phase (if one exists). This type of error occurs when the programmer uses an incorrect assumption in the program. This can happen, for instance, in a program that adds withdrawal amounts to a current balance, instead of subtracting them.

❑ **Processing invalid data**: This type of error occurs when the program accepts invalid data. An example of this would be a library checkout program that accepts a book's return date as February 29, 2003, in which case, you may not have to return the book for a while!

While this is far from being a complete list of all possible logical errors, it should give you a feel for what to look out for when testing your code.

Try It Out   Generate a Runtime Error

1. Open `compilationerror.aspx` in Web Matrix, go to the All Window, and make the following change to the case of the `if` statement:

```
public void CompleteOrder(Object sender, EventArgs e)
{
    if (txtQuantity.Text == "")

    {
      lblOrderConfirm.Text = "Please provide an Order Quantity.";
    }
    else if (Convert.ToInt32(txtQuantity.Text) <= 0)
    {
      lblOrderConfirm.Text = "Please provide a Quantity greater than 0.";
    }
    else if (Convert.ToInt32(txtQuantity.Text) > 0)
    {
        lblOrderConfirm.Text = "Order Successfully placed.";
    }
}
```

2. Save the file as `runtimeError.aspx`.

3. View the `runtimeError.aspx` file using the browser. Provide a non-numeric value, such as ABC, to the order quantity textbox, and click the **Complete Order** button. Figure 14-4 shows the result:

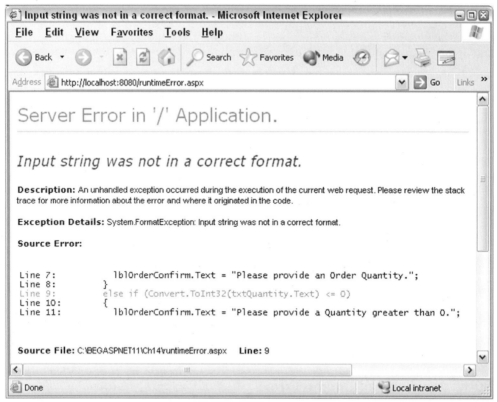

Figure 14-4

How It Works

Our control block validates input for null values, and for numeric values that are equal to or less than zero. It does not check input for other non-numeric input values. The code generated a runtime error when the `ConvertTo.Int32()` function tried to convert a non-numeric entry to an integer field. The process of checking for this type of errors is called validation. To validate the data entry values, your control block should have an extra couple of lines as follows:

```
else if (Convert.ToInt32(txtQuantity.Text) <= 0)
   {
     lblOrderConfirm.Text = "Please provide a Quantity greater than 0.";
   }
```

Let's take a closer look at validating user input.

Trapping Invalid Data

Testing your code by supplying both legal and illegal values is crucial for the proper functioning of your program. Your program should return expected results when providing legal values, and handle errors when supplied with illegal values. In this section, we'll talk about ways to handle the illegal values supplied to your program. We have two objectives here:

❑   Prevent the occurrence of errors that may leave you with many disgruntled users

❑   Prevent your program from accepting and using illegal values

There are two main techniques used to fulfill these objectives: *manual trapping* and *using validation controls*.

Manual Trapping

When building the application, you could create *error traps* to catch illegal values before they get into the page execution, where they might halt the execution of the page or provide invalid results. How do you block illegal values from sneaking into page processing? Let's develop a page that accepts order quantity from the user.

Try It Out   Catching Illegal Values

1.   Open `runtimeError.aspx` in Web Matrix and make the following changes in the All Window:

```csharp
<%@ Page Language="c#" Debug="true" %>
<script Language="c#" runat="server">
void CompleteOrder(object sender, EventArgs e)
  {
    if (txtQuantity.Text!= "")
    {
      if (!(Char.IsNumber(txtQuantity.Text,0)))
      {
        if (txtQuantity.Text.Substring(0,1) != "-")
        {
          lblOrderConfirm.Text =
                    "Please provide only numbers in Quantity field.";
        }
        else
        {
          lblOrderConfirm.Text =
                    "Please provide a Quantity greater than 0.";
        }
      }
      else if (Convert.ToInt32(txtQuantity.Text) == 0)
      {
        lblOrderConfirm.Text = "Please provide a Quantity greater than 0.";
      }
      else if (Convert.ToInt32(txtQuantity.Text) > 0)
      {
        lblOrderConfirm.Text = "Order Successfully placed.";
      }
    }
    else
    {
      lblOrderConfirm.Text = "Please provide an Order Quantity.";
    }
  }
</script>
<html>
<head>
    <title>Manual Trapping Example</title>
  </head>
```

2. Save the file as `manualtrapping.aspx`.

3. Load this file using your browser. Figure 14-5 shows the result of providing an order quantity of `10`:

Figure 14-5

4. Supply different values to the order quantity textbox and check whether the page behaves as expected.

How It Works

Notice that we have added an extra directive to the page calls:

```
<%@ Page language="C#" Debug="true" %>
```

This will enable us to view detailed error messages throughout the course of the chapter. How this works will become clearer as we progress.

We are using two `Label` controls: a `TextBox` control and a `Button` control. The first `Label` control is the label for the order quantity textbox:

```
<asp:Label text="Order Quantity" runat="server" />
```

The second label control called `lblOrderConfirm` is used to display a message after processing the order, indicating whether the order was successfully placed or not:

```
<asp:Label id="lblOrderConfirm" runat="server"/>
```

The textbox accepts an entry from the user – the order quantity:

```
<asp:TextBox id="txtQuantity" runat="server" />
```

The button calls the `CompleteOrder()` function when clicked:

```
<asp:Button id="btnComplete_Order" Text="Complete Order"
        onclick="CompleteOrder"
```

```
runat="server"/>
```

Within the `CompleteOrder()` function, we create a series of checks to avoid illegal values. First, we check for 'no entry' to the textbox:

```
if (txtQuantity.Text!= "")
{
...
}
else
{
  lblOrderConfirm.Text = "Please provide an Order Quantity.";
}
```

This is followed by the numeric check and checks to ensure that the quantity is greater than zero:

```
if (!(Char.IsNumber(txtQuantity.Text,0)))
{
  if (txtQuantity.Text.Substring(0,1)!= "-")
  {
    lblOrderConfirm.Text =
                  "Please provide only numbers in Quantity field.";
  }
  else
  {
    lblOrderConfirm.Text =

                        "Please provide a Quantity greater than 0.";
  }
}
else if (Convert.ToInt32(txtQuantity.Text) == 0)
{
  lblOrderConfirm.Text = "Please provide a Quantity greater than 0.";
}
```

Finally, the code for accepting the order:

```
else if (Convert.ToInt32(txtQuantity.Text) > 0)
{
  lblOrderConfirm.Text = "Order Successfully placed.";
}
}
```

Using Validation Controls

The second technique is to use one or more of several validation controls provided by ASP.NET (refer to *Chapter 10* for a detailed discussion on validation controls.)

Validation controls are used to validate user input. For instance, you could use the `RequiredFieldValidator` control to ensure that users enter a value to a textbox. By doing this, you could avoid runtime errors that occur because of your program using a null (unknown value), when it is expecting an 'entry' from the user.

By using one of the many validation controls provided by ASP.NET, you could present the users with a message informing them about the incorrect value supplied, and the value your program is expecting. This prevents the program from processing an illegal value and developing an error.

Let's look at an example to demonstrate how to use these controls. We'll use the `RequiredFieldValidator` to ensure that the user provides a value for the `Order Quantity` field.

Try It Out   Using RequiredFieldValidator

1. Open `manualtrapping.aspx` (from the previous exercise) in Web Matrix, and make the following changes in the All Window:

```
<form method="post" action="usingvalidationcontrol.aspx" runat="server">
  <asp:Label text="Order Quantity" runat="server" />
  <asp:TextBox id="txtQuantity" runat="server" />
  <asp:RequiredFieldValidator ControlToValidate="txtQuantity" runat="server"
          ErrorMessage="Please enter a value in the Order Quantity Field">
  </asp:RequiredFieldValidator>
  <br />
  <asp:Button id="btnComplete_Order" Text="Complete Order"_
                              onclick="CompleteOrder" runat="server"/>
  <br>
  <asp:Label id="lblOrderConfirm" runat="server"/>
</form>
```

2. Save this file as `usingvalidationcontrol.aspx`.

3. Use your browser to open `usingvalidationcontrol.aspx`. If you try to complete the order without entering anything, you're presented with the request that you see in Figure 14-6:

Figure 14-6

How It Works

In this example, we have used a `RequiredFieldValidator` control. The `ControlToValidate` property is used to specify the control that we are validating:

```
<asp:RequiredFieldValidator ControlToValidate="txtQuantity" runat="server"
```

In this case, we are validating the `order quantity` textbox. The ErrorMessage property is used to provide an error message when the user does not enter a value to the order quantity field.

```
ErrorMessage="Please enter a value in the Order Quantity Field">
```

The validation control saves us the extra second guessing of typical mistakes a user might make.

System Errors

These errors are generated by ASP.NET itself. They may be due to malfunctioning code, a bug in ASP.NET, or even one in the CLR. Although you could find this type of error, rectifying it is usually not possible – particularly if it is an ASP.NET or CLR error.

Other errors that can be placed in this category are those that arise due to the failure of a Web server or component, a hardware failure, or a lack of server memory.

When an error occurs in an ASP.NET page, the error details are sent to the client. However, ASP.NET by default shows detailed error information only to a local client.

A local client is a browser running on the same machine as the Web server and therefore only viewable by the site administrator. For instance, if you create the ASP.NET examples in this book on a machine running a Web server, and access them using a browser on the same machine (as you would do with Web Matrix), then the browser is a local client. If this was deployed on a network using IIS, you might see the error, but other users on the network would just receive a generic "something's wrong" kind of message.

So, the fact that ASP.NET sends detailed information about errors to local clients is actually very helpful to the developer during the development phase.

Finding Errors

Having adopted the good coding practices and different techniques to trap invalid data in our programs, why are we still talking about finding errors? Even after taking precautions, our program might still end up with an error page. It could be because we did not cover all possible error scenarios in our testing (point the fingers at the testers), or another program did not behave as expected (refer it to the other team) or worse, the server administrators did not set up the server right (blame it on the network administrators).

However well you plan, it is difficult, if not impossible, to catch every bug in advance. So, what do we do if our well-constructed code still doesn't work? We will discuss this topic next.

Let's go back to the local client scenario. ASP.NET displays a *call-stack* when a runtime error occurs. A call-stack contains a series of function calls that lead up to an error. Before you do this, delete (or rename) any `web.config` files residing with your samples; otherwise all errors generated will be handled by this file.

Let's create a page that causes a runtime error.

Try It Out   Viewing the Call-Stack

1.   Open Web Matrix and create a file called `callStack.aspx`. Then type the following code into the All Window:

```csharp
<%@ Page Language="c#" Debug="true" %>
<script language="c#" runat="server">
  void CreateRunTimeError()
  {
    int[] array = new int[5];
    int arrayIndex = 5;
    array[arrayIndex] = 5;

    Response.Write("This should never be reached");
  }
</script>

<%
  CreateRunTimeError();
%>
```

2.   Save the file and open it in your browser. You should see something like Figure 14-7 (as long you haven't got a `web.config` file in the same folder as the .aspx file):

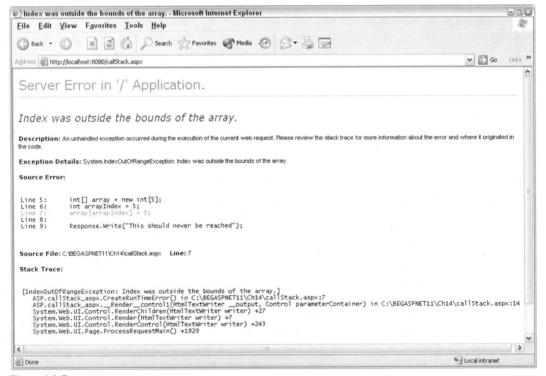

Figure 14-7

How It Works

In the block of code we entered, we set up an array of five elements, numbered from 0 to 4, and tried to access an element with the number 5, which is an element beyond the end of the array:

```
int[] array = new int[5];
int arrayIndex = 5;
array[arrayIndex] = 5;
```

On running this code, an error was generated when the program tried to execute an integer data type containing a string. We were presented with the error page above. The error page contains different sections, such as Exception Details (we'll discuss exceptions shortly), Source Error, Stack Trace, and so on. The Stack Trace contains the call-stack that says that the value we are trying to assign to an integer variable is not valid. If you look through the call-stack, you can see the series of functions that led to the exception.

The information provided under the Source Error section is useful in locating the line in which the error occurred. The display of this information is controlled by the Debug mode.

Debug Mode

If Debug mode is enabled, the Source Error section of the error message is displayed as part of the error message that pinpoints the location in the code that generated the error. If Debug mode is disabled, the Source Error section is not displayed.

Now the question is: where and how can we set the value for Debug mode?

It can be set in two different places. The first place should be familiar as we have used it twice already within this chapter. You can set it at every page within the Page directive at the top of the page, as shown below:

```
<%@ Page Debug="true" %>
```

To disable it, you can set it to false:

```
<%@ Page Debug="false" %>
```

If the Debug mode is set like this (at the page level), the setting is applied *only* to that specific page.

Let's return to our previous example, and disable the Debug mode at the page level:

Try It Out   Disable the Debug Mode

1. Open the callstack.aspx file in Web Matrix, and in the All window, insert the following line at the top of the page – don't replace the existing declaration:

```
<%@ Page Language="C#" Debug="false" %>
```

2. Save the file as debugmode.aspx and access the page using the browser. You will see an error page as shown in Figure 14-8:

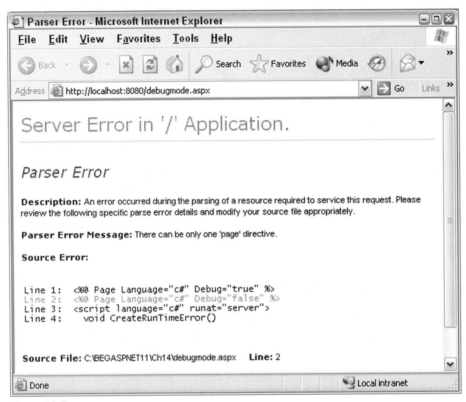

Figure 14-8

How It Works

We disabled the Debug mode in our debugmode.aspx by adding the following line at the top of the page:

```
<%@ Page Debug="false" %>
```

On running our new file in the browser, we saw a new error message. Under the **Source Error** section, there are instructions to enable the Debug mode for displaying the source code that generated the exception, but the actual source code is not there.

As mentioned a moment ago, there are two ways to set the Debug mode. The second way is to set it at the *application level*, using the <compilation> configuration section in the configuration file (see *Chapter 15*).

Setting the `Debug` mode at the application level will display the **Source Error** section in the error message for all the files under the application. This has a performance overhead though, so before moving your application to a production environment, make sure you disable the `Debug` mode.

Tracing

When developing an application, we execute the page at different levels of development, and for effective debugging, we always need to see the values assigned to variables and the state of different conditional constructs at different stages of execution. In ASP, developers used the ubiquitous `Response.Write` statement to display this information. The downside of this is that while completing the application development, the developer had to go to every page and either comment or remove the `Response.Write` statements they created for testing purposes. ASP.NET provides a new feature to bypass all of this. It is the `Trace` capability.

The Trace feature provides a range of information about the page, including request time, performance data, server variables, and most importantly, any message added by the developers. It is disabled by default. Like the `debug` mode, tracing can be either enabled or disabled at either the page (or the application) level. We'll now consider these levels in more detail.

Page-Level Tracing

Tracing can be enabled at the page level to display trace information using the `Page` directive's `Trace` attribute, as shown below:

```
<%@ Page Trace = "true" %>
```

Tracing can be disabled using:

```
<%@ Page Trace = "false" %>
```

When tracing is enabled, the trace information is displayed underneath the page's contents. Let's create a simple ASP.NET page with a `TextBox` and a `Label` control, and enable tracing at the page level.

Try It Out   Enabling Trace at the Page Level

1.   Open Web Matrix, create a page called `pageleveltracing.aspx`, and type in the following code to the All Window:

```
<%@ Page Trace="true"%>
<html>
  <head>
    <title>Page Level Tracing</title>
  </head>
  <body>
    <form method="post" action="pageleveltracing.aspx" runat="server">
    <asp:label text="Name" runat="server" />
    <asp:textbox name="txtName" runat="server" />
    </form>
  </body>
</html>
```

2. Save this file and view it using the browser as shown in Figure 14-9:

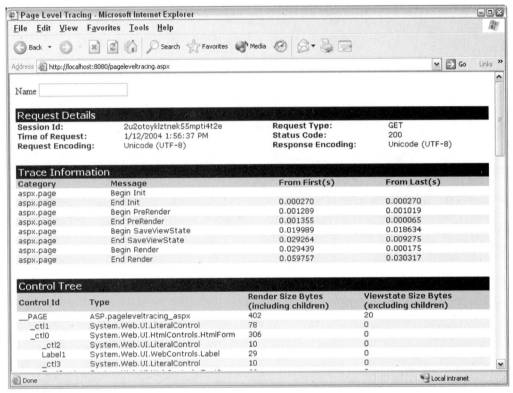

Figure 14-9

How It Works

First, we enabled the page trace with the line:

```
<%@ Page Trace="true"%>
```

We then created a textbox with some text beside it. What we got was the textbox plus a whole load of tracing. Let's look at each section of the trace output to get a fuller understanding of what they display:

❑ **Request Details**: This section contains information pertaining to the page request, such as the Session ID for the current session, the request type (whether it is GET or POST), the time at which the request was made, the encoding type of the request among others, as shown in Figure 14-10:

Request Details					
Session Id:	chuwlnihzidnb245sx3bi221		Request Type:		GET
Time of Request:	1/12/2004 12:21:14 AM		Status Code:		200
Request Encoding:	Unicode (UTF-8)		Response Encoding:		Unicode (UTF-8)

Figure 14-10

❑ **Trace Information**: This is the section in which the actual trace information is displayed along with the messages written by developers. As shown in Figure 14-11, this section displays the category, the message, the time since the first message, and the most recent message displayed:

Trace Information			
Category	Message	From First(s)	From Last(s)
aspx.page	Begin Init		
aspx.page	End Init	0.000269	0.000269
aspx.page	Begin PreRender	0.001251	0.000982
aspx.page	End PreRender	0.001326	0.000075
aspx.page	Begin SaveViewState	0.021493	0.020167
aspx.page	End SaveViewState	0.038247	0.016754
aspx.page	Begin Render	0.038373	0.000126
aspx.page	End Render	0.041535	0.003162

Figure 14-11

❑ **Control Tree**: This section displays details about the different controls used in the page. The details include the ID provided for the control, the type of control used, and its position among other controls, as shown in Figure 14-12:

Control Tree			
Control Id	Type	Render Size Bytes (including children)	Viewstate Size Bytes (excluding children)
__PAGE	ASP.pageleveltracing_aspx	378	20
__ctl3	System.Web.UI.LiteralControl	85	0
__ctl0	System.Web.UI.HtmlControls.HtmlForm	271	0
__ctl4	System.Web.UI.LiteralControl	7	0
__ctl1	System.Web.UI.WebControls.Label	17	0
__ctl5	System.Web.UI.LiteralControl	7	0
__ctl2	System.Web.UI.WebControls.TextBox	49	0
__ctl6	System.Web.UI.LiteralControl	6	0
__ctl7	System.Web.UI.LiteralControl	22	0

Figure 14-12

❑ **Cookies Collection:** This section displays all cookies used in the page. Figure 14-13 shows only the SessionID because it is the only member of the cookies collection used in our page:

Cookies Collection		
Name	Value	Size
ASP.NET_SessionId	chuwlnihzidnb245sx3bi221	42

Figure 14-13

❑ **Headers Collection**: As shown in Figure 14-14, this section displays the various HTTP headers sent by the client to the server, along with the request:

Headers Collection	
Name	Value
Connection	Keep-Alive
Accept	image/gif, image/x-xbitmap, image/jpeg, image/pjpeg, application/vnd.ms-excel, application/vnd.ms-powerpoint, application/msword, application/x-shockwave-flash, */*
Accept-Encoding	gzip, deflate
Accept-Language	en-us
Host	localhost:8080
User-Agent	Mozilla/4.0 (compatible; MSIE 6.0; Windows NT 5.1; .NET CLR 1.1.4322)

Figure 14-14

❑ **Server Variables**: This section displays all the members of the Server Variables collection as shown in Figure 14-15:

Server Variables	
Name	Value
ALL_HTTP	HTTP_CONNECTION:Keep-Alive HTTP_ACCEPT:image/gif, image/x-xbitmap, image/jpeg, image/pjpeg, application/vnd.ms-excel, application/vnd.ms-powerpoint, application/msword, application/x-shockwave-flash, */* HTTP_ACCEPT_ENCODING:gzip, deflate HTTP_ACCEPT_LANGUAGE:en-us HTTP_HOST:localhost:8080 HTTP_USER_AGENT:Mozilla/4.0 (compatible; MSIE 6.0; Windows NT 5.1; .NET CLR 1.1.4322)
ALL_RAW	Connection: Keep-Alive Accept: image/gif, image/x-xbitmap, image/jpeg, image/pjpeg, application/vnd.ms-excel, application/vnd.ms-powerpoint, application/msword, application/x-shockwave-flash, */* Accept-Encoding: gzip, deflate Accept-Language: en-us Host: localhost:8080 User-Agent: Mozilla/4.0 (compatible; MSIE 6.0; Windows NT 5.1; .NET CLR 1.1.4322)
APPL_MD_PATH	
APPL_PHYSICAL_PATH	C:\BEGASPNET11\Ch14\
AUTH_TYPE	
AUTH_USER	
AUTH_PASSWORD	
LOGON_USER	
REMOTE_USER	
CERT_COOKIE	
CERT_FLAGS	
CERT_ISSUER	
CERT_KEYSIZE	
CERT_SECRETKEYSIZE	
CERT_SERIALNUMBER	
CERT_SERVER_ISSUER	
CERT_SERVER_SUBJECT	
CERT_SUBJECT	
CONTENT_LENGTH	0

Figure 14-15

Now that we've introduced the information displayed in the trace page, let's talk about techniques used to write a message to the Trace Information section, and get updates on what goes on behind the scenes as your code is executed.

Writing to the Trace Log

Each ASP.NET page provides a `Trace` object that can be used to write messages to the trace log. You can use two methods to write messages to the trace log:

❑ `Trace.Write()`

❑ `Trace.Warn()`

The messages are only displayed when tracing is enabled.

Both methods are used to write messages to the trace log, but when using the `Trace.Warn()` method, the messages are displayed in red. You may want to use `Trace.Warn()` for writing (and highlighting) unexpected results or incorrect values for variables in your program. Let's create an example that shows how to use these methods.

Try It Out Writing to the Trace Log

1. Open Web Matrix, create a file called `writetotrace.aspx`, and type the following code into All Window:

```
<%@ Page Trace="true"%>
<script Language="c#" runat="server">
  void WriteToTrace()
  {
    // This is where messages are written to Trace Log
    // Syntax as follows:
    // Trace.Write ["Category", "Message to be displayed"];
    // Trace.Warn ["Category", "Message to be displayed"];
    int intCounter=1;
    Trace.Write("FirstCategory", "Variable is initialized");
    while (intCounter > 10)
    {
      intCounter++;
    }
    if(intCounter < 10)
    {
        Trace.Warn("ErrorCategory", "Value of intCounter is not incrementing");
    }
  }
</script>
<%
  WriteToTrace();
%>
```

2. Save this file and open it in your browser. The message we wrote using the `Trace.Warn()` method is shown in Figure 14-16. It's the ErrorCategory line and is displayed in red:

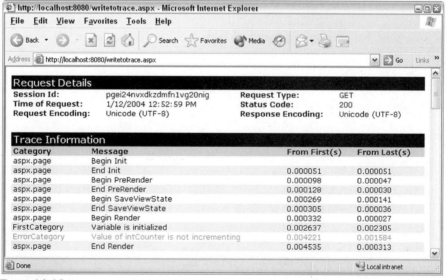

Figure 14-16

How It Works

The first thing we do is declare `intCounter` (which we're using as a label) as an integer data type, and assign a value of 1 to it:

```
int intCounter=1;
```

We write a message to the trace log, which says our variable has been initialized:

```
Trace.Write ("FirstCategory", "Variable is initialized");
```

The next three lines of code constitute a loop, so that while `intCounter` is greater than 10, it will be incremented:

```
while (intCounter > 10)
{
   intCounter++;
}
```

This looks like a programming error. As we initialized `intCounter` to 1, it cannot be greater than 10. We then introduce our `Trace.Warn()` statement that displays a warning message if `intCounter` is less than 10 (which it is). This is what we want because, in order for the loop to work, `intCounter` must be greater than 10:

```
if(intCounter < 10)
{
    Trace.Warn("ErrorCategory","Value of intCounter is not incrementing");
}
```

Note that we've specified category information in both, `Trace.Write()` and `Trace.Warn()`, methods.

Application-Level Tracing

As stated earlier, tracing can also be enabled or disabled at the application level, in which case the tracing information is processed for all the pages under the application.

A page-level trace setting always overrides the application-level trace setting. For instance, if tracing is enabled at the application level but disabled for a page, then the tracing information will not be displayed for that page.

Application-level tracing is set using the `<trace>` section in the configuration file (`web.config`) discussed earlier. The following is an example of the `<trace>` section:

```
<configuration>
  <system.web>
    <trace enabled="true" requestLimit="10" pageOutput="true"
    traceMode="SortByTime" localOnly="true" />
  </system.web>
</configuration>
```

The use of tracing in `web.config` is discussed in more detail in *Chapter 15*.

Trace.axd: The Trace Information Log

When application-level tracing is enabled (there has to be a `web.config` file present for this – you can copy the previous code and save it as `web.config` just to test it), the trace information is logged to the `rrace.axd` file. This file can be accessed using the URL for your application, followed by `trace.axd` – for example, http://yourwebservername/applicationname/trace.axd

Figure 14-17 shows how the `trace.axd` file looks in the browser, after another browser has made a request to `manualtrapping.aspx` and received a response from the server:

Figure 14-17

`trace.axd` provides a summary of each page requested, and a View Details hyperlink takes you to the trace information page for that particular screen.

Handling Errors

We've seen the kind of errors that can occur, how to avoid them, and how to find them if things do go wrong. But what if the errors just won't go away; annoyingly, this happens all the time! Don't worry though, because there is a way of dealing with this – we can use an error handling technique to catch them. Even though we can't write a 'magical' program to fix all the bugs on the fly, we can let users know that there is a bug and not to worry if things don't look right. In this section, we will talk about different error handling techniques that can be used to catch errors.

On Error Goto?

If you have a background in Visual Basic, you might be asking yourself whether you can use syntax like `On Error Resume Next` in C#, and the short answer is, no you cannot! C#'s built-in error handling syntax is based on *structured exception handling*. Structured exception handling in C# does not allow you to simply skip the line of code producing the error and proceed with the next one. Such a function is OK for a script-based application such as a traditional ASP page, but for the object-oriented world of C# and ASP.NET, you need something more robust. Structured exception handling also largely replaces the crude error handling offered by `On Error Goto Label` syntax as well. C# also does not have any equivalent to the Visual Basic `Err` object.

Structured Error Handling

We have already come across structured exception handling in this book wherever we have actually needed it:

❑ We used it to deal with situations where conversion between data types might fail and generate a run-time error.

❑ We mentioned it as a means of dealing with situations where conversion between object types might fail and generate a runtime error.

❑ We used it when dealing with databases. Runtime errors can occur for many reasons including the unavailability of the database, trying to access a non-existent data field, or trying to update a read-only data field.

In all cases, we referred to this point in the book where we look closely at implementing error handling. However, to provide a complete picture of what C# error handling can achieve, we are going right back to the basics.

So what do we mean by structured error handling? Pretty much just that: handling errors via a particular structure. Lines of code are grouped together, and different handlers are provided to handle different errors within those groups. The following list shows the sequence of events that take place when using structured error handling:

1. We execute one or more lines of code in a group. They might execute without an error, or they might generate one or many different kinds of errors.

2. If errors are generated, a handler (which you will have defined) corresponding to the error will be called. If there is no error, no handler will be called.

> **You can also define a generic handler that handles any errors for which you did not define a specific handler.**

Two important things need to be done for effectively using structured error handling:

❑ Creating a group of lines or a block of code.
❑ Creating handlers for the different kinds of errors that could occur when the code block is executed.

Before launching into this subject, we need to introduce the concept of exceptions.

Exceptions

An *exception* is any error condition or unexpected behavior that occurs during the execution of a program, and consequently disrupts the normal flow of execution – in fact, the term is just shorthand for *exceptional event*. If an error occurs within a method call, the method creates an *exception object* and hands it off to the runtime system. This object contains information detailing the type of exception that was raised and the state of the program at the time.

> **Depending on whether the exception stems from the program itself or from the CLR, you may or may not be able to recover from the exception. While you can recover from most application exceptions, you can seldom recover from a runtime exception.**

The exception event is thrown by the code that calls the event. The code can either catch the exception (and try to handle the problem), or pass it on up to the code that called that code, and so on up the invocation stack. If it reaches the top of the stack without being caught by a handler somewhere along the way, the program will crash. Before talking about how to handle exceptions, we'll briefly introduce you to the exception class, and its properties.

The Exception Class

.NET Framework provides a `System.Exception` class, which acts as the base class for all exceptions. The `Exception` class contains properties that aid our understanding of the exception. The following table summarizes the different properties within `Exception` class:

Property	Description
StackTrace	This property contains the stack trace (which shows the sequence of nested function calls your program has executed.) This can be used to determine the location of the error occurrence.
Message	This property contains a message about the error.
InnerException	This property is used to create and store a series of exceptions during exception handling. For example, imagine if a piece of your code threw an exception. The exception, and its handler, could be stored in the `InnerException` property of that handler. You could then reference the exception, see how it was handled, and, based on that information, perhaps create a more effective handler. This can be very useful when you are reviewing the execution of a piece of troublesome code. `InnerException` can also be used to store an exception that occurred in a previous piece of code.
Source	This property contains information about the application that generates the error.
TargetSite	This property contains information about the method that throws the exception.
HelpLink	This property is used to provide the URL for a file containing help information about an exception that occurs.

The two important exception classes that inherit from `System.Exception` are `ApplicationException` and `SystemException`. The `SystemException` class is thrown by the runtime while the `ApplicationException` class is thrown by an application. Let's now look at some actual code that makes structured error handling possible.

Using try...catch...finally

The general C# syntax for error handling is as follows:

```
try
{
   // statement or statements which might fail at runtime
}
catch (Exception e)
{
   // error handing block
}
catch
{
   // optional second error handling block
}
finally
{
   // Code must be run regardless of what happens above
}
```

Let's explain what each block means.

The `try` block contains all the code that might cause a runtime exception. This can be a single line of code or multiple lines. There is not much more to say on this, as there are no parameters to consider, nor any limitations on the code you can wrap in a `try` block. However, a `try` block by itself is not valid code and immediately after the closing brace, you must have a `catch` (or `finally`) block to handle any exceptions that could be raised. Therefore, the code construct that fulfils the minimum requirements for structured exception handling would look like this (we have seen many instances of this earlier on tin this book):

```
try
{
   // statement or statements which might fail at runtime
}
catch (Exception e)
{
   // error handing block
}
```

Multiple catch Blocks

A `try` block can be followed by more than one `catch` blocks. We said earlier on, that you can write exception handlers that respond to different types of errors as well as a general purpose error handler, that is able to deal with any error at all. In C#, this is achieved by stacking `catch` blocks one after another. If an exception is thrown from the `try` block, the code will pass the `Exception` object created down the chain of `catch` blocks until there is a match. On the other hand, if there is no match, the exception is passed to the.NET runtime and you will get an unhandled exception error page as we saw earlier.

> Any variables declared in the code blocks in C# are local in scope, so if you want variables to be available to the try, catch, and finally blocks, they must be declared before the try block starts.

Let's illustrate this by using some pseudo-code:

```
try
{
  // Error generated here, Exception object created
}
catch (SystemException e)
{
  // If Exception type matches SystemException, then this code is run
}
catch (Exception e)
{
  // If Exception type matches Exception, then this code is run
}
// If Exception doesn't match either SystemException or Exception, then code
// execution is aborted
```

One important thing to note here is that only one catch block is executed at any one time, and this is the very first one that matches the exception object type being thrown. Therefore, you have to be careful when implementing more than one handler. Error handlers of specific nature should always come before any general error handler. We have already mentioned three types of the Exception object: Exception, ApplicationException, and SystemException; the last two are derived from the first. The correct sequence for the catch blocks is as follows:

```
try
{
  // Error generated here, Exception object created
}
catch (SystemException s)
{
  // If Exception type matches SystemException, then this code is run
}
catch (Exception e)
{
  // If Exception type matches Exception, then this code is run
}
```

The catch block dealing with objects of the derived class, SystemExeception, comes first and the one dealing with the base Exception object comes last. If you reversed the two, the code will not compile:

```
try
{
  // Error generated here, Exception object created
}
catch (Exception e)
{
  // If Exception type matches Exception, then this code is run
}
```

```
catch (SystemException se)
{
  // If Exception type matches SystemException, then this code is run
}
```

Why is this code wrong? The `catch` block that is executed as the result of an error is the very first one that matches the exception object type. The first catch block in the above code would thus be called for *any* .NET exception that is thrown, including system exceptions. In other words, if a `SystemException` is thrown, it will be caught by the `catch (Exception e)`, because it is first in the list, and because derived exception types can be caught by error handlers matching the base `Exception` type. Therefore, the second and more specific error handler can never be executed because it is unreachable code. The compiler will flag this up as an error.

The rule is that you place all error handlers in order, from the most specific to the least specific. So, does that mean that code blocks preceded with `catch (Exception e)` always come last in the set? Well, no – you can define a `catch` block that is even more general that this one. The `catch (Exception e)` block can deal with any .NET-related exception but it cannot deal with any exceptions thrown by objects outside .NET, such as the ones from the Windows operating system (OS). To trap any error at all, regardless of its origin, C# allows you to use a `catch` with no parameter at all:

```
catch
{
  // Code here
}
```

As this type of `catch` block is as general as you can get, it has to be placed at the very end of a sequence of `catch` blocks.

What You Can Put in a catch Block

There is no limit to what you can put in a `catch` block. Normally, you would generate some message to inform the user that something exceptional had occurred or write the information to an error log. Alternatively, you could add some recovery code to deal with the error and bring the application back to a normal state, without the user even knowing that anything happened at all. In most cases, you will want to make use of the contents of the exception object that was created when the exception was thrown.

The general `Exception` object only provides general information on an error, which may or may not be useful to you. A more specific exception object that uses one of the derived classes would contain more specific information about the error, which would also make it easier to deal with. For this reason, it is always best to include as many specific error handlers as you deem reasonable, when you know beforehand what kind of exceptions are likely to occur.

The following code example would display the contents of the `Message` property of an `IndexOutOfRangeException` object:

```
catch (IndexOutOfRangeException e)
{
  Response.Write (e.Message)
}
```

The general-purpose error handler should only be used if you do not know what type of exception is likely to occur, or as a catch-all error handler for any unlikely exceptions. You can also use this error handler if you are only outputting a simple error message:

```
catch (Exception e)
{
  Response.Write("You must type your name in the box");
}
```

Here the compiler may warn you that you are not using the Exception object e (it's not necessary that you *have* to use this). If you want to eliminate this compiler warning altogether, you can use the ultimate general-purpose error handler:

```
catch
{
  Response.Write("You must type your name in the box");
}
```

Because the latter error handler receives no error information at all, you cannot retrieve any error-specific information.

finally Block

The finally block, if defined, will be executed either after the error has been handled, or after the code in the try block has been executed, depending on whether an error occurred or not. The finally block is typically used to do cleanup tasks, such as releasing resources, closing objects, and so on. The syntax is very simple:

```
finally
{
  // Clean-up code here for example calling Close() on previously opened
objects
  // for example database connections
}
```

Generating Exceptions Using throw

Up until now, we have assumed that we only handle exceptions that are thrown by the .NET runtime and that we create error handlers that are matched to the various exception objects that could be produced. We have even considered exceptions that are thrown by code outside the control of the .NET runtime. However, we can take control of the exception generation process ourselves by manually generating an exception in response to a given set of conditions. Any code can be configured to generate an exception, and the syntax for doing this is as follows:

```
if (something happens)
{
  throw new Exception("An error has occurred");
}
```

An exception is generated whenever the above condition evaluates to true and will contain the message An error has occurred. If left alone, the program execution will immediately terminate, therefore the code containing the `throw` statement should be enclosed in a `try` block, and followed by an appropriate `catch` block. However, this need not be the case.

A `throw` statement could well be included in a function without any `try` and `catch` blocks defined at all. This means that the function call itself must be placed in a `try` block, and the code calling the function must take responsibility for handling any error that could be generated by the function. Say we have a function like this:

```
double MayThrowError(double a, double b)
{
   if(b == 0)
   {
      throw new DivideByZeroException();
   }
   return a/b;
}
```

Here, if we pass zero as the second parameter, we will get an exception that is not handled in the function itself, and must be handled by the calling code. Because you know what type of exception will be thrown – you created it in the first place – you can implement a `catch` block that matches it:

```
try
{
   double result = MayThrowError(50,0);
}
catch (DivideByZeroException dbz)
{
   Response.Write(dbz.Message);
}
```

Let's consider a different scenario. Rather than creating a function that contains a `throw` statement, you might have called it from an external class. And it's also conceivable that you do not know that the chosen function throws an exception, until it actually happens! Therefore, it is normal for the documentation for a class to inform you whether an exception could be thrown by a function, and if so, what kind. If you should go on to create a function for general use that can throw an exception, you should inform your potential users of this in order to prevent them from receiving a nasty surprise!

Another way of manually generating exceptions is by using the `checked` keyword. It is applied to a statement that can fail, to make sure that a runtime exception is thrown. We saw this when considering overflows of variable types, but it can also be applied to other potential problem areas such as data type conversions. If you use `checked` in your code, you must also use `try...catch` blocks.

Now we've done the theory, let's try an example.

Try It Out Using try...catch...finally

1. Create a new file called `structuredErrorHandling.aspx` in Web Matrix and add the following code within the All Window:

```
<script Language="C#" runat="server" >
```

```
     void StructuredErrorHandling ()
     {
       try
       {
         int [] array = new int[9];
         for(int intCounter=0; intCounter <= 9; intCounter++)
         {
           array[intCounter] = intCounter;
           Response.Write("The value of the counter is:" + intCounter +
                                                   "<br>");
         }
       }

       // Handler for index out of range exception

       catch (IndexOutOfRangeException ex)
       {
           Response.Write("Error Occurred"+ "<br>" + ex.ToString() + "<br>");
       }

       // Handler for generic exception

       catch (Exception e)
       {
           Response.Write("Generic Error Occurred" + "<br>");
       }
       finally
       {
           Response.Write("The Page Execution is completed" + "<br>");
       }
     }
   </script>

   <%
     StructuredErrorHandling();
     Response.Write("Function call completed" + "<br>");
   %>
```

2.   Save this file and load it in your browser. Figure 14-18 shows the result:

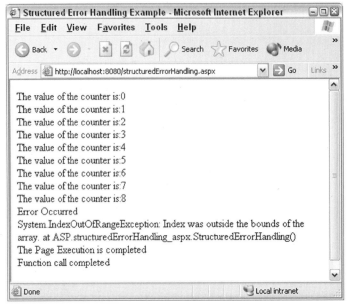

Figure 14-18

How It Works

In the `StructuredErrorHandling()` function, the `try` block encloses all the code we want to execute. We create an integer array and we attempt to loop through it:

```
void StructuredErrorHandling ()
{
  try
  {
      {
    int [] array = new int[9];
    for(int intCounter=0; intCounter <= 9; intCounter++)
    {
      array[intCounter] = intCounter;
      Response.Write("The value of the counter is:" + intCounter + "<br>");
    }
  }
}
```

We have made a deliberate mistake in the code, in that we are attempting to loop through ten elements in an array whereas there actually are only nine. An exception will be thrown.

There are two `catch` blocks defined. One for the expected `IndexOutOfRangeException` object:

```
catch (IndexOutOfRangeException ex)
{
  Response.Write("Error Occurred"+ "<br>" + ex.ToString() + "<br>");
}
```

The other one is a generic catch-all handler, which should not be executed in this code, but is there just as a precaution:

```
catch (Exception e)
{
    Response.Write("Generic Error Occurred" + "<br>");
}
```

The `finally` block is there just to confirm that it was actually run:

```
finally
{
    Response.Write("The Page Execution is completed" + "<br>");
}
```

At the end, once the function has been called, a line is sent to inform the user that the whole function is complete:

```
Response.Write("Function call completed" + "<br>");
```

Nested Try Blocks

Structured exception handling can be extended to allow for multiple levels of error handling using nested `try` blocks. This enables you to exert more control over the error handling process than can be achieved using a single `try` block. You can do two things with nested `try` blocks that may not be achievable using just one. You can modify the type of exception thrown, and you can enable different types of exception to be handled in different places in your code. The syntax for implementing nested `try` blocks looks like this:

```
try
{
  // main try code block [1]
  try
  {
    // code block that needs closer attention [2]
  }
  catch (SystemException se)
  {
    // [3]
  }
  catch (ApplicationException ae)
  {
    // [4]
  }
  finally
  {
  }
  // more code
}
catch
{
  // main catch block code [5]
```

```
    }
    finally
    {
    }
```

This is a very simplified representation as there are only two `try` blocks (there can be any number of them). The inner block has two `catch` blocks and a `finally` block, the outer one has one `catch` block and a `finally` block.

This is how it works. If the code at the point marked `[1]` fails, then the `catch` block marked `[5]` will be called upon to handle it. This corresponds with the behavior already outlined for a single `try` block. In case of a failure occurring before the inner `try` block starts, the page will not even be aware that the inner `try` block exists, as all code from the point where the exception occurs is ignored.

If, however, the code in the inner `try` block fails, marked by `[2]`, then control passes to `catch` blocks `[3]` or `[4]`, which will process the error. Then the inner `finally` block is executed and the code execution continues as normal until the end of the outer `try` block, where the outer `finally` block is executed.

This is all well and good, but what if none of the inner `catch` blocks can handle the error? What happens then? Well, the .NET runtime will keep looking for a handler to deal with the exception generated. It will run the code in the inner `finally` block before leaving the outer `try` block (passing over any code that occurs after the end of the inner `try` block). The set of `catch` blocks following the outer `try` block are examined for a match and, if there is one, then the code for that particular `catch` block is executed. If even at this point there is no match, the outer `finally` block is run and control passes to the .NET runtime.

So what happens if the code in the `catch` blocks `[3]` and `[4]` fails? We have not considered this before in this section, but code can fail even in error handlers! In such situations, .NET runtime will, in the first instance, look for an error handler in any `catch` block associated with the outer `try` block (block `[5]` in this case).

This passing around of exception objects between `catch` blocks can actually be used to our advantage. We have said before, that the benefit of using nested `try` blocks is that you can modify the exception that was originally thrown. You might want to do this because the exception object that was thrown might not be the root cause of the problem; you might want to look at other possibilities.

So if you have code like that shown in the following snippet and an `ApplicationException` is thrown, it will be caught by the appropriate `catch` block. However, on further investigation, you might find that the real problem lies with a missing file. Then, you can generate a new exception to deal with this situation by using `throw`. In the code, the line marked in bold achieves this. The new exception is thrown with an appropriate message as well as a reference to the original `ApplicationException` stored in the `InnerException` property:

```
try
{
    // main code block [1]
    try
    {
        // code block that needs closer attention [2]
    }
    catch (SystemException se)
```

```
    {
        // [3]
    }
    catch (ApplicationException ae)
    {
      if (something happens)
      {
      // [4]
        throw new FileNotFoundException("File does not exist", ae);
      }
    }
    finally
    {
    }
    // more code
  }
catch
{
  // [5]
}
finally
{
}
```

If, however, you want manually to re-throw an exception from a `catch` block without modifying it, you can use the `throw` keyword by itself:

```
catch (ApplicationException ae)
{
  if (something happens)
  {
  // [4]
    throw;
  }
}
```

This code passes control back to the outer `try` block where its can be dealt with by any of its associated `catch` blocks. This method enables the same exception to be handled by more than one error handler. You might be thinking that this is all a bit complicated, but nested `try` blocks are actually more common than you realize. This is because nested `try` blocks do not have to be in the same code block at all; they don't even have to be in the same class. When you call a function `A()` from within a `try` block, the function itself might include a `try` block of its own. Any exception thrown by `A()` that is not handled by `A()`, will be caught by the error handlers in your code.

> The exception handler might not be defined in your class at all – it might be a .NET Framework base class function; the rules for passing exceptions around are handled by the .NET Framework and so are not dependent on the way the code is structured. Indeed, it is possible for code written in Visual Basic .NET to throw an exception that is then handled by code written in C#.

Handling Errors Programmatically

We can now handle errors using `try...catch` blocks, but some exceptions may still sneak through. ASP.NET provides us with two more methods that can be used to handle any errors that are unaccounted for, and provide a friendly message to the user, instead of the default runtime error screen.

The two methods are:

- ❑   Page_Error()
- ❑   Application_Error()

Page_Error()

The Page class provides this method. (Refer to *Chapter 10* for more information on the Page class and its members.) The Page_Error() method can be used to handle errors at the page level. Every time an unhandled exception occurs, this event is called.

To see how it works, let's take our previous example and modify it to use the Page_Error() method. Here, we created an error by storing a string to an integer datatype, and we used the Try statement to handle exceptions. This time, we'll just use the Page_Error() method to handle the exception:

Try It Out   **Using Page_Error()**

1.   Open structuredErrorHandling.aspx in Web Matrix, and make the following adjustments within the All Window:

```
<script Language="c#" runat="server">
  void PageLevelErrorTest()
  {
    // Remove opening try
    int[] array = new int[9];
    for(int intCounter=0; intCounter <= 9;intCounter++)
    {
        array[intCounter] = intCounter;
        Response.Write("The value of the counter is:" + intCounter + "<br>");
    }
    // Remove catch and finally blocks
  }
  void Page_Error(object sender, EventArgs e)
  {
    Response.Write("Error occurred: " + Server.GetLastError().ToString());
    Server.ClearError();
  }
  void Page_Load()
  {
    PageLevelErrorTest();
  }
</script>
<%
  PageLevelErrorTest();
  Response.Write("Function call completed" + "<br>");
%>
```

2.   Save the file as pageLevelError.aspx, and open it in your browser. You should see something like Figure 14-19:

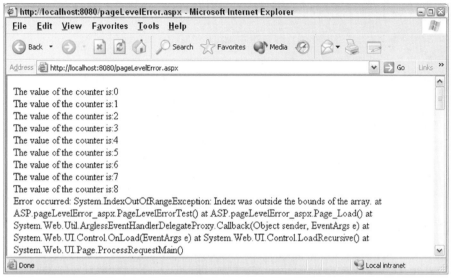

Figure 14-19

How It Works

We already know about the first half of this code, as it is the same as for the previous example. However, it's the `Page_Error()` function that we're interested in:

```
void Page_Error(object sender, EventArgs e)
```

Within the `Page_Error()` method, we write a message to the user to say that an error has occurred, and get detailed error information from the server using the `GetLastError()` method of the `Server` object:

```
Response.Write("Error occurred: " + Server.GetLastError().ToString());
```

After displaying the message, we free up the server by using the `ClearError()` method of the `Server` object.

The `Page_Error()` method is called whenever an unhandled exception is thrown within the page. This method could be used to catch the error, log the error to a log file, notify the administrator of the error using e-mail, or store the error information to a database. We will talk about this in the *Notification and Logging* section.

Application_Error()

This too can be used to handle any errors unaccounted for. The `Application_Error()` method is similar to the `Page_Error()` method – that are if it is enabled, it is called whenever an unhandled exception is thrown, from *any page under the application*. This method is part of the `global.asax` file. Another similarity with the `Page_Error()` method is that `Application_Error()` can also be used to log the errors to a log file, notify an administrator using e-mail, or store the error information to a database.

The following example shows the usage of this method:

```
void Application_Error(object sender, EventArgs e)
{
  //Handle the Error
  //Provide code to log the error or send an email
}
```

Error Notification and Logging

In this section, we will talk about the techniques that are used to log errors to the Windows event log, and notify a site manager or administrator of the occurrence of the error.

Customized Error Messages

The next question is: what if the development server is on a different machine? ASP.NET allows you to specify whether you want the detailed message to be displayed on the local client, on remote clients, or both. You can specify this information using the `<customErrors>` section in the Web configuration file, `web.config`. We'll discuss the `web.config` file later in the book (see *Chapter 15* for more details); for now, just create a new file in your application folder called `web.config`, so that you can demonstrate how to handle custom errors. The following example shows a sample setting for the `<customErrors>` section:

```
<configuration>
  <system.web>
    <customErrors defaultRedirect="userError.aspx" mode="On">
    <error statusCode="404" redirect="PagenotFound.aspx" />
    </customErrors>
  </system.web>
</configuration>
```

> All settings in **web.config** file have to be enclosed with **<configuration>** and **<system.web>** tags. In addition, make sure that you copy the upper and lower case of this code exactly as **web.config** is case-sensitive.

As shown, the `<customErrors>` configuration section has two attributes. The first is the `defaultRedirect` attribute, and specifies the URL for the page to be redirected to when an error occurs. The above configuration setting will redirect the user to a default error page, `userError.aspx` when an error occurs.

The second attribute is the `mode` attribute, which takes three values: `On`, `Off`, and `RemoteOnly On`, specifies that the custom error is enabled; the users will be redirected to the custom error page specified in the `defaultRedirect` attribute. `Off` specifies that the custom error is disabled; the users will *not* be redirected to a customized error page, but to a general non-informative one. `RemoteOnly`, the default setting, specifies that only remote (and not local) clients should be redirected to the custom error page.

The `<customError>` configuration section contains an `<error>` sub tag, which is used to specify error pages for different errors. In the above example, the `PagenotFound.aspx` page has been specified as the error page when HTTP 404 error occurs. You could provide multiple `<error>` sub tags for different error codes.

Let's create the two friendly error pages, `userError.aspx` and `PagenotFound.aspx`, specified in the configuration file.

Try It Out Creating Error Pages

1. Create a Web configuration file in `BegASPNet11/ch14`. To do this, go to Web Matrix and choose the **Web.config** option in the third row of the **Add New File** dialog. Don't worry if there is already a `web.config` file there; it is OK to overwrite it.

2. Delete all of the code that is automatically generated, as it only needs to consist of the following `<customErrors>` section, which you should type in as follows:

```
<configuration>
  <system.web>
    <customErrors defaultRedirect="userError.aspx" mode="On">
    <error statusCode="404" redirect="PagenotFound.aspx" />
    </customErrors>
  </system.web>
</configuration>
```

3. Create the `userError.aspx` page. Open up Web Matrix, and enter the following code into the All Window:

```
<html>
  <head>
  <title> Friendly Error Page</title>
  </head>
  <body>
  <h2> An error has occurred in executing this page. Sorry for the
  inconvenience. The site administrator is aware of this error occurrence.
  </h2>
  </body>
</html>
```

4. Create the `PagenotFound.aspx` page. Create another file in Web Matrix and enter the following code into the All Window:

```
<html>
  <head>
  <title> Friendly Error Page</title>
  </head>
  <body>
    <h2> Sorry, the resource you are requesting is not available. Please
    verify the address.
    </h2>
  </body>
</html>
```

5. Load the `userError.aspx` file, using your browser. Figure 14-20 shows the `userError.aspx` file (and not the detailed error message):

Figure 14-20

6. Try to access a file that does not exist in your application folder. Type into the URL address section of your browser something like `thispagedoesntexist.aspx`. Figure 14-21 shows the result of accessing a file that is not found in the application (what you see is the file with the friendly error message and *not* the default Page not found message from the Web server):

Figure 14-21

How It Works

We created a `<customErrors>` section in the Web configuration file. This section pointed to the correct file. We did this by setting the default error page displayed to `userError.aspx`, and the error page for status code 404 to `PagenotFound.aspx`:

```
<customErrors defaultRedirect="userError.aspx" mode="RemoteOnly">
  <error statusCode="404" redirect="PagenotFound.aspx" />
</customErrors>
```

Once this was done, we created our own text for the error messages in `userError.aspx` and `PagenotFound.aspx` files. If we had been using a pre-existing `web.config` file, we would have also had to ensure that `<customErrors>` was set to `On`, so that our new error pages were sent to the local browser. Otherwise, we wouldn't have been able to view them when we triggered them by using files containing mistakes.

In the example, we saw how to redirect users to a friendly error page using the different attributes in the `<customErrors>` section of `web.config`. There is also a way to redirect users to *different* error pages based on which page the error has occurred on. You can do this by using the `ErrorPage` property in the `Page` directive as shown below:

```
<% @ Page ErrorPage="ErrorPage.aspx" %>
```

If you have this directive in `runtimeerror.aspx`, the users will be redirected to `ErrorPage.aspx` when an error occurs in `runtimeerror.aspx`.

Now let's go back to the local client scenario. ASP.NET displays a call-stack (a series of function calls that lead up to an error) when a runtime error occurs. Before doing this, we suggest you delete the `web.config` file; if you don't, all errors generated will be handled by this file.

Writing to the Event Log

We now know that any exceptions that are not handled can call the `Application_Error()` and `Page_Error()` methods. There is another step we can take in handling these unforeseen errors, which involves finding out when they occurred, or logging them, as this could provide vital clues as to how we handle them in the future.

For instance, say a customer who is ordering a few items from your online shopping center receives an error that the order could not be completed. The site manager should be able to see that an error has occurred, so they can take steps to avoid this error in the future. To achieve this, errors can be logged in to the Windows event log where they can be reviewed on a periodic basis. Depending on the nature of the application, the event log could be reviewed every hour, day, or week.

System.Diagnostics Namespace

The tool that the.NET Framework provides for us here is the `System.Diagnostics` namespace. This namespace contains classes that can be used for reading and writing to event logs. Before using the class for accessing event logs, we have to import the `System.Diagnostics` namespace into the program, as follows:

```
<%@ Import Namespace="System.Diagnostics" %>
```

EventLog Class

We use the `EventLog` class to read and write to the event log. We can create a new log, or write entries to an existing log.

First, you need to create a log that you can write to, and then specify an event *source*. A source is a string identifying an individual entry to the log. Creating an event source opens some space in the log for the entry to be recorded. The `CreateEventSource()` method can be used to create both a source and a log. In the following example, we create a log called `MyApplicationLog`, and a source called `MyApplicationSource`.

To actually write an entry to the log, we use the `WriteEntry()` method, and as in our last example, provide detailed error information by using the `GetLastError()` method of the `Server` object.

Try It Out   Writing to the Windows Error Log

1.   Type the following code into Web Matrix All Window:

```c#
<%@ Import Namespace="System.Diagnostics" %>
<script Language="c#" runat="server" >

  void EntrytoLog()
  {
    int[] array = new int[9];
    for(int intCounter=0; intCounter <= 9;intCounter++)
    {
        array[intCounter] = intCounter;
        Response.Write("The value of the counter is:" + intCounter + "<br>");
    }
  }
  void Page_Error(object sender, EventArgs e)

  {
    string errorMessage = "Error occurred" + Server.GetLastError();
    Server.ClearError();
    string LogName = "MyApplicationLog";
    string SourceName = "MyApplicationSource";
    if (!(EventLog.SourceExists(SourceName)))
    {
        EventLog.CreateEventSource(SourceName, LogName);
    }

    // Insert into Event Log;
    EventLog MyLog = new EventLog();
    MyLog.Source = SourceName;
    MyLog.WriteEntry(errorMessage, EventLogEntryType.Error);
  }

</script>

<%
  EntrytoLog();
%>
```

2.   Save this file as `entryToLog.aspx` and load it in the browser. After the page has loaded, you will see the screen shown in Figure 14-22:

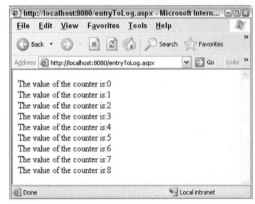

Figure 14-22

3. It's not really the display we interested in, but the fact that it was written to a log. To view the contents of the log, you will need to open the Event Viewer. Click Start from the Windows tool bar, and select Settings. Select Control Panel and double-click on the Administrative Tools icon. This will launch the Administrative Tools window. Double-click on the Event Viewer icon to open the Event Viewer window. Figure 14-23 shows the Event Viewer:

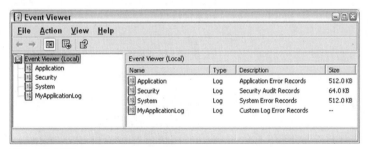

Figure 14-23

4. Double-click on the MyApplicationLog (listed under the Name column after System Log) to open it. You will see the Error entry that we made. Figure 14-24 shows the entry:

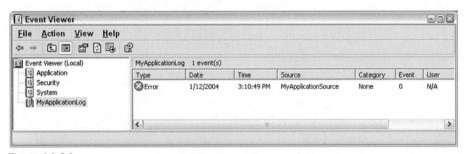

Figure 14-24

5. Double-click on the Error entry to open the Event Properties window, as shown in Figure 14-25. This shows the date and time at which the entry was made, and the description we provided using the `WriteEntry()` method:

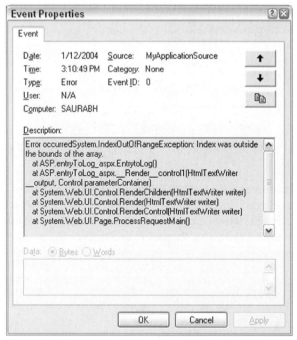

Figure 14-25

How It Works

As before, the main function in the code creates an array of nine elements and attempts to loop through ten. After this, you create the `Page_Error()` function. You start by creating the `errorMessage` variable as a string, and supply it with a line of text to display along with error information from the server. Finally, erase the error from the server:

```
void Page_Error(object sender, EventArgs e)
{
   string errorMessage = "Error occurred" + Server.GetLastError();
   Server.ClearError();
```

Next we define the name of our log, and this particular source of the error, but before creating them, we check to see if the source already exists:

```
string LogName = "MyApplicationLog";
string SourceName = "MyApplicationSource";
if (!(EventLog.SourceExists(SourceName)))
{
   EventLog.CreateEventSource(SourceName, LogName);
}
```

If the source does not already exist, we proceed to create the log object and set the Source property before displaying the error message:

```
// Insert into Event Log;
EventLog MyLog = new EventLog();
MyLog.Source = SourceName;
MyLog.WriteEntry(errorMessage, EventLogEntryType.Error);
```

In the above example, we have used the EventLog class to make an entry to the log file using the Page_Error() method. Alternatively, you could use this class within the Application_Error() method in global.asax. Doing this will create an entry to the log files for any unhandled errors occurring in any of the pages within the application.

Mailing the Site Administrator

In the last example, we made an entry to a log file after the occurrence of an error. In a real world scenario, a Web site manager or administrator could review this log file at regular intervals. However, this may not be prudent for certain applications. Depending on the nature of the application, the manager or administrator may need to be informed of an error right away. To do this, we could notify the site administrator by sending an e-mail with the details of the error as soon as it occurs.

System.Web.Mail Namespace

The .NET Framework provides a namespace with a set of classes to do this. The System.Web.Mail namespace contains three classes that can be used to create and send an e-mail using SMTP:

❑   MailMessage

❑   MailAttachment

❑   SmtpMail

Before using these classes in our page, we need to import the System.Web.Mail namespace, just as we did with the System.Diagnostics namespace in the last example. Let's look at our three classes in more detail.

MailMessage

The MailMessage class provides properties that are used to create an e-mail. The following table lists the name and purpose of some of the more commonly used members of this class:

Name	Use
From	This property specifies the sender's e-mail address
To	This property specifies the recipient's e-mail address.
Subject	This property specifies the subject line for the e-mail message.
Body	This property is used to set the body of the e-mail message.

The syntax for using this class is as shown in the following code

```
mailMessage.From = "senders email address";
mailMessage.To = "recipients email address";
mail.Message.Subject = "subject line";
mailMessage.Body = "body of email message";
```

MailAttachment

This class contains members that are used to create an attachment that is to be sent with the e-mail.

Name	Use
Encoding	This property specifies the type of encoding of the e-mail attachment.
Filename	This property specifies the file name of the mail attachment.

SmtpMail

This class provides properties that are used to send an email using the SMTP Service. The method we are interested in, at the moment, is the Send() method of this class. This method is used to send an email, and the code looks like this:

```
SmtpMail.Send(mailMessage);
```

To show you how a working piece of code based on the System.Web.Mail namespace, would look, we have modified the previous example so that it sends an email instead of writing to the log file:

```
<%@ Import Namespace="System.Web.Mail" %>
<script language="c#" runat="server" >
  void sendMailTest()
  {
    int[] array = new int[9];
    for(int intCounter=0; intCounter <= 9;intCounter++)
    {
      array[intCounter] = intCounter;
      Response.Write("The value of the counter is:" + intCounter + "<br>");
    }
```

```
    }

    void Page_Error(object sender, EventArgs e)
    {
      string errorMessage = "Error occurred" + Server.GetLastError();
      Server.ClearError();

      // Create an email message
      MailMessage newMail = new MailMessage();
      newMail.From = "fromaddress@yourserver.com";
      newMail.To = "administrator@yourserver.com";
      newMail.Subject = "Error Occurred";
      newMail.Body = errorMessage;
      // send the mail to the administrator.
      SmtpMail.Send(newMail);
    }
</script>
<%
  sendMailTest();
%>
```

This code allows email to be sent to the administrator of the server in the event of an error being generated. We haven't stepped through this code in the Try It Out fashion, because unless you have a working SMTP server on your machine, it won't send emails from or to your address.

Summary

In this chapter, we talked about error handling techniques that can be used when developing ASP.NET applications. We discussed the different kinds of errors that can occur, techniques for handling errors (including the new tracing features), handling exceptions using structured error handling, and finally, techniques to log the error messages to a log file and notify the site administrator through email.

We saw that adopting good coding practice helps reduce the number of errors in your code, and that the time spent in testing helps us create handlers for recurring errors before the application is moved to the production environment. Using different error handling techniques helps us to develop applications with fewer bugs, which are, therefore, more successful and competitive.

Exercises

1. How are parser errors different from compilation errors? Is there any difference between the ways in which they are displayed by ASP.NET?

2. Here are three code snippets – what is wrong with each section and what type of error does it contain? How would you fix it?

❑ **Section A:**

```
<html>
  <head>
```

```
    <title>Syntax Error Example </title>
  </head>
  <body>
    <form method="post" action="syntaxerror.aspx" runat="server">
    <asp:TextBox id="txtQuantity" runat="Server />
    </form>
  </body>
</html>
```

❑   **Section B:**

```
<script language="C#" runat="server">
void Page_Load()
{
int intCounter, intLoop;
intCounter=0;
intLoop=0;
while (intCounter<10)
{
    intLoop = intLoop +1;
}
}
</script>
```

❑   **Section C:**

```
<script language="C#" runat="server">
void Page_Load()
{
  string a;
  int b;
  string c;
  a = "Hello";
  b = "World";
  c = a + b;
}
</script>
```

3.   Create a form with four textboxes and a submit button. Make the first textbox accept a user name, the second accept an email address, the third accept a phone number, and the last accept the user's gender. Use validation controls to make sure there are no blank entries, that you can only enter numbers into the phone field, and that you can only enter a number between 1 and 140 in the age field. Also, but not necessarily with validation controls, make sure that the gender textbox only accepts male or female and that the email address contains a "@". In what ways could this form be improved further?

4.   Write a `try..catch` error handler that will handle errors specifically for a divide by zero exception.

Hint: We haven't mentioned the specific class involved, you can find a list of classes using the class browser.

5.   Create a custom error page for an HTTP 403 error Access is forbidden. and get it working for this chapter's code folder.

15

Configuration and Optimization

ASP.NET makes important and dramatic changes to configuration management. With ASP, a lot of configuration was done via the Web server's interface, whereas in ASP.NET, the configuration information is located within XML files that are separate from the Web server. These configuration files are directly accessible from ASP.NET and offer the user greater control over the workings of both the Web server and the Web page. They eliminate the need to restart your Web server after configuration changes are made, because once you alter the configuration files and recompile your application code, the change has already been made. In addition, you don't have to worry about whether you are running Web Matrix or IIS; you have the ability easily to alter the configuration settings.

With the greater level of customization that we can exercise over our applications, it is crucial that our code runs quickly and efficiently. In addition to the configuration aspects, optimization of your code is equally vital to ensure that everything runs as expected on the Web server. Up until now, we've only really been concerned with demonstrating a particular concept and the ways it can be used, but from now on, we need to be concerned with the efficiency of our code too.

This chapter will cover how to configure your applications in ASP.NET, and how to increase the performance of your pages through general code optimization techniques. We will consider the effects of installing .NET Framework 1.1 as it doesn't replace the old version of the .NET Framework but runs alongside it. We will also look at other aspects of optimization to improve security, user-friendliness, and to make debugging and managing applications easier.

In particular, this chapter covers:

- ❑   The structure and function of the configuration files, `machine.config` and `web.config`
- ❑   Customization of the `machine.config` and `web.config` files
- ❑   Using caching to improve server performance
- ❑   Monitoring the resources used by an application and gathering basic operation statistics

These advanced topics are covered in Professional ASP.NET 1.1, Wiley ISBN: 0-7645-5890-0.

Configuration Overview

IIS has long been a powerhouse for ASP and continues that role in ASP.NET. In the earliest days of ASP, IIS offered only limited functionality beyond the ability to switch its Web serving capabilities on and off. This is because initially IIS was only expected to render static HTML pages. Everything was different about it, right down to the name. IIS used to stand for *Internet Information Server*. However, just like the jump from the early browsers that couldn't display tables or frames to the multimedia-saturated monsters we see today, IIS has had to adapt to the changing environment and the changing needs of its users.

It quickly grew to control many of ASP's features via a point-and-click interface, such as those normally accessed by the `Server` and `Response` objects, so a name change was in order. To alter aspects of the Web server's operation in ASP, you could point and click via IIS's management console and then restart the IIS service to refresh and resume operations. You could assign permissions for different users and implement security policies. IIS was able to handle e-commerce transactions and much more than it was ever designed for. However, if you were running ASP via *Personal Web Server* (*PWS*), your ability to make changes was severely restricted by the rudimentary nature of the interface, which offered you little more than a Stop/Start button.

ASP.NET has made configuration even more powerful and flexible by removing the reliance on the Web server front-end by the adoption of XML-based configuration files. These files can be used to configure any component of ASP.NET by editing the file in a text editor. You just need to write a piece of code to explain how you'd like ASP.NET to perform a certain operation, and then configure ASP.NET to run your code instead of its built-in code. You no longer have to worry about understanding IIS and its different settings, because now you can alter the code itself.

You're not restricted to just defining configuration settings at design or run time, either. You can add or change them at any time. The new configuration settings you supply will simply be activated, with no loss of efficiency for the server.

This chapter will look at two configuration files:

- ❑   **The machine configuration file**: `machine.config`
- ❑   **The application configuration file**: `web.config`

> The .NET Framework has two other configuration files, which are beyond the scope of this book. They are the security configuration files, `enterprisesec.config` and `security.config` that deal with the tiers of a Web server's security policy.

Let's look at how you can view configuration files using Internet Explorer.

Browsing .config Files

The configuration files are stored as XML documents in plain text format. This means you can view them with any text editor. When viewed in the Internet Explorer, you have the ability to expand and collapse different nodes of the document to make the tree easier to read. To view a configuration file, type its location into Internet Explorer's address bar.

A Quick Word on .NET Framework Versions

Before looking at the `machine.config` file, you need to ascertain the exact location of the configuration file on your machine and its version. This book assumes that you are using .NET Framework 1.1.

> **When .NET Framework 1.1 is installed on a machine that already has .NET 1.0, the older installation is *not* removed automatically. To remove the older version, you need to uninstall it manually.**

Having .NET 1.0 installed along with .NET 1.1 is not a problem though, because .NET gives you the ability to run an application against a particular version of the Framework. As the .NET Framework evolves, certain aspects of a class could be removed entirely. This may cause older applications built with a particular version of the framework to malfunction. If you have more than one version of `machine.config` on your machine, you need to ascertain exactly which version of the Framework is Web Matrix using, and therefore which version of the file you need to use.

It is already mentioned in *Chapter 1* that you need to alter settings in the `WebServer.exe.config` file. It's possible (although unlikely) that you didn't do this and got this far. However, in this chapter it will be essential to change this file if you have both versions installed. So, if you haven't already changed the settings, find `Webserver.exe.config`, which should be located at `C:\Program Files\Microsoft ASP.NET Web Matrix\v.0.6812` (the version number is liable to change). Open it in Web Matrix and add the following settings after the `</configSections>` and before the `<runtime>` section, roughly around line 17:

```
<startup>
    <supportedRuntime version="v1.1.4322" />
</startup>
```

Save the changes and restart the Web Matrix Web server.

Finding the Correct machine.config File

Right then – now that we have ensured that everybody is using the same version, let's now look at the `machine.config` file. You will find this file at the following location:

```
%SystemRoot%\Microsoft.NET\Framework\v1.1.4322\CONFIG\machine.config
```

> **If you have both versions of the Framework installed, you will find a second `machine.config` at this location:**
> `%SystemRoot%\Microsoft.NET\Framework\v1.0.3705\CONFIG\machine.config`.
> **Ignore this version, as it is now redundant for the examples in this book.**

Copy this file and save it as `machine.config.xml` anywhere on your system, and then open it in your browser. You'll see your `machine.config` file displayed in the same way as an XML document. If you collapse the major nodes, you'll get a graphical display of the basic elements as shown in Figure 15-1:

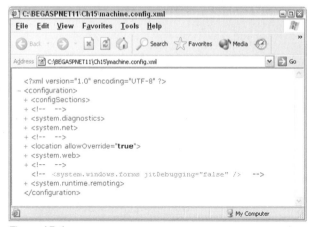

Figure 15-1

> Do not rename the original `machine.config` – ASP.NET relies on this file for its configuration, and will not run properly without it!

The Configuration Files

Your system will have only one `machine.config` file per installation of the .NET Framework, but it could possibly contain many `web.config` files. `machine.config` contains machine-specific settings that ASP.NET needs to function, whereas `web.config` contains configuration information for a *specific* Web application. The `web.config` settings can override default functionality defined in the `machine.config` file to provide a customized environment for each application.

The configuration sequence of events runs as follows. When a page is initialized, the information in `machine.config` is read. Once this has been done, ASP.NET descends to the next level of the hierarchy and reads the individual `web.config` files stored in your Web application's root directories. These files supply additional configuration information to augment or override settings inherited from `machine.config`. Then, ASP.NET descends further to the next level a+nd reads the `web.config` files stored in your application's child directories below the root. These are used to augment or override information given either in `machine.config` or in the root `web.config`. Next, any `web.config` files in subdirectories below this level are read and acted upon in a similar manner.

This will continue until all `web.config` files in the tree have been processed. Some of your directories may not have a `web.config` file. In this case, they will inherit their settings from the closest configuration file node.

This can be seen more clearly in Figure 15-1, which shows the virtual directories in IIS. Don't worry if you are using Web Matrix – this diagram is purely for illustrative purposes and only demonstrates the hierarchical organization of the `.config` file.

A well-structured setup would store the general settings that are to be taken into account at a machine level in the `machine.config` file, and then override them when necessary by using `web.config` files specific to the application page or pages. This approach is beneficial because if any changes need to be made to the general structure of your application, you would only need to alter the `machine.config` file. Likewise, if an individual page needs special settings to function, it can be placed in a child directory with its own `web.config` file. Any changes you make there will affect just that page and not your whole application or machine.

At runtime, ASP.NET uses the information provided by the configuration files to compute the settings for each application resource. The settings are then cached (covered later in the chapter) to allow faster access on subsequent calls. ASP.NET can detect changes made to the configuration files while the Web server is running and can apply these changes immediately without requiring the server to be stopped or rebooted.

Configuration files are protected from unauthorized snooping because both Web Matrix and IIS are automatically configured to prevent HTTP access to them. A server error will be returned if any attempt is made to browse these files over HTTP, even if the file does not exist. You can try this for yourself by directing your browser to http://localhost/web.config, where you will see an error message as depicted in Figure 15-2:

Figure 15-2

You'll get the same result if you try to browse to `global.asax` or any file that has the following extensions: `.ascx`, `.cs`, `.csproj`, `.vb`, `.vbproj`, and `.webinfo`. This is because all these files are set up in the same way

Configuration File Rules

Let's look at the basic rules of XML that apply to the configuration files:

❑ They must have a single unique root element that encloses all other elements within it. The root element for both `machine.config` and `web.config` is `<configuration>`.

❑ Elements must be enclosed between the corresponding start (`<tag>`) and end (`</tag>`) tags. These tags are case-sensitive, so `<Tag>` and `<tag>` will be treated differently.

❑ Any attributes, keys, or values must be enclosed in double quotes: `<add key="data" />`.

❑ Elements must be nested and not overlap.

In the `.config` files, you will also find that a couple of rules of thumb follow. Note that these are general methods (not XML-related):

❑ Tag names and attribute names are camel-cased; in other words, the first character of a tag name is lowercase and the first letter of any subsequent concatenated word is uppercase.

❑ Attribute values are Pascal-case, that is, the first character is uppercase and the first letter of any subsequent concatenated word is also uppercase. Exceptions to this are `true` and `false`, both of which are lowercase.

> **Be very careful when editing configuration files, as they affect your server's behavior – always make a backup before modifying them.**

Configuration File Format

Now that we've refreshed our memory about the basic XML rules that apply to configuration files, let's look at the way these files are structured.

As the .NET Framework uses a set of XML classes to access and alter the configuration files, it forces developers to use a common structure for each of the configuration files. The XML structure is most noticeable in `machine.config`, where all the XML elements are declared and their values set. The `web.config` file is a smaller file because it only contains a subset of the settings already found in `machine.config`.

The configuration files are structurally divided into two main areas:

❑ **Declarations**: Individual classes are defined to manipulate information. This section is delimited by `<configSections>` tags.

❑ **Settings**: Values are assigned to the classes declared in the first section. This section is delimited by `<sectionGroup>` tags.

In `web.config` files, we can override the values of classes defined in the `machine.config` file. Within these two main groups are several subgroups that divide the information into manageable chunks. Let's now consider the `system.web` group, because this is the only section that contains the ASP.NET-specific material.

Figure 15-3 shows a screenshot of the declarations section, with the `system.web` group expanded:

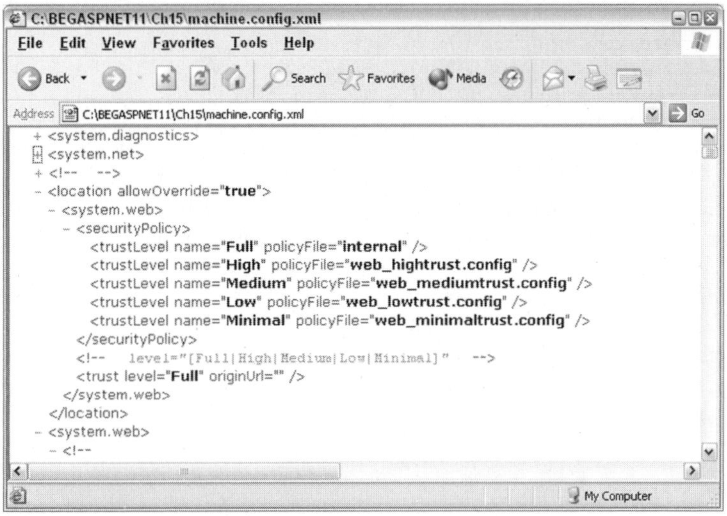

Figure 15-3

Beneath the declarations sections in the hierarchy, you will find a settings section. This section establishes the attributes and properties for each of the declared classes, such as `CustomError`. The settings of the elements don't have to be declared in the same order as they are found in the `<configSections>` tags, but there must be settings defined for every handler declared, otherwise exceptions will be thrown when applications are run.

> All tags must be properly closed and nested, and any values specified must fall within the correct range.

The Structure of the Configuration Files

As mentioned earlier, the structures of `machine.config` and `web.config` are similar. In fact, the `web.config` file is strictly a subset of the `machine.config` file. To explain the subset division, let's first consider the `machine.config` file.

machine.config

A typical `machine.config` file has the following outline:

```
<?xml version="1.0" encoding="UTF-8" ?>
<configuration>
    <configSections>
    </configSections>
    <appSettings>
    </appSettings>
    <system.diagnostics>
    </system.diagnostics>
    <system.net>
```

```
      </system.net>
      <system.web>
      </system.web>
      <system.runtime.remoting>
      </system.runtime.remoting>
   </configuration>
```

The different sections deal with matters such as the manner in which settings are specified at runtime and the settings used to define the elements required for tracing and routing.

Most of the settings within the `machine.config` file have some preliminary explanation or examples within comment tags demonstrating the use of the element involved. For example, under the `pages Attributes` section, you'll find the following:

```
<!-- pages Attributes:
  buffer="[true|false]"                     // Default: true
  enableSessionState="[true|false|ReadOnly]"   // Default: true
  enableViewState="[true|false]"            // Default: true
  enableViewStateMac="[true|false]"         // Default: false
  smartNavigation="[true|false]"            // Default: false
  autoEventWireup="[true|false]"            // Default: true
  pageBaseType="[typename]"        //Default: System.Web.UI.Page
  userControlBaseType="[typename]"//Default: System.Web.UI.UserControl
-->
<pages buffer="true" enableSessionState="true" enableViewState="true"
       enableViewStateMac="true" autoEventWireup="true" />
```

This example should give you a reasonable idea about how each of the settings work, and how they can be specified. The top-level `system.net` section deals with .NET network class settings, while the `system.web` section deals with all the ASP.NET class settings. We're only interested in the `system.web` section because it deals specifically with ASP.NET configuration and controls all of the aspects of the behavior of a typical ASP.NET application.

The Settings of system.web

There are over thirty settings in the `system.web` section. Some of the more commonly used settings are:

❑   **Page settings**: Allows a user to alter options related to the ASP.NET page, such as Web page buffering

❑   **Session-handling**: Handles options related to sessions, such as the length of a session or whether cookie-less support should be enabled

❑   **Application settings**: Allows a user to create name-value pairs within this section and access data from within a specific application

❑   **Tracing**: Sets the level to which execution should be traced (used in debugging)

❑   **Custom errors**: Allows a user to create error pages for particular situations or change settings altering whether users can see different types of error messages

❑   **Web services**: Stores options that affect the operation of the Web service such as the method of transmission of the Web service (HTTPGET, HTTPPOST, or SOAP)

❑ **Security**: Alters security-related aspects such as modes of authentication, encryption, user access and so on

❑ **Compilation**: Provides options for setting/altering the default language for ASP.NET as well as the way in which the page is compiled

❑ **Globalization**: Contains options to specify the character encoding to be used in the requests to and responses from the server

❑ **General settings**: Contains general information relating to the request and options affecting what happens to the page at runtime

There is a great deal more structure and detail in these files than we've covered here. Our aim has been to give you a general idea of what these files are and what they look like, so that when we move on to the next section you'll be able to find your way around and tune your system.

web.config File

As `web.config` files govern the settings of specific applications, they are much smaller than the `machine.config` file.

The sections of a typical `web.config` file are as follows:

```
<?xml version="1.0" encoding="utf-8" ?>
<configuration>
  <system.web>
    <compilation  />
    <customErrors  />
    <authentication />
    <trace  />
    <sessionState  />
    <globalization  />
  </system.web>
</configuration>
```

Here you find only the `<system.web>` section present within the `<configuration>` element that has a much reduced set of elements. You can deduce from this that it is possible to set only these attributes independently for each application.

In the next section, we will have a quick overview of five of the most useful settings and point out some simple alterations that you can make to improve the functioning of your Web application. In particular, we will look at: general configuration settings, page configuration, application settings, custom errors settings, and trace settings.

General Configuration

This section of the configuration files contains general application configuration settings, such as the interval for which a request is processed before it times out, the maximum size of a request, and whether or not to use a fully qualified URL when re-directing pages. Using these settings, you can control some specific aspects of application execution. They are contained within the `<httpRuntime>` tags and occur within the `<system.web>` tags. Here's how you'd set them up in your `web.config` file:

```
<configuration>
  <system.web>
    <httpRuntime executionTimeout="120"
    maxRequestLength="8192"
    useFullyQualifiedRedirectUrl="false"
    />
  </system.web>
</configuration>
```

Let's look at these settings in more detail:

❑   `executionTimeout`: Controls the time in seconds for which a resource is allowed to try to execute before ASP.NET cancels (times out) the execution of the request. The default value is 90 seconds. If you know that a process (such as a complex database query) is likely to take longer than 90 seconds to execute, you should increase this value. This is a very useful feature because if your database returns an error during the code's execution, ASP.NET will know how long to wait before delivering an error message – it will not wait forever!

❑   `maxRequestLength`: Specifies the maximum length of a request. The default value is 4MB. If you think that the content requested from the application would be larger than 4MB (4096 KB), you need to increase this value. If the content requested never exceeds a lesser value, use that value instead. If your code has a bug, this setting will prevent it from dumping great quantities of data on a client, as it will stop transmission of data when it hits the `maxRequestLength` limit. It also prevents a client from requesting too much information at once and hogging the server's processing time at the expense of other users.

❑   `useFullyQualifiedRedirectUrl`: This setting is not often used. One example of when you need to use this parameter is when you are working with mobile controls. It indicates whether client-side redirects are fully qualified, or whether relative redirects should be used (which is the default). Certain mobile controls require that you use fully qualified redirects.

There are also settings such as `minFreeThreads`, `minLocalFreeThreads`, `appRequestQueueLimit`, and `enableVersionHeader`, but these are beyond the scope of this book. If you wish to learn more about these, we recommend reading up Professional ASP.NET 1.1, Wiley ISBN: 0-7645-5890-0.

Page Configuration

Page configuration settings give us control over the default behavior of ASP.NET pages. This can include specifications about whether we should buffer output before sending it, and whether or not session state is enabled for pages within your application. The information is housed within the `<pages>` element in your configuration files. Here's how you'd set it up in your `web.config` file. All values are set to their default values:

```
<configuration>
  <system.web>
    <pages buffer="true"
    enableSessionState="true"
    enableViewState="true"
    autoEventWireup="true" />
  </system.web>
</configuration>
```

Let's take a closer look at what these settings do:

❑ buffer: Indicates the code execution processing mode. When it is set to true, all code is executed before any HTML data in the page is rendered. When it is set to false, all code is rendered as it executes. For example, you could turn off buffering if you're running a complex data query that returns results with a slight delay between each record. You could display such a table line by line while the page is loading, so that the user is aware that something is happening.

❑ enableSessionState: Indicates whether server session variables are available. The default value is true, enabling session state. To disable it, set its value to false. We recommend that you set it to true only if you need to use session variables in your page, as disabling session state improves performance.

❑ enableViewState: Indicates whether server controls should maintain state when the page request ends. This is a global setting for all server controls used on the page. You can, however control the ViewState setting of individual server controls by changing the property value. When EnableViewState is set to true, the server controls maintain state (they 'remember' their value). This is the default setting. If it is set to false, the server controls don't maintain state. Setting it to true hampers performance, so do it only if you need your controls to maintain state.

❑ autoEventWireup: Indicates whether ASP.NET fires page events such as the Page_Load() automatically or not. The default setting is True. Changing it to false allows custom assemblies to control the firing of page events. The default setting for Visual Studio .NET IDE is false, as it uses an internal mechanism to control event firing. If you are not using VB.NET, you should leave it at the default true.

Application Settings

Application settings allow us to store application configuration details in configuration files without the need to write custom section handlers for them. The data is stored in the form of key-value pairs. You've come across them earlier in the book, so we won't linger too long on them. Here we have a typical add key:

```
<add key="XMLFileName" value="myXmlFileName.xml" />
```

You can see that the add tag has both a key attribute and a value attribute. The key attribute is like the name of the variable and the value attribute can be whatever you wish to set it to. In this example, you are assigning the key XMLFileName a value of myXmlFilenName.xml, just like the line XMLFileName = "myXmlFileName.xml" would in ASP.NET code.

We can use key-value pairs to store the connection string for database access. This connection string typically contains the database user ID and password that can be accessed from within applications. This is a great benefit; configuration files are not accessible over HTTP so it keeps your database connection strings (and other such important aspects) away from prying eyes. Here's how you'd set it up in web.config:

```
<configuration>
 <appSettings>
 <add key= "DSN"
```

```
        value="server=LSERV; uid=user; pwd=password; database=data" />
    </appSettings>
    </configuration>
```

Here a key called DSN is being added to the table, and the values in the value attribute are being associated with it. We can now access this information from inside our application. This is done in your ASP.NET script as follows:

```
    strDataSource = ConfigurationSettings.AppSettings("DSN")
```

Custom Errors

While developers do their best to ensure their pages are thoroughly tested before they are deployed in a full application, errors still occur. When a page has errors that are caught during compilation by a .NET Framework compiler (remember that ASP.NET pages are compiled), ASP.NET generates a syntax error report with information about the error and sends this information to the browser. On the other hand, if an error occurs while a page is being executed, ASP.NET sends a *stack trace* containing information about the error to the browser. This stack trace contains information about what was going on when the error occurred. While this information is convenient for the developer to debug his code, it's not something you'd want visitors to your site to see. The stack trace can reveal detailed information about how your code works, thus potentially allowing malicious users to find loopholes and exploit them.

That aside, we don't want this information to be displayed to users of our application because this 'raw' information will disconcert them and bring the quality of our coding into question. It'll spoil your client's experience. Furthermore, they have no way of finding out whether the error is in the application or their computer. Therefore, if there is a friendly message in plain English, with a look and feel similar to your site, the users will know that there is a problem and that the problem is not with the client machines, but with the application. This means it is far better for us to make some changes to the way our application handles errors, so that the user can be redirected to some place else on the site.

You can configure custom error pages for your application using the <customErrors> section of your web.config file inside the <system.web> tags:

```
<customErrors
    defaultRedirect="url"
    mode="On|Off|RemoteOnly">
    <error statusCode="statuscode" redirect="url"/>
</customErrors>
```

Let's look at the important settings in this section:

❏   defaultRedirect: Used to specify the default URL to which the browser is redirected if an error occurs. This allows your application to recover if a page fails by sending your users elsewhere, so that they're not confronted with a broken page.

❏   mode: Indicates whether custom errors are On, Off, or RemoteOnly. On shows your custom error to everyone when it occurs, regardless of where they are. Off never shows a custom error to anyone, and RemoteOnly shows your custom error to browsers that are not located on your server.

You'll need to set mode to On in order to test your custom error pages (unless you've access to a browser off the server). After this, we recommend you change it to RemoteOnly, so that your users will see the custom error page while you'll get the standard error page with all the debugging information that it contains.

❑   error subtags: Can appear as often as required throughout your custom error element. They are used to define special conditions above and beyond the redirect we set up with the defaultRedirect value. They are assigned an HTTP status code that they react to and a redirect URL if that status code occurs. This gives you the flexibility to react to different errors differently; for example, reacting to 404 Page Not Found and 403 Access Forbidden errors differently.

By default, the customErrors configuration option for ASP.NET is set to RemoteOnly, which means that detailed ASP.NET error information is only shown at the server end and remote users are directed to a custom error page. However, since no redirect page is specified as the defaults, the redirection won't work until you set it up in web.config:

```
<configuration>
  <system.web>
    <customerrors
      defaultRedirect = "customerror.aspx"
      mode = "RemoteOnly"
    />
  </system.web>
</configuration>
```

Trace Settings

Chapter 14 discussed how tracing was a very useful feature that enables you to follow the execution of your code and review it afterwards. It helps you tighten up loose code and fix bugs. Tracing can also be set up in your web.config files as shown here:

```
<configuration>
  <system.web>
    <trace
      enabled="true"
      requestLimit = "10"
      pageOutput="false"
      traceMode="SortByTime"
      localOnly = "true"
    />
  </system.web>
</configuration>
```

When we set up tracing in this way (the default value for trace inherited from machine.config is false), we can view our trace output using a special tool called trace.axd. This file is a log file that can be used to store the trace results for the last page viewed. It can be called from your browser in the directory for which you have enabled tracing. This method is useful if you don't want to display the actual trace information at the bottom of your page, but want to keep a record of it in a separate file that is overwritten each time a page is called. Setting the `pageOutput` directive to `true` appends this information back to the bottom of your page.

The options for the `web.config` file are:

- ❏ `enabled`: Switches tracing on when set to `true` and off when set to `false` at the application level. When it is switched off, you can still set traces for individual pages using the `page` directive. By default, this is set to `false` in `machine.config`.

- ❏ `requestLimit`: This is the total number of trace requests to maintain for viewing later with `trace.axd`. By default, it is set to 10.

- ❏ `pageOutput`: Allows you to specify whether you want trace information to be displayed on every page. When it is set to `true`, the tracing information is added to every page. By default, it is set to `false`.

- ❏ `traceMode`: Allows you to specify if the trace information is to be sorted by time or by category. If you sort by category, it will be group information based on the system and `Trace.Write()` settings. By default, this is set to `SortByTime`.

- ❏ `localOnly`: Specifies that only requests made through http://localhost/ will be allowed to see the trace information and is set to `true` by default. This prevents users from viewing trace information, while letting you see exactly what's going on at the same time.

You can embed `Trace.Write` statements in your code to provide useful information about debugging your pages. If you turn tracing off for the page, these statements get hidden and need not be removed as they do not affect the final page output. However, if you find that your application isn't performing as it should, all you need to do is re-enable tracing and these statements can be used again.

Performance Optimization

Some of the options discussed in the previous section help in improving your system's security (storing database connection strings using configuration files). Others increase user-friendliness (creating customized error pages). Some simply improve the speed at which your applications perform (enabling page buffering while disabling session state will speed up your pages).

Let's focus on some more ways to make your application perform faster.

Caching

Caching is the process of storing frequently accessed Web pages or data. The data can then be accessed from the cache faster than from its original location. What effect does this have on you? Well, imagine that you're working on your home PC and it's connected to the Internet via a modem. When you browse a Web page for the first time, you may find that the page takes a while to load. Subsequent visits to that page may well be a lot quicker, because the page has been cached on your machine. Similarly, if a person on a corporate network visits a Web site, the page may take a while to load. But, if someone else visits the same page, depending on the settings on the network, they may find the page loads a lot more quickly because a network proxy has cached it. Caching is used by ASP.NET to store frequently used portions of ASP.NET pages on the Web server so they don't need to be compiled every time a page is accessed.

However, you probably don't want certain items to be cached indefinitely – for example, if you're running a news site, you want the content on your site to be refreshed at regular intervals to display any new news items. Depending on the nature of your news, you might want it to refresh every half an hour, ten minutes, or even every minute. Any requests that get served during the cached period see the same page. After the cache duration expires, the old cache content is destroyed and a new page is retrieved from its original location and cached once again. Simply checking for an absent item in a cache causes the recreation of data in the cache. This content is then cached for the required duration and the cycle starts again.

Setting an appropriate time period for cache expiry is very important. A list of cities or ZIP codes won't need a short expiration period, while a list of clients or a product list will need regular refreshing over relatively short periods of time.

> **Keep in mind that anything you place in the cache consumes memory, so use this feature judiciously.**

Let's look at the three types of caching that you can set up. These are:

- ❑ Output caching
- ❑ Fragment caching
- ❑ The Cache object

Output Caching

Output caching allows caching of any response generated by any request for any application resource. It is very useful when you want to cache the contents of an entire page. On a busy site, caching frequently accessed pages for even as little as a minute, can result in substantial performance gains. While the page lives in the output cache, additional requests for that page are served from the cache without executing and recompiling the code that created the page. Output caching is especially useful for static pages on busy sites.

The complete syntax for the `OutputCache` directive is as follows:

```
<%@ OutputCache Duration="#ofseconds" Location="Any | Client |
    Downstream | Server | None" VaryByControl="controlname"
    VaryByCustom="browser | customstring" VaryByHeader="headers"
    VaryByParam="parametername" %>
```

Let's look at the parameters of this directive in detail:

- ❑ `Duration`: Specifies the duration in seconds that the content should be cached for.
- ❑ `Location`: This is used to specify the locations at which pages can be cached. When set to `Server`, only the server running the application is allowed to cache the page. The `Downstream`

setting implies that any intervening network proxies are allowed to cache a copy of the page. When set to `Client`, the browser is allowed to cache the page locally. When set to `Any`, any of these caches may be used. Alternatively, you could specify a setting of `None`, which prevents caching from being used.

❑   `VaryByControl`: Allows controls to be cached on the server, so that they do not have to be rendered every time a page is requested. Using this parameter caches the specified control as it appears on the page. For example, if you have a control that displays a list of news items, these could be cached for ten minutes simply by caching the control.

❑   `VaryByCustom`: Allows you to specify whether you want to create different cache versions for different browsers, or to vary by a specified string. If this parameter is given the value `browser`, different caches are created by browser name and major versions, which allows you to have different cached versions of a page for each page. This is particularly useful when you need to target output differently for different browsers or different devices. It allows you to specify in detail the parts of a page that you want to cache. If the browser is given the setting `CustomString`, then you can use `VaryByCustom` to distinguish between different versions of cached pages by using the `Vary` HTTP header's content. It works by matching any word you store there against a semicolon-separated list contained within `VaryByCustom`. Whenever `VaryByCustom` finds a match, it will cache a new version of the page.

❑   `VaryByHeader`: Enables you to cache pages by different HTTP headers by using a semicolon-separated list. When this parameter is set to cache multiple headers, the output cache will contain a different version of the requested document for each specified header.

❑   `VaryByParam`: Allows you to vary the caching requirements by specific parameters in the form of a semicolon-separated list of strings. By default, these strings correspond to a querystring value or to a parameter sent via the `POST` method. When this parameter is set to multiple values, the output cache will contain a different version of the requested document for each specified value. Possible values include `none`, `*`, or any valid querystring or `POST` parameter name. This attribute is required when you output cache ASP.NET pages (or user controls). A parser error will occur if you don't include it. If you want the complete page cached at all times then set the value to `none`. If you want to have a new output cache created for each of the possible setting of the parameters, then set the value to `*`.

Let's take a look at how this works in a simple example.

Try It Out   **Output Caching**

1.   Open Web Matrix, create a new ASPX file, and call it `Servertime.aspx`. Type the following code into the All window:

```
<%@ Page Language="C#" %>
<script  runat = "server">
string ServerTime()
{
   return System.DateTime.Now.ToLongTimeString();
}
</script>

The time on your web server is : <% Response.Write(ServerTime());%>
```

2. This code displays the current time on your Web server. Call it up in your browser and verify that the code is working as depicted in Figure 15-4. After a couple of seconds, click your browser's Refresh button and watch the numbers change:

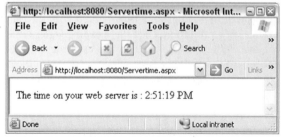

Figure 15-4

3. Now add the following page directive at the top of your code:

```
<%@ OutputCache Duration="60" VaryByParam="none" %>
<%@ Page Language="C#" %>
<script  runat = "server">
  string ServerTime()
  {
    return System.DateTime.Now.ToLongTimeString();
  }
</script>

The time on your web server is : <% Response.Write(ServerTime());%>
```

4. Save your file as `CachedServerTime.aspx` and call it up in your browser again. To begin with, everything looks the same – the code displays the time as before. But when you click the refresh button, the time doesn't change and remains the same. In fact, it will remain the same for 60 seconds. Try it and see!

How It Works

The `Servertime.aspx` code example is very simple. It runs a function called `ServerTime()` on your server to get the server's time, and then returns it formatted as a string. This returned information is then displayed on the screen using a line of HTML and some inline ASP.NET tags:

```
string ServerTime()
{
  return System.DateTime.Now.ToLongTimeString();
}

The time on your web server is : <%=ServerTime %>
```

This code does not specify that the page should be cached, so the server processes it freshly each time the page is called. When you click your browser's Refresh button, it processes the code and gives you the newly processed result. The time changes every time you press the Refresh button.

When the following page directive is added, this is no longer the case:

```
<%@ OutputCache Duration="60" VaryByParam="none" %>
```

We're instructing the server to cache the output generated by your request for a period of 60 seconds. Any subsequent page requests within that period will be served with the cached version, so the displayed time will remain the same until the cached page expires, after which it is processed afresh. The VaryByParam attribute you saw earlier is set to none in this example, meaning that the same page will be delivered from the cache regardless of the parameters delivered with the request (although our example is quite basic, and as a result, doesn't have any parameters).

Fragment Caching

This allows the caching of sections of a response generated by any request that includes user controls. Sometimes it's not practical to cache an entire page, (for example, if you've got a section for advertisements on a page, or some personalization features that have to be unique to every user). In such cases, you may still want portions of the page to be cached and the remainder to be generated programmatically for each user. For such pages, it is worthwhile to create user controls that do not change, so that they can be created once and cached for a defined time period.

For example, to cache all the controls defined in an ASCX (user control) source file, just include this directive in the control itself:

```
<%@ OutputCache Duration="60" VaryByParam="none" %>
```

You don't have to place the OutputCache directive in the page in which the controls are called (the ASPX page). All other controls included in the ASCX will automatically be cached for 60 seconds.

If you want to cache each of the possible variations of your control's properties, you need to use this directive:

```
<%@ OutputCache Duration="60" VaryByParam="*" %>
```

The asterisk (*) directs the output cache to cache a page for every parameter property returned by your control.

The Cache Object

The third and most complex method of caching is to use the ASP.NET Cache object. Unlike the first two methods of caching, the Cache object doesn't store pages. Instead it stores data that is frequently viewed and doesn't change often between views.

The Cache object came into being as developers continually used the Application object as a cache. This was because ASP provided little support for caching mechanisms above and beyond the Application and Session objects. When developers used the Application or Session objects, they had to write code to manage the creation and disposal of the data. In ASP.NET, advanced caching capabilities were introduced in the form of a programmable Cache object. Efficient use of ASP.NET's caching capabilities can allow you to balance the use of resources such as PC memory and database connections against the need to generate client pages quickly.

The Cache object provides a temporary repository for information along with the ability to refresh the cache (and to expire old information depending on different policies). The first policy is based on a date or timestamp – when a particular date or time is reached, the cache is expired. The second involves linking the cache to a file and expiring it if the file is updated or amended in any way. The third policy is to link the cache to another cache via a master key, and then expire the items in all linked caches if an item changes in just one of them. As the Cache object has quietly sneaked in through the backdoor in ASP.NET, we'll take a little time discussing it now.

Cache Creation

When creating a cache, you'll find the Cache object uses the same syntax as the other ASP objects:

```
Cache["NewCache"] = "Confidential Information";
```

Here we create an instance of the Cache object called NewCache and store the value Confidential Information in it. It's more effectively used when it's storing objects though. If we created an Addressbook class that contains the name, address, phone, and email properties, we could store the contents of this class in our cache as follows:

```
AddressBook newAddressBook = new AddressBook();
newAddressBook.name = "Rheingold Cabriole";
newAddressBook.address = "673 Chellingworth Place, Morningtown";
newAddressBook.email = "Rheingold.Cabriole@fabemails.com";
newAddressBook.phone = "333-444-555";
Cache["address"] = newAddressBook;
```

One major application of the Cache object is using it to store datasets. For example, the Cache object could point to the contents of an XML document, such as the following address.xml file:

```
<?xml version="1.0"?>
<address>
  <name> Rheingold Cabriole </name>
  <address>673 Chellingworth Place, Morningtown </address>
 <email>Rheingold.Cabriole@fabemails.com</email>
 <phone>333-444-555</phone>
</address>
```

If this was saved on the root of the C:\ drive, then the following code could be used to store it in the Cache object:

```
DataSet XMLFileDataSet;
XMLFileDataSet.ReadXml("C:\\address.xml");
Cache["XMLDoc"] = XMLFileDataSet;
```

This is known as the *implicit* method of insertion, where key-value pairs are inserted into the cache – the key being XMLDoc and the value being the contents of XMLFileDataset. However, there is also another method of insertion, known as *explicit* insertion. To do an explicit insert, use the Cache.Insert() method to add the XML file you created:

```
DataSet XMLFileDataSet;
XMLFileDataSet.ReadXml("C:\\address.xml");
Cache.Insert("XMLDoc", XMLFileDataSet, null);
```

It does exactly the same thing as the implicit method, but uses a more powerful syntax. You might notice that there is a third argument present in the method, null. This third parameter allows us to specify a parameter setting up a dependency (in this example we set it to nothing). Dependencies allow us to create expiration policies for the cache. We're also not just restricted to inserting datasets; we can add files or any other objects or items that don't change regularly. Let's now talk about retrieving information from the cache.

Cache Data Retrieval

When retrieving information, all you need to do is follow the exact reverse of the procedure we just outlined. With the AddressBook class, you'd create an instance of the class and read the contents of the cache into it:

```
AddressBook newAddressBook = new AddressBook();
newAddressBook = (AddressBook)Cache.Item["address"];
```

We cast the cache data into something that can be stored in the AddressBook class; you have to ensure that you store the contents of a class into a class of the correct type.

You could then display the contents of the Cache object in a Label control called MyLabel1 as follows:

```
myLabel1.Text = newAddressBook.Name + "<br>" + newAddressBook.Address + "<br>"
                + newAddressBook.Phone + "<br>" + newAddressBook.Email;
```

Due to the transient nature of caches, it is a good practice to first check if anything is present in the cache:

```
if (!(Cache.Item("address") == null))
{
  newAddressBook = (AddressBook)Cache.Item["address"];
  myLabel1.Text = newAddressBook.Name + "<br>" +
  newAddressBook.Address + "<br>" + newAddressBook.Phone + "<br>" +
  newAddressBook.Email
}
else
{
  mylabel1.Text = "Cache is Empty";
}
```

Having seen how we can place and retrieve items from the cache, it's time to move on to the crux of the tutorial – how things can be removed from the Cache object.

Cache Data Removal

To remove items from the Cache object, you just need to use the Cache.Remove[] method:

```
Cache.Remove["address"];
```

However, this would mean using the Cache object just like an Application object and nullifying the main advantages that the Cache object enjoys over the Application object – expiration policies. It is more beneficial to be able to tell the Cache object when or under what circumstances to expire the contents of the cache.

Expiring Information in the Cache

There are three common ways in which information can be expired and we shall look briefly at each of them:

- ❑ **Timestamp expiration**: Information is deleted when a pre-specified time or date is reached.
- ❑ **File dependency**: Information is expired when a specified file is updated or amended in some way.
- ❑ **Key dependency**: Cache items are commonly linked together and when information is expired in one cache, it is desirable that information in the linked cache should be cleared. This linking can be achieved via a set of cache keys.

Timestamp Expiration

The most straightforward type of expiration policy is via a timestamp. There are two ways in which cached information can be removed via a timestamp. The first is by the setting an absolute date or time when the cache must expire. The second is by the means of a timescale within which the cache must be updated. For instance, you can specify that a cache needs to be updated 30 minutes after the object was last updated or accessed.

The absolute method of expiration takes two extra arguments. One is for the absolute time of expiration and the second specifies the time within which the cache must have been last visited. To insert our XML file into the cache and expire it in five minutes time, you use the following code:

```
Cache.Insert("XMLDoc", XMLFileDataSet, null, DateTime.Now.AddMinutes(5),
             TimeSpan.Zero);
```

The syntax for Cache.Insert() is as follows:

```
Cache.Insert(FileName, DataSet, Dependency, DateTime, TimeSpan);
```

The five parameters specified here are:

- ❑ FileName: Name of the XML document
- ❑ DataSet: Name of the DataSet
- ❑ Dependency Type: The type of dependency
- ❑ DateTime: Date and time at which the cache should expire
- ❑ TimeSpan: The period of time that should elapse after the cache was last accessed for the cache to expire

After specifying the file name and DataSet contents, the dependency type is set to null, as there are no dependencies. We use the AddMinutes() method to specify a time 5 minutes in advance of the current time. As we don't wish to expire the cache if it isn't updated, the second argument is set to

`TimeSpan.Zero`, which is the syntax used to indicate that we don't wish to use a time period within which the cache must have been last updated.

When specifying a time within which the cache must have been visited, the method looks very similar; it's just that we tweak the last two argument's values as follows:

```
Cache.Insert("XMLDoc", XMLFileDataSet, null, Cache.NoAbsoluteExpiration,
             TimeSpan.FromSeconds(300));
```

Here the absolute expiration value is set to `NoAbsoluteExpiration` (in other words it will never expire) while the maximum value is set to 300 seconds (5 minutes) from when the cache was last refreshed. In this way the cache, will expire when it hasn't been accessed within the last five minutes. If it is accessed again (even at 4 minutes 59 seconds), it will have a lifespan of 5 minutes. This is called *sliding time expiration*.

File Dependency

With a *file dependency*, things get a little more complex. You have to create a `CacheDependency` object. This object is given an argument that specifies the file that you wish to associate with your cache. We can set up this dependency by creating an instance of the `CacheDependency` object and reading the filename into it. We must then read the contents of the file into a `DataSet`:

```
CacheDependency FileDepend = new CacheDependency("C:\address.xml");
DataSet XMLDataSet;
XMLDataSet.ReadXml("C:\address.xml");
Cache.Insert("address", XMLDataSet, FileDepend);
```

Instead of setting the third argument to `null` as in the time expiration policy, we set it to the name of our `CacheDependency` object. Thus the contents of the cache expire whenever the file is amended. We can demonstrate the use of file dependency now. In the next Try-It-Out, we will cache an XML document relating to our fictitious entrant, Rheingold Cabriole, and then change the document and use a file dependency to force the expiration of the contents of the cache.

Try It Out Creating a File Dependency

1. Open up Web Matrix and create an XML document called `address.xml` in the `C:\BegASPNet11\Ch15` folder. Enter code as follows:

```
<?xml version="1.0"?>
<address>
  <name>Rheingold Cabriole</name>
  <address>673 Chellingworth Place, Morningtown </address>
  <phone>333-444-555</phone>
  <email> Rheingold.Cabriole@fabemails.com</email>
</address>
```

2. Create the following ASP.NET page and name it `cachefile.aspx`:

```
<%@ Page Language="C#" Debug="true" %>
<%@ Import Namespace="System.Data" %>
<%@ Import Namespace="System.Xml" %>
```

```
<html>
<head>
<script runat="server">

public void Create(Object sender, EventArgs e)
{
  DataSet XMLFileDataSet = new DataSet();
  XMLFileDataSet.ReadXml("C:\\BegASPNet11\\ch15\\address.xml");
  CacheDependency filedependency = new
                  CacheDependency("C:\\BegASPNet11\\ch15\\address.xml");
  Cache.Insert("address",XMLFileDataSet, filedependency);
  mylabel1.Text="Cache Full";
}

public void Display(Object sender, EventArgs e)
{
  DataSet myAddressBook = new DataSet();
  if (Cache["address"] == null)
  {
    grid1.DataSource = null;
    grid1.DataBind();
    mylabel1.Text = "Cache Empty";
  }
  else
  {
    myAddressBook = (DataSet)Cache["address"];
    grid1.DataSource = myAddressBook;
    grid1.DataBind();
  }
}

</script>
</head>
<body>
  <form id="form1" runat="server">
   <asp:label id="mylabel1" runat="server" />
   <asp:datagrid id="grid1" runat="server" />
   <br/>
   <input type="submit" Value="Create Cache" OnServerClick="Create"
          runat="server" />
   <input type="submit" Value="Display Cache" OnServerClick="Display"
          runat="server" />
  </form>
</body>
</html>
```

3. Run this on your browser and press the Create Cache button, followed by the Display Cache button. You will see the screen depicted in Figure 15-5:

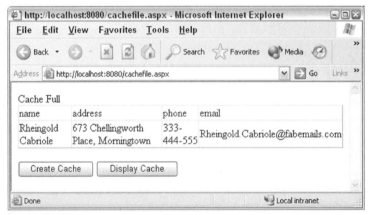

Figure 15-5

4. Keeping the browser open, go back and change the code in `address.xml` to read as follows:

```
<?xml version="1.0?>
<address>
<name>Rheingold Cabriole</name>

<address>135 Tabletop Drive, Workville </address>

<phone>333-444-555</phone>
<email>Rheingold.Cabriole@fabemails.com</email>
</address>
```

5. Save it and go back to the browser and click the Display Cache button only (without refreshing). View the browser and you will see the screen depicted in Figure 15-6:

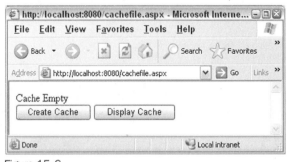

Figure 15-6

As you have updated the file, it automatically expired the contents of the cache. You must then reload the cache object using the Create Cache button to see the updated contents.

How It Works

Basically, the code is very straightforward. For the event code for the **Create Cache** button, we create a `DataSet` and read into it the contents of the `address.xml` file:

```
DataSet XMLFileDataSet = new DataSet();
XMLFileDataSet.ReadXml("C:\\BegASPNet11\\ch15\\address.xml");
```

We then create a `CacheDependency` object and link it to this file:

```
CacheDependency filedependency = new
CacheDependency("C:\\BegASPNet11\\ch15\\address.xml");
```

After this we create an `address` item using the `DataSet` and `filedependency`, and set the `Label` control text to `Cache Full`:

```
Cache.Insert("address",XMLFileDataSet, filedependency);
mylbel1.Text="Cache Full";
```

For the code for the **Display Cache** button, we create a new `DataSet` called `Addressbook` and then check to see if there is an item present in the cache:

```
DataSet myAddressBook = new DataSet();
if (Cache["address"] == null)
```

If there is no item, we bind the grid to nothing and display `Cache empty`:

```
grid1.DataSource = null;
grid1.DataBind();
mylabel1.Text = "Cache Empty";
```

If there is an item in the cache, we convert it into a `DataSet` and bind it to our `DataGrid` control:

```
else
{
    myAddressBook = (DataSet)Cache["address"];
    grid1.DataSource = myAddressBook;
    grid1.DataBind();
}
```

It's only a simple usage, but we can see how the `Cache` object can be used to monitor an XML document and see when it has been changed so as to update the cache with every change. In fact, in this example the cached object is created from an XML file and file dependency is also placed on the same XML file. It is also possible to cache content from a different file, and expire the cache based on updates made to another file – the cache need always be dependent on the same source file.

It is possible to use file and key dependencies together, so that if the contents of one file changed and several files were affected, all files could be expired automatically from all linked caches. This is beyond the scope of our tutorial, but you now have a solid grounding in the fundamentals of the `Cache` object.

Key Dependency

The last method of expiration is key dependency. It is similar to file dependency, but is slightly more complex. It is known as key dependency because it is based upon a key rather than the cached item itself. If you wanted to expire something from the cache when another related item in the cache had been changed, you would use a key dependency to do this. It is done in two stages:

- ❑ Creation of the key based upon a cached item
- ❑ Mapping the key to another dependent item

For instance, if you had an address and a phone number for that address in the cache, and if the address changed, you'd want the phone number changing in all likelihood. You could use a key dependency to do this.

The following code would create a key dependency:

```
Cache["addressKey"] = "1273 Abledown Road ";
string[] keydepend;
keydepend[0] = "addressKey";
CacheDependency keydependency = new CacheDependency(null, keydepend);
Cache.Insert("phone","123-456-789", keydependency);
```

We create a cache item for the phone and link this to a cache item for the address. This means that if the phone item changes, the address item should also be expired. You don't have to restrict yourself to creating one key dependency, you could create many dependencies so that other details such as fax number and zipcode are removed automatically when the address item in the cache is changed.

To create a key dependency, once again we have to create a `CacheDependency` object, but this time we pass it two parameters. The first parameter is left blank deliberately, because it is normally used to pass a filename or path and this information isn't needed here. Then we can insert a name/value pair into the `Cache` object along with an argument that specifies our `CacheDependency` key. So in effect, when we create a second cache item, we add the `CacheDependency` key to specify a link to the first cache item. The second parameter passed is an array containing the dependency key, the key itself being the name of the first cache we created (`address`). Let's develop a fully working example based on key dependency.

Try It Out   Creating a Key Dependency

Let's create an ASPX page with three buttons, one that fills the cache with two items, one that displays the contents, and one that removes one of the cache items.

1. Open Web Matrix, create an ASP.NET page called `cachekey.aspx` and enter the following code into the All view, removing all existing code:

```
<%@ Page Language="c#" Debug="true" %>
<html>
  <head>
    <script runat="server">

    public void Create(Object sender, EventArgs e)
    {
      Cache["address"] = "444 Horror House";
```

```
      string[] keydep;
      keydep = new string [1];
      keydep[0] = "address";
      CacheDependency keydependency = new CacheDependency(null, keydep);
      Cache.Insert("phone","123-456", keydependency);
      mylabel1.Text="Cache Full";
    }

    public void Display(Object sender, EventArgs e)
    {
      if (Cache["phone"] == null)
      {
        mylabel1.Text = "Cache Empty";
      }
      else
      {
        mylabel1.Text = "Address:" + Cache["address"] + "<br>Phone: " +
                        Cache["phone"];
      }
    }


    public void Change(Object sender, EventArgs e)
        {
          Cache.Remove("address");
          mylabel1.Text = "Address removed";
        }
  </script>
</head>
<body>
  <form id="form1" runat="server">
    <asp:label id="mylabel1" runat="server" />
    <br/>
    <input type="submit" Value="Create Cache" OnServerClick="Create"
          runat="server" />
    <input type="submit" Value="Display Cache" OnServerClick="Display"
          runat="server" />
    <input type="submit" Value="Change Cache" OnServerClick="Change"
          runat="server" />
  </form>
</body>
</html>
```

> Take care that `Cache["address"]` and `keydep(0)="address"` both have the same case, otherwise you will get an error.

2. Run this page in the browser and you should see the screen depicted in Figure 15-7. Click on the **Create Cache** and **Display Cache** buttons in turn:

Figure 15-7

3. You can see quite clearly that there are two items in the cache. Press **Change Cache** followed by **Display Cache**, and you will see that nothing is in the cache now as shown in Figure 15-8:

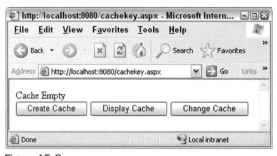

Figure 15-8

How It Works

Our **Create Cache** event handler starts by creating a `Cache["address"]` item:

```
Cache["address"] = "444 Horror House";
```

Next we create a key dependency based on `Cache["address"]`:

```
string[] keydep;
keydep =  new string [1];
keydep[0] = "address";
```

We create a second cache item `phone` and link it to the first and display the message **Cache Full**:

```
CacheDependency keydependency = new CacheDependency(null, keydep);
Cache.Insert("phone","123-456", keydependency);
mylabel1.Text="Cache Full";
```

The `Display()` method just checks to see if there is anything in the cache phone item and if present, displays it; it displays the message **Cache Empty** if nothing is found:

```
public void Display(Object sender, EventArgs e)
```

```
    {
      if (Cache["phone"] == null)
      {
        mylabel1.Text = "Cache Empty";
      }
      else
      {
        mylabel1.Text = "Address:" + Cache["address"] + "<br>Phone: " +
                        Cache["phone"];
      }
    }
```

The third event handler deletes one of the cache items. Pressing the Change Cache button removes the address item only:

```
public void Change(Object sender, EventArgs e)
{
  Cache.Remove("address");
  mylabel1.Text = "Address removed";
}
```

However, when we press Display Cache, we check only the contents of the phone item:

```
...
if (Cache["phone"] == null)
{
    mylabel1.Text = "Cache Empty";
}
...
```

Nothing is displayed in the output; the key dependency has ensured that both items have been deleted from the cache.

Cache Priorities

Apart from the expiration policies, it is also possible to set the relative importance of items within the cache to each other, so that items can be quickly dumped if memory is low or if performance is really dragging. When you create an item, there are a couple of extra arguments you can add, which specify in relative terms the priority of a cache item and how slowly that priority should decline:

```
Cache.Insert("XMLFile", XMLDataSet, null, DateTime.Now.AddMinutes(5),
TimeSpan.Zero, CacheItemPriority.High, CacheItemPriorityDecay.Slow);
```

The items in the cache can be set to the priorities: Low, BelowNormal, Normal, AboveNormal, High, and NotRemovable. The speed at which they decay can be set to Fast, Medium, Default, Slow, or Never. This means that the cache expiration can be determined separately from the expiration policies of the system, if necessary, and the contents of the caches can be managed dynamically.

The Cache object offers a lot of features above the Application object, such as the creation of dependencies on files or other caches as well as the setting of priorities. It's possible to link file dependencies and key dependencies, so that when an item in one file changes, a whole load of files can be expired from the cache. Judicious use of this object in place of the Application object could make your applications a whole lot faster and more efficient.

Tips and Tricks

No configuration guidelines would be complete without offering a list of optimization tips. Here's a brief listing of the tips and examples included in the Microsoft QuickStart samples. If you've not got these installed, they're available from the following sites:

- ❑ http://www.gotdotnet.com/quickstart/aspplus/
- ❑ http://docs.aspng.com/quickstart/aspplus/default.aspx
- ❑ http://aspalliance.com/quickstart/aspplus/
- ❑ http://www.dotnetjunkies.com/quickstart/default.aspx

Don't worry if you don't understand them all! They are included here so that you can refer back to them throughout your development as a programmer. Think of them as a quick reference guide that you'll still be able to use as a refresher in the years to come.

To round off this chapter, let's look at a few tips you could use to optimize the performance of your application and use configuration settings to your benefit:

- ❑ **Disable session state when not needed**. Maintaining session state consumes memory and processing time. If you don't need to recall or modify session variables in a page, disable session state for that page.

- ❑ **Choose your session state provider carefully**. If you are running just one Web server, the fastest and most economical mode of maintaining state is 'in-process'. Only if you are running a Web farm on more than one machine should you even consider using SQL Server or the State Server.

- ❑ **Avoid excessive round trips to the server**. Round tripping to the server takes time and server resources. You should make a round-trip to the server only when storing or retrieving data. You can program your controls to generate client-side code, and still use ASP.NET's efficient server controls. Use client-side processing to save server-processing time as much as you can.

- ❑ **Use `Page.IsPostback` to avoid extra work on a round trip**. For example, you can use `IsPostback` to determine whether a `DataSet` needs to be generated. Generating data is expensive in terms of processing time. Generating one query on first access and another one on a `POST` can cost you processing time.

- ❑ **Use server controls sparingly and appropriately**. Even though server controls are very cool and afford you incredible event-handling capabilities, a simple rendering using `Response.Write` for simple displays will be far more efficient.

- ❑ **Avoid excessive server control ViewState**. The more data you're passing back and forth between the client and the server, the larger the ViewState gets, and the longer it takes for the more resources you're consuming. Like session state, turn this feature off if you don't need to keep state on a page.

- ❑ **Use `System.Text.StringBuilder` for string concatenation**. When you modify a string object using the traditional concatenation methods, you add a new string object for every modification made. This adds up! The new `StringBuilder` object is much more efficient because you use only one object no matter how many modifications you perform on the string.

❑ **Use the page `Strict` setting**. The line `<%@ Page Language="C#" Strict="true" %>` can be your best friend! This forces early-binding of your code, which in turn forces your code to be more efficient. In other words, all of the variables are checked to see if they have been declared up front. By having correct typing enforced you prevent costly, inefficient, late-binding (waiting until a variable is used before checking to see it is bound to a data type). A side benefit is that `Strict` forces you to declare your variables, preventing misplaced values in your code.

❑ **Use SQL stored procedures for data access**. In the .NET Framework, the `SqlConnection` class allows you to have even larger performance gains, since it can actually execute native SQL Server code. Not only do you gain the speed of stored procedures, they also are natively executed. Performance gains are estimated at 200 to 300% over `OleDb` or `Odbc` connections!

❑ **Use `SqlDataReader` for a fast-forward, read-only data cursor**. `SqlDataReader` provides what is known in the ASP world as a 'firehose' cursor, which is much faster than other cursors available. In addition, `SqlDataReader` reads data directly from a database connection using *Tabular Data Streams* (*TDS*), and allows you to bind server controls directly to data.

❑ **Use caching features wherever possible**. In high-traffic situations, caching data can save you a lot of processing time, since the data will be served from RAM instead of using precious processing cycles.

❑ **Enable Web gardening for multiprocessor computers**. Enabling the use of all processors available makes sense, since the more the processing power available to your applications, the more efficient your Web server will be.

❑ **Do not forget to disabled debug mode**. Having a compiler watching for errors is the most expensive process that a processor can undertake! Never enable debugging in a production environment!

Summary

This chapter has covered a lot of ground in the vast topic of configuration and optimization. We looked at `machine.config` and `web.config` and saw how they were structured and their settings were hierarchically inherited. Then we looked in more detail at some of the specific settings within those files that you could use to improve the performance, security, and user-friendliness of your applications.

Next, we moved on to look at how we could increase our Web server's performance through the use of output and fragment caching so that our pages didn't need to be compiled as frequently, before looking at how the Cache object can be used to store information that is frequently visited. We also looked at various methods of expiring caches by specifying dependencies. The chapter concluded with a list of recommended performance optimization tips.

Exercises

1. If you didn't know how to set a particular element in the `.config` file, where would you look to find them?

2. Create a "friendly" custom error page for a File Not Found error and set the relevant `.config` file so that it appears whenever a 404 error message is generated.

3. Create a page with two Label controls that both display the time and create an output cache that lasts for 30 minutes and caches just one of the controls.

4. Create a cache that stores the following information "MyFavouriteColour = Orange" and expires the cache if it hasn't been updated for 3 minutes.

5. Create a cache that will expire whenever the contents of one of three files, XMLDoc1.xml, XMLDoc2.xml, and XMLDoc3.xml is changed. Note they can all contain the following code:

```xml
<?xml version="1.0"?>
<address>
 <name>Rheingold Cabriole</name>
 <address>673 Chellingworth Place, Morningtown </address>
 <phone>333-444-555</phone>
 <email> Rheingold.Cabriole@fabemails.com</email>
</address>
```

16

Web Services

In the days before the Internet, if you wanted to research a subject, you would visit a library to find a book on the topic, or browse the relevant periodicals to find the latest articles. While this is still quite possible (if you like that sort of thing), it isn't usually necessary. As the Internet connects computers containing all sorts of different data sources, it frequently provides us with a one-stop shop for whatever information we might need. In a sense, the Internet has become a 'virtual library' for Web users.

Over the years, Web developers created isolated Web applications and would often produce code that merely duplicated what many other programmers had already done elsewhere. To overcome this, many developers began using technologies (such as COM and DCOM) that would allow them to build code components once and bundle them up so they could be shared across multiple applications by many developers. However, in practice, these components had some fundamental drawbacks. They had to be physically distributed, and then explicitly registered on each user's machine. It was possible to share logic, but it wasn't easy.

The next step was using the infrastructure to make specific bits of the information available without requiring a user to download a whole component or application. The ASP.NET *Web services* model provides a simple, straightforward way to do this. For example, if a developer wanted a weather forecast for their flight simulator, or the latest currency rates for their economic models, rather than having to program the logic, or download a component, they can access the relevant Web service and glean the necessary information for their own application. Web services enable developers to share application logic and therefore reduce the overall amount of code duplication. They also provide us with the ability to easily access information from different sources because Web services make information available as pure text. Web services truly make the Web a 'virtual library' for Web developers. This chapter will show how easy it is to create and use ASP.NET Web services. The topics covered are:

- ❑ What a Web service is, and its role in the .NET Framework.

- ❑ How to create and use a Web service.

- ❑ How to describe a Web service's behavior using WSDL.

- ❑ How users can discover which Web services are available using UDDI.

- ❑ What you need to consider when building a Web service.

What Is a Web Service?

Technically speaking, a Web service is a component of the programmable application logic that can be accessed using standard Web protocols. It's quite similar to the server controls considered earlier on in the book. The major difference is that it lets you access all of its functionality across the Web, whereas server controls only access functionality on the "*local*" Web server. For example, if I browsed a calendar control, this would be all done on the local Web server, whereas if I accessed a stock price, this could come from any remote Web site that exposed stock prices as a Web service. In principle, anyone who can browse the Web can see, and use a Web service.

Think of a Web service as a 'black box' resource that accepts requests from a consumer (an application running on the Web client), performs a specific task, and returns the results of that task. In some respects, a search engine such as Google (www.google.com) is a kind of Web service – you submit a search expression, and it compiles a list of matching sites, and returns the list to your browser.

Currently, the term Web service is something of a buzzword within the sphere of software development thanks to a number of new protocols that have opened up the scope of what we can expect Web services to do. XML plays a central role in all these technologies, and *XML Web Services* are something you can expect to hear a great deal about, now and well into the future.

Most of the time, you'll find that when people talk about Web services, they're implicitly referring to XML Web services. This is now so prevalent that many people believe that all Web services use XML by definition.

There's a very important distinction between a Web service like Google and the kind of XML Web service that will be discussed here: on Google, *you* submit the search expression, and read the list of sites that are sent back. The browser provides you with a textbox, and parses the response stream so that it looks nice –it doesn't actually *understand* the information you've submitted, let alone the HTML that Google sends back.

If you're using an XML Web service, you can assume the results will be returned as some kind of XML document, with information that's explicitly structured and self-describing. It's therefore quite straightforward to write a program that interprets these results and perhaps even uses the results to formulate a new submission.

ASP.NET makes it very easy to build XML Web services, and just as easy to use them. Ultimately you only need to reference the Web service in your code, and you can use it just as if it were a local component. As with normal components, you don't need to know anything about how the service functions, only the tasks it can do, the type of information it needs to do them, and the type of results you'll be getting back.

You can use Web service methods to do just about anything from adding two numbers together to writing information to a database. The logic they use can be as simple or as complex as we need it to be.

Let's create a simple Web service to demonstrate just how easy it is.

Try It Out **Creating Our First Web Service**

In this example, we'll make a Web service that takes a string input and returns a greeting that includes the name specified in the input.

1. Open up Web Matrix and choose the XML Web service option. Create a file called `greetings.asmx` and enter Greetings into the Class textbox and Ch16 into the namespace textbox, as shown in Figure 16-1:

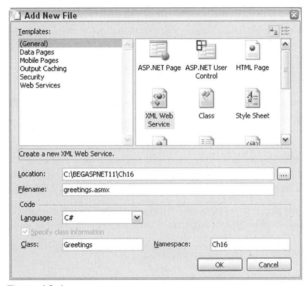

Figure 16-1

2. In the window that opens up, add the following code:

```
<%@ WebService Language="c#" Class="Greetings"%>
using System;
using System.Web.Services;
using System.Xml.Serialization;
public class Greetings
{
  [WebMethod]
  public string Hello(string strName)
  {
    return "Hello, " + strName + ". Have a great day!";
  }
}
```

3. Open the file in your browser, and you should see something like Figure 16-2:

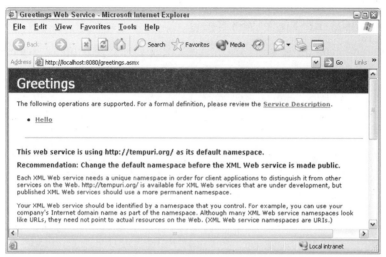

Figure 16-2

4. Following the Hello hyperlink, this page will also include a warning message about using the http://tempuri.org default namespace. It will also display information on how to use the Web service directly from SOAP, and from HTTP GET and HTTP POST requests.

5. Click on the bulleted Hello hyperlink – this is the name of the method defined in the Greetings class. A new page will be displayed that allows us to enter a name as shown in Figure 16-3:

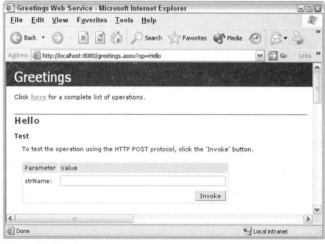

Figure 16-3

6. Enter your name in the textbox adjacent to the Name parameter, and hit the Invoke button to call your Web service's Hello method. The screen shown in Figure 16-4 should now appear in a new browser window:

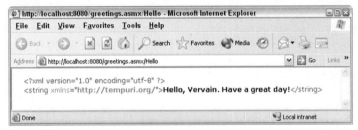

Figure 16-4

7. That's it! The Web service is now working on our local machine.

How It Works

The first line shows that the Web service is written in C#. We also declare our class name as `Greetings`, which will be important when a consumer wants to use it:

```
<%@ WebService Language="c#" Class="Greetings"%>
```

The next lines give us access to objects that are needed to build a Web service:

```
using System;
using System.Web.Services;
using System.Xml.Serialization;
```

Next, we have some logic to actually define the Web service's functionality. Within the `public class Greetings` declaration (notice the name here matches the one in the `WebService` declaration), we define a `Hello` function that simply returns a string based on the parameter `strName`. We prefix this method declaration with a `[WebMethod]` attribute – this is how we specify that it's to be exposed as a Web method, making the function visible to the outside world:

```
public class Greetings
{
  [WebMethod]
  public string Hello(string strName)
  {
    return "Hello, " + strName + ". Have a great day!";
  }
}
```

With just a few lines of code, we've created a functioning Web service. We didn't need to specify a format for the result, or write any code to handle any network connections. We didn't even have to register it on the client – all we needed to know was the URL.

To conclude the first example, let's touch upon the warning message that appeared on the first page of the Web service. It reads as follows:

This Web service is using http://tempuri.org/ as its default namespace. Recommendation: Change the default namespace before the XML Web service is made public.

This warning means that if you do not make a practice of changing this namespace, your Web service will be organized within the default `tempuri.org` namespace, which can become difficult to manage if there are multiple developers on a project who all use this default.

Namespaces were discussed in detail back in *Chapter 7*, but let's recap here. A namespace allows us, as developers, to organize our programming components into categories. For instance, imagine multiple Web services that perform various tasks for specific parts of an application. If you were working on a 'Purchasing' module for an accounting system, you could specify a `Purchasing` namespace within all of your Web service files pertaining to purchasing-related tasks.

That way, if you have a Web service called `Reporting`, and Joe, in the 'Accounts Receivable' module, has a similarly named service, you can declare your namespace (in applications that use it) as `Purchasing.ReportingWS`. Joe can declare his namespace as `AccountsReceivable.ReportingWS`, and the two will not conflict.

Now, let's take a look at how the requests and responses are sent to and from a Web service.

HTTP, XML, and Web Services

Chapter 3 discussed the basic mechanism by which information is passed back and forth across the Web. We can pop a URL in our browser's address bar and request a Web page from a remote server. We also pointed out that ASP.NET Web services rely on the same mechanism – namely the HTTP Request-Response system. All the information submitted to a Web service is sent as an HTTP Request. Likewise, any information received from the Web service is via HTTP Response (see Figure 16-5):

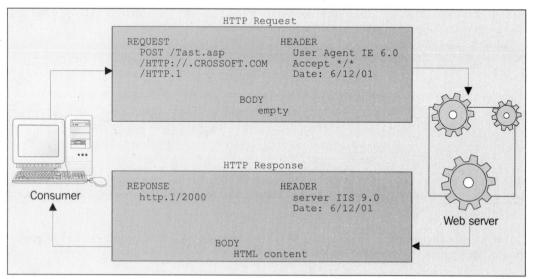

Figure 16-5

You've already seen that a typical Web service operates by accepting input from a consumer, and using it to produce a result that is sent back to the consumer as XML. When a consumer makes use of Web service logic, it takes the form of an HTTP Request – that's why it's so easy to access from a Web browser, which is tailor-made for such requests. An HTTP Request consists of packets of information that are sent to the Web service (wherever it may reside). These packets contain:

❑ Vital information such as the Web service's URL and the fact that we're submitting a Request (that is, initiating a data exchange that requires a Response, rather than simply Responding to someone else's Request).

❑ Details regarding the amount of information being sent.

❑ The type of document we require back from the Web service.

❑ Information about the consumer, the request date, general configuration statistics, and the data itself.

The Web service will return an HTTP Response with:

❑ A return address for the consumer, and the fact that it's submitting a Response and hence doesn't expect any further action from the recipient.

❑ A success or failure status code indicating whether or not the Web service received a valid Request from the consumer.

❑ Configuration information.

❑ Any appropriate data.

We can transmit HTTP Requests and Responses between a Web service and a consumer as many times as we like, depending on how the interaction between the two has been designed.

So, how exactly does the submitted data get wrapped up in this bundle of HTTP information? As discussed in *Chapter 3*, there are two ways to submit information within an HTTP Request, using the GET and POST methods respectively – let's do a quick recap.

HTTP GET

This is the simplest way to send data to the client, and probably the most familiar to users of the Web. Simple, unstructured information is bundled in with the page as a sequence of *name-value pairs*. These pairings are a simple way to combine all the values into a single string. We can use the Request.QueryString collection in our ASP.NET code to access these name-value pairs on the server.

When you tested the Greetings.Hello Web method, the built-in testing mechanism provided by ASP.NET used HTTP GET to submit the string Vervain to the Web service. Here's the actual GET request that your browser used to access the Web service:

```
GET /BegASPNET11/Ch16/greetings.asmx/Hello?Name=Vervain HTTP/1.1
Host: localhost
```

It specifies the GET method, states the requested page (including the directory path) along with your query string, and declares that it has structured the HTTP Request according to version 1.1 of HTTP. It then states the name of the host to which it wants the request submitted – in this case, the local machine. The resource requested is:

```
/BegASPNET11/Ch16/greetings.asmx/Hello?Name=Vervain
```

This path along with the `Host` value to get a full URL:

```
localhost/BegASPNET11/Ch16/greetings.asmx/Hello?Name=Vervain
```

The corresponding Response simply specifies the content type we're returning (`text/xml`) along with the character set and content length. The body of the Response also contains the XML we saw earlier:

```
HTTP/1.1 200 OK
Content-Type: text/xml; charset=utf-8
Content-Length: 112
<?xml version="1.0" encoding="utf-8"?>
<string xmlns="http://tempuri.org/">
Hello, Vervain. Have a great day!</string>
```

> Notice that the Response contains our desired message within a **<string>** tag, which is the return type specified in the function.

The Response from the server is a `200` message, which is the HTTP's success message.

> Another common return code is **404**, which indicates 'File not found'. Our HTTP Response from the server can also give us information such as the Web server software, the number of bytes to expect, content type, and the type of cookie that will be set.

Note that it's very easy to make a new request to our Web service by simply editing the query string in the browser's address bar. You might like to try calling up your page again as follows:

http://localhost/BegASPNET11/Ch16/greetings.asmx/Hello?Name=my%20fine%20fellow

HTTP POST

While HTTP `GET` uses the end of the URL to pass its information from resource to resource, HTTP `POST` uses the body of the Request to carry the same name-value pairs. You can retrieve these values using the `Request.Form` collection in ASP.NET. If you use the `POST` method to send the information, it means that the information isn't visible in the URL. This provides a slightly more secure method, since it is possible to manipulate the name-value pairs when using the `GET` method, by just typing names and values into the query string in the address bar.

Here is an example of an equivalent `POST` message being sent to the Web server:

```
POST /57084/ch16/greetings.asmx/Hello HTTP/1.1
Host: localhost
Content-Type: application/x-www-form-urlencoded
```

```
Content-Length: 15
Name=Vervain
HTTP/1.1 200 OK
```

This time, the HTTP Request specifies the POST method before stating the page requested and the HTTP version. It states the host name and content type (usually this is application/x-www-form-urlencoded) and the content length, which now tells the server how many bytes of name-value pairs are there. This is followed by the name-value pairs themselves placed on a separate line. The corresponding response from the Web server is exactly the same as you saw when using the GET method, returning a simple XML document in the Response body, along with the result that our Web method placed inside a <string> element.

That's all well and good so far, but using either HTTP POST or GET is rather limiting. Since we ultimately want to use these Web methods to replace various local method calls in applications, we surely need to be able to pass data sets and other complex objects.

This is where XML comes into the picture. XML plays a vital role in Web services, as it allows us to send simple, structured, self-describing data between many different computer platforms and setups.

Web services, therefore, use XML to describe data sent from the consumer, as well as data being returned. It can also be used to describe the parameters that a Web service expects, and how to find information on Web services that is available to consumers on the Internet. We will look into these topics in detail later in the chapter.

While XML is very easy to read and understand – handy when you debug the code – it can often be verbose. This is because even the simplest of data exchanges requires a significant amount of description (since while exchanging all types and structures of data, we must cater to the lowest common denominator). With a common protocol (HTTP/ HTTPS, or even SMTP) and a common language (XML) that transcends individual machine platforms and operating systems (OSs), Web services can be a potentially powerful tool

However, a drawback is that the common protocol HTTP was only designed for calling up Web pages, and returning information as HTML. Web services were built with the aim of returning more complex information than just Web pages. To handle the call and response of Web services, another protocol was needed.

Simple Object Access Protocol (SOAP)

The *Simple Object Access Protocol* provides an effective way to call Web services remotely and to return information either in the form of numeric, string variables, datasets, images, or even files. It wraps up the information inside an XML element known as a *SOAP envelope*, and frees us from most of the structural limitations imposed by the HTTP methods discussed earlier. You can send a request and also receive a response using a SOAP envelope. Here's what a SOAP envelope making a request looks like:

```
POST /57084/ch16/greetings.asmx HTTP/1.1
Host: localhost
Content-Type: text/xml; charset=utf-8
Content-Length: length
SOAPAction: "http://tempuri.org/Hello"
```

```
<?xml version="1.0" encoding="utf-8"?>
<soap:Envelope
    xmlns:xsi="http://www.w3.org/2001/XMLSchema-instance"
    xmlns:xsd="http://www.w3.org/2001/XMLSchema"
    xmlns:soap="http://schemas.xmlsoap.org/soap/envelope/">
  <soap:Body>
    <Hello xmlns="http://tempuri.org/">
      <Name>Vervain</Name>
    </Hello>
  </soap:Body>
</soap:Envelope>
```

The submitted string value Vervain is held in a <Nazme> element (identifying the specific parameter being specified in the Web method call) and this is nested within a <Hello> element (identifying the name of the method called). Admittedly, at this stage it hardly looks more complex than our previous Requests, but that's largely due to the fact that you're only passing a single string value. Once you start sending more complex items of data there will be more to see. When items such as data sets are sent, the SOAP envelope needs to be larger and more detailed to describe the information contained within.

Apart from being somewhat more explicit about your request, this approach also allows you to submit data in a well defined structure. Even if you wanted to submit a huge array of complex data objects, the flexibility inherent within this SOAP envelope allows you to do it. Although the SOAP Request is submitted as part of an HTTP POST Request, it's totally separate and selfcontained.

> **As SOAP allows us to use other protocols, we're not tied to HTTP as a transport protocol. For example, it's quite possible to send this envelope to the Web service via SMTP (that is, simply e-mail it to the Web service). While this is a fascinating and extremely useful option, it's beyond the scope of this book. If you're interested in finding out more about this topic, refer** *Professional ASP.NET 1.1 (Wrox Press, ISBN 0-7645-5890-0).*

The SOAP response takes a form similar to our request:

```
HTTP/1.1 200 OK
Content-Type: text/xml; charset=utf-8
Content-Length: length
<?xml version="1.0" encoding="utf-8"?>
<soap:Envelope
    xmlns:xsi="http://www.w3.org/2001/XMLSchema-instance"
    xmlns:xsd="http://www.w3.org/2001/XMLSchema"
    xmlns:soap="http://schemas.xmlsoap.org/soap/envelope/">
  <soap:Body>
    <HelloResponse xmlns="http://tempuri.org/">
      <HelloResult>Hello, Vervain. Have a great day!</HelloResult>
    </HelloResponse>
  </soap:Body>
</soap:Envelope>
```

You can see that the Response string is the result of a call to the Hello method. Again, this result could just as easily take the form of some sort of structured data, and isn't tied to the HTTP response in any way.

When you use Web services within your ASP.NET logic, SOAP is used as the default protocol. Although it seems a little more bulky than the other options, it's the only mechanism that makes it possible to use Web methods directly, in a flexible manner , and seamlessly from within the code.

Building an ASP.NET Web Service

Let's take a more detailed look at putting a Web service together. We'll also begin to explore the possible uses for Web services.

You can define a Web service by simply writing a few lines of code and placing them inside a file with a .asmx extension. This extension tells Web Matrix that a Web service is being defined. You can create a Web service just like a standard ASP.NET page, using Web Matrix (as we did earlier in the chapter) or any text editor. A Web service must contain four essential parts:

❑ Processing directive.

❑ Namespaces.

❑ Public class.

❑ Web methods.

Let's look at each of these in turn.

Processing Directive

Within the empty ASMX file (the required file type for an ASP.NET Web service page), you must let the Web server know that you're creating a Web service. To do this, enter a directive at the top of your page with the following syntax (in fact, Web Matrix creates this automatically based on the information submitted in the startup dialog):

```
<%@ WebService Language="language" Class="classname"%>
```

This statement appears at the top of an ASP.NET source file to tell the .NET Framework about any settings or constraints that should be applied to whatever object is generated from the file. In this case, the directive tells the compiler the language in which the Web service is written, and the name of the class in which it is defined. This class might reside in the same file, or within a separate file (which must be in the \bin directory, immediately beneath the Web application root in which the Web service lives).

Namespaces

You can make use of other file's logic within your ASMX page by specifying appropriate namespaces. In this case, you can use the C# using command:

```
using System;
using System.Web.Services;
using System.Xml.Serialization;
```

Web services require importing these namespaces as an absolute minimum, because they contain the classes needed for Web services to handle network connection issues and other OS-related tasks.

Public Class

A `public class` acts as a container for the methods in our Web service:

```
public class ClassName
{
   ...
}
```

> **The name of this class is effectively the name of the Web service. Therefore, it should correspond to the Class value specified in the processing directive.**

Essentially, we're just defining an object whose methods will be exposed over the Web. This will ultimately allow us to make remote method calls over the Internet. To our server, these calls look like method calls to the same machine where the consuming application resides.

Web Methods

The methods exposed for consumption over the Internet are known as *Web-callable methods* or simply *Web methods*. By definition, a Web service will expose one or more Web methods – of course it can have other non-Web methods as well, and these can be protected as needed so that consumers cannot use them directly. The syntax varies slightly depending upon the language used, but they all tend to follow a similar structure. In C#, it is as follows:

```
[WebMethod]
public string Hello(string strName)
```

> **We only place the `WebMethod` declaration before the functions that we wish to expose to consumers. Those without this declaration cannot be seen.**

`WebMethod` attribute can take parameters of its own. Thus you can set various properties that modify the activity of the attribute. This allows us to customize our Web methods in various ways; for example, we can use `CacheDuration` to set the number of seconds for which the `WebMethod` will cache its results. If a consumer requests a result from the Web Service within the time specified in this attribute, `WebMethod` will retrieve the cached copy of these values instead of retrieving them from the original source:

```
[WebMethod(CacheDuration:= 5)]
public string Hello(string strName)
{
   ...
```

For more information on `WebMethod` attributes, such as `CacheDuration`, please visit: www.microsoft.com/library/default.asp.

When you build a Web service, a lot of time will be spent creating a Web method for the Web service. It is possible to include more than one Web method in an ASMX file, as you'll see in the next example.

Try It Out Creating a Web Service with Multiple Web Methods

This Web service contains four Web methods that convert inches to centimeters, centimeters to inches, miles to kilometers, and kilometers to miles.

1. Create an XML Web service in Web Matrix called `measurementconversions.asmx` and enter MeasurementConversions as the class, Ch16 as the namespace, and add the following code:

```
<%@ WebService language="C#" class="MeasurementsConversions" %>

using System;
using System.Web.Services;
using System.Xml.Serialization;
public class MeasurementsConversions
{
    [WebMethod(Description="Convert Inches To Centimeters")]
    public decimal InchesToCentimeters(decimal decInches) {
      return decInches * 2.54m;
    }
    [WebMethod(Description="Convert Centimeters to Inches")]
    public decimal CentimetersToInches(decimal decCentimeters) {
      return decCentimeters / 2.54m;
    }
    [WebMethod(Description="Convert Miles to Kilometers")]
    public decimal MilesToKilometers(decimal decMiles) {
      return decMiles * 1.61m;
    }
    [WebMethod(Description="Convert Kilometers to Miles")]
    public decimal KilometersToMiles(decimal decKilometers) {
      return decKilometers / 1.61m;
    }
}
```

2. Call it up in your browser and you should see something like Figure 16-6:

Figure 16-6

Let's look at the code for a moment. We'll get back to the testing of our Web service after this.

How It Works

In this example, we created a Web service that converts between Imperial (English) measurements and Metric measurements. The first line tells us that the file is a Web service written in C#. We have a class name of MeasurementConversions that will be used by consumers to make references to the Web service:

```
<%@ WebService language="C#" class="MeasurementsConversions" %>
```

Next, we import the namespace that allows us to refer to Web service objects without using fully qualified names:

```
using System;
using System.Web.Services;
using System.Xml.Serialization;
```

We then name our class to match the processing directive class name. We'll need to know this when we are ready to make remote calls to the Web service through a consumer:

```
public class MeasurementConversions
```

Finally, consider the actual Web methods. These are separate functions that can be called within a Web service to return a result. The first Web method receives a Decimal value in inches and converts it to a Decimal value in centimeters using the standard conversion formula. The second receives a Decimal in centimeters and converts it to inches in the same manner:

```
[WebMethod(Description="Convert Inches To Centimeters")]
public decimal InchesToCentimeters(decimal decInches) {
    return decInches * 2.54m;
}
[WebMethod(Description="Convert Centimeters to Inches")]
public decimal CentimetersToInches(decimal decCentimeters) {
    return decCentimeters / 2.54m;
}
```

The third and fourth Web methods perform similar conversions from miles to kilometers and kilometers to miles respectively:

```
[WebMethod(Description="Convert Miles to Kilometers")]
public decimal MilesToKilometers(decimal decMiles) {
    return decMiles * 1.61m;
}
[WebMethod(Description="Convert Kilometers to Miles")]
public decimal KilometersToMiles(decimal decKilometers) {
    return decKilometers / 1.61m;
}
```

We've now created a complete Web service by using the processing directive, adding namespaces, and creating Web methods. Now the big question is 'How do we know it works?' It's time to put it through its paces.

Testing Your Web Service

To test Web services, all you need is an Internet connection and a browser. In the browser address bar, just enter the URL of the Web service in the following format:

http://[path]/[webservice].asmx

The first time the Web service is accessed, the code will compile on the Web server, and a new browser window will appear containing some very helpful diagnostic information. This Web service Description page allows us to impersonate a consumer and enter input values to send to the Web service. The page contains the following information about the Web service:

❑ **Web method names**: Names of the Web service's Web-callable functions.

❑ **Request parameters**: The names of all the inputs that the Web service expects a consumer to supply.

❑ **Response Type**: The data type of the result sent by the Web service to a consumer (such as `integer`, `string`, `float`, and `object`).

❑ **Fields**: These can be used to enter test values.

You'll also see the following message at the top of the test page:

The following operations are supported. For a formal definition, please review the Service Description.

The *Service Description* is a comprehensive technical description of all the functionality exposed by the Web service. You'll be taking a closer look at it later on in the chapter. For the time being, we're only interested in testing our Web service. Let's now go back and see what happens when we test our `measurementconversions` Web service.

Try It Out Conversions Test Page

1. Assuming your browser is still open, just click on the MilesToKilometers hyperlink and enter a test value of 60 in the decMiles value field, as shown in Figure 16-7:

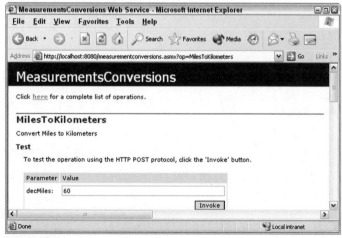

Figure 16-7

2. Click Invoke, and a new browser window appears, containing our result in kilometers in XML format. This is shown in Figure 16-8:

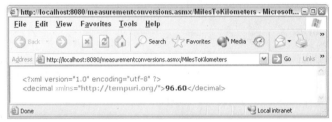

Figure 16-8

3. In the original .asmx page, click on the word here at the top of the test page, and you'll return to the original test screen. You can now repeat this procedure for the other methods shown on the page.

How It Works

When we browse to the test page, we see a screen containing the name of our Web service and underneath it, a list of the methods that it exposes. These method names are hyperlinks. When we click on MilesToKilometers, the Web method test section will appear in the browser window. We are given the name of the parameter (decMiles), and an associated field to enter the test value.

> The data type for `MilesToKilometers` is a decimal. This is the value that our `measurementconversions` Web service expects from a consumer.

Once the value is entered, we can press the Invoke button to execute the Web method. By doing this, we are impersonating a consuming application. The entered test value (60) is passed using HTTP as a request, to the `MilesToKilometers` Web method. The value will be multiplied by 1.61 and returned as a decimal. The result is in XML.

You might say, "Sure, our test page tells *us* what the Web service's expectations are. But how would a consumer know what they are?" This consumer might not necessarily be another user, it could be an application and then the expectations need to be explicitly defined.

The next section discusses how to know what a Web service requires, what it produces, and how a consumer can communicate with it.

Using Your Web Service

As you've learned, it's essential for consumers to know what parameters to send to a Web service and what values to expect it to return. To accomplish this, a *Web service Description Language (WSDL)* file is used. This is an XML file that defines how the interaction between a Web service and its consumer will occur. WSDL is a standard managed by the W3 standards organization, and you can find more details about it at http://www.w3.org/TR/wsdl.

The impact of this WSDL standard is enormous. WSDL is able to define all the interactions of a Web service regardless of whether the service is running in ASP.NET or Java, and regardless of whether it is running on Windows or UNIX.

It means that in future you won't need to be concerned with whether our services, or languages, are compatible across platforms. This would allow us to concentrate on the real issue of writing robust and functional code. WSDL will take care of declaring the interaction for us.

For instance, if a Web service expects two specific parameters and returns a single value, the WSDL defines the names, order, and data types of each input and output value. Since we know where to find the Web service using its URL, we don't need to know the physical location or the internal logic of the Web service. With WSDL, we have all the information necessary to begin making use of the Web service functionality within our applications. It's really that simple!

Let's take a quick look at what a WSDL contract looks like using our `MeasurementConversion` Web service.

Try It Out   Viewing the WSDL Contract

1.   Enter the path http://localhost/measurementconversions.asmx in your browser's address bar and click on the Service Description hyperlink at the top of the page. You should see a screen similar to Figure 16-9:

Figure 16-9

How It Works

As you can see, there's a lot of information in here and this is just the collapsed view! Our Web method message names along with the various HTTP GET, HTTP POST, and SOAP message structures are displayed. These message formats contain the requirements for a consumer to know what parameters are needed to communicate with a Web service using each message structure.

At the top, the following declaration indicates that the WSDL file is in XML format:

```
<?xml version="1.0" encoding="utf-8" ?>
```

Below that declaration is the `<definitions>` element, which contains various namespaces. Most of these namespaces make a reference to SOAP, which we discussed earlier. These must be included in the file for SOAP to work correctly:

```
<definitions xmlns:http="http://schemas.xmlsoap.org/wsdl/http/"
xmlns:soap="http://schemas.xmlsoap.org/wsdl/soap/"
xmlns:s="http://www.w3.org/2001/XMLSchema" xmlns:s0="http://tempuri.org/"
xmlns:soapenc="http://schemas.xmlsoap.org/soap/encoding/"
xmlns:tm="http://microsoft.com/wsdl/mime/textMatching/"
xmlns:mime="http://schemas.xmlsoap.org/wsdl/mime/"
targetNamespace="http://tempuri.org/"
xmlns="http://schemas.xmlsoap.org/wsdl/">
```

Next, the `<types>` element defines each of the data types that the Web service expects to receive and return after completion. This is very complex, and almost a science in itself. It is written in *XML Schema Definition (XSD)* language. You can't see the definitions in the screenshot as its section is collapsed (like the others). All you need to do is click on the node in Internet Explorer in order to view them.

After this are the various one-way transmissions from a consumer to the Web service and back again. Our Web method message names are in here, and the various SOAP message structures are laid out. For example, on expanding the `<message>` element, we can see the `InchesToCentimeters` Web method message structures for SOAP:

```
<message name="InchesToCentimetersSoapIn">
<part name="parameters" element="s0:InchesToCentimeters" />
</message>
<message name="InchesToCentimetersSoapOut">
<part name="parameters" element="s0:InchesToCentimetersResponse" />
</message>:
```

In short, this file contains all of the information necessary to communicate with our Web service. Now that you've seen the process of building and communicating with XML Web services in detail, let's create something a bit more complex.

The next example will accept a value, and return a result using ADO.NET to retrieve data from an Access database.

Try It Out   ISBN Search Web Service

Let's create a Web service that returns the title of a book, based on an ISBN that the consumer provides. This will allow our librarian to add a function on the library's Web page that enables users to search by consuming this Web service.

This particular service will access a database of books. The database contains information on ISBN and book titles. Once the details are received from the database, the results will be inserted into a `DataReader` and returned to the consumer in XML.

This example uses the `Library.mdb` Access database, which you can download along with the code samples for this book from www.wrox.com. You should ensure that the file is in the same location as the Web service that you create.

1. Create an XML Web service called `ISBN.asmx` in Web Matrix, entering **ISBN** as the class name and **Ch16** as the **Namespace**.

2. Add the following `using` statements to the beginning of the file:

```
<%@ WebService Language="C#" Class="ISBN" %>
using System;
using System.Web.Services;
using System.Xml.Serialization;
using System.Data;
using System.Data.OleDb;
```

3. Add the following code to enable the Web service:

```
public class ISBN : System.Web.Services.WebService
{
  [WebMethod]
  public string BookDetail(string strIsbn)
  {
    return GetBookDetails(strIsbn);
  }
```

4. Enter the following code directly after the `BookDetail` Web method. This function performs the database lookup and returns the book title string:

```
  private string GetBookDetails(string strIsbn)
  {
    OleDbDataReader objLibraryDR = null;
    OleDbConnection objLibraryConn = null;
    OleDbCommand objLibraryCmd = null;
    string strConn = "Provider=Microsoft.Jet.OLEDB.4.0;Data Source=" +
                              Server.MapPath("Library.mdb") + ";";
    string strSQL = "SELECT Title FROM Books WHERE ISBN = '" + strIsbn +
                                                              "'";
    string strBookTitle;
    objLibraryConn = new OleDbConnection(strConn);
    objLibraryCmd = new OleDbCommand(strSQL, objLibraryConn);
    objLibraryConn.Open();
    objLibraryDR =
            objLibraryCmd.ExecuteReader(CommandBehavior.CloseConnection);
    if (objLibraryDR.Read())
    {
      strBookTitle = objLibraryDR[0].ToString();
    }
    else
    {
      strBookTitle = "Book not found in the database";
    }
    objLibraryDR.Close();
    return strBookTitle;
  }
}
```

5. Once you have completed this code entry, test your Web service. Save the file, and then browse to http://localhost/ISBN.asmx.

6. Within the Isbn field, enter the ISBN 0764557076. A new browser window will appear, containing XML shown in Figure 16-10:

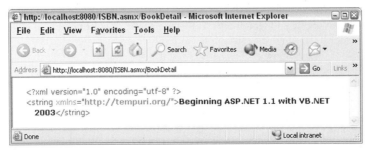

Figure 16-10

How It Works

Our Web service provides what is technically known as a 'level of abstraction'. This means that the code that does the work of finding our information isn't taken care of by the Web-callable BookDetails method. Instead, BookDetails calls another internal function that consumers can't see. This function, GetBookDetails, does the work of finding the book information, and then returns it to BookDetails, which returns it to us:

```
[WebMethod]
public string BookDetail(string strIsbn)
{
   return GetBookDetails(strIsbn);
}

private string GetBookDetails(string strIsbn)
{
   ...
}
```

This is done because the job of the GetBookDetails function remains the same, regardless of the source making the request. The same function may be called from a non-Web service source. Also, we certainly wouldn't want to maintain two separate functions that do the same thing, the difference being only the [WebMethod] declaration.

We're using ADO.NET to connect to the Library.mdb database, retrieve a book title from its Books table based on the ISBN, and store it in a string variable. Keeping the data request simple, we define a connection string (Conn), and then open the connection to the database (with LibraryConn):

```
objLibraryConn = new OleDbConnection(strConn);
objLibraryCmd = new OleDbCommand(strSQL, objLibraryConn);
objLibraryConn.Open();
```

Using the `LibraryCmd` object, we execute the query for a specific ISBN, placing the results in the `LibraryDr` DataReader. Then we close the connection:

```
objLibraryDR =
        objLibraryCmd.ExecuteReader(CommandBehavior.CloseConnection);
```

We then check whether a row was returned, by calling the `Read` method of our `DataReader`, `LibraryDr`. If it returns `true`, we take the first column (column zero, the `Title` column of the database) from the `DataReader` and place it into `BookTitle`. If it returns `false`, we know that the book was not found, and we place a 'not found' message in the title value. Then we close our `DataReader` and return the book title string:

```
if (objLibraryDR.Read())
    {
      strBookTitle = objLibraryDR[0].ToString();
    }
    else
    {
      strBookTitle = "Book not found in the database";
    }
    objLibraryDR.Close();
    return strBookTitle;
```

For more information on working with data sources, please refer to *Chapters 8* and *9*.

Consuming a Web Service

You've created some Web services from start to finish using a variety of technologies. The next step is to understand how to include this functionality within a consumer application. To do this, you must first create an interface that will allow the consumer to see all of the Web-callable methods and properties exposed by the Web service. This saves the headache of ensuring that your parameters are the correct type and having to create our own protocol request and response handlers. This interface is called a Web service *proxy*.

How Does a Proxy Work?

A proxy resides on the consumer's machine and acts as a relay between the consumer and the Web service. When building a proxy, we use a WSDL file (we'll examine the source shortly) to create a map that tells the consumer what methods are available and how to call them. The consumer then calls the Web method that is mapped in the proxy, which in turn, makes calls to the actual Web service over the Internet. The proxy (and not the consumer) handles all of the network related work, the sending of data, as well as managing the underlying WSDL. When we reference the Web service in the consumer application, it looks as if it's part of the consumer application itself. Figure 16-11 illustrates this process:

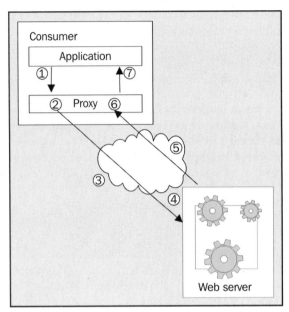

Figure 16-11

The function works as follows:

1. The application executes a function in the proxy code, passing any appropriate parameters to it, without being concerned that the proxy is going to call a Web service.

2. The proxy receives this call, and formulates the request that will be sent to the Web service, using the parameters the consumer has specified.

3. This function call is sent from the proxy to the Web service. This call can be within the confines of the same machine, across a *Local Area Network (LAN)*, or across the Internet. The method of calling remains the same.

4. The Web service uses the parameters provided by the proxy to execute its Web-callable function and build the result in XML.

5. The resulting data from the Web service is returned to the proxy at the consumer end.

6. The proxy parses the XML returned from the Web service to retrieve the individual values generated. These values may be as simple as integers and strings, or they may define more complex data types.

7. Your application receives the expected values from the proxy function, completely unaware that they resulted from a Web service call.

To make use of a Web service from an ASP.NET page, your proxy must be created and compiled appropriately. You can create a proxy to a Web service using either Web Matrix or a command line tool called WSDL.exe provided in the .NET Framework SDK. Both of these methods make use of WSDL to create a proxy, built in the language of your choice. We'll create a new ASP.NET application, which will access our new ISBN Web service using Web Matrix as it is easier to use.

Creating a Proxy

Building a proxy is a two-step process:

1. Generate the proxy source code automatically.
2. Compile the proxy into a runtime library.

Try It Out Accessing the ISBN Web Service from an ASP.NET Page

In this example, you will build the proxy and a simple page for retrieving book titles from the ISBN Web service, demonstrating how quickly your Web service applications can be up and running.

1. Open the ISBN.asmx file you just created in Web Matrix.
2. Go to the Tools menu and select Web service Proxy Generator.
3. Fill in the dialog that appears, as shown in Figure 16-12:

Figure 16-12

4. You've created the proxy class in C#, and defined the ISBNService namespace. By selecting a namespace, you will be able to reference your proxy class from within your consuming application. The proxy is contained in a file called ISBNProxy.cs. At the same time, Web Matrix has also performed the second stage. It has taken the ISBNProxy.cs and compiled it to create a DLL file that can be referenced within the code. Once this process is finished, you should see the dialog shown in Figure 16-13:

Figure 16-13

5. Now that we have a proxy class and a DLL. We're ready to make use of the ISBN Web service from within an ASP.NET page. We'll call the `BookInfo.aspx` page, and use it to call the Web-callable function `BookDetail` in `ISBN.asmx`. By using a proxy, the reference to the function's namespace will appear as if it was a function within the same page. So, create a new ASPX file called `BookInfo.aspx` in Web Matrix, in the folder `C:\BegASPNET11\Ch16`.

6. Click on the All window and enter the following code:

```
<%@ Page Language="C#" Debug="true"%>
<%@ Import namespace="ISBNService" %>
<script Language="C#" runat="server">
private void RetrieveBook(object sender, EventArgs e)
{
  ISBNService.ISBN ws = new ISBNService.ISBN();
  lblBookTitle.Text = ws.BookDetail(txtISBN.Text);
}
</script>
<html>
  <body>
  <form id="Form1" method="post" runat="server">
      Enter an ISBN number to search on:
      <br />
      <asp:TextBox id="txtISBN" runat="server"></asp:TextBox>
      <br />
      <asp:Button id="Button1" runat="server" Text="Submit" _
          OnClick="RetrieveBook"></asp:Button><br />
      <asp:Label id="lblBookTitle" runat="server" Width="152px" _
                      Height="23px"></asp:Label>
  </form>
  </body>
</html>
```

7. Save the file and run it in your browser. You should see the screen shown in Figure 16-14:

Figure 16-14

8. Enter an ISBN that we know is in the `Books` table, like the ISBN for this book (0764557084) and you'll see something like Figure 16-15:

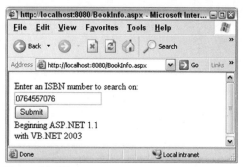

Figure 16-15

9. Now try an ISBN that you know will not be found, to ensure that the proxy is actually working; see Figure 16-16:

Figure 16-16

How It Works

Before Web Matrix came along, we had to use `WSDL.exe` to generate a proxy class and use a command line compiler to compile the proxy class, and to create the `ISBNProxy.dll`. This is no longer the case as we can use Web Matrix to perform these two distinct operations in one step. Set the options in the dialog as follows:

❑ **WSDL URL**: The location of the Web service.

❑ **Namespace**: The name by which you can reference the Web service in your ASP.NET code.

❑ **Language**: The language the proxy class should be generated in.

❑ **OutputDirectory**: The place where both the proxy class and the assembly should be placed.

❑ **SourceFile**: The name of the proxy class.

❑ **GenerateAssembly**: The name of the DLL.

These options ensured that we create the DLL so that it works correctly, and can be added to our ASP.NET page.

In our ASP.NET page, we made use of Web Form controls. These controls – `<asp:TextBox>`, `<asp:Label>`, and `<asp:Button>` – make up the simple form that makes a very specific call to the `BookDetail` function.

Upon clicking the **Submit** button, the `RetrieveBook` event fires, as specified in the `OnClick` attribute of `<asp:Button>`:

```
<asp:Button id="Button1" runat="server" Text="Submit"
            OnClick="RetrieveBook" /></asp:Button>
```

Within the `RetrieveBook` function, first of all, we create an instance of the proxy class that we'll be using:

```
ISBNService.ISBN ws = new ISBNService.ISBN();
```

Then it's simply a matter of calling the `BookDetail` function of the `ws` object. Remember the previous example where we created the Web method:

```
[WebMethod]
public string BookDetail(string strIsbn)
{
   return GetBookDetails(strIsbn);
}
```

Here we are actually accessing the same Web Method from our ASPX page. `ISBNService.ISBN` refers to our automatically created DLL file, which is used to communicate with the ASMX Web service file created from the previous example. So once we've created our `ws` object using the DLL, we can use all the Web methods of the object as though they were normal methods.

With a single line of code, we pass the string contents of `txtISBN.text` to the Web service and receive the book title, placing that string into the label `lblBookTitle.text`:

```
lblBookTitle.Text = ws.BookDetail(txtISBN.Text);
```

Once again, this example proved the simplicity and power of Web services.

Creating a Web Service for the Wrox United Application

The process for creating a Web service, although relatively easy, can be quite lengthy. So far the examples have been kept as simple as possible. In fact, the previous example might seem like a long winded way to go about just returning a single string from our database. The power of Web services lies in the ability to return more complex items than just single items of data.

We'll now build a Web Method that links back to the Wrox United application and use it to return a set of results. In fact, the Web service will prompt you for the name of a team, scour the database for the score from the most recent game, and return that to the user. For the sake of simplicity and compatibility, we'll still take these results and output them as a single string. However, this string will be created from a concatenation of both integer and string values that have been gleaned from the database. It is possible to return this information as a dataset. There isn't a standard way to return a dataset, so by returning our information as a string, we make it easily consumable to users on all platforms, because a dataset on Windows can be completely different from a dataset returned by a database on a UNIX server.

Before building the Web method though, we're going to add a results page to the Wrox United application. This page's functionality is unrelated to Web services, so let's see how it works. We'll borrow some of the data-reading routines from this page and use this within our Web method to extract a single result from the database.

Try It Out   Adding a Results Page

1. Open up Web Matrix and create a new `.aspx` page called `results.aspx`.

2. Next, download the code for `results.aspx` from http://www.wrox.com – we're not going to reproduce it here as it is over five pages long!

3. Alter the `navbar.ascx` navigation bar, so that it points to the new `results.aspx` page. Amend the code as follows:

```
...
<p>
    <asp:HyperLink id="lnkGames" runat="server"
     NavigateUrl="Default.aspx">Upcoming Games
     </asp:HyperLink>
</p>
<p>
    <asp:HyperLink id="lnkResults" runat="server"
    NavigateUrl="results.aspx">Results
     </asp:HyperLink>
</p>
<p>
    <asp:HyperLink id="lnkChat" runat="server"
    NavigateUrl="Chat.aspx">Chat
     </asp:HyperLink>
</p>
...
```

4. Now, open the Wrox United Application and browse to the `results.aspx` page, as shown in Figure 1617:

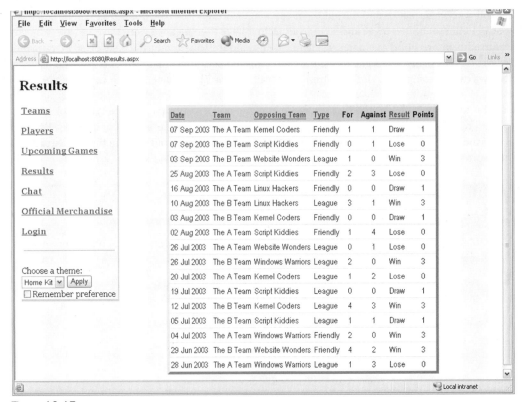

Figure 16-17

5. You can now see a complete list of the results of the games played. If you click on the column heading, it will sort the results by the appropriate column.

How It Works

We're only going to look at the data reading routine in the `TeamResults` function. We create a seemingly massive variable query string that takes an enormous SQL statement. The SQL statement isn't as scary as it looks:

```
string queryString = "SELECT [Games].[Date], [Games].[WroxGoals], " +
                     "[Games].[OpponentGoals], [Teams].[TeamName], " +
                     "[Opponents].[OpponentName], [GameTypes].[GameType],"+
                     "[Games].[GameID] [GameTypes]" +
                     "FROM [Games], [Teams], [Opponents]," +
                     "WHERE (([Games].[WroxTeam] = [Teams].[TeamID]) AND " +
                     "([Games].[OpposingTeam] = [Opponents].[OpponentID])" +
                     "AND ([Games].[GameType] = [GameTypes].[GameTypeID])" +
                     "AND ([Games].[Date] < now())) ORDER BY " +
                     "+ SortExp  + SortDir;"
```

Basically the SQL statement gets the date, opponent goals, team-name, opponent name, type of game and game identifier from the Games table. However, as this information is spread across the Games, Teams, Opponents, and GamesType tables, we have to perform joins to the Games table to extract this information. If you're not familiar with SQL don't worry, you don't need to be. You just need to understand that this query (a slightly modified version) will form the heart of our Web service, as this is exactly the information we need to extract. The only difference is that we want to extract only one result as opposed to a whole set of results.

The rest of the code in this function just creates a Command object and supplies the QueryString variable as the CommandText. It then runs the ExecuteReader method and returns the dataset as a DataReader object:

```
System.Data.IDbCommand dbCommand = new System.Data.OleDb.OleDbCommand();
dbCommand.CommandText = queryString;
dbCommand.Connection = dbConnection;

dbConnection.Open;
System.Data.IDataReader dataReader =
  dbCommand.ExecuteReader(System.Data.CommandBehavior.CloseConnection);
return dataReader;
}
```

This is exactly what we'll be doing .

Try It Out   Creating The Web Service

1. Open Web Matrix and create a new latestscore.asmx XML Web service with the class name as **LatestScore** and the namespace as **WroxUnited**.

2. Add the following code into the window making sure that it replaces all of the default code created by Web Matrix:

```
<%@ WebService language="c#" class="LatestScore" %>
using System;
using System.Web.Services;
using System.Xml.Serialization;
using System.Data;
using System.Data.OleDb;
using System.Configuration;
//Inherit the WebService class that provides all the built-in features
//that are needed to create a Web Service.
public class LatestScore : System.Web.Services.WebService
{
    [WebMethod]
    public string ReturnScore(string Team)
    {
        return GetLatestScore(Team);
    }
    private string GetLatestScore(string Team)
```

```
{
        //Declare the database access objects
        OleDbDataReader LibraryDr;
        OleDbConnection LibraryConn;
        OleDbCommand LibraryCmd;

        //Declare the connection string that grants access to the database
        string Conn = ConfigurationSettings.AppSettings["ConnectionString"];

        //Declare the SQL that will be executed.
        string SQL = "SELECT [Games].[WroxGoals], [Games].[OpponentGoals], "+
                "[Opponents].[OpponentName], [Games].[Date] "+
                "FROM [Games], [Teams], [Opponents] "+
                "WHERE ((([Games].[WroxTeam] = [Teams].[TeamID]) AND "+
                "([Games].[OpposingTeam] = [Opponents].[OpponentID]) AND "+
                "([Teams].[TeamName] = \"" + Team + "\")) "+
                "ORDER BY [Games].[Date] DESC";
        string MaxDate,LatestScore, WroxGoals, OpponentGoals, TeamName,
          OpponentName;

        //Open the connection to the database.
        LibraryConn = new OleDbConnection(Conn);
        LibraryCmd = new OleDbCommand(SQL, LibraryConn);
        LibraryConn.Open();
        LibraryDr = LibraryCmd.ExecuteReader(CommandBehavior.CloseConnection);

        if (LibraryDr.Read())
        {
            MaxDate = Convert.ToString(LibraryDr["Date"]);
            WroxGoals = Convert.ToString (LibraryDr["WroxGoals"]);
            OpponentGoals = Convert.ToString (LibraryDr["OpponentGoals"]);
            OpponentName = Convert.ToString (LibraryDr["OpponentName"]);
            LatestScore = MaxDate + " - " + Team + " " + WroxGoals + " " +
                        OpponentName + " " + OpponentGoals;
        }
        else
        {
            //A row was not returned; this book does not exist.
            LatestScore = "The team cannot be found in the database";
        }

        LibraryDr.Close();
        return LatestScore;
    }

}
```

3. You can now test the Web service to see if it is working correctly. Go to
http://localhost/latestscore.asmx and browse the LatestScore link that appears, as shown in Figure
16-18. You should be asked for a single parameter – the team. This can be either The A team or
The B Team:

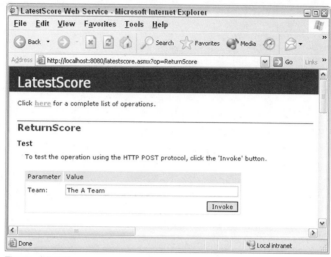

Figure 16-18

4. When you invoke this service, you should see the result shown in Figure 16-19:

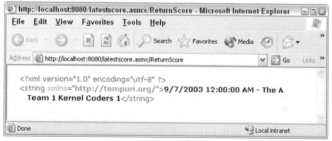

Figure 16-19

5. You'll get the score from the A Team vs Kernel Coders match that was played on the 7th of September. Go back to the `results.aspx` page and sort the columns by date. At the foot of the screen as shown in Figure 16-20, you'll see that this is indeed the most recent match played:

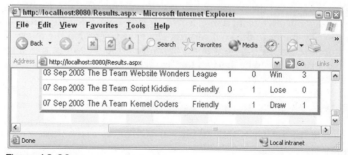

Figure 16-20

Go back and check the Web service for the B team and you'll see the result against the Script Kiddies, which is a 0-1 loss.

How It Works

Our Web service has a single Web Method that calls the `GetLatestScore` function and supplies it with a single parameter: the team name:

```
[WebMethod]
public string ReturnScore(string Team)
{
    return GetLatestScore(Team);
}
```

The `GetLatestScore` function does all the work. We start by initializing three objects that will return the data from the database: `OleDbDataReader`, `OleDbConnection`, and `OleDbCommand` .

```
OleDbDataReader LibraryDr;
OleDbConnection LibraryConn;
OleDbCommand LibraryCmd;
```

Next we create a connection string to the database, using the `AppSettings` from our `Web.Config` file:

```
string Conn = ConfigurationSettings.AppSettings["ConnectionString"];
```

The following line should also be familiar – it's where we create the query string that will be used to extract our results from the database:

```
string SQL = "SELECT [Games].[WroxGoals], [Games].[OpponentGoals], "+
        "[Opponents].[OpponentName],[Games].[Date] FROM "+
        "[Games], [Teams], [Opponents] WHERE ((([Games].[WroxTeam] = "+
        "[Teams].[TeamID]) AND ([Games].[OpposingTeam] = "
        "[Opponents].[OpponentID]) AND ([Teams].[TeamName] =  \"" +
        "Team + "\")) ORDER BY [Games].[Date] DESC";
```

What's different here is that we have added a clause that orders the columns returned by the final date. SQL provides its own parameters for returning maximum values, but in our case, it's easier to "cheat" by just sorting the data ourselves into the order that we want and then taking the last value only. This variable contains a query that gets the goals, opponent's goals, opponent team's name, and game date from the database, so it's a little bit simpler than the one used in `results.aspx`.

We create a condition so that only teams that match the team name supplied in the `Team` variable are returned. So if we have supplied the A Team, then it will only return the A team's results. In fact, we don't even need to return our own team name, as we already have been supplied that by the user, when they entered the team parameter to the Web service. Once we've created the query, we need to create a set of variables to store each of the different items of information in. Notice that they are all created as strings, although they don't have to be; it's just that we want to concatenate the information into one big string and it's easier to do it this way:

```
string MaxDate,LatestScore, WroxGoals, OpponentGoals, TeamName, OpponentName;
```

We open a connection to the database, and supply our SQL query to the `Command` object and run it against the database:

```
LibraryConn = new OleDbConnection(Conn);
LibraryCmd = new OleDbCommand(SQL, LibraryConn);
LibraryConn.Open();
LibraryDr = LibraryCmd.ExecuteReader(CommandBehavior.CloseConnection);
```

Now we're going to "cheat" to keep the code short. As mentioned in results.aspx, we return a dataset. Now in the last example, we performed a check for a single row of data. If we're returning a dataset, then more than a single row is returned. However, to avoid having to create an array of information, most of it unwanted, we read each row into the variables, and then overwrite each row:

```
if (LibraryDr.Read())
    {
        MaxDate = Convert.ToString(LibraryDr["Date"]);
        WroxGoals = Convert.ToString (LibraryDr["WroxGoals"]);
        OpponentGoals = Convert.ToString (LibraryDr["OpponentGoals"]);
        OpponentName = Convert.ToString (LibraryDr["OpponentName"]);
```

So the first row will read the dates, goals, and name information into our four variables. However, as pointed out earlier, we sorted the information in the SQL query. We sorted our information in ascending order, by date, and restricted it to the results of only one team. Thus, we know that the last line of information in the dataset must be the most recent line. Plenty of information is read into the variables, but it is overwritten. Only the most recent set of information is kept. As data readers move through datasets sequentially, and we have already sorted the dataset into ordered data, we know that only information from the last row – the one with the most recent date – is stored.

We concatenate this into the LatestScore variable:

```
LatestScore = MaxDate + " - " + Team + " " + WroxGoals + " " + OpponentName +
              " " + OpponentGoals;
```

We perform a check to make sure that the DataReader isn't empty. It would be empty only if someone supplied a team name that wasn't found in the database. Just in case this is true, the LatestScore variable is supplied with an appropriate message instead:

```
        else
        {
          //A row was not returned; this book does not exist.
          LatestScore = "The team cannot be found in the database";
        }
```

Lastly, we close the DataReader and return the contents of the function to the Web method:

```
        LibraryDr.Close();
        return LatestScore;
```

It's now a straightforward task to create a proxy client using the same method from our ISBN example and change the class so that it queries the ReturnScore Web method instead. We're not going to supply the code here to do that, but instead leave that as an exercise for the reader to complete, as the code changes needed are minimal and WebMatrix can do most of the work for you.

We have a Web service that takes a team name and returns as a string, the date of the latest game played by the team and the score for that team. That information is widely available to be used in anybody's application now, and not just ours. But how would someone else go about discovering this information so as to be able to use it?

Web Service Discovery

As you begin to build Web Service-integrated applications, it will become increasingly important to locate services that provide the functions you need, or alternatively post your own Web services so that others can make use of them. *Universal Description, Discovery, and Integration (UDDI)* is a Microsoft backed initiative that allows you to do this.

Whenever an industry initiative gains the support of several major players, it will usually become mainstream. For this reason, UDDI is positioned to dominate the Web service discovery field in the future. The UDDI service (accessible from http://uddi.microsoft.com or http://www-3.ibm.com/services/uddi/) lets businesses register themselves and list their existing Web services at no charge. Anyone can browse and search the UDDI database for a service that may suit their needs. UDDI provides information such as contact details (address, phone number, e-mail address, Web site), business details (DUNS number and industry sector), and a discovery URL for each service. WSDL is a key component of the UDDI project.

By using http://uddi.microsoft.com/, you can search for businesses that provide Web services, select the WSDL appropriately, and build your proxies (see Figure 16-21):

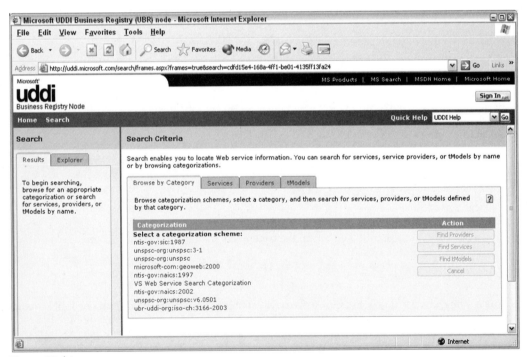

Figure 16-21

Securing a Web Service

Whether your Web service is made available on a subscription basis or is completely free to the public, it is important to consider security. The reasons for securing Web services can range from simple usage logging to strict access control. If your Web service provides a very useful feature (of course it will!), it's helpful to keep track of who's using it. While you can log the usage of a Web service that provides privileged information, more stringent security measures should be taken to make sure that the use of your Web service is consistent with your purposes.

There are many options for securing Web applications and services. The following are the most common techniques and will be discussed over the next sections:

❑ **Username-password**: Used to provide custom database based access control. This is an authentication service.

❑ **Secure Sockets Layer (SSL)**: Used to ensure that the data transfer across the Web is encrypted. However, it does not protect access to the Web service itself.

❑ **IP address restriction**: Used to specify valid IP addresses that can access the service. However, you need user's authentication even if the IP is the same.

❑ **Web services Enhancements**: A toolkit from Microsoft that adds a whole new set of specifications for making your Web services secure.

Please remember that these methods are not mutually exclusive, and can be combined to provide a higher level of security.

Username-Password Combination or Registration Keys

By requiring either a username-password pair or a registration key code as an input parameter, you can provide a way to track which consumers are using your Web service. A simple database table or XML file containing each username-password pair or registration key code is all that's required to provide this kind of security. Considering that no authentication of the consumer takes place in this scenario, it is very simple for the client to share the username and password (or registration key) with others. However, when the data provided by the Web service is not sensitive or proprietary in nature, this security method provides us with a quick and effective option.

Let's examine how you might apply this type of security to the ISBN Web service.

Try It Out   Securing a Web Service with Username and Password

You will be using the `security.mdb` database (provided with the code for this book and can be downloaded from http://www.wrox.com/). This contains a very simple `Users` table consisting of usernames and passwords. Ensure this database is in the same location as the `isbn.asmx` file created earlier. Our security will only attempt to match details from the user with an entry in the `security` database.

1. Re-open the ISBN Web service (`isbn.asmx`) in Web Matrix, and make the following modifications to the `BookDetail` Web method:

```
[WebMethod]
public string BookDetail(string strIsbn, string strUsername, string
      strPassword)
{
  OleDbDataReader objSecurityDR = null;
  OleDbConnection objSecurityConn = null;
  OleDbCommand objSecurityCmd = null;
  string strConn = "Provider=Microsoft.Jet.OLEDB.4.0;Data Source=" +
                    Server.MapPath("Security.mdb") + ";";
  string strSQL = "SELECT Username FROM Users WHERE username = '" +
                    strUsername + "' AND password = '" + strPassword + "'";
  objSecurityConn = new OleDbConnection(strConn);

  objSecurityCmd = new OleDbCommand(strSQL, objSecurityConn);
  objSecurityConn.Open();
  objSecurityDR =
            objSecurityCmd.ExecuteReader(CommandBehavior.CloseConnection);
  if (objSecurityDR.Read())
  {
     objSecurityDR.Close();
     return GetBookDetails(strIsbn);
  }
  else
  {
     objSecurityDR.Close();
     return "Login to library failed.";
  }
}
```

2. Save the result as `ISBNSecurity.asmx`. Notice that no changes have been made to the `GetBookDetails` function, as the core functionality of retrieving the book title from the database hasn't changed. The goal in this scenario is to provide a gatekeeper that prevents access to the internal logic if the consumer's username and password pair is not found in the database.

3. Browse to the `ISBNsecurity.asmx` Web service to test this newly applied security. You will now see two extra textboxes: one for `strUserName` and one for `strPassword`, as shown in Figure 16-22:

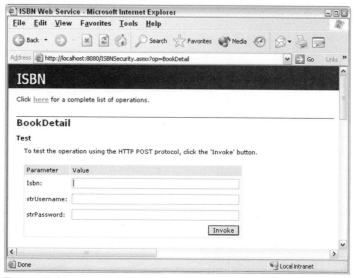

Figure 16-22

4. If you put in a number without specifying the correct security details, you will get the response shown in Figure 16-23:

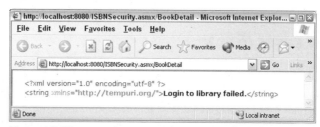

Figure 16-23

The only entry in our security database has the username `librarian` and the password `secret`. This is the only user that is permitted to access our Web service. However, you can add more registered users by modifying the `Users` table.

How It Works

We have used nearly the same logic validating the login as previously used in `GetBookDetails` to look up a book. By adding this logic to the Web-callable `BookDetail` function, we completely prevent access to the internal `GetBookDetails` function if the login fails. First, we create a connection to the security database and run the SQL command that retrieves the username if the user name and password supplied to the Web service match any of those in the database.

```
string strConn = "Provider=Microsoft.Jet.OLEDB.4.0;Data Source=" +
                    Server.MapPath("Security.mdb") + ";";
string strSQL = "SELECT Username FROM Users WHERE username = '" +
```

```
                              strUsername + "' AND password = '" + strPassword + "'";
        objSecurityConn = new OleDbConnection(strConn);
        objSecurityCmd = new OleDbCommand(strSQL, objSecurityConn);
        objSecurityConn.Open();
        objSecurityDR =
        objSecurityCmd.ExecuteReader(CommandBehavior.CloseConnection);
```

Now, if anything is returned, we run the `BookDetails` function and return the answer to the Web method:

```
if (objSecurityDR.Read())
    {
        objSecurityDR.Close();
        return GetBookDetails(strIsbn);
    }
```

However, upon failure to login correctly, we return a simple string:

```
else
    {
       objSecurityDR.Close();
       return "Login to library failed.";
    }
```

If the username and password combination is successfully located in the database, the result of the `GetBookDetails` function is returned just as before.

Secure Sockets Layer (SSL)

The most common method of securing information on the Web is the Secure Sockets Layer (SSL). When you make an online purchase, you'll typically see a lock or key icon displayed in the browser's status bar to let you know your communication is secure. Information passed between the browser and the Web site travels in an encrypted form. In the case of Web services, applying SSL ensures that the data traveling between the consumer and the endpoint is encrypted hence difficult to intercept.

SSL has no effect on the integrity of the data provided by your Web service. When a value is returned to the consumer, it remains the same regardless of the encryption used in its transportation. The only downside is that it affects the overall performance of your site, as more processing is required. You can get more information about verifying your identity for use with SSL from a Certificate Authority like Verisign (www.verisign.com). We discuss SSL in more detail in the next chapter.

IP Address Restriction

Maintaining an IP address list of all registered users can help control the use of a Web service. This approach presents a number of potential issues, the greatest being the never-ending maintenance of IP address ranges for each client. IP address restriction can take place at both hardware and software levels. A hardware application of this security typically involves firewall restrictions to specific IP addresses. Restricting IP access using software security often involves keeping a database table of clients and another with associated IP addresses.

Each time a Web service is accessed, you can get the client's IP address (using the HTTP headers) and confirm that it exists in the security tables. If a match is located, the Web service executes normally. Another option for software-based IP-address security is at the Web server level. Most Web server software permits any number of IP addresses to be restricted or enabled. Within IIS, it's as simple as selecting the properties of a given site and changing the IP restrictions. Since maintaining IP addresses of clients can be terribly cumbersome, as well as overly restrictive (if a consumer's IP address changes frequently), this option is generally not recommended.

Web Services Enhancements (WSE)

The Web services Enhancements (*WSE*) toolkit is a set of classes that allow developers to build Web services using specifications from the *Global XML Architecture* (*GXA*). The GXA specs are a set of specifications that cover security, Web service discovery, routing, and attachments that were developed jointly by Microsoft and IBM with the aim of building a framework by which all Web services would be developed in the future. The largest part of the WSE is the WS Security specification, and this contains classes that can enable you to use authorization and authentication (both discussed in the next chapter) with your Web services, as well as being able to sign and verify services and details for their encryption.

The WSE toolkit can be downloaded for free from http://msdn.microsoft.com/webservices/. Further discussion of WSE is beyond the scope of this book.

Other Web Services Considerations

Web services are bringing about a major paradigm shift, not seen since the early days of the Internet. Because of this, it's important to recognize that these new conveniences have their own set of advantages and disadvantages. We won't talk about all the ways to avoid the pitfalls (which would require a book in itself), but will consider some of key issues.

Network Connectivity

A few years ago, the idea of calling a remote function and retrieving a value from it seemed unlikely. Now that we have Web services, this newfound ability to use or purchase a given function from any organization on the Web causes us to think about the issue of Internet connectivity. It's important to realize that as must your company's Internet connection be reliable, so should your Web service provider's connection. Furthermore, if a Web service requires any additional Internet resources, their service vendor's network must also be stable. There are many potential failure points in this arrangement. Often, this can be compounded if a Web service provider hesitates, or refuses, to disclose who *their* providers are, since they don't want you going directly to them!

Asynchronous Method Calls

Since SOAP can be transported using SMTP (the e-mail protocol), we can write Web services that make use of asynchronous method calls. Asynchronous communication is a sort of disconnected, two way interaction that doesn't require an immediate response. Most programming deals with synchronous communication, where you call a function and wait for it to complete and return a value:

```
Distance_To_Rome = DistanceBetween("Los Angeles", "Rome", "meters");
```

In a situation like this, our application will not continue until the `DistanceBetween` function completes its logic and returns a value, which is placed in `Distance_To_Rome`. While this suits our needs most of the time, it is not always appropriate, especially when dealing with Web programming.

Batch processing, slowing down of applications, and anticipated disconnections are three situations where we should consider the possible advantages of asynchronous communication. The great news is that your Web service need not be tailored specifically for synchronous or asynchronous communication; this is the proxy's duty.

The following C# code snippet illustrates how you might implement asynchronous function calls, using events:

```
...
DistanceBetween("Los Angeles", "Rome", "meters");
...
private void DistanceBetween_CalculationComplete(integer Distance)
{
    Distance_To_Rome = Distance;
}
...
```

If the application contains code such as this, we will issue a request to `DistanceBetween` to calculate the distance between two cities, and then move on with our code. When the `DistanceBetween` object completes its calculation, it fires the `DistanceBetween_CalculationComplete` event, which allows us to handle the returned value without making the rest of the application wait.

Because we can call a remote function without the need for an immediate response (without breaking an application), our applications can support longer time intervals and handle poorer network conditions, such as dial-up situations. In the case of SMTP, the SOAP request is packaged in an e-mail format and delivered to a mailbox on the server, just as if it were an e-mail composed and addressed to another individual. The specification for SOAP over SMTP defines a process of retrieving this message from the mail server, executing the function required, and mailing the SOAP results to the consumer, again using SMTP.

Service Hijacking (or Piggybacking)

Once your Web service is available to the public, you may attract a client who is particularly interested in the service you provide. They're so interested, in fact, that they consider wrapping your powerful Web service inside one of their own and representing it as their own product. Without security safeguards in place (and legal documents as well), a client may repackage your Web service as if it were their own function, and there's no way for you to detect that this is being done (though you may become suspicious by examining your usage log when your client who occasionally uses your Web service suddenly shows an enormous increase in activity). Given the level of abstraction that Web services provide, it would also be nearly impossible for any customers of your unethical client to know who really owns the functionality.

Some organizations use a combination of usage logging and per-use charges. In my opinion, a smarter way to avoid piggybacking is by using false data tests. Within your Web service, you could create an undocumented function that creates a result that only *your* logic could produce. You would then be able to determine whether this code is really yours and the client is piggybacking the Web service, or if the client is truly using its own logic.

An example of implementing a false data test would be a Web service that provides book information for a given ISBN. As in the ISBN Web service, we may return some arbitrary details if a certain ISBN is provided and is not associated with a real book. If the ISBN ABCDEFGHI were entered, special codes or copyright information could be sent as the resulting book title. You could then test this on the piggybacking company suspected of stealing your Web service. Since this hidden functionality would not be published, it would provide a great way to prove that a company was reselling your Web service's logic without your legal approval.

Provider Solvency

Since the Web service model is a viable solution, you're probably eager to add its functionality to your core information systems and mission-critical applications. As Web services become more and more interdependent, it becomes increasingly necessary to research the companies from whom you consume Web services. You'll want to make sure these providers have what it takes to remain in business. UDDI goes a long way towards helping you with this research by providing company information for each registered Web service provider (including their DUNS number).

In the business world, nothing seems to impact and force sweeping changes more than insolvency, and if you find yourself in the unfortunate circumstance of lost functionality due to a bankrupt Web Service provider, you'll realize how painful the hurried search for a new vendor can be (with little room to bargain with your ex-service's competitors). Although the initial work can be a bit tedious, it is important to consider whether a potential Web service vendor will still be in business five years from now.

The Interdependency Scenario

The basis for all these and other Web service considerations is the issue of interdependency. It's possible that you wake up a given morning, start an application that has worked for years, and find that the Web service that it relies on is no longer available.

To some extent, thanks to the UDDI search capabilities, you can investigate and assess potential providers, but at the end of the day a degree of faith needs to be put into the services of each provider you choose to consume.

Summary

In this chapter, you've seen that a Web service exposes its functions as a service that other applications can use. We began by discussing what a Web service is and how it is used. We recapped XML and HTTP and their uses within the Web services architecture. We then delved into the process of building Web services, and creating and compiling a Web service proxy. You learned how to use Web services in an application by incorporating a defined namespace and making use of its methods. Afterwards, we saw how to discover what Web services we have available to consume, and finally, considered some of the ways to make a Web service secure.

As .NET makes programmatic interfaces over the Web more commonplace, you'll gradually be able to see applications sharing and building upon the contributions made by the community of Web service providers. Web services will provide a powerful means of seamlessly assembling applications that can span multiple platforms and languages. For the user, a transition is on the horizon from the browser to the more specific applications that make use of Web services. For the developer, ASP.NET Web services will make the Internet a programmer's toolbox, with a greater assortment of tools than ever before.

Exercises

1. Explain the role of the Simple Object Access Protocol (SOAP) in Web services.

2. What is the purpose of the WSDL file?

3. How would you locate a Web service that provides the functions you require?

4. Create a Web service with a class name of `circles`, that calculates the area of a circle, the circumference of a circle and the volume of a sphere. (Area = $(Pi)r^2$; Circumference = $2(Pi)r$; Volume of a sphere = $4/3(Pi)r^3$.)

5. Create a Web service that connects to the Northwind database and returns employee's addresses based on their last names.

6. Create an ASP.NET page containing a drop-down listbox in which a user can select names of Northwind employees to return their addresses.

7. Secure the Northwind employee Addresses Web service so that no unauthorized users have access to it.

17

ASP.NET Security

As soon as you start making information available on the Web, you've got to stop and ask yourself, "Who do I want seeing this?" Chances are that unless you actively do something to protect your site's resources, they'll be available to anyone who cares to look for them. Unlike corporate intranets, the Web is a public forum; many people out there could be interested in what your ASP.NET pages have to offer. You need to take considered action to prevent your pages and Web services being used and consumed by people who have not been authorized to do so.

Fortunately, there are many ways of controlling who's looking at your information. However, security doesn't stop with access policies; it's equally important that the applications you write are themselves secure. It's no good having a secure authentication procedure if your homepage has a list of the users' passwords on it, or if a password entered by a user is stored in a non-encrypted form by the ASP.NET page.

Security is about the strict enforcement of such access policies and about common sense. If you were asked to create a secure application, you might face situations where the users and administrators themselves don't update their passwords, choose passwords that are easy to crack, don't patch their servers with the latest Windows updates, or don't use firewalls to protect their systems. How can you effectively deal with this? You must be aware of the situation your application is likely to be deployed in, the kind of people who are likely to access it, and the kind of system it is likely to be maintained on. A secure system requires careful planning and you have to be certain of these issues when storing confidential and valuable information within the application.

This chapter covers the most common and effective ways of creating secure applications. In addition, we will also discuss some guidelines and best practices. However, our usage of Web Matrix will restrict what we *can* demonstrate.

Specifically, this chapter will cover:

❑   What is security?

❑   Forms authentication

❑   Forms database authentication and authentication against our case study

❑   Authorization

❑   SSL and encryption

What Is Security?

First of all let's discuss what security actually is.

> **Security is a process that protects private property from the general public, and permits access based only upon being able to verify that each individual's identity is in accord with the access permissions granted to him or her.**

For example, you protect the possessions in your home by fitting a lock to your front door. You will be able to decide who has access to your property, and who does not (provided you give the key only to the approved people). Further, you could fit a different lock on the door of your study, and place a second set of *access permissions* with regard to who could enter that area.

The ASP.NET Security Model

When you are implementing a security solution, the first thing you need to consider is the type of security most appropriate for your site. This will depend on the type of resources that you're exposing to users (whether your data is sensitive, or you just want to keep a track of who's viewing what) and the nature of the users that visit your site.

Many sites traditionally feature three levels of *user security*:

❑   **Anonymous Users**: For anyone visiting the site

❑   **Registered Users**: For users who have logged into the site with a user name and password

❑   **Administrators**: For users who have logged into the site with an administrative username and password

Having levels of user security on your site is a very powerful tool. It allows you to grant people access to your site without giving them "carte blanche" to go anywhere they like.

Preventing anonymous access to key areas of your site is one of the simplest ways to reduce the likelihood of people viewing information that they are not authorized to view. By restricting access to just a select set of registered users and administrators, you can drastically cut down on the number of people that can view specific areas of your site. However, sites such as www.usatoday.com are happy to allow anonymous access. It is the nature of their business to let people pop in and read the newspaper without having to give details about who they are.

You should choose a level of security that is appropriate for your site, and perhaps combine the three levels to create a complete solution. For example, www.amazon.com allows you anonymous access to browse its products, but requires you to be a registered user to place an order or request account information.

Apart from general security, we're also interested in how security measures are applied in the .NET Framework. In ASP.NET, the process of securing an application is split into two separate (but related) stages:

❑ **Authentication**: The process of checking whether users are who they claim to be. The process of authentication involves requesting details (such as a user name and password and maybe even a zip code or mother's maiden name) from a user. These details are then checked against a relevant authority, such as a database or a Windows domain server.

❑ **Authorization**: The process of granting a user (or a group of users) the permission to use a resource, or denying them access to a resource or a group of resources.

Primarily, this chapter will cover authentication. We will also cover authorization and look at a simple *tiered* approach to building Web sites, so as to allow normal users to see one level of the site, and an administrator to see another. We'll add a simple authentication and authorization system to the Wrox United application later in the chapter.

Lastly, we'll look very briefly at an issue that affects both of these processes – *encryption*. Encryption is the practice of using mathematical formulae to scramble information and make it unreadable to anyone who might intercept it. There are several types of encryption, all of which require the use of shared secret information between the Web site and the intended recipient. This information is known as a *key*. As discussed in earlier chapters, the HTTP protocol sends information as pure text, so if someone was able to intercept an HTTP request or response that hadn't been encrypted, they'd be able to read the details contained within. These could range from usernames and passwords to credit card details and account numbers.

In ASP.NET, encryption is typically implemented through the use of the *Secure Sockets Layer* (*SSL*), which is used to encrypt the information that you are passing back and forth and protect it from eavesdroppers. However, the task of building secure Web sites can be a lengthy one, and as it requires the IIS Web, server we're not going to cover it in detail. We recommend that anyone setting out to build a secure Web site refer to other more detailed texts on encryption, because its complexities are beyond the scope of this book.

Authentication

There are several methods of authenticating whether visitors to your site have permission to access the information that they are requesting. There are four types of authentication:

❑ **Forms-based authentication**: A powerful and flexible means of taking control of the presentation of your security features to the user. We'll discuss how you can use this to authenticate user details stored both in `web.config` and in a database.

❏ **Basic authentication**: A simple method of verifying users, mostly used for customization options, rather than restricting access.

❏ **Integrated Windows authentication**: A very simple, quick, and easy means of authenticating users, but can only be used with Internet Explorer browsers higher than version 5.0.

❏ **Passport authentication**: Microsoft also has its own separate and centralized authentication service. It provides a single login for all registered member sites of http://www.passport.com and is in use on sites such http://www.ebay.com. To implement it on your server you would require the Passport SDK to be downloaded first, which in turn requires IIS.

Unless you are using IIS, you will only have access to forms-based authentication. This isn't an issue to worry about though. Forms-based authentication provides all of the aspects needed for good security. Also as demonstrated in the first chapter, Web Matrix isn't a Web server that is intended for deployment over networks. By default, you can view pages on the Web Matrix server only via the machine that is actually running the server. Web Matrix's limited security options are not a problem because no one else outside has access to the machine anyway.

Lastly, basic and integrated Window authentication have serious limitations with regard to the way they present themselves to your users, and the kind of information you can use with them (all your users need accounts in the Windows user account database). Thus, we will concentrate on forms-based authentication.

Implementing Forms-Based Authentication

Forms-based authentication uses cookies. When a user logs into your ASP.NET application using forms-based authentication, ASP.NET issues an *authentication cookie* that will be sent back and forth between the server and client during the ensuing Web requests. If the authentication cookie is *persistent*, a copy will be stored on the user's hard drive and whenever they revisit your ASP.NET application, they can be pre-authenticated based on it, until the cookie expires. If the authentication cookie type is *non-persistent*, the authentication cookie will be destroyed at the end of each browser session. In this case, when they visit your ASP.NET application again, you can't pre-authenticate them and they will have to provide their credentials all over again.

You can use persistent and non-persistent cookies very flexibly. Whenever you log in on most sites, such as www.amazon.com, there will be a link beneath the password text box labeled Remember my password. If you check this box during login, it will place a persistent cookie on your local computer and will be able to pre-authenticate you on your subsequent visits to the site. If you don't check it, then a non-persistent cookie is used and you'll have to login each time you visit.

You'll be pleased to hear that forms-based authentication is also easy to implement. All you have to do is create a configuration file (`web.config`), a login page to accept (and then verify) the credentials from the user, and a default page where you'll display the content you wish to restrict. Let's look at how this is used.

In the following example, we'll create a form that accepts two pieces of information from the user via two ASP.NET textbox server controls – the first will be the username and the second their password. For good measure we'll also include some validation controls to make sure that the boxes are not left blank. An additional validation control will display any messages there may be from the server-side code.

Finally, we'll add a button server control to allow us to submit the form using the `Login_Click()` event.

We'll send this to a form that will display the username of the currently logged in user, the type of authentication that we've used, and an option for them to logout.

Try It Out Forms-Based Authentication

1. Create a folder called `Ch17` under the path `C:\BegASPNET11\` and within this folder, create a new `web.config` file.

2. Overwrite the automatically generated code as follows, save the file and close it:

```
<configuration>
  <system.web>
    <authentication mode="Forms">
      <forms name=".WroxDemo" loginUrl="login.aspx"
      protection="All" timeout="60" />
    </authentication>
    <machineKey validationKey="AutoGenerate" decryptionKey="AutoGenerate"
     validation="SHA1"/>
    <authorization>
      <deny users="?" />
    </authorization>
  </system.web>
</configuration>
```

In authentication mode="Forms", Forms is case-sensitive.

3. Next create a file called `login.aspx` in the `Ch17` folder, and insert the following code in the All window:

```
<%@ Page Language="C#" %>
<%@ import Namespace="System.Web.Security " %>
<script runat="server">

  void Login_Click(Object Src, EventArgs E)
  {
    if (txtEmail.Text == "Wrox" && txtPwd.Text == "MyPass")
    {
      FormsAuthentication.RedirectFromLoginPage(txtEmail.Text,false);
    }
    else
    {
      lblLoginMsg.Text = "Use Wrox as user name and MyPass as password.
                          Please try again";
    }
  }

</script>
<html>
<head>
</head>
<body>
    <form runat="server">
      <h1>Using Form-Based Authentication with Pre-Defined Credentials
```

```
        </h1>
        <hr />
        Users Name:<br />
        <asp:textbox id="txtEmail" runat="server"></asp:textbox>
          <font color="red" size="2">*</font>
        <br />
        Password:<br />
        <asp:textbox id="txtPwd" runat="server"
                     TextMode="Password"></asp:textbox> 
        <font color="red" size="2">*</font>
        <br />
        <asp:Label id="lblLoginMsg" runat="server" forecolor="Red" font-
                     name="Verdana" font-size="10"></asp:Label>
        <br />
        <asp:button id="btnLogin" onclick="Login_Click" runat="Server"
                     Text="Login"></asp:button>
    </form>
</body>
</html>
```

4. Save the file and close it.

5. Create another new file called `default.aspx`. Add the following code into the All window of this file:

```
<%@ Import Namespace="System.Web.Security " %>
<html>
<head>
<script language="C#" runat=server>
  void Page_Load(Object S, EventArgs E)
  {
    lblUser.Text = User.Identity.Name;
    lblType.Text = User.Identity.AuthenticationType;
  }

  void Logout_Click(Object S, EventArgs E)
  {

    FormsAuthentication.SignOut();
    Server.Transfer("login.aspx");
  }
</script>
</head>
<body>
<form runat="server">
    <font face="Verdana" size="4" color="navy">
    <b>Forms Authentication</b></font><hr>
    <table border=1 bordercolor="#FFFFFF" bgcolor="Silver"
    cellspacing=0 cellpadding=4>
      <tr>
        <td><b>Current Users Name</b></td>
        <td><asp:label id=lblUser runat=server/></td>
      </tr>
      <tr>
        <td><b>Current Authentication Type</b></td>
        <TD><asp:label id=lblType runat=server/></TD>
      </tr>
    </table>
  <asp:button text="Logout" OnClick="Logout_Click" runat=server/>
```

```
    </form>
    </body>
    </html>
```

6. When you request `default.aspx` from the browser, you should automatically be redirected to the login page shown in Figure 17-1:

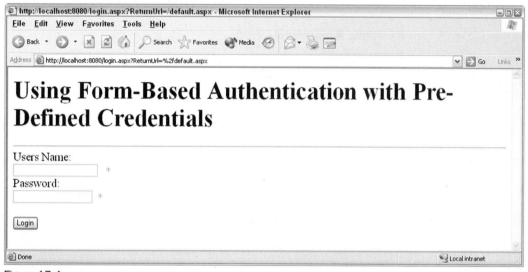

Figure 17-1

7. If you enter the login credentials incorrectly, you will receive the (rather insecure) error shown in Figure 17-2:

Figure 17-2

641

8. If you login correctly (taking care to enter the user name and password in the correct case) you will be granted access to the restricted page as shown in Figure 17-3:

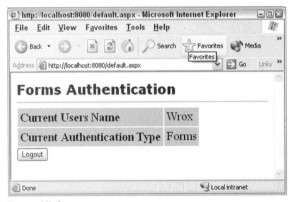

Figure 17-3

Hardcoding login details, as we have done here, within this file is not recommended.

How It Works

When the browser requests the `default.aspx` file, the Web server first checks to see if we've logged in. Since we haven't, it serves us with the `login.aspx` page instead and passes the authentication request to the ASP.NET runtime. This reads the `web.config` file and discovers that we're using forms-based authentication. The runtime will then look for the authentication cookie named in the `web.config` file (in the `name` element of the `<forms>` tag). Note that in this file, we are using the `:<forms>` tag to set the forms authentication properties.

```
<authentication mode="Forms">
  <forms name=".WroxDemo" loginUrl="login.aspx"
  protection="All" timeout="60" />
</authentication>
```

The following table describes the possible attributes for the `<forms>` tag:

Attribute	Description
Name	Name of the authentication cookie. If you are hosting more than one ASP.NET application from your Web server, make sure you give different names to each of the authentication cookies that you're using.
LoginUrl	The login page to which unauthenticated users should be redirected. This `loginUrl` can be on the same server, or a different one. If the `loginUrl` is on a different server then both servers should use the same `decryptionKey` parameter in the `machineKey` tag.

Attribute	Description
Protection	This attribute is used to protect the authentication cookie. The `protection` attribute has four possible values: `All`, `Encryption`, `Validation`, `None`. Validation is the process of checking that the value decoded using the user key matches the value when decoded using the server's key – we look at it later in the chapter. When you set the value as `All`, both validation and encryption will be performed against the authentication cookie to protect it. For validation and decryption, the values specified in the `validationKey` and `decryptionKey` of the `machineKey` tag will be used. The `All` value is the default and suggested value for this parameter. When you set the value to `None`, the cookie will be transferred between the client and the server as plain text and you can turn off the encryption and validation with the `machineKey` tag. When you set the value as `Encryption`, the cookie will be decrypted as per the value specified in the `decryptionKey` of the `machineKey` tag and the content of the cookie will not be validated. When you set the value as `Validation`, the cookie will be validated, when received from the client, as per the value specified in the `validationKey` of the `machineKey` tag and the content of the cookie will not be encrypted and decrypted.
Timeout	The timeout value for the cookie to expire. The default value is 30 minutes.
slidingExpiration	This can be set to `true` or `false`, and is by default set to `false`. If it is set to `true`, then it indicates that the value in the timeout is to be renewed, whenever another request is made that accesses the cookie.

Next, the `<machineKey>` tag configures the encryption, decryption, and validation level for the authentication cookies. These values can be set for the machine-level, site-level, and application-level. The value can't be set for the sub-directory level. The `<machineKey>` tag supports three attributes. Don't worry if these attributes don't make much sense now; we will talk about encryption later in the chapter.

Attribute	Description
validationKey	Specifies the validation key to be used when validating the authentication cookie data. The possible values for this element are either `AutoGenerate` or a manually assigned key.
	The minimum and maximum length of the key should be 40 characters (20 bytes) and 128 characters (64 bytes). `AutoGenerate` is the default.
decryptionKey	Specifies the encryption key to be used when validating the authentication cookie.
	Permitted values are the same as for `validationKey`.
validation	Specifies the type of encryption used for the data validation. The possible values are SHA1, MD5, and 3DES.
	SHA1 and MD5 are hashing algorithms, and 3DES is an algorithm used to encrypt and decrypt data.

The `<authorization>` tag is used to enable or disable access to an application. It can contain the following tags, which in turn have their own attributes:

Tag	Description
Deny	This can take three attributes:
	USER – the user name can be set to a particular user name or * (meaning all) or ? (meaning anonymous users)
	ROLE – this describes a particular role such as an administrator
	VERB – this can be set to a particular type of request such as HTTP GET or HTTP POST.
Allow	This can take three attributes:
	USER – the user name can be set to a particular user name or * (meaning all) or ? (meaning anonymous users)
	ROLE – this describes a particular role such as an administrator
	VERB – this can be set to a particular type of request such as HTTP GET or HTTP POST.

The <authorization> tag can be used to deny or allow access to particular users, groups of users, or types of request, within the section of the file. An authentication cookie is only issued if it meets the requirements of this section.

If an authentication cookie is present, the ASP.NET runtime checks the protection attribute of the <forms> element, and takes appropriate action based on its value. The protection attribute's settings of validation, encryption, or none, are all connected to the <machineKey> settings. So if the protection attribute is set to encryption, ASP.NET will check the web.config <machineKey> tag for the encryption setting. Validation forms the first level of protection and then encryption can form the second level if needed.If the cookie is valid, the requested page will be served back to the client. If the authentication cookie is not present (or invalid), the runtime will transfer the browser to the login page.

We specified the following in the web.config file:

```
<authorization>
  <deny users="?">
</authorization>
```

This means that anonymous users are redirected to the login page.

The page URL holds a QueryString called ReturnUrl with a reference to the previous page (default.aspx) that we requested from the Web server. That's how the RedirectFromLoginPage() method of the FormsAuthentication class knows where to transfer the browser back to once the user has successfully logged in. When you click the Login button without entering the username and password, the validation controls display their error messages (refer to *Chapter 14* for more information on this topic.)

login.aspx

Let's look at the logic in the <script> block in the login.aspx file.

Firstly, we compare the txtEmail textbox value with the hardcoded value (Wrox), and the txtPwd textbox value with the hardcoded value (MyPass):

```
void Login_Click(Object Src, EventArgs E)
{
  if (txtEmail.Text == "Wrox" && txtPwd.Text == "MyPass")
  {
```

If the values match, we call the RedirectFromLoginPage() method of the FormsAuthentication class. This method takes two parameters: the username and whether the cookie used is persistent or not. As the attribute for this is set to false, our cookie will be non-persistent:

```
FormsAuthentication.RedirectFromLoginPage(txtEmail.Text,false);
```

If the login details don't match these values, we display a message via the lblLoginMsg label to the user telling them to use Wrox as the username and MyPass as the password with the following code:

```
else
{
```

```
        lblLoginMsg.Text = "Use Wrox as user name and password as MyPass.
                    Please  try again";
    }
  }
</script>
```

default.aspx

When using forms-based authentication, the authentication via login is only necessary when somebody who hasn't been identified tries to access the protected resource. The following code just displays the user name and authentication type as we saw in Figure 17-3:

```
<script language="C#" runat=server>
  void Page_Load(Object S, EventArgs E)
  {
    lblUser.Text = User.Identity.Name;
    lblType.Text = User.Identity.AuthenticationType;
  }
```

Then we add a `Logout` button to log the user out and redirect them back to the login page:

```
  void Logout_Click(Object S, EventArgs E)
  {
    FormsAuthentication.SignOut();
    Server.Transfer("login.aspx");
  }
</script>
```

When we click this button, the `SignOut()` method of the `FormsAuthentication` class is called. This will remove the authentication cookie from the client regardless of the persistence of the cookie. The user is then transferred back to the login page.

Forms-Based Authentication Using a Database

Forms-based authentication is a very flexible and secure approach to authenticating users. However, the previous example had a major weakness – authentication took place against values hardcoded into the ASPX file. While this is fine for demonstration purposes, it is no good at all for production environments. We'll fix this weakness in the following authentication example.

Try It Out Authenticating against a Database

For this example, you'll need to download the `WroxDBAuth.mdb` database that's available with this book's code samples on www.wrox.com.

1. Create a new folder called `DB` in `C:\BegASPNET11\Ch17` and place the `WroxDBAuth.mdb` database in it.

2. Create a `web.config` file containing the following information and place it in the `Ch17` folder, overwriting the previous one:

```
<configuration>
  <system.web>
```

```
        <authentication mode="Forms">
          <forms name=".WroxDemo2" loginUrl="login.aspx"
          protection="All" timeout="20" />
        </authentication>
        <authorization>
          <deny users="?" />
        </authorization>
      </system.web>
</configuration>
```

3. Modify the login.aspx file used in the previous example from the All window and save it:

```
<%@ Page Language="C#" %>
<%@ Import Namespace="System.Web.Security " %>
<%@ Import Namespace="System.Data.OleDb" %>
<html>
<head>
<script language="C#" runat=server>
  void Login_Click(Object Src, EventArgs E)
  {
  string strConn ="PROVIDER=Microsoft.Jet.OLEDB.4.0;DATA SOURCE=" +
                      Server.MapPath("DB\\WroxDBAuth.mdb") + ";";
  OleDbConnection Conn = new OleDbConnection(strConn) ;
  Conn.Open();

  string strSQL = "SELECT Pwd FROM Tbl_MA_Users WHERE Email = '" +
                                      txtEmail.Text + "'";
  OleDbCommand Cmd = new OleDbCommand(strSQL,Conn);

  //Create a datareader, connection object

  OleDbDataReader Dr =
      Cmd.ExecuteReader(System.Data.CommandBehavior.CloseConnection);

  //Get the first row and check the password.
  if (Dr.Read())
  {
    if (Dr["Pwd"].ToString() == txtPwd.Text)
    {
      FormsAuthentication.RedirectFromLoginPage(txtEmail.Text, false);
    }
    else
    {
      lblLoginMsg.Text = "Invalid password.";
    }
  }
  else
  {
    lblLoginMsg.Text = "Login name not found.";
    Dr.Close();
  }
}
</script>
...
```

4. Don't do anything to the `default.aspx` page from the previous example; it doesn't need changing at all for this one. Call up the `default.aspx` page in your browser and enter the login credentials as shown in Figure 17-4:

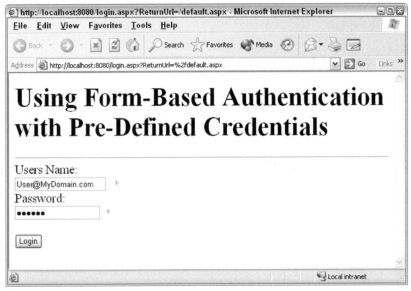

Figure 17-4

The login details from the database are **User Name** = `User@MyDomain.com` and **Password** = `MyPass` or **User Name** = `NewUser@MyDomain.com` and **Password** = `MyPass`. Either of these will work.

5. If you've entered the details correctly, you'll be shown the `default.aspx` page as depicted in Figure 17-5:

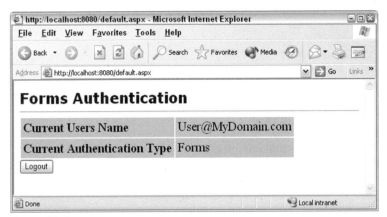

Figure 17-5

6. If you make a mistake, you'll be shown the `login.aspx` page again as shown in Figure 17-6, with an error message highlighted in red:

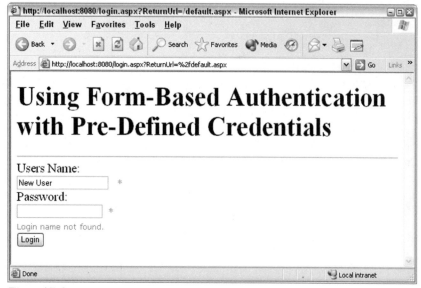

Figure 17-6

How It Works

The `login.aspx` page is the only one that has changed substantially from the previous example.

First of all, we include the `"System.Web.Security"` and `"System.Data.OLEDB"` namespaces for Security and Microsoft Access data access respectively:

```
<%@ Import Namespace="System.Web.Security" %>
<%@ Import Namespace="System.Data.OLEDB" %>
```

After the `Login_Click()` event, we build a connection string for the Access database and declare an `OLEDBConnection` object to connect to the Access database and open the connection:

```
string strConn ="PROVIDER=Microsoft.Jet.OLEDB.4.0;DATA SOURCE=" +
                        Server.MapPath("DB\\WroxDBAuth.mdb") + ";";
OleDbConnection Conn = new OleDbConnection(strConn) ;
Conn.Open();
```

Then we build a dynamic SQL statement into the `strSQL` variable, before creating an `OLEDBCommand` object by passing the dynamic SQL statement and the `OLEDBConnection` object to its constructor:

```
string strSQL = "SELECT Pwd FROM Tbl_MA_Users WHERE Email = '" +
                                    txtEmail.Text + "'";
   OleDbCommand Cmd = new OleDbCommand(strSQL,Conn);
```

Next, we create an `OLEDBDataReader` object and initialize it with the executed result of the `OLEDBCommand` object. We specify the `CommandBehavior` as `CloseConnection`. This makes sure that when we close the `OLEDBDataReader` object, the associated database connection will be closed.

```
OleDbDataReader Dr =
        Cmd.ExecuteReader(System.Data.CommandBehavior.CloseConnection);
```

Next, we must read the first record from the `OLEDBDataReader` object and compare the username and password with that entered by the user. If there are no rows in the `OLEDBDataReader` object, then the e-mail address entered by the user doesn't exist in the database (if it did, it would have been selected.) As there can only be one unique e-mail address per entry, our database query can only return one row at maximum. If no rows are returned, we display the error message Login name not found. in the label control. If the password doesn't match, we display the error message Invalid password in the label control. If they both match we then transfer the user to the page that they originally requested:

```
//Get the first row and check the password.
if (Dr.Read())
{
  if (Dr["Pwd"].ToString() == txtPwd.Text)
  {
    FormsAuthentication.RedirectFromLoginPage(txtEmail.Text, false);
  }
  else
  {
    lblLoginMsg.Text = "Invalid password.";
  }
}
```

After looking at some simple authentication pages, we're now nearly ready to see how we can integrate an authentication process into the existing Wrox United application, and see how it can be used to affect the functionality offered to the user. Before we do this, let's look at the associated process of authorization.

Authorization

As you have seen by now, it's possible to deny users access to all files on my Web site via the deny section, or allow individual users access. You might just be wondering now, "... but what if I want to allow users to access only *parts* of my Web site?"

For example, what if you wanted to allow access to your site in general, but you have an "admin" section that you want to keep private to everybody except the administrators? It is possible to use `web.config` to provide a solution once again, by introducing some simple authorization. It was mentioned earlier that authorization is the process of checking whether a particular user should be granted or denied permission to a particular resource. This means by default, authentication must have already been performed before we first authorize a user. If you think about it, this is logical, as we have to confirm *who* a user is *before* we can check what things they are allowed to see.

In previous examples, you were actually using authorization to provide access to the applications, but rather than doing any checking, you were just letting all users though, and granting them full authorization. However, just about all security systems will need to be more sophisticated than this. You'll probably only want to let a few users have authorization to certain areas and deny the same to others.

So let's see how our `web.config` file can be changed to allow access to only the `User@MyDomain.com`, and deny the other account `NewUser@MyDomain.com`.

Try It Out   Authorization for User@MyDomain.com

1. Go to Web Matrix, open the `web.config` file, and change the following highlighted code:

```
<configuration>
  <system.web>
    <authentication mode="Forms">
      <forms name=".WroxDemo" loginUrl="login.aspx"
      protection="All" timeout="60" />
    </authentication>
    <machineKey validationKey="AutoGenerate" decryptionKey="AutoGenerate"
     validation="SHA1"/>
    <authorization>
      <deny users="?" />
      <deny users="NewUser@MyDomain.com " />
      <allow users="User@MyDomain.com" />
    </authorization>
  </system.web>
</configuration>
```

2. Go back and run `default.aspx` again and enter the details for `NewUser@MyDomain.com`. This time, it directs you straight back to the login page. However, if you supply the details for `User@MyDomain.com`, it works just fine.

How It Works

In the `web.config` file, we've put in two extra lines:

```
<deny users="NewUser@MyDomain.com " />
<allow users="User@MyDomain.com" />
```

The first denies access to our `NewUser` account, while the second allows access to our `User` account. The line preceding these extra lines makes sure that no anonymous users are allowed access:

```
<deny users="?" />
```

We can use authorization to allow or deny access to our application for specific users.

You might even wish to go further and allow all users access to one section of your site and deny them access (and force them to login) to say an admin area. First, create a separate subfolder underneath your main application. For example, if you had all your examples in `C:\BegASPNET11`, you could create a folder `C:\BegASPNET11\admin`. Then, to allow preferential or selective access, you can split the `web.config` file into two separate sections. If you look at the previous examples, you can see that we have denied access to all users:

```
<configuration>
  <system.web>
    <authentication mode="Forms">
      <forms name=".WroxDemo" loginUrl="login.aspx"
      protection="All" timeout="60" />
    </authentication>
    <machineKey validationKey="AutoGenerate" decryptionKey="AutoGenerate"
     validation="SHA1"/>
    <authorization>
        <deny users="?" />
    </authorization>
  </system.web>
</configuration>
```

However, to enable access to the main site and deny access only to the files contained within the `admin` folder, you could change the file as follows:

```
<configuration>
  <system.web>
    <authentication mode="Forms">
      <forms name=".WroxDemo" loginUrl="login.aspx"
      protection="All" timeout="60" />
    </authentication>
    <machineKey validationKey="AutoGenerate" decryptionKey="AutoGenerate"
     validation="SHA1"/>
    <authorization>
        <allow users="?" />
    </authorization>
  </system.web>
  <location path="admin">
    <system.web>
      <authorization>
          <deny users="?" />
      </authorization>
    </system.web>
  </location>
</configuration>
```

First, we've changed the authorization tags in the main part to allow access to the main site, and then added a new section under the `<location>` tag. The `<location>` tag has a `path` attribute, which is set to the name of the folder that is to be denied access to. Then we have a new set of `<system.web>` tags. This is a vital feature. The `<location>` tag can only be set outside the `<system.web>` section, but inside the configuration tags. It contains a `<system.web>` section that only applies to that one folder. Inside the new `<system.web>` section is a set of `<authorization>` tags and a `deny` attribute, that takes precedence in the `admin` folder, over the previously specified ones.

It was mentioned in *Chapter 15* that the `web.config` settings take priority over `machine.config` settings. Here the principle is the same – the settings for the individual folder in the location tag take precedence over the settings for the main site.

With these settings, we can now deny or allow users access to only specific parts of our site. Let's see a practical demonstration in the next example, where we add authentication to the WroxUnited application.

Authentication in Wrox United

We'll add a password login system to the Wrox United application, which we created over the course of *Chapters 10* to *13*. This will enable a user to log in to the application. It will then detect whether a user is an administrator or not, and if so, will display an extra panel in the user control navigation bar which will allow administrators to see special links that are hidden from users.

However, the Wrox United application isn't a members-only club; it's something that all people should have access to. Therefore, we only want to block access to the administration section.

We can achieve this by adding forms-based authentication to the `web.config` file, and then by adding a login page (as in our previous examples), but only allowing access to the login page via the main navigation bar. We'll use the same forms-based authentication process as in the previous example and show how it neatly dovetails with the existing application functionality. We'll then add a login panel to the NAVBAR control and some code behind to generate the panel contents. We'll also add a Logout button.

Try It Out   Adding a Login Page to WroxUnited

1. Create a new `web.config` file and add the following code over the auto-generated code and save the file in the `WroxUnited` folder:

```
<configuration>
<appSettings>

    <add key="ConnectionString" value="Provider=Microsoft.Jet.OLEDB.4.0;Ole DB
Services=-4;Data Source=C:\BegASPNET11\WroxUnited\Database\WroxUnited.mdb" />

  </appSettings>
    <system.web>
      <authentication mode="Forms">
        <forms name=".WroxUnited"
               loginUrl="admin\login.aspx"
               protection="Validation"
               timeout="999999" />
      </authentication>
      <authorization>
         <allow users="*" />
      </authorization>
    </system.web>
  <location path="admin">
    <system.web>
```

```
         <authorization>
           <allow users="*"/>
           <deny users="*" />
         </authorization>
      </system.web>
   </location>
</configuration>
```

2. Next create an `admin` folder and download `playeradmin.aspx`, `teamadmin.aspx`, and `gamesadmin.aspx` into the folder.

3. Now, in the `admin` folder, create a login form called `login.aspx` with two text boxes called `UserName` and `UserPass`, a button called `LoginBtn`, and a label called `Msg`:

```
<html>
<head>
    <link id="css" href='<%= Session["SelectedCss"]%>' type="text/css"
rel="stylesheet" />
</head>
<body>
    <form runat="server">
        <WROXUNITED:HEADER id="HeaderControl"
                           runat="server"></WROXUNITED:HEADER>
        <h2>Login Page
        </h2>
        <table width="800">
          <tbody>
            <tr>
              <td style="VERTICAL-ALIGN: top; WIDTH: 165px">
                <WROXUNITED:NAVBAR id="NavBar"
                              runat="server"></WROXUNITED:NAVBAR>
              </td>
              <td style="VERTICAL-ALIGN: top">
                <table>
                  <tbody>
                    <tr>
                      <td>
                          Username:</td>
                      <td>
                        <asp:TextBox id="UserName"
                                runat="server"></asp:TextBox>
                      </td>
                    </tr>
                    <tr>
                      <td>
                        Password:</td>
                      <td>
                          <asp:TextBox id="UserPass" runat="server"
                                TextMode="Password"></asp:TextBox>
                      </td>
                    </tr>
                  </tbody>
                </table>
                <asp:button id="LoginBtn" onclick="LoginBtn_Click"
```

```
                                                runat="server"
                                                text="Login"></asp:button>
                                <p>
                                        <asp:Label id="Msg" runat="server"
                                                        forecolor="red"></asp:Label>
                                </p>
                        </td>
                </tr>
        </tbody>
        </table>
    </form>
</body>
</html>
```

4.   Add the following code in the Web Matrix **Code** window:

```
private void LoginBtn_Click(object Sender, System.EventArgs e)
{
  System.Data.IDataReader PlayersDB;
  PlayersDB = Players();
  while (PlayersDB.Read())
  {
    string PlayerLogin = Convert.ToString(PlayersDB["SiteLogin"]);
    string PlayerPassword = Convert.ToString(PlayersDB["SitePassword"]);
    string AdminLevel = Convert.ToString(PlayersDB["AdminLevel"]);

    if (UserName.Text == PlayerLogin && UserPass.Text == PlayerPassword)
    {
        HttpCookie UserNameCookie = new HttpCookie("UserNameCookie");
        UserNameCookie.Value = UserName.Text;
        Response.Cookies.Add(UserNameCookie);

        HttpCookie UserLevelCookie = new HttpCookie("UserLevelCookie");
        UserLevelCookie.Value = AdminLevel;
        Response.Cookies.Add(UserLevelCookie);

        FormsAuthentication.RedirectFromLoginPage(UserName.Text, true);
    }
    else
    {
      Msg.Text = "Invalid Credentials: Please try again";
    }

  }

  PlayersDB.Close();
}

public System.Data.IDataReader Players()
{
  string connectionString =
                    ConfigurationSettings.AppSettings["ConnectionString"];
  System.Data.IDbConnection dbConnection = new
                    System.Data.OleDb.OleDbConnection(connectionString);
```

```
      string queryString = "SELECT [Players].[SiteLogin], " +
              "[Players].[SitePassword], [Players].[AdminLevel] FROM [Players]";

  System.Data.IDbCommand dbCommand = new System.Data.OleDb.OleDbCommand();
  dbCommand.CommandText = queryString;
  dbCommand.Connection = dbConnection;

  dbConnection.Open;
  System.Data.IDataReader dataReader =
          dbCommand.ExecuteReader(System.Data.CommandBehavior.CloseConnection);

  return dataReader;
}
```

5.   In the All window, add the two registration tags to the top of the code after the `<@Page>` tag:

```
<%@ Register TagPrefix="WroxUnited" TagName="Header" Src="..\header.ascx"%>
<%@ Register TagPrefix="WroxUnited" TagName="Navbar" Src="..\navbar.ascx"%>
```

6.   Next, add the login details to the navigation bar. Open `navbar.ascx` and add the following code to the existing code in the HTML window:

```
  <p>
      <asp:HyperLink id="lnkMerchandise" runat="server"
                      NavigateUrl="Merchandise.aspx">Official
                      Merchandise</asp:HyperLink>
  </p>
  <asp:panel id="pnlLogin" runat="server" visible="true">
      <p>
          <asp:HyperLink id="lnkLogin" runat="server"
                  NavigateUrl="\admin\login.aspx">Login</asp:HyperLink>
      </p>
  </asp:panel>
  <hr width="95%" />
  <br />
  <p>
      Choose a theme:<br />
      <asp:DropDownList id="ddlTheme" runat="server">
      <asp:ListItem Value="WroxUnited.css" Selected="true">Home Kit
      </asp:ListItem>
      <asp:ListItem Value="WroxUnited2.css">Away Kit</asp:ListItem>
      </asp:DropDownList>
      <asp:Button id="btnApplyTheme" onclick="btnApplyTheme_Click"
                  runat="server"
                  Text="Apply">
      </asp:Button>
      <br />
      <asp:CheckBox id="chkRememberStylePref" runat="server" Text="Remember
                  preference">
      </asp:CheckBox>
  </p>
      <asp:panel id="pnlEdit" runat="server" visible="false">
      <hr width="95%" />
```

```
        <br />
        <p>
            Login Details:
            <asp:Label id="lblStatus" runat="Server"></asp:Label>
        </p>
        <asp:Button id="btnLogout" onclick="btn_Logout" runat="server"
                        Text="Logout"></asp:Button>
    </asp:panel>
</div>
```

7. Now, add both the following functions to the **Code** window of `navbar.ascx` in Web Matrix:

```
private void Page_Load()
{
string check = Request.ServerVariables["APPL_PHYSICAL_PATH"];
if (Request.IsAuthenticated == true){
 pnlEdit.Visible = true;
 pnlLogin.Visible = false;
 lblStatus.Text = "<br>You are logged in as: " +
 Request.Cookies["UserNameCookie"].Value;
 if (Request.Cookies["UserLevelCookie"].Value == "Admin" &&
     check.Substring(check.Length-11)=="WroxUnited\\")
 {
   lblStatus.Text += "<br><br><a href='\\admin\\playeradmin.aspx'>Player
                        Admin Page</a><br>";
   lblStatus.Text += "<br><a href='\\admin\\teamadmin.aspx'>Team Admin
                        Page</a><br>";
   lblStatus.Text += "<br><a href='\\admin\\gamesadmin.aspx'>Games Admin
                        Page</a><br>";
 }
 else if (Request.Cookies["UserLevelCookie"].Value == "Admin" &&
         check.Substring(check.Length-6) =="admin\\")
 {
   lblStatus.Text += "<br><br><a href='playeradmin.aspx'>Player Admin
                        Page</a><br>";
   lblStatus.Text += "<br><a href='teamadmin.aspx'>Team Admin
                        Page</a><br>";
   lblStatus.Text += "<br><a href='gamesadmin.aspx'>Games Admin
                        Page</a><br>";
 }
public void btn_Logout(object sender, System.EventArgs e)
{
    string check = Request.ServerVariables["PATH_INFO"];
    FormsAuthentication.SignOut;
    pnlLogin.Visible= true;
    pnlEdit.Visible=false;
    if (check.Substring(check.Length-10)=="admin.aspx")
    {
      Response.Redirect("\\default.aspx");
    }
    else
    {
      Response.Redirect("\\default.aspx");
    }
}
```

8. Open `default.aspx` and go to the login page via the new link as shown in Figure 17-7:

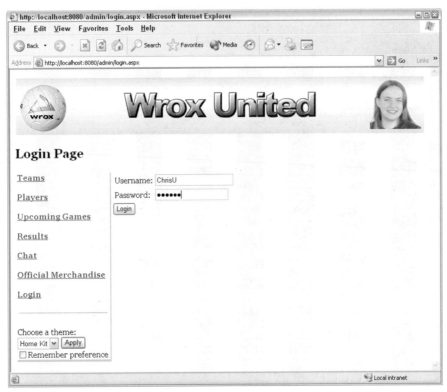

Figure 17-7

9. Login with the username ChrisU and the password secret, and scroll down to see the login details panel on the navigation bar as shown in Figure 17-8:

Figure 17-8

10. Click on the Player Admin Page link. As you can see in Figure 17-9, you have access to the administration screen and can make changes by adding and deleting new players:

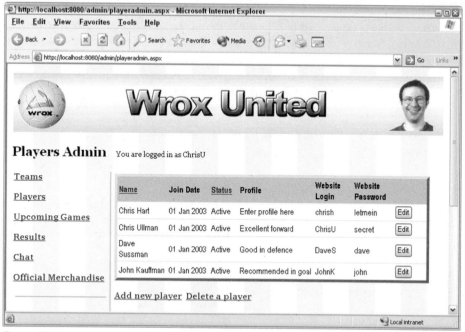

Figure 17-9

11. Scroll down the page and click on the logout button at the bottom of the login details panel. You're redirected back to the login page. This time enter the details DaveS and the password dave, and scroll down once logged in to arrive at the view depicted in Figure 17-10:

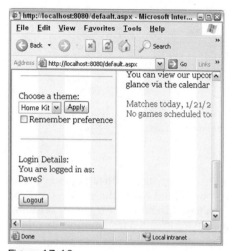

Figure 17-10

This time you can't see any links, just the user details. You should be unable to use the admin links. However, entering the URL would still take you to the relevant page; we haven't shut that door!

How It Works

The login system is able to offer a two-tiered view of the site because our code is able to detect who the user is from the user details, authorize them, and then offer a different view of the Web site. If you go to WroxUnited database and check the Players table, you should find that:

SiteLogin	SitePassword	AdminLevel
ChrisU	Secret	Admin
DaveS	Dave	User

Let's go back to the code we created. The web.config file is almost identical to the one in the *Authorization* section. We use forms-based authentication and allow access to the main site using the <allow user="?"> tag, but we redirect access to the login.aspx page for the entire contents of the admin folder. We deny authorization to any anonymous user, using the ?:

```
          <authentication mode="Forms">
            <forms name=".WroxUnited"
                          loginUrl="admin\login.aspx"
                          protection="Validation"
                          timeout="999999" />
          </authentication>
          <authorization>
            <allow users="*" />
          </authorization>

      </system.web>
  <location path="admin">
    <system.web>
          <authorization>
            <allow users="*"/>
            <deny users="?" />
          </authorization>
    </system.web>
  </location>
```

The web.config file handles most of the security.

login.aspx

The login page is where the authentication against the WroxUnited.mdb takes place. The HTML part of it is of no interest to us; it's the code-behind where the work is done. We have two functions. The first is activated when the user clicks on the Login button. We start by creating an instance of a data reader called playersDb, and then read in information from it by calling the IDataReader function:

```
private void LoginBtn_Click(object Sender, System.EventArgs e)
```

```
{
  System.Data.IDataReader PlayersDB;
  PlayersDB = Players();
  while (PlayersDB.Read())
  {
```

We are interested in are the SiteLogin, the SitePassword, and the AdminLevel. We create three variables to store each of the items in as they are read back from the WroxUnited database:

```
string PlayerLogin = Convert.ToString(PlayersDB["SiteLogin"]);
string PlayerPassword = Convert.ToString(PlayersDB["SitePassword"]);
string AdminLevel = Convert.ToString(PlayersDB["AdminLevel"]);
```

Next we check if the username and password match a record in the database:

```
if (UserName.Text == PlayerLogin && UserPass.Text == PlayerPassword)
{
```

If they do, we create two cookies. The first cookie stores the corresponding user name in a cookie called UserNameCookie, with no expiry date specified:

```
HttpCookie UserNameCookie = new HttpCookie("UserNameCookie");
UserNameCookie.Value = UserName.Text;
Response.Cookies.Add(UserNameCookie);
```

The second cookie stores the corresponding admin level in a cookie called UserLevelCookie, also with no expiry date specified:

```
HttpCookie UserLevelCookie = new HttpCookie("UserLevelCookie");
UserLevelCookie.Value = AdminLevel;
Response.Cookies.Add(UserLevelCookie);
```

We then authenticate the login and redirect the user back to the original URL they requested:

```
FormsAuthentication.RedirectFromLoginPage(UserName.Text, true);
```

If we don't have any matches for the UserName and Password in the Players table in the WroxUnited database, we display an appropriate message, refusing them entry and urging them to try again:

```
else
{
  Msg.Text = "Invalid Credentials: Please try again";
}

}
```

We finish the function by closing the Players table. , we call the iDataReader function. This function creates an instance of a DataReader object and populates it with the results of the following SQL query:

```
string queryString = "SELECT [Players].[SiteLogin]," +
        "[Players].[SitePassword], [Players].[AdminLevel] FROM [Players]";
```

This SQL query returns the site login, password, and admin level for every player in the `Players` table. This is the information against which we check the contents of the `textname` and `password` textboxes in the `Login_Click()` function.

Basically, the `login.aspx` page checks a user's entry credentials and either allows them to move on to the default page, or stops them at the login page depending on whether they enter valid details. If they do enter valid details, the username and admin level are stored in two cookies for use in the next section of the code.

Navbar.ascx

In the navigation bar, we created an extra `<asp:panel>` that contained a button and a label control. By default, the panel was made invisible:

```
<asp:panel id="pnlEdit" runat="server" visible="false">
```

This is because we wanted to enable it only once someone had correctly logged in. Behind the `<asp:panel>` are functions. The first is a `Page_Load()` function, which is executed whenever the navigation bar is loaded. When the bar is loaded, we check to see if the user has been authenticated:

```
private void Page_Load()
{
   string check = Request.ServerVariables["APPL_PHYSICAL_PATH"];
   if (Request.IsAuthenticated == true)
   {
```

If the user has been authenticated, the panel is made visible and the Login link is made invisible:

```
pnlEdit.Visible = true;
pnlLogin.Visible = false;
```

The *only* place this panel shouldn't be visible is on the login page. To get to the main application, someone needs to have logged in correctly. Also, we set the contents of the label control here. First we display the name of the contents of our `UserNameCookie`:

```
lblStatus.Text = "<br>You are logged in as: " +
Request.Cookies["UserNameCookie"].Value;
```

Then we check if the user is an administrator, by checking the contents of the `UserLevelCookie`. If the user is an administrator, we display three extra links to the admin control in our login panel. However we have a small problem here. These files are already in the `admin` folder. So we stick a `\admin` in front of our ASPX page name. However, if we are in the `admin` folder already, then this will stick an extra `admin` in front of our `admin` folder: for example, `admin\admin`. This would cause a file not found error. So we have to check to see our location in the application as well:

```
if (Request.Cookies["UserLevelCookie"].Value == "Admin" &&
    check.Substring(check.Length-11)=="WroxUnited\\")
{
    lblStatus.Text += "<br><br><a href='\\admin\\playeradmin.aspx'>Player
                      Admin Page</a><br>";
    lblStatus.Text += "<br><a href='\\admin\\teamadmin.aspx'>Team Admin
```

```
                                          Page</a><br>";
        lblStatus.Text += "<br><a href='\\admin\\gamesadmin.aspx'>Games Admin
                                          Page</a><br>";
    }
    else if (Request.Cookies["UserLevelCookie"].Value == "Admin" &&
             check.Substring(check.Length-6) =="admin\\")
    {
      lblStatus.Text += "<br><br><a href='playeradmin.aspx'>Player Admin
                                          Page</a><br>";
      lblStatus.Text += "<br><a href='teamadmin.aspx'>Team Admin Page</a><br>";
      lblStatus.Text += "<br><a href='gamesadmin.aspx'>Games Admin
                                          Page</a><br>";
    }
  }
}
```

We use a pruned version of the server variable's APPL_PHYSICAL_PATH to determine whether we are in the WroxUnited folder or the admin folder. If it's located in C:\BegASPNET11\WroxUnited, for example, we need to add an admin folder to our ASPX admin page links. If this variable contains C:\BegASPNET11\WroxUnited\admin, we are already in the admin folder, and we can create a link straight to our ASPX admin page just by mentioning the page name. In other words, the links would read if we were in WroxUnited:

```
Href="Admin\playeradmin.aspx"
Href="Admin\teamadmin.aspx"
Href="Admin\gamesadmin.aspx"
```

While if we were located in the admin folder they would just read:

```
Href="playeradmin.aspx"
Href="teamadmin.aspx"
Href="gamesadmin.aspx"
```

We create three links, and add them to the control's text property to send them straight to the screen.

The second function just handles the logout process. This is triggered when the logout button is pressed, and it simply uses the FormsAuthentication.SignOut method to automatically revoke authentication. We make the login panel invisible and the login link visible on the navigation bar. Then as we no longer want the user to be logged in, we redirect them to the login page:

```
public void btn_Logout(Object sender, EventArgs e)
{
  string check = Request.ServerVariables["PATH_INFO"];
  FormsAuthentication.SignOut();
  pnlLogin.Visible= true;
  pnlEdit.Visible=false;
  if (check.Substring(check.Length-10)=="admin.aspx")
  {
    Response.Redirect("..\\default.aspx");
  }
  else
  {
```

```
        Response.Redirect("default.aspx");
    }
```

There is one little caveat here; if we are in the `admin` section, the URL back to the home page is once again slightly different (it has an extra `admin` folder in). Aswith the `APPL_PATH` variable, we use the `PATH_INFO` server variable to determine whether or not we are in the admin folder. If we *are* in such a folder, we jump up one in the hierarchy; if we are *not*, we can go straight back to the home page. And there you have it, we have used authentication to create a very simple two-tiered approach to our Wrox United application. Let's now quickly consider *encryption* of data on the Web and how it works with authentication.

Encryption Using SSL

The amount of business conducted over the Internet has grown exponentially. This business, known as *e-commerce*, comprises of online banking, online brokerage accounts, and Internet shopping. Today you can book plane tickets, make hotel reservations, rent a car, transfer money, and buy clothes using your PC. Unfortunately, this convenience comes at a price. Simply entering your credit card number on the Internet leaves you wide open to fraud as your information can be intercepted and read. This is because when information is transmitted between the client and server via the HTTP protocol, it is sent as normal text that could be viewed by anyone who is trying to *listen in* on the transactions you make.

You can use encryption to code the message. In encryption, the sender of the message uses a secret key to scramble (or encrypt) the message and the receiver needs the same key to be able to unscramble and understand. However, this method, known as *secret-key encryption* has a drawback. The sender and receiver must agree on the secret key without anyone else discovering it. Anyone who intercepts the key in transit can decipher and read the encrypted messages.

In more recent times, secret-key encryption has been replaced with a method called *public-key encryption*. This method gives each user a pair of keys: a *public* key and a *private* key. Each person's public key is made available to public but the private key is kept under wraps. It works along these lines: if a user named Vervain wanted to send an encrypted message to another user named Rheingold, he can look up Rheingold's public key in a directory, and use it to encrypt the message before sending it. Rheingold can then use his own private key to decrypt the message and read it. This means that it's possible for anybody to send an encrypted message to Rheingold using the public key, but only Rheingold can use the private key to decrypt and read the message.

In ASP.NET, SSL is used to encrypt information that you send over to the server (not just your credit card number, but the entire message) with a public key system. The server then receives this data, decrypts it, and proceeds with the transaction without fear of your personal information being used by the wrong people. The SSL protocol uses *hashing keys* to encrypt the message, and authenticating servers before data is exchanged by the higher-level application. It maintains the security and integrity of the transmission channel by using encryption, authentication, and message authentication codes. SSL uses sophisticated hashing algorithms like MD5 and SHA1, which are very tough to break. You can enable SSL in forms-based authentication very simply by using the `requireSSL` attribute. This was introduced in ASP.NET 1.1. By default, it is set to `false`, but if changed to `true` in `web.config`, it sets a secure property in ASP.NET. The browser connected to it will return a cookie only if it is using SSL.

Try It Out Enabling SSL

You cannot create an SSL link with Web Matrix (it can only be done in ASP.NET with IIS, and this is beyond the scope of the book) but you can prevent your normal user from logging in by altering the `requireSSL` attribute, which is what we'll do now.

1.   In `web.config` created in the forms authentication databases example, add the attribute as:

```
<configuration>
  <system.web>
    <authentication mode="Forms">
      <forms name=".WroxDemo2" loginUrl="login.aspx"
      protection="All" timeout="20"
     requireSSL="true" />
    </authentication>
    <authorization>
      <deny users="?" />
    </authorization>
  </system.web>
</configuration>
```

2.   Now go back to `default.aspx` and try to login now via http://localhost/default.aspx and supply the correct credentials. You'll find that instead of letting you in, it dumps you back to the login screen.

How It Works

This example code won't allow us access to our main `default.aspx` page in any circumstances, because we are using a straight http:// link, which, as we've just stressed, sends requests and receives responses in pure text. We would have to enable a secure http link to do this, but it isn't possible to enable a secure link with Web Matrix, as Web Matrix isn't intended to be deployed in a production setting. To identify a secure link, the URL would have to be prefixed with https://, and Internet Explorer would have a small lock icon in the bottom right hand corner as shown in Figure 17-11:

Figure 17-11

Typically you supply sensitive details over a secure https:// link. Enabling SSL via the `requireSSL` attribute forces users to use the secure link. When you connect to a secure Web server using SSL, the server sends a certificate to you. This certificate is created by one of many *Certificate Authorities* (*CAs*):

❑   **Verisign:** http://www.verisign.com

❑   **Belsign:** http://www.belsign.be

❑   **Xcert:** http://www.xcert.com

These businesses provide a validation service performing a yearly validation to check if the business is a legitimate functioning one. So when you log on, you can be confident that a CA on your behalf has checked the business. Once the browser receives the certificate, it extracts a public key, which can be used to encrypt or decrypt information. To create a secure link using SSL, you would need to be using

IIS. We don't really need to go any further into this complicated process, but it gives you a feel for how standard secure transactions are conducted on the Internet. Further discussion of SSL is beyond the scope of this book, but you could find out more about if from a CA such as www.verisign.com. You can also buy an SSL certificate to prove your server's identity.

Summary

In this chapter we've covered a few of the most important aspects of basic ASP.NET security.

We looked at how we can secure our applications flexibly using the more complex method of forms-based security that allows us to build our own user interfaces, and how we can improve upon the basic ideas of this approach by storing the user's details in a database. We then looked at how the associated process of authorization could be used to restrict access to specific areas of the site, or to specific users. We created a login panel for the Web site, with a simple two-tier system for normal users and for administrators. Lastly, we touched upon the idea of encryption and finally we talked about the basic premises upon which SSL works.

With security, we complete our tour of ASP.NET. We've covered a lot of subjects within this book, and hope that you've enjoyed it. If you're wondering what to do next, go back and learn each of the subjects the chapters focused on in more detail. Each chapter forms a stepping-stone from which you can go on to build sections of your own applications. Application building is something that can only be learned from experience. You can go back and add extra sections to the application presented in this book. We provide some extra pages on the Web site. Try adding those to the application. You can then customize it and play around with the code. See what effects you can have by tweaking it.

Next, you can try building your own applications from scratch. It can be quite daunting at first, but you've already covered all of the main areas, so you've no need to worry. Base your own applications on the framework presented here, and don't be afraid to experiment. ASP.NET is a powerful tool and takes time to master. It's also something you can develop an individual approach for. We've presented a recommended way to do it, but within this framework there is plenty of room for you to create your own approach. Most of all, have fun. Happy developing!

Exercises

1. What is the difference between authorization and authentication?

2. Create an application that uses forms-based authentication that requires a username, password, and a zip code before you can go to the main login page. Hardcode the username, password, and the zip code. Call it `zipcodelogin.aspx`.

3. Upgrade the application from Exercise 2 to use the `WroxAuth.mdb` used in this chapter.

4. Create an account for a user named `John@MyDomain.com`, but deny him access in `web.config`. What happens when you try to log in as him? Can you think of a way of displaying a message to accompany this?

5. Create a new page called `newpage.aspx` on the example, and use `web.config` to ensure that only John has access to it. *HINT: Create a subfolder for this page.*

Exercise Solutions

Chapter 2

This chapter discusses the structure of an ASP.NET page and the way that it functions in relation to the .NET Framework.

Exercise 1

Describe what the .NET Framework provides for programmers.

Solution

The .NET Framework offers the following:

- ❑ A single tool for creating Windows-based applications and Web-based applications
- ❑ Object Oriented Programming (OOP), which simplifies application development
- ❑ Reduction in the number of lines of code required to achieve a task
- ❑ Ability to use multiple languages within a single application
- ❑ Tools to automatically accommodate devices beyond the desktop, including PDAs, mobile phones, and wrist PCs.

Exercise 2

Which encompasses more code, a class or a namespace?

Solution

A namespace is made of one or more classes, so a namespace is larger.

Exercise 3

The ASP.NET module of code adds on to which part of Windows?

Solution

The ASP.NET module of code adds on to IIS Web server.

Exercise 4

What special modifications must be made to the browser on the client-side in order to view an ASP.NET page?

Solution

None – a browser (by definition) displays HTML, and ASP sends out pure HTML. No special tags, software or plug-ins are required on the browser.

Exercise 5

Why does an ASP.NET page get compiled twice?

Solution

The first time, the page gets compiled to the Intermediate Language, which compiles as much of the code as possible except for those that are dependent on the specific capabilities of a server. The second time, the code is compiled to the CLR to make optimal use of the server resources that will actually host the page.

Exercise 6

Why does the first display of an ASP.NET page take several seconds but subsequent views appear in only milliseconds?

Solution

The first time the page is requested, it must be compiled to the CLR which isn't necessary on subsequent requests.

Exercise 7

What two attributes should always be included in all ASP.Net Web controls?

Solution

Always include the `runat="server"` and `ID="MyControlName"` attributes in all ASP.Net Web controls.

Chapter 3

This chapter discusses the use of variables for holding data in C#.

Exercise 1

Explain the difference between `<form>` and `<form runat="server">` and describe how each is handled.

Solution

The HTML `<form>` tag provides space for user input and any input is sent back to the server without specific instructions for handling the input. The ASP.NET tag `<form runat="server">` will send the information back to an IIS .NET server that is able to handle many basic functions of the user's input.

Exercise 2

What is a variable and how is it related to data types in C#?

Solution

A variable is a place to temporarily hold information that can be used in the code. All variables in C# must be declared as a datatype, a designation that identifies the kind of information the variable holds.

Exercise 3

Use string, numeric, and date variables to create an ASPX file that displays your name, age, and date of birth.

Solution

See file `57084_Ch03_Ans03.aspx`, available with the code download:

```
<%@ Page Language="C#" Debug="true" %>
<script runat="server">

  void Page_Load()
  {
    if (Page.IsPostBack)
    {
      string  strName;
      byte bytAge;
      DateTime datDOB;

      strName = txtName.Text;
      bytAge = Convert.ToByte(txtAge.Text);
      datDOB = Convert.ToDateTime(txtDOB.Text);

      lblOut.Text = "Your Name is " + strName;
      lblOut.Text += "<br>Your Age is " + Convert.ToString(bytAge);
```

```
        lblOut.Text += "<br>Your Birthdate was " + Convert.ToString(datDOB);

    }    //End if (Page.IsPostBack)
}    //End Page_Load()

</script>
<html>
    <head>
    </head>
    <body>
      <form runat="server">
        Please enter your Name:
        <asp:TextBox runat="server" ID="txtName"/><br/>
        Please enter your Age: <asp:TextBox runat="server" ID="txtAge"/><br/>
        Please enter your Date of Birth:
        <asp:TextBox runat="server" ID="txtDOB"/><br/>
        <asp:Button runat="server" Text="Submit"/><br/>
        <asp:Label runat="server" ID="lblOut"/><br/>
      </form>
    </body>
</html>
```

Exercise 4

Arrange the following into groups of Numeric, Textual, and Miscellaneous data types. Rank the Numerics according to the size number they can hold. Give an example of a value and use for each.

Integer, Char, Byte, Uint, Short, Boolean, String

Long, Sbyte, Float, Double, Ushort, Date, Decimal, Ulong

Solution

The data types can be grouped in the following manner:

❑ **Numeric (small to large):**

   ❑ Byte and sbyte are good for people's ages or school grade levels

   ❑ Integer and uint can be used for storing numbers such as quantity of goods sold if the amount does not go over 2 billion and does not have decimals

   ❑ Short could be used for the quantity of goods sold that needs decimals but does not go over 32,000

   ❑ Ushort would be useful for storing the back log of sold items, providing the values do not go lower then 65,000

   ❑ Long and Ulong could hold distances to stars in kilometers

   ❑ Decimal could hold the value of an exchange rate to several dozen decimal places

  ❑ Float could hold the exact amount of load on a structural beam (including the decimal value)

  ❑ Double could hold a representation of ? to hundreds of decimal places

❑ **Text (small to large):**

  ❑ Char could hold the value for a single Chinese character that represents a person's family name

  ❑ String could hold a person's family name in a western language

❑ **Miscellaneous:**

  ❑ Boolean could hold a true if a box in a form has been filled in

  ❑ Date can hold a person's date of birth or the date when an order is shipped

Exercise 5

Create an array containing five of your favorite singers. Concatenate the elements of your array into one string and, after the opening sentence "My 5 favorite singers are:", display them using the <asp:label> control.

Solution

See file 57084_Ch03_Ans05.aspx, available with the code download:

```
<%@ Page Language="C#" Debug="true" %>
<script runat="server">
    void Page_Load()
    {
        if (Page.IsPostBack)
        {
            String[] strSingers = new String[5];

            strSingers[0] = txtSinger0.Text;
            strSingers[1] = txtSinger1.Text;
            strSingers[2] = txtSinger2.Text;
            strSingers[3] = txtSinger3.Text;
            strSingers[4] = txtSinger4.Text;

            lblOut.Text = "Your names of your favorite singers are:";
            lblOut.Text += "<br>" + strSingers[0];
            lblOut.Text += "<br>" + strSingers[1];
            lblOut.Text += "<br>" + strSingers[2];
            lblOut.Text += "<br>" + strSingers[3];
            lblOut.Text += "<br>" + strSingers[4];

        }     //End if (Page.IsPostBack)
    }   // End  Page_Load

</script>
<html>
    <head>
```

```
    </head>
    <body>
      <form runat="server">
        Please enter the names of your five favorite singers<br>
        <asp:TextBox runat="server" ID="txtSinger0"/>
        <asp:TextBox runat="server" ID="txtSinger1"/><br/>
        <asp:TextBox runat="server" ID="txtSinger2"/>
        <asp:TextBox runat="server" ID="txtSinger3"/><br/>
        <asp:TextBox runat="server" ID="txtSinger4"/><br/>
        <asp:Button runat="server" Text="Submit"/><br/>
        <asp:Label runat="server" ID="lblOut"/><br/>
      </form>
    </body>
</html>
```

Exercise 6

Describe a situation in which you would use each of the following and state why that choice is the best:

❏ Arrays

❏ Arraylists

❏ Hashtables

❏ Sorted lists

Solution

❏ **Arrays**: Storing the words of a document while looking for patterns in phrasing. This is a situation where we need a high processing speed but do not need to sort or add to an index.

❏ **Arraylists**: Creating a list of items in an order. At the beginning of the order we are not sure how many kinds of items there will be. Speed is an issue, but we the flexibility of adding any number of items is of higher importance.

❏ **Hashtables**: Storing country names and codes and reading the names by referring to the codes. Hashtables are best because they avoid the use of a numbering index system, we can use the country codes directly for indexing.

❏ **Sorted lists**: Displaying a glossary of abbreviations in alphabetically ascending or descending order. A sorted list allows you to use abbreviations to read the list and avoid a numeric index.

Chapter 4

This chapter looks at the key building blocks of C# in the context of an ASP.NET page.

Exercise 1

In each of the following Boolean expressions, identify the integer values for A for which each expression will evaluate to true, as well as those for which each will evaluate to false:

Solution

You can test your answers using the page named `57084_Ch04_Ans01.aspx` in the download files.

1.   `NOT A=0`

True for all integers except 0.

Without the `NOT`, the answer would be only zero. When we add the `NOT`, it reverses to be all numbers except zero.

2.   `A > 0 OR A < 5`

True for all integers.

The left side alone would be true for all integers greater than zero (only zero and negative integers would be false). The right side includes all integers that are less than five, including zero and negative integers. With the OR clause an integer has to be within one of the two expressions in order for the whole expression to be true. When we combine these two sets of answers we get all integers. (The integers 1 to 4 are included by both expressions)

3.   `NOT A > 0 OR A < 5`

True for integers 5 and below. Integers 6 and above will evaluate to false.

The issue here is precedence between the `NOT` and `OR`. The `NOT` is only applied to the expression on the left of the `OR`. Think of this problem as `(NOT A > 0) OR (A < 5)`. On the left we have true for any numbers that are not greater then zero, so true is for zero and negative numbers. On the right we have true for any number that is less then five. With the two sides of the `OR` combined, we have true for all negative numbers and zero and positive numbers up to 5. Numbers greater than and including 6 are true for neither side and thus resolve to false.

4.   `A > 1 AND A < 5 OR A > 7 AND A < 10`

True for 2,3,4, 8, and 9 only.

Like the last problem, the issue is to establish the precedence of the operators. Think of this as `(A > 1 AND A < 5) OR (A > 7 AND A < 10)`. On the left of the `OR` we can see that only integers 2,3, and 4 would fit both criteria. On the right side of the `OR` the situation is similar; only 8 and 9 meet both criteria. When you consider the `OR` you have to combine those two answer sets.

5.   `A < 10 OR A > 12 AND NOT A > 20`

True for all integers 9 and below (including zero and negatives) and for 13 through 20 inclusive. False for 10, 11, 12, and all integers above (and inclusive of) 21.

Think of this problem with some parentheses. The `OR` is the last to be evaluated, so our parentheses are `(A < 10) OR (A > 12 AND NOT A > 20)`. First look at the right side of the `OR`. Integers must meet both tests when there is an `AND` clause so that would be 13 through 20 are true. Now look at the left side of the `OR`. Any number less then 10 will be true. The final answer is the combination of those two answer sets.

Exercise 2

Suggest a loop structure that would be appropriate for each of the following scenarios and justify your choice:

Solution

1. **Displaying a set of items from a shopping list stored in an array**

This depends on whether we know the array is full or not. We can get the value of the upper bound of an array, but it is harder to know if all of the members have values. In most cases, we would use a `while` loop.

2. **Displaying a calendar for the current month**

We can know how many days are in a month, so we know how many loops we will have to perform before we start looping. Therefore, we can use the `for` loop.

3. **Looking through an array to find the location of a specific entry**

Assuming that we do not know the number of members when we start the loop it is best to use a `while` loop. If we can find out the number of members before the loop starts, we can use a `for` loop.

4. **Drawing a chess board using an HTML table**

Before we start the loop, we know a chess board is 8 by 8 squares, so we can use a `for` loop. You can access the code file named `57084_Ch04_Ans2.aspx` for code that generates a chess board.

Exercise 3

Write a page that generates a few random numbers between two integers provided by the user in textboxes.

Solution

See file `57084_Ch04_Ans03.aspx`, available with the code download:

```
<%@ Page Language="C#" Debug="true" %>
<script runat="server">

    void Page_Load()
    {
        if (IsPostBack)
        {
            lblOut.Text = "";
            Random MyRand = new Random();
            byte intOutputCounter;
            for (intOutputCounter=1; intOutputCounter< 11; ++intOutputCounter)
            {
                lblOut.Text += "<br>";
                lblOut.Text += Convert.ToInt32((Convert.ToSByte(txtHigh.Text) -
                               Convert.ToSByte(txtLow.Text)) *
                               MyRand.NextDouble() +
                               Convert.ToSByte(txtLow.Text));
            }           // end loop
        }               //End If
    }                   //end Page_Load()

</script>
```

```
<html>
    <head>
    </head>
    <body>
     <form runat="server">

     Please enter integers for range of random numbers. <br>
     Lowest number (min = -128):
     <asp:TextBox runat="server" ID="txtLow" Text="-5"/><br>
     Highest number (max = +127):
     < asp:TextBox runat="server" ID="txtHigh" Text="+5"/><br/>
     <asp:Button runat="server" Text="Submit"/><br/>
     <asp:Label runat="server" ID="lblOut"/><br/>
     </form>
    </body>
</html>
```

Chapter 5

This chapter covers the basics of functions and their implementation in ASP.NET using C#.

Exercise 1

Determine whether a function will return a value for each of the following scenarios and justify your choice:

Solution

❑ **Calculate the due date of a book being checked out of a library**: The function should return a value because we will execute some code and return a value (the due date).

❑ **Find out on which day of the week (Monday, Tuesday, and so on) does a certain date fall in the future**: The function should return a value because we will execute some code and return a value (the day of the week).

❑ **Display a string determined by the marketing department and stored in a text file in a label**: The function should not return a value because we will only execute some code to perform an action.

Exercise 2

List where and when are values held when a variable is used as a parameter passed by value. Do the same for a variable for a variable that is a parameter passed by reference.

Solution

Passing a parameter by value holds the value in the original place *and* in the function. So while the function is running, two copies of the value exist of which *one* may be modified in the function. The copy in the function will be destroyed when the function finishes executing.

Passing a parameter by reference holds the value in only one place. Changes made to the value during the function will affect the sole copy and will be useable by both the function and the calling code. Although the function will stop using the value when it finishes executing, the value will persist in the calling code.

Exercise 3

Write a function that generates a set of random integers. Build an ASP.NET page that allows you to enter the lower and upper bounds, and generate a set of random numbers within that range.

Solution

The ASP.NET page could be written as follows (available in the code download as 57084_Ch05_Ans03.aspx:

```
<%@ Page Language="C#" Debug="True" %>
<script runat="server">

void Page_Load()
{
    if (IsPostBack)
    {
        /* The easiest way to see if people have written numbers in the
           textbox is to try and convert them to integers as required.
           If an error occurs, they aren't. We use the try catch to write
           them a note to use numbers. See Chapter 14 on handling errors for
           more on the try catch statement */
        try
        {
            int Bound1 = Convert.ToInt32(txtBound1.Text);
            int Bound2 = Convert.ToInt32(txtBound2.Text);
            int NumberOfNumbers = Convert.ToInt32(txtQty.Text);

            /* Check first if the numbers are the same. If they are, tell the
               user off. If not, find out which is larger and pass that as the
               upper bound to RowOfNumbers. Pass the other number as the lower
               bound. */
            if (!(Bound1 == Bound2))
            {
                if (Bound1 < Bound2)
                {
                    RowOfNumbers(Bound1, Bound2, NumberOfNumbers);
                }
                else
                {
                    RowOfNumbers(Bound2, Bound1, NumberOfNumbers);
                }
            }
            else
            {
                lblOut.Text = "<hr>The two numbers must be different!";
            }
        } // end of try statement
```

```
                catch
                {
                    lblOut.Text = "<hr>Please enter three numbers. No tricks now!";
                }
        }    // End of if postback
        CleanUI();
}

/*
    Cleans up the input boxes after the random numbers have been displayed
*/

void CleanUI()
{
    txtBound1.Text = "";
    txtBound2.Text = "";
    txtQty.Text = "";
}

/*
    Generates a random number. Uses a seed value to make sure the number is
    random each time.
*/

int GenerateRandomNumber(int LowerBound, int UpperBound, int seed)
{
    Random objRandom = new Random(seed);
    int RandomNumber = objRandom.Next(LowerBound, UpperBound);
    return RandomNumber;
}

/* Generates the row of as many numbers as requested*/

void RowOfNumbers(int LowerBound, int UpperBound, int Quantity)
{
    lblOut.Text =  "<hr>" + Quantity.ToString() +
                    " random numbers between " + LowerBound.ToString();
    lblOut.Text += " and " + UpperBound.ToString() + " inclusive: ";

    for (int i=1; i<=Quantity; i++)
    {
      lblOut.Text += GenerateRandomNumber(LowerBound, UpperBound,
                    i).ToString();
      lblOut.Text += "   ";
    }
}
</script>

<html>
<head>
    <title>Random Number Generator</title>
</head>
<body>
    <form runat="server">
```

```
            Number 1:
            <asp:TextBox id="txtBound1" runat="server"></asp:TextBox>
            <br />
            Number 2:
            <asp:TextBox id="txtBound2" runat="server"></asp:TextBox>
            <br />
            Quantity of Numbers:
            <asp:TextBox id="txtQty" runat="server"></asp:TextBox>
            <br />
            <asp:Button id="Button1" runat="server" Text="Submit"></asp:Button>
            <br />
            <asp:Label id="lblOut" runat="server"></asp:Label>
        </form>
</body>
</html>
```

Chapter 6

This chapter discusses how ASP.NET revolves around an event-driven model, how things occur in strict order, and ways in which the ASP.NET page can react to user intervention. The solution files for some of the exercises are too long to be included here – these have been put up for download on the Wrox Web site.

Exercise 1

Explain why event-driven programming is such a good way of programming for the Web.

Solution

Event-driven programming is a good way of programming for the Web because it mirrors user interaction with Web pages.

Exercise 2

Modify an HTML form to add a set of ASP.NET Server Controls so that the information in the form is retained when the submit button is pressed.

Solution

The following code solves this problem (available in the code download as 57084_Ch06_Ans2.aspx):

```
<%@ Page Language="C#" %>
<html>
<head>
    <title>Chapter 6 Question 2 Solution</title>
</head>
<body>
    <form runat="server">
        <p>
```

```
                    Please enter your name:
                    <asp:TextBox id="txtName" runat="server"></asp:TextBox>
        </p>
        <p>
            What would you like for breakfast?
            <asp:CheckBoxList id="cblWhatToEat" runat="server">
                <asp:ListItem Value="Cereal">Cereal</asp:ListItem>
                <asp:ListItem Value="Eggs">Eggs</asp:ListItem>
                <asp:ListItem Value="Pancakes">Pancakes</asp:ListItem>
            </asp:CheckBoxList>
        </p>
        <p>
            When would you like breakfast?
            <asp:RadioButtonList id="rblWhenToEat" runat="server">
                <asp:ListItem Value="Now">Now</asp:ListItem>
                <asp:ListItem Value="Later">Later</asp:ListItem>
            </asp:RadioButtonList>
        </p>
        <p>
            <asp:Button id="Button1" runat="server"
                        Text="Place Your Order"></asp:Button>
        </p>
    </form>
</body>
</html>
```

Exercise 3

Add a Page_Load() event handler to the ASPX code you've just created for *Exercise 2*, to confirm the selections made in the following format:

Thank you very much _____.

You have chosen _____ for breakfast. I will prepare it for you _____.

Solution

The required changes are highlighted below.

```
<%@ Page Language="C#" %>
<script runat="server">

    void Page_Load()
    {
        if (IsPostBack)
        {
            lblConfirmation.Text = "Thank you very much "
                                   + txtName.Text + ".<br />";
            lblConfirmation.Text += "You have chosen " +
                cblWhatToEat.SelectedValue + " for breakfast. ";
            lblConfirmation.Text += "I will prepare it for you " +
                rblWhenToEat.SelectedValue + ".";
        }
```

```
        }

</script>
<html>
<head>
    <title>Chapter 6 Question 3 Solution</title>
</head>
<body>
    <form runat="server">
...
...
            <asp:Button id="Button1" runat="server"
                        Text="Place Your Order"></asp:Button>
        </p>
        <p>
            <asp:Label id="lblConfirmation" runat="server"></asp:Label>
        </p>
    </form>
</body>
</html>
```

Exercise 4

Create a very basic virtual telephone using an ASPX file that displays a textbox and a button named Call. Configure your ASPX file so that when you type a telephone number into the textbox and press Call, you are:

❑ Presented with a message confirming the number you are calling

❑ Presented with another button called Disconnect, which when pressed, returns you to your opening page, leaving you ready to type another number

Solution

The following code will generate these results for you (also available as 57084_Ch06_Ans4.aspx):

```
<%@ Page Language="C#" %>
<script runat="server">

    void DialNumber(object sender, EventArgs e) {
        lblConfirmation.Text = "Dialling " + txtPhoneNumber.Text;
        btnDisconnect.Visible = true;
    }

    void DisconnectNumber(object sender, EventArgs e) {
        lblConfirmation.Text = "";
        btnDisconnect.Visible = false;
    }

</script>
<html>
<head>
    <title>Chapter 6 Question 4 Solution</title>
```

```
    </head>
    <body>
        <form runat="server">
            <p>
                Number to Dial:
                <asp:TextBox id="txtPhoneNumber" runat="server"></asp:TextBox>
                <asp:Button id="btnCall" onclick="DialNumber"
                            runat="server" Text="Call"></asp:Button>
            </p>
            <p>
                <asp:Label id="lblConfirmation" runat="server"></asp:Label>
            </p>
            <p>
                <asp:Button id="btnDisconnect" onclick="DisconnectNumber"
                            runat="server" Text="Disconnect"
                            Visible="False"></asp:Button>
            </p>
        </form>
    </body>
</html>
```

Chapter 7

This chapter introduces concepts such as properties, methods, constructors, collections, and overloading by making use of examples related to real-world objects.

Exercise 1

In our examples, we've modelled some simple characteristics of real world objects, such as animals. Think about other real world objects that when turned into classes would be useful in programming.

Solution

You've probably used one of these objects without thinking about it. What happens when you go to the supermarket? You put items in a shopping basket. Ever bought anything online? How many of those online sites have a shopping basket? Yep, pretty much all of them. In fact, the shopping basket is one thing where the concept maps really well from the real world into the virtual one.

Creating a shopping basket in .NET is actually a little more complex than you'd think because it has to contain multiple items. You don't know in advance the number of items people will put into it, therefore you can't define properties for each item. What you need is a collection of some sort which expands as items are added. There are several collections supplied in the `System.Collections` namespace. It's worth experimenting with them.

Exercise 2

In the `Animal` class where the `Walk()` method accepts an argument of type Integer, expand this to use it as the speed of walking. Think about how you'd store that speed and what you could do with it.

Solution

Storing the speed internally in the class can be achieved simply by declaring a private variable, and modifying the `Walk()` method:

```
private int _Speed;

public string Walk(int Direction) {
    _Speed = Direction;
    if (Direction > 0)
        Return _Name +
                ": you are now walking backwards at a speed of " + _Speed;
    else
        Return _Name +
                ": you are now walking forwards at a speed of " + _Speed;
}
```

What you could also consider is providing a property to access or set the speed. Other options include adding methods to speed up and slow down the speed. For example:

```
public void SpeedUp(int SpeedUpBy) {
  _Speed += SpeedUpBy;
}

public void SlowDow(int SlowDownBy) {
  _Speed -= SlowDownBy;
}
```

Exercise 3

Taking the results of *Exercise 2*, think about how you'd add validation to the speed to ensure that it doesn't exceed some set limits.

Solution

The interaction between methods and properties can be seen very clearly when we need to validate values. Consider the addition of speed to our `Person` class, which can be set via three methods: `Walk()`, `SpeedUp()`, and `SlowDown()`. If you want to ensure that the speed never exceeds the range -100 to 100, where would you do this? Should you do this in each method that accesses the _Speed variable? No, because you don't want to have lots of repeated code. Remember how we said encapsulation is one of the key points of classes – we should encapsulate the speed as a property and do the checking there:

```
public int Speed {
  get {
    return _Speed;
  }
  set {
    if (Value < -100)
      _Speed = -100;
    else
      _Speed = Value;
```

```
    if (Value > 100)
      _Speed = 100;
    else
      _Speed = Value;
  }
}
```

All accesses to the _Speed variable should be replaced with the property name:

```
public string Walk(int Direction) {
  Speed = Direction;
```

If you don't want to expose the speed as a public property you can make it private:

```
private int Speed {
```

You still get the advantages of encapsulation but without exposing the property.

Exercise 4

Describe the main differences between inheritance and interfaces. When would you use one over the other?

Solution

The main difference between inheritance and interfaces is that interfaces don't implement any functionality. They only define what the class must implement and not how it is done. Inheritance on the other hand provides a way to supply implementation to classes that inherit from a base class. It's important to understand this difference and understand where you'd use one method over another.

Interfaces are good if you need to define the structure of a class for others to implement – perhaps in a team environment where you are writing common routines and require certain features to be present on the objects that will use those routines. Inheritable classes are good when you have to supply functionality to multiple child classes. The ASP.NET Server controls are a perfect example, where much of the implementation is provided in the base WebControl class. An interface wouldn't be any use because each control would then have to implement the same functionality.

Exercise 5

Create a class called PieceOfString with a single read / write property (of type int) called Length. Create an instance of the class and set Length to 16. Now you can answer that age old question, "How long is a piece of string?"

Solution

OK, OK, so it's not a real exercise. But I thought it was funny!!!

Chapter 8

This chapter looks at the use of the `Connection` and `Command` objects for opening data sources and retrieving information into `DataSets`.

Exercise 1

In this chapter, we created a page that showed the products for a single selected category. Try and think of ways to enhance this to show products for either a selected category or all categories.

Solution

The simplest solution to this would seem to be adding another button to fetch all of the products. However, this isn't the best approach because it can easily confuse the user. The best approach is to have a dropdown list showing all categories. Two things are required to implement this: you need to add the All Categories selection to the list and you need to customize the data retrieval so that it fetches all rows.

The first part is fairly simple, as we can simply add a new item to the list after we add the categories from the database. We can't add it to the list before this because if we bind data to the list, the manually added item would get overwritten. Our code now becomes:

```
void Page_Load(Object Sender, EventArgs e) {

  if (!Page.IsPostBack) {
    lstCategory.DataSource = GetCategories();
    lstCategory.DataValueField = "CategoryID";
    lstCategory.DataTextField = "CategoryName";
    lstCategory.DataBind();
    lstCategory.Items.Add(new ListItem("<all categories>", "-1"));
  }
}
```

This works by adding a new `ListItem` to the `DropDownList` control. Every item in the list is a `ListItem` that is contained within an `Items` collection. So we create a new `ListItem` (the arguments are the text and the value), and add it to the collection. This item appears at the end of the list.

To handle this `ListItem`, you can use the `GetProducts()` function. We can automatically build an SQL string with the placeholder and parameters, but these aren't required if we are showing all products. Since we've added the `ListItem` with a value of -1 (which isn't a real `CategoryID`) we can use that to change our SQL string:

```
System.Data.DataSet GetProducts(int categoryID) {
  string connectionString = "Provider=Microsoft.Jet.OLEDB.4.0; " +
        "Ole DB Services=-4; Data Source=C:\\BegASPNET11\\" +
        "data\\Northwind.mdb";
  System.Data.IDbConnection dbConnection =
        new System.Data.OleDb.OleDbConnection(connectionString);

  string queryString;
  if (categoryId == -1){
    queryString = "SELECT [Products].[ProductName], " +
```

```
            "[Products].[QuantityPerUnit], [Products].[UnitPrice], " +
            "[Products].[UnitsInStock] FROM [Products]";
    }
    else {
        queryString = "SELECT [Products].[ProductName], " +
            "[Products].[QuantityPerUnit], [Products].[UnitPrice], " +
            "[Products].[UnitsInStock] FROM [Products] " +
            "WHERE ([Products].[CategoryID] = @CategoryID)";
    }
    System.Data.IDbCommand dbCommand = new System.Data.OleDb.OleDbCommand();
    dbCommand.CommandText = queryString;
    dbCommand.Connection = dbConnection;

    if (categoryID != -1) {
        System.Data.IDataParameter dbParam_categoryID =
                new System.Data.OleDb.OleDbParameter();
        dbParam_categoryID.ParameterName = "@CategoryID";
        dbParam_categoryID.Value = categoryID;
        dbParam_categoryID.DbType = System.Data.DbType.Int32;
        dbCommand.Parameters.Add(dbParam_categoryID);
    }
    System.Data.IDbDataAdapter dataAdapter =
            new System.Data.OleDb.OleDbDataAdapter();
    dataAdapter.SelectCommand = dbCommand;
    System.Data.DataSet dataSet = new System.Data.DataSet();
    dataAdapter.Fill(dataSet);

    return dataSet;
}
```

Here, we simply create a different SQL string if we are showing products for all categories. If the `CategoryID` is not −1, it implies that a category has been selected so we add the `Parameter`.

Exercise 2

In *Exercise 1* we encountered the problem of wanting to bind data from a database to a `DropDownList` as well as manually adding an entry, where adding the manual entry could only be done at the end of the list. You could use techniques shown in this chapter or using techniques that have not yet been covered. Try and code the solution using the known technique, but see if you can think of a way to solve it with code we haven't covered yet.

Solution

The first solution to this problem is to not use data binding; simply add the data manually. We could do this by not using a `DataSet` and using a `DataReader` instead, looping through all of the records. This would allow you to manually add a category first, and then all of the data. For example, assuming our `GetCategories()` function returns a `DataReader`, we could do this as follows:

```
void Page_Load(Object sender, EventArgs e) {

    if (!Page.IsPostback) {
        lstCategory.Items.Add(new ListItem("<all categories>", "-1"));
```

```
        System.Data.IDataReader dr = GetCategories();

        while (dr.Read())
          lstCategory.Items.Add(new ListItem(dr["CategoryName"].ToString(),
                                      dr["CategoryID"].ToString())))
    }
}
```

Here, we simply add all of the items from the `DataReader` in the same manner as for the **All Categories** item.

The other solution to this would be to add the item to the first row of the data in the `DataSet` and then use the existing data binding. This is more difficult to achieve and we are not going to cover this solution here.

Chapter 9

Exercise 1

Load a `DataSet` using the `Shippers` table from the `Northwind` database and add the following data into it:

❑   **Company Name**: FastShippers

❑   **Phone**: (503) 555-9384

Solution

This isn't too hard and can easily be done in the `Page_Load()` method of an ASP.NET page:

```
string connectionString;
string strSQL;
DataSet data = new DataSet();
OleDbConnection dbConnection;
OleDbDataAdapter dataAdapter;
OleDbCommandBuilder commandBuilder;

// set the connection and query details
connectionString = "Provider=Microsoft.Jet.OLEDB.4.0; " +
                    "Data Source=C:\\BegASPNET11\\data\\Northwind.mdb";
strSQL = "SELECT * FROM Shippers";

// open the connection and set the command
dbConnection = new OledbConnection(connectionString);
dataAdapter = new OledbDataAdapter(strSQL, dbConnection);

// fill the dataset with the data
dataAdapter.Fill(data, "Shippers");
```

```
// add a new row to the table
DataTable  table;
DataRow newRow;

table = data.Tables["Employees"];
newRow = table.NewRow();
newRow["CompanyName"] = "FastShippers";
newRow["Phone"] = "(503) 555-9384";
table.Rows.Add(newRow);
```

Exercise 2

Using the `CommandBuilder` object, create an `InsertCommand` to insert this new data.

Solution

Create an `OleDbCommandBuilder` object, use the `GetInsertCommand()` method, and send the changes back to the database:

```
// create the other commands
commandBuilder = new OleDbCommandBuilder(dataAdapter);
dataAdapter.InsertCommand = commandBuilder.GetInsertCommand();

// update the database
dataAdapter.Update(data, "Shippers");
```

Notice that we didn't specify other commands, as we are only adding a row of data. If we had changed a row or deleted one, then those changes would be reflected in the database as we haven't specified the `UpdateCommand` or `DeleteCommand`.

Exercise 3

Using direct SQL commands, change the phone number of `FastShippers` to `(503) 555-0000`.

Solution

This is quite similar to the previous examples, only in those we added a row. In this case, we use the SQL `UPDATE` command to set the `Phone` column to the value of the supplied parameter.

```
string connectionString = "Provider=Microsoft.Jet.OLEDB.4.0; " +
        "Data Source=C:\BegASPNET11\data\Northwind.mdb";
OleDbConnection dbConnection = new OleDbConnection(connectionString);
dbConnection.Open();

string commandString = "UPDATE Shippers SET Phone = @Phone " +
                          "WHERE CompanyName = 'FastShippers'";

OleDbCommand dbCommand = new OleDbCommand(commandString, dbConnection);

OleDbParameter firstNameParam =
        new OleDbParameter("@Phone", OleDbType.VarChar, 24);
firstNameParam.value = "(503) 555-0000";
```

```
dbCommand.Parameters.Add(firstNameParam);

dbCommand.ExecuteNonQuery();

dbConnection.Close();
```

Exercise 4

Use the Web Matrix Data templates to create an Editable `DataGrid`. Have a look at the code and see how many familiar techniques you see.

Solution

This uses many advanced features of the `DataGrid`, but the ADO.NET code is similar to what you've been working with. Take the `DataGrid_Update()` method for example, which caters for new and updated data. It either builds a SQL `INSERT` or `UPDATE` statement, uses `Parameters` to set the values, and then uses the `ExecuteNonQuery()` method of the `DataAdapter` to send changes back to the database.

The `DataGrid_Delete()` method does a similar thing, constructing a SQL `DELETE` statement.

The `AddNew_Click()` method uses an interesting technique – it adds a new row to a table but doesn't update the database. Instead, it sets a flag indicating that a new row is being added. This means that the user can modify the data in the new row, or even cancel the addition before sending changes to the database.

Chapter 10

This chapter explains how ASP.NET server controls derive their properties and methods from the various classes and objects that make up the .NET Framework. This chapter is where you see the Wrox United application taking shape.

Exercise 1

Consider a use for an HTML tag with `runat="server"` in the Wrox United application in place of one of the existing Web controls and explain why the HTML control is able to achieve the same result as the Web control.

Solution

You can make this change in several places in `Default.aspx` – for example, the `asp:Hyperlink` controls could be replaced with HTML anchor tags with a `runat="server"` attribute. You could also change the panel which displays match details and replaces it with a `<div>` tag:

```
<div id="pnlFixtureDetails" runat="server" visible="false">
  <asp:Repeater id="MatchesByDateList" runat="server">
    <headertemplate>
    . . .
```

```
        </headertemplate>
        <itemtemplate>
        ...
        </itemtemplate>
        <separatortemplate>
        ...
        </separatortemplate>
    </asp:Repeater>
</div>
```

This works because the only property of the `Panel` control used in this example is the `Visible` property; a property that is available to all server controls, including HTML controls. A `<div>` is a direct replacement for a `Panel` in this case.

Exercise 2

Add another event handler to the `Teams.aspx` page that reacts to the selection of a player's name and takes the reader to the `Players.aspx` page.

Solution

Add the following event-handling code to `Players.aspx`:

```
void PlayersList_ItemCommand(object sender, RepeaterCommandEventArgs e)
{
  if(e.CommandName == "ShowPlayers")
  {
    Response.Redirect("Players.aspx");
  }
}
```

Change the HTML as follows:

```
<asp:Repeater id="PlayersList" runat="server"
              OnItemCommand="PlayersList_ItemCommand">
  <ItemTemplate>
    <asp:linkbutton
          text='<%# DataBinder.Eval(Container.DataItem, "PlayerName") %>'
          style="color:darkred"
          runat="server" width="120" CommandName="ShowPlayers" />
      
    <asp:Label
          text='<%# DataBinder.Eval(Container.DataItem, "PositionName") %>'
          id="playerposition" runat="server" />
    <br />
  </ItemTemplate>
  <headerTemplate>
    Players in: <%= selectedTeam %>
    <hr color="#b0c4de" width="250px" />
  </headerTemplate>
  <footerTemplate>
    <hr color="#b0c4de" width="250px" />
  </footerTemplate>
```

```
</asp:Repeater>
```

Exercise 3

Amend the code in Default.aspx so that if a user selects a date in the calendar for which there are no matches, nothing is displayed in the panel.

Solution

There are two ways you can achieve this result. The first of these is to modify the EventCalendar_SelectionChanged() event handler as follows:

```
public void EventCalendar_SelectionChanged(object sender, EventArgs e)
{
  if (DateList[EventCalendar.SelectedDate] != null)
  {
    MatchesByDateList.DataSource = GamesByDate(EventCalendar.SelectedDate);
    pnlFixtureDetails.Visible = true;
    MatchesByDateList.DataBind();
  }
  else
  {
    pnlFixtureDetails.Visible = false;
  }
}
```

Alternatively, you can change how non-match days are rendered in the calendar:

```
public void EventCalendar_DayRender(object sender, DayRenderEventArgs e)
{
  if (DateList[e.Day.Date] != null)
  {

    e.Cell.Style.Add("font-weight", "bold");
    e.Cell.Style.Add("font-size", "larger");
    e.Cell.Style.Add("border", "3 dotted darkred");
    e.Cell.Style.Add("background", "#f0f0f0");

    // ensure match dates are hyperlinks
    e.Day.IsSelectable = true;
  }
  else
  {
    e.Cell.Style.Add("font-weight", "lighter");
    e.Cell.Style.Add("color", "DimGray");

    // ensure non-match dates are not selectable
    e.Day.IsSelectable = false;
  }
}
```

Using the `IsSelectable` property, we can control whether or not a date is selectable. Setting this to `false` means that non-match days are not rendered as hyperlinks and therefore, will cause the panel to not be displayed. The code in the following chapters uses this property to achieve this result.

Exercise 4

Have a go at customizing `Players.aspx`: change the field that displays the name of the player into a hyperlink that, when clicked, will reveal a panel lower down on the page that lists the team or teams that the selected player is a member of. You will find that the `Fields` editor of the `MxDataGrid` is very useful for this (select the `Fields` property builder when you are in the **Design** view). You need to ensure that the clicking of the player name is handled correctly. You also need to add another method to extract team information (you may find that the `DataReader` that returns the list of teams from the `Teams.aspx` page is useful here).

Solution

First, we need to change the `BoundField` into a `ButtonField`:

```
<Fields>
  <wmx:BoundField Visible="False" DataField="PlayerID"></wmx:BoundField>
  <wmx:ButtonField DataTextField="PlayerName"
    HeaderText="Name" CommandName="ShowPlayer"></wmx:ButtonField>
  <wmx:BoundField DataField="Profile" HeaderText="Profile"></wmx:BoundField>
  <wmx:BoundField DataField="JoinDate" HeaderText="Join Date"
    DataFormatString="{0:d}"></wmx:BoundField>
</Fields>
```

Notice we set a `CommandName` property on the field as well to be able to intercept and handle commands. Let's now add a repeater that will show the teams for a particular player:

```
<p>
  <asp:Repeater id="TeamList" runat="server" Visible="False">
    <ItemTemplate>
      <asp:Label
            style="color:darkred"
            text='<%# DataBinder.Eval(Container.DataItem, "TeamName") %>'
            runat="server" width="120" />
        
      <asp:Label
            text='<%# DataBinder.Eval(Container.DataItem, "PositionName") %>'
            id="playerposition"
            runat="server" />
      <br />
    </ItemTemplate>
    <headerTemplate>
      <%= selectedPlayer %>'s Teams:
      <hr color="#b0c4de" width="250px" />
    </headerTemplate>
    <footerTemplate>
      <hr color="#b0c4de" width="250px" />
    </footerTemplate>
  </asp:Repeater>
```

```
  </p>
```

The resultant page looks almost identical to the repeater from the `Team` page.

We also need to tell the `DataGrid` that we'll be writing an `ItemCommand()` event handler for it:

```
<wmx:MxDataGrid id="MxDataGrid1" runat="server"
    BorderStyle="None"
    BorderWidth="1px"
    DataKeyField="PlayerID"
    CellPadding="3"
    BackColor="White"
    AllowPaging="True"
    DataMember="Players"
    AllowSorting="True"
    BorderColor="#CCCCCC"
    DataSourceControlID="AccessDataSourceControl1"
    AutoGenerateFields="False"
    OnItemCommand="MxDataGrid1_ItemCommand">
```

Now, in the **Code** view, we need to change the whole page script:

```
private string selectedPlayer;

void Page_Load()
{
  Page.DataBind();
}

private void MxDataGrid1_ItemCommand(object sender,
  MxDataGridCommandEventArgs e)
{
  if (e.CommandName.Equals("ShowPlayer"))
  {
    LinkButton thing = (LinkButton)e.CommandSource;
    selectedPlayer = thing.Text;

    TableCell cell = (TableCell)e.Item.Controls[0];

    int SelectedPlayerID = int.Parse(cell.Text);

    TeamList.DataSource = GetTeamsByPlayer(SelectedPlayerID);
    TeamList.DataBind();
    TeamList.Visible = true;
  }
  else
  {
    TeamList.Visible = false;
  }
}

private System.Data.IDataReader GetTeamsByPlayer(int playerID)
{
```

```
      string connectionString =
        ConfigurationSettings.AppSettings["ConnectionString"];
      System.Data.IDbConnection dbConnection =
        new System.Data.OleDb.OleDbConnection(connectionString);

      string queryString = "SELECT
        [Players].[PlayerName],[Positions].[PositionName],[Teams].[TeamName]
        FROM [Players], [Positions], [PlayerTeam], [Teams]
        WHERE (([PlayerTeam].[PlayerID] = [Players].[PlayerID])
        AND ([PlayerTeam].[Position] = [Positions].[PositionID])
        AND ([PlayerTeam].[TeamID] = [Teams].[TeamID])
        AND ([Players].[PlayerID] = @PlayerID))";
      System.Data.IDbCommand dbCommand = new System.Data.OleDb.OleDbCommand();
      dbCommand.CommandText = queryString;
      dbCommand.Connection = dbConnection;

      System.Data.IDataParameter dbParam_teamID =
                                    new System.Data.OleDb.OleDbParameter();
      dbParam_teamID.ParameterName = "@PlayerID";
      dbParam_teamID.Value = playerID;
      dbParam_teamID.DbType = System.Data.DbType.Int32;
      dbCommand.Parameters.Add(dbParam_teamID);

      dbConnection.Open();
      System.Data.IDataReader dataReader =
        dbCommand.ExecuteReader(System.Data.CommandBehavior.CloseConnection);

      return dataReader;
}
```

The `GetTeamsByPlayer()` method is a very simple alteration of `GetPlayersByTeam()` from the `Teams` page. The really tricky part on this page is that we need to obtain the ID of the player that the user selects. In the `Team` page, that was easy – we packaged up each team's ID as the `CommandArgument` for the `LinkButton` in the teams `DataList`. But a `DataGrid` won't let us do that, so we need to find another solution. Remember the fields we set up on the players `DataGrid`? At the left hand side there was an invisible column that contained the player ID. This is how we get it:

```
      TableCell cell = (TableCell)e.Item.Controls[0];
      int SelectedPlayerID = int.Parse(cell.Text);
```

Chapter 11

This chapter deals with tracking users across pages and looks at the ASP.NET objects that are used to enable this feature.

Exercise 1

Add some text, **Current Topic**, and a `Label` control to the `Chat.aspx` page above the main chat box, which contains the text of the current topic (stored in the `Application` object). Add some default topic text to the `Global.asax` file and also another box and button to the page, allowing you to change the current topic.

Solution

You should start this exercise by adding the text and `Label` control to the top of the page. This is a simple addition that you can do either in the Design view, HTML view, or the All view.

❑   In Design view, type some text directly below the sub-heading that says Current topic:.

❑   Drag a `Label` control onto the page and set its `ID` to `lblCurrentTopic`.

Alternatively, enter the following code below the sub-heading:

```
<h2>Online Chat</h2>
Current topic:  
<asp:Label id="lblCurrentTopic" runat="server">
</asp:Label>
<br />
. . .
```

In `Global.asax`, you need to enter code that will store the details of the default topic when the application is first started:

```
public void Application_Start(Object sender, EventArgs e)
{
   Application["ChatLog"] = "Hello, and welcome to the Wrox United Chat page!";
   Application["CurrentTopic"] = "General free-for-all chat!";
}
```

Back in `Chat.aspx`, add the following line to the `Page_Load` event handler:

```
void Page_Load()
{
   txtChatBox.Text = (string)Application["ChatLog"];
   lblCurrentTopic.Text = (string)Application["CurrentTopic"];
}
```

You can run the page at this stage and the default topic, 'General free-for-all chat!', will be displayed at the top of the page.

To make this exercise interactive, you need to add a couple of controls and another event handler. Below the two buttons, you need to add another row to your table.

❑   In the first cell, enter some text to tell the user what to do (for example, Enter a new topic).

❑   In the next cell, drag a `TextBox` control into the cell and name it `txtTopic`.

❑   Add another row and in the first cell, enter a non-breaking space. In the second, add a button control with its `ID` set to `btnUpdateTopic`. Double-click this button to wire up an event handler for the click event.

Alternatively, enter the following code:

```
    <asp:Button id="btnPost" onclick="btnPost_Click" runat="server"
        Text="Post message"></asp:Button>
    <asp:Button id="btnClearLog" onclick="btnClearLog_Click" runat="server"
        Text="Clear log"></asp:Button>
      <hr />
    </td>
  </tr>
  <tr>
    <td width="150">
      Enter a new topic:
    </td>
    <td>
      <asp:TextBox id="txtTopic" runat="server" MaxLength="100" width="402px">
      </asp:TextBox>
    </td>
  </tr>
  <tr>
    <td>
       
    </td>
    <td>
      <asp:Button id="btnUpdateTopic"
            onclick="btnUpdateTopic_Click" runat="server" text="Update Topic">
      </asp:Button>
    </td>
  </tr>
```

Finally, you need to add some code to update the contents of the `Application` object when the button is clicked:

```
void btnUpdateTopic_Click(object sender, EventArgs e)
{
  Application["CurrentTopic"] = txtTopic.Text;
  lblCurrentTopic.Text = (string)Application["CurrentTopic"];
  txtTopic.Text = "";
}
```

Exercise 2

Add the session initialization code from the stylesheet example to your `Global.asax` file.

Solution

You'll recall that, during the CSS example, the following code was included in the `Page_Load()` method of `Default.aspx`:

```
if (Session["SelectedCss"] == null)
{
  if (Request.Cookies["PreferredCss"] == null)
  {
```

```
        Session["SelectedCss"] = "WroxUnited.css";
    }
    else
    {
        Session["SelectedCss"] = Request.Cookies["PreferredCss"].Value;
    }
}
```

This code can be shortened considerably by adding the following statement to the `Global.asax` file:

```
public void Session_Start(Object sender, EventArgs e)
{
    System.Collections.Hashtable basketTable =
        new System.Collections.Hashtable();
    Session["Basket"] = basketTable;

    Session["SelectedCss"] = "WroxUnited.css";
}
```

The code in `Page_Load()` method can now be changed to the following:

```
if (Request.Cookies["PreferredCss"] != null)
{
    Session["SelectedCss"] = Request.Cookies["PreferredCss"].Value;
}
```

Exercise 3

Add a link to the `Merchandise.aspx` page from the front page of the site, and then apply the stylesheet used in the `Default.aspx` page to all the other pages in the site. You will need to add the `<link ... >` tag to the `<head ... >` section of each page and you will need to ensure that the session initialization code is correctly configured in the `Global.asax` file from the previous exercise.

Solution

Adding the link to the `Default.aspx` page is quite simple – just add the following code to the list of links:

```
<p>
    <asp:HyperLink id="lnkMerchandise" runat="server"
            NavigateUrl="Merchandise.aspx">
        Merchandise
    </asp:HyperLink>
</p>
```

Now you can add the `css` link to each of the other pages in the site:

```
<head>
    <link id="css" href='<%= (string)Session["SelectedCss"] %>'
        type="text/css" rel="stylesheet" />
</head>
```

Having said this, it's not always quite as simple as it looks – take a look at the output of `Teams.aspx` when using the Away scheme and you'll notice that the red links remain red, because the color was hard-coded when the page was created. You need to remove the color information from the tag:

```
<asp:linkbutton
        text='<%# DataBinder.Eval(Container.DataItem, "TeamName") %>'
        CommandArgument='<%# DataBinder.Eval(Container.DataItem, "TeamID") %>'
        id="TeamNameLink"
        style="color:darkred"
        runat="server"
        CommandName="ShowTeam" />
```

Once you delete the `style="color.darkred"` attribute, the links will inherit the styling defined for all hyperlinks.

`Players.aspx` has some additional styling that will need to be amended. The font color and header bar are blue and since the theme for the site is red, white, and black, these colors need altering. First, delete all the hard-coded styles from the control – you may find that the Properties pane is the most useful tool for this.

Next, you can add some custom styling. Here is some CSS code you can add to `WroxUnited.css`:

```
.datatablebody {
  background-color:"#ffffff";
  color:black;
  font-size:smaller;
}

.datatablebody td{
  padding:3;
}

.datatablehead {
  background-color:"#c0c0c0";
  color:black;
  font-weight:bold;
}

.datatablehead td{
  padding:3;
}
```

Once these styles are added, you can apply them to the control:

```
<ItemStyle cssclass="datatablebody"></ItemStyle>
<HeaderStyle font-bold="True" cssclass="datatablehead"></HeaderStyle>
```

Chapter 12

This chapter covers the concepts of user controls and code-behind. The first three exercises for this chapter don't really have any new type code to them; it's only practicing adding user controls to pages and switching to using code-behind. The completed code for these pages is available for download from the Wrox website.

Exercise 1

Add the header control and navigation bar control to each page in the site. Remember to add the following code at the top of each page:

```
<%@ Register TagPrefix="WroxUnited" TagName="Header" Src="Header.ascx" %>
<%@ Register TagPrefix="WroxUnited" TagName="NavBar" Src="NavBar.ascx" %>
```

Solution

Refer 57084_Ch12_Ans01.aspx for the code for this question.

Exercise 2

Move the C# code for each page (visible in the Code view in Web Matrix) into an associated code-behind file, making sure each control has a corresponding declaration in the code-behind file.

Solution

See 57084_Ch12_Ans02.aspx for the solution.

Exercise 3

Move the C# code from the navbar.ascx control (containing an event-handler) into an associated .cs code-behind file, following the same technique as you used for the other pages on the site.

Exercise 4

Create a user control for the Merchandise.aspx page that enables you to easily add new items to the list. You will need to copy a row of the table from Merchandise.aspx into a new ASCX user control file. Make the properties on the image and button controls generic and add some public properties to programmatically set the values on each Web control in the user control.

Firstly, here's some code (currently in Merchandise.aspx) that could be placed in the control:

```
<tr>
  <td>
    <asp:Image id="imgCap" runat="server" Height="100px"
      ImageUrl="images/shirt.gif" Width="100px"></asp:Image>
  </td>
  <td>
    The Wrox United shirt, available in one size only</td>
  <td>
    <asp:Button id="btnBuyShirt" onclick="AddItemToBasket" runat="server"
      Width="100px" CommandArgument="Shirt" Text="Buy a shirt!"></asp:Button>
```

```
    </td>
  </tr>
```

If you change the `ImageUrl` of the image, the `Text` of the button, and the `CommandArgument` to empty strings `""`, then you can set those in the `Page_Load()` event. Consider the earlier example – the word `"Shirt"` features in all three of these attributes, so you could add a property like the following to store the name of the item (in this case, shirt), then use this value to construct the appropriate values for these attributes:

```
private string _itemName = "";

public string ItemName
{
  get{ return _itemName;  }
  set{ _itemName = value; }
}
```

Here's an example of using this property to update another private variable. This could be used, for example, to provide a default image name:

:

```
if (_imageName == "")
{
  _imageName = _itemName + ".jpg";
}
```

You would also need to move the `AddItemToBasket()` function to the control because the buttons now reside within this control. Since the name of the session is globally available, it's possible to set or update session values from the control just as easily as from a page.

You will need three properties in all. The first, `ItemName` is shown above. You can include an optional `ImageName` property to override the default value (in case you want to use a `.gif`, for example). Finally, you need to store the text that describes the item in a `Text` property and include the value stored in this property in the page using the following syntax:

```
<td><%=Text%></td>
```

All that remains then is to add the item to the page:

```
<WroxUnited:Product id="Shirt" runat="server"
  ItemName="Shirt"
  ImageName="shirt.gif"
  Text="The Wrox United shirt, available in one size only"/>
```

Solution

Firstly, the HTML of the `Product.ascx` user control:

```
<tr>
  <td>
```

```
      <asp:Image id="image1" Width="120px" ImageUrl="<%=imageLink%>"
        Height="120px" runat="server"></asp:Image>
  </td>
  <td>
    <%=Text%></td>
  <td>
    <asp:Button id="button1" onclick="AddItemToBasket" Width="100px"
                                    runat="server"
      Text="<%=buttonText%>"
      CommandArgument="<%=ItemName%>"></asp:Button>
  </td>
</tr>
```

Next, the code for the `Product.ascx` user control:

```csharp
using System;
using System.Web;
using System.Web.UI;
using System.Web.UI.WebControls;
using System.Web.Caching;
using System.Collections;
using System.Configuration;

namespace WroxUnited
{
  public class Product : UserControl
  {
    public Image image1;
    public Button button1;

    private string _itemName = "";

    public string ItemName
    {
      get{ return _itemName;  }
      set{ _itemName = value; }
    }

    private string _imageName = "";

    public string ImageName
    {
      get { return _imageName;  }
      set { _imageName = value; }
    }

    private string _text = "";

    public string Text
    {
      get { return _text;  }
      set { _text = value; }
    }

    public void Page_Load()
    {
```

```
      if (_imageName == "")
      {
        _imageName = _itemName + ".jpg";
      }

      string imageLink = "images/" + _imageName;
      string buttonText = "Buy the " + _itemName + "!";

      image1.ImageUrl = imageLink;
      button1.Text    = buttonText;

    }

    public void AddItemToBasket(object sender, EventArgs e)
    {
      System.Collections.Hashtable basketTable = (Hashtable)Session["Basket"];

      if (basketTable[_itemName] == null)
      {
        basketTable[_itemName] = 0;
      }

      int itemCount = (int)basketTable[_itemName];
      basketTable[_itemName] = itemCount + 1;

    }
  }
}
```

In `Merchandise.aspx` add the following:

```
<%@ Register TagPrefix="WroxUnited" TagName="Product" Src="Product.ascx" %>
...
<table width="600">
  <WroxUnited:Product id="Shirt" runat="server"
    ItemName="Shirt"
    ImageName="shirt.gif"
    Text="The Wrox United shirt, available in one size only"/>
  <WroxUnited:Product id="Hat" runat="Server"
    ItemName="Hat"
    ImageName="hat.jpg"
    Text="The official Wrox United hat!"/>
  <WroxUnited:Product id="Mascot" runat="Server"
    ItemName="Mascot"
    ImageName="mascot1.jpg"
    Text="The Wrox United cuddly mascot - a must-have for the younger
          supporters!"/>
  <WroxUnited:Product id="Plate" runat="server"
    ItemName="Plate"
    ImageName="team_s_b.gif"
    Text="This is a strange square collector's plate of the team!"/>
</table>
```

Exercise 5

Move the new code in `Product.ascx` into a code-behind file.

Chapter 13

This chapter covered how to compile a .NET assembly and use it from within our ASP.NET page. It also discussed the encapsulation of business logic into a reusable component.

Exercise 1

Build a data access component that connects to the `Travel.mdb` access database and retrieves data about the weather at that location (filtered by location). You may find the following SQL useful:

```
SELECT [Locations].[LocationName], [Locations].[CurrentTemperature],
   [WeatherTypes].[WeatherType]
FROM [Locations], [WeatherTypes]
WHERE (([WeatherTypes].[WeatherTypeID] = [Locations].[CurrentWeather])
AND ([Locations].[LocationName] = @LocationName))
```

If you use the Web Matrix **SELECT Data Wizard**, you can create a method called `GetWeatherByCity()` that takes the `LocationName` as a parameter, and returns a `DataReader`.

Exercise 2

Add another method called `GetCities()` to this data access component, which selects all the `LocationNames` from the database and returns a `DataReader`.

Solution (1 and 2)

Once you have created the two methods using the data wizards in Web Matrix, all that remains is to ensure that everything is in place for compilation. Note that we've used the `BegASPNET` namespace and a Class named `TravelData` – these will come handy for the rest of the exercise solutions. The following code is available in the file called `DataAccessCode.cs` in the code download.

```
// DataAccessCode.cs
//

using System;

namespace BegASPNET
{

  public class TravelData
  {
    public TravelData()
    {
    }

    public System.Data.IDataReader GetWeatherByCity(string locationName)
```

```
    {
      string connectionString =
        "Provider=Microsoft.Jet.OLEDB.4.0; Ole DB Services=-4;
         Data Source=C:\\BegASPNET11\\Chapter13Code\\Exercises\\travel.mdb";
      System.Data.IDbConnection dbConnection =
        new System.Data.OleDb.OleDbConnection(connectionString);

      string queryString =
        "SELECT [Locations].[LocationName], [Locations].[CurrentTemperature],"+
        "[WeatherTypes].[WeatherType] "+
        "FROM [Locations], [WeatherTypes] "+
        "WHERE (([WeatherTypes].[WeatherTypeID] = " +
        "[Locations].[CurrentWeather])" +
        "AND ([Locations].[LocationName] = @LocationName))";
      System.Data.IDbCommand dbCommand = new System.Data.OleDb.OleDbCommand();
      dbCommand.CommandText = queryString;
      dbCommand.Connection = dbConnection;

      System.Data.IDataParameter dbParam_locationName =
        new System.Data.OleDb.OleDbParameter();
      dbParam_locationName.ParameterName = "@LocationName";
      dbParam_locationName.Value = locationName;
      dbParam_locationName.DbType = System.Data.DbType.String;
      dbCommand.Parameters.Add(dbParam_locationName);

      dbConnection.Open();
      System.Data.IDataReader dataReader =
        dbCommand.ExecuteReader(System.Data.CommandBehavior.CloseConnection);

      return dataReader;
    }

    public System.Data.IDataReader GetCities() {
      string connectionString =
        "Provider=Microsoft.Jet.OLEDB.4.0; Ole DB Services=-4;
         Data Source=C:\\BegASPNET11\\Chapter13Code\\Exercises\\travel.mdb";
      System.Data.IDbConnection dbConnection =
        new System.Data.OleDb.OleDbConnection(connectionString);

      string queryString = "SELECT [Locations].[LocationName] FROM " +
                           "[Locations]";
      System.Data.IDbCommand dbCommand = new System.Data.OleDb.OleDbCommand();
      dbCommand.CommandText = queryString;
      dbCommand.Connection = dbConnection;

      dbConnection.Open();
      System.Data.IDataReader dataReader =
        dbCommand.ExecuteReader(System.Data.CommandBehavior.CloseConnection);

      return dataReader;
    }
  }
}
```

We'll see how to compile this file along with the two server controls once after we have seen the solutions for the next two exercises.

Exercise 3

Create a simple custom control that has a temperature property, which takes the temperature in Celcius and renders a string of text that displays the temperature in both Celcius and Fahrenheit:

```
Fahrenheit temperature = Celsius temperature * (9/5) + 32
```

The control should render a `<span>` tag that has a `style=color:<color>` attribute that can be used to change the color of the text for different temperature ranges. If the temperature is below 0 degrees Celcius, you should make the text blue, above 30 degrees it should be red, and all others should be orange.

Solution

The code for this control isn't too different from the code we used in the chapter. In the following code, you'll see that there are two properties in this control, one for Celcius and one to convert that value into Fahrenheit. The `Render()` method then creates a `<span ... >` control when the control is rendered. Notice that we've used a string formatter to render the control exactly as we intended (adding a degrees symbol after each temperature value. This file is called `57084_Ch13_Ans03.cs` in the code download:

```csharp
using System;
using System.Web;
using System.Web.UI;

namespace BegASPNET
{

  public class TemperatureControl : Control
  {
    private double _tempInCelcius;

    public double TempInCelcius
    {
      get{return _tempInCelcius;}
      set{_tempInCelcius = value;}
    }

    public double TempInFahrenheit
    {
      get {return _tempInCelcius * (9.0 / 5.0) + 32.0;}
      set {_tempInCelcius = (value - 32.0) * (5.0 / 9.0);}
    }

    protected override void Render(System.Web.UI.HtmlTextWriter writer)
    {
      string color;

      if (_tempInCelcius <= 0.0)
      {
```

```
      color = "blue";
    }
    else if (_tempInCelcius >= 30.0)
    {
      color = "red";
    }
    else
    {
      color = "orange";
    }

    writer.Write("<span style='color:");
    writer.Write(color);
    writer.Write("'>");

    writer.Write("{0:##0.#}&deg;C ({1:##0.#}&deg;F)", TempInCelcius,
      TempInFahrenheit);
    writer.Write("</span>");
  }
 }
}
```

Exercise 4

Create another control that takes the code built in the first two examples to produce a composite control that displays temperature data stored in the database for a specific city. Your control should render the following output:

❑   The name of the city

❑   The temperature at the specified city (use an instance of the control created in the previous example)

❑   An image control <ASP:Image ...> that displays one of a series of images (available in the code download for this chapter) that represents the style of weather currently being experienced at the specified city – for example, an image of a cloud if the weather is overcast

Solution

This control only has one property, the name of the city to display. The tricky bit is to get it to render the output we're after. In the following code, you'll see that the output will be rendered in an HTML table. Also, notice also that it's very simple to nest the first control within this control. This file is called 57084_Ch13_Ans04.cs in the code download:

```
using System;
using System.Web;
using System.Web.UI;
using System.Web.UI.WebControls;
using System.Web.UI.HtmlControls;
using System.Data;

namespace BegASPNET
{
```

```
public class CityWeatherControl : Control
{
  private Label _cityNameLabel = new Label();
  private TemperatureControl _temperatureControl = new TemperatureControl();
  private Image _weatherImage = new Image();
  private TravelData _travelData = new TravelData();

  private string _city;

  public string City
  {
    get{return _city;}
    set{_city = value;}
  }

  protected override void CreateChildControls()
  {
    Controls.Clear();

    IDataReader cityData = _travelData.GetWeatherByCity(City);

    try
    {
      if (cityData.Read())
      {
        double currentTemperature = (int)(cityData["CurrentTemperature"]);
        string weatherType = (string)(cityData["WeatherType"]);

        _cityNameLabel.Text = City;
        _temperatureControl.TempInCelcius = currentTemperature;
        _weatherImage.AlternateText = weatherType;
        _weatherImage.ImageUrl = weatherType + ".gif";

        Table layoutTable = new Table();

        TableRow topRow = new TableRow();
        TableRow bottomRow = new TableRow();

        TableCell cell1 = new TableCell();
        cell1.Controls.Add(_cityNameLabel);

        TableCell cell2 = new TableCell();
        cell2.Controls.Add(_weatherImage);
        cell2.RowSpan = 2;

        topRow.Cells.Add(cell1);
        topRow.Cells.Add(cell2);

        TableCell cell3 = new TableCell();
        cell3.Controls.Add(_temperatureControl);

        bottomRow.Cells.Add(cell3);

        layoutTable.Rows.Add(topRow);
```

```
        layoutTable.Rows.Add(bottomRow);

      Controls.Add(layoutTable);
    }
    else
    {
      Literal errorLiteral = new Literal();
      errorLiteral.Text = "No data available for city " + City;

      Controls.Add(errorLiteral);
    }
  }
  finally
  {
    cityData.Close();
    cityData.Dispose();
  }

  ChildControlsCreated = true;
    }
  }
}
```

These three components now need to be compiled. In the download for these solutions, you'll find that there's a file called `Compile.bat` that contains the following code:

```
CD C:\BegASPNET11\Chapter13Code\Exercises
md bin

csc /t:library /r:System.dll,System.Data.dll,System.Web.dll
/out:bin/TravelSite.dll DataAccessCode.cs TemperatureControl.cs
CityWeatherControl.cs
pause
```

This code will compile all three components into an assembly called `TravelSite.dll`. They are all based in the same namespace, so this is a fairly logical thing to do in real life applications.

Exercise 5

Finally, add the following to an ASP.NET page:

❑   Add a drop-down `ListBox` and bind it to the `DataReader` returned by the `GetCities()` method in the data access component. Enable auto-postback for this control so that a postback occurs whenever the selection changes.

❑   Add a copy of the weather control created in the previous exercise to the page, and pass the name of the currently selected city to the control for displaying the weather for that city.

Solution

All that remains is to add the `CityWeatherControl` to a web page. In this page, we've used a drop down `ListBox` for selecting a city, which automatically posts back to the server to refresh the page. This page is called `travel.aspx`:

```
<%@ Page Language="C#" %>
<%@ Register TagPrefix="TravelControl" Namespace="BegASPNET"
        Assembly="TravelSite" %>
<%@ import Namespace="BegASPNET" %>
<script runat="server">

  void Page_Load()
  {

    if (!Page.IsPostBack)
    {
      TravelData data = new TravelData();
      System.Data.IDataReader reader = data.GetCities();
      ddlLocations.DataSource = reader;
      ddlLocations.DataValueField = "LocationName";
      ddlLocations.DataTextField = "LocationName";
      ddlLocations.DataBind();
    }
    CityWeather.City = ddlLocations.SelectedItem.ToString();
  }

</script>
<html>
<head>
</head>
<body>
  <form runat="server">
    <asp:DropDownList id="ddlLocations" runat="server" AutoPostBack="True">
    </asp:DropDownList>
    <br />
    <TRAVELCONTROL:CITYWEATHERCONTROL id="CityWeather" runat="server" />

  </form>
</body>
</html>
```

As long as you have the images in the same directory as the ASPX page, you should be able to see the results of your efforts.

Chapter 14

This chapter explains the steps you can take to debug your code, minimize errors, handling errors as well as how to recover when things go wrong.

Exercise 1

How are parser errors different from compilation errors? Is there any difference between the ways they are displayed by ASP.NET?

Solution

When a page has errors that are caught during compilation by a .NET Framework *compiler* (remember that ASP.NET pages are compiled), ASP.NET generates a syntax error report with information about the error and sends this information to the browser. When an error occurs while a page is being executed, it gives rise to a *parser error*. The difference is that ASP.NET sends a *Stack Trace* to the browser; it that contains information about what was going on when the error occurred.

Exercise 2

Here are three sections of code – what is wrong with each section and what type of error does it contain? How would you fix it?

❑ Section A:

```
<html>
  <head>
    <title>Syntax Error Example </title>
  </head>
  <body>
    <form method="post" action="syntaxerror.aspx" runat="server">
    <asp:TextBox id="txtQuantity" runat="Server />
    </form>
  </body>
</html>
```

❑ Section B:

```
void Page_Load()
{
  int intCounter, intLoop;
  intCounter=0;
  intLoop=0;
  while (intCounter<10)
  {
    intLoop = intLoop +1;
  }
}
```

❑ Section C:

```
  <script language="C#" runat="server">
void Page_Load()
{
    string a;
    int b;
    string c;
    a = "Hello";
    b = "World";
    c = a + b;
}
</script>
```

Solution

The sections, the errors they would generate, and a possible solution have been provided as follows:

❏ In section A, see the following line:

```
<asp:TextBox id="txtQuantity" runat="Server />
```

It is missing a closing quotation mark after `Server`.

❏ Section B is an infinite loop. We check the contents of `intCounter` to see if it has reached 10, but increment the variable called `intLoop`:

```
while (intCounter<10)
{
    intLoop = intLoop +1;
}
```

To correct this, change `intLoop` to `intCounter` (or vice versa).

❏ In section C, b is declared as an integer, yet a string value is read into it:

```
int b;
...
b = "World";
```

b should be declared as a string.

Exercise 3

Create a form with four textboxes and a submit button. Each of the textboxes accepts a user name, an email address, a phone number, and the user's gender. Use validation controls to make sure that there are no blank entries, that you can only enter numbers into the phone field, and that you can only enter a number between 1 and 140 in the age field. Also, but not necessarily with validation controls, make sure that the gender textbox only accepts male or female and that the email address contains the '@' character. In what ways could this form be improved further?

Solution

The code should read as follows (available in the code download as `57084_Ch14_Ans03.aspx`:

```
<form method="post" action="usingvalidationcontrol.aspx" runat="server">

  <asp:Label text="Name" runat="server" />
  <asp:TextBox id="txtUserName" runat="server" />
    <asp:RequiredFieldValidator ControlToValidate="txtUserName" runat="server"
          ErrorMessage="Please enter a value in the Name Field">
    </asp:RequiredFieldValidator>

  <asp:Label text="Email" runat="server" />
  <asp:TextBox id="txtEmail" runat="server" />
    <asp:RequiredFieldValidator ControlToValidate="txtEmail" runat="server"
```

```
                    ErrorMessage="Please enter a value in the Email Field">
          </asp:RequiredFieldValidator>
          <asp:RegularExpressionValidator   ControlToValidate="txtEmail"
            ValidationExpression="^\w+[\w-\.]*\@"
            ErrorMessage="This isn't a valid email address!"
            runat="server" />

      <asp:Label text="Age" runat="server" />
      <asp:TextBox id="txtPhone" runat="server" />
          <asp:RequiredFieldValidator ControlToValidate="txtPhone" runat="server"
                    ErrorMessage="Please enter a value in the Phone Field">
          </asp:RequiredFieldValidator>
          <asp:CompareValidator id="numbervalidatior"
            ControlToValidate="txtPhone"
            Type="Integer"
            Operator="DataTypeCheck"
            ErrorMessage="You must enter a number!"
            runat="server" />

      <asp:Label text="Age" runat="server" />
      <asp:TextBox id="txtAge" runat="server" />
          <asp:RequiredFieldValidator ControlToValidate="txtAge" runat="server"
                    ErrorMessage="Please enter a value in the Age Field">
          </asp:RequiredFieldValidator>
          <asp:RangeValidator id="Range1"
                    ControlToValidate="txtAge"
                    MinimumValue="1"
                    MaximumValue="140"
                    Type="Integer"
                    EnableClientScript="false"
                    Text="The value must be between 1 and 140!"
                    runat="server"/>

      <br />
      <asp:Button id="btnComplete_Order" Text="Submit Form"
                              onclick="Submit Form" runat="server"/><br>
      <asp:Label id="lblOrderConfirm" runat="server"/>
    </form>
```

There are many ways that this could be improved; here are a few:

❑ The email address could be checked to see that it took a format text@text.text, or you could even check to see if it was a valid email. There are plenty of pre-written regular expressions for email validation. You can download some from http://www.regexplib.com/.

❑ You could use an authentication tool such as *Passport* to check these details and not worry about the user having to input them! You should be aware that there isn't a set of hard and fast rules when creating forms, just that some ways of doing things will be more sensible than others.

Exercise 4

Write a try...catch error handler that will handle errors specifically for a divide-by-zero handler (as we did for invalid casts).

Hint: We haven't mentioned the specific class involved, you can find a list of classes using the class browser.

Solution

There are many ways of doing this, as long as you include a `DivideByZeroException`. Here is a suggested method, complete with an example divide-by-zero error (available in the code download as `57084_Ch14_Ans04.aspx`:

```csharp
<script language="C#" runat="server" >
void StructuredErrorHandling()
{
  try
  {
    int a;
    int b
    int c;
    a=1;
    b=0;
    c=a/b;
  }
//Handler for DivideByZero Exception
  catch (DivideByZeroException excep)
  {
    Response.Write ("Error Occurred"+ "<br>" + excep.ToString + "<br>");
  }
  finally
  {
    Response.Write ("The Page Execution is completed" & "<br>")
  }
  }
}
</script>
```

Exercise 5

Create a custom error page for an HTTP 403 error **Access is forbidden** error and get it working for this chapter's code folder.

Solution

The following section should go in `web.config` in the `ch14` folder:

```xml
<configuration>
  <system.web>
    <customErrors defaultRedirect="userError.aspx" mode="On">
    <error statusCode="403" redirect="PageForbidden.aspx" />
    </customErrors>
  </system.web>
</configuration>
```

The page `Forbidden.aspx` can just say something like:

```
<html>
  <head>
  </head>
  <body>
    <h1> You are not allowed access to this page.</h1>
  </body>
</html>
```

Chapter 15

This chapter explains how ASP.NET applications can be managed from a series of XML configuration files.

Exercise 1

If you didn't know how to specify a particular setting of an element in the config file, where would you look to find them?

Solution

In the machine.config file itself, which has examples of how to use many of the commonly used settings.

Example 2

Create a *friendly* custom error page for a file not found error and set the relevant config file so that it appears whenever a 404 error message is generated.

Solution

The following section should go in web.config in the ch14 folder:

```
<configuration>
  <system.web>
    <customErrors defaultRedirect="userError.aspx" mode="On">
    <error statusCode="404" redirect="PageNotFound.aspx" />
    </customErrors>
  </system.web>
</configuration>
```

The page PageNotFound.aspx can just say something like:

```
<html>
  <head>
  </head>
  <body>
    <h1> Sorry but this page cannot be found on our web server.</h1>
  </body>
</html>
```

Example 3

Create a page with two `Label` controls that both display the time, and create an output cache that lasts for 30 minutes and caches just one of the controls.

Solution

When using fragment caching, you cache only in the ASCX file; so create an ASPX page that isn't cached containing two user controls:

```
<%@ Page Language="C#" %>
<%@ Register TagPrefix="l1" TagName="mylabel1" Src="label1.ascx" %>
<%@ Register TagPrefix="l2" TagName="mylabel2" Src="label2.ascx" %>
<script runat = "server">
  string ServerTime()
  {
    return ServerTime = System.DateTime.Now.ToLongTimeString();
  }
</script>
  <l1:mylabel1 text="ServerTime()" runat="server"/>
  <l2:mylabel1 text="ServerTime()" runat="server"/>
```

Then create two ASCX files, and cache only one of them. Consider `Label1.ascx`:

```
<%@ OutputCache Duration="1800" VaryByParam="none" %>
<asp:label id="mylabel1" text="ServerTime()" runat="server"/>
```

`Label2.ascx`:

```
<asp:label id="mylabel2" text="ServerTime()" runat="server"/>
```

Exercise 4

Create a cache that stores the following information `"MyFavouriteColour = Orange"`, and expires it if it hasn't been updated for three minutes.

Solution

The following lines of code serves this purpose:

```
Cache.Insert("MyFavoriteColor", "orange", null, DateTime.Now.AddMinutes(3),
NoSlidingExpiration);
```

Exercise 5

Create a cache that will expire whenever the contents of one of three files – `XMLDoc1.xml`, `XMLDoc2.xml`, and `XMLDoc3.xml` – change. They all contain the following code:

```
<?xml version="1.0"?>
<address>
  <name>Rheingold Cabriole</name>
  <address>673 Chellingworth Place, Morningtown </address>
```

```
    <phone>333-444-555</phone>
    <email> Rheingold.Cabriole@fabemails.com</email>
</address>
```

Solution

```
DataSet XMLFileDataSet = New DataSet();
XMLFileDataSet.ReadXML("C:\\BegASPNet11\\ch15\\address.xml");
CacheDependency filedependency1 = New
              CacheDependency("C:\\BegASPNet11\\ch15\\xmldoc1.xml");
CacheDependency filedependency2 = New
              CacheDependency("C:\\BegASPNet11\\ch15\\xmldoc2.xml");
CacheDependency filedependency3 = New
              CacheDependency("C:\\BegASPNet11\\ch15\\xmldoc3.xml");
Cache.Insert("address",XMLFileDataSet, filedependency1);
Cache.Insert("address",XMLFileDataSet, filedependency2);
Cache.Insert("address",XMLFileDataSet, filedependency3);
```

Chapter 16

This chapter teaches you how to expose functionality from your Web site to others as a Web service.

Exercise 1

Explain the role of the Simple Object Access Protocol (SOAP) in Web services.

Solution

SOAP is the protocol with which functions are called remotely in Web services.

Exercise 2

What is the purpose of the WSDL file?

Solution

The WSDL file is an XML file that specifies the parameters that are used in the Web services. With this file, consumers know what parameters to send to the Web service and the values they will receive.

Exercise 3

How would you locate a Web service that provides the functions you require?

Solution

To locate a Web service, you can use the UDDI service. Businesses register their Web services on the UDDI database, which can then be searched for a service that suits your needs.

Exercise 4

Create a Web service with a class name of circles that calculates the area and circumference of a circle and the volume of a sphere.

* Area = (Pi)r2

* Circumference = 2(Pi)r

* Volume of a sphere = 4/3(Pi)r3.

Solution

See 57084_Ch16_Ans04.asmx available in the code download:

```
<%@ WebService Language="C#" Class="Circles"%>

using System.Web.Services;
public class Circles
{
  [WebMethod] _
  public decimal Areaofcircle(Decimal radius)
  {
     return radius*radius*3.142;
  }

  [WebMethod] _
  public decimal CircumferenceofCircle(Decimal radius)
  {
    return 2 * 3.142 * radius;
  }

  [WebMethod] _
  public decimal VolumeofSphere(Decimal radius)
  {
     return (4 / 3) * 3.142 * radius * radius * radius;
  }
}
```

We create a WebMethod to calculate each of these values. Each method takes one parameter –the circle radius – and returns one value. They are all encapsulated within the public class Circles.

Exercise 5

Create a Web service that connects to the Northwind database and returns employees' addresses based on their last names.

Solution

See 57084_Ch16_Ans05.aspx:

```
<%@ WebService Language="C#" Class="Addresses" %>

using System.Web.Services;
```

```
using System.Data;
using System.Data.OleDb;

public class Addresses :System.Web.Services.WebService
{

  [WebMethod] _
  public string NorthwindAddresses(string strLastName)
  {
    return GetAddress(strLastName);
  }

  private string GetAddress(string strLastName)
  {
    OleDbDataReader objDataReader;
    OleDbConnection objConnection;
    OleDbCommand objCommand;
    string strConn = "Provider=Microsoft.Jet.OLEDB.4.0;Data
                      Source=C:\\BegASPNET\\ch16\\Northwind.mdb;"
    string strSQL = "SELECT Address FROM Employees WHERE lastName = '" +
                    strlastName + "'";
    string strAddress;

    objConnection = New OleDbConnection(strConn);
    objCommand = New OleDbCommand(strSQL, objConnection);
    objConnection.Open();
    objDataReader = objCommand.ExecuteReader(CommandBehavior.CloseConnection);

    If (objDataReader.Read())
    {
      strAddress = objDataReader(0);
    }
    else
    {
      strAddress = "Address not found in the database";
    }
    objDataReader.Close();

    return strAddress;
  }

}
```

We create two methods, one that returns the address (from Northwind), and the other that connects to the database and queries it for a given address (GetAddress). GetAddress() creates a connection and uses a single line of SQL to return a matching address. If no matches are found, you display an appropriate message instead. We create a DataReader and read the data into this object, and return the first occurrence in the DataReader as our string.

Exercise 6

Create an ASP.NET page containing a drop-down ListBox in which a user can select names of Northwind employees to return their addresses.

Solution

```csharp
<%@ Page Language="C#" Debug="true"%>
<%@ Import namespace="AddressService" %>

<script language="C#" runat="server">
private void RetrieveAddress(System.Object sender, System.EventArgs e)
{
  AddressService.Addresses adr = New AddressService.Addresses();
  lblAddress.Text = adr.NorthwindAddresses(Request.Form("list"));
}
</script>
<html>
  <body>
    <form runat="server">
      <asp:dropdownlist id="list" runat="server">
      <asp:listitem>Davolio</asp:listitem>
      <asp:listitem>Fuller</asp:listitem>
      <asp:listitem>Leverling</asp:listitem>
      <asp:listitem>Peacock</asp:listitem>
      <asp:listitem>Buchanan</asp:listitem>
      <asp:listitem>Suyama</asp:listitem>
      <asp:listitem>King</asp:listitem>
      <asp:listitem>Callahan</asp:listitem>
      <asp:listitem>Dodsworth</asp:listitem>
      </asp:dropdownlist>
      <asp:Button id="Button1" runat="server" Text="Submit"
                  onClick="RetrieveAddress"></asp:Button><br />
      <asp:Label id="lblAddress" runat="server" />
    </form>
  </body>
</html>
```

Here, we created an instance of our proxy class that will call our WebMethod and then we read the returned value into the `Text` property of our `Label` control. We create a separate server-side `DropDownList` control and only call our Web Method when a selection has been submitted.

Exercise 7

Secure the `Northwind` employee `Addresses` Web service so that no unauthorized users have access to it.

Solution

```csharp
using System.Data;
using System.Data.OleDb;

public class Addresses : System.Web.Services.WebService
{
  [WebMethod] _
  public string NorthwindAddresses(string strLastName, string strUsername,
string  strPassword)
```

```
{
  OleDbDataReader objSecurityDR;
  OleDbConnection objSecurityConn;
  OleDbCommand objSecurityCmd;

  string strConn = "Provider=Microsoft.Jet.OLEDB.4.0;Data Source=";
      strConn += Server.MapPath("Security.mdb") + ";";
  string strSQL = "select Username from Users where username = '";
          strSQL += strUsername + "' and password = '" + strPassword + "'";

  objSecurityConn = New OleDbConnection(strConn);

  objSecurityCmd = New OleDbCommand(strSQL, objSecurityConn);
  objSecurityConn.Open();

  objSecurityDR =
  objSecurityCmd.ExecuteReader(CommandBehavior.CloseConnection);

  if (objSecurityDR.Read())
  {
    objSecurityDR.Close()
    return GetAddress(strLastName)
  }
  else
  {
    objSecurityDR.Close();
    return "Login to Northwind Employees Directory failed.";
  }
}

public string GetAddress(string strLastName)
{
  OleDbDataReader objDataReader;
  OleDbConnection objConnection;
  OleDbCommand objCommand;
  string strConn = "Provider=Microsoft.Jet.OLEDB.4.0;Data
  Source=C:\\BegASPNET\\ch16\\Northwind.mdb;"
  string strSQL = "SELECT Address FROM Employees WHERE lastName = '" +
                  strlastName + "'";
  string strAddress;
  objConnection = New OleDbConnection(strConn);
  objCommand = New OleDbCommand(strSQL, objConnection);
  objConnection.Open();
  objDataReader = _

   objCommand.ExecuteReader(CommandBehavior.CloseConnection);

  if (objDataReader.Read())
  {
    strAddress = objDataReader[0];
  }
  else
  {
    strAddress = "Address not found in the database";
```

```
    }

  objDataReader.Close();
  return strAddress;
  }

 }
```

In this answer, we merely add the code from the security section of the Web services chapter that checks a security database before giving someone access to our Web meethods.

Chapter 17

Exercise 1

What is the difference between authorization and authentication?

Solution

Authentication is the process that verifies if a user is who they claim they are, while authorization is the process of checking whether a particular user has access to a particular resource.

Exercise 2

Create an application that uses forms-based authentication and requires you to enter a username, password, and zip code before you can go to the main login page. Hard code the username, password, and the zip code. Call it `zipcodelogin.aspx`.

Solution

The `web.config` file should be changed as follows:

```
<configuration>
  <system.web>
    <authentication mode="Forms">
      <forms name=".WroxDemo" loginUrl="login.aspx"
      protection="All" timeout="60" />
    </authentication>
    <machineKey validationKey="AutoGenerate" decryptionKey="AutoGenerate"
     validation="SHA1"/>
    <authorization>
      <deny users="?" />
    </authorization>
  </system.web>
</configuration>
```

The `login.aspx` file should contain the following code:

```
<%@ Import Namespace="System.Web.Security " %>
```

```
<html>
<head>
<script language="C#" runat=server>
 void Login_Click(System.Object Src, EventArgs E)
 {
   if (txtEmail.Text == "Wrox") && (txtPwd.Text == "MyPass") &&
                                  (txtZipCode.Text = "12345")
   {
      FormsAuthentication.RedirectFromLoginPage(txtEmail.Text,false);
   }
   else
   {
      lblLoginMsg.Text = "Use user name, password and zip as " +
                      "Wrox, MyPass and 12345 . Please try again";
   }
 }
</script>
</head>
<body>
  <form runat="server">
    <h1>Using Form based Authentication<BR>with Pre-Defined Credentials</h1>
    <hr>
    Users Name:<br />
    <asp:textbox id="txtEmail" runat=server /> 
    <FONT SIZE=2 COLOR="RED">*</FONT>
    <br />Password:<br />
    <asp:textbox TextMode="Password" id="txtPwd" runat=server />
     <FONT SIZE=2 COLOR="RED">*</FONT>
    <br />

    <asp:textbox id="txtZipCode" runat=server />
     <FONT SIZE=2 COLOR="RED">*</FONT>
    <br />

    <asp:Label  id="lblLoginMsg" ForeColor="Red" Font-Name="Verdana"  Font-
    Size="10"
    runat=server />
    <b />
    <asp:button  id="btnLogin" Text="Login" OnClick="Login_Click" runat=Server
 />
  </form>
</body>
</html>
```

Exercise 3

Upgrade the application from Exercise 2 to use the WroxAuth.mdb used in this chapter.

Solution

First, add an extra field to the database for zip code and insert 12345 for each record in it. Then change the login.aspx file as follows:

```
<%@ Page Language="C#" %>
<%@ Import Namespace="System.Web.Security " %>
<%@ Import Namespace="System.Data.OleDB" %>
<script language="C#" runat=server>
void Login_Click(System.Object Src, System. EventArgs E)
{
string strConn ="PROVIDER=Microsoft.Jet.OLEDB.4.0;DATA SOURCE=" &
server.mappath("DB/WroxDBAuth.mdb") + ";";
    OLEDBConnection Conn = New OLEDBConnection(strConn);
    Conn.Open();
    string strSQL = "SELECT Pwd FROM Tbl_MA_Users WHERE Email = '" +
                    txtEmail.Text
                    + "'" + "ZipCode = '" + txtZipCode.Text + "'";
    OLEDBCommand Cmd = New OLEDBCommand(strSQL,Conn);
    //Create a datareader, connection object
    OLEDBDataReader Dr =
    Cmd.ExecuteReader(System.Data.CommandBehavior.CloseConnection);
     //Get the first row and check the password.
    if (Dr.Read())
    {
      if (Dr("Pwd").ToString == txtPwd.text)
      {
        FormsAuthentication.RedirectFromLoginPage(txtEmail.Text, false);
      }
      else
      {
        lblLoginMsg.text = "Invalid password.";
      }
    else
    {
      lblLoginMsg.text = "Login name not found.";
    }
    Dr.Close;
}
</script>
```

Exercise 4

Create an account for a user named 'John@MyDomain.com', but deny him access in web.config. What happens when you try to log in as him? Can you think of a way of displaying a message to accompany this?

Solution

Trying to log in as 'John@MyDomain' com bounces you back to the login page without an error message. You could use the login process with an exception handler, and if it returns to the login page, you could handle the exception and display an error.

Exercise 5

Create a new page called newpage.aspx on the example, and use web.config to ensure that only John has access to it.

HINT: Create a subfolder for this page.

Solution

Place newpage.aspx in the admin folder and then change web.config as follows:

```
<configuration>
  <system.web>
    <authentication mode="Forms">
      <forms name=".WroxDemo" loginUrl="login.aspx"
      protection="All" timeout="60" />
    </authentication>
    <machineKey validationKey="AutoGenerate" decryptionKey="AutoGenerate"
     validation="SHA1"/>
    <authorization>
      <allow users="?" />
    </authorization>
```

Web Matrix Quick Start

To write ASP.NET pages, you can choose from several software tools. They range from the simple Notepad to the powerful and expensive (Visual Studio .NET). In this book, we use a tool called *Web Matrix*, because it is easy to learn, powerful enough, and most importantly, free. If you haven't used Web Matrix before, this appendix will lead you through the basics in about an hour. We assume that you have downloaded and installed the software as described in *Chapter 1*.

This appendix will cover:

- ❑ ASP.NET Web Matrix and its uses
- ❑ Starting Web Matrix
- ❑ The screen
- ❑ Entering code
- ❑ Saving and viewing pages
- ❑ Reusing code
- ❑ Class browser

What Is Web Matrix?

Web Matrix is a *development environment*. This basically means it helps you to write new software (in this case, the ASP.NET pages). Web Matrix helps application development by providing:

- ❑ A group of tools that reduce the amount of typing needed to create a page
- ❑ Several ways to view your Web pages during development
- ❑ *Workspace*, a small Windows Explorer-like interface that lets you view the pages in your site

❑ Automatic color-coding within your code to identify keywords, comments, and other kinds of code

❑ A simple server that can compile and display pages in the same way as the more complex IIS or .NET Framework

In short, Web Matrix is a great tool that can support almost everything we do in this book.

Web Matrix is developed and distributed under a different model from most development tools. It is an *Open Source* tool, which means that anybody can see and improve the code that makes the tool. There is no charge for getting or using ASP.NET Web Matrix. Many add-ins and changes for this product are expected in the next few years.

For this book, we selected ASP.NET Web Matrix as our editor for the following reasons:

❑ It is free, an important factor for many students starting in ASP.NET

❑ It is small and simple, making it easy to download and install

❑ Its interface is very similar to Visual Studio .NET, which you may need to use in the future.

Although the best things in life are free, that is not necessarily the case with development tools. There are some serious limitations to ASP.NET Web Matrix, particularly if you have used a more advanced tool such as Visual Studio or Visual Studio .NET:

❑ *IntelliSense*, a Visual Studio tool that uses pop-ups to help in function and statement completion, is missing in Web Matrix.

❑ There is no F1 option for quick help.

❑ Web Matrix does not have collaborative tools to help teams of programmers.

❑ The basic coding model is not code-behind (which we encourage you to use in the later part of the book). Web Matrix generates inline code.

❑ You do not get line-by-line error checking like in Visual Studio .NET (a big help if you are prone to typing and syntax mistakes).

❑ Web Matrix does not have a built-in debugger, watch windows, or immediate windows, all of which are useful troubleshooting tools available in Visual Studio.

❑ As you develop more complex pages, you might have to manually compile assemblies using the DOS command line. Some of these features may be implemented in future versions of Web Matrix as people create different add-ins.

Overall, ASP.NET Web Matrix is a fine choice for a beginner. When you want to work faster and on larger projects, you can upgrade to Visual Studio .NET.

Starting ASP.NET Web Matrix

First download and install ASP.NET Web Matrix as described in *Chapter 1*. If it is already running, then exit the software. Before starting ASP.NET Web Matrix, create your `BegASPNET11` folder as described in *Chapter 1*. Within that folder, create a `MatrixPractice` folder and then start ASP.NET Web Matrix. After it loads, you get a wizard to create a new document. For now, change the location to the nascent `MatrixPractice` folder and then change the filename to `NewFile`. You do not need to type an extension.

Keep all other options the same, especially the selection of Template = General, and in the top right graphical selector keep the choice of an ASP.NET page. Click OK to create the page. You will see a window with the title `NewFile.aspx`. Double-click on the title bar to maximize the window.

The Screen

Let's start with a quick tour of the areas on the screen. The Web Matrix screen looks similar to Figure B-1:

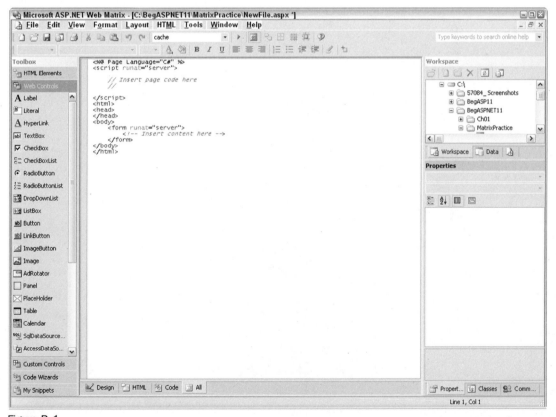

Figure B-1

The screen has six broad regions. First is the menu toolbar as shown in Figure B-2. This has the standard File, Edit, Window, and Help options as well as some choices discussed later in this appendix.

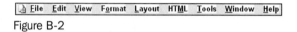

Figure B-2

There are one or more toolbars below the menu as shown in Figure B-3. Again, many of these tools are familiar to you from other Windows applications. We will cover most of the new ones in this tutorial.

Figure B-3

To the left is a Toolbox with five subsections (as seen in Figure B-4), which shows an expanded view of the Web Controls toolbox: HTML Elements, Web Controls, Custom Controls, Code Builders, and My Snippets. Click on one of these to expand a group of options.

Figure B-4

The center of the screen is the *Page Space*, where you type in the code for the page. Later we will discuss the four tabs at the bottom that change the view between Design, HTML, Code, and All as shown in Figure B-5:

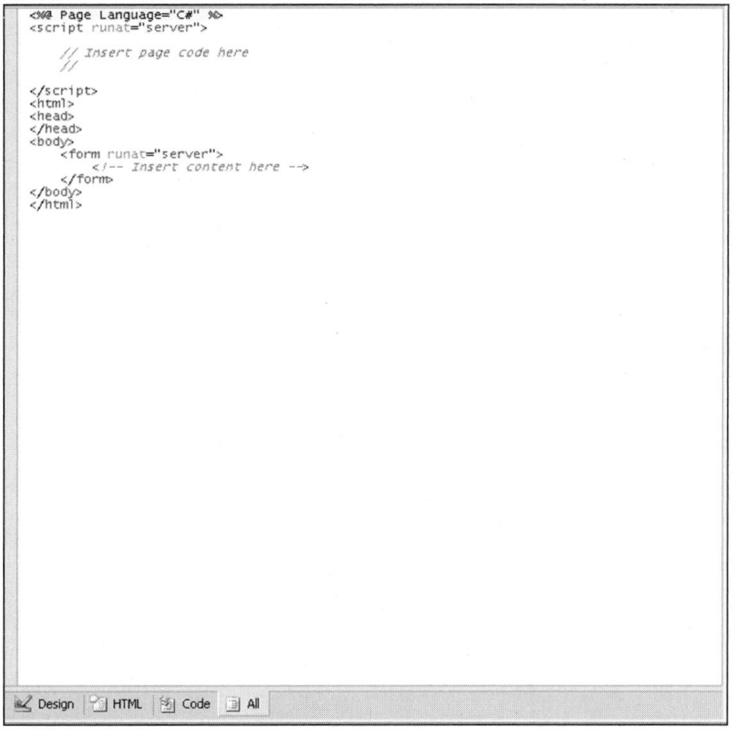

```
<%@ Page Language="C#" %>
<script runat="server">

    // Insert page code here
    //

</script>
<html>
<head>
</head>
<body>
    <form runat="server">
        <!-- Insert content here -->
    </form>
</body>
</html>
```

Design | HTML | Code | All

Figure B-5

The *Workspace* is similar to Windows Explorer as you can see in Figure B-6. You should see all currently connected drives, local and networked. This area of the screen can switch to display available database connections by clicking on the Data tab:

Figure B-6

The Properties space at the bottom-right can display one of three sets of information: properties, the class browser, or a connection to the ASP.NET Web Matrix community. When you first open your page, the Properties box will be empty as shown in Figure B-7:

Figure B-7

When you have controls on your Web pages, you will be able to select a control and view its properties as shown in Figure B-8:

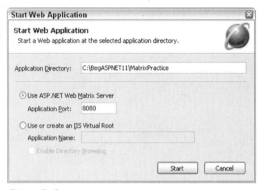

Figure B-8

Each area can be resized. In addition, the toolbar can be removed completely by hitting F2. Now that you know your way around the screen, let's begin to use Web Matrix to create ASP.NET Web pages.

How to Enter Code

You can add code to an ASP.NET page in four ways:

❑ Web Matrix automatically generates some code on your page. You have already observed this technique when you created the `NewFile.aspx` (Figure B-1) file. The automatic code includes a page designator (in yellow), the `<script>` and `<form>` tags, and dividers for the HTML, head, and body of your page.

❑ You can type code directly into the page space at the center of the screen. Notice the four tabs at the bottom of the page space. If you click on All, you will see the page presented in the same way as if you were working in Notepad.

❑ You can add code using the Toolbox on the left side. Position your insertion bar on the page, open a group in the Toolbox, and double-click an option. Under Web Controls there are ASP.NET-enabled controls, and under HTML Elements there are various tags.

❏ You can select a control and make changes in the **Properties** table. Code will be written or re-written automatically to the page.

In the following *Try It Out*, we will try adding code to our page in each of the four possible ways:

Try It Out **Code Entry**

1. Open `NewFile.aspx` and choose the **All** view. Observe that ASP.NET Web Matrix has already entered some standard code. That is the first method of code entry.

2. Position your text insertion cursor just after the `<body>` tag, and type a simple line of text to practice the second code-entry method:

```
<body>
    Text for the page
    <form runat="server">
```

3. Now position cursor in the `<form>` tag. You can keep the green comments or delete them – it doesn't matter. In the Toolbox, expand the **Web Controls** and double-click on **TextBox**. The code for the textbox is inserted in the page, demonstrating the third code entry method.

4. At the bottom of the page space, click on the **Design** tab. Select the new textbox with a single click. When selected, there are eight gray handles around the object. The **Properties** section at the lower right corner of the screen shows the table of properties for the textbox. (You may want to drag up the top of this area to see more of the table.) Scroll down to the **Width** property and in the right hand side column, type the number 50 and press Enter. Note the change in textbox size. Switch back to the **All** view and observe the change to the `TextBox` tag in the form. That was the fourth way to enter code, using the **Properties** box. There is no need to save the page after entering the properties.

We have just demonstrated all four ways to enter text: automatically, by typing, by clicking a control in the **Toolbox**, and by changing a value in the **Properties** table.

Saving and Viewing Pages

Pages are saved in the same way as in all Windows applications, by going to **File | Save | Save As**. Always save files before attempting to view them in your browser. A common mistake is to make changes to a page and view it without saving. The changes are not visible and you can easily get frustrated. Also be sure that if you save a page called `MyPage1` with a new name (say, `MyPage2`), then switch to the browser, double check that you are looking at `MyPage2` and not the original version.

A list of pages is visible in the Workspace in the right central area the screen. This area requires manual refreshes using the tool provided. Select a folder (not a file) prior to clicking on the refresh icon.

As with all document windows within application windows, you can maximize or minimize your page window. Multiple pages can be open at once and they can be tiled or cascaded using the **Window** menu.

Most programmers adjust the sizes of areas to suit the amount of screen they want to devote to code and to the various tools.

You can work on pages in one of two modes, depending on whether or not you want Web Matrix to revise your code to conform to XHTML standards. These revisions will not affect the appearance of the page in the browser; it just changes the indenting, tabs, returns, and the use of closing tags.

❑ Design Mode will have code layout revised to meet the XHMTL standards.

❑ Preview Mode leaves your spacing, indents, tabs, and returns as is.

The Web Matrix mode can be set using Tools | Preferences | WebEditing | General. If you select Preview Mode, the formatting will never change. If you pick Design Mode, the code will be reformatted. Within Design Mode, you can start your pages in either the Design view (which means they will be automatically reformatted to XHTML before being displayed to you) or you can set the pages to open by default in Source (the Code) view. The word *design* is used two ways. Design *mode* reformats code layout to meet XHTML standards. The Design *view* is a way to look at a page. In either case, your change to the mode only takes effect the next time you open a page; it does not apply to currently open page windows.

> **If you don't want XHTML reformatting, use the Preview Mode. If you use the Design view, select a default of Preview and don't switch to Design view manually. If you *do* want reformatting to XHTML format and want the design tools, use the Design Mode.**

You have six options for viewing your work in the page screen. Four are available in Design Mode and two in Preview Mode. In the Design Mode, you will find:

❑ The Design view that shows the page similar to how it will appear in a browser. In this view, you can use various layout tools, such as absolute position. A page shown in Design view will *always* be reformatted to XHTML.

❑ The All view that shows all of the code on the page.

❑ The HTML view that shows only the non-script part of the page – the HTML tags.

❑ The Code view that shows only the script part of the page.

The Preview Mode supports two other types of views:

❑ The Preview view is similar to Design view in that it shows approximately what the page will look like in a browser. The Toolbox is not available, but you can type in text.

❑ The Source view displays all of the code and the toolbox is available.

None of these view options will display the result of executing code. For example, if you set the text of a label in the code of the `Page_Load()` event procedure to `Bingo`, you would still see the default label text in all the preceding views.

To run scripts, you must actually serve the page through IIS+ASP.NET or a substitute. Web Matrix includes a substitute (similar to the classic ASP Personal Web Server). To run a page, first save it (Ctrl+S) then strike F5 or select View | Start. Web Matrix will provide a Start Web Application dialog box for which you can accept the default port. We recommend that you change the application directory to the root of your project, C:\BegAspNet11 as shown in Figure B-9. Now you can serve pages from anywhere in your Web application.

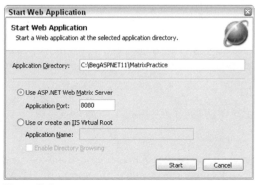

Figure B-9

Your computer will start a server process and display your page. Its scripts will be processed. You will see a pop-up notice stating that the service has started along with an icon in the tray as shown in Figure B-10. Once the server is running, you can view other pages without restarting the server.

Figure B-10

Try It Out Formatting Modes, Views, and Serving Pages

In this exercise, we will look at a simple page in various views and in a browser. In each case we will pay attention to our capabilities to work on the page.

1. Start Web Matrix but don't create a new file. Choose the Design Mode | Source setting by going to Tools | Preferences | Web Editing | General. Note that in Design Mode, your code will be reformatted to XHTML whenever you view a page in the Design view.

2. In the MatrixPractice folder create a file named Exercise-Views.aspx. Double-click the title bar to maximize the page. Confirm that you are in the All view. You can leave the green comments or delete them.

3. Staying in All view, add a `<title>` into the header. Then type View Exercises in the `<body>` section. Position your cursor within the `<form>` tag and use the toolbar to add a label within the form. Add an attribute for ID="lblTest". Change to the Design view, select lblTest, and change its Text property (in the property box) to Default text. Save the file. You have now added code to your page in several ways, and the section of interest in the All view should be as follows:

```
<body>
    View Exercises
    <form runat="server">
        <asp:Label id="lblTest" runat="server">Default Text</asp:Label>
    </form>
</body>
```

4. Now let's experiment with the feature that reformats to XHTML. In the All view, change the style in which the tags are typed as follows. Start by removing the spaces to the left of the `<asp:Label...>` tag. Then change the label to the single tag form. Your label tag should look like the following:

```
<form runat="server">
    <asp:Label id="lblTest" runat="server"/>
</form>
```

5. Switch to the Design view and back to All view. Note that whenever you switch to the Design view, the formatting of your code is changed to conform to XHTML standards.

6. Close the page. Change your preference to Preview Mode and reopen the page. There are now two different views available: Preview and Source. Note that in Preview Mode there is no reformatting to XHTML. Also, in Preview Mode, you lose the toolbox and most of the icons on the toolbars.

7. Close the page, change your preference back to Design Mode | Source, and reopen the page. Staying in the All view, type the following between the `<script>` tags. Pay careful attention to the punctuation. This script code (as you will learn when you read the early chapters of the text) changes the text in lblText when a server serves the page:

```
<script runat="server">
    void Page_Load()
    {
        lblTest.Text = "New Text";
    }
</script>
```

8. Switch to HTML view; you will only see the non-script part of the page. Switch to the Code view and you will see just the code. Switch to the Design view. Note that even though we have the new line of code in the script, the label's text does not change. Scripts are only executed (carried out) when the page is actually served by a server; in Design and Preview views it is only being displayed within ASP.NET Web Matrix.

9. With the page open in any mode and any view, click F5 to start the ASP.NET Web Matrix server and see the page in your browser. Accept the port, but change the Application Directory to `C:\BegAspNet11`. It could take up to two minutes for the server to start and prepare the page. Note that when you view the page in your browser, the server is actually serving it and thus the script is run and the text of the label changes.

Reusing Code

You will probably find yourself using the same small section of code on many pages. You can write it once, save it in Web Matrix, and then drag and drop it into subsequent pages. Once it is written, select the code and drag it into the toolbox category named **My Snippets**. After this, you can right-click and rename the snippet. To insert a snippet into a new page, merely position the page cursor and double-click on the snippet's name in the toolbox. Select the text with your mouse cursor in the ASPX code on the left edge of the lines so that you are selecting whole lines. Selecting partial lines leads to formatting inconsistencies when you later paste the code.

In the following exercise, you will create a snippet to put a title in your pages.

Try It Out   Saving and Using Snippets

1. Open Web Matrix. In the workspace, select `C:\BegASPNET11\MatrixPractice`. Right-click and choose **Add New File**. In the top left corner, ensure that **Templates: (General)** is selected, and on the right side, the **ASP.NET Page** icon is selected. Confirm that the location is `C:\BegASPNET11\MatrixPractice`, then enter the file name as `SnippetSource.aspx`. The page should open in the page space; double-click on its title bar to maximize the page.

2. Switch to the **All** view using the tab at the bottom and add a title as follows:

```
<html>
<head>
  <title>Example</title>
</head>
<body>
```

3. Select the entire title line by clicking in the left margin and then drag the selection to the **My Snippets** section of the **Toolbox**. Right-click on the new snippet in the toolbox and rename it `Title`.

4. Now that our model of code is saved, we can customize the actual title in this page, as follows:

```
<head>
  <title>Snippet Source Example</title>
</head>
```

5. Now let's use the snippet in a new page. Create a new page named `SnippetTarget.aspx` following the same actions as in Step 1 of this *Try It Out*. Position the insertion bar after the head tag and then double-click on the **Title** snippet in the **Toolbox**. Finish the job by adding the text `Snippet Target` to the `<title>` of `SnippetTarget.aspx`.

Class Browser

In Visual Studio .NET you automatically get a display of various options as you type (IntelliSense). But in Web Matrix you have to find the names of those properties and their values on your own. The process is somewhat cumbersome and non-intuitive. After a few months of writing pages, the lack of intellisense may be the number one reason you pay the money for Visual Studio .NET.

The names of properties and their values are held in the *class browser*. It shares screen space with the properties window in the lower right of the Web Matrix screen. Click on the **Classes** tab, and then you will probably want to make the window wider and higher while you use it. F2 toggles the **Toolbox** on and off to make more room. In the class browser, you will see a list of the names of classes, many of which will be completely foreign to your experience. Let's run through an example that shows how to use the tool.

Some of these examples use vocabulary and theory covered in the book, so if you've just started reading, you may have to follow the steps without a complete understanding of the terminology.

The technique to use the class browser consists of five steps:

1. In the Properties window, switch to the Class tab

2. Expand a class until you see the object of interest, and then double-click on the object to open its description in the central screen

3. In the central screen, expand the members of the object until you see the item of interest

4. Double-click on that item to see a description

5. Click on the hyperlink to read further documentation

Note that when you open a class browser page, it is a sister to your ASP.NET pages in the center of the screen. You can switch between the windows with **Ctrl+F6** or by going to **Windows** and then selecting your page. You can also tile the ASP.NET page and the class browser page.

In this exercise, we will use the class browser to see if we can set the Text property of a checkbox to a certain alignment.

Try It Out   Class Browser Property Look-Up

1. Create a page named `ExerciseClassBrowser1.aspx` in your `MatrixPractice` folder. Add an `asp:CheckBox` (from the **Toolbox Web Controls**). Be sure you use **CheckBox**, and not **CheckBoxList**. Now you need to find out if you can align the text.

2. Open the class browser by selecting the **Class** tab at the lower right. Recall that all `<asp: >` controls are part of the ASP.NET Web Controls class. Find that class in the list (near the top) and expand it by clicking on the + sign. In the list you see your `<asp:CheckBox>`. Double-click on it to open information on the control in the central part of the screen. On the left is a tree that gives you options to view the properties, methods, and other members of the **CheckBox** control. If you expand **Properties**, you see a **TextAlign** property available (see Figure B-11):

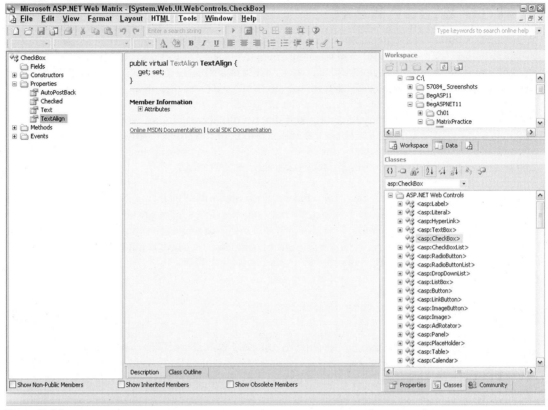

Figure B-11

3. To know the syntax and possible values, double-click on the `TextAlign` property in the left side of the page (Figure B-11) and you get some details in the center panel. These details are not of much use so click on the link to read MSDN documentation on the Web.

4. The Web page gives many details that are of little use to you. However, if you scroll down you can see an example that shows the proper syntax. Near the top of the page is a section on property values with a link that takes you to a table of values, including `Left` and `Right`.

5. Now that you know that the `asp:CheckBox` control supports alignment of text and have learnt the acceptable values, add the following to your page. Remember to use Ctrl+F6 to switch between the ASPX page and the class browser information page. Take a look at the **Design** view or **Preview** view in the tab at the bottom of the page space. Change the `TextAlign` value to `right` to see the difference:

```
<form runat="server">
  <asp:CheckBox id="CheckBox1"
      runat="server"
      textalign="right">
  </asp:CheckBox>
</form>
```

What to Study Next

Web Matrix is introduced in detail through a free on-line book in PDF format. You can access the book by going to Help | Help Topics, and then scrolling down to Finding Answers and clicking the link to the book. There is also a guided tour of ASP.NET Web Matrix available on the same page. Additional resources are listed in the Web Community option tab below the Properties area.

ASP.NET Web Matrix offers many layout options that we did not cover here because they are not germane to the coding focus of this book. It is well worth your time to learn about absolute position, alignment, snap-to-grid, and making controls the same size. All of these options are only available in the Design view when the page is in Design Mode (they rely on XHTML).

Another important feature is the find and replace facility under the Edit menu. Find... is invaluable when trying to locate a given variable on a page. Likewise, you can save a lot of time by using Replace... when you have to change a variable name. This also prevents mistakes while retyping manually. Many times you will be working on pages on a remote site and transferring the pages using FTP. ASP.NET Web Matrix workspace supports FTP connections to look like a local drive.

Summary

ASP.NET Web Matrix is a free tool for developing ASP.NET Web pages. However, ASP.NET Web Matrix has limitations, including lack of tools that speed page development and reduce the number of errors. ASP.NET Web Matrix also lacks troubleshooting and debugging tools. The logical upgrade path is Visual Studio .NET.

The ASP.NET Web Matrix environment includes panes displaying tools, properties of objects, an explorer-like view of your site, and a central area called the page space, where you type. The Toolbox actually has five or more toolboxes overlaid.

You can enter code by typing, by double-clicking a tool icon, or by pasting a saved snippet of code. The characters of your page will automatically color-code according to their purpose. Code is edited and saved in essentially the same way as when you work with Word.

You can work in one of two modes. The Design mode will reformat your code to meet the XHTML standards. Although the reformatting does not affect functionality, it changes tabs and enters, and may add certain closing tags. The other mode, Preview, does not change your code but does limit the tools ASP.NET Web Matrix makes available. You can view the page space using one of five options, ranging from just the code, to just the user interface, to a preview of the entire page.

By clicking F5 you can start the ASP.NET Web Matrix Web server to enable you to view a page without actually serving it on a dedicated server. Once the Web server is started, Web Matrix allows you to create, serve, and browse a page all on one machine.

Code that you write and expect to reuse on other pages can be saved to the My Snippets toolbar. A double-click on a saved snippet makes a copy into the current page at the location of the insertion bar.

Web Matrix includes a class browser that provides the members of almost all objects. The class browser can be difficult for programmers new to .NET, but as your knowledge increases, the class browser can prove to be very useful.

The Wrox United Database

Starting from *Chapter 10* in this book, we worked through examples that were based around a fictitious soccer league team called Wrox United. These examples relied on a database for match and team information. In this appendix, we'll look at:

❏ How the Wrox United database is structured

❏ Downloading the database from the Wrox Web site and preparing it for use

The Database Design

As we've seen in the examples in *Chapters 10* to *13*, the Wrox United database has several different tables that store data about teams, players, matches, and much more. Let's take a look at a diagram of the database. The Figure C-1 was produced in the Relationships view in Microsoft Access:

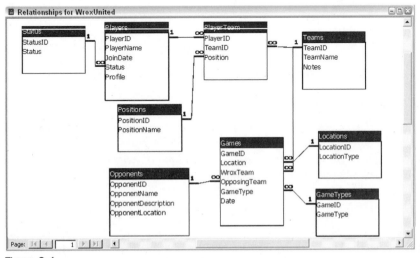

Figure C-1

Let's look at each of the different tables in turn, and see what columns they contain.

Players

This table holds the details for each player in the club. These players can be members of one or more teams and can play in different positions. The `Players` table holds the core information for each player and the foreign key information to link to the `Status` table, which means that each player can be flagged as active, injured, or retired. This is a one-to-many relationship, where each player can be one of many possible status types.

Column	Type	Description
PlayerID	Integer / AutoNumber Primary Key, Unique	Unique identifier for each row in the database, generated automatically by the database whenever a new row is inserted.
PlayerName	String / Text, 50 characters	The name of the player.
JoinDate	DateTime	The date that the player joined the club.
Status	Integer / Number Foreign Key (to the StatusID column on the Status table)	A link to the Status table, used for specifying whether a player is active, injured, or retired.
Profile	String / Text, 255 characters	A brief description of the player.
SiteLogin	String / Text, 20 characters	A login name used to access restricted parts of the site.
SitePassword	String / Text, 20 characters	A password used to access restricted parts of the site.

Primary key-foreign key one-to-many relationships are a core part of relational database design, and enable us to minimize repetition of data in the database. It also aids consistency, and avoids several different variations of the same data being stored.

For example, without this relationship, we could include a Status column in the Players table to store text describing the active status of a player. This is a fine solution if you have tight control over the data that's inserted into the database, but if you allow users to enter custom strings of text for the values in this column, you could end up describing a player as being injured using the text "injured", "Injured", "sick", or "ill" instead of simply selecting the Injured status from the Status table.

Status

The `Status` table stores the availability and status information that each player can select from or specify. The available status types in the samples provided in the code download are `Active`, `Injured`, or `Retired`. However, you can enter whichever type you like in your database.

Column	Type	Description
StatusID	Integer / AutoNumber Primary Key, Unique	Unique identifier for each row in the database, generated automatically by the database whenever a new row is inserted.
Status	String / Text, 50 characters	Description of the status (injured, active, retired). Each player in the Players team has to select one of these values.

Teams

The `Teams` table stores information about each team in the Wrox United club. The name of the team and any associated notes can be stored here.

Column	Type	Description
TeamID	Integer / AutoNumber Primary Key, Unique	Unique identifier for each row in the database, generated automatically by the database whenever a new row is inserted.
TeamName	String / Text, 50 characters	The name of the team.
Notes	String / Memo	Description of the team, plus any additional information that may be useful. This field is long enough to hold several thousand characters of data.

PlayerTeams

This is a join table between the `Players` table and the `Teams` table. One player can be in many teams, and each team consists of many players. In this situation, we have a many-to-many relationship, and thus need to include a join table between these two tables to store information about both sides. In this way, the `PlayerTeams` table now stores many *unique* combinations of players and teams (hence if you were one of the players, you could join Team A only *once* but you could *also* join Team B).

The other item of interest in this table is the `Position` column, which is a foreign key link to the `Positions` table. This enables you to specify the position for each player in a given team.

Column	Type	Description
PlayerID	Integer / Number Part of Primary Key	Link to the ID of the Player.

Column	Type	Description
TeamID	Integer / Number Part of Primary Key	Link to the ID of the Team. Used together with the `PlayerID` column, the Primary Key constraint specifies that each combination of `PlayerID` and `TeamID` must be unique.
Position	Integer / Number Foreign Key (to the `PositionID` column on the `Position` table)	Used to specify, for each combination of Player and Team, the position the player plays in on that team.

Positions

This table stores details of the available positions that a player can assume in a particular team.

Column	Type	Description
PositionID	Integer / AutoNumber Primary Key, Unique	Unique identifier for each row in the database, generated automatically by the database whenever a new row is inserted.
PositionName	String / Text, 50 characters	Name of a position (left wing, defence, and so on).

Games

The `Games` table stores information about each match, including who is playing the match, where the match will take place, what type of match it is, when the match is scheduled, and the score, when known. Many columns in this table are foreign keys to other tables, reusing data and centralizing information where possible.

Column	Type	Description
GameID	Integer / AutoNumber Primary Key, Unique	Unique identifier for each row in the database, generated automatically by the database whenever a new row is inserted.
Location	Integer / Number Foreign Key (to the `LocationID` column on the `Locations` table)	Used to choose a location for the game, from the list defined in the `Locations` table (for example, home or away.)

Column	Type	Description
WroxTeam	Integer / Number Foreign Key (to the TeamID column on the Teams table)	Link to the Teams table to select which Wrox team is participating in the game.
OpposingTeam	Integer / Number Foreign Key (to the OpponentID column on the Opponents table)	Link to the Opponents table to select which opposing team is participating in the game.
GameType	Integer / Number Foreign Key (to the GameTypeID column on GameTypes table)	Link to the GameTypes table to select the type of game (for example, a friendly or league match.)
Date	DateTime	The date of the match.
WroxGoals	Integer / Number	The number of goals scored by the Wrox team.

GameTypes

This table is used to store the 'type' of games – for example, friendly or league.

Column	Type	Description
GameTypeID	Integer / AutoNumber Primary Key, Unique	Unique identifier for each row in the database, generated automatically by the database whenever a new row is inserted.
GameType	String / Text, 50 characters	The type of a match, for example, friendly or league.

Locations

This table stores types of location for a game – for example, home or away.

Column	Type	Description
LocationID	Integer / AutoNumber Primary Key, Unique	Unique identifier for each row in the database, generated automatically by the database whenever a new row is inserted.

Column	Type	Description
LocationType	String / Text, 50 characters	The type of location (for example, home or away.)

Opponents

The Opponents table stores details of the other teams in the league, and details of where they are based.

Column	Type	Description
OpponentID	Integer / AutoNumber Primary Key, Unique	Unique identifier for each row in the database, generated automatically by the database whenever a new row is inserted.
OpponentName	String / Text, 50 characters	The name of the opponent.
OpponentDescription	String / Memo	A description of the opponent that could be used, for example, to describe their strengths and weaknesses.
OpponentLocation	String / Text, 50 characters	The name of the home location of the opponent.

Fans

This table is completely standalone compared to the other tables. It has only one column and is used for storing email addresses of fans. You could expand this table to store more details about each of the fans registered in the database. Since email addresses are unique to an individual (in most cases), we can make this column the primary key for the table without the need for an additional key column.

Column	Type	Description
FanEmail	String / Text, 255 characters Primary Key, Unique	The email address of a fan. Since email addresses are individual, this field can be given a unique constraint and assigned as a primary key for the table.

Installing the Database

The quickest and simplest way to obtain a copy of this database is to download and install the appropriate database from the code download section of this book on http://www.wrox.com/. Access and MSDE are quite different in structure, so the process for installing each of them is also different. Let's look at how to install the Access version of the database first.

Installing the Access Database

Access is a simple database storage format. It's not designed for heavy usage, or for storing large amounts of data. However, for small database projects, it's very easy to use and distribute.

To install this database, obtain a copy of `WroxUnited.mdb` from the code download for this book, and save it in the appropriate folder on your hard drive. As long as the path to the `.mdb` file is specified correctly in your connection string, you will be able to read data from the database.

There is, however, one adjustment you will need to make if you want to make changes to the database programmatically. Once you have downloaded the database, you need to right-click on the database file and select Properties to get the dialog shown in Figure C-2:

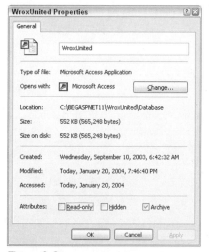

Figure C-2

Ensure that the Read-only checkbox is unchecked, and you will be able to make modifications to the contents of the database.

Installing the MSDE Database

MSDE databases are more tricky to install than Access databases, but since they are based on the more powerful SQL Server database engine, they are much more robust and scalable.

MSDE databases are registered with the MSDE database server. The main database data file has a file extension of .mdf, and it has a corresponding log file with an extension of .ldf. To install the database, you need to have copies of the WroxUnited.mdf and WroxUnited_log.ldf files from the code download section.

> You must have a copy of MSDE/SQL Server installed before you can install the WroxUnited MSDE version of the database. SQL Server is a full-scale product that is available for purchase or as part of some MSDN subscription options. MSDE is a free download from Microsoft and is the same as SQL Server, but with a more restrictive license. For more information, you can consult the Microsoft Web site (http://www.microsoft.com). Alternately, you can download MSDE from http://www.asp.net/msde/default.aspx?tabindex=0&tabid=1.

The easiest and most reliable way to install a new MSDE database from these two files is as follows:

1. Open up Web Matrix and switch to the Data view in the pane at the top right. In here, click the Add Database Connection button, which is the second button from the right in the top panel of buttons (see Figure C-3):

Figure C-3

2. In the window that appears, create a new MSDE database as shown in Figure C-4:

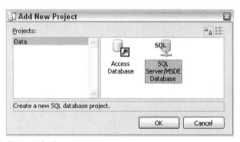

Figure C-4

3. A dialog will pop up asking for the name of the database. Click the Create a new database link at the bottom of the dialog as shown in Figure C-5:

Figure C-5

4. Finally, when prompted, enter WroxUnited as the name for the new database and click OK as shown in Figure C-6:

Figure C-6

5. You will now see the new empty database appear in the Data pane as in Figure C-7:

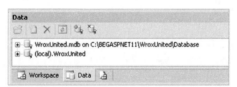

Figure C-7

6. This is where the fun begins – close down Web Matrix. Now, on the bottom right of your screen – your system tray – you will see a SQL Server/MSDE icon with a green arrow next to it (you may have to click the round button with an arrow in it, to unhide the SQL Server icon). Right-click this icon and select MSSQLServer – Stop as shown in Figure C-8:

Figure C-8

7. Once the service has stopped, open an Explorer window, and navigate to C:\Program Files\Microsoft SQL Server\MSSQL\Data.

This location may be slightly different on your system. If, for example, you are running a named instance of SQL Server, you will need to navigate to the MSSQL$InstanceName *directory.*

8. In this folder, you need to replace the two WroxUnited files (`WroxUnited.mdf` and `WroxUnited_log.ldf`) with the files available in the code download as shown in Figure C-9:

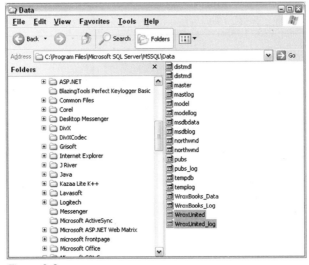

Figure C-9

9. Once you have done this, restart your SQL Server (again, by right-clicking on the icon in the System Tray), and then reopen Web Matrix. Note that it may take a couple of moments for your SQL Server to restart completely (hover your mouse over the icon in the System Tray for the exact status of the service – once it says Running - \\MachineName - MSSQLServer, you know that the service has fully restarted.

10. Expand the (local).WroxUnited node in the Data pane in Web Matrix, and the tables should have been imported successfully as shown in Figure C-10:

Figure C-10

Web Application Development Using Visual Studio .NET

This appendix is a brief overview of the key elements of Visual Studio .NET that you can use to create Web applications. You should work through the examples in Chapters 10-13 to understand the sample application demonstrated in this appendix, and to understand the programming concepts we'll be using.

Visual Studio .NET is a huge tool. In the same way that you can start using Microsoft Word as a beginner one day and still be learning about its many different features several years later, Visual Studio .NET has numerous wizards and tools available if you know where to look. This appendix concentrates on the core features that you'll use as a Visual Studio .NET Web developer.

Visual Studio .NET comes in many different packages. The lowest end, designed for developers on a budget, is the language-specific edition (Visual C# Standard or Visual Basic .NET Standard). Those with MSDN subscriptions or larger wallets may use Visual Studio .NET Professional or Visual Studio .NET Enterprise Architect. Each edition has a different subset of features available. The language editions are not only language-specific, but also have the following key restrictions:

❑ No option to create Class Library or Server Control projects.

❑ No option to modify the structure of SQL databases (to create or edit tables in the Data Explorer). However, you can still view information in the database.

There are ways around each of these limitations – you can add classes to other projects (as we will do in this appendix) for adding compiled data access components or server controls to your Web applications. You can even modify the structure of SQL Server databases in Visual Studio .NET by using the SQL window and executing SQL commands directly against the database. However, a better idea is to edit databases using Web Matrix – it's a free tool, and you can edit existing databases or even create new databases using the Web Matrix Data pane.

> In this appendix, all of the exercises will assume that you only have Visual C# .NET Standard Edition. This will ensure that you can try out these exercises for yourself on any of the Visual Studio .NET range of products.

In this appendix, we'll recreate some of the functionality built across *Chapters 10-13* of this book, concentrating on how to achieve similar results using the Visual Studio .NET environment and associated tools. We'll look at:

- ❑ Creating a Web application project, and the files that are created by default.
- ❑ Visual Studio .NET's Solution and Project based architecture.
- ❑ The main features of the environment that you'll need to be familiar with.
- ❑ Adding HTML and Web controls to pages and adding some interactivity.
- ❑ Creating custom user controls and adding them to pages.
- ❑ Moving data access code into a separate class file (a technique that can be duplicated for any custom server controls you may need to write).

We won't be discussing how any of the code in this appendix works, because this is covered in depth in the earlier chapters.

Creating a Web Application Project

Open up Visual Studio .NET and create a new **ASP.NET Web Application** by clicking on either the **New Project** button on the Start page, or by selecting File | **New Project** from the main menu as shown in Figure D-1:

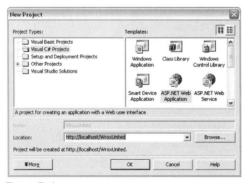

Figure D-1

Name the new project `WroxUnited` and click **OK**. Wait a few moments for Visual Studio .NET to create the new project and you will end up with the screen as shown in Figure D-1:

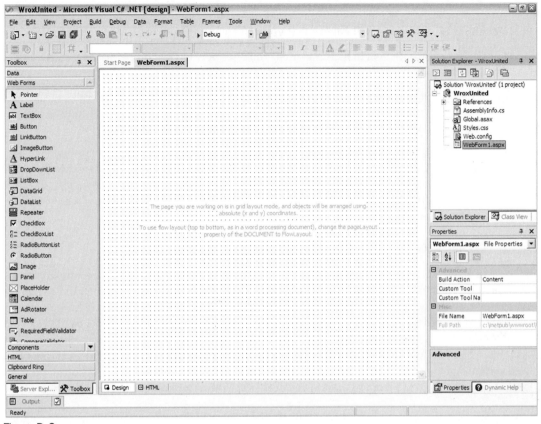

Figure D-2

Features of the Visual Studio .NET Environment

❑ **Solution Explorer**: Contains the root Solution and any sub-projects represented in a hierarchical (tree) arrangement. Because we only created a project, a root solution was created automatically. This is where you can double-click files to open them, right-click to rename them, or select different views on the same file.

❑ **Toolbox**: Contains all the controls you'll need to use to create Web pages – simply drag and drop, or double-click, to add each control.

❑ **Server Explorer** (not shown): Clicking the tab for the Server Explorer opens up another hierarchical tree representation of the server – you can use this to create connections to databases and view data held in these databases.

❑ **File Selector Tabs**: Contains a corresponding tab for each open file – simply click to make the selected file visible.

❑ **Properties Pane**: Contents change dynamically to reflect the properties available to the currently selected object. These properties change dynamically. In the screenshot shown in figure D-2, the properties for the Web page itself are visible. Try clicking on items in the Server Explorer to view properties on each item in there. Later on, you'll see how to view properties on controls and edit them in this pane.

❑ **HTML / Design View**: Switch between the Design Surface or HTML view of a web page, similar to the behaviour seen in Web Matrix. Code view can be displayed by right-clicking on a page in server explorer and clicking View Code.

❑ **Design Surface**: In Design view, you can drag and drop controls from the toolbox onto the page. By default, elements are placed using absolute positioning (wherever you place them, they stay, and have x and y coordinates to place them on a page). Normally, we use Flow view (like in Web Matrix by default) to add controls to the top left of a page and work downwards, then use tables to arrange elements.

Visual Studio .NET Solutions and Projects

When you develop Web applications in Visual Studio .NET, you need to move conceptually from creating individual files to creating Web projects. You can create many different *projects*, and combine them into a *solution*. A solution is a collection of related projects. For example, you may have a solution that contains four projects. One project could be a Web application that is accessed by general visitors to a site. Another project could be a Web application that has user or role level access restrictions (an administration site that updates the application created in the first project). The third project could be a web service that exposes some of the functionality from the central web server, and the fourth project could be a setup project that can be used to install all of the other applications onto a Web server.

If you create a new project, without first creating a blank solution, a solution file will be created at the same time, and stored in a central location. By default, solution files for Web applications are created in the \My Documents\Visual Studio Projects\ folder., hence you will find a folder within this location called WroxUnited that contains WroxUnited.sln and WroxUnited.suo. A .sln file is the solution file, and contains information about which projects exist within the solution. A .suo stores user preferences associated with the solution, including information on which files were open in the editor when you last opened the solution.

In contrast, all ASP.NET code associated with a project (and each individual project file) will be created within your web root by default (c:\Inetpub\wwwroot\). If you look at the C:\Inetpub\wwwroot\WroxUnited folder on your system, you'll see (among other files) WroxUnited.vbproj. This is the project file for the web application.

One Visual Studio .NET solution can consist of one or many projects. The solution file itself (the .sln) is a simple text file that describes which projects exist in the solution, and information about how they are compiled. Creating a new project without first creating a solution means that a new solution file will be created. However, you may prefer to first create a new blank solution and then add new projects to that central solution (for example, having a solution called "BigWebSite", consisting of several projects including "SitePages" and "Administration Site" projects).

A project can be a member of more than one solution – the solution is simply a handy way of collecting together related projects so that the appropriate projects are all loaded when you open a solution in Visual Studio.

Files in a Web Application Project

By default, Visual Studio .NET will create many files whenever a new Web application is created including the following:

❑   A `Default.aspx` web page (or web form, as Visual Studio .NET refers to it).

❑   A relatively empty `web.config` file containing basic site configuration options.

❑   A relatively empty `Global.asax` file containing event handler placeholders to which you can later add code.

❑   A `Styles.css` template stylesheet that you can use, if you choose, to instantly add some style to your pages.

❑   An `AssemblyInfo.cs` file that you'll rarely (if ever) need to amend in order to customize how your applications work.

You will also notice that the Solution Explorer contains a References tab that contains the names of various DLL files that are referenced whenever Visual Studio .NET compiles your code.

Visual Studio .NET only uses the code-behind method of creating Web applications, so although you can't see it by default, `Default.aspx` has an associated code-behind file called `Default.aspx.cs`.

Working with Web Pages

In the Solution Explorer, right-click on `WebForm1.aspx` and rename it to `Default.aspx`. Then, click on the design surface and look at the Properties pane. Find the entry for pageLayout and change it to Flow Layout as shown in Figure D-3:

Figure D-3

Now let's add some basic content. In the toolbar just above the main pane is a drop-down box, much like in Web Matrix, where you can select a text style. Select Heading 1 from this menu as shown in Figure D-4:

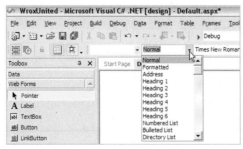

Figure D-4

Type in Wrox United as the header and press Enter. We'll be replacing this later with a user control, but for now, it helps to have a placeholder heading to identify the page.

Next, place your cursor directly below this heading, then select the Table menu and select Insert | Table to add a table that we can use to arrange the items on the page that appear below the heading as shown in Figure D-5:

Figure D-5

Add a table that has 1 row, 2 columns, and is 800 pixels wide as shown in D-6:

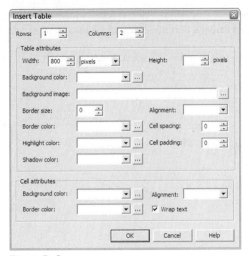

Figure D-6

Click inside the first cell and set its width to 580px in the Properties pane, then enter some Heading 2 style text that says Welcome to the Wrox United Web Site! as shown in Figure D-7:

Figure D-7

Next, click to place the cursor in the second cell. From the Toolbox, ensure that the Web Forms controls are visible (click on the Web Forms bar if they aren't and they'll pop into view). Double-click a Label control in the toolbox, then a TextBox, followed by a Button, and finally a RegularExpressionValidator (you may have to scroll down to see this control using the down arrow at the bottom right of the active control toolbox).

For each of these controls, name them `lblRegister`, `txtEmailAddress`, `btnRegister`, and `validEmail` respectively. Set their text properties as shown in Figure D-8:

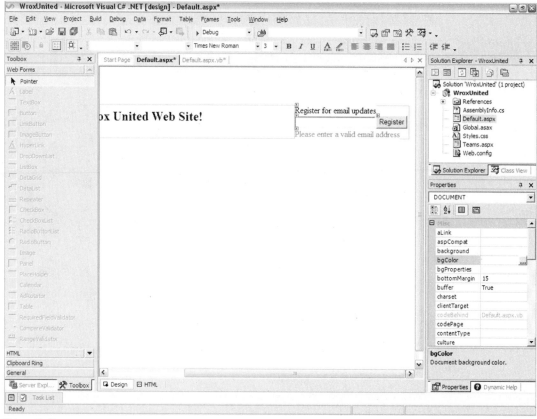

Figure D-8

Make sure you set the ControlToValidate property of the RegularExpressionValidator control to the textbox control (txtEmailAddress).

You need to select an appropriate validation expression for the validator control. In the Properties pane, select the ValidationExpression property, and click the ... icon. In the dialog that appears, select the Internet Email Address expression and click OK:

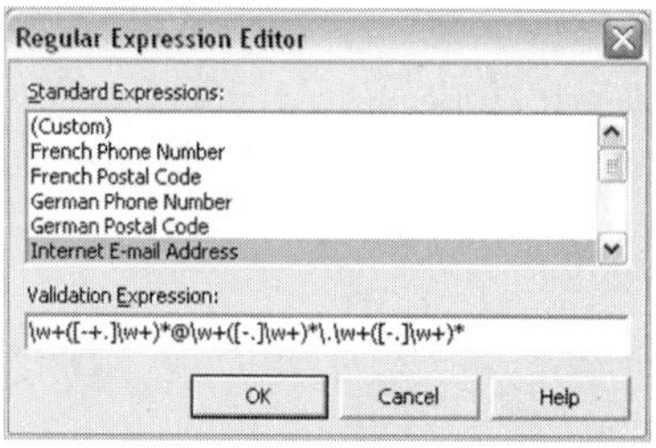

Figure D-9

Compiling and Running Pages

This process is very simple to initiate – just click the Start button (the Play button on the main toolbar) to run the page. Whereas Web Matrix simply ran the page, allocating a port if necessary, Visual Studio .NET actually compiles the pages in the application, and you'll see this compilation process in action as shown in Figure D-10:

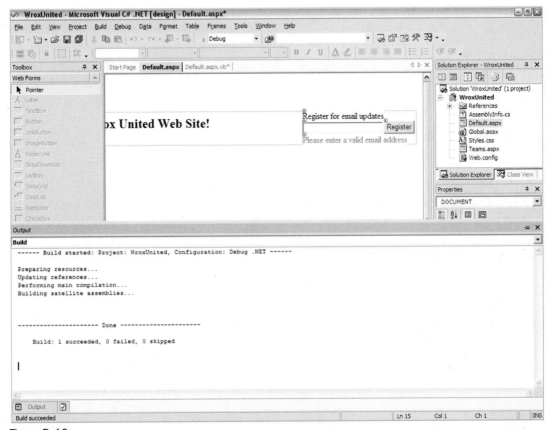

Figure D-10

The Output tab will pop up whenever you compile and run your applications. If any errors occur, you'll see them in here, and in the Tasks tab as well (located next to the Output tab at the bottom of the screen). We'll see this in action later on.

Once the page has loaded, you will find that, without entering any code, you can see the validation control in action as shown in Figure D-11:

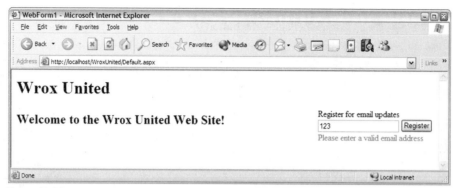

Figure D-11

Adding Code to the Code-Behind Class

It's time to add some code to the page. The simplest way to display the code-behind file for this page is to double-click the `Button` control as shown in Figure D-12:

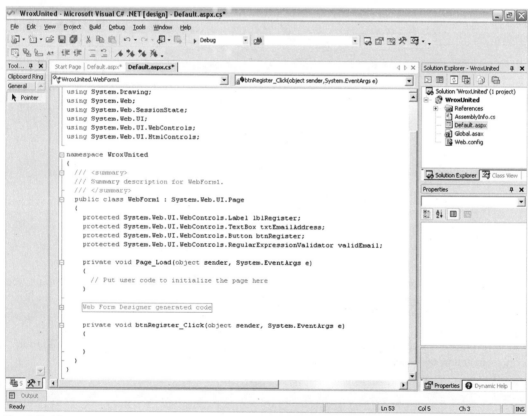

Figure D-12

Notice that, similarly to Web Matrix, a `Click` event handler method signature has been generated automatically in response to double-clicking the button.

Features of Code View

Notice the + and – signs next to each method. If you click on these, you'll see them expand and contract the code contained within them – this makes it much easier to navigate through big code blocks.

Notice the gray box labelled **Web Forms Designer Generated Code** – this contains code that is created for you behind the scenes to relate the controls on the page to the code-behind file (as we saw in *Chapter 12*). This appears in a gray box because the code within it is in a region. You can add custom regions to your code files by adding the following lines at the top and bottom of the section you want to add to a region:

```
#region My Region
...
// Code to be contained in region goes here
...
#endregion
```

Once you add these statements, you can expand and contract the code contained between these two tags using the + and – boxes next to the `#Region` line.

Adding Code to Methods

If you refer back to the version of `Default.aspx` in Chapter 11, you may recall adding code that reacts to a user clicking the Register button on the page. Take the body of the `btnRegister_Click` method from the Chapter 11 version of `Default.aspx` the in Chapter 11 and paste it in to VS.NET. Add the highlighted lines to the sub, either by copying and pasting or typing (we'll discuss what happens when you type in code in just a moment):

```
private void btnRegister_Click(object sender, System.EventArgs e)
{
    string FanEmail = txtEmailAddress.Text;

    //Check whether the email address is already registered
    //If not, we need to register it by calling the AddNewFanEmail() method
    if (!CheckFanEmailAddresses(FanEmail))
    {
      AddNewFanEmail(FanEmail);
    }

    // Email has been registered, so update the display and attempt write to a
    //cookie
    txtEmailAddress.Visible = false;
    lblRegister.Text = "You have successfully registered for email updates";
    btnRegister.Visible = false;

    HttpCookie EmailRegisterCookie = new HttpCookie("EmailRegister");
    EmailRegisterCookie.Value = FanEmail;
    EmailRegisterCookie.Expires = DateTime.Now.AddSeconds(20);
    Response.Cookies.Add(EmailRegisterCookie);
}
```

Notice that we haven't defined two important data-access functions yet, and these have been underlined for us using blue squiggly lines. Also, the code has been highlighted appropriately as shown in Figure D-13:

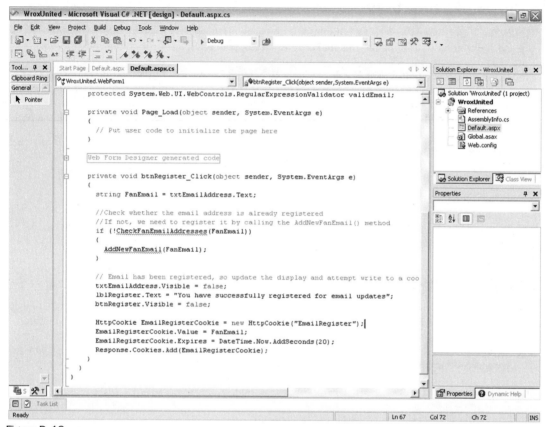

Figure D-13

We need to add the code that accesses the database in order to add a new user to the database, depending on whether their email address has already been added to the database or not. However, unlike Web Matrix, there aren't any useful data wizards on the left – unfortunately, we have to add the code by hand, but don't worry, because Visual Studio .NET has a useful feature known as *IntelliSense* that makes it all very easy. This will be discussed shortly. Let's look at the two methods we need to add.

> In this example, we will connect to the SQL Server version of the WroxUnited database, created in the previous appendix. For installation instructions and more details, please refer to *Appendix C*.

Let's amend the code slightly from the way it is presented in the chapters (because we will be using the SQL Server version of the database in this appendix), we will need to add the following code. For the CheckFanEmailAddresses function:

```csharp
public bool CheckFanEmailAddresses(string fanEmail)
{
  string connectionString =
ConfigurationSettings.AppSettings["ConnectionString"];
  System.Data.IDbConnection dbConnection =
    new System.Data.SqlClient.SqlConnection(connectionString);
  string queryString = "SELECT COUNT([Fans].[FanEmail]) FROM [Fans]" +
                       " WHERE ([Fans].[FanEmail] = @FanEmail)";
  System.Data.IDbCommand dbCommand = new System.Data.SqlClient.SqlCommand();
  dbCommand.CommandText = queryString;
  dbCommand.Connection = dbConnection;
  System.Data.IDataParameter dbParam_fanEmail =
    new System.Data.SqlClient.SqlParameter();
  dbParam_fanEmail.ParameterName = "@FanEmail";
  dbParam_fanEmail.Value = fanEmail;
  dbParam_fanEmail.DbType = System.Data.DbType.String;
  dbCommand.Parameters.Add(dbParam_fanEmail);
  int result = 0;
  dbConnection.Open();
  try
  {
    result = (int)dbCommand.ExecuteScalar();
  }
  finally
  {
    dbConnection.Close();
  }

  if (result > 0)
  {
    return true;
  }
  else
  {
    return false;
  }
}
```

And for the `AddNewFanEmail` function:

```csharp
public int AddNewFanEmail (string fanEmail)
{
  string connectionString =
            ConfigurationSettings.AppSettings["ConnectionString"];
  System.Data.IDbConnection dbConnection =
    new System.Data.SqlClient.SqlConnection(connectionString);

  string queryString = "INSERT INTO [Fans] ([FanEmail]) VALUES (@FanEmail)";
  System.Data.IDbCommand dbCommand = new System.Data.SqlClient.SqlCommand();

  dbCommand.CommandText = queryString;
  dbCommand.Connection = dbConnection;

  System.Data.IDataParameter dbParam_fanEmail =
    new System.Data.SqlClient.SqlParameter();
  dbParam_fanEmail.ParameterName = "@FanEmail";
  dbParam_fanEmail.Value = fanEmail;
  dbParam_fanEmail.DbType = System.Data.DbType.String;
```

```
dbCommand.Parameters.Add(dbParam_fanEmail);

int rowsAffected = 0;
dbConnection.Open();
try
{
  rowsAffected = dbCommand.ExecuteNonQuery();
}
finally
{
  dbConnection.Close();
}
return rowsAffected;
}
```

Just try typing in the first line of one of the methods, and press ctrl+space after the opening bracket and you'll see that Visual Studio .NET will try to help you as shown in Figure D-14:

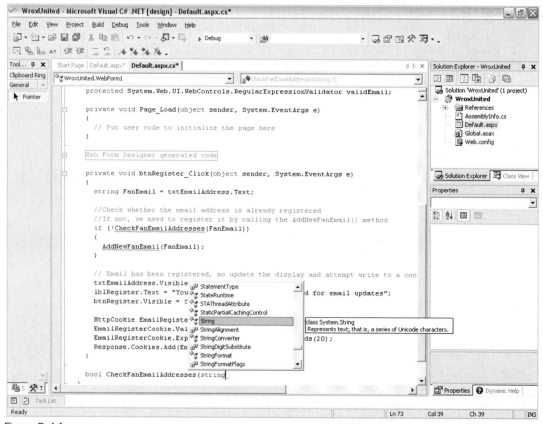

Figure D-14

Complete writing the first line, press Return, and add the opening and closing curly braces. You'll notice now that you can expand and collapse the method, which will be useful once you have many different methods in the code. You'll find that these kind of features save you a lot of time! Continue to add the code for these two methods and see what happens as you type – IntelliSense will pop up with helpful suggestions with each line you add. To accept a suggestion, either click on the appropriate suggestion from the list, scroll through the list using up or down, and press Tab or Enter when the appropriate statement is highlighted. To request IntelliSense, just use the ctrl+space combination as before.

There's one thing left to do before the page can run – we need a connection string! Open the web.config that is created by default (double-click on it from the server explorer) and add the following code to the top:

```xml
<?xml version="1.0" encoding="utf-8" ?>
<configuration>
  <appSettings>
    <add key="ConnectionString"
      value="server='(local)'; trusted_connection=true; integrated
      security=SSPI; database='WroxUnited'" />
  </appSettings>
  <system.web>
...
```

You should see the screen as shown in Figure D-15:

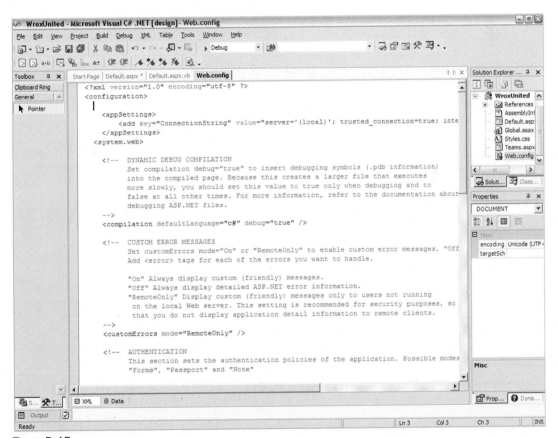

Figure D-15

Finally, add another using statement to the top of the page:

```
using System;
...
using System.Web.UI.WebControls;
using System.Web.UI.HtmlControls;
using System.Configuration;
namespace WroxUnited
{
```

You can now run the page again, enter an email address as shown in Figure D-16, and add it to the database:

Figure D-16

When you click the button, the display will change accordingly as shown in Figure D-17:

Figure D-17

Notice that invalid email addresses will cause the validation control to fire as seen in Figure D-18:

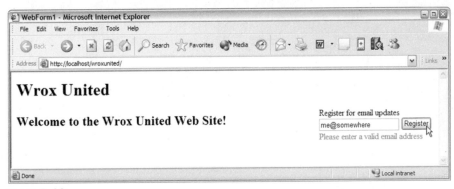

Figure D-18

Styling Controls and Pages in Visual Studio .NET

So far, we've not looked at the HTML source for the page. You can do this by clicking the HTML tab at the bottom of the main design area. In here, you'll see the HTML representation of all of the controls mixed in with the default HTML code for the page.

Let's add a stylesheet to the application to give it a more familiar look and feel. Right click on the WroxUnited project (the entry just below the main root Solution 'WroxUnited' node in the tree), and select Add | Add New Item from the context menu as shown in Figure D-19:

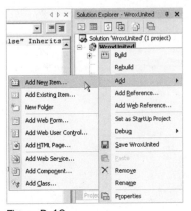

Figure D-19

In the popup dialog that appears, scroll down the types of files until you find a .css, and enter WroxUnited as the name for the .css file as shown in Figure D-20:

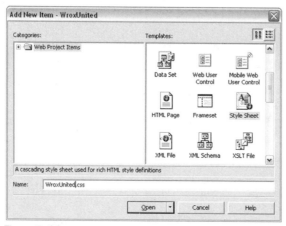

Figure D-20

Note there's a `Styles.css` stylesheet that's created by default with every new Web project. If you look at this file, you'll see a wide range of styles that you can use 'out of the box' for new Web applications. Since you already have all the styling needed for the current version of the Wrox United application, you can remove this file from the project. If you right-click on this file, you can either select **Exclude From Project** or **Delete**. **Exclude From Project** will remove the entry in the solution file for this file, but will leave the physical file on your file system. **Delete** will permanently delete the file.

Back in the editor, you will see the newly-created stylesheet displayed in code form. To the left is the CSS tree – select the **Body** style node and click the **Build Style...** button directly above this panel. This is shown in Figure D-21:

Figure D-21

The style builder dialog will pop up as shown in Figure D-22. This is what you can use to apply a wide range of styling attributes to the `body` element:

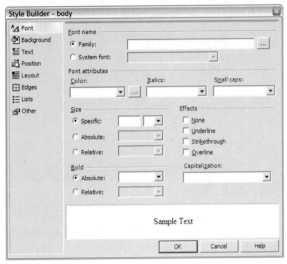

Figure D-22

You may recall that the CSS we used for the body element in *Chapter 11* was as follows:

```
BODY {
  background-image:url(images/background.gif);
  color:"#000000";
  font-family: georgia;
}
```

Let's build the style using the dialog. Set the Color to be black, then you could either enter the name Georgia in the Family box as shown in Figure D-23:

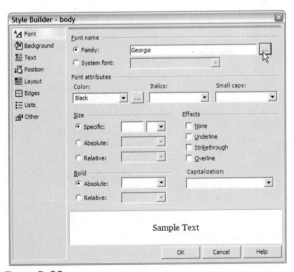

Figure D-23

Or click the ... button to launch the **Font Picker** as shown in Figure D-24:

Figure D-24

To select a background image, you first need to exit this dialog, so click OK. Now in the Solution Explorer, right-click on WroxUnited project and select **Add Folder**, name it **Images**. Highlight the folder, right-click and select **Add Existing Item** to get the screen shown in Figure D-25. Select `background.gif` from the Images folder of the Wrox United application built in *Chapters 10-13* of the book (it's a very small GIF file that, when repeated, applies a set of pale vertical stripes to the page, a bit like a soccer shirt!):

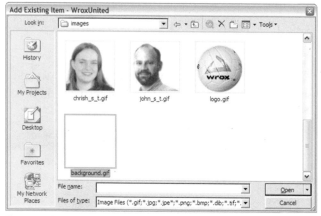

Figure D-25

You should now have Figure D-26 in the Solution Explorer:

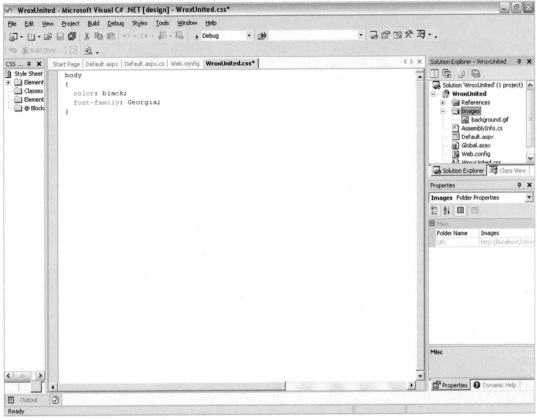

Figure D-26

Back in **Style Builder** for the `body` tag, select the **Background** icon on the left, and then click the ... button next to the background image box as shown in Figure D-27 to select the image:

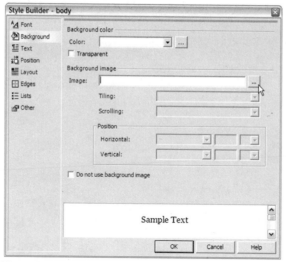

Figure D-27

Select the image from the dialog as shown in Figure D-28:

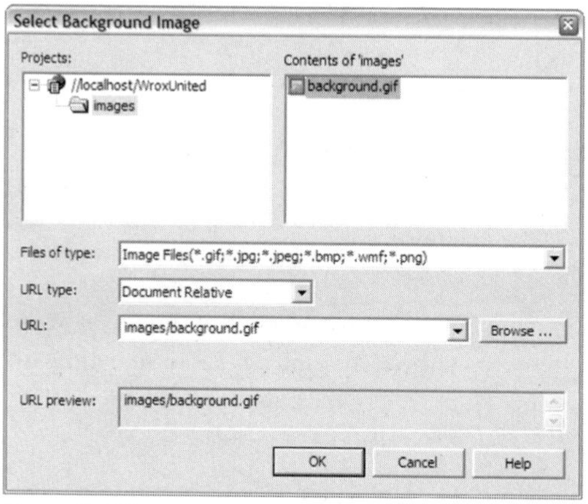

Figure D-28

Click **OK** twice to exit the **Style Builder** and the style will be built successfully. You can either build the rest of the styles in this manner, or you can copy in the rest of the stylesheet from the code from the rest of the book. For now, let's just add the code for the a tag. The original code for this was as follows:

```
a {
  color:"#8b0000";
  font-weight:bold;
}
```

Right-click on the Elements node in the CSS Browser and select Add Style Rule. Select the A tag as shown in Figure D-29 and click OK:

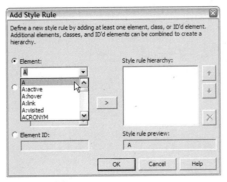

Figure D-29

Back in Code view, if you attempt to type in the style, IntelliSense will help you as shown in Figure D-30:

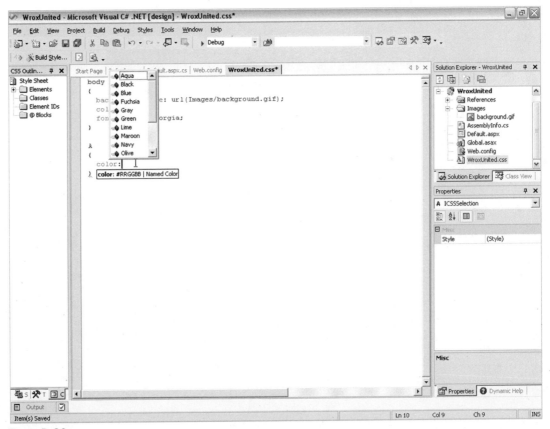

Figure D-30

> If ever IntelliSense disappears, you can view it by pressing Ctrl+Space.

Working in HTML View

Once you have built the basic stylesheet, you need to add it to the page. In the `<head>` section of the page (shown in HTML source view), add the `<link ... >` tag as shown below:

```
<meta name="vs_targetSchema"
      content="http://schemas.microsoft.com/intellisense/ie5">
<link rel="stylesheet" id="css" type="text/css" href="WroxUnited.css" />
</head>
```

You could change the `href` to point to a Session object, like we did in *Chapter 11*, but we'll not be implementing that in this example.

While you're in HTML view, change the `<title>` element of the page as shown below:

```
<head>
  <title>Welcome to Wrox United</title>
```

This will ensure that the title bar of the page will have some more useful text in it for visitors to the site.

Switching back to Design view, you'll see the stylesheet has been applied as shown in Figure D-31:

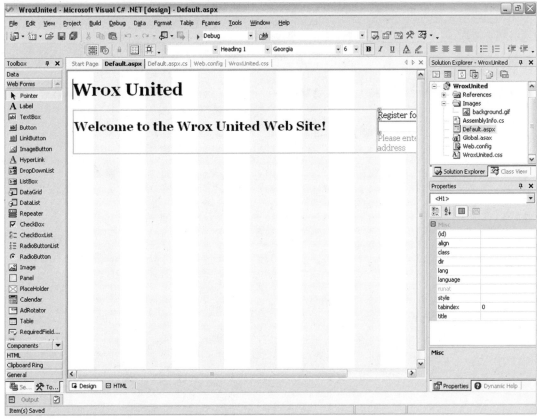

Figure D-31

Creating User Controls

It's time to replace the temporary header text in the page with a header control. Adding a user control is again performed via the Solution Explorer. Right-click on the WroxUnited project and select Add | Add Web User Control... as shown in Figure D-32:

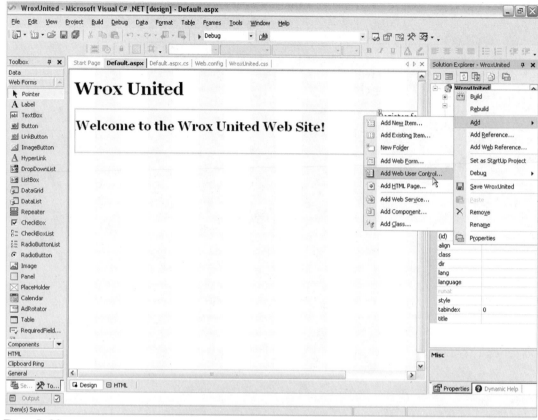

Figure D-32

Name this control `Header.ascx` as shown in Figure D-33:

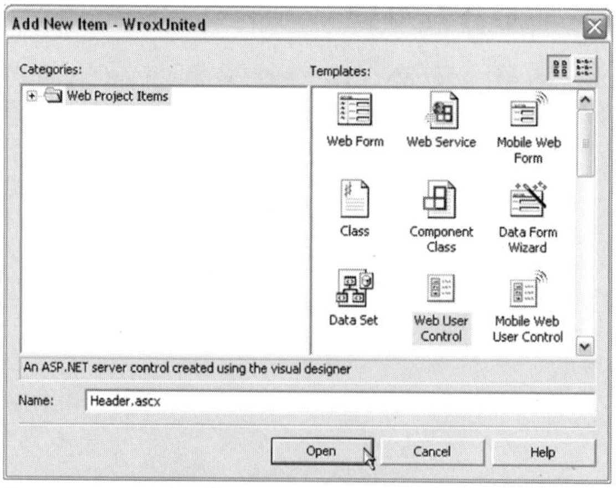

Figure D-33

The code used in the earlier chapters to create this control can be entered in HTML view, but first, you need to add the images that we'll need. Right-click on the images folder and add the following files:

- ❑　`headbg.gif`.
- ❑　`logo.gif`.
- ❑　`teamlogo.gif`.
- ❑　`chrish_s_t.gif`.
- ❑　`chrisu_s_t.gif`.
- ❑　`dave_s_t.gif`.
- ❑　`john_s_t.gif`.

You can make multiple selections by holding down Ctrl when you click on each file.

Add a table to the header control that is 100% wide, with one row and one column. Delete the standard values for the spacing and border attributes as shown in Figure D-34:

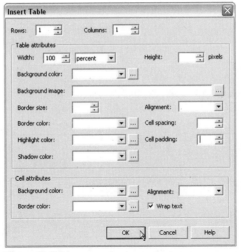

Figure D-34

For the row in this table, switch to HTML view and add a Style attribute. As you type, IntelliSense will offer the Style Builder as shown in Figure D-35, so click on this as it appears:

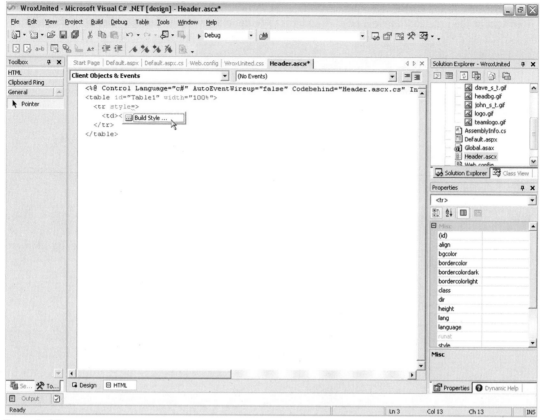

Figure D-35

In the style builder, select the `headbg.gif` image as shown in Figure D-36, to use as the background for this row:

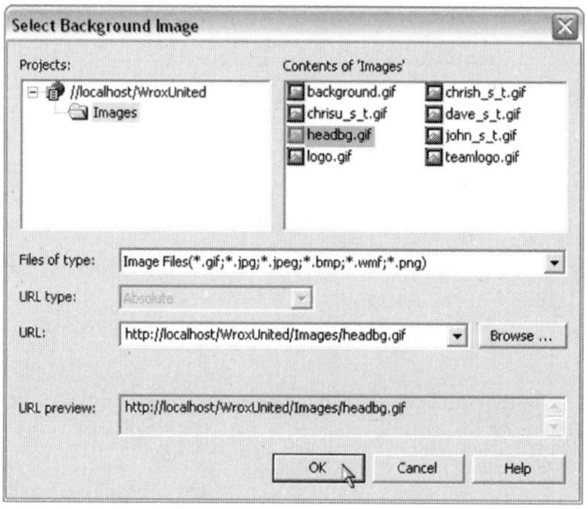

Figure D-36

Once this style has been added, you can add the inner table. You don't need to be in Design view for this – you can add a table in just the same way from HTML view. Position your cursor between the `<td>` and the `</td>` and use the Table | Insert | Table... command from the main menu as shown in Figure D-37:

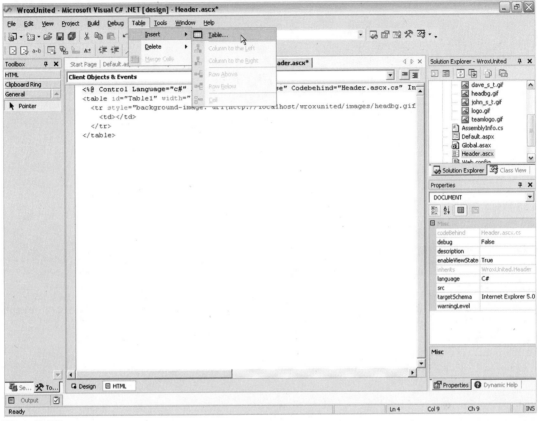

Figure D-37

Add a table that is 800 pixels wide, with one row and three columns. Again, delete the standard values for the spacing and border attributes as shown in Figure D-38:

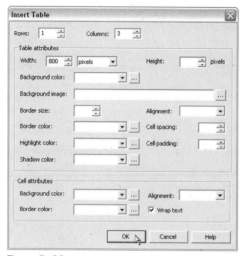

Figure D-38

Formatting Blocks of Code

I often find Visual Studio .NET a bit messy at times – after adding this table, you can see that the code generated on my system was hardly tidy. In my default preferences (you can specify your own preferences via Tools | Options from the main menu) I specified that I wanted all tags to be in lowercase when editing HTML code, and I wanted to use two spaces indentation for all lines of code, yet the editor added the code shown in Figure D-39:

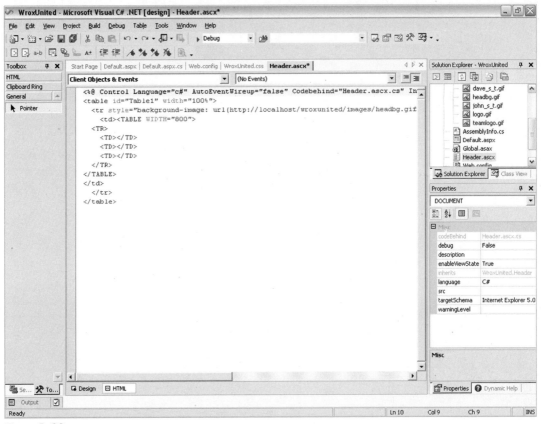

Figure D-39

The solution to this problem is to select all the code and use the Edit | Advanced | Format Document menu option. After running this, my code was spaced out a bit better, and my preferred capitalization rules were followed as can be seen in Figure D-40:

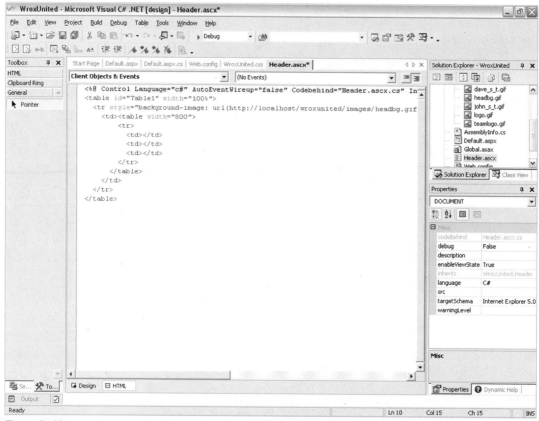

Figure D-40

You will find that the results of this will vary according to the default preferences you have on your system, but once you have set up the defaults as you like them, you'll find that this feature can be very handy!

Developing the User Control

In this table, set the row and cell attributes as shown in the code below. Leave the last cell empty for the moment:

```
<tr style="VERTICAL-ALIGN: middle">
  <td style="TEXT-ALIGN: left" width="200">
    <a href="default.aspx"><img src="images/logo.gif" border="0" /></a>
  </td>
  <td style="TEXT-ALIGN: center" width="400">
    <img src="images/teamlogo.gif" />
  </td>
  <td style="TEXT-ALIGN: right" width="200">
```

```
        </td>
      </tr>
```

If you switch back to Design view, you'll see that the page taking shape as shown in Figure D-41:

Figure D-41

Recall from the chapters that the header control had an `AdRotator` control that displayed different pictures of authors each time the page was requested. It's now time to add the `AdRotator` to the page. Either drag and drop this control into the right-most cell, or click to position your cursor in this cell and double-click the `AdRotator` control to add it to the page. This is shown in Figure D-42:

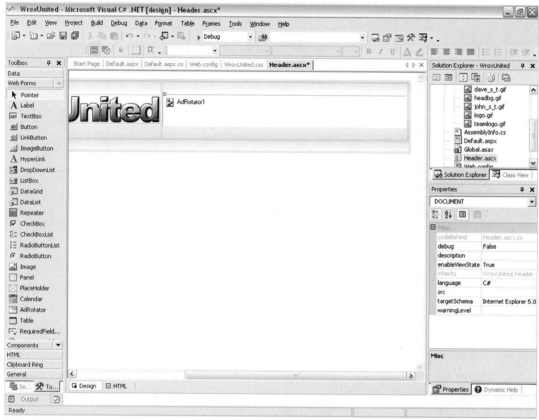

Figure D-42

By default, the control is created with standard width and height attributes. To fit our images, you should change these attributes in the `Properties` pane so that the width is 100 pixels and the height is 95 pixels. To select the source for the `AdRotator` control, you need to first create the XML source file.

Creating an XML File

Right click on the `WroxUnited` project and create a new file. In the dialog that appears (shown in Figure D-43), create a new XML file and call it `faces.xml`:

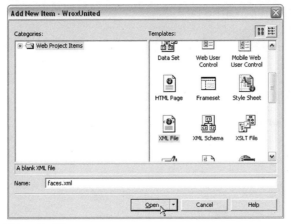

Figure D-43

In the newly created file, enter the code that we used previously and save the file:

```xml
<?xml version="1.0" encoding="utf-8" ?>
<Advertisements>

  <Ad>
    <ImageUrl>images/chrish_s_t.gif</ImageUrl>
    <NavigateUrl>players.aspx</NavigateUrl>
    <AlternateText>Player: Chris Hart</AlternateText>
    <Impressions>80</Impressions>
    <Keyword>ChrisH</Keyword>
  </Ad>

  <Ad>
    <ImageUrl>images/chrisu_s_t.gif</ImageUrl>
    <NavigateUrl>players.aspx</NavigateUrl>
    <AlternateText>Player: Chris Ullman</AlternateText>
    <Impressions>80</Impressions>
    <Keyword>ChrisU</Keyword>
  </Ad>

  <Ad>
    <ImageUrl>images/dave_s_t.gif</ImageUrl>
    <NavigateUrl>players.aspx</NavigateUrl>
    <AlternateText>Player: Dave Sussman</AlternateText>
    <Impressions>80</Impressions>
    <Keyword>Dave</Keyword>
  </Ad>

  <Ad>
    <ImageUrl>images/john_s_t.gif</ImageUrl>
    <NavigateUrl>players.aspx</NavigateUrl>
    <AlternateText>Player: John Kauffman</AlternateText>
    <Impressions>80</Impressions>
```

```
      <Keyword>John</Keyword>
    </Ad>

  </Advertisements>
```

That's all you need to do to create an XML file. Notice that with each element, Visual Studio .NET assists you by adding closing tags.

Back in the `header.ascx` file, head to the Properties for the advertisement file again. Select the `AdvertisementFile` attribute and click on the ... button that appears. In the popup dialog shown in Figure D-44, select the `Faces.xml` file and click OK:

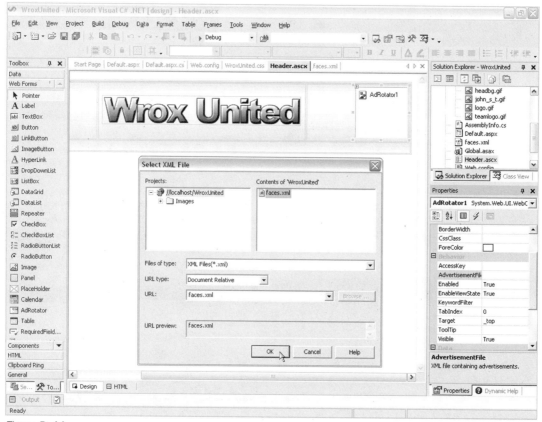

Figure D-44

The header needs one last thing before it's finished, and that's the custom text. In HTML view, add the following code to the bottom of the control (below the last `</table>` statement):

```
<h2><%= PageTitle %></h2>
```

Finally, right-click on `Header.ascx` and select **View Code**. You are now in the code-behind page for the header control. Add the following line of code directly above the `Page_Load` sub, as shown in Figure D-45:

```
public string PageTitle = "";
```

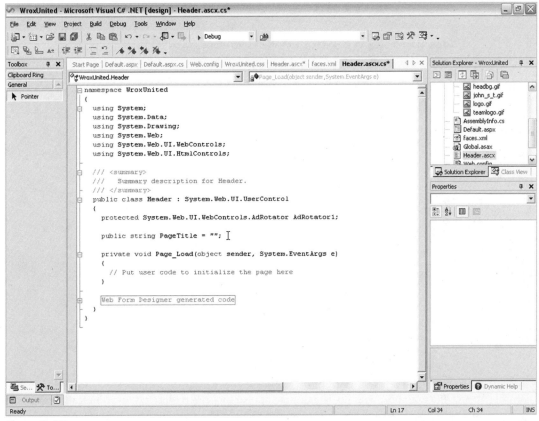

Figure D-45

Time for a quick **File** | **Save All** and that's the control done! Time to add it to the page!

Adding a User Control to a Page

Switch to the **Design** view for `Default.aspx`. Click and drag `Header.ascx` from the **Solution Explorer** onto the page, right before the main header. This is shown in Figure D-46:

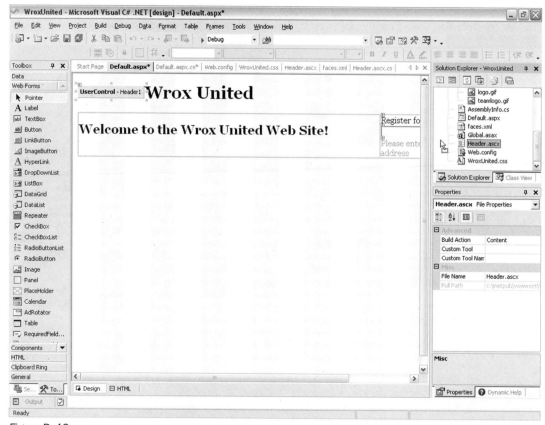

Figure D-46

You'll notice that this will add the control its reference to the HTML of the page. Also, notice that the control appears as a gray box, with no design-time appearance (Web Matrix, you will recall, provided a sample of the appearance of each user control as it was added to a page).

The newly added control is added with a default `TagName` of `Header` and `TagPrefix` of `UC1`. You can change this prefix to `WroxUnited` (if you prefer) by editing the HTML of the page. Since we need to tidy up this page in any case, let's do that now. Amend the highlighted lines of code (notice that you need to remove the `<h1>` tag and the default header text):

```
<%@ Register TagPrefix="WroxUnited" TagName="Header" Src="Header.ascx" %>
<%@ Page Language="vb" AutoEventWireup="false" Codebehind="Default.aspx.vb"
    debug="true" Inherits="WroxUnited.WebForm1"%>
...
  <body>
    <form id="Form1" method="post" runat="server">
      <WroxUnited:header id="Header1" runat="server">
      </WroxUnited:header>
```

```
        <table id="Table1" cellspacing="0" cellpadding="0" width="800"
border="0">
  ...
```

The `PageTitle` attribute isn't used on this page, but it exists for use on other pages where the email update registration box doesn't appear.

Running the page now will produce a more familiar screen, as shown in Figure D-47:

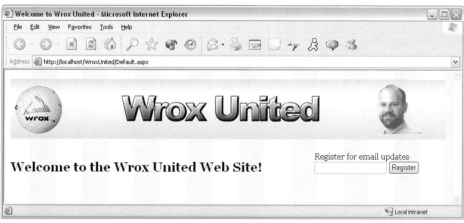

Figure D-47

Adding Custom Classes

It's time to look at adding a data access component. Right-click on the `WroxUnited` project and select Add New Item.... In the dialog shown in Figure D-48, select the `Class` template, and name the file `DataAccessCode.cs`.

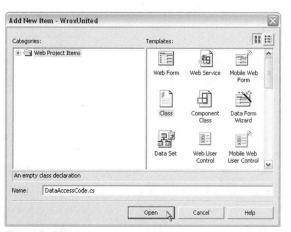

Figure D-48

In the code, add some `using` statements at the top of the code:

```
using System;
using System.Data;
using System.Collections;
using System.Configuration;
```

Now cut and paste over the data access methods from the `Default.aspx.cs` code-behind page that we produced earlier. Figure D-49 shows the code so far. Again, notice that the + and – icons on the left can be clicked to expand or contract blocks of code to make it easier to see which methods exist in the code:

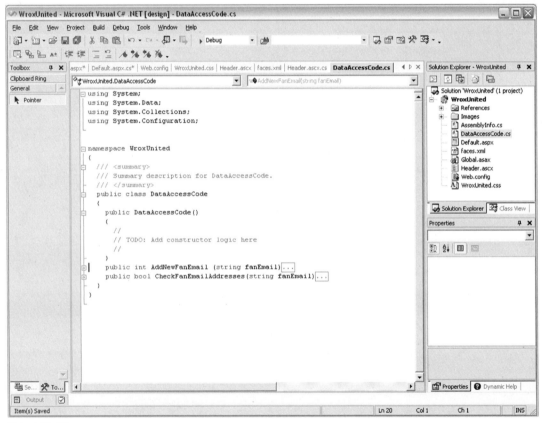

Figure D-49

Back in the code-behind for `Default.aspx`, we've managed to break the code by removing the two data access methods. If you select Build | Build WroxUnited, you'll see Visual Studio attempt to compile the project, but this process will now fail. The blue squiggly underlines in Figure D-50 indicate method calls that VS.NET can no longer find:

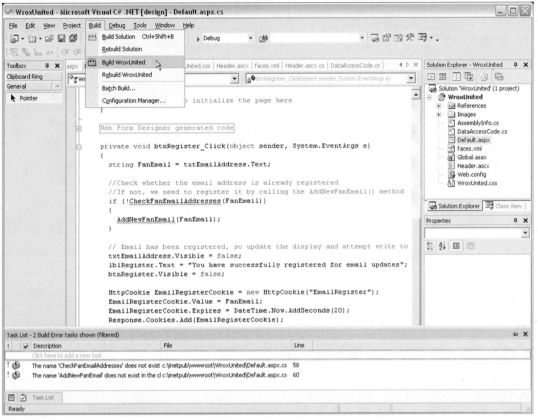

Figure D-50

Add the following line of code directly above the `Page_Load` method:

```
public DataAccessCode Data = new DataAccessCode();
```

Then prefix each underlined method with `"Data."`. The code should now be able to locate the methods in question. Notice that as you do this, IntelliSense locates the list of available methods in this class and gives you hints about what their signatures look like. This is shown in Figure D-51:

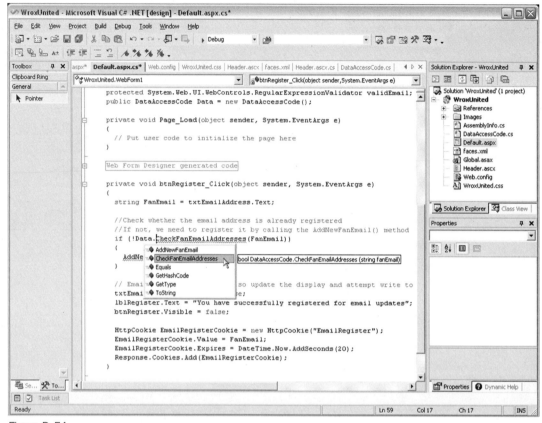

Figure D-51

Complete adding each method call with the Data object prefix, and you will be able to run the page, which should look and feel the same as before.

You can duplicate this methodology to create custom server controls in exactly the same way.

Professional and higher editions of Visual Studio .NET allow you to create entire custom class library projects and custom server control projects, but this functionality isn't available in the Standard language-specific editions.

Working with Databases Using the Server Explorer

If you click the Server Explorer tab (at the bottom of the Toolbox), you can see the database connectivity functionality of Visual Studio .NET. By default, this will look at little empty. Click on the Connect to Database button to add a new connection, as shown in Figure D-52:

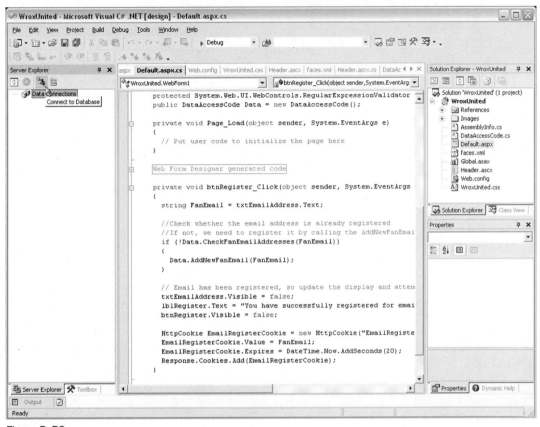

Figure D-52

In the dialog that appears, select your SQL Server database server, and then select the WroxUnited database from the list as shown in Figure D-53:

Figure D-53

In the Server Explorer, you will now see the newly added database connection in the list. Expand this connection, and double-click the Games table to view the contents of the table as shown in Figure D-54:

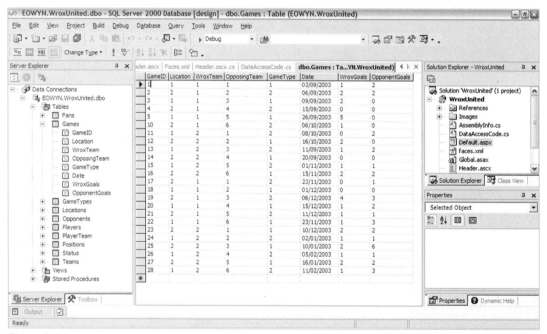

Figure D-54

In Standard edition, you can edit the data contained in the table, but cannot edit the structure of an existing table or create a new table. However, you can enter SQL as shown in Figure D-55, and if you know how to write SQL, you can enter any valid SQL statement, including CREATE TABLE, DROP TABLE, or even CREATE DATABASE statements:

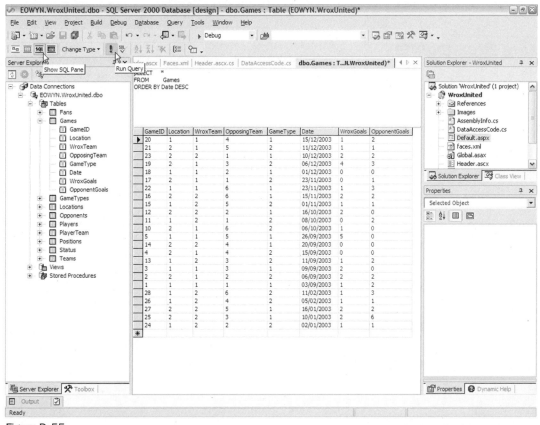

Figure D-55

If you are using Professional or higher editions of Visual Studio .NET, you can simply right-click on a table and create a new table, or alter the design of a table using the context menu. You can also create stored procedures and views in this way.

Debugging in Visual Studio .NET

One of the most powerful and indispensable features of Visual Studio .NET is its ability to debug code and fix errors. First, we'll look at break points and stepping through code line-by-line at run-time to fix run-time errors or exceptions, then we'll look at fixing errors at compile time.

> You can only debug if the compilation mode of your solution is set to **Debug** (see the drop down box next to the Run button on the main toolbar). Once you finish debugging and are ready to deploy your site, set this to Release – you'll notice a significant performance boost on higher-traffic sites because debug code is much more processor intensive. If you're not debugging, turn it off!

Using Breakpoints

In `Default.aspx.cs` (the code-behind for the web page), click in the margin next to one of the lines of code, for example, the first line of code in the event-handler for the clicking of the button on the page shown in Figure D-56:

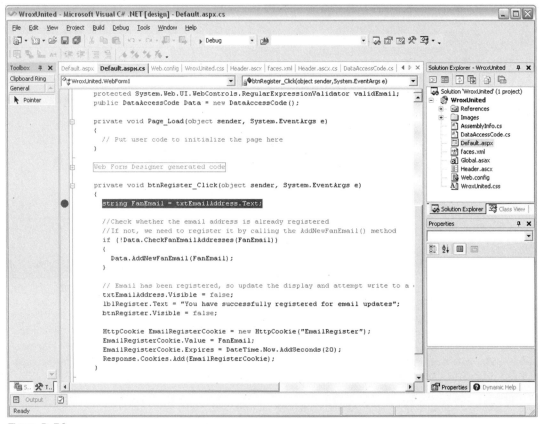

Figure D-56

This has added a breakpoint to the code, which means that when that line of code is processed, you can step inside and see what's happening. To demonstrate this, run the page – notice that when you click the button on the page, you automatically switch back to the screen shown in Figure D-57:

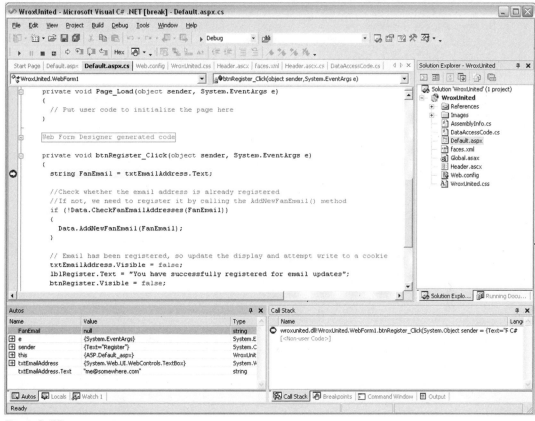

Figure D-57

At the bottom left of the screen, you can see the value entered into the textbox when the button was clicked. You can watch the values of controls on the page using this window. You can step through this code line by line to see what happens when each line of code is run by pressing F11. When you reach a method call, you can either press F11 to jump into the code where that method is defined and watch as the code in that method is executed line by line (*Step Into*), or you can press F10 to *Step Over* this method and continue with the next line of code in the current code block.

Pressing the Start button again will continue execution of the page, taking you back to the browser window, as if no interruption had occurred. This feature is particularly useful when fixing broken code. All you have to do is add a break point before the piece of code that is broken and step into the code, watching to see where the code breaks. This will often give you a clear idea as to why the code is not running as expected.

Fixing Design-Time Errors

You will often find that errors at design time will prevent a page from compiling correctly. For example, if you forgot to prefix one of the methods on the page with the Data. object reference, you would see an error message when you tried to run the page, as shown in Figure D-58:

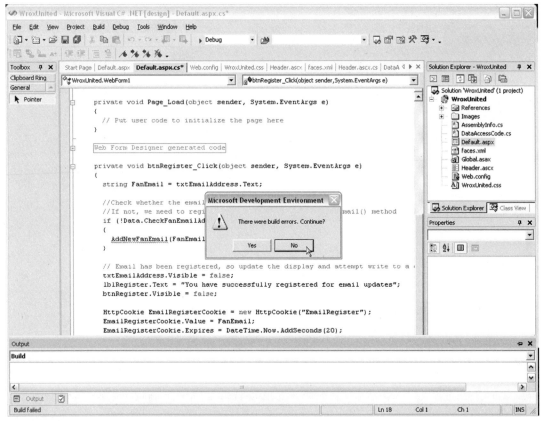

Figure D-58

If you click No, you will see an entry in the Task list shown in Figure D-58. It will give you a hint as to why the code would not compile:

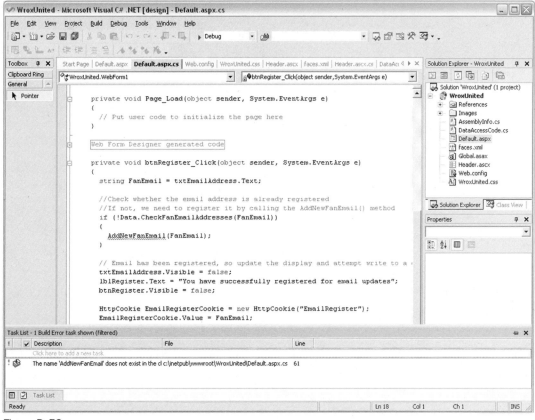

Figure D-59

It's now fairly obvious that the compiler can't deduce where the `AddNewFanEmail` method is declared, but once you add the `Data.`, prefix, it'll soon find what it's looking for.

Suggested Exercises and Further Reading

After completing this appendix, you will probably feel a bit more confident with creating web applications in Visual Studio .NET. The best way to increase your confidence further is to try out adding more controls and pages yourself. You may want to try to implement the whole of the Wrox United application in Visual Studio .NET – this would give you experience of working with many different controls in the Visual Studio .NET environment, as well as programming with many different ASP.NET techniques.

Visual Studio .NET is a large product, so if you really want to learn more about this tool, visit http://msdn.microsoft.com/vstudio/using/.

Installing and Configuring IIS

The installation processes for IIS on Windows 2000 Professional, Windows XP Professional, or Windows Server 2003 don't differ significantly. The main difference is that Windows 2000 installs IIS 5.0, while Windows XP Professional Edition installs IIS 5.1, and Windows Server 2003 installs IIS 6.0. The options for installing are exactly the same; the only thing that might differ is the look of the dialog boxes.

> **You cannot install IIS on Windows XP Home Edition. It will only work on Windows XP Professional.**

Before you install it though, it's worth noting that you might not have to do much in this initial stage, as it's possible you're already running IIS. We'll describe a process for checking whether this is the case as part of the installation process. Note that to install anything (not just ASP.NET, but *literally anything*) on Windows 2000, XP, and 2003 you need to be logged in as a user with administrative rights. If you're uncertain about doing this, please consult your Windows documentation. Right, let's get started!

Try It Out   Creating a Virtual Directory and Setting Up Permissions

1. Go to the control panel (Start | Settings | Control Panel) and select the Add/Remove Programs icon. The dialog will appear, displaying a list of your currently installed programs as shown in Figure E-1:

Figure E-1

2. Select the Add/Remove Windows Components icon on the left side of the dialog to get to the screen that allows you to install new windows components:

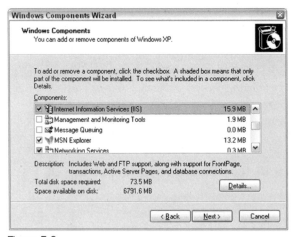

Figure E-2

3. Locate the Internet Information Services (IIS) entry in the dialog, and note the checkbox that appears to its left. Unless you installed Windows 2000 or XP via a custom install and specifically requested IIS, it's most likely that the checkbox will be unchecked.

4. If the checkbox is unchecked, check it and click Next on the screen shown in Figure E-2 to load Internet Information Services. You might be prompted to place your Windows 2000 or XP installation disk into your CD-ROM drive. It will take a few minutes to complete. Then go to Step 5.

OR

If the checkbox is checked, you won't need to install the IIS component – it's already present on your machine. Go to the *Working With IIS* section instead.

5. Click on the Details button – this will take you to the dialog shown in Figure E-3.

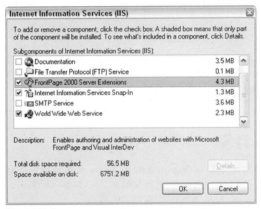

Figure E-3

6. There are a few options here for the installation of various optional bits of functionality. For example, if the World Wide Web Server option is checked then your IIS installation will be able to serve and manage Web pages and applications. If you're planning to use FrontPage 2000 or Visual Studio.NET to write your Web page code, then you'll need to ensure that the FrontPage 2000 Server Extensions checkbox is checked. The Internet Information Services Snap-In is also very helpful, as you'll see later in the chapter, so ensure that this is checked too; the other options (although checked here) aren't necessary for this book:

How It Works

IIS starts up automatically as soon as its installation is complete, and thereafter whenever you boot up Windows. Thus you don't need to run any startup programs or click on any short cuts.

IIS installs most of its components on your hard drive, under the \WinNT\system32\inetsrv directory; however, we are more interested in the \InetPub directory that is also created at this time. This directory contains subdirectories that will provide the home for the Web page files that we create.

If you expand the InetPub directory, you'll find that it contains several subdirectories:

❑ \iissamples\homepage contains some examples of classic ASP pages.

❑ \iissamples\sdk contains a set of subdirectories that hold classic ASP pages which demonstrate the various classic ASP objects and components.

❑ \scripts is an empty directory, where ASP.NET programs can be stored.

❑ \webpub is also empty. This is a special virtual directory, used for publishing files via the Publish wizard. Note that this directory only exists if you are using Windows 2000 Professional Edition.

❑ \wwwroot is the top of the tree for your Web site. This should be your default Web directory. It also contains a number of subdirectories that contain various bits and pieces of IIS. This directory is generally used to contain subdirectories that hold the pages that make up our Web site – although, in fact, there's no reason why you can't store your pages elsewhere. The relationship between physical and virtual directories is discussed later in this appendix.

❑ \ftproot, \mailroot and \nntproot should form the top of the tree for any sites that use FTP, mail or news services, if installed.

❑ In some versions of Windows, you will find a \AdminScripts folder that contains various script files for performing some common 'housekeeping' tasks on the Web server, allowing you to stop and start services.

Working with IIS

Having installed IIS Web server software, you'll need some means of administering its contents and settings. In this section, we see the user interface that is provided by IIS.

In fact, some versions of IIS provide two user interfaces, the *Microsoft Management Console (MMC)* and the *Personal Web Server (PWS)* interface (which is just included for those people familiar with PWS from Windows 98 and looking to migrate to IIS). Let's look at MMC, as the other interface is now obsolete.

The Microsoft Management Console (MMC)

The best part of MMC is that it provides a central interface for administrating all sorts of services that are installed on your machine. We can use it to administer IIS. In fact, when we use it to administer other services, the interface looks roughly the same. The MMC is provided as part of the Windows 2000 operating system – in fact, the MMC also comes with older Windows server operating systems.

The MMC itself is just a shell – on its own, it doesn't do much at all. If you want to use it to administer a service, you have to add a *snap-in* for that service. The good news is that IIS has its own snap-in. Whenever you need to administer IIS, simply call up the Internet Services Manager MMC console by selecting Start | Control Panel | Administrative Tools | Internet Services Manager:

Figure E-4

Having opened the IIS snap-in within the MMC, you can perform all of your Web management tasks from this window as seen in Figure E-4. The properties of the Web site are accessible via the Default Web Site node. We'll be using the MMC more a little later in the chapter.

Testing Your Installation

The next thing to do is test the Web server to see if it is working correctly, and serving pages as it should be. We've already mentioned that the Web services should start as soon as IIS has been installed, and will restart every time you start your machine. In this section, we'll try that out.

In order to test the Web server, we'll start up a browser and try to view some Web pages that you know are already placed on the Web server. In order to do that, you need to type a URL (Uniform Resource Locator) into the browser's Address box, as you often do when browsing on the Internet.

What URL do you use in order to browse to your Web server? If your Web server and Web browser are connected by a local area network, or if you're using a single machine for the Web server and the browser, then it should be enough to specify the name of the Web server machine in the URL.

Identifying Your Web Server's Name

By default, IIS will take the name of your Web server from the name of the computer. You can change this in the machine's network settings. If you haven't set one, then Windows will generate one automatically – note that this automatic name won't be terribly friendly; probably something along the lines of P77RTQ7881. To find the name of your own Web server machine, select Start | Settings | Network and Dial-up Connections or Start | Settings | Control Panel | System (depending on which operating system you are using – if it isn't in one, try the other) and from the Advanced menu select Network Identification. This tab will display your machine name under the description Full computer name as shown in Figure E-5:

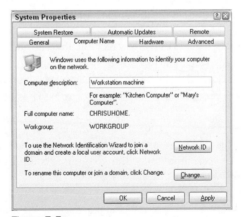

Figure E-5

My machine has the name chrisuhome, and (as you can see here and in Figure E-4) my Web server has adopted the same name. On a computer within a domain, for example a WROX_UK domain, it would be like WROX_UK/chrisuhome. However, this doesn't alter operation for ASP.NET. Browsing to pages on this machine across a local area network (or even from the same machine), I can use a URL that begins http://chrisuhome/…

There are a couple of alternatives if you're using the same machine as both Web server and browser. Try http://127.0.0.1/…. Here, 127.0.0.1 is a default that causes requests to be sent to a Web server on the local machine. Alternatively, try http://localhost/… where localhost is an alias for the 127.0.0.1 address. You may need to check the LAN settings (in your browser's options) to ensure that local browsing is not through a proxy server (a separate machine that filters all incoming and outgoing Web traffic employed at most workplaces, but not something that affects you if you are working from home).

> **Throughout the book, in any examples that require you to specify a Web server name, the server name will be shown as localhost, implicitly assuming that your Web server and browser are being run on the same machine. If they reside on different machines, then you simply need to substitute the computer name of the appropriate Web server machine.**

Managing Directories on Your Web Server

Before installing ASP.NET, you need to make one last pit stop in IIS. This is because when you run your ASP.NET pages, you need to understand where to place your pages, and how to make sure you have the permission to access them. As this is governed by IIS, let's look at it now.

These days, many browsers are sufficiently advanced that you can use them to locate and examine files and pages that exist on your computer's hard disk. For example, you can start up your browser, type in the physical location of a Web page (or other file) such as C:\My Documents\mywebpage.html, and the browser will display it. However, this isn't real Web publishing at all.

First, Web pages are transported using HTTP protocol. Note that the http:// at the beginning of a URL indicates that the request is being sent by HTTP. Requesting C:\My Documents\mywebpage.html in your browser doesn't use HTTP, and this means that the file is not delivered and handled in the way a Web page should be. No server processing is done in this case. HTTP is discussed in *Chapter 2*.

Second, consider the addressing situation. The C:\My Documents\mywebpage.html string tells us that the page exists in the \My Documents directory of the C: drive of the hard disk of the machine on which the browser is running. In a network situation, with two or more computers, this simply doesn't give enough information about the Web server.

However, when a user browses (via HTTP) to a Web page on some Web server, the Web server will need to work out where the file for that page is located on the server's hard disk. In fact, there's an important relationship between the information given in the URL, and the physical location (within the Web server's file system) of the file that contains the source for the page.

Virtual Directories

So how does the relationship between the information given in the URL, and physical location work? It works by creating a second directory structure on the Web server machine, which reflects the structure of your Web site.

The first directory structure is what you see when you open Windows Explorer on the Web server – these directories are known as *physical directories*. For example, the C:\My Documents folder is a physical directory.

The second directory structure is the one that reflects the structure of the Web site. This consists of a hierarchy of *virtual directories*. We use the Web server to create virtual directories, and to set the relationship between the virtual directories and the real (physical) directories.

When you try to visualize a virtual directory, it's probably best not to think of it as a directory at all. Instead, just think of it as a nickname or alias for a physical directory that exists on the Web server machine. The idea is that when a user browses to a Web page that is contained in a physical directory on the server, they don't use the name of the physical directory to get there. Iinstead, they use the physical directory's nickname.

To see how this might be useful, consider a Web site that publishes news about different sporting events. In order to organize his Web files carefully, the Webmaster has built a physical directory structure on his hard disk, which looks like Figure E-6:

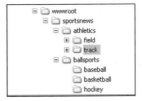

Figure E-6

Now, suppose you visit this Web site to get the latest news on the javelin event in the Olympics. If the URL for this Web page were based on the physical directory structure, the URL for this page would be something like this:

http://www.oursportsite.com/sportsnews/athletics/field/javelin/default.asp

That's okay for the Webmaster, who understands his directory structure; however it's a fairly unmemorable Web address! So, to make it easier for the user, the Webmaster can assign a virtual directory name or alias to this directory – it acts just like a nickname for the directory. Here, let's suppose we've assigned the virtual name javelinnews to the C:\inetpub\...\javelin\ directory. Now, the URL for the latest javelin news is:

http://www.oursportsite.com/javelinnews/default.asp

By creating virtual directory names for all the directories (such as baseballnews, 100mnews, 200mnews, and so on) it's easy for the user to type in the URL and go directly to the page they want:

http://www.oursportsite.com/baseballnews/default.asp

http://www.oursportsite.com/100mnews/default.asp

http://www.oursportsite.com/200mnews/default.asp

Not only does this save the user from long, unwieldy URLs – it also serves as a good security measure, because it hides the physical directory structure from all the Web site visitors. This is good practice; hackers may be able access your files if they knew what the directory structure looked like. Moreover, it allows the Webmaster's Web site structure to remain independent of the directory structure on the hard drive – so he can move files on his disk between different physical folders, drives, or even servers, without having to change the structure of his Web pages. There is a performance overhead to think about as well, as IIS has to expend effort translating the physical path. It can be a pretty costly performance-wise to have too many virtual directories.

Let's have a crack at setting up our own virtual directories and permissions (please note that these permissions are set automatically if you use the FrontPage editor to create a new site – so don't use FrontPage to set up this site for you unless you know what you're doing).

Try It Out Creating a Virtual Directory and Setting Up Permissions

It's time to create our own virtual directory. We'll use this directory to store the examples that we'll be creating in this book. We don't want to over complicate this example by creating lots of directories, so we'll demonstrate this by creating a single physical directory on the Web server's hard disk, and using the IIS admin tool to create a virtual directory and make the relationship between the two:

1. Start Windows Explorer and create a new physical directory named BegASPNET11, in the root directory of your hard drive. For example, C:\BegASPNET11 as shown in Figure E-7:

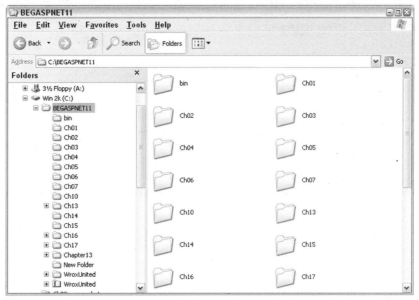

Figure E-7

2. Next, start up the IIS admin tool (using the MMC, as described earlier). Right-click on Default Web Site, and from the menu that appears select New | Virtual Directory. This starts the Virtual Directory Creation Wizard, which handles the creation of virtual directories for you and the setting up of permissions as well. You'll see the splash screen first as shown in Figure E-8. Click on Next:

Figure E-8

3. Type BegASPNET11 in the Alias text box as shown in Figure E-9; then click Next:

Figure E-9

4. As shown in Figure E-10, click on the Browse button and select the directory C:\BegASPNET11 that you created in Step 1. Then click Next:

Figure E-10

5. Make sure that the Read and Run scripts checkboxes are checked, and that the Execute checkbox is empty. Click on Next in Figure E-11, and in the subsequent page click on Finish:

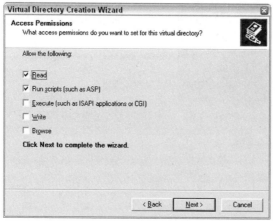

Figure E-11

6. The BegASPNET11 virtual directory will appear on the tree in the IIS admin window as shown in Figure E-12:

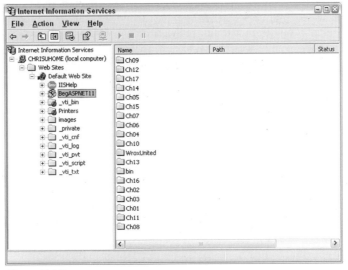

Figure E-12

How It Works

You just created a physical directory called BegASPNET11. This directory has been used throughout the book to store our code examples. The download files from www.wrox.com are also designed to follow this structure. Within this directory we recommend that you create a subdirectory for each of the chapters in order to keep things tidy (this needn't be a virtual directory – just a physical one.)

You've also created a virtual directory called **BegASPNET11** as an alias for the physical BegASPNET11 directory. If while creating *Chapter 1* examples you place the ASP.NET files in the physical C:\BegASPNET11\ch01 directory, you can use the browser to access pages stored in this folder. You'll need to use the URL http://my_server_name/BegASPNET11/ch01/...

Also you note that the URL uses the alias /BegASPNET11; IIS knows that this stands for the directory path C:\BegASPNET11. When executing ASP.NET pages, you can reduce the amount of typing you need to do in the URL, by using virtual directory names in your URL in place of the physical directory names.

We also set the permissions read and run – these must be set or the IIS security features will prevent you from running any ASP.NET pages. The **Execute** checkbox is left unselected as allowing others to run applications on your own machine is a sure way of getting viruses or getting hacked. We'll take a closer look at permissions now, as they are very important. If you don't assign them correctly you may find that you're unable to run any ASP.NET pages at all. Worse still, anybody can access your machine, and alter (even delete) your files via the Web.

Permissions

As you've just seen, we can assign permissions to a new directory as you create it, by using the options offered in the Virtual Directory Wizard. Alternatively, you can set permissions at any time, from the IIS admin tool in the MMC. To do this, right-click on the BegASPNET11 virtual directory in the IIS admin tool, and select Properties. You'll get the dialog shown in Figure E-13:

Figure E-13

Access Permissions

The four checkboxes on the left (see Figure E-13) govern the types of access for the given directory and dictate the permissions allowed on the files contained within that directory. Let's have a look at what each of these options means:

❑   **Script source access**: This permission enables users to access the source code of an ASP.NET page. It's only possible to allow this permission if the Read or Write permission has already been assigned. But we generally don't want our users to be able to view our ASP.NET source code, so we would usually leave this checkbox unchecked for any directory that contains ASP.NET pages. By default, all directories created during setup have Script Source Access permission disabled. You should leave this as is.

❑   **Read**: This permission enables browsers to read or download files stored in a home directory or a virtual directory. If the browser requests a file from a directory that doesn't have the Read permission enabled, then the Web server will simply return an error message. Note that when the folder has Read permission turned off, HTML files within the folder cannot be read; however, ASP.NET code within the folder can still be run. Generally, directories containing information that you want to publish (such as HTML files, for example) should have the Read permission enabled, as we did in our earlier example.

❑ **Write**: If the write permission on a virtual directory is enabled, then users will be able to create or modify files within the directory, and change the properties of these files. This is not normally turned on, for reasons of security and we don't recommend you alter it.

❑ **Directory browsing**: If you want to allow people to view the contents of the directory (that is, to see a list of all the files that are contained in that directory), check the Directory Browsing option.

If someone tries to browse the contents of a directory that has Directory Browsing enabled but Read disabled, then they will receive the message seen in Figure E-14:

Figure E-14

> For security reasons, we recommend disabling this option unless your users specifically need it – such as when transferring files using FTP (file transfer protocol), from your Web site.

Execute Permissions

There's a dropdown list box near the foot of the Properties dialog, labeled Execute permissions – this specifies what level of program execution is permitted on pages contained in this directory. There are three possible values here – None, Scripts only, or Scripts and Executables:

❑ Setting Execute permissions to None means that users can only access static files, such as image files and HTML files. Any script-based files of other executables contained in this directory are inaccessible to users. If you tried to run an ASP.NET page, from a folder with the permission set to None, you would get the following – note the Execute Access Forbidden message in the page shown in Figure E-15:

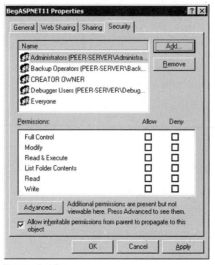

Figure E-15

❑ Setting Execute permissions to Scripts Only means that users can also access any script-based pages, such as ASP.NET pages. So if the user requests an ASP.NET page that's contained in this directory, the Web server will allow the ASP.NET code to be executed, and the resulting HTML to be sent to the browser.

❑ Setting Execute permissions to Scripts and Executables means that users can execute any type of file type that's contained in the directory. It's generally a good idea to avoid using this setting, in order to prohibit users from executing potentially damaging applications on your Web server.

For any directory containing ASP.NET files that you're publishing, the appropriate setting for the Execute permissions is Scripts Only. There is one last bit about directory that needs pointing out though for users of Windows 2000.

Configuring Directory Security in Windows 2000

If you're running Windows 2000 Server, you might have one extra bit of configuration to do. In ASP.NET all ASPX pages run under a special user account named ASPNET. For security reasons this account has restricted permissions by default; ordinarily, this isn't a problem. The database samples in this chapter use Access. When updating data in a database Access creates a separate file (with a .ldb suffix), which holds the locking information. These are the details that stores who is updating records, and the locking file is created and removed on demand.

The security problem encountered is that we are running pages under the ASPNET account, which doesn't have write permissions in the samples directory. Consequently, any ASP.NET pages that update a sample Access .mdb database will fail. Setting the write permission is simple – just follow these steps:

1. In Windows Explorer, select the BegASPNET11 directory, where the samples are located.

2. Using the right mouse button, select the Properties menu option, and from the Properties dialog that appears, select the Security tab as shown in Figure E-16:

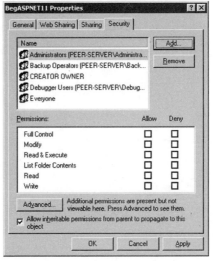

Figure E-16

3. Click the Add button to display the Select Users or Groups dialog. In the blank space enter ASPNET and click the Check Names button. This checks the name you've entered and adds the machine name to it:

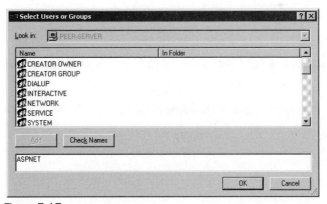

Figure E-17

4. Click the OK button to return to the Properties dialog, and you'll see that the ASPNET user is now shown in the list of users. In the Permissions area, at the bottom of this screen, select the

Write permission and tick it. This gives the ASPNET user write permission to the BegASPNet11 directory tree:

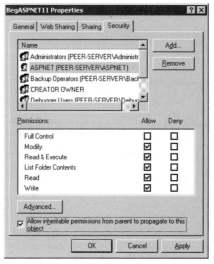

Figure E-18

5. Click the OK button to save the changes, and to close the dialog.

The security issue arises only if you need write access to a directory, in the same manner as required by our examples (which use Access). Most production Web sites wouldn't use Access as their database store, since Access isn't designed for a high number of users. In these cases SQL Server would be a more likely choice. The .NET SDK documentation has examples of connection strings for SQL Server.

Browsing to a Page on Your Web Server

You can test the installation by viewing some classic ASP pages hosted on your Web server, by browsing to them with your Web browser. Let's test out this theory by viewing our default home page, which is http://localhost and should appear something like Figure E-19 (this was taken on Windows XP Professional, so it might appear a little differently):

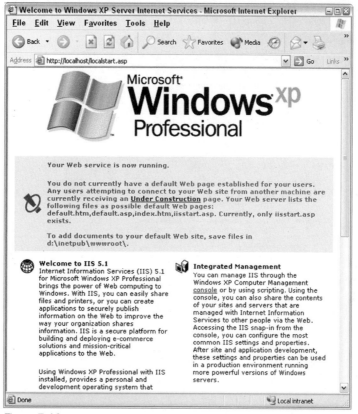

Figure E-19

If you see the screen as shown in Figure E-19, it means the install has worked and you can jump back to *Chapter 1* and the section on creating your first ASP.NET page.

What Do You Do if This Doesn't Work?

If it's not working correctly, then you are most likely to be greeted with the screen similar to Figure E-20:

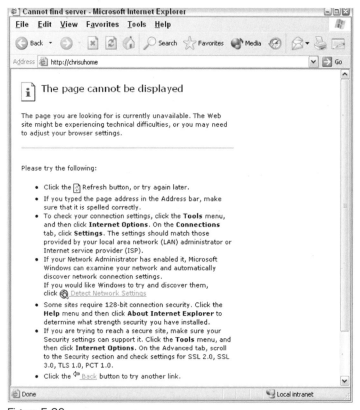

Figure E-20

If you get this page, it can mean a lot of things; however, one of the most likely problems is that your Web services under IIS are not switched on. To switch on Web services, you'll first need to start the IIS admin snap-in that we described earlier in the chapter (select Start | Run, type MMC and hit OK; then select Open from the MMC's Console menu and locate the `iis.msc` file from the dialog. Alternatively, just use the shortcut that you created there).

Now, click on the + of the root node in the left pane of the snap-in, to reveal the Default sites. Then right-click on Default Web Site, and select Start as shown in Figure E-21:

Figure E-21

If it's still not working then here are a few more suggestions, which are based on particular aspects of your PC's setup. If you're running on a network and using a proxy server (a piece of software that manages connections from inside a firewall to the outside world – don't worry if you don't have one, they're mainly used by big businesses), there's a possibility that this can prevent your browser from accessing your Web server. Most browsers will give you an opportunity to bypass the proxy server.

❏   If you're using Internet Explorer, you need to go to View | Internet Options (IE4) or Tools | Internet Options (IE5/IE6) and select the Connections tab. In IE5/IE6 press the LAN Settings button and select Bypass the proxy server for local addresses. In IE6, this section forms part of the Connections dialog and can be accessed by pressing the LAN settings dialog as shown in Figure E-22:

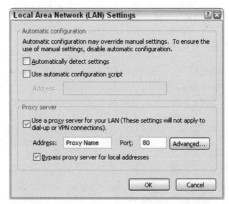

Figure E-22

❑ If you're using Netscape Navigator (either version 4.*x* or 6.*x*) and you are having problems then you need to turn off all proxies and make sure you are accessing the Internet directly. To do this, select Edit | Preferences; in the resulting dialog select Advanced | Proxies from the Category box on the left. Then on the right, select the Direct Connection to Internet option, and hit OK. Although you won't be browsing online to the Internet, it'll allow Netscape Navigator to recognize all variations of accessing local ASP.NET pages – such as http://127.0.0.1, http://localhost, and so on.

If you get the message displayed in Figure E-23, it means the install has succeeded but you have some old install files on your machine:

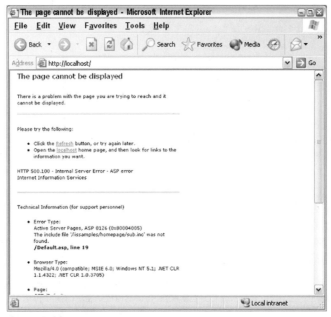

Figure E-23

This may happens if you have an old installation of Visual Studio. To get rid of this, simply go to `C:\inetpub\wwwroot`, delete the `default.asp` file, and then run http://localhost. What is happening is that IIS will use `default.asp` as the home page, and not IIS's home page `localstart.asp`. If there is no `default.asp` then IIS will automatically use `localstart.asp`.

Alternatively if you have customized `default.asp`, just go to http://localhost/localstart.asp to see that IIS has in fact installed correctly. So, you can jump back to *Chapter 1* and build an ASP.NET page and all the examples will work just fine.

Lastly, if your Web server is running on your home machine with a modem, and you get an error message informing you that your Web page is offline, this could in fact be a misperception on the part of the Web server.

This can be corrected by changing the way that your browser looks for pages. To do this, select View | Internet Options (IE4) or Tools | Internet Options (IE5/IE6), choose the Connections tab and select Never dial a connection.

Of course, you might encounter problems that aren't covered here. In this case, the chances are that they would be related to your own particular system setup. We can't possibly cover all the different possible configurations here; but if you can't track down the problem, you may find some help at one of the Web sites and newsgroups listed in *Chapter 15*.

Index

A Guide to the Index

The index is arranged hierarchically, in alphabetical order, with symbol preceding the letter A. Most second-level entries and many third-level entries also occur as first-level entries. This is to ensure that users find the information they require however they choose to search for it.

Symbols

(negation) operator, 114
- (subtraction) operator, 114
!= inequality operator, 119
* (multiplication) operator, 114
/ (division) operator, 114
/t, /target switch
  see target switch
@ character, 260
\ character, 260
^ (exponential) operator, 114
+ (addition) operator, 114
< Less than operator, 118
<% %> delimiters, 47
<= Less than or equal to operator, 118
== equality operator, 118
> greater than operator, 118
>= greater than or equal to operator, 118
3-tier application design, 464
  application layer, 464, 465
  data layer, 464, 465
  fitting the layers together, 465
  presentation layer, 464

A

abstraction, objects, 217
access permissions, 814
AccessDataSourceControl control
  see also MxDataGrid control
  ConnectionString attribute, 254
  data grid example, 254
  SelectCommand attribute, 254

Add () method
  ArrayList class, 104, 106
  caching, dependencies, 414
  DataRow object, 295
  Hashtable class, 107
addition (+) operator, 114
administrators, user security level, 636
ADO and ADO.NET compared, 289
ADO.NET, 245
  ADO, compared to, 289
  data access classes, 269
    relationship diagram, 271
  disconnected model, 289
  ISBN search Web service example, use in, 612
  namespaces, 269
  .NET Framework, database connection for, 39
  parameters collection, 272
  Web services, using within, 610
AdRotator control, 353
  see also rich controls
  simple header control example, use within, 443
  user control, used in example of, 441
  Wrox United example, Visual Studio .NET, 785
allow sub-tag, authorization tag, 644
AllowPaging property, DataGrid control, 342
AllowSorting property, DataGrid control, 341
AlternatingItemStyle property, DataGrid control, 342
AND (&&) logical operator, 120
  see also logical operators
  implementation example, 122
    code workthrough, 124
    page view, 124
  operator precedence, 121
anonymous users,user level security, 636

application configuration file, 562

application design, 465
3-tier application design, 464
structuring process, 466
user controls, 465

application exceptions, 536

application layer, 3-tier application design, 465

application level tracing
Trace.axd file, information storage within, 534
web.config file, setting within, 534
<trace> section, 534

application logic layer
3-tier application design, 464
determining location, 466

application settings, configuration files
key-value pairs, information storage in, 571
web.config file, within, 571

Application_Error() method, 549
event logs, making entries within, 557
handling errors programatically, 547

ApplicationException class
Exeption class, inheritance from, 537
nested try block, handing using, 546

applications, 382
see also caching; cookies; sessions
ASP.NET, reacting to events within
Global.asax file, using, 410
Chat page, state usage within, 409
database, state management using, 420
definition, 404
disadvantages, 419
operation mechanism, 405
usage guidelines, 419
ViewState, state management using, 420
web.config file, configuration information in, 381

arithmetic operators, 113
Tax calculation example, 115-118
code workthrough, 117
Label control, use of, 117
modulo, use of, 117
postback, use of, 117
TextBox control, use of, 117
mathematical precedence, 114
types, 114

ArrayList class
Add() method, 104, 106
advantages, 103
definition, 103
disadvantages, 104
implementation example, 105-106
Insert() method, 104, 106

new keyword, creating objects using, 104
syntax, 104

arrays
advantages, 102
Array class, 100
declaration, 98
declaring, 98
disadvantages, 103
implementation example, 99–101
code workthrough, 100
error handling, 100,101
Page_Load() method, use of, 100
page view, 100
postback, use of, 100
IndexOf() method, 100
multi-dimensional arrays, 101
using, 99

ASCX files, 451

ASP (Active Server Pages)
ASP.NET, compared to, 9, 561, 562
introduction, 1

ASP.NET
advantages, 1
ASP, compared to, 9, 561, 562
C#, use of, 10
Cache object, 578
configuration files, 561
control-based, event-driven architecture, 313
cross language compatibility, 1, 481
custom controls, 489
database binding, 51
databases, ease of use with, 1
definition, 9, 11
dependencies, handling, 413
dynamic content, 1, 64
events, 191
calculator example, 206
definition, 192
event driven programming model, 191, 192
Page class, handling using, 197
types, 193
form definition, 61
<form> tag, 64
HTML
seperating code from, 49
mixing with, 49
HTTP, compared to, 64
IIS
compatibility, 803
installation, 12

installation, 11
  .NET Framework installation, 14
  pre-requisites, 12
  Web Matrix installation, 15
introduction, 1
native languages, 9
.NET Framework
  composition, 36
  using features of, 1, 9
  versioning, 13
operating systems compatibility, 11
operation mechanism, 63
Page class, 324
page lifecycle
  handling control events, 325
  page cleanup, 325
  page disposal, 325
  page initialization, 324
  page loading, 325
  page prerendering, 325
  page rendering, 325
  Postback data loading, 324
  ViewState loading, 324
server-side processing, 8, 10, 11
sessions
  default information storage with, 395
  storing user information in, 381
test page example, 26–29
  code workthrough, 28
  Now() method, use of, 28
tracing, 195
troubleshooting, 28
  additional problems, 33
  blank page, 31
  Page Cannot Be Displayed error, 29
  Page Cannot Be Found error, 30
  referencing problems, 28server error, 32
  sever control mistyping, 31
  Web page unavailable while offline message, 31
VB.NET, default language, 43
ViewState, 205
Web controls, 315
Web Matrix
  application development using, 15
  Class Browser, 735
  code entry, 730
  development screen, 727
  error handling, 738
  installation, 15

  introduction, 725
  layout options, 738
  references for usage, 738
  reusable code, using, 735
  saving pages, 731
  starting, 727
  usage advantages/disadvantages, 726
  viewing pages, 731
Web pages, inserting code into, 42
  <script> tag, using, 42
  inline code blocks, using, 47
  Inserting ASP.NET code example, 44
  server controls, using, 49
XML, 1
  binding to, 54
  Web services, ease of use in, 594
ASP.NET pages
  compilation errors, 572
  custom errors, 572
  execution errors, 572
  IIS, role of, 41
  importing namespaces, 40
  operation mechanism, 41
  saving, 42
ASP.NET security
  see security
ASP.NET Web controls
  see Web controls
ASP.NET Web services
  see Web services
ASPX page
  code-behind files, use of, 466
  components, 432
  Register directive, 440
assemblies
  assembly, compiling to, 472
  components, use of, 463, 470
  definition, 466
  HelloWorld example, 474–476
    code workthrough, 474
  main parts
    assembly manifest, 466
    MSIL code, 466
    page view, 474
  pre-compilation, 470
  simple component example, 467–470
    code workthrough, 468, 469
  web.config file, accessing using, 477
assembly manifest, 466
  see also MSIL

assignment (+=) operator, string concatenation, 118
assignment (=) operator, 114
asynchronous method calls, 631–632
authentication
  see also security
  cookies, 638
  database , use with, 646
  definition, 637
  Login page, Wrox United example, 660
  System.Web.Security namespace, 649
  types
    Basic, 638
    Forms-based, 637
    Integrated Windows, 638
    Passport, 638
  user authentication, 637
authorization
  see also security
  definition, 637
  login example, within, 651
  selective folders, 651
  web.config configuration file, using, 650
authorization tag, web.config configuration file
  definition, 644
  allow sub tag, 644
  deny sub tag, 644
AutoEventWireup parameter, configuration settings, 571
auto-generated commands example, 298-302
  code workthrough, 300
  DeleteCommand property, use of, 301
  InsertCommand property, use of, 301
  page view, 299
  SelectCommand property, use of, 300
  UpdateCommand property, use of, 300
automatic browser detection, Web controls, within, 320
automatic value caching, HTML server controls, 318
AutoPostback property, 326

B

BackColor attribute, Label control, 66
base class library, .NET Framework
  definition, 39
  namespaces, 39
Basic authentication, 638
basic controls
  see intrinsic controls
binding, 591
  see also early binding
binding Web pages to database, 51
black box concept, Web services, 594

block level variables, 90-91
Body property, MailMessage class, 558
boolean data types, 90
brackets
  see parentheses
branching structures
  see also jumping structures; looping structures
  definition, 125
  expressions, 128
  if else statement, 125
  if statement, 129
    implementation example, 134
    structure, 129
    types, 129
    usage table, 132
  switch statement
    implementation example, 141
    structure, 138
  table of uses, 127
breakpoints, debugging, 798
browsers, 23
buffer parameter, configuration settings, 571
Button control, 332, 618
  see also intrinsic controls
  calculator example, use in events, 210
  events, use with, 199
  Hyperlink control, compared to, 331
  manual trapping example, use within, 522
  Web controls, ASP.NET, 319
Byte data type, 86

C

C#
  @ character, 260
  \ character, 260
  \\ character, 260
  ASP.NET, use in, 10
  collections, 103
  constants, 96
  control structures, 125
    branching structures, 125
    jumping structures, 126
    looping structures, 126
  conversion functions, 97
  data types
    numeric, 86
    other, 89
    text, 88
  definition, 11

Err object, absence of, 535
int variable, 82
On Error Resume Next statement, absence of, 535
strongly typed language, 81
stronly typed language, 59
Visual Basic.NET
  compared to, 481
  cross language compatibility, 477
cache key example, 587–89
  code workthrough, 588
  page view, 588
cache object, 579
  cache priorities, 589
  creation, 579
    Cache.Insert() method, 580
    explicit insertion of key-value pairs, 580
    implicit insertion of key-value pairs, 579
  data removal, 580
  data retrieval, example, 580
  dataset storage, 579
  expiration policies, 581
    file dependency, 581, 582
    key dependency, 581, 586
    timestamp expiration, 581
Cache.Insert() method
  cache object, creation, 580
  syntax, 581
  timestamp expiration, setting, 581
caching, 382, 413
  see also applications; cookies; sessions
  automatic value caching, 318
  cache object, 578
  dependencies, 413
    Add() method, addition using, 414
    Insert() method, addition using, 414
  expiration, setting, 415, 575
  fragment caching, 578
  output caching, 575
  performance optimization, 575, 591
  retrieving data, 414
  syntax, 414
  usage guidelines, 419
  WroxUnited example, use within, 415–418
    code workthrough, 417
    Calendar controls, use of, 416, 418
    Hashtable object, use of, 417
    page view, 417
CacheDuration attribute, 604
calculator example, 206–211
  Button controls, event calling using, 210
  code workthrough, 210

page view, 207
switch statement, using, 211
viewstate, source view using, 208
Calendar controls
  see also rich controls
  custom calendar example, 503
  definition, 353
  Event calendar, use in, 358
  implementation example, 354
  OnDayRender property, 359
  OnSelectionChanged attribute, 365
  properties
    FirstDayOfWeek, 353
    SelectionMode, 353
    SelectMonthText, 353
    SelectWeekText, 353
  Wrox United example,
    caching, 416, 418
    Style sheets, use within, 423, 428
call stack
  definition, 525
  runtime errors, viewing, 525
    implementation example, 526–527
case sensitivity, elements, 566
catch block
  contents of, 540
  example, 539
  Exeption/SystemException class, sequence of error handling, 539
  multiple catch blocks, 538
  parameterless catch blocks, 540
Certificate Authority, verification, 665
char data type, 89
character, 260
Chat page, Wrox United example, 405-410
  code workthrough, 408
  Global.asax, global settings using, 411
  navigation user control example, applying, 449
  Page_Load() method, use of, 408
  page view, 407
  posting new messages, 408
  refreshing page content, 409
  setting chat log length, 409
  simple header control example, applying, 445
  testbox properties, 408
CheckBox control, 79, 332
  see also intrinsic controls
  Class Browser, Web Matrix, implementation example, 736
  parameters, Web controls, implementation example, 171,172

CheckBox control (continued)
  RadioButton control, compared to, 79
  syntax, 79
  Web controls, ASP.NET, 319
CheckBoxList control, 79, 353
  see also rich controls
  implementation example, 80-82
    code workthrough, 81
    page view, 81
  syntax, 79
checked statement, exceptions, 542
class browsers, 40
Class Browser, .NET Framework, 243
Class Browser, Web Matrix
  implementation example using CheckBox control,
    736–738
  introduction, 735
  usage technique, 736
Class Libraries, .NET Framework, 36
classes
  see also objects
  class browser, viewing using, 40
  class definition, 39
  constructor methods, 221
    initializing objects, 226
    overloading, 226
  creation, 218
    first class example, 218–24
  definition, 216
  inheritance,
    advantages, 233
    implementation example, 234–238
  interfaces
    definition, 237
    guidelines, 242
    implementation example, 238
    methods & properties implementation, 241
    types, as, 241
  methods, 227
    first class example, 227
    overloading, 229
    static methods, 231
  namespaces declaration, compared to, 475
  settings section, attributes & properties, 221, 567
  static properties, 231
ClearError() method, Server object, 549
client browsers, 5, 808
client-server relationship, Web pages, 62
client-side dynamic Web pages
  see also sever-side Web pages
  coding problems, 7

  disadvantages, 7
  operation mechanism, 6
  server-side dynamic Web pages, compared to, 9
CLR (Common Language Runtime), 482
  definition, 38
  JIT compiler, use of, 38
  .NET Framework, composition, 36
CLS (Common Language Specification), 36, 38
  see also MSIL
code breakage, good coding practice, 513
code comments, good coding practice, 512
code view features, Visual Studio .NET, 763
code wizards, Web Matrix, 262
  implementation example, 262–269
    code workthrough, 265
    DataSet object, use of, 267, 269
    OleDbDataAdapter data adapter, use of, 268
    page view, 265
    WHERE Clause builder section, 266
code-behind, 451
  ASPX pages, use within, 466
  deploying files, 451
  reusable assemblies, 451
  simple code-behind example, 452–457
    code workthrough, 454
    inheritance, 454
    namespace handling, 455
    page view, 454
  usage guidelines, 456
  user controls, use within, 466
  Visual Studio .NET
    default use within, 459
    Web applications development, 757
    web forms applications within, 451
  Wrox United example, applying to, 457–459
  Wrox United example, Visual Studio .NET, 762
coding
  see good coding practices
collections
  ArrayList
    Add () method, 104
    advantages, 103
    definition, 103
    disadvantages, 104
    implementation example, 105
    Insert() method, 104
    new keyword, creating objects using, 104
    syntax, 104
  definition, 103
  Hashtables

advantages, 106
definition, 106
disadvantages, 106
implementation example, 108
key-value pairs, adding, 107
syntax, 107
SortedList class
definition, 110
syntax, 110
columns attribute, Textbox control, 75
COM DLLs, .NET DLL files compared to, 434
Command class
ADO.NET, data access classes, 269
code wizards, implementation example, 268
command execute example, 307–310
code workthrough, 309
ExecuteNonQuery() method, use of, 310
database binding example, 53
database updation, 307
properties
CommandText, 271
Connection, 271
command execute example, 307–310
code workthrough, 309
ExecuteNonQuery() method, use of, 310
page view, 309
Parameters, setting, 309
CommandArgument property, LinkButton control, 339
CommandBuilder, 298
auto-generated commands example, 298-301
code workthrough, 300
DeleteCommand property, use of, 301
InsertCommand property, use of, 301
page view, 299
SelectCommand property, use of, 300
UpdateCommand property, use of, 300
SelectCommand property, based on, 298
CommandText property
DataTable object, use within, 284
OleDbCommand object, 272
CommandType property, OleDbCommand object, 272
CompareValidator control, 372
compiling
see also MSIL
assembly/library file, producing, 472
compilation errors, 514, 516
definition, 37
executable file, producing, 472
IL, use of, 470
interpreted code, 37

JIT (Just-In-Time) compiler, 38, 470
pre-compiled code, 37
process mechanism, 37, 470
switches, 472
target switch, 473
types, 37
components, 431
assemblies, use within, 463
benefits of using, 434
compiling, example, 469-470
cross-language compatibility, 482
custom controls, compared to, 490
data access, 482
definition, 432
documenting, 489
encapsulation, 432
HelloWorld example, 474–476
internal workings, 434
Internet Explorer Address bar, 433
MS Office Save As dialog, 433
objects, compared to, 432
rapid application development, 435
resuable visual components, 489
separation of presentation and functionality, 434
simple component example, 467–470
System.Data.dll component, 489
third party applications, imported, 434
Visual Basic .NET, writing using, 477
Web pages, accessing by, 476
Windows explorer Address bar, 433
components, reusable code
code-behind, 431
definition, 431
user controls, 431
composite controls, 490
custom calendar example, 499–506
code workthrough, 502
page view, 502
definition, 499
System.Web.UI.Control namespace, inheritance from, 499
<configSections> tags, configuration file format, 566
configuration errors, 514
configuration files, 564
<configSections> elements, 566
<sectionGroup> elements, 566
application configuration file, 562
configuration settings
application settings, 571
custom errors, 572
general configuration settings, 570

configuration files (continued)
  page configuration settings, 570
  customizing ASP.NET, 562
  declarations section, 566
  defining configuration settings, 562
  determining correct settings, 565
  guidelines, 566
  IIS, virtual directories, 565
  important blocks examined, 569
  inheritance, 564
  machine.config file, 562, 563
  security configuration files, 562
  security of, 565
  settings section, 566
  settings list, system.web group, 568
  structure, 566
  system.web group, 566
  viewing, 562
  XML
    configuration files based on XML, 562
    element rules, 565
<configuration> root element, 566
Connection class
  ADO.NET, data access classes, 269
  ConnectionString property, 271
  database binding example, 53
  OleDbConnection object, 270, 271
  SqlConnection object, 270
Connection property, OleDbCommand object, 272
ConnectionString attribute
  AccessDataSourceControl control, 254
  Web services example, used in, 624
ConnectionString property
  Connection Class, 271
  Data Source controls, 367
constants, 97
Const keyword, 97
constraints, DataSet class, 295
construct closure errors, 514
constructor methods, 221
  first class example, use within, 226
  HelloCS() method, 469
  initializing objects, 226
  New() method, 480
  overloading, 226
  signatures, 226
continuation character, Visual Basic .NET, 481
control structures, 125
  branching structures
    definition, 125
    expressions, 128

    if statement, 129
    if...else statement, 125
    switch statement, 126
  choice of usage, 127
  jumping structures, 159
    definition, 126
    functions, 159
    procedures, 127
  looping structures, 126, 144
    do...while statement, 144, 151
    for statement, 126, 144
    foreach...in statement, 126, 144, 154
    usage table, 144
    while statement, 126, 144, 148
  table of uses, 127
Control Tree section, page level tracing, 531
control-based, event-driven architecture, ASP.NET, 313
controls
  ASP.NET, control based architecture within, 313
  HTML/Web controls compared, 201
  server controls, 313
    HTML server controls, 313
    Web controls, 313
Convert class
  conversion functions, 97
  implementation example, 97
cookies, 381, 382
  see also applications; caching; sessions
  BBC news site example, 383
  definition, 383
  deleting, 385
  disadvantages, 385, 419
  displaying information within, 383
  expiry limit, 385
  Forms-based authentication, use within, 638
  login example, 642
  Login page, Wrox United example, 661
    UserLevelCookie, 661
    UserNameCookie, 661
  non-persistent, 638
  operation mechanism, 384
  persistent, 638
  time frame, setting, 385
  usage guidelines, 393, 419
  WroxUnited example, use within, 386–393
    code workthrough, 391
    checking user registration, 387, 388
    confirming presence of cookies, 390
    expiry limit, 390
    Now property, setting expiry limit using, 392

Page_Load() method, use of, 393
page view, 390
Style sheets, use within, 422, 428
registering the user, 388
Cookies Collection section, page-level tracing, 531
CreateEventSource() method, EventLog class, 553
CSS (Cascading style sheets)
custom calendar example, 502
Web control properties, adding using, 321
Wrox United example, use within, 421–429
code workthrough, 427
page view, 426
Wrox United example, Visual Studio .NET, 769
custom calendar example, 499–506
code workthrough, 502
Calendar control, use of, 502
CSS, use of, 504
Hashtable object, use of, 503
page view, 502
custom controls, 489
components, compared, 490
composite controls, 490, 499
creating, 490
data access components, compared to, 490
definition, 490
match of the day example, 491–99
code workthrough, 494
data access component, adding, 497
overriding, 496
System.Web.dll, referencing, 498
reusability, 498
page view, 494
System.Web.UI.Control namespace, inheritance from,
490, 495
System.Web.UI.WebControl namespace, inheritance from,
495
user controls, compared to, 490
<customErrors> element
ASP.NET page execution errors, 572
defaultdirect attribute, 550
error handling, notification and logging, 549
<error> subtag, 550
implementation example, 549
mode attribute, 550
custom errors, configuration files, 572
<customErrors> element, 572
RemoteOnly setting, 573
defaultRedirect parameter, 572
error parameter, 573
mode parameter, 572

web.config file, within, 572
customized error messages, 550
<customErrors> element, 550
implementation example, 551
Page not found error example, 551
User error example, 547–549
CustomValidator control, 372

D

data access components, 482
custom controls, compared to, 490
match of the day example, 497
Wrox United example, use within, 482–489
code workthrough, 488
page view, 487
data binding, 341
Data explorer, Web Matrix, 251
data grid example, 253–56
databases, accessing, 251
data grid example, 253
AccessDataSourceControl control, use of, 254
code workthrough, 254
page view, 254
MxDataGrid control, use of, 254
data layer, 3-tier application design, 464, 465
data rendering controls, 316
data binding, 341
templates, 341
types
DataGrid, 341
DataList, 341
Repeater, 341, 343
Data Source controls, Web Matrix, 367
properties, 367
Wrox United example, Players page, 369
data types, C#
numeric
byte, 86
decimal, 87
double, 87
integer, 86
long, 86
short, 86
single, 87
other
boolean, 90
date, 89
textual
char, 88
string, 88

DataAdapter class
  ADO.NET, data access classes, 269
  auto-generated commands example, 298-302
    code workthrough, 300
    DeleteCommand property, use of, 301
    InsertCommand property, use of, 301
    page view, 299
    SelectCommand property, use of, 300
    UpdateCommand property, use of, 300
  data source updation, 297
  database updation, 288
  database updation example, 302–307
    code workthrough, 305
    page view, 305
  Fill() method, 284
  Parameters object, implementation example, 277
  properties
    DeleteCommand, 271, 301
    InsertCommand, 271, 301
    UpdateCommand, 271, 300
    SelectCommand, 271, 298, 300
database binding example, 51–54
  see also XML binding example
  code workthrough, 53
  Command object, use of, 53
  Connection object, use of, 53
  DataGrid object, use of, 53
  Page_Load() method, use of, 53
  page view, 52
  strConnect variable, 53
database connection strings
  application settings, 571
  security, 571
database updation example, 302–307
  code workthrough, 305
  page view, 305
databases
  ASP.NET
    binding within, 51
    easy storage using, 1
  complex files, 248
  data storage, 247
  Forms-based authentication, use with, 646
  normalization, 249
  Primary key/foreign key one-to-many relationships, 742
  tables, used in example, 248
  transactions, 306
  updation, 288
    Command class, using, 307

  data source updation, 297
    implementation example, 302–7
  Web Matrix Data explorer, use of, 251
  Web pages, storage within, 247
  Wrox United example
    database design, 741
    installing Access database, 747
    installing MSDE database, 747
  Wrox United example, Visual Studio .NET, 794
DataGrid class
  database binding example, 53
  properties
    AllowPaging, 258
    AllowSorting, 259
    CurrentPageIndex, 259
    OnPageIndexChanged, 258
    OnSortCommand, 259
    PageSize, 258
  XML binding example, 56
DataGrid control
  DataList control, interchangability with, 343
  definition, 341
  implementation example, 342
  properties, 341
DataList control, 342
  DataGrid control, interchangability with, 343
  definition, 341
  ItemTemplate element, 339
  OnItemCommand property, 349
  Repeater control, compared to, 352
  SeperatorTemplate element, 339
  Teams page, Wrox United example, use within, 333, 339
  templates
    AlternatingItemTemplate, 343
    EditItemTemplate, 343
    FooterTemplate, 343
    HeaderTemplate, 343
    ItemTemplate, 343
    SelectedItemTemplate, 343
    SeperatorTemplate, 343
DataReader class, 278
  ADO.NET, data access classes, 269
  implementation example, 279–281
  ISBN search Web service example, 610
  latest score Web service, use in, 625
  OleDbDataReader object, 280
  Results page, Wrox United example, 621
  SqlDataReader object, 280
DataRow class, 285
  Add() method, 295
  Delete() method, 296

Rows collection, 285
Tables and Rows example, 286–288
    code workthrough, 287
    page view, 287
DataSet class, 278, 283
ADO.NET, data access classes, 269
binding multiple tables, 285
code wizards, implementation example, 267, 269
constraints, 295
data fetching, 284
data source updation, DataAdapter class, 297
database updation, 288, 289
DataRow object, 285
DataTable object, 284
Sort Page example, use in, 261
System.Data namespace, 267
Tables and Rows example, 286–288
    code workthrough, 287
    page view, 287
XML binding example, 56
DataTable class, 284
binding multiple tables, 285
CommandText property, use of, 284
DataSet, fetching data for, 284
NewRow() method, 294
Select() method, 295
Tables and Rows example, 286–288
    code workthrough, 287
    page view, 287
date data types, 89
DateTime class
event handler, creation example, 323
Expires property, 392
Now() method, 323
ToLongTimeString() method, 323
ToShortDateString() method, 323
DayRender() method, Event calendar, Wrox United
    example, 357
Debug mode
disabling at page level, example, 527
performance optimization tips, 591
setting at application level, 528
setting at page level, 527
source errors, displaying using, 527
debugging, 509
RemoteOnly value, mode parameter, 573
XML in Web services, 601
decimal data type, 87
declarations section
<configSection> element, 566
configuration files, 566
system.web group, 567

decryptionKey attribute, machineKey tag, 644
defaultdirect attribute, <customErrors> element, 550
defaultRedirect parameter, configuration settings,
    572
<definitions> element, 610
Delete() method, DataRow object, 296
DeleteCommand property, auto-generated commands
    example, 301
deny sub-tag, authorization tag, 644
dependencies, caching, 413
addition of
    Add() method, using, 414
    Insert() method, using, 414
file dependency, 582
Design Mode, Web Matrix, 732
Design Surface feature, Visual Studio .NET, 756
directives
namespace importing, 40
processing directives, Web services, 603
directories
management of, 808
physical directories, 809
security setting, 816
virtual directories, 809, 810
directory browsing access, access permission, 815
disconnected model, ADO.NET, 289
division (/) operator, 114
division by zero errors, 519
DLL (Dynamic Link Libraries), 433
COM DLLs, 434
ISBN search Web service example, 617
.NET DLLs, 434
Registry, locating within, 476
system files, 433
System.dll file, 472
System.Web.dll, 498
do...while statement, 151
see also looping structures
implementation example, 153-155
    code workthrough, 153
    page view, 153
syntax, 151
usage table, 144
double data type, 87
DropDownList control, 69, 332
see also intrinsic controls
attributes
    id, 71
    method, 71
    name, 71
for statement, implementation example, 147

DropDownList control (continued)
HTML form control, compared to, 69
if statement, implementation example, 135
implementation example, 69–72
  code workthrough, 71
  id attribute, setting, 71
  page view, 70
  runat=server attribute, setting, 71
  viewstate, setting, 71
Parameters object, implementation example, 275
using, 69

Duration property
fragment caching example, 578
OutputCache directive, 575

dynamic Web pages
ASP.NET, creation using, 1
client-side model
  disadvantages, 7
  operation mechanism, 6
server-side model, 7

E

early binding, performance optimization tips, 591
e-commerce, 664
editing data example, 289–297
row addition, 291
  Add() method, use of, 295
  code workthrough, 294
  NewRow() method, use of, 294
  page view, 292
row deletion, 291
  code workthrough, 294
  Delete() method, 296
  page view, 294
row editing, 292
  code workthrough, 295
  page view, 292
  Select() method, use of, 295
elements
  <configuration> root element, 566
  <customErrors> element, 572
  <httpRuntime> element, 570
  <pages> element, 570
  case sensitivity, 566
Email updates, Wrox United example,, 373–377
  code workthrough, 376
  page view, 376
  RegularExpressionValidator control, use of, 376
enabled parameter, tracing, configuration files, 574

EnableSessionState parameter, configuration settings, 571
EnableViewState parameter, configuration settings, 571
EnableViewState property, Data Source controls, 367
encapsulation, 431
  objects, within, 217
  public methods and properties, 432
Encoding property, MailAttachment class, 558
encryption, 664
  cookies, first level of security with, 645
  definition, 637
  e-commerce, importance in, 664
  hashing algorithms, 665
  keys, use of, 637
  public-key encryption, 665
  secret-key encryption, 664
  SSL, use of, 637, 665
enterprisesec.config file, security, 562
Err object, absence in C#, 535
error handling, 509
  custom errors, configuration files, 572
  Debug mode, 527
    disabling at page level, 527
    setting at application level, 528
    setting at page level, 527
  exceptions, 536
  finding errors, 525
  logical errors, 514, 518
  notification and logging, writing to event logs, 553
  programmatically, 547
    Application_Error() method, 547, 549
    Page_Error() method, 547
  specific error handlers, using, 540
  structured error handling, 536
  syntax errors, 514
  system errors, 525
  tracing, page level, 529
  unstructured error handling, 535
error parameter, custom errors, configuration settings, 573
ErrorPage property, Page directive, 553
Event calendar, Wrox United example, 354–360
  code workthrough, 358
  Calendar controls, use of, 358
  DayRender() method, 357
  hashtables, use of, 359
  Page_Load() method, 357
  page view, 358
event driven programming, 192

event handlers
creation example, 322–324
definition, 193
documenting code, 200
functions, compared to, 193
implementation example, 201–203
  Web matrix Properties section, adding event handlers
    using, 202
page lifecycle, within, 326
Page_Load() method, 198
Prerender event handler, 404
Teams page, Wrox United example, 350
Web controls, adding events to, 200
Web pages, use within, 322
event logs
Application_Error() method, using, 557
error handling,notification and logging, 553
implementation example, 554–557
Page_Error() method, using, 557
System.Diagnostics namespace, use of, 553
EventLog class, System.Diagnostics namespace
CreateEventSource() method, 553
WriteEntry() method method, 553
events
ASP.NET, event driven architecture within, 313
calculator example, 206–211
  Button controls, event calling using, 210
  code workthrough, 210
  page view, 209
  switch statement, using, 211
  viewstate, source view using, 208
definition, 192
event driven programming, 192
event handlers, 193
event-driven programming, 191
HTML server controls, processing within, 317
objects, describing characteristics, 216
operation mechanism, 192
page lifecycle
  handling control events, 326
  Init event, 324
  Load event, 325
  PreRender event, 325
  Unload event, 325
page loading mechanism, 197
  implementation example, 198
  methods used, 198
postback, implementation example, 202-205
sessions & applications, handling, 410

Global.asax file, using, 410
types, 193
  HTML events, 193
  page events, 197
Web controls, 199
  adding events, 200
  attributes, adding as, 200
  HTML events, compared to, 199
Web pages, use within, 322
Windows Operating System, 193
Exception class, System namespace, 537
properties
  HelpLink, 537
  InnerException, 537
  Message, 537
  Source, 537
  StackTrace, 537
  TargetSite, 537
exceptions
definition, 536
checked statement, generation of, 542
documentation of classes, 542
.NET Framework, handling by, 547
throw statement, generation using, 541
try . . catch . . . finally statements, 537
  implementation example, 542–544
Exception class
ApplicationException class, inheritance for, 537
catch block, exeption catching using, 539
SystemException class, inheritance for, 537
execute permissions
None, 815
Scripts and Executables, 816
Scripts Only, 816
ExecuteNonQuery() method
command execute example, 310
database updation, 307
OleDbCommand object, 272
ExecuteReader() method, OleDbCommand class, 272
ExecuteScalar() method, OleDbCommand class, 272
**executionTimeout parameter, general configuration
    settings, 570**
expiration policies
cache priorities, 589
file dependency
  concept, 582
  implementation example, 582-585
key dependency
  concept, 581, 586
  example, 586–589
timestamp expiration, 581

Expires property, DateTime class, 392
exponentiation (^) operator, 114
expressions, branching structures, 128

F

Fans table, Wrox United example, 746
file dependency
  cache object, expiration policies, 582
  implementation example, 583–586
    code workthrough, 585
    page view, 584
  key dependencies, linking with, 589
File Selector Tabs feature, Visual Studio .NET, 755
Filename property, MailAttachment class, 558
Fill() method, DataAdapter class, 284
finally block, 541
  see also try...catch...finally statement
firehose cursor, performance optimization tips, 591
first class example, 218–24
  code workthrough, 220
  constructor methods, use of, 226
  Label controls, use of, 223
  methods, defining, 228–231
  page view, 220
    code workthrough, 229
    page view, 229
    Response.Write statement, use of, 230
  new keyword, use of, 226
  Page_Load() method, use of, 223
  private variables, use of, 221
  properties setting, 221
  public variables, 221
  read-only property, use of, 224
Fixture details, Wrox United example, 360–366
  code workthrough, 364
  page view, 364
  Panel controls, use of, 364
  Repeater controls, use of, 364
FooterStyle property, DataGrid control, 342
for statement, 126
  see also foreach...in statement; while statement
  implementation example, 145
    code workthrough, 146
    DropDownList control, use of, 147
    IsPostback property, use of, 147
    page view, 147
  Label control example, use within, 144
  structure, 144
  usage table, 144

foreach...in statement, 126, 155
  see also for statement; while statement
  syntax, 155
  usage table, 144
ForeColor attribute, Label control, 66
Foreign key, 250
<form> tag
  ASP.NET, form controls, 64
  authentication cookie, use in, 2nd level 642
  runat=server attribute, 64
  web.config configuration file
    loginUrl attribute, 642
    Name attribute, 642
    Protection attribute, 643
    slidingExpiration attribute, 643
    Timeout attribute, 643
formatted code, good coding practice, 511
forms
  see Web forms
Forms.Authentication.SignOut method, 664
FormsAuthentication class
  RedirectFromLoginPage method, 645
  Signout() method, 646, 664
Forms-based authentication, 637
  cookies, use of, 638
  database, use with, 646
  login example, 639–646
    cookies, checking for, 642
    databases, using, 646–650
    login page creation, 639
    main page creation, 640
    selective folder authorization, 650
    SSL, use of, 664
    user authorization, 650
    web.config file creation, 639
  Login page, Wrox United example, use in, 660
  SSL, enabling, 665
    login example, 665
    requireSSL attribute, 665
  web.config configuration file, use of, 638
  Wrox United example, 653
fragment caching, performance optimization, 578
From property, MailMessage class, 557
functions, 43, 159
  calling, 173
    returning value as argument for another function, 174, 180
    returning value as expression in control structure, 174, 180
    returning value into a variable, 174, 179

returning value into value of objects property, 174, 179

calls, 162

defining, 161

  simple function example, 161

event handlers, compared to, 193

functions with return values example, 175–181

  code workthrough, 178

  page view, 178

  string concatenation, use of, 179

modularization, 160

parameters, use of, 164

  implementation example, 165–169

  parameter matching, 168

  syntax, 165

return keyword, returning values using, 172

usage guidelines, 163

Visual Basic .NET, 480

G

Games table, Wrox United example, 744

GameTypes table, Wrox United example, 745

garbage collector, .NET Framework, 403

  Merchandise page, Wrox United example, use within, 403

general configuration settings, configuration files, 570

  <httpRuntime> element, 570

  executionTimeout parameter, 570

  maxRequestLength parameter, 570

  useFullyQualifiedRedirectUrl, 570

  web.config file, within, 570

get statement, properties, 221

GetLastError() method, Server object, 549

  event logs, detailing information from, 554

global variables, 96

Global.asax file

  definition, 410

  Visual Studio .NET web application development, 757

  Wrox United example, global settings within, 411–413

good coding practice, 510

  amend identified error conditions, 510

  code breakage, 513

  code comments, 512

  converting variables to the correct data types, 512

  documenting code, 510

  formatting code, 511

  identify potential problem areas, 510

  structuring code, 511

Greetings example, Web services, 595–598

  code workthrough, 597

  HTTP GET method, use of, 599

  page view, 596

GXA (Global XML Architecture) specifications

  WSE toolkit, use with, 631

H

handling errors programatically

  Application_Error() method, 547

  Page_Error() method, 547

hashing algorithms, 644

hashing algorithms, SSL, 665

Hashtable class

  Add() method, 107

  advantages, 106

  custom calendar example, 503

  definition, 106

  disadvantages, 106

  Event calendar, Main page, Wrox United example, 359

  implementation example, 108-110

    code workthrough, 109

    IsPostBack property, use of, 109

    page view, 109

  key-value pairs, adding, 106

  syntax, 107

Headers Collection section, page level tracing, 531

HeaderStyle property, DataGrid control, 342

Height attribute, Label control, 66

HelloCS() method, 469

HelloWorld example, 474–476

  code workthrough, 474

  component compiling, 472

  Label control, use of, 475

  Page_Load() method, using, 475

  page view, 474

  Visual Basic .NET, writing using, 478–482

    code workthrough, 480

    page view, 480

HelpLink property, Exception class, 537

hidden form fields, ViewState, information storage within, 420

high level programming languages, 37

HTML (Hyper Text Markup Language)

  ASP.NET

    mixing with, 49

    separating code from, 49

    separation from ASP code in, 9

  disadvantages, 4

  postback, lack of support for

    explanation, 202

    implementation example, 203

  security, lack of adequacy, 5

  Static Web pages, use within, 2

HTML events, 193
implementation example, 193
Web control events, compared to, 199
HTML form controls
ASP.NET server controls, compared to, 64
DropDownList control,compared to, 69
HTML forms, 60
definition, 60, 61
form controls, 60
Web form, compared to, 61
HTML server controls, 313
advantages, 316
definition, 316
features
automatic value caching, 318
custom attributes, 318
event processing, 317
Programmatic Object Model, 317
validation, 318
HtmlControl class, functionality derived from, 317
runat=server attribute, concept and example, 316-317
Web controls, ASP.NET, compared to, 201, 318
HTML Web services
XML Web services, compared to, 594
HTML/Design View feature, Visual Studio .NET, 756
HtmlControl class
HTML server controls, providing functionality to, 317
HTTP (Hyper Text Transfer Protocol), 23
ASP.NET, compared to, 64
configuration files, security, 565
cookies, Request/Response mechanism within, 384
disadvantage, 63, 382, 601
HTTP Request, 62
HTTP Response, 62
Request-Response system, 62
security, problems with, 637
stateless, 63
Web server, accessing, 808
Web services, use of HTTP within, 599
Web pages, accessing, 808
HTTP Error 403 (Page cannot be displayed), 24, 29
HTTP Error 404 (Page cannot be found), 30, 600
HTTP GET method, 599
Greetings example, use within, 599
HTTP Request, 599
HTTP Response, 600
HTTP POST method, 600
HTTP Request, 600
example, 600
name-value pairs, passing on, 601
HTTP Response, 601

HTTP Request
HTTP GET method, 599
HTTP POST method, 600
Web services, use within, 599
HTTP Response
HTTP GET method, 600
HTTP POST method, 601
<httpRuntime> element, settings, 570
Hyperlink control
see also intrinsic controls
Button control, compared to, 331
Web controls, ASP.NET, 331

I

id attribute
databases, providing details for, 254
DropDownList control, implementation example, 71
Label controls, ASP.NET server controls, 66
if else statement, 125
see also branching structures
if statement
see also branching structures
alternate usage example, 137
disadvantage, 138
implementation example, 134–139
code workthrough, 135
DropDownList control, use of, 134
IsPostback property, use of, 136
Label control, use of, 137
Next() method, Random object, use of, 136
page view, 135
nested if statements, 137
structure, 128
types
if() statement, 129
if() {} statement, 129
if()...else if() statement, 131
if()...else statement, 130
usage table, 132
if(!Page.IsPostBack) construct, 326
if() {} statement, 129
example, 130
syntax, 130
usage table, 132
if() statement, 129
usage table, 132
if()...else if() statement, 131
example, 131
syntax, 131
usage table, 132

if()...else statement, 130
example, 131
syntax, 130
usage table, 132
IIS (Internet Information Services)
ASP.NET, role in, 41, 562, 733
history, 562
InetPub directory, 805
installation, 803–6
installation testing, 807
operating system compatibility, 803
MMC, working with, 806
permissions, 814
security of configuration files, 565
virtual directories, 565, 810
versioning, 5
Web server
installation testing, 818
managing directories, 808
name identification, 807
Windows operating system, versioning within, 803
IL (Intermediate Language)
see also MSIL
compilation process, 470
Image control, intrinsic controls, 332
ImageButton control, rich controls, 353
incorrect code syntax errors, 514
incorrect output errors, 519
IndexOf() method, Array class, 101
InetPub directory, IIS, 805
inheritance
configuration files, within, 564
implementation example, 234–238
interfaces, functionality compared to, 237
objects, within, 218
simple code-behind example, 454
stylesheet information, an example, 448
Injection Attacks, SQL, 277
inline code blocks, 47
disadvantage, 49
implementation example, 48
use in example, 50
InnerException property, Exception class, 537
Insert () method
ArrayList class, 104, 106
caching, dependencies, 414
InsertCommand property
auto-generated commands example, 301
DataAdapter class, 271
Inserting ASP.NET code example, 44–47
code workthrough, 46

<script> tag, use of, 47
inline code blocks, using, 48
Page_Load() method, use of, 47
page view, 46
Response.Write statement, use of, 47
runat= server attribute, HTML server controls, 47
installation, .NET Framework, 13
.NET Framework Redistributable, using, 14
troubleshooting, 15
installation, ASP.NET, 11
MDAC, 12
operating systems compatibility, 11
pre-requisites, 12
installation, Web Matrix, 15, 16–18
instances, 216
int variable, C#, 82
integer data type, 86
Integrated Windows authentication, 638
IntelliSense, Visual Studio .NET, 726
Wrox United example, VS.NET, 764
interfaces
definition, 237
guidelines, 242
implementation example, 238–241
code workthrough, 239
defining properties, 240
page view, 239
inheritance, functionality compared to, 237
methods & properties implementation, 242
types, as, 241
interpreted code, 37
intrinsic controls
definition, 331
types
Button, 332
CheckBox, 332
DropDownList, 332
Hyperlink, 332
Image, 332
Label, 332
ListBox, 332
Panel, 332
RadioButton, 332
Table, 332
TableCell, 332
TableRow, 332
TextBox, 332
invalid data errors, 519
manual trapping, example, 521–523
validation, 520
validation controls, reducing using, 523

IP address restriction, security, 630

IP address restriction, Web services security, 627, 630

ISBN search Web service example, 610–613

accessing from ASP.NET page, 615–618

code workthrough, 612

page view, 612

  code workthrough, 617

  DLL creation, 617

  page view, 617

ADO.NET, using, 612

DataReader object, use of, 610

Username password, using, 627–30

  code workthrough, 629

  page view, 628, 629

IsPostback property, 275, 590

DropDownList control, implementation example, 72

for statement, implementation example, 147

Hashtable class, implementation example, 109

if statement, implementation example, 136

performance optimization tips, 590

Page_Load() method, 325

postback, use for, 205

procedure-level variables, implementation example, 95

switch statement, implementation example, 143

ItemStyle property, DataGrid control, 342

ItemTemplate element, DataList control, 339

Label control, use with, 339

LinkButton control, use with, 339

J

JIT (Just-In-Time) compiler, 38

compilation process, 470

CLR, 38

jumping structures, 159

see also branching structures; looping structures

functions, 159

procedures, 127

table of uses, 127

K

key dependency, 586

cache key example, 586

  code workthrough, 588

  page view, 588

file dependencies, linking with, 589

syntax, 586

keys

see encryption

keyword errors, combining or splitting between languages, 514

L

Label control, 332, 618

see also intrinsic controls

control attributes, 65

definition, 65

first class example, 223

HelloWorld example, use within, 475

if statement, implementation example, 137

implementation example, 67–69

  code workthrough, 67

  for statement, use of, 144

  page view, 67

  Text attribute, modifying, 68

ItemTemplate element, use within, 339

Login page, Wrox United example, navigation bar, 662

manual trapping example, use within, 522

runat=server, attributes id, 66

simple function example, 162

Tax calculation example, 117

Text property, 66, 456

  Merchandise page, Wrox United example, 401

variables, implementation example, 85

syntax, 66

language attribute, Page directive, 43

latest score web service

code workthrough, 624

DataReader object, use of, 625

page view, 623

Results page, Wrox United example, 621–625

layers, 3-tier application design, 464

library files

see assemblies

LinkButton control, 353

see also rich controls

CommandArgument property, 339, 349, 350

CommandName property, 349, 350

ItemTemplate element, use within, 339

ListBox control, 332

see also intrinsic controls

definition, 72

implementation example, 72–74

selectionmode attribute, 73

syntax, 73

Web controls, ASP.NET, 319

local variables

see procedure-level variables

localhost

Web server, accessing, 23, 808, 818

localOnly parameter,

tracing, configuration files, 574

Location property, OutputCache element, 576

Location table, Wrox United example, 745

<location> tag, web.config configuration file, 652

logical errors, 514

call stack, viewing using

implementation example, 526–527

Stack Trace section, 527

invalid data errors, manual trapping, 520

runtime error example, 519

types, 518

logical operators

definition, 119

implementation example, 122–125

operator precedence, 121

syntax errors, 121

login example, security, 639–646

cookies, checking for, 642

databases, using, 646–650

System.Data.OLEDB namespace, use of, 649

System.Web.Security namespace, use of, 649

login page creation, 639

code workthrough, 645

databases, using, 647, 649

page view, 641

RedirectFromLoginPage method, use of, 645

main page creation, 640

code workthrough, 646

page view, 642

databases, using, 647

Signout() method, use of, 646

selective folder authorization, 651

SSL, use of, 664

user authorization, 651

web.config file, creation, 639, 642

Login page, Wrox United example, 653–664

administrator level page view, 659

authentication, with cookies, 661

code workthrough, 660

navigation bar, 662–664

page view, 658

Label control, using, 662

Page_Load() method, using, 662

Panel control, creation using, 662

Signout() method, use of, 664

user level page view, 660

web.config configuration file, authentication using, 660

LoginUrl attribute, <forms> tag, 642

long data type, 86

looping structures, 144

see also branching structures; jumping structures

do...while statement, 144

implementation example, 151

syntax, 151

for statement, 126, 144

Label control, implementation example, 145

implementation example, 147-149

structure, 143

foreach...in statement, 126, 144, 155

syntax, 154

table of uses, 127

usage table, 144

while statement, 126, 144, 148

implementation example, 150

syntax, 148

M

machine code, 37

machine.config file, 562

configuration sequence of events, 564

contents, 564

examining, 563

important blocks examined, 569

.NET Framework, versioning, 563

overriding other machine.config file settings, 565

structure, 567

page settings, 568

web.config file, overridden by, 564, 566

machineKey tag, web.config configuration file

attributes

decryptionKey, 644

validation, 644

validationKey, 644

definition, 643

MailAttachment class

properties

Body, 558

Encoding, 558

Filename, 558

From, 558

Subject, 558

To, 558

System.Web.Mail namespace, 557

MailMessage class, System.Web.Mail namespace, 557

Main page, Wrox United example, 328–331

code workthrough, 330

components, encapsulating data access code into, 482–489

page view, 330

  code workthrough, 488

  page view, 487

custom calendar example

  code workthrough, 502

  page view, 502

custom calendar example, applying, 499

Email updates, 373–377

  code workthrough, 376

  page view, 376

Event calendar, 354

  code workthrough, 358

  Calendar controls, use of, 358

  DayRender() method, use of, 357

  hashtables, use of, 359

  Page_Load() method, use of, 357, 359

  page view, 358

Fixture details, 360–366

  code workthrough, 364

  page view, 364

  Panel controls, use of, 364

  Repeater controls, use of, 364

match of the day example, 491

  code workthrough, 494

  data access component, adding, 497

  overriding, 496

  page view, 494

  System.Web.dll, referencing, 498

navigation user control example, applying, 446

simple header control example, applying, 445

Teams page, linking to, 340

match of the day example, 491–499

code workthrough, 494

data access component, adding, 497

Main Page, Wrox United example, 491

overriding, 496

page view, 494

System.Web.dll, referencing, 498

mathematical precedence, operators, 115

maxRequestLength parameter, general configuration setting, 570

MD5 encryption algorithm, 665

MDAC (Microsoft Data Access Components)

ASP.NET installation pre-requisite, 12

installation, 13

site for downloading, 12

MeasurementsConversion example, 605–607

code workthrough, 606

namespaces, defining, 606

page view, 605

Public Class, naming, 606

testing, 607–8

web methods, defining, 606

WSDL, contracts, 609

Menu section, Web Matrix, 728

Merchandise page, WroxUnited example, 396–405

code workthrough, 400

page view, 399

Page_Load() method, use of, 401

reference types, working with, 402

Repeater controls, use of, 401, 404

Message property, Exception class, 537

methods

see also functions

classes, defining within, example of, 227

consolidation, overloading, 230

keeping names unique, 469

objects, describing characteristics, 216

overloading, 229

signatures, 230

static methods, 231

static keyword, 231

Microsoft Access

Web Matrix, lack of support for queries by, 253

mistaken assumption errors, 519

MMC (Microsoft Management Console)

IIS, working with, 806

permissions, 814

service snap-ins, 806

Windows operating system, within, 806

mode attribute, <customErrors> element, 550

mode parameter, configuration settings, 573

modularization

advantages, 160

best practices, 188

definition, 160

modulo (%) operator, 114

Tax calculation example, 117

while statement, implementation example, 154

MSDE (Microsoft Data Engine), Wrox United example, 747

MSIL (Microsoft Intermediate Language)

see also assembly manifest; CLS

CLS, generation from, 38

definition, 37, 466

.NET Framework, composition, 36

multi-dimensional arrays, concept and example, 101-102

multiplication (*) operator, 114

MxDataGrid control, 366

see also AccessDataSourceControl control

attributes, 255

data grid example, 254

Players page, Wrox United example, use within, 369

properties used, 370

style elements, 255

N

Name attribute, <forms> tag, 643

name value pairs

HTTP POST method, passing on using, 601

Web services, use within, 599

namespaces

class declarations, compared to, 475

definition, 39

documentation, 243

importing, using directives, 40

MeasurementsConversion example, defining within, 606

.NET Framework, within, 243

syntax, 603

System namespace, 41

Web services

components, 603

used in, 598

navigation user control example, 446–451

code workthrough, 450

Chat page, Wrox United page, applying to, 450

page view, 450

Main page, Wrox United example, applying to, 446

page view, 448

negation (-) operator, 114

.NET assemblies

see assemblies

.NET Framework

ADO.NET, database connection using, 39

advantages, 36

ASP.NET, feature usage within, 1, 9

assemblies, 463

base class library, 39

class browser, 40

Class Browser, 243

CLS, definitions for, 36

COM DLLs, DLL files compared to, 434

composition

ASP.NET, 36

Class Libraries, 36

CLR, 36

languages, 36

MSIL, 36

Web services, 36

cross language compatibility, 481

definition, 35

exeption handling, 547

garbage collector, 403

important aspects, 36

introduction, 1

installation, 14

namespaces, 39, 243

.NET Framework Redistributable, 14, 41

.NET Framework SDK, 40

objects, 216, 217

OOP, implementation using, 38

QuickStart tutorials, 40

System.dll file, 472

System.Data.dll component, 489

troubleshooting of installation, 15

versioning, 14, 563

Web controls, features used in, 320

.NET Framework 1.1

Web Matrix, setting for use with, 19

.NET Languages

.NET Framework, composition, 36

brief introduction, 36

nested try blocks, 545

ApplicationException object, handling, 546

implementation example, 545

network connectivity, 631

new keyword

first class example, 226

objects, initializing, 226

New() method, constructor, as, 480

NewRow() method, DataTable object, 294

Next() method, Random object, 136

no-existent object errors, 519

nondescript variable names, 90

normalization

definition, 249

keys, 250

ordering system example, 249

NOT (!) logical operator, 120

see also logical operators

implementation example, 123

operator precedence, 121

notification and logging errors, 552

customized error messages, 549

<customErrors> element, 549

Page not found error example, 550

User error example, 547–549

event logs

notification and logging errors (continued)
Application_Error() method, using, 556
implementation example, 553–556
Page_Error() method, using, 556
System.Diagnostics namespace, use of, 553
mailing the site administrator, 557
Now property, DateTime class
Wrox United example, cookies, use within, 392
Now() method, Date time class
ASP.NET, test page example, 28
event handler, creation example, 323
numeric comparison operators, 119
numeric data types
see also data types, C#
byte, 86
decimal, 87
double, 87
integer, 86
long, 86
short, 86
single, 87

O

objects
see also classes
abstraction, 217
built-in with ASP.NET, 39
classes, 39, 216
components, compared to, 432
definition, 38, 215
describing characteristics
events, 216
methods, 216
properties, 216
encapsulation, 217, 431
inheritance, 218, 232
advantages, 233
implementation example, 234–38
initializing with new keyword, 226
instances, 216
namespaces, 243
OOP, 38, 216
polymorphism, 217
String example, 216, 217
variables, 216, 217
OleDataAdapter object, 278
OleDbCommand object, 271
methods
ExecutableNonQuery, 272

ExecuteReader, 272
ExecuteScalar, 272
properties
CommandText, 272
CommandType, 272
Connection, 272
Parameters, 272
OleDbConnection object, 270
OleDbDataAdapter data adapter, 261
OleDbDataReader object, 650
On Error Resume Next statement, absence in C#, 535
OnSelectionChanged attribute, Calendar controls, 365
OOP (Object Oriented Programming), 38
advantages, 38, 39
classes, 216
instances, 216
.NET Framework, implementation within, 38
operator precedence, logical operators, 120
operators
arithmetic operators, 114
assignment (=) operator, 114
definition, 113
logical operators, 1209
mathematical precedence, 114
modulo operators, 116
numeric comparison operators, 119
Tax calculation example, arithmetic operators, 114
string concatenation, 118
Opponents table, Wrox United example, 746
options
see switches
OR (||) logical operator, 120
see also logical operators
implementation example, 123
operator precedence, 121
ordering system example, normalization, 248, 249
other data types, 89
boolean, 90
date, 89
out parameter
see also passing parameters by reference; passing
parameters by value
definition, 181
example, 182
implementation example, 183–187
code workthough, 185
page view, 184
output caching
see also caching
example, 576

OutputCache directive, syntax, 575

performance optimization, 575

Servertime example, 577–578

  code workthrough, 578

  page view, 577

OutputCache directive

Duration property, 575

Location property, 575

VaryByControl property, 576

VaryByCustom property, 576

VaryByHeader property, 576

VaryByParam property, 576

overloading, methods, 168

consolidation, concept and example, 230

disadvantage, 230

first class example, use within, 229

signatures, defining, 230

overriding, match of the day example, 496

P

Page class

ASP.NET, page lifecycle, 324

event handling, 197

IsPostback property, 275, 590

  DropDownList control, implementation example, 72

  for statement, implementation example, 146

  Hashtable class, implementation example, 108

  if statement, implementation example, 136

  performance optimization tips, 590

  Page_Load() method, 325

  postback, use for, 205

  procedure-level variables, implementation example, 96

  switch statement, implementation example, 143

methods

  Page_Error, 547

  Page_Init, 324

  Page_Load, 325

  Page_PreRender, 325

  Page_Unload, 326

properties

  ErrorPage, 552

  SortField, 259

  Trace, 529

page configuration settings, configuration files, 571

AutoEventWireup parameter, 571

buffer parameter, 571

EnableSessionState parameter, 571

EnableViewState parameter, 571

web.config file, within, 570

Page directive, 43

page initialization, configuration sequence of events, 564

page level tracing

Control Tree section, 531

Cookies Collection section, 531

Headers Collection section, 531

Server Variables section, 532

Trace Information, 531

page lifecycle, ASP.NET

methods

  Page_Init, 324

  Page_Load, 325

  Page_PreRender, 325

  Page_Unload, 325

operation mechanism, 324

  handling control events, 325

  page cleanup, 325

  page disposal, 325

  page initialization, 324

  page loading, 325

  page prerendering, 325

  page rendering, 325

Postback data loading, 324

ViewState loading, 324

Page not found error example, 547–549

  <customErrors> element, use of, 552

Page_Error() method, Page class

event logs, making entries within, 557

error handling, programmatically, 547

implementation example, 547–549

  code workthrough, 548

  page view, 548

Page_Init() method, Page Class

events, page loading mechanism, 198

page lifecycle, ASP.NET, 324

Page_Load() method, Page class, 43, 72, 325

  <script> tag, working with, 47

arrays, implementation example, 100

Chat page, use within, 408

database binding example, 53

Event calendar, Main page, Wrox United example, 357, 359

event handlers, use as, 198

events, page loading mechanism, 198

first class example, 223

functions with return values example, 178

HelloWorld example, use within, 475

implementation example, 325

implementation uses, 326

Inserting ASP.NET code example, 47

Page_Load() method, Page class (continued)
  IsPostback property, 325
  Login page, Wrox United example, navigation bar, 662
  Merchandise page, WroxUnited example, use within, 401
  page lifecycle, ASP.NET, 325
  Parameters object, implementation example, 275
  parameters, implementation example, 168
  Players page, Wrox United example, use within, 371
  procedure-level variables, implementation example, 96
  simple function example, 163
  Sort Page example, 259
  Wrox United example
    cookies, use within, 390, 393
    Style sheets, use within, 422
  XML binding example, 56
Page_PreRender() method, Page class
  page lifecycle, ASP.NET, 325
Page_Render() method, Page class
  events, page loading mechanism, 198
Page_Unload() method, Page class
  definition, 326
  events, page loading mechanism, 198, 199
  implementation example, 327
  page lifecycle, ASP.NET, 325
pagelets
  see user controls
pageOutput parameter, tracing, configuration files, 574
<pages> element, page configuration settings, 570
Panel control, 332
  see also intrinsic controls
  Login page, Wrox United example, navigation bar, 662
parameters
  definition, 164
  functions, use with, 164
    implementation example, 165–169
    matching contents of, 168
    syntax, 165
  out parameter
    definition, 181
    implementation example, 183
  passing by reference
    definition, 181
    implementations example, 183
  passing by value
    definition, 181
    implementation example, 183
  Teams page, Team players listing, 352
  Web controls, referencing, 169, 170–172
  Width parameter, 167

Parameters object
  command execute example, 309
  definition, 272
  filtering queries, 277
  implementation example, 165–69
    code workthrough, 275
    DataAdapter object, use of, 277
    DropDownList control, use of, 275
    Page_Load() method, use of, 275
    page view, 275
  Parameters collection, 272
  properties, 277
Parameters property, OleDbCommand object, 272
parentheses, mathematical precedence, 115
parsers, 42
parser errors, 515
passing parameters by reference
  see also out parameter; passing parameters by value
  definition, 181
  implementation example, 183-187
    code workthough, 185
    page view, 184
  passing parameters by value, compared to, 186
passing parameters by value
  see also out parameter; passing parameters by reference
  definition, 181
  implementation example, 183–187
    code workthough, 185
    page view, 184
  passing parameters by reference, compared to, 186
Passport authentication, 638
  see also authentication
  authentication site of microsoft, 638
performance optimization, 561, 574
  Cache object, 578
  caching, 574
    fragment caching, 578
    output caching, 575
  disconnected model, ADO.NET, 289
  references, 590
  tips, 590
  tracing, 573
permissions
  access permissions, 814
  directory security, 816
  execute permissions, 815
  IIS admin tool, setting within, 814
  virtual directories, creation, 812
physical directories
  virtual directories relationship, 809

Players page, Wrox United example, 367–372
  code workthrough, 369
  DataSourceControl, use of, 369
  MxDataGrid control, use of, 369
  Page_Load() method, use of, 371
  page view, 369
Players table, Wrox United example, 742
PlayerTeams table, Wrox United example, 743
plus (+) operator, string concatenation, 118
polymorphism, objects, 217
Position table, Wrox United example, 744
postback, 325
  arrays, implementation example, 100
  ASP.NET, page lifecycle, 324
  definition, 202
  implementation example, 203–205
    ASP.NET page view, 204
    code workthrough, 205
    No postback in HTML page view, 203
    viewstate, viewing information using, 205
  IsPostBack property, using, 205
  runat=server attribute, usage with, 202
  Tax calculation example, 117
pre-compiled code, 37
  see also interpreted code
Prerender event handler
  Merchandise page, Wrox United example, 404
presentation layer, 3-tier application design, 464, 465
Preview Mode, Web Matrix, 732–733
Primary key, 250
Primary key/foreign key one-to-many relationships,
    database design, 742
private variables
  first class example, 221
  properties, working with, 223
procedure-level variables, 92
  implementation example, 92–96
    code workthrough, 95
    IsPostback property, use of, 96
    Page_Load() method, use of, 96
    page view, 95
processing directive
  syntax, 603
  worked example, 606
  Web services, components, 603
Programmatic Object Model, HTML server controls, 316
projects, Visual Studio .NET, 756
  see also solutions, Visual Studio .NET

Properties Pane feature, Visual Studio .NET, 754
Properties section, Web Matrix, 729
properties, classes, 221
  get statement, 221
  private variables, working with, 223
  read-only, example, 222
  set statement, 221
  write-only, 224
Protection attribute, <forms> tag, 643
provider solvency using UDDI, 633
Public Class
  syntax, 604
  MeasurementsConversion example, defining within,
      606
  Web services, components, 604
public keys/private keys, 665
public methods, encapsulation of objects, 432
public properties, encapsulation of objects, 432
Public Sub New() method, a constructor, 454
public variables, example, 220
public-key encryption, 665

Q

QueryString collection, Request object, 599

R

RadioButton control, 77
  see also intrinsic controls
  Checkbox control, compared to, 79
RadioButtonList control, 78
  see also rich controls
  implementation example, 78–79
    code workthrough, 79
    page view, 78
    SelectedItem.Value property, use of, 79
  parameters, implementation example, 167
  SelectedItem.Value property, 142
  switch statement, implementation example, 143
  syntax, 76
Random object
  if statement, implementation example, 136
  Next() method, 136
RangeValidator control, 372
rapid application development, 435
read access, access permission, 814
read-only property, classes, 224
RedirectFromLoginPage method, 645

reference types
Merchandise page, WroxUnited example, 402
Register directive
TagName attribute, 440
TagPrefix attribute, 440
registered users,user security level, 636
Registry, 476
DLL files, locating, 476
XCopy deployment, 476
RegularExpressionValidator control, 373
ControlToValidate property, 760
Email updates, use within, 376
properties, 374
ControlToValidate, 376
ErrorMessage, 376
validation expressions, 377
Wrox United example, Visual Studio .NET, page creation, 759
RemoteOnly attribute, <customErrors> element, 573
render code block
see inline code block
rendering, of Web controls, 313
Repeater control
see also data rendering controls
DataList control, compared to, 352
definition, 341
Merchandise page, Wrox United example, use within, 401, 404
Team players listing, Teams page, Wrox United example, 349
templates, use within, 343
Request Details section, page level tracing, 530
Request.Query collection, HTTP requests, 599
requestLimit parameter, tracing, 574
RequiredFieldValidator control, 373
ControlToValidate property, 524
ErrorMessage property, 524
validating illegal data, 524
System.Web.UIWebControls namespace, 523
Response.Write statement
disadvantage in testing, 529
first class example, methods, 230
Inserting ASP.NET code example, 47
response-request mechanism, 599
return keyword, functions, 172
reusable code, 431
ASPX pages, 432
code-behind, 451

COM and DCOM, 593
components, 431
encapsulation, 431
modularization, use within, 160
rapid application development, 435
usage guidelines, 456
user controls, 435
Web Matrix, using within, 735
Web services, 593
rich controls, 316
definition, 352
types
AdRotator, 353
Calendar, 353
CheckBoxList, 353
ImageButton, 353
LinkButton, 353
RadioButtonList, 353
rich object model, Web controls, 320
root element, configuration files rules, 566
rows attribute, Textbox control, 75
Rows collection, 285
runat= server attribute, HTML server controls, 316
implementation example, 317
Inserting ASP.NET code example, 47
tag to control conversion, 318
runat=server attribute
ASP.NET server controls, attributes, 65
databases, providing details for, 254
DropDownList control, implementation example, 71
<form> tag, 64
Label controls, ASP.NET server controls, 66
postback, usage with, 202
runtime errors
see logical errors
runtime exceptions, 536

S

Sbyte data type, 86
Script source access, access permission, 814
<script> tags
inserting ASP.NET code, 42, 44
Page_Load() method, working with, 47
<sectionGroup> tags, configuration file format, 566
security, 635
access policies, 635
authentication, 635, 637
authorization, 637
configuration files, 565
database connection strings, 571

definition, 636

directories, within, 816

encryption, 637, 664

HTML, lack of adequacy within, 5

user level security, 636

virtual directories, advantage of, 810

Web services, of, 627, 635

security, Web services, 627

security.config file, 562

Select() method, DataTable object, 295

SelectCommand attribute

AccessDataSourceControl control, 254

Data Source controls, 367

SelectCommand property

auto-generated commands example, 300

CommandBuilder, basis for, 298

DataAdapter class, 271

SelectedItem.Value property

DropDownList control, implementation example, 73

RadioButtonList control, implementation example, 79

SelectedValue property, 276

selectionmode attribute, ListBox control, 73, 74

Send() method, SmtpMail class, 558

SeperatorTemplate element

DataList controls, 339

Repeater controls, Wrox United example, 365

server controls, 49

definition, 313

HTML server controls, 313

mixing HTML and ASP.NET code, 49

performance optimization tips, 590

seperating ASP.NET and HTML, 49

Web controls, 313

Server Explorer, Visual Studio .NET, 755

example, 794

server hits, performance optimization tips, 590

Server object

ClearError method, 549

GetLastError() method, 549, 554

Server Variables section, page level tracing, 532

server-side dynamic Web pages, 7

see also client-side dynamic Web pages

advantages, 8

ASP.NET, processing model within, 8

client-side dynamic Web pages, compared to, 9

operation mechanism, 7

Servertime example, 577–578

code workthrough, 577

page view, 577

service hijacking, 632

sessions, 381, 382

see also applications; caching; cookies

adding data to, 395

ASP.NET

default information storage within, 395

reacting to events within, 410

database, state management using, 420

definition, 393

operation mechanism, 394

session scope, web.config file, 381

session state, performance optimization tips, 590

Sessions class, 395

usage guidelines, 419

uses, 393

ViewState, state management using, 420

Wrox United example

Merchandise page, using session state within, 395

Style sheets, use within, 422, 427

set statement, properties, 221

settings section

<sectionGroup> element, 566

classes, establishing attributes & properties for, 567

configuration files, 566

important blocks examined, 569

SHA1 encryption algorithm, 665

Shared keyword, static methods, example, 232

short data type, 86

signatures, methods

overloading, defining using, 230

Signout() method, FormsAuthentication class, 646

Login page, Wrox United example, navigation bar, 664

simple code-behind example, 452–457

code workthrough, 454

inheritance, 454

namespace handling, 455

page view, 454

simple function example, 161–64

code workthrough, 162

Label control, use of, 162

Page_Load() method, use of, 163

page view, 162

simple header control example, 440–446

AdRotator control, use of, 443

chat page, Wrox United example, applying to, 445

code workthrough, 443

creating .ascx file, 443

Main page, Wrox United example, applying to, 445

page view, 442

simple user control example, 437–40
  code workthrough, 439
  page view, 439
single data type, 87
site administrator mailing, 557
sliding time expiration, 582
slidingExpiration attribute, <forms> tag, 643
SmtpMail class, example, 558
SmtpMail class, System.Web.Mail namespace, 558
SOAP SOAP (Simple Object Access Protocol), 601
  ASP.NET Web services, default protocol for, 603
  delayed response, 632
  envelope, 601
SOAP envelope, 601
  HTTP Request, not tied to, 602
  HTTP Response, not tied to, 602
  implementation example, 601
    request code, 601
    response code, 602
  usage flexibility, 602
Solution Explorer, Visual Studio .NET, 755
solutions, Visual Studio .NET, 756
Sort Page example, 257–262
  code workthrough, 258
  DataSet object,use of, 261
  OleDb class, use of, 258
  OleDbDataAdapter data adapter, use of, 261
  Page_Load() method, use of, 259
  page view, 258
  SortField property, use of, 259
  String.Empty element, 260
SortedList class
  definition, 110
  syntax, 110
SortField property, Sort page, example, 259
Source property, Exception class, 537
SQL (Structured Query Language)
  Injection Attacks, 277
  stored procedures, 251
  tables, linking of, 251
  VS.NET, modifying server database using, 753
SqlConnection object, 270
SqlDataReader class, System.Data.SqlClient
  performance optimization tips, 590
SSL (Secure Sockets Layer)
  Certificate Authority, verifying identity using, 665
  encryption, implemented within, 637, 665
  Forms-based authentication, use in, 664
    login example, 665

  requireSSL attribute, 665
  hashing keys, using, 665
  Web services security, within, 627, 630
StackTrace property, Exception class, 537, 572
stateless protocol, 382
static methods
  definition, 231
  static keyword, 231
Static Web pages
  see also dynamic Web pages
  definition, 2
  disadvantages, 4
  dynamic features, lack of, 5
  HTML, use of, 2
  implementation example, 2
  operation mechanism, 3
Status table, Wrox United example, 742
stored procedures
  advantages, 251
  definition, 251
  performance optimization tips, 590
strConnect variable, database binding, 53
string concatenation
  assignment (+=) operator, using, 118
  definition, 118
  functions with return values example, 179
  performance optimization tips, 590
  plus (+) operator, using, 118
string variables/data type, 88
String.Empty element, Sort Page example, 260
StringBuilder class, System.Text namespace, 590
strong typing, C#, 82
structured code, good coding practice, 511
structured error handling
  definition, 536
  exceptions, 536
  try . . . catch . . . finally statements, 538
  usage methods, 535
Subject property, MailMessage class, 558
subroutines, Visual Basic .NET, 480
subtraction (-) operator, 114
switch statement, 126, 138
  see also branching structures
  calculator example, 211
  case statement, 139
  implementation example, 143–144
    code workthough, 142
    IsPostback property, use of, 143
    page view, 142

RadioButtonList control, use of, 143
numeric comparison operators, lack of support for, 143
structure, 138
switches, 472
syntax errors, 514
common mistakes, 514
compilation errors, 514
example, 516
configuration errors, 514
parser errors, 514
system errors
definition, 525
local client, viewable only on, 525
System namespace
DateTime class, 323
Exeption class, 537
System.Collections namespace
ArrayList class
Add() method, 103, 105
advantages, 102
definition, 102
disadvantages, 103
implementation example, 104–105
Insert() method, 103, 105
new keyword, creating objects using, 103
syntax, 103
Hashtable class
Add() method, 106
advantages, 105
custom calendar example, 503
definition, 105
disadvantages, 105
Event calendar, Main page, Wrox United example, 359
implementation example, 107–109
key-value pairs, adding, 106
syntax, 106
SortedList class, 109
System.Data namespace, ADO.NET, 269
System.Data.dll component, 489
System.Data.OleDb namespace
ADO.NET, classes contained for, 269
login example, databases, 649
System.Data.SqlClient namespace
ADO.NET, classes contained for, 269
SqlDataReader class, 591
System.Diagnostics namespace
event log, writing to, 553
EventLog class, 553
System.dll file, component compiling, 472

System.Text namespace, StringBuilder class, 590
System.Web group
configuration files, 566
declarations section expanded, 567
settings list, 568
system.web tag, web.config configuration file,
authorization sub-tag, 652
deny attribute, 652
System.Web.dll, example of use, 498
System.Web.Mail namespace
MailAttachment class, 558
MailMessage class, 558
site administrator, mailing, 557
SmtpMail class, 558
System.Web.Security namespace, example, 649
System.Web.UI.Control namespace
composite controls, inheritance to, 499
custom controls, 489, 490
components, compared, 490
creating, 490
data access components, compared to, 490
definition, 490
inheritance to, 495
match of the day example, 491–499
reusability, 498
user controls, compared to, 490
System.Web.UI.HtmlControls namespace, HtmlControl
class, 317
System.Web.UI.WebControls namespace
custom controls, inheritance to, 499
RequiredFieldValidator control, 523
SystemExeption class
catch block, exeption catching using, 539
Exeption class, inheritance from, 537

T

Table control, intrinsic controls, 332
TableBox control, intrinsic controls, 332
TableCell control, intrinsic controls, 332
TableRow control, intrinsic controls, 332
Tables and Rows example, 286–88
code workthrough, 287
page view, 287
Tables collection, 284
tables, databases
definition, 248
normalization, 249
ordering system example, 248
SQL, linking using, 251

tables, Wrox United example

Fans, 746

Games, 744

GameTypes, 745

Locations, 745

Opponents, 746

Players, 742

PlayerTeams, 743

Position, 744

relationship diagram, 741

Status, 742

Teams, 743

TagName attribute, Register directive, 440

TagPrefix attribute, Register directive, 440

target switch, compilation options, 473

TargetSite property, Exception class, 537

Tax calculation example, 115–118

code workthrough, 117

Label control, use of, 117

modulo operators, use of, 117

page view, 116

postback, use of, 117

TextBox control, use of, 117

Teams page, Wrox United example, 332–340

code workthrough, 339

components, encapsulating data access code into, 482–489

page view, 338

code workthrough, 488

DataList control, use of, 333, 339

Main page, linking to, 340

Team players listing, 343–352

code workthrough, 349, 350

event handlers, using, 350

page view, 349

parameters, use of, 352

Repeater control, use of, 349

Teams table, Wrox United example, 743

template pages, Web Matrix, 256

Sort Page example, 257–262

code workthrough, 258

DataSet object,use of, 261

OleDb class, use of, 258

OleDbDataAdapter data adapter, use of, 261

Page_Load() method, use of, 259

page view, 258

SortField property, use of, 259

String.Empty element, 260

templates

DataList control, use within

AlternatingItemTemplate, 343

EditItemTemplate, 343

FooterTemplate, 343

HeaderTemplate, 343

ItemTemplate, 343

SelectedItemTemplate, 343

SeperatorTemplate, 343

definition, 341

Repeater control, use within, 343

test page example, ASP.NET, 26–29

testing Web services, 607

Text attribute, Label controls, 66, 456

Merchandise page, Wrox United example, 401

textual data types, 88

string, 88

char, 89

Textbox control, 618

see also intrinsic controls

attributes

columns, 75

rows, 75

textmode, 75

definition, 75

events, use with, 199

implementation example, 74–76

code workthrough, 77

page view, 75

manual trapping example, use within, 522

multiline setting, 76

Tax calculation example, 116

Web controls, ASP.NET, 319

textmode attribute, Textbox control, 74

throw statement

exeptions, generating, 541

syntax, 541

try...catch...finally statements, use with, 541

tiered access to Web sites

see authorization

Timeout attribute, <forms> tag, 643

timestamp expiration, cache object, 581

Cache.Insert() method, setting using, 581

sliding time expiration, 582

To property, MailMessage class, 558

ToLongTimeString() method, Date time class, 323

Toolbox feature, Visual Studio .NET, 755

Toolbox section, Web Matrix, 728

MySnippets option, reusable code using, 735

example, 735

Web Matrix, code entry, 730

ToShortDateString() method, Date time class

event handler, creation example, 323

Trace attribute, Page directive, 529

Trace class
  Warn() method, 532, 534
  Write() method, 532
  writing to the trace log, 532
trace element, Page directive, example, 195
trace log, Trace class, writing using methods of, 532
<trace> section, application level tracing, 534
  example, 534
Trace.axd file, 535, 573
Trace.Write() method, Page directive, 197, 574
traceMode parameter, tracing, configuration files, 574
tracing, 195, 529
  application level tracing, 534
  configuration files, within
    enabled parameter, 574
    localOnly parameter, 574
    pageOutput parameter, 574
    requestLimit parameter, 574
    traceMode parameter, 574
  page level tracing, 529
    Control Tree section, 531
    Cookies Collection section, 531
    Headers Collection section, 531
    implementation example, 529–32
    Request Details section, 530
    Server Variables section, 532
    Trace information section, 531
  performance optimization, 573
  trace element, Page directive, 195
  trace log, writing to, 532
  Trace.Write() method, 574
  web.config file, 573
  writing to the trace log, 532
transactions
  definition, 306
  operation mechanism, 306
try . . . catch . . . finally statements
  catch blocks
    contents of, 540
    example, 539
    exeption handling, 540
    multiple catch blocks, 538
    parameterless catch blocks, 540
  exceptions, catching, 538
  finally block, 541
  implementation example, 542–544
  nested try blocks, 544
  syntax, 538
  throw statement, use with, 541
  try block, 538

try block, 538
  concept, 538
  implementation example, 542–544
type mismatch errors, 519
typo errors, 514

U

UDDI (Universal Description, Discovery, and Integration)
  provider solvency, 633
  solving interdependency, 633
  Web services, locating, 626
  WSDL, use of, 626
UpdateCommand property
  auto-generated commands example, 300
  DataAdapter class, 271
URL (Uniform Resource Locator), 27
  Web Server, for, 807
useFullyQualifiedRedirectUrl parameter, general configuration setting, 570
user controls
  application design, 465
  code-behind files, use of, 466
  custom controls, compared to, 490
  definition, 435
  mechanism of working, 436
  navigation user control example, 446–451
    Chat page, Wrox United page, applying to, 449
    Main page, Wrox United page, applying to, 446
  simple header control example, 440–446
    AdRotator control, use of, 443
    code workthrough, 443
    page view, 442
  simple user control example, 437–440
    code workthrough, 439
    page view, 439
  tag libraries, using, 440
  usage examples, 436
  usage guidelines, 437
  Wrox site example, 435
  Wrox United example, Visual Studio .NET
    developing user controls, 784
    user control creation, 777
User error example, 547–549
  <customErrors> element, use of, 552
user level security
  administrators users, 636
  anonymous users, 636
  registered users, 636
user security levels, 636

user sessions
  see sessions
Username password, Web services security, 627
  ISBN search Web service example, 627–630
    code workthrough, 629
    page view, 628, 629
username-password, security technique
  worked example, 627
Ushort data type, 86

V

validation
  cookies, first level of security with, 645
  definition, 643
  good coding practice, 512
  hashing algorithms, 644
  HTML server controls, within, 318
validation attribute, machineKey tag, 644
Validation controls, 316
  advantages, 372
  definition, 372
  invalid data errors, eliminating, 523
    example, 524
  types
    CompareValidator, 372
    CustomValidator, 372
    RangeValidator, 372
    RegularExpressionValidator, 373
    RequiredFieldValidator, 373
validationKey attribute, machineKey tag, 644
variable scope, 91
  block level variables, 91
  global variables, 96
  procedure-level variables, 92
variables
  assigning values, 85
  conversion functions, 97
  declaration, 90
    example, 83
    guidelines, 82-90
    nondescript variable names, effect of, 90
  definition, 82
  example using, 83
  implementation example, 83–86
    code workthrough, 85
    compilation error page view, 85
    Label control, use of, 85
    page view, 84
  naming conventions, 90

  objects, as, 216, 217
  public variables, 220
  scope, 91
VaryByControl property, OutputCache directive, 576
VaryByCustom property, OutputCache directive, 576
VaryByHeader property, OutputCache directive, 576
VaryByParam attribute, OutputCache directive, 576
  fragment caching example, 578
  Servertime example, 578
ViewState, 318
  ASP.NET, page lifecycle, 324
  definition, 71
  DropDownList control, implementation example, 71
  performance optimization tips, 590
  postback, implementation example, 205
  hidden form fields, information storage using, 420
  state management, 420
virtual directories
  creation, 810–813
    IIS admin tool, using, 810
    permissions, setting, 812
  definition, 808
  IIS
    configuration files, 564
    security within, 810
  Web server, within, 808, 809
Visible attribute, Label control, 66
Visual Basic .NET
  ASP.NET, default language for, 43
  C#
    compared to, 481
    cross language compatibility, 477
  class definitions, 480
  components, writing, 477
  continuation character, 481
  functions, 480
  HelloWorld example, within, 478–482
    code workthrough, 480
    page view, 480
  subroutines, 480
Visual Interdev, 5
Visual Studio .NET
  code block formatting, 782
  code view features, 763
  code-behind
    default use of, 459
    web forms applications using, 451
  features, 755
  IntelliSense tool, 726, 764
  introduction, 753

language edition drawbacks, 753
projects, 756
reference reading, 801
solutions, 756
SQL, modifying server database of, 753
Web applications development
code-behind, use of, 757
generated files, 757
Web Matrix, compared to, 459, 726
Wrox United example, 754
adding code to code-behind class, 762
adding code to methods, 763–769
custom classes, using, 791–794
databases, working with, 794–797
debugging, 797–801
page compiling, 761–762
page creation, 757–761
stylesheets, use of, 769–776
user control creation, 777–782

W

Warn() method, Trace class
trace log, writing to, 534
writing to the trace log, 532
Web applications, 381
COM and DCOM, 593
information storage, 382, 404
applications, 382
caching, 382, 413
cookies, 382, 383
sessions, 382, 393
Visual Studio .NET, development using
code-behind, use of, 757
generated files, 757
Web controls, 9, 313, 315
attributes
id, 65
runat=server, 65
intrinsic, 316, 331
Button control, 319
CheckBox, 319
CheckBoxList, 78
Label, 65
ListBox, 319
RadioButton, 76
RadioButtonList, 76
TableCell, 332
Textbox, 74, 319
automatic browser detection, 320

data rendering controls, 316, 341
DataGrid, 341
DataList, 341
Repeater, 341
definition, 319
events, 199
adding events, 200
attributes, adding as, 200
HTML events, compared to, 199
event handling, 322
HTML
form controls, compared to, 64
server controls, compared to, 201, 318
Hyperlink control, 331
inheritance, 320
modifying, 68
.NET Framework, features drawn from, 320
parameters, as, 169, 170–173
postback, 202
properties, 320
AutoPostBack, 326
CSS stylesheet, adding, 321
implementation example, 321
rendering, 314
rich controls, 316
AdRotator, 353
Calendar, 353
CheckBoxList, 353
ImageButton, 353
LinkButton, 353
RadioButtonList, 353
rich object model, 320
Validation controls, 316, 372
CompareValidator, 372
CustomValidator, 372
RangeValidator, 372
RegularExpressionValidator, 373
RequiredFieldValidator, 373
variables, assigning values using, 84
Web forms
composition
ASP.NET code, 61
HTML templates, 61
definition, 60
HTML forms, compared to, 61
information transmission, 59
uses, 60
Web services proxy example, use in, 618
Web gardening, performance optimization tips, 591

Web Matrix
Microsoft Access, lack of support for queries in, 253
ASP.NET
  application development for, 15
  installation, 15
built-in class browser, 41
Class Browser, 735
  implementation example, 736
  usage technique, 736
code entry, example, 730-731
code wizards, example, 262-269
configuring for.NET Framework 1.1, 118
Data explorer, 251
  data grid example, 253
  databases, accessing, 251
Data Source controls, 367
  properties, 367
  Wrox United example, Players page, 369
development screen, 727
  Menu section, 728
  page view, 727
  Properties section, 729
  Toolbox section, 728
  Workspace section, 729
error handling, 738
event handler, implementation example, 201–203
installation, 15, 16–18
introduction, 5, 725
layout options, 738
MxDataGrid control
  attributes, 255
  data grid example, 254
  Players page, Wrox United example, 369
  properties used, 370
  style elements, 255
.NET Framework versioning, 563
Properties section, 202
references for usage, 738
reusable code, using, 735
saving pages, 731
starting, 727
template pages, 256
usage advantages/disadvantages, 726
viewing pages, 731
  Design Mode, 732
  Preview Mode, 732
Visual Interdev, inspired by, 5
Visual Studio .NET, compared to, 459
Web server
  built-in feature, 5
  introduction, 725

  limited security options, 638
  page loading, example, 733
  starting, 20–24
  troubleshooting, 24
Web services proxy, in example, 614, 616
Web methods
CacheDuration attribute, 604
MeasurementsConversion example
  code workthrough, 606
  namespaces, defining, 606
  page view, 605
  Public Class, defining, 606
syntax, 604
Web services, components, 604
Wrox United example, use within, 618
Web pages, 60
accessing pages locally, 808
ASP.NET, dynamic content creation using, 1
browsers, role of, 23
client-server relationship, 62
components, accessing, 476
databases, storage using, 247
definition, 60
dynamic Web pages, 6
  client-side model, 6
  server side model, 7
HTTP, access role of, 808
inserting ASP.NET code, 42
  inline code blocks, using, 47
  Inserting ASP.NET code example, 44
  server controls, using, 49
static Web pages
  definition, 2
  disadvantages, 4
  implementation example, 2
  operation mechanism, 3
Web Server, placed within, 60
Web server
ASP.NET, server error, 32
client browsers, 5
common types, 5
definition, 5
HTTP Error 403, 24
IIS, 5
  managing directories, 808
  name identification, 807
  testing installation, 807
installation testing, 818
  Internet Explorer, troubleshooting within, 821
  Netscape Navigator, troubleshooting within, 822
  other errors, 822
  page not found error, 819

localhost, access using, 23
virtual directories, 809
    example, 809
Web server, Web Matrix, 5
introduction, 725
limited security options, 638
page loading, example, 733
starting, 20–25
troubleshooting, 24
Web service Description page, 607
Web service proxy, 613
creating, 615
definition, 613
operation mechanism, 613
WSDL, managing, 613
Web services, 593
ADO.NET, using, 610
asynchronous method calls, 631
black box concept, 594
components, 603
    namespaces, 603
    processing directives, 603
    Public Class, 604
    Web methods, 604, 605
consuming, 613
    accessing the ISBN Web service from a ASP.NET page,
        615
    proxy, using, 613
definition, 594
Discovery, 626
Greetings example, 595–598
    code workthrough, 597
    page view, 596
HTML Web services, 594
HTTP Request-Response system, 598
    HTTP Request information, 599
    HTTP Response information, 599
interdependency, 633
ISBN search Web service example, 610–613
    code workthrough, 612
    page view, 612
namespaces, use of, 598
.NET Framework, use of, 36
network connectivity, 631
provider solvency, 633
security, 627
    common techniques, 627
    IP address restriction, 630
    registration keys, using, 627
    SSL, using, 630
    WSE toolkit, using, 631

service hijacking, 632
sharing application logic, 593
SOAP, 601
SOAP, default protocol for, 603
UDDI, locating using, 626
Web controls, compared with, 594
Web server installation testing, 818
    Internet Explorer, troubleshooting within, 821
    Netscape Navigator, troubleshooting within, 820
    other errors, 820
    page not found error, 818
Web service Description page, 607
Wrox United example
    applying to, 618
    latest score web service, 621
    Results page, creation of, 619
WSDL file, 608
XML, use of, 599
    usage advantages, 601
    Web services, 594
XSD, writing data types using, 610
Web services security, 627
web.config configuration file, 562
application level tracing, settings for, 534
application settings, 572
AppSettings, used in example, 624
assemblies, accessing in other locations, 477
    example, 477
authorization tag, 644
authorization, use within, 650
configuration sequence of events, 564
contents, 564
custom errors, 572
    <customErrors> element, 550
error handling, 525
<forms> tag, 642
Forms-based authentication, 638, 639
    Wrox United example, 653
general configuration settings, 570
latest score web service, within, 624
location tag, 652
login example, 642
login page example
    authentication against database, 646
    user authentication, 639, 642
    user authorization, 651
Login page, Wrox United example, 653–664
    administrator level page view, 659
    authentication, 661
    code workthrough, 660
    navigation bar, 662–664

web.config configuration file (continued)

    page view, 658

    user level page view, 660

    web.config configuration file, authentication using, 660

  machineKey tag, 643

  machine.config file, overriding settings of, 564, 566

  overriding other web.config file settings, 564

  page configuration settings, 570

  structure, 569

  system.web tag, 652

    authorization sub-tag, 652

    deny attribute, 652

  tracing, 573

web-callable methods

  see Web methods

Website references (URL)

  Certification Authority, SSL, 630

  class browser, 40

  UDDI service, 626

WHERE Clause builder section

  AND Clause button, 266

  code wizards, Web Matrix, 266

  Parameters object, implementation example, 276

while statement, 126

  see also for statement; foreach..in statement

  implementation example, 150

    code workthough, 151

    modulo (%) operator, using, 154

    page view, 150

  infinite looping problem, 149

    example, 148

  syntax, 148

  usage table, 144

Width attribute, Label control, 66

Windows 2000 operating system

  directory security, 816

Windows operating system

  ASP.NET, compatibility with, 11

  event driven model, 193

  IIS

    versioning of, 803

    compatibility, 803

  MMC, 806

Workspace section, Web Matrix, 729

  saving pages, 731

write access, access permission, 814

Write() method, Trace class

  writing to the trace log, 532

WriteEntry method method, EventLog class, 554

write-only property, classes, 224

Wrox United Application

  authentication, adding to, 653

  creating a Web service for, 618

Wrox United example, 314

  caching, using, 415–418

    code workthrough, 417

    Calendar controls, use of, 416, 418

    Hashtable object, use of, 417

    page view, 417

  Chat page

    code workthrough, 408

    page view, 407

    posting new messages, 408

    refreshing page content, 409

    setting chat log length, 409

    simple header control example, applying, 445

    testbox properties, 408

  code-behind, applying, 457–59

    code work through, 458

  cookies, using, 386–394

    code workthrough, 391

    checking user registration, 387

    confirming presence of cookies, 390

    expiry limit, 391

    Page_Load() method, use of, 390

    page view, 390

    registering the user, 388

  database design, 741

    Fans table, 746

    Games table, 744

    GameTypes table, 745

    installing Access database, 747

    installing MSDE database, 747

    Location table, 745

    Opponents table, 746

    Players table, 742

    PlayerTeam table, 743

    Position table, 744

    Primary key/foreign key one-to-many relationships, 742

    relationship diagram, 741

    Status table, 742

    Teams table, 743

  database structure, 327

  Forms-based authentication, use of, 653

  global settings, 411–413

    Global.asax, using, 411

  Login page, 653–64

administrator level page view, 659
  authentication, 661
  code workthrough, 660
  navigation bar, 662–664
  page view, 658
  user level page view, 660
  web.config configuration file, authentication using, 660
Main page, 328–31
  adding Web controls, 329
  browser code view, 331
  code workthrough, 330
  components, encapsulating data access code into, 482
  composite controls, using, 499
  Email updates, 373–377
  Event calendar, 354
  page view, 330
  Fixture details, 360
  setting Web control properties, 329
  Teams page, linking to, 340
  Web Matrix HTML code view, 330
  Web Matrix, creating new page using, 328
Merchandise page, using session state within, 396–405
  code workthrough, 400
  page view, 399
opening page view, 314
Players page, 367–372
  code workthrough, 369
  DataSourceControl, use of, 369
  MxDataGrid control, use of, 369
  Page_Load() method, use of, 371
  page view, 369
Results page, 619–621
  code workthrough, 620
  page view, 620
simple header control example, 440–446
  AdRotator control, use of, 443
  code workthrough, 443
  page view, 442
Style sheets, 421–429
  Calendar controls, use of, 423, 428
  code workthrough, 427
  cookies, use of, 422, 428
  Page_Load() method, use of, 422
  page view, 426
  sessions, use of, 422
  Sessions, use of, 427
Teams page, 332–340
  code workthrough, 339

components, encapsulating data access code into, 482
  DataList control, use of, 333, 339
  Main page, linking to, 340
  page view, 338
  Team players listing, 343–352
Web services, applying, 618
Wrox United example, Visual Studio .NET, 754
  adding code to code-behind class, 762
  adding code to methods, 763–769
  custom classes, 791–794
  databases, working with, 794–797
  debugging, 797–801
    breakpoints, using, 798
    design-time errors, fixing, 799
  page compiling, 761–762
  page creation, 757–761
    RegularExpressionValidator control, use of, 759
  stylesheets, use of, 769–776
    HTML view, adding in, 776
  user controls
    adding control to page, 789–791
    creation, 777–782
    development, 784–786
    XML file creation, 786–789
WSDL (Web services Description Language), 608
  contracts, 609
    MeasurementsConversion example, 609
  elements
    <definitions> element, 610
    <types> element, 610
  UDDI, key component of, 626
  Web service, defining interactions for, 608
  Web service proxy, handling by, 613
WSE (Web services enhancements) toolkit, 627, 631
  GXA specifications, 631
  WSE toolkit, 631
WS-Security specification, 631

X

XCopy deployment, 476
XML (eXtensible Markup Language)
  ASP.NET
    binding to, 54
    configuration files, basis for, 5621
    configuration files, structure in, 566
    user control, used in example of, 440

XML (eXtensible Markup Language) (continued)
Web services
  usage advantages, 601
  use within, 599
Wrox United example, Visual Studio .NET, 784
XML binding example, 54–57
see also database binding example
code workthrough, 55
DataGrid object, use of, 56
DataSet object, use of, 56
Page_Load() method, use of, 56
page view, 55
XML element rules, 564
XML Web services, 594
see also Web services.
ASP.NET, easy deployment using, 594
HTML Web services, compared to, 594
XSD (XML Schema Definition)
Web service data types, writing, 610